THE
SEA-HUNTERS

*The New England Whalemen
During Two Centuries
1635-1835*

EDOUARD A. STACKPOLE

J. B. LIPPINCOTT COMPANY

PHILADELPHIA   NEW YORK

LIBRARY OF CONGRESS CATALOG CARD NUMBER 52-13734

THE SEA-HUNTERS

To My Wife
FLORENCE TUPPER BROWN STACKPOLE

Acknowledgment is gratefully extended The John Simon Guggenheim Foundation and The American Philosophical Society for grants which made possible the writing of this book.

CONTENTS

7

PART FOUR

THE SEA-HUNTERS AT THE OCEAN'S FRONTIERS

PART FIVE

THE AMERICAN WHALEMAN BECOMES A PATHFINDER IN THE GREAT OCEANS

ILLUSTRATIONS

9

Captain Timothy Folger, of Nantucket

> *Captain Folger (1732-1814) drew the first chart of the Gulf Stream. He was a direct descendant of Peter Folger who moved to Nantucket in 1663. Captain Folger left the island for Dartmouth, Nova Scotia, in 1785, later settling in the whaling colony at Milford-Haven, Wales. This portrait by J. S. Copley was painted in 1764 and is in the Collection of the Metropolitan Museum of Art, New York City.*

A Chart of the Gulf Stream

> *This chart was copied by Benjamin Franklin from a drawing of the Gulf Stream by Captain Timothy Folger and was engraved in France. Reproduced from plate in the* Transactions of the American Philosophical Society, *Vol. II (1786), facing page 330.*

Whaling in the South Seas

> *This is a reproduction of an engraving from the painting by the French artist, Le Breton. Courtesy of Harry Shaw Newman, The Old Print Shop, New York City.*

Killing Sea-Elephants on Desolation Island

> *One of the rare drawings made by W. T. Peters in 1848. Peters afterward went to Japan on the Perry Expedition. From the original drawing owned by Mrs. Lincoln Ceely, of Nantucket.*

View in Otaheite—Matavi Bay

> *From a drawing by an unknown whaleman found in the logbook of the whaleship* Columbia, *of Nantucket, Captain Abbott, 1860-62.*

The Whaleship *Syren,* of London, England

> *Under Captain Frederick Coffin, of Nantucket, this ship was first on the "Japan Grounds," with the* Maro, *of Nantucket, Captain Joseph Allen, in May-June 1821. Painting by the English artist Walters in 1823. Original is in the possession of the Nantucket Whaling Museum.*

View of the Antarctic Continent

> *From a sketch by Lieutenant Charles Wilkes, leader of the U. S. Exploring Expedition, 1838. Reproduced from engraving in* Narrative of the United States Exploring Expedition During the Years 1838, 1839, 1840, 1841 *by Wilkes.*

Contemporary Log

> *A list of "Reefs and Islands in the South Pacific not laid down in the charts," by Frederick Taylor, Mate of the* Zenas Coffin, *of Nantucket, from the log of her 1832-35 voyage.*

Gathering "Terrapin" at the Galàpagos Islands

> *Reproduced from a contemporary engraving (1813) of painting by J. W. Clark.*

Chart and View of Pitcairn Island

> *Reproduced from engraving in Delano's* Voyages and Travels, *Boston, 1867.*

Ship *Edward Carey,* of Nantucket, off Norfolk Island, December 8, 1856

> *A resort of whaleships from the early 1800's, Norfolk Island (between New Zealand and Australia on the whaler's routes) was at one time the home of descendants of the* Bounty *mutineers, removed there by the British government when Pitcairn Island became overpopulated. Original drawing from ship's log is in the possession of the Nantucket Whaling Museum.*

PART ONE

The American Whaleman
Is Born

chapter i

WHALING ALONGSHORE

There is the green pasture where our children's children will go for their bread.

—Old Nantucket Saying

THE ONCE EXTENSIVE and important industry known as the American whale fishery had its beginnings in the early days of the English colonies along the New England coast. It attained its greatest growth in the eighteenth and nineteenth centuries which saw the birth and expansion of our nation. It passed into oblivion with the early years of our own twentieth century.

The first whale catchers in the Americas were the Indians. Perhaps the earliest description of the aborigines' method of capturing the whale, was given by Captain George Waymouth, the English navigator, in 1605:

One especial thing is their manner of killing the whale which they call a powdare; and will describe his form; how he bloweth up the water; and that he is twelve fathoms long [about 70 feet]; that they go in company of their king with a multitude of their boats; and strike him with a bone made in fashion of a harping iron fastened to a rope; which they make great and strong of bark of trees, which they veer out after him; then all their boats come about him as he riseth above water, with their arrows they shoot him to death; when they have killed him and dragged him to shore, they call all their chief lords together and sing a song of joy; and those chief lords, whom they call sagamores, divide the spoil and give to every man a share, which pieces are distributed, they hang up about their

15

houses for provisions; and when they boil them they blow off the fat and put their pease, maize and other pulse which they eat.[1]

Nine years later in 1614, the redoubtable Captain John Smith reported sighting large numbers of whales cruising along the New England coast.[2] In 1635, Richard Mather wrote that he had seen "mighty whales spewing up water in the air like the smoke of a chimney, and making the sea about them white and hoary."[3]

In a narrative attributed to a certain Mount, printed in the nineteenth book of *Purchas: His Pilgrimes,* is a most interesting passage concerning the *Mayflower,* then anchored in Cape Cod Bay in a "harbour wherein a thousand sail of ships may ride safely,"[4] a few days before the eventful disembarking at Plymouth in November 1620. The passage reads:

> And every day we saw whales plying hard by us; of which in that place, if we had instruments and means to take them we might make a very rich return, which to our grief we wanted. Our master and his mate, and others experienced in fishing, professed we might make three or four thousand pounds worth of oil. They preferred it before Greenland whale-fishing, and purpose the next winter to fish for whale here.[5]

Although the Indian probably taught the white settlers the art of harassing a stranded whale, it does not follow that his primitive methods were always used thereafter. The whale fishery was an established craft in Europe long before the first settlers came to America, and there was certainly considerable knowledge among these white men as to the catching of whales.

Scammon's belief that the colonists followed the Indian method up to the early 1700's cannot be sustained as *Purchas* gives an account of English lines being used on "harping irons" as early as 1613.[6] It is possible, however, that the use of drags or "droges"—thick boards or blocks of wood bent on the whale lines and tossed into the sea to serve as a check to the whale's progress—were adapted from the Indians.

Perhaps the Indians' greatest contribution, following their first instructions to the settlers in driving ashore or killing a stranded whale, was in their capacity as whalemen. They served as lookouts atop a hill or on a spar set up along the shore, and as crewmen in a whaleboat. In confirming a law regarding employment of Indians, passed

by the town of Southampton in 1672, Governor Lovelace further stipulated: ". . . that whosoever shall Hire an Indyan to go a-whaling, shall
not give him for his Hire above one Trucking Cloath, Coat, for each
whale hee and his Company shall kill, or halfe the Blubber, without
the Whale Bone under a Penalty herein exprest: Upon Consideration
had there upon, I have thought good to allow of the said Order, and
do hereby Confirm the same. . . ." [7]

Zaccheus Macy, the Nantucket Quaker boatbuilder and bonesetter,
one of the earliest of the island's historians, tells a significant story of
the settlers and the island Indians. "It happened once," he wrote,
"when there were about thirty boats about six miles from shore, that
the wind came around to the northward, and blew with great violence,
attended with snow. The men all rowed hard, but made little headway. In one of the boats were four Indians and two white men. An
old Indian in the head of the boat, perceiving that the crew began to
be disheartened, spoke out loud in his own tongue and said . . . 'Pull
ahead with courage; do not be disheartened; we shall not be lost now;
there are too many Englishmen to be lost now.' His speaking in this
manner gave the crew new courage. They soon perceived that they
made headway, and after a long rowing they got safe on shore." [8]

Just how many American Indians shared in the rise of the industry,
as members of boat crews or on whaling vessels, will probably never
be known. But the red men from Long Island, Cape Cod, Martha's
Vineyard and Nantucket made good whalemen. Melville's *Moby Dick*
has immortalized the Gay Head Indian. Obed Macy is good authority
for stating in his *History of Nantucket* that the native aborigines soon
became experienced whalemen, conversant with all the details of the
business. [9]

Macy also relates that the first whale taken at Nantucket, was called
a "scrag," which had come into the harbor and was there three days
before the settlers (only recently arrived on the island) devised a harpoon, wrought by one skilled in blacksmithing, and attacked and
killed the whale. [10] Such an incident indicates that the commonly held
opinion that the white man emulated the native Indian methods of
attacking and capturing Leviathan is wrong and that the Indian had
to learn the European way of approaching and killing the whale.

The early records of Massachusetts reveal that the first whales "cut in" for their oil by the colonists were drift whales, already dead. After whales were discovered more or less stranded in shoal water they were pursued and killed, and their oil and bone utilized. Among early colonial laws were those which gave one third of such whales to their finder, one third to the town, and the remaining third to the church.

In 1688, Secretary Edward Randolph, one of the King's Commissioners sent to investigate economic conditions in the colonies, wrote home from Massachusetts Bay: "New Plymouth Colony have great profit by whale killing. I believe it will be one of our best returns, now beaver and peltry fale us." [11] This same colony in 1690 appointed "Inspectors of Whales" for the "prevention of suits by whalers." The rules included four regulations for the viewing and recording of whales found cast ashore, as well as for their proper disposition and, in the case of a whale found ashore, warned against "cutting or defacing a whale before being viewed." [12]

Boston was the chief trading center for whale oil in those times. According to the Massachusetts State Archives, the sloops *Mary* and *Society,* Captain Richard Gardner, and *Dolphin,* Captain Peter Coffin, were registered as of Nantucket in 1698.[13]

The settlers on Long Island brought their customs and laws with them when they left Massachusetts Bay, but they went further and developed the first organized system for taking whales sighted alongshore. In 1644, they ordered townships divided into four patrols of eleven persons each. Two at a time were selected for cutting up each whale taken. Cutters received double share, older inhabitants received one share. It was later decreed that whoever discovered a stranded whale should be rewarded with five shillings—but no reward came to the man sighting a beached whale on Sunday.[14]

Southampton had been settled in 1640 by colonists from Lynn in the Massachusetts Bay Colony and the settlers were quick to take advantage of the numerous whales which appeared off the Long Island ocean beaches. The early records of both Southampton and Easthampton reveal the growing importance of the whale-oil trade, and the custom of embarking on "boat-expeditions" which camped on shore at night, was introduced by 1650.

In a petition presented to the Court at Whitehall in 1672, the towns of Southampton, Easthampton and Southwold, set forth that "they had spent much time and pains, and the greatest part of their estates, in settling the trade of whale-fishing in the adjacent seas, having endeavored it alone these twenty years but could not bring it to any perfection till within these 2 or 3 yeares last past. . . ." This would indicate that the industry in this section began about 1650. The petition further stated that the Dutch, then in control at New York, "threaten to cut down their timber which is but little they have to Casks for oyle. . . ."[15]

The trade in oil from Long Island was with Boston and Connecticut, and this was always a source of trouble to the New York Colony authorities. Governor Lovelace, of New York, appointed two commissioners to investigate the taking of drift whales without proper report,[16] and it is probable that many captors decided not to share their whale with the authorities. Certain it is that the eastern Long Islanders were closer to the Connecticut folk than to the New York government.

It is significant, also, that when the Dutch secured control of New York again, from July 1673 to November 1874, they received a petition from the towns of Southampton, Easthampton, Southwold, Seatoocock and Huntington with ten requests relating to local government. The only item not granted was the one requesting: "That there be free liberty granted ye 5 towns aforesaid for procuring from any of ye united Colonies (without molestation on either side:) warpes, irons, or any other necessaries for ye comfortable carring on the whale design."[17]

Howell, in his *History of Southampton,* questions why the Dutch chose to snub the request of the provision for a "few whale-irons and necessary tackle for capturing the whales which happened along the coast."[18] The answer becomes clear when it is remembered that the English and Dutch were the chief rivals in the European whale fishery, and the Dutch were loath to encourage further rivalry from the English colonial settlements.

An interesting chapter in Long Island history resulted from the attempt of the ambitious Governor Robert Hunter, in the early 1700's, to secure revenue from the whalemen of the east end by decreeing that one twentieth of all oil and bone taken be delivered to him in New York. The doughty whaleman-citizen, Samuel Mulford, chosen to represent the communities and inspired by the hereditary rights of Englishmen, fought the Royal Governor through the colonial Assembly, the High Court, and even to the London Privy Council chambers. Eventually, he secured the rights of the settlers to be "governed by the Constitution of English Government." It is a remarkable story and entirely prophetic.[19]

The success of expeditions alongshore influenced the Nantucketers to undertake whaling as a business. Both Obed Macy and Alexander Starbuck, historians of whaling, believe it was in furtherance of this plan that, in 1672, a certain James Lopar was invited to "Engage to carry on a design of Whale Catching on the Island of Nantucket, that is the said James, Engaged to be a third in all respects, and some of the Town Engage Also to carry on the other two thirds with him in like manner." A company was formed and Lopar granted ten acres of land, cattle and sheep pasturage, provided he "follow the Trade of Whaling on the Island two years in all the season thereof. . . ."[20]

That Lopar ever followed through with the bargain is doubtful. The Nantucketers continued anxious to get the best instruction in whaling which they could obtain and so, in 1690, invited Ichabod Paddock of Cape Cod to settle among them and instruct them in the best manner of killing whales and extracting oils. As the Paddock name soon became identified with the island, and as Zaccheus Macy states that the Cape Codder did accept the invitation, there is good reason for believing the islanders secured an excellent and experienced whaleman as a teacher and townsman.[21]

De Crèvecoeur, during a visit to Nantucket recorded (though considerably later) the type of shore-station which no doubt had typified the early whaling lookouts all along the New England coast:

> The South side of the Island [Nantucket] was divided into four equal parts, and each part was assigned to a company of six, which, though much separated, still carried on their business in common! In the middle of this distance they erected a mast, provided with a sufficient number of rounds, and near it they built a temporary hut where five of their assistants lived, whilst the sixth from his high station carefully looked toward the sea in order to observe the spouting of whales.[22]

After the capture, the whale's body was towed to the beach where a "crab," or shore winch, was set into operation, so that the blubber would be "cut in" and stripped from the body, then boiled, or "tryed out," in large iron pots ashore. For years the shore tryworks were used. The first cruises off the shoals resulted in the blubber being cut from the whale, put into casks and brought home for trying out the oil.

The Nantucket town records of March 1694, reveal that a local by-law prescribed a penalty for cutting any wood (cedar) unless it was "for whale bots or the like."

By such diligent pursuit of whaling in season and the cod fishery, Nantucketers soon made a speedy advance as a town and a port.

In the late decade of the old century and the first years of the 1700's, the Nantucket fleet grew rapidly, revealing the growing importance of the whaling industry as it gradually centered at Nantucket and Dartmouth.

Only scattered accounts still exist to give fragmentary statements of these early days of pioneer whaling in America. Some of these came from Salem and Philadelphia, as well as from Nantucket and Martha's Vineyard.

Salem had become interested in whaling in the early years of the industry.

Felt, in his *Annals of Salem,* mentions a petition of James Lopar in 1688, in which he asked the colonial government of Massachusetts for a patent for making oil. In this petition he claims to have been engaged in the whale fishery for twenty-two years.[23]

According to a letter written in 1690 by a Major John Higginson to his brother in the East Indies, Salem had been exporting "whale and other fish oil and whale bone." And in another letter, Higginson stated: "In the year 1689, when this war [French and Indian War] first broke out, I had attained a competent estate, being as much concerned in the fishing trade as most of my neighbors, but since that time have met with considerable losses . . . of sixty-odd ketches . . . about six are left." [24] Salem did not follow up its bay whaling, but after a long lapse did engage in deep-sea whaling from 1821 to 1840.

Two Salem merchants "concerned in severall whale voyages," in

March 1692, protested the "unjust dealing" of the inhabitants of certain Cape Cod ports when two whales (harpooned by the Salem men, and which temporarily escaped the final killing), were afterwards "unjustly detained" by the Cape men who found them, despite the telltale evidence of harpoon, warp, etc.[25]

The *Boston Gazette* of May 11, 1742, stated:

> Philadelphia, April 19—The beginning of April came ashore. . . . eastward of Cape May a dead whale about 4½ foot bone, with a hole in her supposed to have been made by an iron. And about the middle of the month, another about 40 miles of the Cape, with 2 or 3 irons in her, a valuable fish. . . . This is mentioned that the persons who struck the said whales and have right to them, may know where to make their claims.

Although in the same advantageous position off the coast, the people of Martha's Vineyard did not take up the whale fishery in the same progressive manner as the Nantucketers. This was not wholly strange. On the Vineyard, the rich soil supported farming which Nantucket could not match, and so the Vineyarders were not so completely dependent on the sea as were the Nantucketers.

However, both had similar experiences in shore whaling, with the Vineyarders taking whales several years before Nantucket was settled. Under date of April 13, 1653, it was ordered by the Edgartown authorities that whales were "to be cut up freely, four men at one time and four men at another, and so every whale, beginning at the east end of the Town." [26] One Indian sachem in selling his land reserved the right to "four spans around the middle of every whale that comes upon the shore." [27] Other records show the prevalence of shore whaling at the Vineyard, and its inhabitants early shared in the marketing of the oil. Lookouts and tryhouses became a part of the landscape; proprietors transferred rights "of fish and whale" with their deeds to land.

Apparently, the first Vineyard whaler of note was John Butler. For some time prior to 1700, he carried on whaling in the shoals and kept his tryhouse busy. An Edgartown record shows him to have made several catches between 1702-03.[28] But the people of the island as a whole were slow to follow the inspiring example of the Nantucketers and organize a fleet of deep-sea whalers. In fact, it was in 1738 that

Captain Joseph Chase, of Nantucket, moved to Edgartown and with his sloop, the *Diamond,* went whaling off in "ye deep." [29] A wharf and tryhouse were erected. But Starbuck states this was not successful and that similar discouraging results followed when James Claghorn, in 1741, and John Harper, in 1742, attempted to develop the industry there.

But while there were comparatively few Vineyard whaling sloops in those early days, compared with Nantucket and Dartmouth, there were many Vineyard men in the crews of sloops from neighboring ports. Among the Vineyard captains who took out vessels (probably from Edgartown) was Captain Peter Pease. As master of the *Susanna* and *Lydia,* he made voyages from the Grand Banks to the West Indies. One of his entries, as of 1763, records him at Barbados, where he was forced to heave-to at the harbor entrance. A shot from the fort crossed his bow "for not dousing his foresail at the sight of the King's colors. Next morning went to the Captain of the fort to make restitution for the shot, and to pay the anchor money." [30]

From the log of the *Betsy,* of Dartmouth, on the Grand Banks in 1761, at least two Vineyarders are identified among the Yankee whalemen "spoken." These were Peter Pease and Shubael Dunham, the latter of Tisbury. But what they lacked in ships and warehouses, the Vineyarders made up in men, for the island, like Nantucket, was a nursery of seamen. And in the early years of the next century, Edgartown, or Old-Town as it was affectionately known, became a valuable port of clearance and entry for those Nantucket whaleships, deep-laden, which could not get over the shoal or bar at their home-harbor entrance.

But to return to the beginnings of the eighteenth century. The transition from shore whaling to organized sea voyages was gradual but steady. These ventures into deep-sea voyaging became profitable particularly to the little colony of Englishmen on the Island of Nantucket, for here the embryo whalemen were geographically situated as if on a mother-ship anchored in the Atlantic.

chapter ii

〰〰〰

THE WHALEMAN SAILS OUT
INTO "YE DEEP"

The Spermacetti Whale found by the Nantucketers, is an
active, fierce animal, and requires vast address and boldness
in the fishermen.

—Thomas Jefferson

B Y THE EARLY 1700's whalers at Nantucket were fitting out their
sloops for voyages beyond the shoals, some forty to fifty miles
off their island coast, out of sight of land. From its strategic position
in the Atlantic and from the character of its people, Nantucket was
soon to become the forerunner of American whaling. The success of
this persevering settlement brought impetus to the industry and finally gave the islanders the unchallenged leadership. Thus, the history
of American whaling during the eighteenth century is practically the
history of the little colony of whalemen on Nantucket Island.

For half a century after the first English families moved from Salis-
bury and Newbury in Massachusetts Bay Colony (after 1659), the
Nantucket settlement had no established religion. Then, through the
leadership of Mary Coffin Starbuck (the wife of a pioneer whaleman),
the majority of islanders became members of the Society of Friends.
There is something remarkably symbolic in this conversion. It was as
if the islanders, creating as they were the headquarters for American
deep-sea whaling, found in the Quaker faith the perfect union of the
elements of living.

24

Exposed to the dangers of the most hazardous of occupations, it was inevitable that tragedy should strike at some Nantucket homes. In the records of the State House at Boston is a petition from Dinah Coffin, setting forth that "her husband, Elisha Coffin, did on the 27th day of April, *Anno Dom, 1722,* Sail from sd Island of Nantucket in a sloop; on a whaling trip, intending to return in a month or six weeks at most, and instantly a hard and dismal Storm followed; which in all probability swallowed him and those with him up, for they were never heard of." [1] Daily confronting the alternate smiles and frowns of sea and wind they found in the religion of the Friends both a challenge and a comfort.[2]

The fact that the sea was now providing a harvest beyond that to be reaped from the island's sandy soil soon made whaling the sole business of the Nantucketers. The combination of sea, the Quaker religion and whaling gradually created a race of mariners who were to write an American saga unequaled in our maritime history.

When the little settlement called Sherburne, built around the limited harbor at Capaum Pond on the bay side of the island, was removed to a new site beside the "Great Harbor," American deep-sea whaling gradually developed. Here, wharves, warehouses, refineries, and cooper shops soon grew up along the waterfront.

Other seaports did not grasp the opportunity so eagerly accepted by the Nantucketers owing, no doubt, to their pursuit of the cod and mackerel fisheries and to other trades. The islanders became whalemen or adopted trades allied with the industry. Thus whaling became a community enterprise—the riggers, coopers, sailmakers, boatbuilders, blacksmiths, millers and farmers on shore; the shipmasters, steersmen, forecastle hands and shipkeepers at sea. By 1723, the large Straight Wharf in Nantucket Harbor had become the focal point of the industry.[3]

In Europe the Dutch fleet diminished because of the scarcity of whales in Arctic seas off Spitzbergen, and the British fleet also fell off to an alarming degree. Hence, the London market for oil offered rich rewards for colonial whaling. It spurred the American whalers to voyages farther off-shore. As larger sloops were built—generally of sixty to seventy tons burden—courses were laid across Nantucket South Shoal, thence east to Georges Banks, thence to the Gulf Stream.

It was significant that, as Scoresby wrote, "While the subjects of Great Britain performed a voyage so distant and practised arduous operations in the polar regions, the colonists in America had the advantage of conducting the fishery more immediately at home. Hence, we find many notices of their successful labors in this speculation." [4]

Early records show that Benjamin Alford, of Boston, in April 1678, was allowed clearance for a sloop sailing from the "East End of Long Island with her loading of Whale Oyle and whalebone." [5] This was probably one of the first of such shipments to the mother country.

Shore whaling and sea whaling were carried on in conjunction on Nantucket until the mid-1700's. In 1726 shore whaling reached its peak with eighty-six whales taken that year along island shores. Although the bulk of the oil was shipped to Boston, Nantucketers soon realized the need for direct trade with the London market, and in 1720 the ship *Hanover,* Captain Chadder, took a cargo of oil from the island to Britain. The size of the whaling sloops increased from the twenty-five-ton craft of 1690 to 118-ton vessels in 1732, in which year Isaac Myrick built a large vessel on Nantucket. By 1730 the island had twenty-five whaling craft in its fleet and Holmes records the arrival in England of "154 tons of train and whale-oil and 9,200 lbs of bone" which reveals the growing importance of the American whalers. [6]

On Cape Cod, sloops from the towns of Eastham, Provincetown and Chatham pursued the whale fishery with some success. Under date of March 20, 1727, the *Boston News-Letter* says:

> We hear from the Towne of the Cape that the Whale-Fishery among them had failed much this Winter, as it has done for several Winters past, but having found a way of going to Sea Upon that Business, and having had much Success in it, they are now fitting out several Vessels to sail with all Expedition upon that dangerous design this Spring, more (its tho't) than have ever been sent out from among them.

The Long Islanders, first organizers of shore whaling, also went into the off-shore business but not to the extent of the Nantucketers of this early period. Sag Harbor, settled around 1730, soon became the center for sea whaling out of Long Island. Starbuck believed this was done prior to 1760. In that year, three sloops were fitted out by Joseph Conkling, John Foster and others. They were named *Goodluck, Dolphin* and *Success,* and their cruising ground was off soundings in 36° north latitude, between Nantucket Shoals and Bermuda. However, the industry was not extensive enough to rival the Massachusetts ports and it was not until the early 1830's that Sag Harbor actually entered the competitive field with a large whaling fleet.

In 1731, Rhode Island's Assembly authorized a bounty of five shillings for every barrel of whale oil, one penny a pound for bone, and five shillings a quintal of codfish brought into the colony in Rhode Island vessels. The first deep-sea whaler from this colony was the *Pelican,* under Captain Benjamin Thurston, which craft arrived at Newport in 1733 with 114 barrels of oil and two hundred pounds of bone.[7]

In 1712, an event had occurred which was to have a profound and lasting influence on the entire history of the whale fishery. Captain Christopher Hussey, on a whaling voyage in Nantucket South Shoals, was blown far out to sea by a strong gale and when the storm had cleared he sighted a school of whales.[8]

Tradition has it that when Captain Hussey sighted these whales he was surprised by the fact that the creatures had a single bushy spout, which puffed into the air, and then arched forward, instead of having the characteristic forked spout of the familiar right whale. Prompt pursuit and killing of the whale revealed him to be one of that mysterious species known as the "spermaceti." Here was, indeed, the aristocrat of all whales.

This was not the first living sperm whale known to Nantucketers or to other colonists, for that matter. Obed Macy records that early in Nantucket's history a sperm whale was found on the southwestern shore of the island, causing considerable excitement and not a little controversy over its rightful claimants. Not only did its oil prove of exceptional quality but it was discovered, with pardonable wonder, that instead of slabs of whalebone in its mouth, the sperm had a long underjaw with great teeth which fitted into sockets in its tremendous head.

Further it was discovered that in this bulky head was concealed a real treasure—a reservoir of pure spermaceti—contained in the tubular "case," averaging two feet in diameter, about six feet deep. It was at first supposed that this case yielded oil which had medicinal qualities, and Macy states that the credulity of the people was such that the oil was esteemed to be worth its weight in silver.[9]

The commercial value of this sperm oil left nothing to conjecture. It was the best lighting fluid yet discovered. The "head-matter" from the case, which became a waxy substance when exposed to the air, made the finest of candles. The sperm candle was literally a jewel of light.

The manufacture of spermaceti candles became in time a highly important industry. A secret process was used in the manufacture. Benjamin Crabb, of Rehoboth, Rhode Island, established the industry in 1749 and the next year was granted the exclusive right to manufacture the candles in Massachusetts Colony if he would "teach and instruct some of the inhabitants of this province his Art Aforesaid." In 1753 Obadiah Brown, of Providence, engaged Crabb to work for him. Less than a decade later, Brown, Moses Lopez, Collins & Rivera and other New England merchants attempted to establish a monopoly by "cornering" the market for "head-matter" under the name of the United Company of Spermaceti Chandlers. Of course, the chief supply came from the whalers of Nantucket, and as Joseph and William Rotch, the leading merchants there, did not join the enterprise, trouble developed among the factors or agents bidding for the oil. This is best shown by a letter to Lopez at Newport, in which Henry Lloyd of Boston wrote:

> I must caution you against being to nice and critical with the Nantucket men, for I can assure you that nothing can be done with them in that case; the only way is to make the best terms you can with them, whenever you have occasion to purchase; but 'tis in vain to go to them with any measures they don't like.[10]

The secret of the manufacturing process was eventually discovered by merchants at Nantucket and New Bedford, and candle-houses were established at these American whaling centers before the Revolution.

Captain Kit Hussey's taking of the sperm whale from a school of them at sea proved that this type was not such a rarity as was supposed.

The spermaceti's spout was looked for and other island whalemen killed them and brought in rich cargoes.

And now the Nantucketers became the outstanding specialists among the American whalemen. They sought the sperm whale in the Gulf Stream, soon to seek him farther, and later to concentrate almost entirely upon this pursuit until they had relentlessly followed him into the world's most distant seas.

Thus, they founded a great American industry, the most hazardous of any before or since—deep-sea whaling.

chapter iii

~~~

"A PEOPLE STILL IN THE GRISTLE
AND NOT HARDENED INTO MANHOOD"

> *The whaling business is peculiarly an ocean life. The sea,
> to mariners . . . is but a highway . . . but to the whaler it
> is his field of labor. . . .*
> —Obed Macy, *History of Nantucket* [1]

I T DID NOT take many voyages to London to convince the colonial
whale-oil merchants that here was their strongest market. At Nantucket in particular this trade, built up slowly and with true Quaker
cautiousness, brought a steady success. It was early found that return
cargoes of iron ore, hemp, sailcloth and other goods provided important additions to the colonial market, as well as supplying necessary
articles for home manufacture. Profits were not allowed to become
dormant capital; the islanders invested in themselves by building
larger sloops and brigantines.

Already the pioneering instinct of these Nantucket whalemen was
revealing itself. Soon vessels from other ports ventured out into the
"green pastures" of Nantucket South Shoals. Thereupon, with a rest-
less energy which was to characterize them always, the Nantucket
whalemen sailed south along the fringes of the Gulf Stream. Next
they voyaged to the Nova Scotian waters, on to the Grand Banks and
the Strait of Belle Isle. This was the beginning of a pattern closely
adhered to during the next century—the Nantucket pioneers discover-

ing new whaling grounds and their contemporaries following hard in their wake.

Through their combination of shore whaling and sea whaling the Nantucketers were able steadily to increase their fleet. By 1740, some fifty stout sloops of forty to fifty tons burden were bringing in 4,700 barrels of oil valued at about $25,000 to the island so securely situated out in "ye deep." The islanders had sailed far to the north, bringing home reports of whales in such old grounds as the Gulf of St. Lawrence and the Grand Banks, and then revealing that new grounds had been discovered about 1738 in the Strait of Belle Isle, between Labrador and Newfoundland. The *Nightingale,* of Nantucket, Captain Seth Folger, was in the Strait of Belle Isle from April 4 to August 9, 1738.

These colonial sea-hunters began to adopt new methods in the old procedure of capturing and killing the whale. It now became customary to man two boats to each sloop. Rowing until within striking distance, the harpooner threw his "harping-iron" like a javelin into the quarry. "This requires both strength and dexterity," records a contemporary account, "in order to make the wound deep enough and in the most proper place." [2]

When the whale sounded or plunged off on a wild dash for freedom, it was often necessary to make the line of the second boat fast to that of the first. Often eight hundred feet of line would be in use at one time. As the whale rose to the surface the attacking boat approached close enough to allow the officer to thrust the long, razor-edged lance into its vitals. "He spouts out streams of blood," recounted a writer, "and rages most furiously, beating the sea with his tail till it is all of a foam, and the noise of it, may be heard at a great distance, till, having lost his strength, he turns on one side and expires."

The American whaleman was still catching right whales and humpbacks, (a species of whalebone whales) as well as the newly found spermaceti. These first American deep-sea whaling vessels (particularly the Nantucket craft) were manned by a smaller crew than British or Dutch whalers. They were mostly sloops, evolved in the colonies from the single-masted Dutch sloops of the seventeenth century, built for the open sea, between forty and fifty feet long, about fifteen feet beam and drawing six feet of water fully loaded. A square-topsail was a characteristic of these fore-and-aft rigged vessels. Mungo Murray's *Naval Architecture* shows the sturdy lines of these sloops with the tiller, after-cabin-companion, fore-scuttle and barrel windlass abaft the bowsprit bitts as other features.[3]

Obed Macy states these sloops were of about fifty tons to ninety tons burden.[4] Felt's *Annals of Salem* mentions that the sloops carried two whaleboats and thirteen men;[5] the log of the *Phebe,* of Nantucket, in 1750, states the crew was composed of thirteen hands. An account in the *Boston News-Letter* of 1730 relates a whaleboat crew consisted of "a steersmen, a Harpineer, and Four Oarmen."

Important changes took place in the method of trying out a whale. At first it had been the custom after killing the whale at sea to cut off his blubber and pack it into casks, fetching it home for trying out the oil for the refining process. Now brick fireplaces with great iron pots contained therein were set up on board ship, and the whole structure was called the tryworks.[6] These with the two boats were to be the distinguishing mark of a whaler's deck henceforth. The implements for whaling, patterned upon the European model, were changed to an American design.

The old haunts of the European whalemen were being invaded by the Americans. Steadily pushing their way up the coast, the Nantucketers led the fleet into Davis Strait in the early 1730's. A contemporary newssheet shows that among the Boston custom house clearances were several whalemen to the Greenland Grounds. These ships sailed in March or April, returning from September to November. As the Dutch and British rivals sailed into these seas they probably viewed with little alarm these colonial newcomers—not realizing that this was the isolated vanguard of a new and greater breed of whalemen.

In the logbook of the sloop *Seaflower,* Captain Christopher Coffin, is found an excellent recounting of a typical early whaling voyage of the New Englanders to the Arctic.[7] The *Seaflower* sailed from Nantucket June 2, 1752, keeping company with Benjamin Bunker, who soon dropped out of sight in the fog. ". . . We blowed our shell [conch shell] and found him again." On the fourteenth of June, the logkeeper recorded:

These 24 hours a mighty clear N.W. wind in the afternoon and pretty cold in the night—Calm—We sounded in the afternoon and found about 60 fathoms. About 8 o'clock in the morning we saw an Icy Island at first appearance like a Vessel but drawing nigher it appeared in a triangular form and peaked to the very top and white. We Likewise saw two more different shapes. At 12 o'clock sounded and found no Bottom.

The *Seaflower*'s boat crew had a narrow escape one morning. A boat had been launched and was attacking a cow whale and her "yearling," the latter being struck first and killed. Then follows:

At the yearling's side the cow always keeps and presently she was struck likewise. . . . In her flurry she came at our boat and furiously ran over us and overset us and made a miserable wreck of our boat in a moment. A wonder it was we all had our lives spared, tho' the whale had divers warps over her and divers of us were sadly puzzled under water. Yet we were all taken up well and not one hurt, Praise the Lord for his mercies & for his wonderful works to the Children of Men.

Steering north-northeast, the *Seaflower* came up to the land on June 11, but due to a storm, wherein "it rained, thundered and lightened, and was exceeding thick and a bad sea" she stood offshore. Eventually they sighted the Newfoundland shore at the Bay of Bulls and stood alongshore. Running by Cape St. Frances, Captain Coffin crossed Trinity Bay and got into Cataline Harbor, where the Nantucketers "unloaded and ballassed" the sloop. The next stopping place was called "Misketo Cove," and here there was trouble.

. . . The Irishmen cursed us at high rate for they Hate the Whalemen in this Harbour. Here we lay till June 27th, and in that Space of time Rose many an oath of the Paddies & bogtrotters they swearing we should not cut up one whale in the Harbour. But, however, we cut up one or two & then on the aforesaid 27th of June they raised a mob in the evening. (One Pike, an Irishman who called himself Captain of the Harbour, being the Chief Head) and fired upon us but through mercy Hurt no man: So we towed our Vessels out of the Harbour 6 or 7 Sail of us & lay off in the Bay that night & on the next went to Western Bay.

A more sustained effort to reach across the "Western Ocean" (the northern Atlantic), toward new whaling grounds was checked by the wars with France and Spain, between 1741 and 1765, which brought constant menace of capture to the colonial whalemen.

That some should suffer the fate of wartime was, however, certain, and the *Boston News-Letter* in 1744 notes that Captain Rotch, of Nantucket, had arrived in a Cape vessel, reporting the loss of his sloop on a voyage from Nantucket to Boston. A French privateer had chased Captain Rotch inshore at Cape Cod, and he escaped in the sloop's boat with his crew and a few personal belongings, abandoning a cargo of 330 barrels of oil in his vessel. The Frenchman, who displayed English colors in attempts to trick her quarry, afterwards appeared off Nantucket and landed some prisoners taken out of another island craft captured a few days before.[8]

To counteract the effect of these wars the British Parliament in 1748 passed an Act to encourage the whale fishery. Bounties to all ships engaged in whaling during the war were granted, and seamen in the Greenland fishery were exempted from impressment into the naval service. Besides offering premiums on inspections of masts, yards, bowsprits, tar, pitch, duties on foreign-made sailcloth were remitted to whalers. This Act of 1748 also granted a second bounty of twenty shillings per ton for whaling vessels. All colonial whaling craft had to remain in the Greenland fishery from May through August (unless filling sooner) to be eligible for this bounty. Foreign Protestants serving as Greenland whalemen for two years were to be treated as natives.[9]

By 1748 American whaling had become a powerful factor in colonial trade. It was an established industry, and Nantucket, with its fleet of sixty sail, represented the very heart of the enterprise, its annual catch valued at $96,000.

Thomas Hutchinson, Royal Governor of Massachusetts (1771-74), wrote in his *History of Massachusetts* that the increase in the consumption of oil by lamps as well as "divers manufacturies" in Europe has been no small encouragement to the colonial whale fishery. "The flourishing state of the island of Nantucket must be attributed to it," he stated. "The cod and whale fishery, being the principal source of our returns to Great Britain, are therefore worthy not only of provincial but national attention."[10]

And what of these "colonials" who had emerged from their roles as settlers of a new land to become whalemen? No longer were they regarded as mere chasers of whales which had been trapped in shallow waters. They were now the organizers of an important native industry.

In the ship journals of these early whalemen is found that rugged quality which so marked them as true men of the sea. Written in varied hands, each sentence laboriously scrawled with little or no punctuation, these logbooks are not only fascinating for the stark simplicity of their record but for the delineation of the personality of their writers.

A few early sea journals or logbooks fortunately remain to illustrate the times and the type of these men. One of these—perhaps the earliest known—is still in its Nantucket home port. It was kept from 1751 to 1760 by Peleg Folger, of Nantucket, whose first voyage was in the sloop *Grampus,* under Captain Benjamin Bunker.[11]

The sloop sailed from Nantucket early in 1751. There is left in the reader's mind little doubt as to the kind of man Peleg Folger was and of the worth of his log. He prefaced the record as follows:

> Many People who keep Journals at Sea fill them up with some trifles or other. My part I purpose in the following sheets, not to keep overstrict history of every trifling occurrence that happens, only now and then of Some particular affair; and to fill up the rest with subjects either mathematical, theological, Historical, Philosophical, or poetical, or anything else that best suits mine inclination. P. F.

And he adds, for good measure:

> *Qui docet indotoc, licet indoctissimus esset, Ille quoc, breve, ceteria doctior esse Quest.*

which, in literal translation, means: "He who teaches the unlearned may be most unlearned, although he is only a little more learned than the others."

Young Peleg, for he was scarcely eighteen at the time he began his journal, has left us a concise record of a typical Nantucket whaleman "not yet hardened into manhood," and his manuscript is as pithy and revealing as any logbook since written. He continues:

> May 3, 1751—This day we have killed a Spermaceti Whale which is the first we have killed this our first trip, having now been out

above three weeks, for we took our Departure from our Good Isle of Nantucket near about the tenth as near as I can Remember.

And a few days later, he observed:

> May 12—1st day of the week: This Day we are in latitude 38°–27′; having Killed a Blackfish this day. In the morning we Spyed a Sail and Drew up with her but the Clown would not Speak with us. Steering off about SE.

If there was danger from the very business of whaling there was also danger in cruising through the shoals, perilous to navigation at all times. How carefully approaches to the coast were recorded for future use may be noted by reading another entry in Folger's log of *Grampus,* as follows:

> June 18th—Last night at 8 o'clock we had 34 fathoms depth of water, fine Black and white sand; so we kept her N.W. under a Balanc'd Mainsail and Gib till 12 o'clock; then Sounded and found 22 fathoms; So we kept our Luff W by N. till we found 16 fathoms: So we kept her in North till we made Nantucket. We found ourselves to have Been to the Eastward of the South Shoal. As we run Westward we Shoaled our water till we got by the South Shoal to the Westward: so then deepened our water; To the Eastward of South Shoal we found for most part Black and White Sand etc; So now we are to the Southward of Noppodeer [Nobadeer—south shore of Nantucket Island] & hope to Be at our Bar before Sunset: So I hope we Shall Have a good time (*Deo Volente et adjuvante*).

Many of the expressions used by this whaleman-philosopher, who liked so much to quote his Latin, existed among these men of the sea for a century or more. When whaleships sighted each other at sea, they changed courses so as to meet and "speak" each other. These sea conferences might mean a series of hailings across the crested intervening sea, or promptly heaving to and boarding one another for an exchange of news and experiences—this was called a "gam." On another voyage, this time in the *Phebe,* of Nantucket, in July 1751, Peleg Folger recorded: [12]

> July 3—Spoke with Christopher Coffin and our mate Reuben Folger: We had a good breakfast upon meat and Doboys & we are all merry together.

No doubt, in becoming "merry" the rum flowed a little more freely than usual. At any rate, Friend Peleg celebrated the occasion well enough and his observation for the following day is both droll and comforting:

> July 4—Nothing very remarkable these 24 hours, only I like a Dunce forgot myself and rubbed out my Knots, Courses and Winds off the Logbook before I had Set them down on my Reckoning. However, I had cast up my Difference of Lat and Long, So I have not lost my reckoning, yet this was a very careless trick.

He continued with varied entries and expressed the hope that the *Phebe* could get into 36° of latitude to get some sperm whales. This reveals that the sloop was cruising south into the Gulf Stream rather than heading north toward Newfoundland and the privateer-infested seas off Nova Scotia and the Gulf of St. Lawrence. The journal continues:

> July 8—Nothing remarkable these 24 hours only 'tis very hot and no whales to be seen: Much Toil and Labor mortal man is forc'd to Endure & little Profit to be Got by it, & if one grows rich, he often dies as it were in the beginning of his Prosperity: the whole World's a cheat (the Saying is) & he is a fool that hath not a Hand in it: Let all Say as they will, Honesty is the best policy, when all is said that can be said, or done that can be done.

But the gloom engendered from little success and from tumbling about at a considerable distance from home, soon gave way to the excitement of the chase. It was a week before Peleg took up his pen again, and he tells it thus:

> July 14—I have not had time to continue my Journal any longer. Since we have had more business than Common to do, for since July 9th we have killed 2 Spermaceties: So now we have 4 whales. Now for Home, Boys, for we have 70 bbls. in our Hold.

Peleg Folger's next voyage was in the sloop *Mary,* under Captain Richard Pinkham, which sailed March 16, 1752.[13] Two weeks later, far out to sea, he recorded the following:

> March 28th—Nothing Remarkable this Day—only here we are in lat't 39°-0′, all alone by ourselves. It continues to Hold very Rough Weather: No whales nor no Whalemen to be seen—what a Strange

uneven Sort of life a man lives! Kings are always afraid of Being Poisoned and Live in many other Anxieties of Life concerning maintaining and enlarging their Dominions. And the Dukes, Earls, and others are always Concerned in their master's quarrels. As for Merchants and Traders and almost all wealthy men they are always tiezing themselves about adding to their riches or gathering in their Debts. No Sort of Life is free from trouble or whosoever think to live so in this world finds Themselves mistaken. We poor Seamen are many times in Jeopardy of Life by Storms, Tempests, Rocks, Shoals, Pirates, and Whales, and many unhealthey Climates, and more Sorts of men to Deal with of Different Constitutions and Dispositions. . . .

There can be no better description of the adventures of those whalemen of two hundred years ago than that given in the following account:

April 4th—This Day we Spy'd Spermaceties in the morning and toss'd out one Boat (the other being out before after Waggins). So we row'd about a mile and a Half from the Vessel, and then a whale come up under us, & stove our boat very much, and threw us every man overboard Save one. And we all came up and Got Hold of the Boat & Held to her until the other boat (which was a mile and half off) came up and took us in, all Safe, and not one man Hurt, which was remarkable, the boat being threshed to pieces very much. The Same Day we got a Quarter of a Spermaceti with Joseph Swain (who was cruising in company with *Mary*) and Now we Shall be headed homewards pretty soon having but one boat to Help ourselves, which yet was enough to be a means of Saving our Lives, when Stove through Mercy. *Benedic Dominum, a anima mea, & omnia quae sunt inter me, Benedicte Nomen ejus Sanctum.*

On April 6, the sloop "spoke" craft commanded by Edward Starbuck and Thomas Giles, "both good voyages," and three days later two more Nantucket sloops were sighted and spoken—"William Hussey and Francis Swain." In coming in to the coast, the *Mary* first struck soundings in forty-five fathoms, soon after sighting "Martin's Vineyard and No Man's Land," and getting into Holmes Hole the next day.

After a week at home, the *Mary* again set out, and this time spoke five fellow whaling craft when they arrived at 36°–30' (north) latitude. The logbook gives an interesting picture of how a sperm whale was "cut in" and her valuable sperm saved:

May 3— . . . We concluded to keep company with Beriah Fitch (sloop Polly): . . . in the afternoon struck a large spermaceti and killed her and cut off her body blubber the Same Day. . . . We got her between both vessels and got a Barbuckle under her and four tackles and runners to her and hoisted her head about 2 feet above water and then cut a scuttle in her head and a man got in up to his armpits and Dipt out almost 6 Hogsheads of Clear Oyle out of her Case beside 6 more of the Noddle.

The narrator observed, soon after, that "all is not catched that's gaped at," and described sighting a school of sperm and striking two, one of which was killed, "but the other run away with one iron in her tail." An interesting "gam" resulted from sighting another whaler:

May 26— . . . About 12 o'clock we spoke with a Cape man who told us oyle bore a very good price in Boston . . . £140 old tenor per ton to be paid in dollars on the Spot, and the Small pox which hath been in Boston some time still continues very Brief there. It seems to me as if there is nothing but fear and care and trouble on every side. No man can be born and live and die without his Share. And certain it is that in the world we shall have trouble and yet how the fear of Death will terrify poor Mortals! So conclude this Day's remarks hoping all are well at Home, Male and Female, etc.

Fortunately, Peleg Folger's shipmates were also readers of his log-book. One of them wrote at the bottom of a page: "Peleg Folger is a Rum Soull for writing Latin," and, with his conscience probably twitting him, the observer continued: "I fear Peleg Folger will be offended with me writing in his Book, but I will intercede with Anna Pitts in his behalf for Retaliation for the same. Nathaniel Worth."

But Peleg Folger, not yet twenty, did not marry Anna Pitts, and so Nathaniel's intervention went for naught. Perhaps the fact such a match never took place caused Peleg to abandon thoughts of marriage for he remained a bachelor all of his life. When he gave up the sea in his later years, he became a schoolteacher and as "a knowing Folger" proved his kinship to his famous cousin, Benjamin Franklin.

The entry in the log of the *Seaflower* at "Misketo Cove" records as early as 1732 at least one encounter between the Quaker whalemen from Nantucket and the Newfoundlanders. The noisome stench of decaying carcasses of whales was reason enough for trouble, and it is understandable that the Newfoundlanders objected strenuously. Certain regulations were drawn up by Captain John Hamilton of H. M. sloop-of-war *Merlin,* on the Labrador Station in June 1765. All "Whalers from the Plantations" carrying on their business near Labrador were notified they must not leave any of the carcass of a whale within three leagues of shore; that they must not carry any passengers away from Newfoundland or the Labrador coast; must leave the coast before November first; must take no fish other than whale, and must not trade with the French.[14]

Many vessels were in need of taking cod to complete their cargoes, and a *Boston News-Letter* of 1765 reported that the vessels were not only having poor voyages but were "being ill-treated by some of the Cruisers on the Labradore Coast." Colonial whalemen were further warned that they could only cut up their whales in the Gulf of St. Lawrence within an unoccupied area, and were also told they could not winter on the Labrador coast. Governor Hugh Palliser, of the Newfoundland-Labrador territories, also issued decrees discriminating against the colonial whalemen, and accused the provincials of lawless acts on the coast of his territories.[15]

Then came the oppressive Act of Parliament in 1766 which placed a duty on oil and bone from the colonies to England, checking the spread of their voyages, north and south, while arbitrarily prohibiting their trading with other nations. At the same time, residents of Great Britain were granted a bounty for all oil and bone brought into the home market. The American whalemen felt such glaring discrimination was neither reasonable nor wise. They only asked for the same treatment accorded all subjects of the Crown.

The natural result was that some New England whalemen became discouraged and the industry dwindled appreciably. Nantucket, however, had seventy-five vessels in the fishery with 975 whalemen. But the British whalemen could not supply the London market and the merchants, forced to import Dutch oil, petitioned for fair play for the New Englanders.

In 1767, it became necessary for Governor Palliser, responding to pressure from the Ministry, to issue a proclamation announcing: "All vessels from the Plantations employed in the Whale-Fishery" would be encouraged and assisted by the King's officers stationed in "those parts" and would be admitted to that "coast on the same footing as they had ever been admitted in Newfoundland."[16]

In response to such encouragement combined with grants of land, a number of New England families from Plymouth, Cape Cod and Nantucket went up to Nova Scotia to settle around Shelburne and Cape Sable. The whalemen in these groups, despite the fact they were nearer the whaling grounds than at home, were never successful.

Further concessions were made to encourage emigration to Nova Scotia as part of the attempt of Lord Shirley, "the King's only advocate-general in America," to oust the French from that province, this attempt of course being highlighted by the shameful expulsion of the Arcadians. But the provincials in general were not fooled by these late attempts to placate them, for they realized that the home Ministry was anxious only to build up the British whale fishery at the expense of the hardworking colonials. This knowledge forced them to rely on themselves and was of the utmost importance in determining the course of their development.

In 1758 a petition had been sent to the Massachusetts General Court from Nantucket and Vineyard.[17] The petition requested that whalemen be allowed to proceed on their voyages as usual to the west and south of the Virginia Capes until June, as the first part of the whaling season was the "Principal time for making their voyages which, if they lose, the greatest part of the People will have nothing to Purchase the Necessaries of life withal."

The council considered this petition and on April 8, 1758, passed a resolution permitting the Quaker Nantucketers to pursue their voyages "taking the inhabitants of s'd Island in s'd Vessels, and that upon taking any other person with them they be subject to all the penalties of the laws . . . as if they had proceeded without Lease."[18] Here was an unusual use of the potential value of the Nantucket whalemen. It was a recognition justified fully by subsequent events.

Among the first essentials for this self-reliant maintaining of the industry was the necessity of discovering whaling grounds away from the coast of Nova Scotia, and Newfoundland. Cruising far out to sea, and along the Gulf Stream, the New Englanders were forced to make longer voyages.

Again the pioneering Nantucketers led the way. New whaling grounds were opened by them, slowly but steadily. Obed Macy, the Quaker historian, noted that after the Gulf of St. Lawrence had been found to be a whaling ground in 1751, the whalemen sailed to the Strait of Belle Isle, Grand Banks east, then through Davis Strait in 1751 to the island of Disco—beyond 70° north latitude, up Greenland's western, icy shore to Baffin Bay.[19]

In the logbook of the sloop *Greyhound,* of Nantucket, which sailed March 17, 1753, are excellent word pictures of the rigors of a whaling voyage to the Arctic in the fifties.[20] The *Greyhound* was commanded by Captain Richard Pinkham, and was bound for Davis Strait. On her way to the eastward she spoke a whaling sloop from Saybrook, Connecticut, and also a fellow-Nantucketer, Hezidiah Cartwright. An entry for May 10 reads as follows:

> This day spoke with a trading schooner from Montserrat, David Denneck, Master, and went on Board & got two bottles of Rum, & some Limes & some Sugar, oranges, etc. Nothing more very remarkable. We are all in good health as yet.

That these early whalemen were fully aware of the limitations existing in navigation in those days may be deduced from the entry as of May 25:

> Latitude by rec. Mer. drift 61°–Long. 43°–43'. This latitude is true. Long. and mer. drift as near ye truth as may be considering the divers courses we have run while chasing whales & trying out our Blubber.

Running north from the Grand Banks, the *Greyhound* came into the area where the drift ice appeared, carried down by the Labrador current. On May 28 the log reported: "Several Ice Islands of Divers shapes & and one of them we thought to be a mile long and showed itself like Nomansland. . . . It has snow this day as thick as need for."

Sperm whales were taken and the sloop lay-to under a trysail and foresail to try out the blubber. Another Nantucket sloop, with Elisha Coffin in command, hove into sight on June 14— ". . . we mated and killed four Spermaceties between us & saved them." The log further recorded: "The sun sits about this time in this Latitude with us at 8 and rises at 4. The daylight goeth not out of the sky during the whole

24 hours. Pretty cold weather but very comfortable at present. Lat. by observation 58°-22′ north, Long. 51°-45′ west." Compass variation was given at three points. It is of interest to note that there was a chronometer on board, the longitude being noted.

On June 15, 1753, the *Greyhound*'s journalist wrote a concise description of the sloop's rig. The square topsail is mentioned, and the foresail or staysail. His observations of this day provide one of the most delightful entries of the journal:

> First part of this 24 hours calm weather and a jumbling kind of Swell, and we set up our Rigging & Shrouds & mainstay & got down our top-yard lift and served him with Leather where the Spunyarn service was worn off. At 10 P.M. made Sail with the wind S by E. So we ran all night with pleasure. At 10 A.M. it grew very thick of fog and we Brought to under a trisail & Foresail not daring to run we knew not whither among ye Ice or Fog. The weather is freezing cold; Nights short; Sea rowling and Tumbling. The Deep tedious; our cabbin our Delight; the fire pleasant, our allowance to every man on board his belly-full and more too if he wants. Alas, if it were not for hope the heart would fail. Lat. by obs. 57°-57′. Long. 51°-46′. . . . It snowed thick and so no more, only we saw about eight ice islands ye last 24 hours.

The customs of these early Quaker whalemen are characteristically expressed in the words of this journalist. On June eighteenth, the log records that they judged themselves at the mouth of Davis Strait in latitude 60°-22′ north. Carefully the writer states:

> It is now high time for me to Put an End to my Longitudes and Meridian Distances, till we begin to be bound home along. First part of this 24 hours the wind Small. Elisha hove out his boat and came on board of us and we had had pancakes for supper. The Ice Islands are very Plenty hereabouts.

Then came the sober business of whaling, graphically described:

> June 20— . . . We saw Right Whales and our Skipper struck one which stove his boat so that she overset but (through Mercy) they were all taken up Safe and the Whale ran away & soon we struck another which also ran away so there is two shot of craft and a Stoven boat in one day. But Walter will soon mend our boat. So never fear kind Providence!
> June 21st—We saw whales and Elisha [commanding the sloop in

company] Move out his boat and Struck one and we soon made her Spout Blood but she was a long time Dying but at last she Dyed and we got her between both vessels and cut off her Head, the Bone measured 8 feet, 3 inches as being a very Large, deep whale. So it blew up a little chopling & we got our vessels apart, and one Boat's crew went on Board Elisha & rafted some Blubber and we took it on Board our Vessel so they kept cutting upon the whale all the remaining part of the Day.

June 22— . . . Still a-cutting our whale. But the wind blew up so . . . Elisha parted his cable. A large Swell Going hard. Gale at S. E. with rain & Snow, etc. So the whale is gone with about one-third of the blubber. I hope we shall find her again.

June 23—This day a very hard & heavy Gale of wind at SE and SSE and it raised a very Long and high sea (a right Topgallant swell) which lasted all this 24 hours. So we lay to under a trisail and let her Drive and She lay very well and made good weather of it, But we were very uneasy for fear of driving amongst the Ice. . . . Cleaned our whalebone, stowed it away in the run.

It was duly observed that the sun in this latitude 61° north at this time of year "is not 6 hours out of our visible hemisphere and it is not darker at North Sun than it is ½ hour after Sunset at home"; also that "it is very seldom the Sun Shines out all ye day," it being overcast and cloudy.

To give variety to shipboard fare, seabirds called "heights" were killed and made into pies which were washed down by hot chocolate "poured down into our bellies." The flukes of young whales were found to yield good meat to add to the "doboys." This marks the first recorded use of whale steaks on board an American ship.

The *Greyhound* lost sight of her consort, Elisha Coffin's sloop, during a storm. On July 13 spoke with a Scotch whaler from Glasgow, Alexander Carr, commander, who informed them he had fallen in with Jonathan Coffin, of Nantucket, who had gotten 170 barrels. Their consort at length was sighted coming up to them, and Captain Elisha Coffin came on board "and we had a great Plum pudding for dinner. Latter part we spyed whales and killed one large Spermaceti and got her alongside and began to cut." The Nantucketer further commented: "The Scotchman stood away till he had gotten out of sight, he having no luck among the whales." They were in Latitude 61°–12' north on July 17 when they sighted six Dutch whalers, one of which was boarded by Captain Pinkham and his mate. The log keeper noted:

> . . . They had an Indian & his Canoe on board and Intended to carry him to Holland and bring him back next year.

On July 30, 1753, the *Greyhound* headed south on the long voyage home. More sperm whales were taken and the oil extracted in the "tryworks set a-going by a flaming torch under our caboose." On August 29 they sighted land at the Bay of Bulls, Newfoundland, "it being 112 days since we saw land before." After several days here, the sloop headed on a southwest by west course, "so we hope to have a good passage home." On September 22, they struck soundings of Georges Bank in fifty fathoms—"Nantucket bears west 50 leagues." The final entry contains this laconic statement:

> Sept. 24— . . . This day made ye land. About 9:00 o'clock at night we got into our harbor and anchored in the Road . . . & found all our friends well. Laus Deo.

A careful reading of these old logbook records yields something more than the mere noting of course and distance and wind and weather. There are graphic and thrilling encounters with the mighty sperm and eloquent descriptions of the sea. In his log of the sloop *Phebe* for July 30, 1754, the redoubtable Peleg Folger records:

> We struck a large spermaceti & got in three irons [harpoons] and one tow-iron put in by John Way, one of our mates. As soon as the tow-iron went into the whale she gave a flank and went down & coming up again she bolted her head out of the water almost if not quite as far as her fins. And then pitched the whole weight of her head on the Boat—stove ye boat & ruined her and killed the midshipman (an Indian named Sam Lamson) outwright a Sad & Awful Providence.

The *Phebe* was well toward Davis Strait at this time, and the logbook recorded that "the sky glittered with the northern lights appearing very bright and Luciferous, like Streaks of Lightning." A school of sperm whales stirred up considerable activity. One was taken and a day later Peleg recorded the following incident:

> Still cutting our whale. A chopling sea agoing & But little wind; our sloop girded most violently & we parted our Runners twice and

split one of our Runner Blocks & hurt one of our Hands, (splitting his fingers, one of them most sadly) & made most Racking work. About 6 P.M. we unhooked our tackles & runners not daring to cut and Longer for fear of our Lives & Limbs. About 12 at night the wind began to blow Violent hard & Raised a large sea. It both rained & blew as Violently as I think ever I knew it and the Color of the night resembled the Egyptian Darkness. About 3 o'clock we parted our Sheet Cable and Lost our Whale from ye Bow with about half the Blubber on her Body; about 5 in the morning we Blew away our Tri-sail & tore him out of the Bolt ropes & ruined him entirely & then set our Balanced Mainsail, being a Top-Gallant Sea agoing.

That there was more to the life of the whalemen than the hardships of the craft is best shown by this excerpt from Folger's pungent quill-pen.

It feels tiresome & tedious to lay by [under a trisail]. So much rowling and tumbling very uneasily like the conscience of a wicked man. . . . How many are the tedious cares & anxieties of human life? . . . But I carry my discontent about with me for I cannot run away from myself.

The reaction of a young harpooner on a voyage to a new whaling ground is reflected in the log of the *Endeavor* out of Nantucket in 1762.[21] This journalist wrote in a fine hand:

June 16— . . . Foggy, great Plenty of Pinguins, Puffins & other Fowl. Sounded & caught a Codfish but was not certain whether the Grand Bank or Bank next—had no Observation, Caught 11 Codfish which was an agreeable refreshment. . . . Very foggy but the Captain & mate are well acquainted on the Coast but it appears difficult enough to the rest of us.

A week later the logbook keeper's record had the following:

June 22— . . . At 9 P.M. made a school of Spalmicities hove out our boats & struck three of them, sent Two of them Spouting Blood Cil'd one. . . .
. . . We had Whale alongside we Conclude Not to Begin to Cut today their being Such a Large Swell A-going So we caught up our tacles & Runners up and Lye By till better Weather. Middle part had Plenty of rain . . . a bad Sea Going.

The *Endeavor* took her whales on a new whaling ground, between latitude 42° and 44° north, and longitude 40° to 45° west. Several Nantucket sloops had headed east from the Grand Banks to discover that many large schools of whales were swinging away from the Banks and far to the east.

The American deep-sea whaler was emerging from the first experimental eras of his beginnings. He was meeting the swells and smooths of his sea home and becoming an experienced mariner with a growing knowledge of the added hazards of whaling. Having voyaged into the far northern seas he had met the whalemen of Britain and Holland and successfully competed with them. All of this had taken place while he was "still in the gristle and not hardened into manhood." The next phase of his development was of greater importance to himself and to New England than either the colonials or the British ever realized.

chapter iv

~~~ ꭣꮳ ᔛ ꭣꮳ ~~~

BUSINESS ON THE GREAT WATERS

Pray, Sir, what in the world is equal to it? Pass by the other parts, and look at the manner in which the People of New England have of late carried on the whale-fishery?
—Edmund Burke, "Conciliation with America"

WHILE THE MISGUIDED Ministry of George III was unwittingly doing its utmost to foment in the colonies an active resistance against its policies, the resentment in America grew steadily. The economics of the situation—wherein Britain planned that the colonies should be only the supplier of raw materials, to be exchanged in the mother country for manufactured goods—was not a system for a people who knew their own ability. Taxation was but the culmination of a mistaken course of government. The curtailment of American trade was the basic cause of the trouble.

Whale-oil merchants had found steadily increasing profits in their trade with Britain, the Mediterranean ports and the West Indies. The exports of this colonial industry in 1770 included 15,315 pounds of sperm candles to Great Britain and Ireland; some 14,167 pounds to other European ports; 351,625 pounds to the West Indies.[1] Sperm oil continued to be the aristocrat of oils for lighting, and lubricating machinery. Whale oil was a less expensive lighting fluid, and was also used in the making of soap and the finishing of leather and wool products. The colonial whalemen—or more properly the New Englanders—slowly took full control of the London sperm-oil market. From £7 per ton in 1725, the price of oil had risen to £40 a ton in

48

1770.[2] The value of Nantucket's catch in 1771 exceeded £150,000.

It had been the hope of the New England whalemen that the British Ministry would remove the restrictions placed upon them, and a few such indications induced them to return to the northern fishery between 1767 and 1768. Fifty sloops sailed in 1768, most of whom cruised in the Gulf of St. Lawrence and off Newfoundland. Nantucket had eighty vessels, divided between the northern and southern grounds. Ten of this fleet were lost, the majority foundering with all hands; two of them victims of the sudden storms in the Strait of Belle Isle, between Newfoundland and Labrador.

From a logbook kept by Isaiah Eldredge, of Dartmouth, in the sloop *Tryall* which cleared from Nantucket in 1768, there were "about 60 sail of wailmen" in the northern fleet this year. Continually beset by ice while getting to the north in May, the sloops often had to clear their decks of snow which was "almost over-shoes deep." They killed their first whale on July 22, and did not return home until November.[3]

The exact course of one of these is known—Micajah Coffin in another voyage from Nantucket in the *Sandwich,* was off Halifax on the nineteenth of May 1768, and got into Canso the next day.[4] Leaving Canso with the wind east southeast and rainy, he sailed "threw the Gut" and on May 22 "weathered Bud Island & brought too" in a fog. Running northeast, the *Sandwich* sighted Newfoundland on May 25, then headed northwest. By the morning of May 28 they "were close in with the Southeast end of Anticosti Island, at the very mouth of the St. Lawrence River." The course was then changed, the sloop jibing and standing off to beat to windward. By June first the sloop was off Newfoundland again, and here the journal has been mutilated, with the concluding portion ripped out.

Having led the way north, the Nantucketers now began to sail south to the West Indies and the Gulf of Mexico in the search for new whaling grounds made necessary by the scarcity of whales in the old localities as well as by British restrictions on the northern fishery.

The log book of the sloop *Manufacturer,* Captain John Taber, tells that she sailed from Dartmouth (the Acushnet River) in April 1756, came to Nantucket to fit out for whaling, and shipped Zaccheus Gardner as mate on a share or "lay" of one nineteenth. This sloop cruised in latitude 37° north, about halfway between Nantucket and Bermuda.

In their pioneering voyages, the Nantucketers were not always successful but, as Obed Macy tells us, "every new place required experience to teach them how to take advantage of the seasons, the course of the winds and currents as well as the habits of the whales." [5]

Captain Micajah Coffin, of Nantucket, in command of the sloop *Sandwich* sailed April 1762, for the "Bermuda Ground." A curious sequence of entries in the log reveals the singleness of purpose of the typical whaling master.[6] It concerns Paul Swain, who was struck on the head by the main boom on April 15. Two days later Captain Coffin wrote in the sloop's journal:

> . . . Paul continues to complain of a Pain in his head and back, but in hopes it will Pass off in a Day or two we continue our Course Southward to look for Whales.
>
> 18—First day of the week—Lost Ground of the Bank, the wind S. W. Latt'd by Obs. 37° 40' Paul continues to be Poorly—so concludes this Day.
>
> 19— . . . Latt'd by Obs. 36° 48'—Paul Swain no better. . . .
>
> 20— . . . Wind continues (NNE) to blow hard. Paul Swain appears to be lightheaded and Raises Blood. . . .
>
> 21— . . . Spoke Jonathan Moores & Benjamin Bunker. Paul continues of his senses.
>
> 22—Paul very poorly, Raises Blood, slept none last night. At Sunset carried away the Goose Neck of our Boom.
>
> 24— . . . May hew out some cleeks for our Boom, in hopes Paul mends fast Not to Go Home.

But Paul Swain did not improve. The sloop was headed homeward, but whether to get a new boom or to save his life through recuperation on shore is not stated. The sloop records as of May 6: "Got into Nantucket, got our Goose Neck mended and Racked our Mast & carried up Paul Swain."

After taking water aboard, Captain Coffin made ready to sail but "could not Git a hand to suit." Apparently Paul Swain was a harpooner or steersman, and, as the whaling fleet had all departed, a replacement could not be procured on the island. The *Sandwich* sailed for Martha's Vineyard on putting in at Holmes Hole just in time to see the "woods on fire upon the Neck or West Chop." Next morning, they "saw the chimney of Baxter's house Standing and the house Burnt Down."

In May Captain Coffin reported in his journal: "Went on Shore to try to Git a Hand but could Git not one toDay. . . . Being Loth to go out a hand Short I sent Timothy Merry in Quest of one—Just at Night one Came Down of his own accord. I Ship'd him, went on board heft [the anchor] up to Run up to Gay Head to Git his things." There is little doubt but that the new hand was a Gay Head Indian.

At sea once more the *Sandwich* had no sooner arrived at the whaling grounds than she was chased by a privateer. "A Large Ship with a schooner under her Lee Gave us Chase," reads the log books, in May. ". . . We weathered her away about 4 miles. She fir'd a Gun to Leward & heft out an English Ensine . . . we run to ye S. W. att Sunset spoke with Walter Folger."

This Nantucket whaleman told Captain Coffin he had cruised as far south as Barbados. During the next few days the *Sandwich* sighted a dozen whaling sloops and "spoke" nine of them, most of them fellow Nantucketers and all New England craft. Again on May 14, the *Sandwich* was chased by a ship, but she "weathered her away."

A school of sperm was sighted and one was captured, and killed. On May 17, there were fourteen whaling sloops in sight, the latitude then being 35°–50' north. Captain Coffin decided to "mate" with Shubael Pinkham and went on board, "dividing company." The sloop was back in Nantucket by June 6, with her blubber in casks.

A report in the *Boston News-Letter,* dated June 1767, stated that a whaling sloop putting in at Charleston, South Carolina, gave an account of fifty New England whaling craft in the latitude 36° to 44° north. This was probably an average number for the southern fleet at this period.

Roaming the seas, dodging privateers of France and Spain, the New England whalemen gradually lengthened their voyages as they continued to seek new whaling grounds. As early as 1763, they had crossed the Atlantic with the favoring westerly winds. Meeting with considerable success, they cruised first on the African coast off Guinea, thence around the Azores (or the "Western Islands," as they were always called by the whalemen). One vessel, returning from a voyage to these grounds, brought back three hundred barrels of oil.[7]

It appears strange, at first, that with the Azores nearest geographically to the grounds between 36° and 44° north latitude, the whalemen should have gone first to the Gulf of Guinea off the African coast. But it must be remembered that in cruising to the West Indies and South American coast, the American whalemen, following the equatorial counter-current, crossed the mid-Atlantic and worked into the African coastal areas, then two thousand miles nearer these grounds than the Azores, off to the north.

The first navigators to appreciate and utilize fully the mysterious ocean river known as the Gulf Stream were the whalemen. British merchants had been aware that their ships took longer than the colonial vessels to cross the Atlantic Ocean westward. The difference in time ran into weeks. For explanation the British appealed to Dr. Benjamin Franklin, London, before the Revolution.

The redoubtable American scientist promptly called upon his cousin from Nantucket, Captain Timothy Folger, who quickly told him of the influence of the Gulf Stream. Franklin wrote an account of the Stream, containing a chart drawn by Captain Folger.[8]

Several years later (1786) this sketch of the Stream was published with Franklin's article in the *Proceedings of the American Philosophical Society of Philadelphia*. In this article Franklin wrote:

> The Nantucket whalemen being extremely well acquainted with the Gulf Stream, its course, strength, extent, by their constant practice of whaling on the edges of it, from their island quite down to the Bahamas, the annexed draft of that Stream was obtained from one of them, Captain Folger, and caused to be engraved on the old chart in London, for the benefit of navigators by B. Franklin.

But it was many years before the British navigators would admit the counter-strength of this mighty stream—and, as usual, they lost valuable time to their Yankee competitors.

The whalemen had ceased to be mere blubber-hunters. They had become sea-rovers, who by living on the ocean had grown to know much about her customs and moods. They had now become America's first oceanographers.

The discovery of two new whaling grounds occurred during the early 1770's. It is difficult to ascertain the exact dates when these new localities were found, but the customary pursuit down the African coast brought the whaleman to Angola and Walvis (Woolwich) Bay before 1770.[9]

A few years later Admiral Montague, of His Majesty's Navy, informed whaling masters that whales in considerable numbers had been sighted off the Falkland Islands, far in the South Atlantic toward Cape Horn. Freeman, in his *History of Cape Cod,* declares that the first whalers to these grounds were Truro ships—Cape Cod craft. This was in 1774, and Captains David Smith and Gamaliel Collins are cited as the men who made voyages there at the suggestion of the British admiral. But it was written of the Nantucketers in 1772: "Would you believe that they had already gone to the Falkland Islands?" [10]

Along the fringe of the South Atlantic region subsequently known as the River Plate Ground on March 30, 1776, Francis Swain wrote in the log of the brig *Speedwell,* of Nantucket:

> This morning I went out in my boat to the Carcass of a Dead Whale. There was a great number of Albatrosses & I knocked down 52 of them with my lance Pole and haul'd them into the boat, the boat was loaded with them and brought them on board and they proved to be Excellent good Meat.[11]

What would Coleridge's "Ancient Mariner" have thought of Captain Swain? The Nantucketer had not only killed this "great number of Albatrosses" but had eaten them!

In less than a decade, the Nantucket fleet had increased from seventy-eight vessels (in 1762) to one hundred and twenty-five (in 1770). Other ports had also added to their whalemen, with Dartmouth (the district including that township, Fairhaven and the new village of Bedford) leading with some fifty sloops. Wellfleet, the Cape Cod headquarters, had twenty vessels in 1771, and Martha's Vineyard, twelve. Boston, as a port of entry, included fifteen whalers in 1771. No less than nineteen sail of whalemen were cleared from Rhode Island in 1770.[12]

By 1774, the New England whale fishery, representing the bulk of the colonial whaling, was at the high tide of its success. The total number of vessels fitted out annually was probably in excess of 250. Of this total Nantucket manned 150 sloops, schooners and brigs, totaling 15,095 tons. Jefferson's *Report on the State of the Whale-Fishery in Massachusetts, 1771 to 1775,* reveals that the Massachusetts Bay Colony had a fleet of 183 vessels in the northern fishery and 121 in the southern.[13] The attendant industries ashore brought the total of men actually engaged in the industry to some ten thousand. No wonder the British Ministry envied. As Burke aptly reminded, the spirit of these Americans "ought to raise your esteem and admiration." [14]

The new whaling port at Bedford Village had grown rapidly since Joseph Russell, its co-founder, began whaling there in 1765. Several decades later, this port was to wrest the leadership from Nantucket, from which island came Joseph Rotch and others to supply it with leadership.[15]

Across the river, in another advantageous position, the little hamlet of Fairhaven had already started to grow. In 1760, a certain tract of land had been sold here, which included the site of the later town, in which the seller reserved that part of the section "where the Tryhouse & Oyl shed now stands." [16] By 1765, New Bedford had four sloops a-whaling. Prior to 1760, sloops from Dartmouth township often sailed to Nantucket for outfitting.

The settlement of the famed city of New Bedford was directly attributable to the whaling industry. It is strange that the early settlers of the ancient township of Dartmouth established themselves in all other sections before the beginnings of Bedford village, but there is also a definite significance in this fact. The head of the Acushnet had its colony, Bellville, in Oxford village; the Apponaganset region was early settled, as were the sections around Acoaxet or Westport and on Sconticut Neck. It was natural for the farmers to seek the rich lands, although they did have a landing place and carried on coasting trade from Fairhaven village.

At the Acushnet's sea mouth, lay the thickly-wooded shore which rose gradually to the meadows and pasture land beyond. Here in 1761, Joseph Russell, the third generation of that pioneer family in the township, had extensive holdings with neighbor Ephraim Hempton to the north—two large farms stretching for miles. Russell laid out a plan for a village. John Lowden, a shipwright, built not only a house but a wharf.

The year 1765 is a memorable one in New Bedford's history since it marked the date of the arrival of Joseph Rotch, of Nantucket. A man of wealth, but more important a whaling merchant with practical experience at sea as well as ashore, he joined Joseph Russell in a plan to make a whaling port at this strategic place. Russell had the land; Rotch the ships and experience. Both had strong vision. Within ten years they had laid out more streets, erected houses, built ships and fully launched a village founded on the premise of a whaling New Bedford. Among the men coming from Nantucket with Rotch were his nephew Captain Joseph Rotch and Benjamin Taber, a boatbuilder and block-maker. He also built a wharf.[17]

Despite the fact that before New Bedford was settled Fairhaven had fifty years of opportunity to become a great whaling port, it did not so develop until some years after the beginnings of the Russell settlement. Joseph Rotch's acquisition of his Dartmouth land was the beginning of the new era in whaling from the Acushnet. Prospect Hill became Johnnycake Hill. Bedford Village's Four Corners became the foundation of a good-sized city.

In April 1775, within a period of a few days, the news of two historic events reached Nantucket. They were of equal importance to the islanders, although their results were, of course, then unknown. First came the news of the fight at Lexington and Concord.[18] Then the whaleship *Amazon*, Captain Uriah Bunker, arrived with news that a great new whaling ground had been discovered in the South Atlantic and named the Brazil Banks because that coast (thought five hundred miles away) was nearest. It had previously been found that the River Plate and Falkland Island grounds were excellent migratory lanes for whales.

The discovery of these new whaling regions was to have not only a salutory effect upon the industry, but was to provide one of the most unusual and adventurous chapters in our nation's history.

PART TWO

The Whaleman Becomes
a Pioneer Voyager

chapter v

~~~~~~

THE WHALEMEN CREATE
A KINGDOM IN THE SEA

*The Nantucketois, then, were the only people who exer-
cised this fishery to any extent at the commencement of the
late war. Their island, from its barrenness, yielding no subsistence, they were obliged to seek it in the sea surrounding
them. Their economy was more rigorous than that of the
Dutch.*

—Thomas Jefferson [1]

THAT REMARKABLE FRENCHMAN, J. Hector St. John de Crèvecoeur
(whose *Letters From an American Farmer* delighted the essayist
Hazlitt so much that he declared him to be one of the three most noted
writers of the eighteenth century), states in his description of the island and its people: "I want not to record the annals of the island of
Nantucket—its inhabitants have no annals, for they are not a race of
warriors. My simple wish is to trace them throughout their progressive
steps . . . to enquire by what means they have raised themselves from
the most humble, the most insignificant beginnings, to the ease and
the wealth they now possess. . . ." [2]

On the eve of the Revolution, when de Crèvecoeur visited it, Sherburne-Town, the port of Nantucket, contained five thousand people.
Obed Macy, in his history of the island, with justifiable pride, noted
that as the islanders had "centered on one engrossing subject"—whaling—they adopted new improvements and conveniences which enabled
them to pursue the industry with more efficiency than their contempo-

raries. "Time and experience," he observed, "gave them advantages which made it difficult to rival them." [3]

Perhaps the chief reason for the success of the Nantucketers was the rigorous prosecution of their voyages. Another factor was the interwoven business connections. Every family had a part in the voyage, either through the cooper-shops, which made the casks; the blacksmithy, which forged the harpoons and lances, and the iron work; the rope-walks, twisting the cordage; the shipwrights and ship-chandlery shops, which outfitted the craft, or the sail lofts, which cut and sewed the sails—or by being represented on board the ship in the crews or officers posts. Thus, a voyage was a success for all in the measure of their investment, while a poor voyage was never a total loss. [4]

Surely, community enterprise was never more fully exemplified. Theirs was a pride in accomplishment seldom equaled. Frugal to the point of habitual self-denial, confident through the experience of a generation of whalemen, governed by the sober tenets of their Quaker religion, the Nantucketer was the whaling symbol of his time.

In 1774 the Nantucket fleet of 150 sail was providing an income of $500,000 annually; each vessel was bringing in an average cargo of 150 barrels. Some 4,500 inhabitants lived in the confines of a trim Quaker town, built on the slopes of the Wesco Hills, and the harbor held four wharves. The second lighthouse erected in the colonies (originally built in 1746), guarded the entrance at Brant Point. Despite the shoal water and the sand bars across the harbor mouth, there was a steady increase of their shipping. Included were not only the whaleships but packets and sloops which regularly plied to all the leading ports along the coast. Here was a prosperous Quaker kingdom in the sea before the Revolutionary War suddenly burst upon it. [5]

The four wharves of the town fairly bristled with activity. The sturdy, oil-blackened hulls of the whaleships swung at anchor in the harbor or lay alongside the coasting craft at the wharves. Riggers swarmed aloft and outfitters busied themselves stowing down barrels of salt pork, beef, flour, molasses and other staples for the voyage. Stevedores tramped around windlasses heaving out the oil from a newly arrived whaling brigantine, home from the coast of Africa or Davis Strait's arctic seas. Heavy-timbered warehouses stood at the heads of the wharves, containing hundreds of casks of oil, winter or spring strained, carefully packed boxes of sperm-oil candles, that rare light of the century.

Nantucket became a great distributing center for the various kinds of oil and candles, whalebone, and even sealskins. For the products brought in exchange, reshipment to still another port was often necessary. The dim interiors of the great warehouses were fragrant with the mingled odors of stored commodities. Cassia and sandalwood, licorice and spices from the Indies; tea in odd boxes from Canton and Ceylon; molasses in puncheons from Cuba; rum from Jamaica; wine in butts from Madeira; coffee from Arabia; flour from Philadelphia; beef and pork from New York; pitch and tar from North Carolina, and lumber from the Kennebec. And, when the wind shifted to the east, always there was that rare pungent odor like musk of the spermaceti, and the smell of salt from the sea.

It was estimated by Zaccheus Macy that Nantucket whalemen in 1772 obtained annually thirty thousand barrels of oil, the largest percentage of which was shipped to England. Of the 2,800 seamen out of the port, 2,200 were whalemen and the remainder coastwise mariners and sailors in the London trade.[6]

The observation of another visitor to Nantucket in those times is significant. George Churchman, a Quaker, wrote in part:

> Sometimes vessels have sailed Eastward to the Coast of Africa, sometimes to the South Seas, to the Coast of Brazil, the Falkland Islands, &c., and at times Westward through the Gulf of Mexico, to Cape Horn and the Southern Capes of South America. They tell us of one man now alive on this island, who once went with others first to London with another cargo (being successful in the business); then fitted out for the South Seas, where they caught as many whales as made up many hundred barrels of oil before they came home and within the course of one year they ranged the seas into North Latitude as far as 8 degrees and to 52 degrees in South Latitude.[7]

De Crèvecoeur, with complete understanding, stated that despite its populous towns and business establishments, the greatest part of Nantucket's property was "floating at sea." He commented on the fact that the population, for the most part Quakers, had one minister representing the Presbyterians, "the two sects living in perfect peace and harmony," and remarked: "Most of these people are continually at sea, and have often the most urgent reasons to worship the Parent of Nature in the midst of storms which they encounter." [8]

In his tribute to the islanders, whose industry had made Nantucket "the greatest mart for oil, whalebone, and spermaceti on the Continent," De Crèvecoeur further expressed the hope that the citizens would "dwell in uninterrupted peace, undisturbed by the waves of the surrounding element, or the political commotions which sometimes agitate the Continent." [9] Unfortunately, the island was too much a part of the colonial economy to be able to escape the blight and scourge of war.

The first touch of trouble came through the unwilling part which Nantucket played in the Boston Tea Party. In June 1773, the ships *Dartmouth,* of New Bedford, owned by Francis Rotch, and *Beaver,* of Nantucket, owned by William Rotch, took cargoes of sperm whale oil to London. Captain James Hall commanded the *Dartmouth.* The *Beaver* was in charge of Captain Hezekiah Coffin. Francis Rotch had joined his father Joseph Rotch in developing the port of New Bedford. William Rotch the elder of the three sons of Joseph, was still in Nantucket, one of the leading merchants in Massachusetts Bay Colony, and an outstanding member of the Society of Friends. [10]

In London, King George's Ministry was planning an experiment. The British East India Company was in trouble. It had been almost scuttled by dissolute management and thieving agents. Its plight was critical and millions of pounds of tea and other goods lay unsold in its warehouses. Rather than risk the £400,000 received annually from the company, the Ministry proposed a method of salvaging the unwieldy ship. Lord North proposed to sell the tea to the colonists at ten shillings per pound—a price cheaper than that which the smugglers of Dutch tea (then supplying the colonial market) could meet.

But there had been a threepence tax per pound on the tea exported by Britain to America, through regular channels, and the colonists had refused to buy a single pound. "Taxation without representation is tyranny," James Otis had declared, and the colonists had echoed the sentiment.

No amount of logic on the part of the friends of the colonists in Parliament could change the situation. By the Tea Act of 1773, the tax on tea was retained, and the East India Company was permitted to export the tea directly to America without the trouble of selling it first to British merchants. Lord North believed the colonists would buy the cheap tea and forget their pride. His mistake touched off the smouldering spark of active resistance by the Americans.[11]

The East India Company's officials were not at all confident of the result as they prepared to load 1,253 chests of tea for America. They placed 298 chests of tea on four ships chartered for the voyage to Boston—the *Beaver* and *Dartmouth,* having discharged their Nantucket whale oil, cleaned ship and stowed away the tea—the *Eleanor,* Captain James Bruce, and *William,* Captain Lovering, also chartered for the tea fleet. They sailed October 19, 1773. The *Dartmouth,* first to arrive at Boston on November 29, tied up at Griffin's or Liverpool Wharf. The *Beaver* and *Eleanor* arrived a few days later.[12]

The Boston "rebels," led by John Hancock and Samuel Adams, were firmly against the unloading of the tea. It was not only because of the principle of taxation involved but also because they believed the establishment of an East India Company agency in Boston a threat to free enterprise. Massachusetts might consume 2,400 chests of tea each year, but it would not accept one ounce of this tax-ridden tea, even though it be the best Bohea from Amoy.

It is well to note that the consignees of the tea were Joshua Winslow, Richard Clarke & Sons, Benjamin Faneuil, Jr., and Thomas and Elisha Hutchinson, sons of the Royal Governor of Massachusetts, Thomas Hutchinson. Faced by the threats of the "Sons of Liberty," these consignees appeared subsequently to have crept out of the business by refusing to accept the tea from Francis Rotch, the owner of the *Dartmouth,* and Captains Coffin and Bruce, representing the other shipowners.[13]

Throughout the whole affair the Quaker whale-oil merchant, Francis Rotch, then a resident of Bedford, stands out like a beacon in the darkness of the turmoil. He is truly the Forgotten Man of the Boston Tea Party. With coolness and courage he appeared before the assembly of militant Boston patriots, at the Old South Church, on November 30, 1773.

Rotch listened while Sheriff Greenleaf read a special proclamation from Governor Hutchinson, ordering the people to disperse at their peril. This reading was greeted by loud hisses and outcries of derision.

But Rotch had one friend in the Assembly, John Hancock, with whom he had conducted much business. After pledging the assembly that he would seek the proper clearances so that the tea could be returned to London, Rotch of the *Dartmouth* quietly withdrew.[14]

On December 2, Francis Rotch and Captain Hall went out to Castle William, where the consignees had fled for protection and where they "could make such terms with the People as will be the least detrimental to the Company." Captain Hezekiah Coffin, of the *Beaver,* had arrived but "having the Smallpox on board was not permitted to come up to town." [15]

The first question which Francis Rotch proposed in writing to the consignees was: "We are now ready to deliver, are you gentlemen prepared to receive?"

The answer: "We understand there is a large body of people assembled in Boston on the 29th and 30th of November, who voted that the tea ship'd by the East India Company and consigned to us should not be landed, that the duty should not be paid, and that the Tea should be returned on the same ship which brought it out; it also appears by the private proceedings of the assembly that you consented that it should go back in your ship; we also understand that there is continually on board your ship a number of armed men to prevent it being landed. We therefore judge it out of our power to receive it at present, but when it shall appear to you to be practical we will give the necessary orders respecting it." [16]

In response to further questions put by Rotch, the consignees also refused to accept the bill of lading or to pay the £91-17s bill for the freight. Captain James Bruce, of the *Eleanor,* had a similar experience with the consignees.

At a meeting of the people held at the Old South Church on Tuesday evening, December 14, Rotch reported his failure to obtain the necessary papers from the collector of the port. On Thursday the Assembly again met and requested Rotch to seek a pass from Governor Hutchinson for the three ships. The Nantucketer went to Milton, seven miles out of Boston, and was informed by the Royal Governor that the pass could not be granted.

Reporting that evening to the Assembly, Rotch must have exchanged a word with Hancock, because he was not surprised "when the meeting broke up and they immediately went in large numbers to each of the three vessels, turning the Custom House officials ashore and proceeded to hoist the tea on deck, and to break open the chest and then threw overboard into the Dock, until . . . they had completed the destruction of the whole." [17]

It is pertinent to note that one outstanding feature (generally overlooked) of the onslaught of the "Mohawks" on the tea-ships is that not one of the ships was damaged and the only article missing (besides the tea) was a padlock from the *Beaver*, probably lost overboard.

There was a fourth tea-ship bound for Boston—the *William*—which never arrived. Getting off her course in approaching this coast, this ship was wrecked on the "back side" of Cape Cod. But most of the tea was salvaged and taken to Boston where it arrived without molestation! [18]

As for the *Dartmouth* and *Beaver,* they both returned to Nantucket, where they were loaded with oil and again sailed for London, the former arriving the second week in February 1774. On board were several passengers from Boston who had witnessed the Tea Party episode. Captain Hall, Rotch and these Bostonians were summoned to Whitehall by Lord Dartmouth and gave testimony regarding "the late transaction" at Boston.[19]

The record would not be complete without observing that not all of the tea was dumped overboard. Quakers abhor waste and the thrifty Nantucket Quakers saw to it that when the ships arrived home they had some tea on board intended primarily for home consumption. "After all, it was a good Bohea, and would have gone overboard anyway!"

On board the *Beaver* was a set of six Chippendale chairs, purchased in London by Captain Coffin. Four of these chairs are still in existence and, with the shipmaster's miniature and a bill of lading for the tea, represent the only surviving relics of the famous Boston Tea Party.[20]

As a concluding argument to the character bearing of Francis Rotch during the entire affair, witness the fact that he afterwards collected from the East India Company for the freight of the 114 chests of noxious tea! And thus it was tea flavored with whale oil, before it became mixed with salt water, which became the brew that gagged the British Ministry.

chapter vi

~~~~~~

BETWEEN THE DEVIL AND THE DEEP

> . . . *the delegates of this Commonwealth . . . impress Congress with just ideas of the high worth and importance of the Whale Fishery to the United States in general and this State in particular.*
>
> —George Cabot [1]

O N THE WAVE of reaction following the news of the Tea Party came the British Parliament's coercive acts. First (March 1774) was the Boston Port Bill, bottling up this "hot-bed of New England rebels." Immediately, the Boston Committee of Safety issued its appeal for the brother colonies to stand firm. In response, there were demonstrations, relief expeditions of supplies, patriot assemblies, and newspaper articles, all of which had the effect of solidifying the purpose of fighting for the rights of the colonies.

The passage of the Restraining Act early in 1775, not only restricted the trade and commerce of Massachusetts Bay, New Hampshire, Rhode Island and Connecticut to Britain, Ireland and the West Indies, but prohibited the colonial fishing on the Banks of Newfoundland, including, of course, the whale fishery.

In March 2, 1775, the House of Commons was holding a hearing on this proposed "Fishery Bill," a bill designed to cut Massachusetts off from traditional privileges of using the Grand Banks, as well as restraining its trade.

Among those appearing before the House, was Captain Seth Jenkins, of Nantucket. Captain Jenkins told the House that the island had 132 ships in the whale fishery alone, and that 128 of these belonged to members of the Society of Friends called Quakers, that the Nantucketers "went out on the whale-fishery at all seasons of the year, . . . had lately extended their fishery as far as the Falkland Islands, and were sometimes twelve months on the voyage." He went on to state that he had known ships from England come on their coast, in search of whales, but were always unsuccessful in catching them "though the Nantucket men at the same time succeeded well, so much experience is necessary to that business." [2]

Captain Jenkins reported that the Nantucketers received all their manufactures from London, and sent most of their oil to Britain; that, in his opinion, if the whale fishery was prohibited, the inhabitants, from their principles, would suffer so long as they could subsist ". . . but as there was seldom more than 3 months of provisions on the island, they must be obliged to emigrate to the southward, as they would not . . . live under the military government of Halifax."

Many London merchants, together with David Barclay and several prominent English Quakers, actively espoused the colonial cause. The most effective note was sounded in the eloquent speech of Edmund Burke, his "Conciliation with America"—in which he dramatically described the exploits of the whalemen of New England. "Neither the perseverance of Holland, nor the activity of France, nor the dexterous and firm sagacity of English Enterprise ever carried the most perilous mode of hardy industry to the extent to which is has been pushed by this recent People." [3]

But arguments, facts and figures, eloquence—all were in vain. The Restraining Act was passed. Yet it is significant to note that Nantucket was exempted from many provisions of this rancorous act, an admittance on the part of Lord North's Ministry of the importance of the New England whale fishery, of which Nantucket was the acknowledged headquarters.

Then the inevitable clash took place. When the British regulars marched out of Boston early in the morning's darkness of April 20, 1775, they were heading for the hiding place of colonial powder. When they found it, the treacherous stuff blew up in their faces. What had started to be a provincial skirmish had turned into a full-scale revolution.

The Revolutionary War, so precipitately a grim reality, the Nantucketers for the most part thought an unnecessary conflict. The granting of a few seats in Parliament would have forestalled it. Franklin suggested this solution fifteen years before Lexington and Concord; Adam Smith advocated such a concession. The sole outstanding advocate of independence for the colonies early in the trouble was Samuel Adams, who was not in good repute with many of his contemporaries. In Nantucket, a community so closely bound to London by trade and heritage, the idea of rebellion and possible independence was not even considered in 1775.

The echoes of the guns of Lexington and Concord had no sooner died away and the siege of Boston begun than the effect of war began making itself felt among the Nantucket whalemen. Their southern voyages had now taken them far below the equator: this meant some three months to make a passage home. On the eve of the "Boston fighting," as it was termed, Captain Abner Briggs and Christopher Pinkham arrived from the Gulf of Guinea with one hundred barrels of oil each.[4] Five days later, April 29, Captain William Moores in the *Maria* and Captain Uriah Bunker in the *Amazon* arrived with four hundred barrels of oil.[5] Following closely after were sloops from the coasts of Africa, and the Western Islands.

The reputation of Nantucket as a Quaker stronghold made it a haven for those Massachusetts loyalists who dared not stay in their homes around Boston and Salem. The first ship carrying these refugees arrived on April 29 from Salem, with a number of women and children. A small vessel from Salem with one family came on May 4, and on the next day a large ship from the same port landed "50 or 60 passengers," at Nantucket, "several Boston families and some from Salem." Mr. Gayer and his family, Robert Calef's family, Joshua Gardner and family, Mr. Goodale and family. "A Dr. Winship came in another Boston vessel disguised as a seaman."[6]

On May 6, Robert Hussey and Stephen Gardner arrived from Guinea with one hundred barrels each; on May 17, Captain Nathaniel Woodbury came into the harbor, reporting his voyage to Guinea had yielded 180 barrels, and two days later two more of the fleet to the Coast of Africa returned to their home post with cargoes of 250 barrels each.[7]

The pattern of things to come was established barely a month after Lexington and Concord. A young Nantucket woman, with truly loyalist sentiments, then recorded the essential facts:

> May 23—A vessel came in before night with one hundred Provincial Soldiers or upwards. It is said that they have come after a quantity of flour that one Rogers landed here some time ago. They pretend that they have heard that General Gage intended sending for it. They marched off the wharf with drums beating, fifes playing, and colours flying. They have quartered in the stores. God save George the King! [8]

The Continental soldiers remained three days, leaving with a local pilot in a "12-swivel brig," and taking away fifty whaleboats.

The use of whaleboats in wartime was not new to Americans. They had been used by General Abercromby on Lake Champlain in the French wars, by the famous Rogers Rangers and Gage's Light Infantry on Lake George, and Amherst had used no less than ninety of them in his campaigning down the St. Lawrence in 1760, where their advantages in the rough waters of the rapids were of great value.

In the very week of the provincials' raid, three more Nantucket whaleships returned from voyages to the African coast, one of them, Obed Bunker, with a cargo of 260 barrels. Captains Daniel Pinkham and John Bailey arrived from voyages to the West Indies five days afterwards. Two ships in the London trade also arrived in May.[9]

The island's strategic position in the whale fishery, and its non-inclusion in the Restraining Act's octopus-like restrictions, was not for a moment lost on the Provincial Congress. On June 9, 1775, a committee reported to this group on supplies entering Nantucket. In relation to this island the following resolution was passed by the Continental Congress:

> That no provisions or necessaries of any kind be exported to the Island of Nantucket, except from the Colony of the Massachusetts Bay, the convention of which colony is desired to take measure for effectively providing the said island, upon their application to purchase the same, with as much provisions as shall be necessary for its internal use, and no more. The Congress deeming it of great importance to North America, that the British fishery should not be furnished with provisions from this Continent through Nantucket,

earnestly recommend a vigilant execution of this resolve to all committees.[10]

This was followed by an order prohibiting any exports to Nantucket unless it was guaranteed by the islanders that these provisions were for outfitting their own whaleships and not "expended in foreign-consumption"; in other words, for fitting out ships to take oil to Britain.

Kezia Fanning, the diarist, put it in more practical terms.

> July 6—Zeb Coffin arriv'd today from Philadelphia, went after a Load of Flour—the Congress would not suffer him to bring any declaring that we were all Tories at Nantucket.[11]

The selectmen of the town immediately sent a memorial to Congress, requesting that they be relieved of the selection of a representative to the Congress, as "the inhabitants are the greater part of the people call'd Quakers, whose well known principles of Religion will not admit of their taking up arms in a Military way in any case whatever," that they hoped for a "speedy reconciliation to take place" for the mutual benefit of "fellow subjects this, or the other side of the Atlantic"; and that any reports of supplying the British fisheries was "without foundation." [12]

Among those from Boston seeking in Nantucket a haven from war was James Bowdoin and family. He had been a delegate to the first Continental Congress, and his attesting to the truth of the selectmen's memorial had much to do with its favorable reception in Watertown.

A number of permits allowing Nantucket to import provisions were granted by the Committee of Correspondence at Falmouth. The economically besieged islanders, hard-pressed, accepted the situation with characteristic calm. But then Governor Trumbull, of Connecticut, through the General Court, accused the Nantucketers of supplying the British with materials granted for their whaling outfits, which had been obtained from Long Island. Captain Thomas Jenkins had made application to sail for a southern port for provisions he had been unable to get in Massachusetts Bay. At Philadelphia, he was prevented from selling his cargo of whale oil in order to obtain a return cargo of supplies. More and more vessels returned empty after cruises to the Continent. Fuel was getting low and winter was rapidly approaching.[13]

The designation of Nantucket as a loyalist stronghold continued to be stressed, with the result that during September 1775, the General Court of Massachusetts, in issuing permits for vessels to go whaling, stipulated that they must give a bond of £2000 for each vessel and must return their cargoes to some port in this Colony, *the Ports of Boston and Nantucket excepted.*[14]

There was no middle course for the Nantucket whalemen. Whaling was their all—the sum and substance of their existence. In order to sail, they must accept the bond to obtain the permits—or be judged Tories. If they were intercepted at sea by the British blockading fleet they would be seized as rebels. As their entire economy depended upon whaling, the shipowners had no alternative but to fit out their vessels. As their livelihood was on the sea, the whalemen chose the risk of making a voyage, and chance either capture or sinking, rather than to stay ashore and starve.

It was at this point that four prominent whale-oil merchants conceived an idea which they hoped would salvage the whaling industry until the "present unhappy troubles" were resolved. These men were Francis Rotch, of New Bedford (already heard of in the Tea Party episode) and Nantucket; Richard Smith, of Boston; Aaron Lopez, of Newport, and Leonard Jarvis, of Dartmouth.[15]

Aaron Lopez, of Newport, was then in his forty-fifth year, a merchant who had made a fortune in coastwise shipping and trading with the West Indies. Since his arrival in Newport from Portugal in 1750, this interesting man had been closely allied with the whale-oil trade and had many trading ventures with the Rotch and other Nantucket business houses.

During his mercantile life Lopez owned thirty-nine ships and owned parts of sixty-one others. When the British seized Newport, he and his immediate family, with others of his circle, removed to Leicester, Massachusetts. He later supported the rebellious colonies but at this period he was apparently neutral.

Shortly after the prohibiting acts on whaling were passed by the Continental Congress, Francis Rotch and Lopez determined to make an effort to carry on the industry. Their plan was a daring one—to establish a rendezvous for the fleet far from the scene of impending war—at the Falkland Islands in the South Atlantic.

In a letter from Jarvis to Lopez, dated April 5, 1775, it is clearly shown that whaling at the Falkland was then of a few years standing and that prospects of obtaining a good voyage there were excellent.[16] It would further appear that those participating in the venture—Francis Rotch, Jarvis, Lopez and Richard Smith—were men who had done much business together.

The very boldness of the scheme was only one feature; the securing of political backing was another. First, Rotch and Lopez obtained from the General Court of Massachusetts Bay permits to dispatch whaling vessels from New England, the bond set at £2000 for each vessel, "that all the Oyl and bone taken by them in the course of said voyage shall be brought in, & landed in some port or harbour in this Colony, such as they may chus, *except* the Ports of Boston & Nantucket." This blanket permit was granted on August 30, 1775.[17]

That the two merchants had made application for these permits sometime before they were granted is shown by a letter from the London oil merchant George Hayley, written to Aaron Lopez, under date of August 31, 1775: [18]

> I notice part of your whaling vessels are sailed for the Vineyard, and that the others will follow soon. I shall be very happy to hear they have sailed from thence, as the report is they will not be suffered to depart. The same I must say respecting the vessels in which you have taken a concern with Mr. Rotch, whose arrivals here will give me great pleasure as I am not without apprehension of her also being stopped. If she has been suffered to sail, I may be expecting her very soon.

A pertinent record in a diary of the time reveals that Francis Rotch and Lopez had fitted out some twenty sail of ships and brigs at least a month before the permits were received from the Continental Congress! These whaling vessels came from New Bedford, Newport and Nantucket. Because they could no longer outfit in safety at Nantucket the fleet were gathered at the Vineyard, either at Holmes Hole (Vineyard Haven), or Edgartown (Old Town), probably the latter.

Kezia Fanning recorded under August 12, 1775:

> Early this morning the Falmouth (Colonel Otis) company went in boats to the Vineyard to stop Rotch's & Lopuses fleet of whale-men. They have fitted out fifteen or twenty sail of ships, brigs and

other vessels to go to the Falkland Islands a-whaling. Common fame says they intend to go to England with their oil. The Falmouth people were satisfied to the contrary of what they had heard. They returned as they went.[19]

The suspicions of the Continentals were justified. But the whaling interests had little alternative. Neither Francis Rotch nor Aaron Lopez had any idea of how long the Revolution would drag on; more than that, their interest was largely in circumventing the trouble. Therefore, although they had given the masters of the whaleships instruction to bring the oil back to their home port if possible, it was London after all that was the only market available.

Fortunately one set of these instructions to the captains is in existence. It was directed to Captain John Lock, master of the brigantine *Minerva,* dated Newport, September 4, 1775,[20] and indicates the whaling fleet made up of a few vessels at a time probably sailed within several days of that date.

Captain Lock's instructions were to sail for the equator and once "across the equinoxial Line . . . make the best of your way towards the Brazil Coast, touching as little time at any island or port in your way for refreshment . . . as possible." It was noted that "we cannot give you particular directions in this point, not knowing that there may be occasion for your stopping at all . . . not doubting, from the inquiries you have made, of your knowledge and ideas of the voyage you are going upon that you are fully convinced at the necessity of getting upon the Whaling Ground as soon as possible." [21]

It is logical to assume here that the masters of the fleet receiving instructions similar to those presented Captain Lock were advised to get off the coast as quickly as possible. Thus they would avoid British cruisers who might not be pleased with inspecting permits issued by the Massachusetts rebels. But the postscript to the orders: "Should any material accident happen . . . after you get off the Coast . . . we would have at all events to avoid returning to either the American Colonies but to proceed as shall be most convenient to either of the under-mentioned places." [22] These ports were St. Eustatius and Barbados, the West Indies, Cadiz, Lisbon and Gibraltar in Europe, Madeira and Teneriffe in the Canary Islands.

The directions to the captains further observed that it was expected that the ships would reach the "Whaling Grounds at Brazil Banks" some time in November 1775, and it was recommended that they cruise southward after "Spermacitis Whales off and about Soundings until you get in the Latitude of the Falkland Islands."

It was carefully pointed out that seeking a harbor in South America should be avoided. The instructions elaborated on this as follows:

> We think it strictly expedient to forbid your going into any Port or Harbour within 4 Leagues of the Brazil Coast, although in cases of extreme necessity as amount to little short of Life & Death, we have a right of admission into Ports of any foreign Nation, which we are in amity with, still under circumstances which is that of Whaling in Seas adjacent to their territories it may be extremely dangerous to fall into their hands. . . .[23]

That the proponents of the scheme had great hopes the fleet would arrive at the rendezvous is certain, but nothing was left to the chance offered by the possible appearance of a privateer or frigate.

> We would further enjoin you to have no connection with any Portuguese or Spanish vessel in any way whatever, but when you approach any Vessel, we would have you hoist your white Signal at your fore-topgallant mast head & in a few minutes haul it down, & after the same space of time hoist it again & if not we desire you will keep entirely clear of them unless by any other circumstance you can be fully satisfied they are English Whalemen.

From these orders to Captain Lock, it was Rotch's plan to sail for the Falklands on one of the whaleships. The sailing directions to the master of the *Minerva* continued:

> We mean for you to cruise . . . until you have filled your casks, or until by . . . bad weather or accident you have occasion to make some port; you are therefore for many reasons, particularly that of Insurance at all events to proceed for Port Egmont in the Falkland Islands where you are, with all the rest of our Vessels upon these voyages to rendezvous & recruit, & where, if no unforseen accident prevents, you may be assured you will find our own Francis Rotch, with whom you will be able to consult & mutually determine upon what further measure . . . to adopt for the remainder of the voyage.[24]

Another important fact was mentioned. After authorizing the ship-master to winter at the Falklands with Francis Rotch, if the voyage required, it further stipulated that, if there was a prospect of advancing the voyage during the winter by engaging in the "Seal Fishery and other ways, you will not think of rejecting such an opportunity." This is definite proof of Rotch's first-hand knowledge of the value of the sealing here—the first American merchant who so recognized this later important industry.

This American fleet sailing for the Brazil Banks and the Falklands actually totaled sixteen vessels. Francis Rotch had five of his vessels and registered six others with Jarvis. Lopez registered two and William Rotch had the other three.

The subsequent activities of this fleet occupy a period of many years, now and then appearing in some report. The full account of their voyages has never been recounted. For over a century and three-quarters they have been like mystery ships, enveloped in the mists of a forgotten period of the Revolution.

Which ship Francis Rotch embarked on is not known. It must have been his intention to sail first to London and there carefully make arrangements with the Admiralty for the protection of his fleet, then sail for Port Egmont in the Falklands. On the way out of Nantucket Sound his vessel was forced to heave-to by the British ship *Rose*, Captain Wallace, who allowed him to proceed. Rotch had no sooner arrived in London than word reached him that five of his whaleships had been captured off the Azores by two British frigates and taken into Spithead and Portsmouth!

Throughout a life filled with climaxes, Francis Rotch never showed more resourcefulness than at this moment. He immediately (November 29, 1775) sent lengthy petitions to Lord North, and to other officials, requesting the release of his vessels, stating:

> . . . That your petitioners came to London with the Intention of residing here and fitting out such Vessels for the whale fishery as proper men could be obtained for, that they are preparing all sorts of whaling stores to the value of ten thousand pounds to be sent to the Falkland Islands where they have ordered their vessels to rendezvous from whence all the oil and other produce of the Fishery will be shipped . . . Immediately for London; this will be as agreeable to their Interest as to their Inclination, no other market calling for the quantity or affording so good a price for the proceeds of the Sperm Fishery.[25]

The petitioner carefully pointed out the advantages to be gained by Britain, announcing he intended the oil for the mother country. Here was something the Admiralty had hoped for years might develop—a vigorous prosecution of whaling out of home ports. Rotch skillfully pointed out how the valuable sperm whale fishery could be fostered:

> The Americans are universally allowed to be the most resolute & expert in this Branch; for of the various species of whalemen which are known, the English, Dutch and other European nations, who pursue the Whale-Fishery, only kill a particular kind of bone whale (the Right Whale) found in the Greenland and other seas, and as the attack on the other kinds (Sperm Whale and Humpback) requiring more dexterity and being attended with more danger, they do not attempt it. The American on the contrary successfully encounters every kind of whale & *are the only people who kill the Sperm Whale.*

Francis Rotch was astute politically, too. He wrote that the whale fishery, as carried on in the New England provinces, which the petitioners hoped to transfer to London, was certain "to prove of greater utility to Great Britain than the Greenland Fisher," which annually cost the government a considerable sum in bounties. He continued, with marked sagacity:

> Your petitioners, in pursuing their design establishing this value-able fishery from hence, have adopted the only mode in which they could succeed. It was not practicable during the present trouble in America to persuade them to come out here to fit out . . . your Petitioners, after having fitted out our Vessels, being desirous of extending the Commerce from hence, attempted to engage a number of whalemen to come to London to be sent on the Fishery in Vessels purchased & fitted here, but from the Public Clamor very few would be prevailed with. . . . Your Petitioners being the first who dare attempt to establish so valuable a branch of the Fishery in Great Britain without any previous requisition from Government for support, but relying on the attention which the Legislators manifested in favor of the Fishery during last session of Parliament.

Now the secret of the Falklands Fleet was out!

As a powerful addition to his persuasive argument, Rotch played his trump card, stating:

> Your Petitioners further intend to establish the manufacturing of Spermaceti candles in London, a branch which is become of consid-

erable consequence in America, though very little known & but imperfectly executed here, for the purpose Mr. A. Lopez, who is well experienced in the manufactury, they expect is now in Jamaica on his way to London, where he intends residing to superintend the s'd manufactury, which they doubt not on enquiry will be found to merit the countenance of Government.

Lord North's Ministry, although they were slow at deliberating, finally recommended that the Admiralty release the five captured whaleships—the *Harlequin, Falkland, Enterprise, Abigail* and *Minerva*. But the British whaling merchants had to have their compensation. In a letter to Lopez, under date of February 26, 1776, Francis Rotch, after informing him of the success of the petition for the release of the ships, stated:

> By tedious application I got them released . . . but attended with the loss of *all our men,* the replacing of which occasioned such delay and subjected us to the greatest severity of weather almost ever known in England. The Thames was frozen for a month . . . the first three whaleships got to sea before the cold came on. . . .[26]

But he was careful to point out to Lopez another distinct possibility which must be anticipated:

> Should any of our whalemen be seized by the late Restraining Act and carried to any port in the West Indies, you will doubtless direct the Master to make a claim for yourself, as a resident of Jamaica, and for myself, a resident of London, and appeal to the Lord Commissioners as the Act directs and by the claim to England where these claims may be supported and the property saved.

Francis Rotch, thereafter, designated himself a resident of London, "formerly of Boston," and Lopez, a resident of Jamaica, "formerly of Newport," and a certain Richard Smith, "formerly of Boston, now of London." Rotch also wrote Lopez that Smith "by mutual consent is dismiss'd from the concern," and that I must refer you to our mutual friend George Hayley, Esquire, for intelligence of what has been done here."

In their carefully written instructions to the captains of the whale fleet, the owners had stated:

> If . . . you see or speak with & if you should see any Vessels coming this way you must not fail to write in a particular manner to

Aaron Lopez in Newport, Leonard Jarvis in Dartmouth, or William Rotch in Nantucket, as may be convenient, if by chance you should fall in with any vessels bound for England, write in the same manner to George Hayley, Es., Merchant, in London, let him know your particulars & success.[27]

In a second petition to Lord Germaine, one of His Majesty's Principal Secretarys of State,[28] endorsed December 11, 1775, Rotch expressed his satisfaction at the release of the five ships of his fleet, captured near the Azores, and for the "assurance that the others would be protected at sea." He therefore "humbly begged that . . . License and protection may be granted" for *other vessels* to be sent into the southern fishery, "in executing their Laudable design for Establishing the said Fishery from hence."

A "protection" was requested for the *Royal Charlotte,* one hundred tons, Nathaniel Hathaway, master, which had sailed from Newport to Surinam, thence to North Carolina, "for staves for the Fishery and to proceed to the Falkland Islands," and for the sloop, *Sally,* bound on a similar voyage. Further than this, the memorialists informed their lordships that they were "loading sundry Vessels in the River Thames with stores for their Fishery which are near ready to sail for the Falkland Islands. They therefore humbly request your Lordship . . . take into the expos'd state of their property in the enumerated Vessels & their Cargoes into consideration and give such reasonable orders or directions for the security of their property so beneficially employed for this Kingdom as to your Lordship shall appear just & reasonable."

Now came the strangest plays of fortune in this game of whaleships playing hide-and-seek with war.

News arrived constantly of the capture of whaleships by both the Continentals and British. Into the stronghold of the Quakers—Sherburne-Town on Nantucket—came privateers and armed vessels manned by refugees from New York, Connecticut and Rhode Island. The headquarters of the New England whale fishery was blockaded, her ships and sloops cut off, her seamen impressed. There were grave doubts that the southern fleet could escape the blockade. A headquarters for supplies and repair at the Falkland Islands was therefore a most desirable one.

Early in May 1776, Captain Moses Giles arrived from the Brazil Banks with a full ship, and reported the sighting of many schools of sperm whales. In former days this news would have been greeted with a hum of activity in outfitting ships to sail hence; now only a few craft were available. In fact, a number of whaleships were loaded with household goods and oil (as a commodity for barter) and many families were transported to settle "on the Main." Some of these ships sailed to North Carolina, where a colony of Nantucket Quakers had settled a few years before; others went up the Hudson to Dutchess County, Saratoga and other parts of New York State.

There were cases of good fortune. Captain Paul Hussey, returning from "on Brazil," was captured a few days' sail from Nantucket by the H.M.S. *Eagle,* with none other than General William Howe, new commander of the British forces in America, on board. "Gen'l Howe told Hussey he was bound for New York and had full power to settle the controversy, betwix Great Britain and her Colonies, and he was determined to make peace quickly. The General treated him handsomely and he released him." [29] Captain John Gage, bound home from St. Pierre, West Indies, was also taken but released with a warning not to trade with the French.

Two other whalemen got through the blockade, but Captain David Rand, in the *Ranger,* of Nantucket, was not so fortunate. Off Sable Island, the whaleship was taken by H.M.S. *Orpheus,* and during the same month two more Nantucket craft were taken by the same frigate, their crews sent into Halifax to the prison ships. Jonathan Mooers' oil-laden craft was retaken, however (in sight of the Nova Scotian shore) by an American privateer, who obligingly brought Mooers home—but kept the whaleship. This episode was repeated many times. Truly the whaleman was between the devil and the deep.

Captain Barzillai Folger, a whaleman turned by circumstance into a trader, appeared at Nantucket Bar early one morning in March 1777. He had sailed the preceding August for the Brazil Banks. While on the whaling ground he was captured by a British frigate, his crew impressed, and he forced to go also before the mast. It was all according to the provisions of the Restraining Act—any prisoners taken on board an American vessel should be compelled, without distinction of rank, to serve as common sailors on British men-of-war. Even the

English Annual Register for 1776 protested this "refinement in tyranny" wherein these American prisoners, "after being plundered themselves, become accomplices in plundering their brethren!" Some thirty Nantucket whaleships were captured by the British and added to the southern fleet, and another large number pressed into the northern or Greenland fleet.

Slowly but steadily, the New England whale fleet was driven from the sea. The sentiment in behalf of the embattled colonies had gradually grown to become a part of the whaling industry as well. Captain Nathan Folger, taken in his whaleship, when asked what he should choose, imprisonment or the forecastle of a British man-of-war, replied: "Hang me if you will to the yardarm of your ship but do not ask me to be a traitor to my country!" With a dozen other whaling masters, he was put aboard the rotting prison hulks of the *Jersey* and *Rising Sun*. Their fate was shared by hundreds of whalemen, some of whom were penned in British prisons for years.

But what of the whale fleet intended for rendezvous at the Falklands under Francis Rotch's careful supervision? The ships were doing well and news of them gradually came to the attention of Benjamin Franklin and John Adams, American Commissioners in France. Early in 1778, these two farsighted men wrote to the President of Congress, urging the destruction of the British whale fleet on the Coast of Brazil, thus cutting off the English supply of oil and releasing the American crews who were practically prisoners of war, compelled to aid the enemy. But Congress was unable to see the importance of the suggestion, or did not fully appreciate the opportunity.

As early as December 1775, from London, Samuel Enderby the British whaling merchant had written to Nathaniel Wheatley, a strong loyalist of Boston, then residing at Providence, advising him to sell his ships *Triton* and *Pitt* in Nantucket, "although you should have given the Master positive orders to proceed here." [30] Then Enderby requests: "If you come over in the Spring, I would wish you to bring over 30 good whalemen, as I have a grand scheme in view. . . . If you can buy a good vessel of 150 tons to come in, and bring 31 good whalemen, I should think it the best thing you can do. The *Rockingham* and

Union are both sailed for the Brassils as is eight vessels more from here. I have brought Bartlett [Coffin] a fine new ship of 350 tons burthen. . . ."

Again in September 1779, John Adams, writing from his home in Braintree to the Council of Massachusetts Bay, urged that a single frigate or a privateer of twenty guns be sent to where the British "carried on this Fishery to great advantage off of the River Plate, in South America, in the Latitude 35° south and from thence to 40° . . . off and on, about the Longitude 65 West. They are seventeen vessels in this Fishery which all sailed from London in the months of September and October. All the officers and men are Americans." [31] Adams then gave a list of twenty whaling masters—one from Newport, one from Long Island, one from Dartmouth, and seventeen from Nantucket. Three of the craft were in the Greenland fishery. He declared the information that the fleet was protected by a frigate was a forgery. Besides capturing the vessels and releasing their masters, Adams wrote that at least 450 whalemen—"the best kind of seamen"— would be taken out of the hands of the British. He concluded, prophetically:

> I thought it my duty to communicate this intelligence to your Honours, that if so profitable a Branch of Commerce, and so valuable a Nursery of Seamen can be taken from the English, it may be done. This State has a peculiar Right and Interest to undertake the Enterprise, as almost the whole fleet belongs to it. . . .

The letter was reported favorably by a committee—but, like so many good suggestions, in the press of war was overlooked in the flood of mediocre measures. It is ironic that the only effort made to destroy the British whale fishery on the coast was the action of John Paul Jones, who sailed the *Alfred* into Canso Harbor in the early winter of 1776 and burned all the craft and oil of the industry gathered there. Among the crew on board the *Alfred* were several young Nantucket whalemen, active participants in the war. They made valuable pilots.

Aboard the *Providence,* September 4, 1776, Captain Jones wrote to the Marine Commission that he had captured a "Nantucket whaler . . . She appeared . . . to be the property of rank Tories who had ordered their oil to be carried to the London market, and the amount of it to be shipped out in English goods to Nantucket." [32] This whaleship was the *Britannia*.

Reuben Swain wrote General George Washington this same year for permission to request from the British release of his son and two sons-in-law, "taken . . . on their return from a long and tedious whale-voyage on the Coast of Brazil." Two of the Nantucketers had been impressed aboard the British ship-of-war *Greyhound*. The whaleship captured was the *Speedwell*, Captain Obed Bunker.

About the same time, Benjamin Barnard wrote a similar petition, seeking the liberation of a son taken on board the whaler *Mercury*, captured while returning from "on Brazil," and detained on board the frigate *Cerberus*. Thus, the fate of whaleships and their crews.

During 1777 and 1778, while New England's whaling headquarters at Nantucket was blockaded, the other ports gradually abandoned the industry. Several ports on the main soon made privateering a lucrative substitute and the Quakers of Sherburne-Town found it hard to keep more of their young whalemen from becoming involved in the struggle.

On board John Paul Jones's *Ranger* was a crew which Jones later called the best he ever commanded. Twenty of these were Nantucket whalemen. When the dynamic little Scot took over the old East Indianman, the *Bon Homme Richard,* most of these islanders went with him. One of them, Henry Gardner, became his chief gunner, and in later years Gardner named his first whaleship the *Ranger*.

The New England privateers became so numerous that in September 1778, the British organized a punitive expedition along the coast of Connecticut and southeastern Massachusetts. The fleet, dispatched by General Clinton, contained a dozen ships-of-war and six transports, and were ordered to burn out the "rebel nests of privateers" and get all the supplies they could to feed the British troops in New York.

On September 4, the British raiders had reached New London. During the day the vessels sailed up the coast to Clark's Cove, where they anchored, and on that night, in the moonlight, they marched two thousand men over a bridge of boats to the shore, and proceeded across the countryside to the little village of New Bedford. Warned by alarm guns, the inhabitants of the village fled, leaving homes and ships to the invaders. [33]

With deliberate malice the "red-coats" pillaged and looted—then set fire to houses and the ships, tied up at the wharves or anchored in the harbor. Their way lighted by the leaping flames, the raiders made their way to the head of the Acushnet River, then marched down the east side to Fairhaven and Sconticut Point where they spiked the cannon at the little fort which commanded the harbor entrance.

They would have burned the hamlet of Fairhaven but for the courageous stand of Major Israel Fearing and his three hundred men.

When the Britishers embarked several hours later they left behind them the ruins of New Bedford village—eleven houses burned flat, cooper shops, warehouses, ropewalks, candle-house, blacksmith shops—all destroyed. The loss in shipping was devastating—seven ships, one snow, one barque, six brigs, five schooners, eight sloops. This was a blow from which New Bedford only recovered by re-establishment as a whaling port, and this took place five years after the treaty of peace. It meant not only the loss of houses, ships, whaling gear, and supplies of sugar, molasses, flour, cotton, tobacco, rum, etc., but the destruction of the second largest whaling port of its time in New England.

The British raiders were in strength, and they had worked methodically. Leaving Clark's Cove, they crossed Buzzards Bay into Vineyard Sound. A few craft were sent up to Falmouth and Wareham for bits of side-play, the objectives being Martha's Vineyard and Nantucket.

At Tarpaulin Cove, on Naushon Island, where Zacheus Lumbert had built a lighthouse for whalers (lighted by contributions of Nantucket oil), the British had taken fourteen hundred sheep, thirty-five head of cattle, and twenty horses. From small Nonannesset, they took off seventy-five sheep and four calves.

At the Vineyard harbor of Holmes Hole, the raiders' fleet stretched from shore to shore, like a swarm of sea-going locusts. The report from Falmouth's raid was that two sloops and a schooner were taken and one sloop burned. Four vessels were taken at Holmes Hole, and at Edgartown a schooner, and a brig were burned, and twenty-three whaleboats captured.[34]

September 10, 1778, dawned with a summons to Colonel Beriah Norton, head of the Vineyard militia, to come on board. He was ordered to produce all the sheep, cattle and arms which the Vineyard contained. Three island representatives repaired on board the *Carysfort,* Captain Fanshaw's flagship. They were given similar orders plus the remission of public funds—with three o'clock the following afternoon as the deadline.

September 11-12, 1778, were sad days for Martha's Vineyard. A total of ten thousand sheep, three hundred head of cattle and oxen, 388 stands of arms with equipment, and ten thousand pounds sterling in paper (an amount equal to the tax levied by the rebel Congress) was the price demanded by the conquerors.

The British commanders counted their gains and watched the weather. In the turmoil of events, perhaps, no one on either side realized that the future of the American whale fishery hung in balance. The largest port in southeastern Massachusetts, and the headquarters of American whaling—Nantucket—was the next destination of the raiders.

chapter vii

⟨⟨⟨◦⟩⟩⟩

SALVAGING THE SINKING SHIP

... I therefore ... forbid all privateers, armed vessels or bodies of armed men from molesting ... or plundering the inhabitants of said island. ...

> —Sir George Collier, Commanding His Majesty's Ships in North America, 1779

WITH SUCH A PROSPECT, the Nantucketers grimly awaited the arrival of the British raiding fleet. They knew what was in store—the final sacrifice of the remnants of their once-extensive whaling fleet, the last hope for their future.

One of the younger people wrote:

> News came ... of war at the Vineyard burning & destroying there and that they were bound here to destroy the stores and shipping. In consequence of it, people are moving their goods out of town.... Mr. Fanning came down with the mare & calash. . . . The oxen & 2 horses went down in the afternoon to bring up things.[1]

Then occurred a circumstance which was almost miraculous. An east-northeast gale sprang up on the night of September 11, 1779. All the next day it blew steadily. The British fleet at the Vineyard could not, in the narrow confines of the sound, beat against it. On the next day and night the wind continued at almost gale force, forcing the fleet to remain at anchor.

Aboard the British transports, the soldiers grumbled and the sailors of the eleven ships cursed the easterly. In their cramped quarters, the sheep and cattle moaned. The air was foul with their stench. The third day dawned—the wind still as strong from the east. General Sir Charles Grey conferred with Captain Fanshaw, of the frigate *Carysfort,* and with Major John André, the intelligence officer. Orders had arrived from Lord Howe; the expedition was to return to New York— the raid on Nantucket was abandoned. Did not the members of the Society of Friends see in this the hand of God at last coming to their aid? [2]

Heartened by this natural interpretation, the Nantucketers took renewed faith in their position. But this was put to a sore test soon after. A fleet of seven vessels, commanded by the loyalist George Leonard, with Tory refugees, came to the island in April 1779, and raided a number of warehouses, taking along 260 barrels of sperm oil, fourteen hundred pounds of bone, a quantity of iron, and other goods valued at more than $50,000. [3]

Three leading men, William Rotch, Samuel Starbuck and Dr. Benjamin Tupper, were deputized by a town meeting to sail to Newport and New York and petition the British commanders for relief from such depredations. At Newport, the influence of the refugees was almost too much to overcome, but they persevered and won their point. Sailing to New York, they presented their case to Sir Henry Clinton and Commodore Sir George Collier. The latter finally agreed to issue an order forbidding any British armed vessel to molest Nantucket Harbor. At this time, also, the three delegates pleaded successfully for the release of island whalemen held on the prison ships in New York Harbor. [4]

But these negotiations had their own repercussions. The Council of Massachusetts Bay received a letter from the blustering General Horatio Gates, the Continental commander, dated April 16, 1779, accusing Nantucket of treason.

> . . . As the Town of Sherburne is in your State, I doubt not but your Honorable Council will immediately take proper measures to prevent any Separate Treaty being made with the enemy . . . such Things are not only pernicious to the General Confederacy of the United States but traitorous in the Transaction. [5]

The council made formal complaint; the town as formally denied the accusation. Corresponding with the enemy under the circumstances was understandable and the provincial authorities recognized the situation. The town was sternly forbidden to further treat with the enemy, but retaliatory measures were lessened somewhat.

To add to the suffering, the winter of 1780 was one of the most severe ever experienced. Reduced to a state of penury many islanders dug the peat from the swamps for fuel. Men walked about the wharves where the whaleships lay, stripped of running rigging, yards and top-masts, their hatches battened over empty holds. Ice formed all around the island, providing the most effective blockade. Finally the dreadful winter passed.

Sloops formerly used in whaling had been sent into the West India trade. Masters of ships who had been taken and impressed in British ships, were captured by provincial privateers and placed in colonial prisons; others were sent to British prisons in England. Kezia Fanning reported the return of "Nathan and Richard Coffin and a number of others" who had gone to London early in 1779, but who had escaped from prison.[6] These entered the West India trade. Codfish became of considerable importance in this business, with return cargoes of salt, molasses and other commodities. Gradually, this business, too, became the prey of privateers and frigates.

As the war dragged on Major Dimmick, of the Continental garrison at Falmouth, proved a welcome ally. Every month had seen one or two Nantucket craft captured, one of them being ransomed for £250 sterling. Major Dimmick, who was on the island during a privateer raid, turned the tables by organizing a boat's crew to capture the Britisher. In July and October 1781, Dimmick coming to the island, waged a pitched battle with British refugee privateers in this harbor, driving them off and recapturing their prizes.[7]

A dozen former whaling masters, plus as many more owners of ships, sent a petition to the General Court of Massachusetts in the spring of 1780, requesting remuneration for goods taken in these refugee raids. The petition stated, in part:

> . . . at the Commencement of the present war almost the whole (of) their property lay in shipping for the carrying on the Whale Fishery Since which they have Employed them in the West India and other trade till they have almost lost the whole; without the power or Ability to replace them . . . the property taken from your Petitioners by

the Refugees consisting mostly in the article of oyl which was taken during the war, and was almost their whole dependence. . . .[8]

At this same time, Captain Timothy Folger, acting as agent for the townspeople, sought to recover $20,000 worth of property stolen by the refugees and was granted permission by the Massachusetts Council to treat with the British in New York for the recovery of the same. Obed Macy states that Folger, while in New York, attempted to secure permits for Nantucket ships to resume whaling. Although not immediately successful the petition opened the way for subsequent aid by British officials.[9]

Timothy Folger also noted the fact that his friend John Hancock was now governor of the Commonwealth of Massachusetts. In a petition to Governor Hancock and the General Court, the whaling master observed that, "before the unhappy troubles," Nantucket had annually taken from twenty-five thousand to thirty thousand barrels of oil and that they had hoped "in one day to come they may be of some service to the Community, if they are not forced to Abandon the Island for want of subsistence of which there is great danger." [10]

It is evident that the town had resolved to seek aid from both the British and Continentals. One group of men was delegated to treat with the former, another with the latter. In each case, the preservation of the whaling industry was the price offered in payment for full consideration. At last, appreciation for what the island stood for was fully acknowledged, and the islanders' prosecution of the industry again allowed.

A town meeting for October 3, 1780, delegated William Rotch, Samuel Starbuck and Benjamin Hussey to treat with Admiral Digby in New York. In his *Memorandum* William Rotch gives an account of the interview and of the subsequent granting for twenty-five permits for the whale fishery.[11] One of these permits shows that the sloop *Dolphin,* Captain Gilbert Folger, with a crew of twelve men, was permitted to proceed on a whaling voyage provided a certificate of ownership from the selectmen accompanied the permit.[12]

The procurement of Admirality permits gave the islanders a chance to trade again directly with London. One of the first to take advantage of the opportunity was Captain Timothy Folger, who had attempted to get permits through the Massachusetts Council. In the fall of 1781, he had sailed for London on the sloop *Good Intent,* Captain William Mooers, master, carrying a cargo of sperm oil, which, as can be imagined, carried a good price. The sloop returned on December 21, 1781, with packages of dry goods and a ballast of grindstones and coal. Not only was he armed with a permit from Admiral Arbuthnot of H. M. Navy, but he also had a "protection" paper signed by "Cousin" Benjamin Franklin. Four passengers came from England on the *Good Intent*—a craft aptly named.[13]

Immediately, the sloop was chartered to six other islanders for a voyage to Havana, Cuba, loading with codfish and onions. Acting upon information received by some apparent troublemaker, (who smelled whale oil in the hold as well as onions), the Provincial Council at Watertown ordered the naval officer of the port at Nantucket, a certain Ichabod Plaisted, to seize the *Good Intent* for violation of the rule on trading with the enemy. Plaisted went down to the wharf and put two of his men on board as guards. That night, a group of "Riotous persons" appeared out of the darkness, seized and bound the guards, and proceeded to strip the sloop of her sails and some running rigging, to keep her from being carried off. Plaisted wrote for instructions; the owners of the cargo petitioned for a permit to sail with the perishable cargo. After hearing the case, the council peremptorily ordered the petition dismissed, but five days later (January 21, 1782) reconsidered and directed the surrender of the cargo to the alleged owners. The original case against the sloop dragged on, however, for eight more months.[14]

The new year of 1782 for Nantucket opened on a sad note, indeed. With the ending of the old year two brigs anchored in back of the bar. They were Boston craft, manned by Nantucketers, bound on whaling voyages, and they had put in for final visits of the whalemen with their families. On the first day of the year, the commander of one of the brigs, Captain Robert Barker, and six fellow-islanders launched their whaleboat from shore to regain their vessel. A strong wind from the north caused them considerable trouble but they made headway until they reached the shoal water at the bar. Here the boat was seen to overturn and all in the boat were drowned. Two boats from shore put out, but too late to save any of the men.[15]

In a letter to Hezekiah Barnard of Nantucket, in the year 1840,

William Rotch, Jr., revealed that some thirty Nantucket whaleships went out under the "Digby permits" during the period from the fall of 1781 to the early winter of 1782. He also recounted that at least one of the vessels sailed to London with oil under Captain Timothy Folger, and that several Boston men sailed as passengers, including "the late Governor Winthrop, Thomas Jones, —— Hutchinson and others whose names I do not recollect."

But the resumption of the whaling industry was attended with so much danger that the gains to individual merchants was offset by losses in equal proportion. If there was any advantage, it was in the fact that the business of whaling was once again being pursued in New England ships.

It was certain that, once the knowledge was released, this whaling under British permits would bring the wrath of the commanders of the American armed vessels. Seventeen whalers sailed in 1782. The hazards in the game become too great; in order to carry on the business successfully, and save both their livelihood and their homes, the Nantucketers resolved to seek permits from the General Court of the State.

At a town meeting held September 25, 1782, it was voted to send five prominent merchants to the General Court with a memorial. This document set forth the critical situation of the island and begged relief; it acknowledged acts committed through the "influence of the great laws of Self-preservation"; it reminded the state of the "great importance of the Whale-Fishery" to the country; it declared that "if due attention is not paid to this valuable branch, which . . . would appear the most advantageous of any possess'd by the government, it will be intirely lost, if the War continues"; and it prophesied "many of the Inhabitants must quit the Island, not being able even to provide the necessaries for the approaching Winter." [16]

The memorial put its "moving finger" on the great choice which lay in the hands of the provincial authorities when it declared, forth-rightly:

> . . . and the most active in the [Whale] Fishery will probably go to distant Countries, where they can have every encouragement by Nations who are eagerly wishing to embrace so favourable and opportunity to accomplish their desires; which will be a great loss to the Continent in general, but more to this Government in particular.

We beg leave to impress the consideration of this important subject not as the judgement of an insignificant few, but of a town which a few Years since stood the third in Rank, (if we mistake not) in bearing the Burdens of Government; It was then populous and abounded with plenty, it is yet populous but is covered with poverty.[17]

The picture was never more concisely summed up. The members of the House quickly approved the memorial and recommended it be referred to the Congress, and the delegates of the state "use their Endeavors to impress Congress with the just Ideas of the high worth & Importance of the Whale fishery to the United States in general & this State in particular." The Senate at once adopted the report. President Samuel Adams signed it, as did Speaker Nathaniel Gorham, and, of course, Governor John Hancock.

At a town meeting held on November 23, 1782, William Rotch, Samuel Starbuck and Stephen Hussey were delegated to represent Nantucket. Rotch and Starbuck accepted and arrived in Philadelphia in mid-winter. Samuel Starbuck was a staunch loyalist but realized the great urgency of the moment. William Rotch was perhaps Nantucket's greatest citizen, whose exploits will be recounted in another chapter.[18]

At first the island delegates discussed their mission with individual members of Congress, among them General Lincoln, Minister of War, and James Madison, President of the Congress, who appeared "to take in interest in our sufferings" stated Rotch. One of the Massachusetts delegates, Samuel Osgood, showed surprising opposition. William Rotch, recognizing the prejudiced opinion of Osgood, went to his quarters and there conversed with him "about two hours . . ." endeavoring to impress him with the situation, and the necessity of their having his aid of Congress, "but it was apparent Osgood was too opinionated to be easily convinced."

Rotch gives an excellent account of his conclusive reasoning. He wrote in his *Memorandum:*

At last I asked him these questions, which were:

"Is the Whale Fishery worth preserving in this Country?"
"Yes."
"Can it be preserved in the present, state of Things by any place except Nantucket?"

"No."

"Can we preserve it unless you and the British will both give us Permits?"

"No."

"Then pray where is the difficulty?"

Thus we parted.[19]

Rotch reported this conversation to other sympathetic delegates. They proposed that Osgood be shown the memorial prepared by the Nantucketers, and be requested to present it to the assembled Congress. Osgood, admitting the worth of the argument, did just this. The keen incisiveness of this and other arguments overcame all obstacles. The danger of a complete loss of the whale fishery to the United States and the possibility of its being usurped by other nations were too solemn probabilities to be neglected.

And so on March 22, 1783, Congress passed, on its third reading, a resolution authorizing permission for Nantucket to

> . . . receive protection from the Commanding officer of His Britannick Majesty's ships in North America for Their vessels, in the prosecution of said Fishery and such protection shall not operate to the condemnation of said vessels many of the Courts of the Admiralty within the United States aforesaid; provided that every vessel furnish with said protections be provided with a certificate from the Selectmen of said Island; that she is a bona fide the property of the inhabitants of said Island; and provided further that nothing be found on board of her but the necessary whaling utensils, provisions for the voyage, and the products for the fish taken therein, anything in the ordinance Of—against double papers to the contrary notwithstanding.[20]

On that same day, thirty-five licenses were granted for a similar number of Nantucket whaleships. This was only a portion of the great fleet of 132 vessels, of whom Captain Jenkins had spoken before Parliament early in 1775. It took time to refit and provision this remnant of a once proud fleet. But there was now hope—for the first time in eight long years there was recognition of the true value of the American whale fishery.

New England had founded it; the young colonial towns of the coast had nurtured it. Nantucket, through its geographic position and Quaker religion, had created a truly great American industry. Scorned as a neutral or worse during the Revolution, its people had given their answer.

Through those dreary years the islanders had clung to whaling, despite blockade, famine and capture; had clung to the industry so that it became a symbol, an anchor of hope. Their staunchness of soul had fostered it until it was as much a part of them as their Quaker religion. By remaining steadfast, against all odds, they had literally salvaged the whaling industry for the young nation just emerging on the main as the United States of America. Later developments were to justify their faith.

chapter viii

~~~

AMERICAN WHALING IN LIMBO

. . . the whaling industry cannot be preserved in this place . . . ; the only possible remedy is in placing the island and its inhabitants in a state of neutrality.
—Report of Nantucket to Massachusetts General Court.[1]

THE COMING OF PEACE brought with it a great relief and a renewed hope to those whaling men of New England who had long awaited the day. Nantucket worked feverishly to re-establish their sole industry. The nucleus of the fleet, armed with British permits, had already sailed one by one. Many of the older men left on the island, too advanced in years to resume whaling, went into the cod-fishing business. The success of the fish trade with the West Indies during the war induced them to continue it. This had the effect of bringing in supplies needed for outfitting vessels and also for repairing ships, warehouses and houses neglected of necessity during the war.

"About this time," states Obed Macy, "many young men came home from different parts, where they had been confined as prisoners. Some of them had been absent so long, without being heard from, that their connections had relinquished all hope of ever seeing them again." [2]

One of these homecoming events was recorded by Kezia Fanning in her diary:

Shubael Coffin came to the Bar yesterday from London, several of our Nantucket young men came with him that hade been gone some time. Albert Hussey is come; he has been from home 9 years.[3]

Beside the fact that the first whaleships of the 1781-32 fleet began to bring in their oil, it must also be considered that there was some sperm oil in Nantucket, hidden from the prying eyes of spies. This was shown by the fact that a considerable quantity was exported shortly after the opening of the year 1783.[4]

The ship *Bedford,* built in 1765 in the North River of Massachusetts for the Nantucket-to-London trade, was owned by William Rotch, of Nantucket. She had been tied up at Still Dock, Nantucket, during the later years of the war. A permit for the ship to sail was obtained by Rotch from the British Admiral Digby, in New York, in the fall of 1781. The *Bedford* made a good voyage whaling to "the Brazils," returning late in the year 1782. Rotch then loaded the ship with 487 butts of whale and sperm oil and sent her on her historic voyage to London. The command of the *Bedford* was entrusted to a leader in the group of the Rotch fleet shipmasters, Captain William Mooers.

History was in the making as the *Bedford* arrived in the Downs on February 3, 1783. Her appearance in the Thames created a sensation because, as she dropped anchor in the shadow of the Tower of London, she proudly displayed from her masthead the bright new flag of the young United States—the first time the Stars and Stripes had ever been flown in any British port![5]

The *Gentleman's Magazine* of London had a paragraph reporting the incident as follows:

The ship *Bedford,* Captain Mooers, belonging to the Massachusetts . . . was reported at the Custom House the 6th instant. She was not allowed regular entry until some consultation had taken place between the commissioners of the customs and the lords of council, on account of the many acts of parliament yet in force against the rebels in America. She is loaded with 487 butts of whale oil; is American built; manned wholly by American seamen; wears the rebel colors and belongs to the Island of Nantucket in Massachusetts. This is the first vessel which displayed the thirteen rebellious stripes of America in any British Port. The vessel lies in Horsefly Down, a little below the Tower, and is intended to immediately return to New England.[6]

Several days after the *Bedford* sailed from Nantucket, the brig *Industry,* Captain John Chadwick, also loaded with oil, cleared from that island port for Europe. She completed loading her oil at Edgartown and sailed from that port on January 20, 1783. The ship's account reads:

> We Sail'd for Sum port of Europ & after a Long & Tedus Pashege We Got Soundings in the Chanel of England Wher we Spoke With a Dutch Galeot that Told us the Happy News of Pease. the 10th of March We arrived at Portland. Where we ly at our Eas the 24th We Sail'd for London, the 26th We got a pilot off Dover . . . arived att London the 29th.[7]

The Rotch firm also sent out two more craft loaded with whale oil during the opening month of 1783. The *Speedwell,* Captain William Whippey, was cleared for Aux Cayes, but was captured and taken into Jamaica. News of the provisional treaty of peace arrived and Captain Whippey immediately displayed the Stars and Stripes—the first exhibited in the West Indies port. Upon her return home, Captain Whippey took the *Speedwell* to Quebec with whale oil. Here, the Nantucket ship again displayed the flag of the young nation, this for the first time before the old citadel town of French Canada.

The success of these ventures not only helped to rebuild the extensive business of the Rotches (William Rotch lost $60,000 in the Revolution) but encouraged other Nantucket merchants to recoup their lost fortunes. By the fall and early winter of 1783-84 the island's fleet numbered sixty vessels, ships, brigs, brigantines and sloops, as well as numerous coasters.

Now other New England ports began to re-enter the industry. First, Bedford village on the Acushnet (where after the war, Joseph Rotch returned with his son Francis), as befitted a colony of Nantucket, gradually gathered another whaling fleet. Falmouth on the Cape, Boston, Plymouth, Wellfleet; Newport and Bristol, Rhode Island; Sag Harbor on Long Island, and New London, Connecticut, sent out ships.[8]

The whales were found in numbers in all the old whaling grounds. Long immunity from pursuit by the sea-hunters had given the whales opportunity to increase and again they gamboled and spouted in familiar waters and along the Gulf Stream. The ships returned to port with full cargoes.

Following the first flurry of success, the market soon became flooded with oil. Prices fell rapidly; Nantucket, specializing in sperm oil, did not at first feel the depressed market, as most of her oil went to Britain, but soon this, too, met with distress when the Parliament affixed an alien duty of £18 per ton. William Rotch summed up the serious problem, writing in his *Memorandum:*

> This duty had its full force on us. Sperm Oil was sold at Nantucket after the Peace at 17 pound Sterling per ton, which before we were separated was worth nearly 30 pounds Sterling. 25 pounds Sterling was necessary at that time to cover our expenses, and leave a very moderate profit to the Owners. Thus a loss of nearly 8 pounds Sterling per ton attended the business.[9]

To return home with good cargoes of oil and find it a glut on the American market and walled off by a duty from the British was not only discouraging but bewildering. While mainland ports, newcomers to the industry, could fit their ships out in other trades, with supplies for shipment close at hand, Nantucket was bound to sink or swim with its only business.

At length, several town meetings were held, and on March 1, 1785, Nantucket voted to empower a committee "to Prepare and Draw up a memorial to be preferred to the General Court at the next May Session."[10] The report of the committee was read at subsequent town meetings and on May 4, 1785, the town voted:

> That a Neutral State is the most convenient Situation that the Town can be placed in for the Benefit of the Inhabitants thereof under their present Circumstances.[11]

William Rotch, Timothy Folger, Richard Mitchell, Jr., and Josiah Barker were delegated to present the memorial to the General Court. In an extract from "a letter from Nantucket," a mainland newspaper printed the following:

> The island of Nantucket has held two town meetings on the subject of independence, and has adjourned until the first week in April next, to prepare a memorial to be presented to the Government and Council at Boston, setting forth their inability of paying their taxes, and the daily depreciation of the island, and likewise to request a separation from their government to enable them to make a contract with England to carry on the whale fishery free from duty. I doubt not it will be granted: Because they are unable to pay their taxes

by reason of the duty on oil, and the rapid depopulation of monied men; because the whale fishery will be carried into Nova Scotia, and their island left desolate. The advantages set forth are, that it will employ at least one hundred square rigged vessels from this state, and give every man a chance of adventuring under the cloak of Nantucket property. It will employ hundreds of men from the United States, and thousands within [the island]. It will bring an annual profit into this state from their produce, double or treble the amount of their present tax—will make a fund for remittance, and check the growth and interest of Nova Scotia. William Rotch sails for England, in May, who is to be an Embassy to lay the matter before the King and Parliament, provided it succeeds at the Court of Boston.[12]

Fearing a precedent, the Legislature denied the petition.

Having undergone the privations and dangers of war with the hope that peace would restore its former greatness, many of Nantucket's prominent merchants and shipowners grudgingly admitted at last that there was no future for the industry on Nantucket—that they must remove to other parts.

Foremost among those who finally concluded to remove was Captain Alexander Coffin. He had supported the Continental cause in its crucial years, and had carried despatches for the Continental Congress in 1776. He had never seen eye to eye with the neutral policy of Rotch. Captain Coffin, in a letter addressed to Honorable Samuel Adams in Boston, under date of June 8, 1785, wrote that William Rotch was aiding the plans of several to remove from Nantucket to England:

> He [Rotch] is now taking on board a double stock of materials, such as Cedar boards [commonly called boat boards] of which they have none in England, a large quantity of cooper's stuff for casks, &c—neither does he stop there, the house of Rotch have been endeavoring to engage a friend of mine to go to Bermuda to superintend the business at that place. . . . One of the company is now at Kennebeck, contracting with some persons for an annual supply of hoops, staves and other lumber necessary for the business.[13]

The Legislature immediately passed an act prohibiting the export of the articles enumerated by Captain Coffin. Whether there was any intent to transfer Nantucket men and material to Bermuda will never be known. But the plans of Nantucket whaling and William Rotch are known.

A few months later, Captain Coffin, discouraged by the situation at Nantucket, led a party of Nantucketers, combined with parties from Martha's Vineyard and Providence, to form a company and to establish themselves as a whaling colony. This was one of the most unusual emigrations in American economic history.

It had been carefully planned. With the close of the war and the unsettled provisions of the peace, there were several island shipowners and masters who were determined to carry on the whaling industry at a port on the main. Seth Jenkins, London trade skipper, his brother Thomas Jenkins, whale-oil merchant, and Captain Alexander Coffin were the prime movers of the organization, which called itself the "Nantucket Navigators." Marshall Jenkins, of the Vineyard, joined, as did John Alsop, of Providence, with his family, and Nathaniel Green and Hezekiah Dayton. Families from Dartmouth, led by Titus Morgan and John Thurston associated themselves with the group.[14]

A careful search was made for an appropriate port in which they might establish themselves. Apparently, Captain Seth Jenkins and his brother Thomas, who had gone to Providence from Nantucket, and Captain Alexander Coffin were the committee on arranging for the site of settlement. After months of sailing along the coast of Rhode Island, Connecticut and New York, the committee decided on a site one hundred miles up the Hudson River!

The selection was not as strange as it would first appear. From 1779 to 1783, the Hudson River below West Point had been cut off to shipping from out-of-state ports, the British being in possession of New York City. After the announcement of the suspension of hostilities, navigation was resumed. On April 18, 1783, General Heath noted:

> This afternoon the schooner *Lark,* Capt. Cottle of Nantucket, with fish, whale-oil, rum, etc., came up the Hudson to Newburgh! This was the first American vessel which had come up the River since the British took possession of New York in 1776.[15]

The Hudson—commonly called the North River—was no strange seaway to Nantucketers. A number of families had removed to Saratoga County before the Revolution. In 1775, Captain John Worth returned to the island from Saratoga with the intention of resuming whaling, but the times were too dark and he went back to his new home. As the war progressed, Daniel Folger, Latham Bunker and other Nantucket families removed to the upper Hudson valley.[16]

And so Captain Coffin and his associates were well acquainted with the Hudson's potentialities as a waterway. They decided to build their port at the sleepy little Dutch village of Claverach Landing—or Clover Reach—and it was here that Captain Coffin paid, as agent for the Nantucket Navigators, the sum of $10,000 to Peter Hogeboom for his landing stage and store and adjacent property. The first family of the migrants to build a house was that of Captain Seth Jenkins in 1783-84. Mrs. Jenkins (Dinah Folger) moved in early in 1784, with her mother, Dinah Coffin Folger, her eldest son, Robert Jenkins and three other children. John Alsop was the next to erect his house. In the spring of 1784 others arrived, bringing with them portions of their houses from Nantucket, carried on their own sloops and brigs.

It was a well-rounded company: Titus Morgan was a shipbuilder; David Bunker a miller; Peter Barnard a carpenter and shipwright; Captain Stephen Paddock a sailmaker; Thomas Jenkins a ropewalk proprietor, Shubael Worth a schoolteacher. David Lawrence became the Moderator for the Proprietors of Hudson, which was the name decided upon for the new colony. Captain Alexander Coffin stayed on at Nantucket until he had completed his affairs and then joined his associates at Hudson. He sailed from the island on October 9, 1785, taking with him not only his own family, but those of Josiah Coffin, Joseph Barnard, Jared Coffin and a number of others.[17]

Thus it was that these stalwart Nantucketers and their friends built a whaling port up the Hudson River, one hundred miles from salt water (and the same distance from British raiders during the 1812 war). Mingled with the smell of clover on the river banks came the pungent odor of whale oil, mixed with the salty tang of the ships which sailed up from the sea. From under the shadows of the Catskills these ships were to embark for seas and coasts thousands of miles away from this quiet river landing.

The town grew and prospered to an astounding degree. Less than a year after its inception, the first ship was launched, named the *Hudson*—the first of one hundred vessels to be owned by this port. Farmers found sloops ready to take their produce anywhere along the coast. By 1786, four fine wharves, several large warehouses, a ropewalk, sail loft, 150 dwellings, a spermaceti factory, a large distillery, barns and cornsheds had been erected. The waterfront teemed with activity. A rival whaling port now competed with New England.

Alarmed by the removal of the whalemen from Nantucket, the General Court of Massachusetts, in its session of 1785, passed a resolution, stating:

> Whereas this Court, having a due sense of the high worth and importance of the whale fishery, and desirous of its preservation, not only to this state, but to the United States in general; therefore, Resolved that there be paid out of the Treasury of this Commonwealth, the following bounties upon whale oil:
> For every ton of white spermaceti oil, five pounds;
> For every ton of brown or yellow spermaceti oil, sixty shillings;
> For every ton of whale-oil (so called) forty shillings.[18]

This bounty was to be paid to any vessel owned and manned wholly by the inhabitants of the Commonwealth, and landed within the same after January 1, 1786. Certificates of registry were required for inspection by deputy customs officials.

Instead of providing a beneficial effect, the state bounties caused ports to increase their fleets and the market became overstocked. Forced to use tallow candles during the war, many people in America were unwilling to return to the better light offered by whale oil because of the price. Nantucket, again caught between two opposing economic forces—their market in England cut off by duty and the supply brought in by the carefully nurtured British fishery—was the scene of a gradual depression.

Much thought was given also to accepting overtures from France for the removal of Nantucket whalemen to that nation. In a letter to John Jay in November 1788, Thomas Jefferson wrote that France had originally set forth its offer in 1785:

> . . . to tempt the Nantucketois . . . to come to France. The British, however, had in their favor a sameness of language, religion, laws, habits and kindred. . . . In the same year, 1785, while M. deCalone was in treaty with the Nantucketois, an estimate of the commerce of the United States was submitted to the Count de Vergennes, and it was shown that, of three millions of pounds sterling, to which their

exports amounted, one-third might be brought to France and exchanged [for] productions and manufactures, advantageously for both nations.[19]

Whale oil made a most effective medium of exchange. Jefferson also wrote of a letter received in Nantucket from Marquis de La Fayette, written by this famous French-American patriot to "a gentleman in Boston, and transmitted by him to Nantucket. The purpose of this letter was to dissuade them from accepting the British proposals." [20] The tenor of this letter is revealed by an article which appeared in September 1785:

> The Right Honorable Marquis de Lafayette, never ceasing to promote the interests of America, has procured proposals from a company for taking a large quantity of Whale Oil of different qualities from America on very advantageous terms to the shipper, having obtained a remission of all duties in France in their favour, payment to be made in the produce and manufacture of that country.
>
> It is likewise proposed that an American company be formed to avail themselves of the benefit of the plan which promises to much advantage to those who may engage in it, as well as the community from the encouragement it will afford to so important a branch of our commerce as the Whale Fishery. The original articles on the part of the French Company are duly executed and now in the possession of Mr. Samuel Breck, of Boston, who has also a sample of the kind of Whale Oil required. Any gentleman, therefore, who desire to be interested in the business may be informed in the subject by said Breck, at his House nearly opposite the Mall.[21]

Here was an opportunity which was not immediately accepted. There were several reasons for the unwillingness of the New England whalemen to enter into any trade with the French. The chief of the reasons was that the negotiations for the final draft of the treaty with Great Britain were then going on. None other than John Adams (who with Eldridge Gerry had worked manfully for the American equality with England in the fisheries on the Grand Banks) was the ambassador to the Court of St. James's.

No one knew better than Adams that the great value of the fisheries and the whaling industry lay not only in the wealth brought in by them but in the trade advantages offered by Great Britain. In peacetime, these men of the sea were New England's greatest asset; in wartime, they were of inestimable value to our naval strategy. As a nursery for seamen, Nantucket alone offered alluring bait to Britain.

In a letter to the Marquis de Carmarten, dated July 2, 1785, Adams stated, in part:

> . . . No political arrangements having been made both the British and American merchants expected that the trade would have returned to its old channels . . . but they have been disappointed. . . . Cash and bills have been chiefly remitted; neither rice, tobacco, pitch, tar, turpentine, ships, oil nor many other articles, the great sources for remittances formerly can not be sent as heretofore, because of restrictions and duties.[22]

Adams pointed out that when the specie was exhausted, trade would cease. No commercial advantage could be held by Britain and America so long as these conditions obtained, and Adams proposed a treaty of commerce between the two countries.

In the meantime, Britain kept delaying the drawing up of the completed treaty with the new United States, holding up the agreements through clumsy subterfuges. And in this interval the New England whale fishery hung in the balance. Nantucket was to determine much of its fate.

Early in 1785, Samuel Starbuck and Timothy Folger opened negotiations with Governor Parr of Nova Scotia, proposing that the British government support a migration of Nantucket whalemen to that province. This was no new comer of the coast to the whaling islanders. In 1762, some forty-eight Nantucketers, members of the Society of Friends, joining a group from Cape Cod, went up to Barrington, near the southwestern tip of Nova Scotia, and settled.

> That they were Quakers is our chief reason for making a distinction in referring to them, for we have no account of any other Quaker immigration into Nova Scotia and therefore their coming may be properly considered as relating that sect to the history of our province.[23]

The Revolution was a time of suffering for the Barrington settlement, and several vessels were granted permits to trade with Massachusetts Bay. It is known that the brig *Polly,* Captain John Swain, of Nantucket, was given a permit (signed by Speaker John Hancock, of the Massachusetts Bay Congress) to bring provisions to Port Rosenay, Nova Scotia, in 1780, and the brigantine *Mercury,* Captain Hills, put in at Barrington in 1779, and supplied the inhabitants. Richard Pinkham, young Nantucket whaleman, escaping from a British prison ship at Halifax in 1778, made his way down the coast to Barrington, where he walked into a house one day and asked: "How are you, Aunt Nabby?" Shelburne, the neighboring town, was settled by New England loyalists in 1783.[24]

Governor Parr was delighted by the prospect of the Nantucket migration. As Richard Uniacke wrote, a few years later:

. . . I apprehend there was not on the face of the earth a set of People who pursued a single Branch of business with the same spirit of enterprise . . . than the Inhabitants of that Island pursued the Southern Whale Fishery.[25]

Parr laid the proposition before Cumberland, the Provincial Agent, who was equally enthusiastic. He referred to French overtures and wrote:

. . . something was immediately necessary to be done by Government or otherwise this valuable Body of People would be lost to the English People.[26]

Samuel Starbuck sailed to Halifax. His interview with Parr was entirely satisfactory. They would be allowed to import into Nova Scotia the value of their Nantucket properties, converted into commodities, would be granted freedom to carry on their religion as Quakers, would be given British citizenship and thus be allowed to carry on their whale fishery and export their oil duty-free to England.[27] This resulted in the tentative agreement that some forty whalemen with their families would remove to a place called Dartmouth, across the excellent harbor from Halifax. In a letter to Lord Sydney, dated September 20, 1785, Parr wrote that he expected the Nantucketers would arrive very soon.[28]

Returning home, Starbuck gathered his first group of whalemen and on the twentieth of September 1785, he was back at Halifax "with three brigantines and a schooner, with their crews and everything necessary for the whale-fishery." [29] The alacrity with which the Nantucketers had accepted his proposals, convinced Parr that he must strike while the iron was hot.

In a speech before the Assembly of the Province on December 5, 1785, Governor Parr said, in part:

> In respect to the latter [commerce] the Prospect of an establishment of the Whale-Fishery here, particularly affords a well founded expectation of great benefit and advantage—and I am confident you will not fail to give every suitable encouragement to a matter of so much concern. . . .[30]

The Assembly voted £1,500 to build homes for the new settlers, and two thousand acres of land was eventually laid out for them.

The arrival of more Nantucketers gave the new settlement at Dartmouth a thriving appearance. At a point of land, the whalemen built their first warehouse, using the cove, known as Mill Cove, as a basin for their ships. Some 347 tons of sperm oil, belonging to Starbuck & Folger was brought from Nantucket, together with two and a half tons belonging to Gideon Gardner. The whole was shipped immediately to London as Nova Scotia oil—duty-free.

Dartmouth had been named for the settlers from that town and vicinity in old England in 1750. Principally a fishing village, it was a satellite of Halifax, which was originally settled as a stronghold for the British fleet between the French bastion of Louisburg and their fortress at Annapolis. Dartmouth's growth was slow, but the arrival of the Nantucket whalemen gave it a decided impetus. The wharves and warehouses, shipyard and oil manufacturers employed hundreds of native Nova Scotians, thus giving a much-needed revenue to many families in the original settlement.

Word had hardly arrived in England, advising Lord Sydney, the Secretary of State for the Home Department, of proposals to the Nantucket immigrants, than the second group of whalemen arrived. Timothy Folger, who had remained in Nantucket to superintend the embarkation, sailed for Halifax on June 7, 1786, with his family. Forty families, consisting of 164 people, exclusive of 150 whalemen, had removed to Halifax by mid-summer, 1786. The first returns from the fleet were at Dartmouth Cove while the last members of the colony were removing from Nantucket. In a letter written by Dr. J. Brenton, Rector of St. Paul's, Halifax, June 4, 1786, it is stated:

> Our whale-fishery represents an encouraging aspect. The brigs are now arriving deep-laden with oil—a ship and a brig arrived within these two days as deep as they can swim—the Whale-fishery will now go on prosperously.[31]

Richard Cumberland, Provincial Agent in London, was also greatly pleased by the prospect. He wrote the Assembly:

> I observe with great Satisfaction the public Attention which is paid to the important object of Whale Fishery. . . . I have no reason to fear but Government here will take Every prudent Measure for the prosperity of your trade.[32]

But the success of Governor Parr's venture was not greeted by the King's Ministry in England with the recognition it deserved. Lord Sydney not only gave his disapproval bluntly, but informed the astonished Parr of the entire dissatisfaction of the home Government. The fulfillment of Parr's promises to the whalemen, Sydney wrote, could only be accomplished through an Act of Parliament, circumventing the old Navigation Laws, as the granting of British registry to Nantucket ships was not legal. The disapproving Home Secretary continued:

> It may upon this occasion be necessary that I should inform you, for your future guidance, that it is the present determination of Government not to encourage the Southern Whale-Fishery, that may be carried on by Persons who may have removed from Nantucket and other places within the American States, excepting they shall exercise that Fishery directly from Great Britain.[33]

As Parr had seen the great possibilities for the development in Nova Scotia of a second Nantucket, he was at first bewildered, and then, undoubtedly, bitter at the stubborn attitude of Government. There was not only the opportunity for the growth of the industry through the New England migration, but the chance of allying some Halifax merchants in the project. Thomas Cochran, of Halifax, had sent out a whaler in 1784 and he had been successful. His ship was probably manned by Nantucketers. At any rate, the files of *The Nova Scotian* for June 15, 1825, tell of the firm of Cochran & Holmes engaging in the business during the Nantucket colony's activities and following their departure.

An important fact is outlined in a report from Richard Uniacke, Speaker of the Nova Scotian Assembly, to Governor Parr on August 15, 1791:

> Your Excellency availed yourself of the very critical moment in which these People could have been removed into the British dominions and, had you been permitted to have executed the whole of the Plan you had concerted, I submit to your Excellency that I do not exaggerate the event that would have happened when I say that the whole of the prosperity and people of Nantucket would at this day be settled in this Province.[34]

Such a happening would have been a catastrophic blow to American whaling, inasmuch as it would have removed the very heart of the industry. Whether or not the bulk of the whalemen could have been induced to remove to Halifax is something beyond conjecture. The stark facts are that forty families and two hundred whalemen migrated there; that a similar number eventually removed to Hudson, New York; that a large number had interests in British whaling fleets; and that another exodus took place to France with William Rotch. This is evidence enough that a large-scale movement to Dartmouth was not a far-fetched scheme on the part of Governor Parr.

But for the selfish interests of the British whaling merchants, supported by the Ministry and Parliament, the advantage to the British Dominion would have been a vital and decisive move in the world's whaling market.

A total of 2,156 acres was surveyed for the colony, including 556 acres in the heart of the town. The lot lay-outs are interesting. They were laid out in squares from the Cove. The Quaker Meeting House occupied the customary position on the hill overlooking the transported Nantucketers. Even today, the old houses built by the emigrants which still remain may be easily recognized by their typical lines of island architecture.

The memorial of Samuel Starbuck and his son and Timothy Folger, as of June 17, 1786, reveals that *thirty-five Nantucket families* had by that time removed,

... for the purpose of carrying on the whale-fishery, in consideration thereof we move to the Governor and Council that they would Grant to your Memorialists ... the following lands at Wisdom's and King's Grants with the Coves and Nooks of land, that was known by the name of the Common Lotte, containing five hundred and fifty-six acres more or less and likewise, one hundred rods square on the Common beginning. . . .[35]

But what of the Nantucketers, removed to a new land, amid strange faces and customs? In the stark simplicity of their faith, as members of the Society of Friends, they had resolved to exile themselves from their island home. To leave hearthstone and relatives, with little prospect of returning, must have brought forth heartrending scenes. They sailed away, bearing household goods and furniture (and in many cases their new framed houses), on board their own ships. The extraordinary force of their motives for leaving Nantucket must have allied with their Quaker spirit to give them a determination of which strength it is hard to conceive today.

It was in their religion that these exiled Nantucketers found solace. Here was one strong, unbreakable link that bound them with Nantucket and those left behind. One of the first acts was to set up a Dartmouth Monthly Meeting. In this they were aided by the arrival of John Townsend, Shubael Coffin and Joseph Robinson, Jr., in the summer of 1786. The leader, Townsend, kept a journal of the "visit," which reads in part:

> We sailed from Nantucket the 4th, 7 mo. 1786 at Six in the morning and arrived at Hallifax on the 8th following about II oClock in the forenoon: we waited on the Governor & Collector for leave to Anchor informing them we were on a Religious Visit & not on trade, they Received us verry kindly, we then came to Anchor at Dartmouth where some of our Friends were settled & building a Town and went on shore to Saml Starbucks who with his family are settled there, we stayed Meeting with them on First Day and then proceeded for the Island of St. Johns.[36]

Returning from St. Johns, Townsend and his associates again visited Dartmouth:

> We went after Brakefast with Saml Starbuck over to Hallifax and waited on the Governor and Proposed to him our holding a Publick Meeting amongst the Inhabitants at which he seemed will pleased

and readily Granted the Use of the Court House to meet in. Accordingly we appointed a Meeting to be held at II Next day which was large. The Governor and famely with many of the Inhabitants attended.[37]

Townsend visited Shelburne, Nova Scotia, before returning to Nantucket. The result of his visit to the province was the formation of the Dartmouth Monthly Meeting of the Friends, on November 11, 1786, which was petitioned for and granted. This Meeting was a part of the Nantucket Meeting, and when the Dartmouth whalers transferred themselves to Milford Harbor, the records of their Meeting were returned to the Nantucket Meeting. They are still in existence on the island.

The island whalemen were now embarking on a new voyage, stranger than they had ever known. Returning from a voyage "to Brazil" or to Guinea, no more would they sight the familiar outlines of their island home, their long-awaited landfall. They were nomads, maritime rovers—truly men of the sea. Nantucket gave them birth and vocation; Dartmouth provided a livelihood. But the ocean was their home.

The whaling community at Dartmouth, Nova Scotia, was a success from the outset. When the colony was dismantled in 1791, there were twenty-two whaleships out of that port. The first fleet (1785-86) consisted of the *Lively,* Captain John Chadwick; *Romulus,* Captain Pinkham; *Somerset,* Captain Daniel Kelley; *Sally,* Captain Daniel Ray, and *Lucy,* Captain Francis Coffin.

On September 6, 1786, the ship *Lyon* sailed from Halifax for London with 135 tons of sperm, forty tons of black oil and 8,759 pounds of bone. This was worth some £10,000 on the British market. In the first year the venture brought in £14,180. Subsequent years of the Dartmouth fishery yielded as follows:

$$
\begin{aligned}
1786 &— £22,300 \\
1787 &— £27,500 \\
1788 &— £27,000 \\
1789 &— £29,200 \\
1790 &— £31,100 \\
1791 &— £30,000(?) \ [38]
\end{aligned}
$$

In a report on the fishery, to Governor Parr, as of August 15, 1791, Speaker Uniacke made the following comment:

> From two to three hundred men have been employed on a average each year in these Voyages and besides the British Shipping and Seamen which are employed in freighting the oil from Nova Scotia to London there is also a like or greater quantity of British Shipping employed in bringing back from Great Britain the returns for the Oil so shipped, the whole of such returns consist of all kinds of British Manufactures suitable for the Fishery and other consumption of the Province.[39]

The list of masters and ships engaged in the Dartmouth whale fishery is an imposing one. Thirty-two ships were included in the fleet, twenty-eight of which were Dartmouth owned.[40] Nantucket men and ships were now competing with each other out of three different ports—Nantucket, Massachusetts; Dartmouth, Nova Scotia, and Hudson, New York.

The majority of the Dartmouth fleet were brigantines, averaging one hundred tons burden, sailing to the Gulf of Guinea or to the Brazil Banks. Each vessel's commander had a "Mediterranean Pass," which gave them protection as British subjects. The crews numbered on an average of twelve to thirteen hands, and the average catch was about forty-eight tons (of which thirty-two tons were right whale or "black oil"), ten tons sperm oil, the latter bringing £55 a ton and the former £45 per ton. Whalebone averaged between £300 and £500 worth per voyage. These averages were for the year 1788.[41]

According to an advertisement in the *Nova Scotia Gazette,* "Spermaceti, Candles and Strained Oil" were for sale at "Mr. Stewart's, opposite St. Paul's Church, below the parade," and were "products of this Province." In the files of the *Halifax Journal* for April 1788 may be found similar advertisements. From a report of commissioners to Governor Parr in 1788, it was shown that the products of three years voyaging on the part of Nantucketers at Dartmouth had resulted in an export of oil to England totaling a worth of £61,500.[42]

The success of the enterprise was evident on every side at Dartmouth. Mechanics did well and most of the persons connected with the fishery became well-to-do. Many native Dartmouth youths shipped aboard the whaleships. In the files of the *Nova Scotian,* of Halifax, for June 15, 1825, is the following paragraph:

> When the usual period of the arrival of the vessels approached, all persons were filled with expectations and anxiety. The success of each voyage inspired a more than ordinary interest in its result, and their relatives and friends were eager to hear the recital of their adventures, and welcome them to their home after all their toils and dangers.

Here was a familiar pattern. It was, like old Nantucket, still the outstanding example of the sole community enterprise of that island-whaling. Dartmouth had gained much. The provincial Commissioners wisely observed to Governor Parr:

> The Province is now possessed of every kind of artifices necessary to fit out Vessels in the Southern Whale-Fishery, as well as some of the best Navigators that that Island of Nantucket has produced. . . . the great advantage which the Commerce and Navigation of the Mother Country will derive from this Establishment.[43]

In the midst of this turmoil of indecision, with many of their people removed to other ports and others preparing to leave, the Nantucketers tried desperately to maintain American whaling. Late in 1785 word came that their bid for neutrality had been refused. New Bedford, which had abandoned the industry from the early years of the war, now began it again, as did Boston, Newport, Warren, Sag Harbor and New London. The American market was soon glutted; the British market was impossible.

At this time of crisis, the young nation's greatest whale-oil merchant—William Rotch—took an active part in restoring the balance of trade in whale oil. He had always been a staunch advocate, during the war, of maintaining neutrality in Nantucket to preserve the town. When George Churchman was on Nantucket in 1781, he wrote:

> Our valuable Friend, William Rotch, we find, is much esteemed by the people, his neighbors, and others, for his knowledge, prudence, and integrity, who appears to be as a prince on the island.[44]

For three decades, Rotch had aided materially in building Sherburne-Town on Nantucket as the greatest whaling port in the world. His entire career had proved his business acumen, community spirit and loyalty to his religious precepts as a Friend.

The most important fact about William Rotch is that he always had complete faith in the whaling industry as a world commodity. He regarded it as a public utility that belonged to no political regime. His entire career as a merchant evinced his solid faith in the over-all whaling industry so long as there were Nantucket men to supply officers and men for a fleet. It was Rotch who sent whaleships to London, following news of the Peace of 1783, which flew the first American flags in any British port. He soon showed his belief that, as the world's statesmen were unable to return the world's commerce to a logical balance, it was up to the practical merchants to show the way.

For two years, Rotch had tried to keep his business at Nantucket afloat. Now he could see no other alternative "but to proceed to England and endeavor to pursue the industry from there." [45] He had decided on this course after much inner debate. His brother-in-law Samuel Starbuck and colleague Timothy Folger had not been able to persuade him to join in the venture to Dartmouth. Rotch was justly suspicious of the British Ministry. His father, co-founder of New Bedford, who had recently died, had suffered by the British burning of that town. He personally, had little faith in politicians after observing their expediencies.

The Nantucket firm of William Rotch and Sons was left in the hands of his son William, Jr., and his son-in-law Samuel Rodman. This fact, alone, reveals that the elder Rotch never wished to abandon his business in America. He was impelled by a desire to justify his own faith in the whaling industry by establishing himself in Britain. And he was determined to help the Nantucket whalemen by so doing. As the unofficial but authorized ambassador of the whalemen of the island, and of the town, he was entrusted with the mission of placing nothing less than the proposition that Nantucket, as a neutral, separate entity, would enter into a business alliance with Britain—a whaling kingdom trading its only products—men, ships and whale oil.

Embarking in his favorite ship, the *Maria,* with his old skipper, Captain William Mooers in command, William Rotch and his son Benjamin sailed on July 4, 1785. Twenty-three days from Great Point (Nantucket) they warped the *Maria* in at Dover wharf. Following the discharge of her "little freight," the ship was prepared for a whale voyage. Rotch was wasting no further time. The *Maria* sailed within two weeks, bound for the Southern Grounds, "her crew yet remain intire," (as Rotch wrote) although attempts were made to lure them away.[46]

The flurry of the British whaling merchants was not lost on the astute Nantucketer:

> The spirit of whaling seems almost running to a degree of madness, they intend if men can be got to send out 30 ships, but at present there appears no possibility of getting men. Six other ships have arrived: Delano, 85 tons; Bennett, 85; Brown, 77; P.Pease, 77; Gage, 50; Goldsmith, 43.[47]

On his way to London, Rotch, in his *Memorandum,* describes his emotions as, from the eminence of Shooter's Hill, he looked down at the great city sprawling away into distance. "Forcibly feeling the great distance separating me from my family," he wrote ". . . the occasion which drew me there, and the uncertainty of its answering any valuable purpose, I was overwhelmed . . . but reason resumed . . . I was there and something must be attempted." [48] With his son Benjamin, the emissary from Nantucket took lodgings at Thomas Wagstaff's in Grace Church Street.

In London, Rotch learned from Captain Daniel Coffin (just arrived on the brig *Mercury,* from Boston) that the Massachusetts General Court had finally voted a bounty of £6 per ton on sperm oil and had abated certain taxes. He greeted the news with mixed feelings, writing:

> His account is imperfect, I can gain little knowledge from it; it is strange Folger did not write me on the subject, as Coffin informs me he left him in Boston. [Timothy Folger was then heading for Dartmouth. It is probably he did not wish Rotch to learn of the state bounty until the latter had made commitments in Britain]. How far this will be adequate to the expenses of the Fishery, I cannot tell, not knowling what oil is worth in Boston . . . but if sufficient to satisfy our people, it will ease me of a great burthen which I could wish to be clear of, & have only to conduct our own business.[49]

Under date of September 5, 1785, Rotch wrote carefully that he had received another letter from Timothy Folger, from Halifax:

He wrote me very short on subject of his business there, promis'g to give me a full account fr next conveyance . . . ; I suppose by these movements nothing was likely to be done as to setting our Island at Liberty, w'ch if is the case I wish I could have known it in time, that I might have done something here for ourselves, which I avoided purely on acc't of the Island, that I might not by any means put the least discouragement to anything being done here for the Island.

This, at least, explains the mystery of why Rotch did not accept the invitation to go to Dartmouth with his brother-in-law Samuel Starbuck, Sr., and Timothy Folger. Further than this, Rotch clearly shows how deeply he felt under an obligation to relieve the distressed conditions of the Nantucket whalemen. His was a self-appointed task, to which he stoutly adhered. Although astonished by the evidence of an "amazing" business in London's trade—apparently unaffected by the "almost total stagnation of the American trade"—he observed that other nations, envious of the British commerce, were "laying heavy duties on their manufacturers that perhaps in the end may affect her." Rotch also affirmed that there was "little prospect of anything being done by a commercial treaty favorable to America at present" [August, 1785].[50]

In his next letter he wrote: "If we [Nantucket] are placed in a Neutral State . . . I fully believe something may be done." Then his conviction on the Dartmouth migration, and its effect on the political leaders was expressed: "Those concerned in settling in Nova Scotia are powerfully making Interest against us, but as I have had no opportunity of laying our situation before more than two of the Privy Council, I can not form much judgement." His former business associates, the whaling firm of Samuel Enderby & Sons, offered to assist him, "which from some circumstances I believe is real." [51]

Though certain in his own mind about the fate of the Halifax removal, Rotch did not want his son-in-law, Samuel Rodman, to consider himself bound by the ties of family or firm. "If thou, my son Samuel, should find thy way clear to remove," he wrote, "I shall furnish thee with property sufficient to do the business with." [52] Later, he cautioned that "Government here is beginning to view every encouragement given to Nova Scotia as building up the whale-fishery for the United States by collusion or otherwise." [53] Early in 1786, he advised: "Would have you postpone all Halifax matters for the Government is very desirous to get us directly to this country." [54]

Nowhere in our maritime history or in the history of American Whaling can there be a more fascinating chapter than that which details the efforts of William Rotch at this time. With supreme confidence, he set out, on September 6, 1785, on a journey of three hundred miles, along the coast of England, to search for a port where the Nantucketers could re-establish their industry. He wrote of his plans thus:

> Our long journey . . . I heartily wish was over but I think shall be inexcusable to come thus far, and not be able to make some judgment of the propriety of removing to the country if necessity shall urge it (I mean respect'g the suitableness of the different places for the Fishery). I am much urged by all ranks to remove into this Kingdon, yet, I never wish to be compelled at this time of life to take such a Step, though I see no way at present for the Inhabitants to subsist at my native Spot. [55]

The result of his quest was to decide that Falmouth was by far the harbor best suited to the enterprise. Returning to London in November, Rotch then sought an audience with the Chancellor of the Exchequer, William Pitt (the Younger), to learn what encouragement Government would offer.

Pointing out the war waged against the colonies was "predicated upon Revolution"; Rotch reminded the Chancellor that Nantucket had taken no part in the war, but had placed itself in a neutral position and had remained a part of the British Kingdom until separated by the peace. Rotch then gave an account of the distressed condition of the island, which had lost practically its entire whale fleet, to the value of £200,000, many of the ships having been taken unjustly by the British Navy. (Again, the ghostly fleet at the Falklands hove into sight). He then told Pitt that under these conditions, the principal part of the inhabitants must leave the island,

> A part [of the Nantucketers] wish to continue the Whale-Fishery wherever it can be pursued to advantage. Therefore, my chief business is to . . . ascertain if the Fishery is considered an object worth giving encouragement for a removal to England. [56]

Pitt was "struck by astonishment" by this recital, "and acknowledg'd agreeable to my assertion," wrote William Rotch. "I committed our case to writing, and sent it to him." [57] But the Chancellor, harassed by the times, placed the Nantucket proposal before the Privy Council. With admirable patience, William Rotch awaited a reply. Days became weeks, and weeks months, and only a few perfunctory messages were conveyed to the anxious emissary.

After four months had elapsed, Rotch indignantly requested the Council to appoint someone with whom he could treat, "that the matter might be brought to a close." The man selected was Lord Hawksbury, who was described by Rotch, thus: "A greater Enemy of America, I believe could not be found in that body, or hardly in the Nation." [58]

The men met, and Rotch immediately proposed that £20,000 be given for the removal of one hundred Nantucket families. Hawksbury demurred; thought it a great sum; asked what was to come which would demand such a price. Tradition has it that Rotch replied: "I will bring some of the best blood of the island of Nantucket." [59] The aristocracy of whaling had its "knights and squires," as well as haughty Britain.

During the next meeting, Rotch asked liberty to bring in a fleet of thirty Nantucket whaleships. Hawksbury frowned on this, as "the ships should be British built." When Rotch pointed out that the cost of two American ships was not more than one British craft, and that the value of property imported would be doubled in Britain, Lord Hawksbury agreed, but stipulated, "tis the seamen we want." Rotch quickly replied: "Two of our ships will answer your purpose better than one of yours, as they will double the number of seamen, which must be the very thing aimed at." [60]

Lord Hawksbury offered £87-10 for the transportation and settlement of one family. He suggested there might be an opportunity to insert a clause in a Fishery Bill he was drawing up, but Rotch declined to enter into such negotiations. The British were offering privileges only on a positive removal to the kingdom, which Rotch could not and would not offer. At the final meeting Rotch mentioned that France was interested in obtaining Nantucket whale oil. Hawksbury attempted a subterfuge and professed doubt. Rotch then remarked:

". . . I am now determined to go to France and see what it is. If there is any such contract, sufficient to retain us at Nantucket, *neither you nor any other nation shall have us!*" [61]

The two men parted and never met again. Writing to his son William and son-in-law Samuel Rodman, Rotch stated: ". . . I am determined to try all Europe (or rather the most probable port) for an opening for our oils, in which I have a little hope of success, though not a market equal to the Kingdom." [62]

Rotch immediately embarked for Dunkirk (April 1786). While in France, a letter arrived from his friend Alexander Champion announcing, at Lord Hawksbury's request, that the British Fishery Bill had a clause providing for the removal into Britain of forty Nantucket ships instead of the thirty requested by Rotch.

Rotch wrote: "But it was too late."

After his return from Dunkirk in May he was sent by George Rose, one of Pitt's secretaries, who informed him that Pitt had authorized him "to tell you that you shall make your own terms."

Rotch reiterated that it was too late—that he had obtained an agreement with the French which was highly satisfactory; that this was obtained in an interview with the French Ministers after a conference of only five hours; that the die had been cast. Both Secretary Rose and Lord Sheffield interviewed the Nantucketer, hoping for a reconsideration, but Rotch convinced them it was too late. The Parliament Minority group asked for information with which to attack the arrogant Lord Hawksbury but the Quaker whale-oil merchant, possessing a fund of material, declined to divulge the particulars. [63]

The Dunkirk migration was greatly aided by François Coffyn and Captain Shubael Gardner. Rotch wrote after this visit to France: "F. Coffyn, our friend and Assistant, has a great influence at Court & is a deserving man—desire you would present him with a box of good Spermaceti candles by the first oppt." [64]

Captain Gardner and Coffyn visited Paris with the Rotch proposals and were eminently successful. Every request of the Nantucket man was granted.

It was Coffyn who had written (under date of March 10, 1786) from Dunkirk to Captain Shubael Gardner at Nantucket that

... the present distressed situation of your worthy brethren . . . oblig-
ing many to quit their natif-spot . . . has created in me the idea to
procure them an azylum in my own country, where they may not
only find an alleviation of their misfortunes and recuperate their
losses, but also where they may expect that comfort and protection
due to their honest principles. [He continued by stating he was ready
to] make use of all the interest with the King's ministers I was capable of. To make such proposals as were penned by our friend
William Rotch, and which you delivered me in his name on your
arrival from London on November last [1785].[65]

Coffyn enclosed a "Copy of advantages granted to the people of
Nantucket who may wish to settle at Dunkirk, and establish the whale-
fishery." These were altogether liberal and extended privileges, as
well, to those tradesmen allied to the whale fishery. It was stipulated
that negotiations should be carried on with "Mr. Rotch or the Selectmen." [66]

Rotch had now definitely committed himself and his colleagues and
followers to settle, as a group, at Dunkirk. The Nantucket whalemen
were guaranteed free enjoyment of their religion (the principles of the
people called Quakers); entire exemption from military service, "as
they are a peaceful people and do not meddle with the quarrels of
Princes"; and a bounty of 50 livres—or £40 sterling per ton with a
minimum of 20 tons per ship, which must fit out in France.[67]

In an important letter [68] about the successful closing of the deal with
France he announced that he had "especial liberty to ship to France,
say Dunkirk, 250 tons of oil this year, exclusive of what our own ships
or vessels bring in this season, duty-free!" Rotch went on to say: "If
any of our people are minded to put in a quantity they may [be] . . .
consigned to the De Bauque Brothers, Dunkirk. You need not mention this. . . . Ours, with those who ship with us, may reap the advantage and not disclose this *part for the present*. If I live to return, I
will open up the whole business." [69]

He then gave an accounting of the French bounty and requested the
frames for the spermaceti presses be sent, "together with box containing screws with the follower on the plates." He mentions (as an aside)
that he could get ironwork done by an iron foundry firm in London!
The presses were for the manufacturing of sperm-oil candles, and
proved a highly paying side-product.

The agreement was reached early in May 1786. Rotch again sailed for England from whence he wrote the news to Nantucket, instructing the firm to "advise our people not to sell their oil yet at a low price until I write you particulars." As he had written previously, his "hearty desire is not to be obliged to quit the island," and now he observed that he saw a "prospect of our family remaining at Nantucket." [70]

Rotch advised immediate sailing of the Nantucket fleet, "such as are for the Brazils, &c., let them go after Right Whales if they are more plenty than Sperm, which will do best in France." He ordered "all our vessels that are fitted for Whaling into that business," and admonished their shipmasters to return to Nantucket after their voyages to the South Atlantic, then separate their oil and "head-matter" and proceed to Dunkirk for disposal of their cargoes. By ostensibly fitting out at this French export city, the whaleships were entitled "to a bounty on their next voyage." [71]

In a postscript to this letter, Rotch directed:

> When you ship our oil, write to Champion & Dickason [in London] for insurance at & from Nantucket to Dunkirk, with liberty to touch at an adjacent Harbour to fill up, & write them to insure it clear of the risque of the Algerians & other Barbary Cruisers, which will lower the premium, as the risque on that Head is very little.

Rotch was most aware of the soundness of British insurance, as he was of the unsoundness of the policies of the British Ministry in regard to whale oil.

Soon after these arrangements, Rotch sailed for home. Thus Britain lost a great opportunity to establish a whaling colony within their kingdom, under the management of a great leader, a sagacious businessman, with ships manned by the greatest whalemen in the world. Subsequent events proved that many prominent merchants realized the mistake.

None other than Thomas Jefferson, the successor to Franklin as ambassador in France, saw the true picture as Rotch saw it. Writing to John Jay in November 1788, Jefferson commented:

> . . . The French government had not been inattentive to the news of the British, nor insensible to the crisis. They saw the danger of permitting five or six thousand of the best seamen existing to be transferred by a single stroke to the marine strength of their enemy, and

to carry over with them an art which they possessed almost exclusively. The counterplan, which they set on foot, was to tempt the Nantuckois by high offer, to come and settle in France. . . . It became evident that the terms offered to the Nantuckois would not produce their emigration to Dunkirk; and that it would be safest in every event, to offer some other alternative. . . . The obvious one was to open the ports of France to their oils so that they might exercise their fishery remaining in their native country.[72]

William Rotch reached home in January 1787, and his son Benjamin sailed for Dunkirk (February 1787) with the Nantucket group of managers and their families for the French whaling export station. The fundamentals had been well taken care of. William did not rejoin his son in France until August 1790. His arrival was to come in the nick of time.

chapter ix

～～～～

THE WHALING INDUSTRY BELONGS
TO THE WORLD

*In agriculture, then they have no resources, and if that of
their fishery cannot be pursued from their habitations it is
natural that they should seek others from which it can be
followed. . . .*

— Thomas Jefferson's Report on
the Fisheries, January, 1791

B RITAIN'S POLICY of treating with the young United States, following the peace of 1783, was that of a haughty parent with a way-
ward child. The British ports were closed to the trade of the new
confederation of thirteen colonies, as well as to all foreign nations,
unless a duty was paid; the lucrative West India trade was cut off
from this nation by the Navigation Laws. Britain was the great manufacturing country of the world. The new American nation could not
find a balance of trade by seeking French ports—for France did not
meet the demand for manufactured goods.

Retaliation to British discrimination was the natural reaction of the
Americans. But there was no workable plan, as no central government
had the power to promote a policy on which all the states would agree.
In 1784, Congress had tried to pass a navigation law, but the various
states put so many restrictions into it that it was futile. Massachusetts
passed a navigation act of its own, restricting trade with Britain, and
attempted to get other states to enact similar legislation.

John Adams, in Paris, was appointed Minister to England, with instructions to make a commercial treaty and to secure the execution of the peace treaty of 1783. Upon arrival in London in May 1785, he sought first to have Britain state specific reasons for its adamant non-trade policy, and had a long conversation with William Pitt.

Finally the talk came around to the whale fishery, and Pitt inquired: "The Americans . . . cannot think hard of the English for encouraging their own shipwrights, their manufactures of ships, and their own whale-fishery?" [1]

Adams replied that it appeared unaccountable to America that Britain "should sacrifice the general interests of the nation to the private interests of a few individuals interested in the manufacture of ships and the whale-fishery," so far as to refuse remittances from America in the broad trade of the two nations. The failure of the several states to push proceedings in the courts, so that the departed Loyalists could collect debts and property values, was a tender spot.

Pitt referred to the attempts of France to lure to its ports American whaling. Adams retorted that there could be no doubt that "Spermaceti oil might find a market in most of the great cities of Europe which were illuminated at night," as it was superior to vegetable oil—"the Spermaceti oil gives the clearest and most beautiful flame of every substance known in nature." Adams continued, with spirit:

> We are all surprised that you prefer darkness and consequent robberies, burglaries, and murders in your streets to the receiving, as a remittance [for colonial trade] our spermaceti oil. The lamps around Grosvener Square, I know, and in Downing Street, too, I suppose, are dim by midnight, and extinguished by two o'clock in the morning and chase away, before the watchmen, all the villains, and save you the trouble and danger of introducing a new police into the city. [2]

Pitt and his Ministers delayed any compromise. There was too much opposition in the mercantile class of Britain. Such shortsighted policy was simply that of attempting to save shillings and pence by sacrificing pounds sterling in goods. The American trade would simply cease seeking the supply, or turn to other nations. The colonists could not remit with oil, tobacco, ships, pitch, lumber and fish as heretofore because the duties of Britain precluded such trade. They must seek other markets.

With respect to the whale fishery: Even while Pitt and Adams were conferring (August 24, 1785), Starbuck and Folger were embarking for Dartmouth; Alexander Coffin and Seth Jenkins were firmly established in Hudson, New York; and William Rotch had embarked for London. Of equal importance was the fact that even then Britain was luring Nantucket masters and whalemen to take out their ships.

Always poor gamblers, His Majesty's Ministers were now attempting to set up a southern whale fishery, employing capital enough to secure cargoes of whale oil totaling in value £105,000. This was the amount of oil which before the war had been annually shipped to Britain by the Nantucketers, at an average price of £35 per ton—three thousand tons of oil. Allowing that most of this money before the war was expended on British manufactured goods, the gain to Britain from the Nantucket fishery alone had been close to £90,000 annually. In order to duplicate these conditions in post-war times, the British must not only build up a fleet but guarantee this return on the investment before the secondary, yet equally important, trade balance was affected.[3]

Arguments and logic were of no avail. Adams went through two years of it. As he wrote to Jay in November, 1787:

> They [the King's Ministers] will aim at recovering back the western lands, at taking away our fisheries, and at the total ruin of our navigation, at least.[4]

Soon after, Adams, at his urgent request, was relieved of his duties at the Court of St. James's. The British were to procrastinate for another year before they showed definite signs of conciliation with America.

It was about this time (1790) that Charles Francis Greville, Secretary to Lord Grenville and nephew of Sir William Hamilton, with the latter evolved the plan which gave the British Government a rare opportunity—or so they believed. Greville, with Sir William Hamilton, owned considerable land at Milford Haven in Wales. He proposed removing the colony of Nantucketers to Milford Haven. He further proposed removing the entire population of Nantucket, some 4,500 people, together with ships, whaling supplies, houses, and so forth—all to that Welsh port. From the office of the Secretary of State, Lord Grenville, in Britain, an agent named Stokes was sent to Dartmouth to interview the whalemen—principally Samuel Starbuck and Timothy Folger. The terms were of considerable magnitude: the full value of their Dartmouth properties, amounting to £6,000, moving expenses of £55 for each family, and compensation for the time wasted in making the transfer.[5]

Basically this was the British Government's long-cherished plan to establish a whaling port in the British Isles, which would be a true competitor to American whaling. It had received considerable encouragement. The evidence of the Falkland Island fleet of Francis Rotch and Aaron Lopez and the numerous ships in British registry manned by other Nantucketers were all the proof that was needed of the New England whalemen's superiority. When William Rotch had approached the Ministry with a definite plan for removal of a colony of Nantucketers to Britain, the Ministry had hesitated in reaching a decision, so much so that Rotch, disappointed and discouraged, went to France with his proposals. The reason for the delay was that Britain's intermediaries were not fully informed. When they were advised as to the worth of the plan, they tried to get in touch with Rotch. It was too late.[6]

Both Samuel Starbuck and Timothy Folger, the leaders of the Dartmouth Colony, were not averse to the proposal of Government to remove the Dartmouth whalemen to the British Isles. Despite the success of the endeavor, Dartmouth was but a suburb of Halifax, and a rival whaling company had already come into existence across the harbor in the larger city. There is something cryptic in a sentence Starbuck wrote to Greville in reply to the proposal: "I saw before their proposals to come to Dartmouth that Nova Scotia would not hold our Friends." [7] Perhaps he was referring to the plan for more Nantucketers to come to Dartmouth, which Government had checkmated.

In one fell swoop, Lord Grenville hoped to secure a corner on the southern whale fishery by obtaining the great exponents of that fishery —the Nantucketers—lock, stock and barrel!

The completeness of this plan may best be seen by a letter to Lord Grenville, from Charles Francis Greville, under date of February 21, 1791:

My Lord

I beg that you will peruse the enclosure containing conditions on which Sir Wm. Hamilton will comply with the proposals of the Nantucketers from Dartmouth. If approved & transmitted to the Board of Trade, I flatter myself the whole plan will sone come before them —if this National object shall be obtained, much will be due to the attention it has already received, and to the readiness of the different departments to consider it without delay.

I hope you will excuse my stating some observations on the proposals which the Nantucketers settled at Dartmouth transmitted to your Lordship to remove the Whale-Fishery to Milford.

A calculation of the charges to Gov't of removing 30 families with 19 ships (whose complement of seamen is 271), their tonage 1800 tons, fitted for a whale voyage valued at £11-11 p. ton & will ensure a capital of £21000 afloat from Milford Haven within 12 months.

Value of the property in Lands & houses certified by Gov. Parr	£6000
Compensation to Mr. Holmes in transferring his property	£500
Freight of 25 families an average of 7 persons total 175 Persons	£1375
Freight to Mr. Homes for 5 families of 7 persons each-35 persons	£275
	£8150
Deduct the value of property certified above by Gov. Parr — £6000 (which the 25 families offer to convey to Gov't)	
Balance against Government	£2150

The Memorialists compose One Entire Class of Nantucketers, viz., of those who are now entitled to all the privileges of British subjects in their persons & Ships.[8]

Greville was an enthusiastic supporter of "the plan." As agent for his uncle, Sir William Hamilton, he owned the land at Milford Haven.

Here was a Welsh harbor of magnificent proportions (a century and a quarter later it was to be headquarters for the Royal Navy). It was advantageously situated near Bristol and Liverpool in Britain, and Waterford, Cork and Dublin in Ireland. Only a few farmers were the occupants of the lands nearby, good land for dairy, sheep and agricultural products.

Early in 1791, Samuel Starbuck, Jr., sailed for England to meet Greville and see for himself the situation proposed. Two days' travel from London brought him to Haverfordwest, where Greville, who had been staying at Stackpole Court, met him and took him to Milford, eight miles further. The younger Starbuck was quick to catch the possibilities of the location, and the courtesy and interest of Greville won his heart. By the time he had returned to London, the preliminaries were settled. Greville wrote to him, back in Dartmouth, that a goodly number of "Artificers" were available at low prices for erecting habitations, "when your determination is made and the plan settled." [9]

In the year before these events (1790), Sir William Hamilton had an Act passed by Parliament empowering him to lay out docks, quays and roads at Milford and establish a station for carrying the mails to Waterford. Nothing was done, however, in the line of construction, until the Nantucketers from Dartmouth arrived the following year. [10]

Coupled with the excitement of such an historical episode as the settlement of Milford by these island Quakers, is the romance of Emma Hart, the former mistress of Charles Greville and then the consort and new wife of his uncle, Sir William Hamilton. This controversial beauty came to see the new town which the whalemen had built and her escort was none other than Lord Nelson.

In Greville's proposals to the Secretary of State (thence to Chancellor William Pitt), it was pointed out that the settlement of Milford would add to the potential naval strength—the whaling industry being the best nursery possible for seamen—and that it would check foreign competition in the southern whale fishery. Distinguishing his report was a summary of market conditions, as follows:

Port	Number of Vessels	Tons Whale-Oil exported to France West Indies & America	Tons Whale-Oil exported to Great Britain	Tons Spermaceti & Head-Matter exported to France & America	Tons Spermaceti & Head-Matter exported to Great Britain
British Subjects: Halifax & Dartmouth	22	00	1399	00	$1383\frac{1}{4}$
Port of Foreigners: Nantucket	56	1569	00	200	166
New Bedford &	40	100	00	00	600
Vicinity	20	500	00	00	250

Total in 1790:
Nova Scotia = 22 Vessels—1399 tons Whale oil—$1383\frac{1}{4}$ tons Spermaceti [11]
American =   116   "   —2169   "   "   "   —1216   "   "

The value of the Dartmouth Colony was never more clearly shown. Greville was careful to emphasize that the

> Dartmouth Fishery owes part of its success, perhaps, in completing their cargoes, to its present connection with Nantucket as do the American, French & English Whale Fishery in other respects, particularly from the skill of these Nantucketers, who leave the island for the season, & return with their wages and profits to their Families. This accounts for the population of the island not having hitherto decreased in proportion to the decrease of the number of vessels. They consist, according to the census of 1790, of 4500 souls & 56 vessels in the Whale Fishery.[12]

Thus, as the British duty on whale oil had excluded that American product from the British market (allowing only a small quantity from America), the exclusion of all this market would lay up the New England fleet, forcing the Nantucketers, at least, to follow their brethren (upon invitation) and to secure British registry for their ships. The other alternative, Greville pointed out, was for the "Nantucket whalemen to follow Mr. Rotch to France, if they are not conducted by the favor of the British Gov't by Messrs. Starbuck & Folger to Milford." [13]

Pitt and his Ministers were quick to agree; the contract with the Dartmouth group was drawn up and signed. In addition to receiving £55 per family, certain other remuneration was allowed the emigrants and Messrs. Starbuck and Folger, and their wives, were granted life pensions of £150 annually.[14]

In his report to Governor Parr, Richard J. Uniacke wrote, with admirable restraint, in August 1791:

> Whether (I cannot help saying) the mistaken Policy which induced Great Britain to discourage this business [at Dartmouth] still exists or not I will not pretend to say, but at any Rate, I would strongly recommend to your Excellency by every means in your power to procure the active services of these two men [Starbuck and Folger] for the British Government.[15]

During 1792, preparations were completed for the removal of the colony of Nantucketers to Milford from their Nova Scotian home of seven years. When the whaling fleet returned, then began the transfer of household goods, storehouse supplies, whaling craft and other commodities. On the last day of August the fleet departed.

According to records still extant, the fleet of migrating whaler consisted of thirteen ships, manned by 182 men. Of the fifteen families embarking at this time, led by Messrs. Starbuck and Folger, five were shipmasters, five owners and the remainder coopers, sailmakers and boatbuilders, totaling 161 persons. This was the nucleus of the colony —the group which constituted the shore or home end of the movement. Some of the ships were at sea and were to return to Milford after completing voyages begun from Dartmouth. The cost of transporting and payment of property left at Dartmouth totaled approximately $30,000 or £5,985.[16] Greville's later statement showed that nineteen of the twenty-two ships in the Dartmouth fleet were transferred and twenty-five families, totaling 175 persons, would be added to the 271 seamen on the ships.

Over in Dunkirk, France, the leading merchant of Sherburne-Town before the Revolution—William Rotch—in a letter to his son-in-law in Nantucket, wrote in October 1792:

I received last evening a letter from Brother Starbuck. . . . They arrived at Milford the [Sept.] 23rd inst . . . after a passage of 24 days—all well, except the women being much fatigued with the voyage.[17]

The voyage across the Atlantic had taken only three weeks and three days. In that time they had gone from one world to another.

Were Samuel Starbuck and Timothy Folger still as staunch in their loyalty to the Crown? [18] The Dartmouth Meeting of Friends was not certain as to the maneuvering of these two leaders. Its members had seen how politics in high station could organize powerful forces. They looked askance at those who sought such high reward.[19] And did they not feel, as Quakers, that there were those other Nantucketers and Bedforders, who had been loyal to American whaling, who needed help also?

The Nantucket Monthly Meeting of Friends, the parent body for the Dartmouth Meeting, in the summer of 1793, inquired as to the trouble. The reply of the Dartmouth Meeting was interesting. It recounts that upon the appearance of Agent Stokes (Greville's man) from England, "after some days said Inhabitants of Dartmouth convened and agreed that each man's property should be estimated and proposals fixed on which said Inhabitants would be willing to move. . . . Samuel Starbuck proposed that if the above proposals were acceded to, said Inhabitants should one and all go, but if not to their satisfaction all should stay, which he requested each to express their approbation." [20]

Some time later, it was learned that "a private Memorial had likewise gone foreward," and that Starbuck and Folger had both received "partial annuities," although they had "undertaken to negotiate the public business." Upon receipt of this information, the Nantucket Meeting declared it could not grant a certificate to Samuel Starbuck until the embarrassment caused by the accusation was cleared. Certificates as members of the Society of Friends were "granted all except Starbuck." [21]

Around the little cove at Dartmouth, the deserted wharves and warehouses, the empty, simply built homes and the Quaker Meeting House were surrounded by a weird silence. Across the intervening ocean a fleet of fifteen whaleships sailed slowly into a magnificent harbor at Milford Haven. From their decks, the Quaker whalemen and their families looked up at the craggy hills of Wales. This was a new and splendid opportunity; the land was rich, the harbor unexcelled—but would they not have preferred the sandy shores and rolling heath of their real homeland in Nantucket?

The British Government had been shrewd, wise, farsighted. This was the first step in "the plan"; everything bade fair to follow in logical order. Within a half dozen years they would have over one hundred and fifty Nantucket shipmasters alone and some five hundred seamen in their whaleships.

But they had not reckoned with the strongest factor of all. These Nantucket whalemen were the greatest in the world, the chief exponents of their calling. But, as whalemen, they were men of the sea, and *they were bound to Nantucket*—their home—by the same mystic chords which they always felt tugging at their hearts no matter how far away from their island the winds of fate might carry them.

PART THREE

The Struggle for American Supremacy in Whaling

chapter x

꩜

THE "COUP-DE-WHALE"

*England fears no rivals in the whale-fishery but America;
or rather, it is the whale-fishery of America she is endeavoring to possess. . . . France, by her ports and markets, holds
the balance between the two countries.*

—Thomas Jefferson [1]

THE IMPORTANCE of the successful negotiations of William Rotch in France had a twofold effect on the over-all history of whaling. When the lucrative British market was cut off by the prohibitive duty, and the removal of the large colony to Dartmouth appeared to presage disaster for Nantucket and American whaling, there was a gradual departure of whalemen to England to accept offers as captains and officers, shipowners. The news of Rotch's agreement with the French tended to halt subsequent withdrawals from the island. True, about a dozen Nantucket families and some fifty to sixty people removed to Dunkirk (Jefferson gives nine families, but the record of a contemporary Quaker had sixty Nantucketers in Dunkirk). These colonizers were necessary to establish the whaling link between Nantucket and France. The Rotch whaleships constituted the entire Dunkirk fleet.

Thus the great importance of the Dunkirk venture was: First, it created a duty-free market for American whale oil through Nantucket; second, it checked migration of whalemen from Nantucket, as these men could now keep their families at home, although their voyages out of Dunkirk kept them away from home for longer periods. Further, the establishment of the whaling headquarters at Dunkirk was an effective checkmate for the competition from Dartmouth, Nova Scotia—in fact, the two colonies of Nantucketers became the chief competitors for the world market. It was this that had caused the British to take the drastic step of removing the Dartmouth colony to Milford Haven, a move which came, however, too late to enable them to corner the southern whale fishery.

As an immediate result of the Dunkirk agreement, Nantucket gradually regained her leadership in whaling. The creation of an European market for whale oil through Dunkirk had provided the means for the *maintenance of Nantucket as a unit*—a headquarters for American whalemen which served as a nursery for whalemen and seamen, the most expert in the world. As William Rotch knew well, so long as the Nantucketers could keep their families on their native isle, they would continue to whale anywhere in the world, fearlessly, with unlimited courage.

The British, lured by the great advance in sperm oil to £95 per ton during the war, hoped to make great voyages. But they did not realize that the reason for the superiority of the Nantucket whalemen was in their frugality and simplicity of living, in their knowledge of the phases of finding, catching and trying out the whale, and in their system of having all on board share in the proceeds of the voyage—the "lay system." Jefferson, in a letter to John Jay in 1788, remarked that the "Nantuckois" had an "economy more rigorous than the Dutch," and were "more vigilant in seeking it [the whale] and bolder in pursuing it, and parsimonious in all their expenses." [2]

The doldrums of 1783 to 1786 were now succeeded by six years of quick recovery for Nantucket. Compelled to seek new markets for their oil, the Nantucketers discovered that "black-oil" from the right whale—first sold in small quantities in the French and Dutch-owned islands of the West Indies (including a few cargoes smuggled into the British islands)—could also be sold at advantage in France and Holland, as well as in Bremen, Copenhagen, Riga and Kronstadt. Thus, turning from the sperm to the right whale fishery for a few years, the Americans, led by the Nantucketers, speculated successfully with the Europeans so they were able to carry on the industry at a market price of from £14 to £17 a ton. The islanders' frugal economy enabled them to carry on very well at this price.[3]

In 1788, Jefferson pointed out that the British had 314 vessels in the whale fishery, compared to eighty American ships. But most of the British whalers were in the Greenland or the northern fishery, while those in the southern (South Atlantic) fishery, especially the sperm whalers, were in most cases under Nantucket captains and officers.[4]

The basic economic factors in the situation were clear. Whale oil provided the lighting facilities for millions of people; it also entered into the curing of leather and the carding of wool, so that it was a part of the shoe and clothing industry. In exchange for the sale of whale oil there was obtained the produce of thousands of workers in manufactories. By increasing the sale of whale oil the sale of other commodities was increased. The astute Jefferson pointed out that "the interests of the adventurers in the whale-fishery . . . politically considered, may be of more importance to the State than a single laborer or manufacturer, but to make the estimate with the accuracy it merits, we should multiply their numbers in each side into their individual importance and see which predominates." [5]

The success of the Nantucketers in re-establishing the importance of American whaling caused the British Government to again seek a method for transplanting them. A report to the British Secretary of State in 1791 revealed any proposal inducing the Nantucketers to remove should be advanced through the "active services" of Timothy Folger and Samuel Starbuck, then still in Dartmouth, Nova Scotia. It was proposed that these two emissaries should arrange the "gradual removing of such as are willing to engage in the enterprise." [6]

Continuing, the report stated that no other prospect could be seen "but that the Southern Fishery, for want of being pursued in the proper manner, will be lost altogether to British subjects, as this [Dartmouth, Nova Scotia] is the only part of His Majesty's Dominions wherein since the peace it has been carried on to any advantage." [7]

Thus, the Nantucketers, competing with each other, under different flags, were the only ones then successfully pursuing the great southern whale fishery.

Now, the Nantucketers, who manned ships in both the northern and southern fisheries, sought a market for their toil-won oil. Of their voyages, a visitor wrote:

> They tell us of one man . . . on the island, who once went with others first to London in a vessel with a cargo of whale oil; from thence to Greenland and back to London with another cargo (being successful in the business); then fitted out for the South Seas, where success again attended, inasmuch that in the whole they caught as many whales as made up many hundred barrels of oil before they came home and within the course of one year they ranged the seas into North Latitude as far as 80 degrees and to 52 degrees in South Latitude . . .[8]

These whalemen were able to undergo the greatest of hardships but they had to seek a market for their oil—a market greater than what the struggling young states could then present.

But what of the whalemen who were creating an unprecedented "coup-de-whale" in the world's market place?

It has been shown that when the whaleship *Maria* reached Dover early in August 1785, William Rotch immediately fitted her out for whaling. Under Captain William Mooers she sailed August 18, 1785 (less than two weeks after her arrival in England), stopping at Portsmouth "for some things which could not be got ready before detention."[9] Although attempts were made to induce her whalemen to ship on board British craft, William Rotch states that her whole "crew were intire" upon sailing.*

The *Maria* became the first New England registered whaler to sail on a whaling voyage from Britain after the war. Her sailing was delayed by the fact that Barnabas Gardner was laid low with the smallpox. The unlucky man was put ashore at Portsmouth, and the ship sailed to the southwest, for the Brazil Banks.

The *Canton,* also of the Rotch fleet, was reported with 350 barrels of oil by Captain Goldsmith, who had mated with the Nantucket vessel "on Brazil." Captain James Whippey of the *Canton,* in the

---

* While Rotch was in London, three other ships owned by British merchants came in, commanded by Americans—Captain Abishai Delano, Francis Macy and William Goldsmith, all of Nantucket—followed by three other London whaleships, with American masters. They were some of the captains who had taken out the Falkland fleet in 1775.

South Atlantic, was reported (1789) to have intended to sail for the Cape of Good Hope "to winter and stay until next season."[10] This was good news as it gave Rotch a chance to get a word to his fleet in the southern fishery that he was now in England on "the business of all."

To follow William Rotch's close attention to the Nantucket fleet in the southern fishery is to appreciate the tactics of a master strategist in this world market for whale oil. He wrote to France to learn the price of oil and bone, and soon after learned that his ship the *Dauphin,* under Captain Paul Coffin, had put into Dunkirk with twenty-five tons of oil. The *Dauphin* was directed to return to Nantucket for orders. Rotch then ordered the ship *Warwick* to be sent to a European port with a cargo of oil, said port being Dunkirk. He urged that a thousand good whale irons (harpoons) be made for shipment, but that "Smith and Sweet must forge the head a little larger."[11]

The arrival of the whaleship *Mary,* at Dover, under Captain Shubael Coffin, in September 1785, marked the return of another Rotch ship from the Falkland Islands, bringing in forty tons of oil of her own and ninety tons from the United States, another of the Nantucket fleet in those waters of the South Atlantic.[12] The return to England of both the *Canton* and the *Mary* out of Nantucket indicates pretty conclusively that they had specific orders to sail for Britain directly from the South Atlantic Grounds. William Rotch, then, even before his departure from Nantucket, felt that the prospect of negotiating with the British authorities was good—in any event that there would be a sale in the European market.

The *Mary*'s oil was held in customs temporarily on information that she had a greater number of "foreigners" (Americans) on board than the law allowed. William Rotch, apparently representing his brother Francis, pointed out that the *Mary* and the *States* had sailed with the full complement of British seamen but that some had run away, "requiring others to ship—these they took being the very ones they wish to invite into their country."[13] He was also called upon to represent his brother as owner of the ship *Manila,* which had arrived from Halifax with oil.[14]

The *Warwick,* under Captain Christopher Mitchell, bearing the first shipment of oil directly from Nantucket after Rotch's arrival in Eng-

land—the second such cargo in island craft within that time—arrived
in the Downs on October 6, 1785. Rotch promptly got her cargo out
and reloaded her with hemp. He wrote to his firm ". . . see market at
Boston or Providence if it can not be disposed of at Nantucket." He
was "glad to learn" that the new ship *Falkland* (a fitting name, if
ever) and the dependable *Bedford,* had been dispatched whaling. He
commented drily:

> They can send out 12 ships from here with as good head-men as
> can be found anywhere (mostly our former inhabitants).[15]

In his next letter (Dec. 14, 1785), he warned:

> I have been cautious in writing some particulars respecting our
> own bysiness. . . . Notwithstanding I ever mean to conduct myself
> in political matters in a line that will bear the strictest examination.

Another important development of Rotch's stay in Britain was his
announcement that he had "discovered a greater use for several thousand tons of whale-oil hitherto unknown here." He advised his sons
to take: "more care in boiling out the oil, whether Sperm or whale, to
keep the pots clean, and the oil white, which will in the future make
a material advantage worth the attention of all concerned."[16] He was
undoubtedly getting ready to make sperm candles in the location—
wherever it was to be—which developed to be Dunkirk.

The *Maria,* under Captain William Mooers, on leaving England in
the summer of 1785, proceeded on the courses of the whaling ships
in the southern fishery. After some success around the Canaries and
Cape de Verdes, she crossed the equator and cruised to the Brazil
Banks: constantly on lookout, if whales failed to appear in one latitude
they tried another. Frequently they took as many as five whales in a
single school.

Continuing south, the *Maria* soon sighted the Falkland Islands.
Here they came upon another Rotch ship—the *States*—under Captain
Benjamin Hussey. While there, the *Canton,* under Captain James
Whippey, came in (at what is now known as Port Stanley), the three
Nantucket whalers exchanging the news.[17] It was at this time that
Captain Whippey received his orders to sail for Falmouth, England,
instead of Nantucket, at the completion of his voyage.

The Falkland Islands—the first headquarters for the sealer-whalemen —and a spot well-suited as such a rendezvous to this day—are situated some three hundred miles east of the Magellan Straits near the southern extremity of the South American continent. The Falklands have two main islands and many similar ones clustered about them: East Falkland with two fine inlets, Berkley Sound and Port William, and West Falkland or Grand Maloon. Between them is Falkland Sound.

The Falklands were discovered in 1592 by Captain John Davis, the same who had first found Davis Strait in Greenland. Hawkins, de Wert, and Strong later visited them, the latter giving them their present name. DeBougainville, the Frenchman, attempted to colonize them in 1764, but two years later the Falklands were ceded to Spain.

It was Port Egmont, on the small islet called Saunders, off West Falkland, that was the first port or anchorage ground. Commodore Byron had attempted a colony here in 1767 but the venture failed when Spaniards drove them away. Britain took over the ownership of the islands in 1771 by a convention agreement with Spain, but it was the whalemen and sealers who utilized the Falklands for fifty years before a settlement developed there. Here they found the sea-elephant and the seal in quantity and it was here the sealers made their first headquarters.

The stay of the three Nantucket ships at the Falklands was brief, only long enough to procure wood, water and fresh game. The latter was doubly welcome after "salt horse" and other shipboard provisions. Still to the south sailed the *Maria,* almost to Cape Horn (nearly accepting the opportunity of being the first whaleship to round it), taking several sperm whales—a just reward. Now again to the north. The *Maria's* journal states: "off the Falklands once more and almost beat out with rugged weather." [18]

In commenting on this voyage, a half century later, Frederick C. Sanford wrote:

> When the weather and sea made it unsafe to lower a boat they struck whales from the bowsprit of the ship—which is not usual, even at this day—one November 15, 1785, and the other April 27 following.[19]

The *Maria* completed her voyage as she passed along the latitude of the Brazil Banks. Under date of May 1786, the log stated. "We are now going off the coast and homeward bound!" They "touched" at the island of Barbados on June ninth, with the intent of coming to anchor to procure a supply of fresh provisions, but a British fifty-gun ship threatened (with appropriate oaths by the officer of the deck) to "blow the damned Yankees out of the water if they stood in toward the harbor." [20] The *Maria* quickly came about and headed for England, thence to Dunkirk, as ordered, to land the first cargo of oil under the French-Nantucket treaty.

On her return voyage the *Maria* sighted the *Lydia,* Captain Timothy Wyer, another of the Rotch ships; the *Swift,* Captain Barnabas Ray, and *Cumberland,* Captain Jonathan Swain, London ships, both of whose Nantucket masters later joined the Dunkirk fleet; and several Nantucket vessels, commanded by Captains Jonathan Mooers (William Mooers' brother), Stephen Bailey, Thomas Brock, Tristram Pinkham, Elijah Coffin, Seth Coffin (he of the wooden leg, to replace the one carried away by a whale), Solomon Bunker—all of Nantucket— and Captain John Hendricks of Boston.[21]

After fitting out at Dunkirk, the *Maria* sailed again, this time to the northern grounds at Greenland, buffeting those frozen regions of snow and ice, mooring sometimes to the solid ice itself. In a storm, tumbling about among the ice floes, the ship was trapped and the pressure of the field threatened to crunch her staunch hull and did, at length, tear a hole in her bow. Nothing daunted, Captain Mooers and his crew careened the ship sufficiently to get some planking and canvas, soaked with hot tar, over the hole, thus enabling her to sail back to Dunkirk with a full cargo.[22]

In 1799 Benjamin Rotch retired Captain Mooers to the land, placing him in charge of the Nantucket whaling interests at Dunkirk. Here the ancient mariner lived until his death in July 1819. His son, William, Jr., commanded a ship when he was only nineteen years of age.

As for the *Maria,* without the benefit of copper sheathing, she continued her voyaging until 1866—in her eighty-fifth year—when she was condemned in a South American port. She was refitted, but how much longer her career lasted is not known. No whaleship ever had a longer career under the same conditions.

Another of the early Dunkirk sailings of the Rotch fleet of which there is still evidence concerns the *Penelope,* under Captain Tristram Gardner. Also one of the ships which pursued voyages to both the southern and northern whaling grounds, the *Penelope* sailed as far north as 79° latitude, in the locality where ships fitted especially for exploring afterwards penetrated. A few extracts from the *Penelope*'s journal follow:

1788, Mch 22d. Still lying in the Downs, wind N.E. and dirty weather.

April 3d Thursday. First part came to anchor at Brass bay where we found 24 ships laying. Latter part fresh wind at N.N.E., we filling fresh water.

April 9th. Put to sea in company with 4 ships, wind S.E. bound for Greenland.

April 27th. Wind from Northward and moderate, we in a stream of water paying by . . . in the ice with a large fleet of ships in company. So ends this 24 hours.

May 21st. Got fast to a large cake of ice, handed our sails. Latter part still lying by ice, blowing hard . . .

May 23rd. Thick snow storm. Latter part saw whales but could not get at them, some ships in sight.

May 24th. Plenty of snow, beset by ice, ten sail of ships in sight.

June 5th. Saw two wrecks, one was the ship *London* of London, the other a ship belonging to Whitty men saved. The ships lost in last gale.

June 7th. Stuck a whale . . . and draw'd one iron-hard luck.

June 8th Sunday. . . . Killed a ten-ft. bone [mouth bone measurements] whale. Mated with Capt. Mooers and took one, several ships in sight.[23]

In this Greenland fishery were ships of Britain, Holland, France and America. The smaller craft, manned by the Americans, were sheathed with leather, with no extra planking, no reinforced bows. But their commanders had a persevering energy, a wealth of sea experience, and their crews endured the roughs and smooths of their voyages with unparalleled fortitude.

Writing from London, William Rotch informed his family and firm:

> We are now making all dispatch to leave England. The coals and
> Grindstones, with Iron Hoops and some other goods are on board,
> the Hemp and other articles will be forwarded as fast as possible.[24]

Here he showed what sort of goods he had obtained by selling whale
oil. He also directed (in a letter from Dunkirk, October 12, 1790)
that the sloop *Two Friends* be sent to Dunkirk with cedar boards and
oil, and stated that he would send Captain Hayden to Greenland
since "the season is now advanced." [25]

It was at this period that he wrote that the National Assembly

> . . . has . . . issued 12 hundred million livres, which at par exchange
> is 50 million sterling [pounds]. It is an enormous sum & funded in
> the Estates of the Clergy, which is . . . computed to be one-third the
> wealth of the Kingdom & are apt to be sold for this paper only; it
> is made a currency in all cases; this is a master stroke of policy in a
> respect, as there were many people much opposed to the Sale of the
> Clergy's lands, but now being saddled with the paper, funded only
> on these lands, have quite altered their tone, and are as Sanguine as
> any that the Estates ought to be sold & the paper redeemed.[26]

The temper of the times was not lost on William Rotch.

William Rotch was America's pioneer in international industry. He
saw beyond the narrow confines of tariff boundaries, visualized world
trade as a common ground for the peoples of the world—a market
place where freedom to trade could be practiced fully, to the advantage
of all. He wrote:

> I heartily wish there had been more Conciliatory disposition in our
> country at the conclusion of the War, and that the Treaty of peace
> had been fully and amply ratified and complied with on their part.
> I am now convinced in my sentiments when at home that we might
> have been place [d] upon a very easy footing here. But this by some
> would be deemed only the sentiment of Tory, but I can say it is the
> sentiment of one who is a hearty well wisher of both America and
> Brittain.[27]

During the six years (1787-1793) that the Nantucket whalers and
some of their families settled themselves at Dunkirk, a total of forty-
four ships had their export headquarters there. These ships and their
masters (most of them directly from Nantucket, some purchased in

England and France) included some of the pioneer whaleships to the Pacific.

During the years 1787 to 1790, William Rotch remained at Nantucket, spending considerable time in New Bedford, where his son William, Jr., was now launching his own business with his brother-in-law Samuel Rodman. But the senior Rotch was anxious that his son Benjamin should also have the benefit of his presence and counsel. And so on July 7, 1790, he took with him his wife, his daughters Lydia and Mary, and Benjamin's wife and young child and sailed for Dunkirk. The parents of the latter, Eliza Barker Rotch, never forgave William Rotch for taking the young wife to her husband, as Eliza never returned to Nantucket.

At Nantucket in 1791, although only seven ships were actually under French registry, it has been shown that five times that number were in reality getting under way from Nantucket and, through the Dunkirk loophole, bringing back the fortunes of their sea-hunts to the island. The result is clearly evident from the number of vessels fitting out under Nantucket registry in 1789—nearly three times the registered fleet of the year preceding.

Writing to Samuel Rodman in Nantucket, Rotch reported (June 6, 1786) on the progress of the French and British whalemen and then directed:

> We cannot carry on our business without a vessel to run between Dunkirk and America regularly, therefore thou must look out for purchase of a carrying Brig of 150 tons, try to get one built of white oak. If she will make no money she will save some. Take out a new register for the *Ann* in thine and my name [as] of Nantucket.[28]

New Bedford recouped its lost fortunes slowly. It was not until the return of William Rotch to this country in 1794 that she got back to deep-sea whaling in earnest. In 1788 Captain Joshua Delano, of Dartmouth, Massachusetts, made some voyages to the West Indies grounds and to the Gulf of Mexico in the *Rainbow*. Other craft from the Dartmouth district were commanded by George Allen, Benjamin Dillingham, Amos Kelley, Cornelius Butler, Robert Hathaway, David Bennett, Prince Sherman, Thomas Shockley and others.[29] These were necessarily small voyages in sloops, as the Dartmouth men did not have the European market that the Nantucket men enjoyed.

Thus, through the 1787-1790 period, the New England whalemen—in the great majority Nantucketers—found themselves, by the strangest twists of fate, actually competing with other Nantucket whalemen in British duty-protected whaleships. Nevertheless, American whaling had gained that impetus so necessary to give it a fresh start. The foresight and enterprise of William Rotch, and his faithful sons—Benjamin, William, Jr., Thomas—and to his son-in-law Samuel Rodman; the co-operation of Jethro and Richard Mitchell, George Hussey, Paul Gardner, the Macys, and other merchants of Nantucket; and the friendly aid of the Jarvises and Russells of New Bedford; all had provided the opportunity. Now the British Ministry had felt the barbs of American harpoons penetrating the very pocketbooks of His Majesty's realm.

In the report of Uniacke to Parr, at Halifax, in 1791, for transmittal to the Secretary of State and Lords of the Treasury, the recognition of this turn of events was excellently expressed. The Nova Scotian, in viewing the competition in whaling, remarked:

> Instead of the circumstances of these people [the Nantucketers] being distressed, it is rather the reverse—they are at the present Day building many new Ships and extending their Fishery, so that the Terms which some years ago they would with joy have accepted for their removal, I am of the opinion, although they same should be offered with trebel advantage, they would now refuse. Therefore, to make an estimate of the expenses that it would require to remove the whole bulk of the Inhabitants of Nantucket to Great Britain, would be to *calculate on a Sum which no nation could afford to give*.[30]

The price was now beyond even the resources of that mighty country. British whaling had not become the dominant factor in the world market. It had been given the "Coup-de-Whale."

And then came—'round Cape Horn!

chapter xi

꩜

THE WHALEMEN ROUND CAPE HORN

January 25, 1792 ... Cape Horn bearing North by East half
East two hundred and sixty miles ...
—Log of the *Rebecca*

IN THE ANCIENT GRAVEYARD on Nantucket known as Old North is the burial place of Captain Archaelus Hammond, the first man to strike and kill a sperm whale in the Pacific Ocean. It was late in the year 1788 that the English whaleship *Emelia,* owned by the London firm of Enderby & Sons, sailed for the Brazil Banks under Captain James Shields, with Hammond as first mate, both Nantucket men. The *Emelia* arrived late for the Brazil season and sailed south for the Falklands, where whales were no longer plentiful.[1]

The year 1789 now came on, and Mate Hammond suggested that they round the Horn to the Pacific, where—as he had heard from masters of China ships—there were many sperm whale seen. Captain Shields accordingly sailed and, upon rounding the Horn and getting well up the coast of Chile, a school of sperm whales was sighted. Boats were lowered and Mate Hammond's was the first to come up to them. That officer struck and killed his whale and the first sperm was taken in the Pacific.[2]

Success for the *Emelia* was immediate and in 1790 she retraced her course around Cape Horn and returned to London with a full cargo. Her arrival caused a considerable stir among the whalemen. Although the British were quick to take advantage of this pioneering voyage, the American whalers benefited as much and eventually gained more.

145

Dakin, in his *Whalemen's Adventures,* makes much of the *Emelia's* voyage. He quotes a letter written by Samuel Enderby, Jr. (in 1789 he believes) in which that member of the London firm recounts the "purchase of a very fine ship at a great expense to go round Cape Horn. She is now ready to sail; we are the only Owners intending to send a ship on that branch of the Fishery."[3] The Enderbys sought permission from the Admiralty to sail north of the equator in the Pacific if no sperm were found south of "the line." The letter continues:

> On the success of our ships depends the Establishment of the Fishery in the South Pacific as many owners have declared they shall wait to hear whether our ship is likely to succeed. . . . If unsuccessful we shall pay for the knowledge.[4]

Unfortunately there is no date on this letter. Since Dakin mistakenly declares on other occasions that the first whaleships to the southern Atlantic whale fishery were British, and that the "Tea Party Ships" were British whalers,[5] his supposition of the date of this letter may be equally questionable.

What is noteworthy, is that the *Emelia* probably had other Nantucketers on board along with Mate Hammond. Subsequent events indicate this conclusively. First of all, the *Emelia's* return in 1790 brought a change in policy, not only for the British firm of Enderby, but also for that of William Rotch. Because of the Nantucket whalemen involved, the result of this initial voyage to the Pacific almost immediately became more important to the Americans than to the British—the ratio of result being in proportion to the number of American whalemen (Nantucketers) involved.

The best evidence of this natural condition is revealed in the letters of William Rotch from Dunkirk. It is probable that the news of the *Emelia's* voyage 'round Cape Horn reached him at about August 1790, for his letter reveals the fact that he immediately prepared his vessels for the Pacific.[6] The first so dispatched was the *Falkland,* under Captain Obed Paddock.

Rotch wrote to Samuel Rodman as of October 19, 1790:

> . . . Captain Shields and Mate Hammond, who now sail from Here, suppose they spoke Thad. Swain on their return from the South Sea,

I believe a little beyond the Line but being offended that Swain did not shorten sail or some other maneuver that he thought his duty as a seaman.[7]

Something of the importance of the meeting in mid-Atlantic of the *Emelia,* of London, and the *Hope,* of Dunkirk, on that day in 1790, is given in Rotch's letter, with added description of the testiness of those whaling masters.

William Rotch reported that as the *Emelia* and *Hope* passed near each other, Captain Shields hailed the latter, asking for news. Captain Thaddeus Swain did not alter his course, but merely called back that he was forty-six days out of Dunkirk, and asked the other's destination. Shields hallooed that the *Emelia* was bound to London, having came *"from round Cape Horn* with 150 tons sperm oil." [8]

At this news, wrote Rotch, "Swain desired more information" and for the first time "more ships to have further conversation." But Captain Shields angered by Captain Swain's first indication of not appearing to heave the *Hope* to for a "gam" became obstinate in turn and made no effort to bring the *Emelia* about. Captain Swain tried to get his craft alongside the London whaler but "Shields' disgust ran so high" he would not allow the *Hope* to "come up with him," despite the fact he was anxious to know whether England and France were at peace or war.

Rotch continued: "Nor could the importunity of Mate Hammond influence Shields' mulish disposition to stop even to get the intelligence which might have—if a War—been of great advantage to him." The writer went on: "I hope he [Swain] so clearly understood that he [Shields] had been round Cape Horn, as to have taken the same route."

With his usual quick realization of the possibilities of Pacific Ocean whaling, Rotch, in October 1790, dispatched (within a few weeks of their return to Dunkirk) the *Falkland,* Captain Obed Paddock and the *Penelope,* under Captain Isaiah Worth, 'round Cape Horn. A few months earlier, he had ordered the *Maria* to take the opposite route around the Cape of Good Hope to Madagascar Ground (newly identified by the whalemen) and thence "to the eastward if necessary," toward New Holland (Australia). He dispatched the rest of the Dunkirk fleet into the Pacific Ocean.[9]

The first of the Dunkirk fleet to get her oil in the Pacific was the *Falkland,* under Captain Obed Paddock, which returned in December 1791, after a voyage of a year and a half. The next of the Rotch Cape Horners to arrive was the *Harmony,* under Captain David Starbuck, with 350 barrels of sperm oil. In a letter from Dunkirk (February 18, 1792), William Rotch commented: "David Starbuck arrived safe from the Coast of Peru, . . . he brings no account so late as the *Falkland,* having left the Coast before her."

In the next month he wrote:

> The *Canton* is ready [having arrived from Nantucket a few weeks before], the *Ospray* is looked for. Stephen Coleman, son of Christopher, has just got to London, having lost his ship in Delagoa Bay, with 170 tons of whale oil. . . . Silas Jones at Delagoa Bay [in the Rotch ship *Swan*] has lost his second mate, a son of George Bunker, I believe his name was Cromwell, killed by a whale, and has left a widow. . . . Henry Delano, in a London ship (the *Kingston*) has arrived at Falmouth from the Coast of Peru, where he left last 7th mo. [July 1791]. . . . He spoke *Lydia* [Captain Benjamin Clark, of Dunkirk], the *Washington* [Captain Bunker, of Nantucket], *Favourite* [Captain Barnard, of Nantucket] on 15th and 18th of 4th month [April 1791].[10]

There were, then at least nine whaleships in the Pacific early in the year 1792, four from Dunkirk, two from Nantucket, two from London, and one from New Bedford; all but one commanded by Nantucketers.

Two new ships were purchased at LeHavre for the Rotch fleet. One of them, the *William Penn,* given to Captain Obed Fitch, was described by Rotch as ". . . a good ship & I think compleat for whaling will not stand us in more than 45 or 47.000 livres, a little more than £1000 sterling." [11]

The *Penelope* returned from a maiden voyage around Cape Horn under Captain Isaiah Worth early in March 1792. Rotch reported that the *Penelope* had left the Peruvian coast October 20, 1791, "all well except some a little touched with scurvy but capable of duty." Captain Worth had serious trouble when the *Penelope* lost all her rudder except seven feet of its upper end ". . . but I. Worth's ingenuity and the industry of the crew replaced it in 4 days, which served to bring them save into port." [12] Two days before leaving her last cruise in the Pacific, the ship had sighted the *Mary,* another Dunkirk (Rotch) ship, under Captain Coffin Whippey.

The *Mary,* under Captain Whippey, had actually left the Pacific two months before the *Penelope,* but had put in at Rio de Janeiro for provisions. As the latter ship was sheathed with copper, she was a much faster sailer, and arrived at Dunkirk before Captain Whippey's ship.

Enderby & Sons of London, the strongest competitor of America among the British, was working closely with Lord Hawksbury, whom Rotch had so aptly described as "a great foe of America." [13] In a letter from Enderby, Jr., to George Chalmers, dated London, January 17, 1789, he states:

> . . . His Lordship first took the Fishery under his protection in 1785, the year prior to which sixteen Sail of Vessels had been employed in the South Whale Fishery, the value of the oil . . . amounting to between 27 and 28,000 pounds, for which Government paid 18% although the premiums were but £1500 per annum. The number of vessels which returned to that Fishery last year [1788] were 45 sail, the value of the oil £90,599, for which Government have and will pay £63,000, which is not 7% of the whole amount of cargoes of oil. . . . In my opinion, nothing is wanting to make this Fishery compleat but an unlimited right of fishing in all seas; the British Adventures would soon explore the most distant parts and the settlements of New Holland would be often visited as there are many whales in the sea.[14]

It was only through the close and frugal co-operation of the Nantucket fleet at home and the Rotch-Nantucket fleet at Dunkirk that the British challenge was met. Nothing could more graphically illustrate the great advantage of the British than the letter quoted above. Through their bounties for their own whaleships, and their tax on foreign imported oils, the British had a wide margin over the American whalemen in competing for the world market.

It was an unfortunate circumstance to find so many Nantucket whaling masters commanding British ships, and to see the Dartmouth colony of Nantucketers taking the lead in competition with their own people. But this development, in itself, proved to be a blessing in disguise, for when the majority of them returned home they had valuable experience to aid themselves and their owners.

We have already seen how the Rotch fleet benefited by information conveyed by Nantucket whalemen, one to the other, and how Rotch anticipated the British move around the Cape of Good Hope. The *Maria* sailed from Dunkirk in 1790, to go around Good Hope, and it was not until the next year, 1791, that Enderby sent out the ship *William and Ann,* commanded by Captain Eber Bunker, with orders to round the Cape and proceed "to the eastward."

Captain Bunker was one of the many Nantucket men commanding British whalers at this time. He was the first man to take the British whale fishery to the coast of Australia, in November 1791. The British had established a convict colony at Botany Bay on the southeast coast of Australia in 1788, and they often used whaleships to transport convicts on the outward voyage. By 1793 there were twenty British whaleships in the Pacific fishery, most of them going by way of Good Hope.

John Adams, writing from London to his friend James Bowdoin in Boston, on May 9, 1786, warned:

> Mr. Jenkinson, an old friend of the British Empire, is still at his labors. He is about establishing a Bounty upon fifteen ships to the southward, and upon two to double Cape Horn for spermaceti whales. Americans are to take an oath that they mean to settle in England before they are entitled to the Bounty.[15]

From London in September of the same year, Adams wrote to Jefferson, then in France:

> The whalemen, both at Greenland and the southward, have been unsuccessful, and the price of spermaceti-oil has risen about £50 per ton.[16]

The same Mr. Jenkinson appeared when Lord Grenville was negotiating to remove the Nantucket whalemen from Dartmouth in Nova Scotia to Milford Haven, Wales, in 1791. In a letter to Samuel Starbuck, at Dartmouth, Nova Scotia, a certain Thomas Owen, of Waterford, Ireland, mentions that "Jenkinson was sorry that he let him [William Rotch] slip through his fingers by the intermediate application of John Parnell, our Chancellor of Exchequer, then in London. I went in search of Roach but happened to be too late."[17]

Now, with Hawksbury rubbing his hands in anticipation of handsome whale-oil cargoes in British ships and the colony at Milford Haven satisfactorily settled, it appeared that Nantucket's migrating whalemen were going to pull Britain well ahead in the race for supremacy in the whale fishery. But the island home of these men of the sea was still pretty much in the fight for the coveted honors.

All this time, in New England the whale fishery, with Nantucket leading the way, was gaining impetus. In 1788 William Rotch, Jr., had gone to New Bedford leaving Samuel Rodman to represent the Rotch firm in Nantucket. During the years 1788 through 1790 the Nantucket and New Bedford fleets grew rapidly, with the market in France aiding the cause considerably. The manufacture of spermaceti candles created a demand, with large exports to the West Indies. The consumption of oil in America was increased by the gradual discontinuance of tallow candles in the street lighting of the cities and the introduction of machinery and oil-burning lamps.

Jefferson, in his *Report on the Whale-Fishery* from 1787 to 1790 listed Nantucket with eighteen ships in the southern whale fishery and eighteen in the northern, employing 487 seamen, and having a tonnage of 4,050. These ships obtained a total of 12,060 barrels of sperm and right-whale oil. The district of Dartmouth, which included New Bedford, Fairhaven, etc., had forty-five ships in the northern fishery (mostly small sloops) and five in the southern. Their tonnage totaled 3,450, less than the Nantucket total and their complete catch of 4,450 barrels was little better than one-third of the Nantucket total. Cape Cod ports had sixteen ships in the industry and other New England ports scattered numbers, so that 122 American whaleships had a total catch of 21,100 barrels of oil.[18]

Jefferson, then Secretary of State, also stated in his report to the House of Representatives, of February 1, 1791:

These details will enable Congress to see what a competition we have to struggle for the continuance of this Fishery, not to say its increase. Against prohibitory duties in one country, and bounties to the adventurers in both of those which are contending with each other for the same object [Britain and France], ours have no auxiliaries but poverty and rigorous economy. The business unaided is a wretched one. . . . The American Whale-Fishery is principally followed by the inhabitants of the island of Nantucket.[19]

Jefferson's report showed that the thirty-six Nantucket ships had a far greater range than the ships from other New England ports. Voyages now included those into the South Atlantic; those across to Walwis (Woolwich Bay) on the west coast of Africa and around Good Hope to Algoa Bay; those down to the Falklands and along the dangerous shores on the east coast of South America.

When the *Canton,* Captain Coffin Whippey, arrived late in 1790 at Nantucket, from Dunkirk, with the news about the voyage of Captain Shields around Cape Horn, there was immediate action. Six ships, three of them newly built, were fitted out from Nantucket and dispatched " 'round the Horn." The port of New Bedford fitted out the *Rebecca* for a similar voyage.[20]

The first of this Nantucket fleet to double Cape Horn was the ship *Beaver,* under Captain Paul Worth. She left Nantucket in August and early in the year 1792 arrived off Cape Horn, successfully rounding this dangerous island promontory.[21] The *Beaver* was thus the first whaler out of an American port to 'round the Horn and sail into the Pacific. Much has been made of this incident. But, as has already been shown, she was not the first American ship, strictly speaking, so to do, since the *Falkland, Mary, Penelope* and *Harmony* had preceded her out of Dunkirk. The *Beaver* was closely followed by the *Rebecca,* of New Bedford, under Captain Joseph Kersey.[22]

Obed Macy tells us that the *Beaver* was a new ship of 240 tons burden. She carried seventeen men and manned three boats of five men each, which left two men called "shipkeepers," available if all boats were down after whales in favorable weather. The whole cost of her outfit was $10,212.[23]

When fitted for sea, Macy states, the *Beaver*'s principal supplies were forty barrels of salt beef and pork, three and one half tons of bread, thirty bushels of peas and beans, one thousand pounds of rice, twenty-four barrels of flour, forty gallons of molasses and four hundred barrels (total quantity) of iron-hooped casks, and fourteen hundred wooden-hooped. The *Beaver* was not copper-sheathed. She was typical of her sister whaleships of the period. Their speed in sailing when first out of port was about eight knots per hour, having nothing on the bottom but pitch and tar. After six months or so, barnacles and seaweed would begin to accumulate on her hull and a speed of six knots per hour would be the limit.

Whether the *Beaver,* of Nantucket, or the *Rebecca,* of New Bedford, was the first whaleship from an American port to enter the Pacific Ocean from an American port has been for years a moot question. The *Rebecca*'s logbook, however, settles the question by reporting that the *Beaver* was already in the Pacific when she arrived there in March 1792.[24] But there is glory enough for all. The *Rebecca,* of New Bedford, sailed September 28, 1791, and was undoubtedly the first to return, arriving at New Bedford on February 23, 1793, a month before the *Beaver* reached Nantucket on March 25, 1793.[25]

Captain Paul Worth, of the *Beaver,* in a letter to a friend in New Bedford communicated "agreeable intelligence of the success of the whalemen fitted out the season past." The letter was dated from "Martinico" in the West Indies, February 18, 1793, where the *Beaver* had put in for provisions, desperately needed, having been unable to secure a full supply on the coast of Peru. In fact, Captain Worth was boarded by a ship-of-war on that coast and warned not to put in at any port. However, needing fresh provisions, he had entered Callao, the port of Lima, Peru, but was driven out with a peremptory notice that he was likely to be seized if he remained.[26] The Spaniards knew little of the Americans and considered them British subjects, and the war between Britain and Spain was only recently concluded.

The *Beaver* was gone seventeen months. She brought home eleven hundred barrels of sperm oil, worth £30 per ton; 370 barrels of head-matter, worth £60 per ton, and 250 barrels of whale oil, worth £15 per ton. Since her outfitting had cost her $10,212, this gave her a good profit of $20,000 on this maiden voyage.

A recorder wrote of the return on this pioneer whaleship to Nantucket:

> Early in 1793, the news spread that a ship was in sight, supposed to be a "Cape Horner." Every hill top and house-top was occupied to see the welcome ship as most families in the town had near or distant relatives in the fleet. A great suspense pervaded the minds

of the people for several hours, not knowing which of the fleet it could be, as no signal colors were on board of any of the ships. At length, Thaddeus Joy, who was remarkable for noticing the standing of ship's masts and the cut of topsails before sailing, announced from his look-out the ship *Beaver,* Captain Worth. The boys were eager to carry the glad tidings to the wives and families of the officers, for which it was customary to pay $1 to him who first imparted the first news.[27]

Following closely in the wake of the *Rebecca* and *Beaver* was another new ship, the *Washington,* Captain George Bunker. After getting around "Cape Stiff," as the seamen called Cape Horn, he got a full cargo of sperm. Needing provisions, Captain Bunker sailed into Callao and there displayed the first American flag on the west coast of South America. This was in July 1792. As has been stated, the Spaniards, ignorant of the new United States, and only recently ending their war with England, treated this ship as they did the *Beaver.* But although at first they would not allow Captain Bunker to land, they did consent to his putting on board some fresh water, potatoes and other vegetables, and fresh meat and allowed him twenty-four hours at anchor. The *Washington* returned home on April 8, 1793, with eight hundred barrels of sperm oil and four hundred of whale oil.[28]

Next of the fleet to return home from the Pacific was the *Hector* (another new ship, built in 1791), Captain Thomas Brock; with a cargo of seven hundred barrels of sperm and five hundred barrels of whale oil, her arrival date being April 8, 1793, the same as that of the *Washington.* The *Rebecca,* Captain Seth Folger, returned to Nantucket on April 30, 1793, and the *Warren,* Captain Robert Meader, and the *Favourite,* Captain Obed Barnard, followed on the next month, all arriving safely from their Cape Horn voyages.

"In this most perilous expedition," writes a person in the *New Bedford Standard,* signing himself "Nantucket," [29]

The captains, officers and crews were selected as the bravest and most resolute. A station on board the fleet was considered a mark of great bravery, and to double Cape Horn was thought to be very dangerous to life and property (it is still so considered), beside going so far from home. Lord Anson's voyage was read, in which he lost some of his fleet in doubling Cape Horn, which deterred many from the voyage. However, Yankee enterprise, ever on the alert to amass the needful, was not deterred by any accounts of former navigators, of storms and gales off Cape Horn, but went forth boldly for the dreaded Cape.

Two decades later, the famous Captain David Porter, in the U.S. frigate *Essex,* was sailing for Cape Horn and the Pacific. His reaction to the perils of the passage are best shown in his own words, written in his *Journal* as he prepared to get through the Strait of Le Maire:

> I am induced to believe no part of the world presents a more horrible aspect than Staten Land. (that island off the east coast of Tierra del Fuego). The breakers appeared to lie about half a mile from the shore. While we were standing off, the whole sea, from the violence of the current, appeared in a foam of breakers, and nothing but the apprehension of immediate destruction could have induced me to have ventured through it. . . .[30]

When the whalemen sailed 'round the Horn there was only one method of ascertaining the longitude, usually by the taking of lunar observations and the imperfect measure of the log line. Chronometer and sextant were used only by the circumnavigators and were practically unknown at this period. It was the opinion of many merchants on the Continent that the whaleships could not find the Pacific Ocean, the distance being so great. How little these people of the land knew of the men of the sea!

Elijah Durfy, the twenty-two-year-old harpooner of the *Rebecca,* wrote in his journal on December 25, 1791:

> This day being Christmas I set myself down to see how far from Bedford I am by my recning. Our crew are all in good health; the weather very bad and tedious, hard south winds attended with rain, lightning and thunder and hail as oftimes three gales in one week. We get down our top gallant masts almost every other day. We had a fine passage of 88 days without the loss of either men or spars, except the fore top-gallant mast. We are now in latitude of 40° and 53 miles south and longitude 57° and 25 miles west. . . . Five thousand, six hundred and forty miles from New Bedford.
>
> We see plenty of Right Whales and other large fish, no spermaceity as yet on this Coast. We have very favorable news from the Pacific Ocean concerning whales by Prince Coleman of Dunkirk [homeward bound in the *Hope,* a Rotch ship, with 1,500 barrels]

and John Basset of Bristol [England] who informs us that between the Latitude 30° and 8° south [in the Pacific] there is whales enough. We have an account of Thomas Lock, 1600 bbls. [London]; Prince Coleman, 1500 bbls.; Henry Delano, 400 bbls. [in *Countess* of London. These were all Nantucket captains].

Just one month later (January 25, 1792) the journal recorded: "Lat. 60°-10′, Long. 71°-5′. . . . Cape Horn bearing North by East half East two hundred and sixty miles; New Bedford bearing north, ¼ east, six thousand one hundred and fifty miles."

And, six days later: ". . . . At 10 P.M. the wind died away on a sudden and left a most terrible sea which, breaking in our stern, filled our Cabin full of water. The day ended in a most furious gale of wind and hail."

Despite the sudden gales and cold, the *Rebecca* made a good passage around Cape Horn, entering the Pacific and getting in the latitude of the west end of the Strait of Magellan on February 7, 1792. The entry for Feb. 13 reads: "Cleaned ship foreward and aft betwixt Decks, made several fires to dry, smoke and clean the ship to prevent scurvy. . . . So we spend our time sailing along the Coast of South America."

The *Rebecca*'s first Pacific whaling was done on February 21, when her boats lowered to attack a school of sperm. ". . . Lost 7 irons and one lance, one short warp and one boat's warp. Got but one alongside that day, two days later found two more. . . ." Five days later they ". . . made land which is called New Chyna . . . appearing high and craggy . . . lat. 35°-12′ south."

One of the most interesting entries describes the typical inquisitiveness and exploring urge of this first American whalemen in this great ocean. It is a record of March 16, 1792, and Elijah Durfy wrote:

. . . Hauled in with the Land in order to make some Discoveries. I went on Shore with the Captain where we found nothing but rocks, but sailing the Coast a Long one League found a Passage about half a mile wide into the Land. We went in with our boat when to our surprize we found a bay where fifty sail of ships might ride free from Danger. Some dangerous rocks in the passage.

We saw no inhabitants but saw several stone huts, the roofs of which were covered with whale's rib-bones. We saw knives, skins, scrapers, spears, files, paddles, parts which clearly indicated that there was natives nigh at hand. . . . The Land almost perpendicular, near a League high, rocky, dry and barren. . . . This lying in the Latitude of 23 degrees nearly.

Here is an anchorage now called Horseshoe Bay, just below the Bay of Mejillones. A few days later a Spanish brigantine was spoken and the whalers were informed of two watering places in 19°–21′ and 18° south—the "Gully of Victor" and Arica.

Sailing north, the *Rebecca* arrived at the "on-shore grounds" off the Peruvian coast, where other whaleships were sighted. The first vessels met were London whalers, the *Redbridge, Brittania* and *Salander.* One of the ships had its crew "very much troubled with scurvy, which is oftimes the case in these seas, a distemper, the most terrible that human nature is Liable."

It was at this time that the *Rebecca* learned of the *Beaver,* of Nantucket, with 180 barrels of sperm, which had preceded her into this ocean. The New Bedford craft also spoke the *Washington,* Captain Obed Barnard, another Nantucket whaler, which had arrived before the *Rebecca.* Among others of the Cape Horn fleet the long records "speaking" the *Lydia* (a Rotch ship), of Dunkirk, under Captain Benjamin Clark, and the *Countess* of London, in command of Captain Henry Delano, also a Nantucketer. The *Lucy,* of Dunkirk, Captain Robert Trott, had lost a boat's crew and second mate by desertion.

For several days, the *Rebecca* sailed in company with the *Fonthill,* Captain Elisha Pinkham, a London ship with a Nantucket captain. On May 19, the log recorded:

> . . . Saw whales, lowered away our boats and killed two. Struck the third, she stove our boat, killed Elijah Wilcocks, our cooper, and wounded myself, one more, and lost the whale.

Among other ships which hove-to for a gam with the *Rebecca,* were the *Hector,* of Nantucket, with 580 barrels of oil, and the *Warren* and another ship named *Rebecca,* of Nantucket, the latter two having entered the Pacific about the same time the New Bedford whaler rounded the Horn.

This logbook records a total of thirty-nine whaleships in the Pacific in 1792—eight Nantucket craft, twenty-one out of British ports, and nine from Dunkirk. Sixteen of the British ships had American whaling masters, so that out of the entire fleet in the Pacific at this time thirty-three were commanded by Nantucket men. The majority of the officers and harpooners of the British craft were no doubt also American whalemen.[31]

At the same time (1790-1793), there were several other London whaleships in the Pacific, all commanded by Nantucket men and probably manned by Nantucketers. Among these were the *Rattler,* Captain Andrew Swain; the *London,* Captain Joshua Coffin, and the *Kingston,* Captain Henry Delano. The latter, arriving at London in January 1793, reported speaking the *Lydia,* of Dunkirk, and the *Washington* and the *Favourite,* of Nantucket, on the coast of Peru in April 1792. Here were ships from three different ports, with Nantucket men manning all of them.

Fortunately, for the pattern of history, persons interested in American maritime endeavors compiled nearly a century ago the names of Nantucket men who, over a period of thirty years, had commanded whaleships out of British and French ports. They found that a total of 206 captains were so engaged, of whom twenty-four at some time during their lives commanded ships under both British and French flags. Also, many of these masters took out different ships from the same port.[32] If we add the number of American whalemen who served as officers in these ships, it can be easily understood where those thousand whalemen known to have left Nantucket during and just after the Revolution found their employ.

In 1869 a writer in the *Inquirer and Mirror* of Nantucket, identified as William R. Easton, wrote:

> . . . Since that period [the post-Revolutionary War period] the changes in the condition of the Town and its inhabitants has been so great— from a deep gloom occasioned by the war in which the entire whaling fleet, the sole means of support to the inhabitants was destroyed —rising again to a degree of prosperity without precedent . . . seems enough to make an old resident willing . . . to join the fathers who have crossed the flood. . . . There are those now living who have seen fleets of ships from England commanded by Nantucket men . . . in the Pacific. Some of the largest fortunes in England, among the commercial classes, were made in this connection, the Greens, Bennetts, Enderbys, Mellishes, the Quaker Sturges and many others. We were informed in 1855 by Mr. Richard Green, of London, the great capitalist, that his whaling ship, the *Matilda,* was the

last employed on that business from London to the South Sea, and that she was commanded by a Nantucket man. . . . There are many incidents showing the prominent connection of Nantucket with the whale-fishery, infusing, stimulating, directing national wealth far beyond our own borders. We have sent to England and France some of the best seamen that ever trod a vessel's deck and directed its course along the trackless main. Many closed their lives in the foreign land, having married . . . but most of them returned to the old home, or near it, seeking to haul up in a snug harbor in their native land.

Insofar as Nantucket was concerned, the firms of Richard Mitchell & Co., Albert Gardner, Obed & Sylvanus Macy, Paul Gardner, and others recognized the advantage of pursuing the sperm into both the Pacific and Indian oceans. The islanders were too closely allied by ties of blood as well as business to have prevented any free flow of information from both the British and Dartmouth whaling fleets. Nantucket was a clearing house for whaling news as well as whaling men.

But what of the Dunkirk fleet and William Rotch?

The times (1790) presaged the danger of war between Great Britain and France. This would mean the end of the Dunkirk venture.

In Dunkirk, William Rotch, after dispatching his Cape Horn fleet, as has been noted, prepared for their protection. He announced that he would have the *Penelope* sent to America, "to be registered under our New Government [the Constitution having at last been ratified], as her register is of our own State only." [33] He reported that the *Harmony,* Captain David Starbuck, the *Lydia,* Captain Benjamin Clark, the *Ann,* Captain Prince Coleman, the *Ospray,* Captain Benjamin Paddock, the *Good Intent,* Captain John Hawes, and the *Mercury,* Captain Laban Coffin, all representing the Rotch fleet, were in the southern fishery. Three of these at least were Cape Horn whalers. [34]

There was also the danger that the French Ministry would put a duty on the importation of American oil, thus threatening the Nantucket export trade.

Rotch gives a very concise account of this controversy. He wrote to Samuel Rodman describing the meeting of his son Benjamin with the French Committee of Commerce and Agriculture, at which time there was evidence of the opposition by the rape-seed farmers. The rape-seed came from a form of turnip and was used in lamps and other industries, and whale oil had supplanted it. The committee voted to allow the Dunkirk whale-fishery oil and American whale oil to be imported duty-free.[35]

But the most serious trouble came at Benjamin Rotch's meeting in Paris with the Ministers of State, the Marquis de La Fayette and the American Ambassador, Thomas Jefferson. The question came upon the petition from Dunkirk to prohibit "the importation of all foreign whale-oil" into the Kingdom except American oil. William Rotch wrote: "This petition was sent long before the meeting, even when Britain was bringing in her oil so plentifully, and Benjamin at that time insisted upon American oil being admitted."

But a certain powerful French minister "was determined it should not," reported Rotch, "and dashed out the words 'American oil' with his own hand, upon which that general prohibition took place." It was shortly after this, as the elder Rotch wrote, that the general prohibition of American and British oil was put into effect, "though afterwards the *present back door* [Dunkirk] for American oil was opened, and this . . . was done through Benjamin's means." [36]

It took considerable patience and tact on the part of Benjamin Rotch to deal with the French ministers and treat with British business associates—while at the same time keeping on open terms with the astute Jefferson. That the Nantucketer had inherited much of the sagacity of his father is evident from the record of events.

Jefferson accused Benjamin obliquely with being the author of the prohibition of American oil; he denied it and assured the Ambassador he had been the advocate for its admission. This, of course, Jefferson had no way of ascertaining at the time and so "appeared to doubt it."

Benjamin quickly pointed out that the original draft of the agreement, which contained the phrase allowing American oil to come into France duty-free, was available and this showed where the French minister had drawn a line through it. Jefferson then acknowledged the truth of the assertion, "and seemed satisfied and not so reserved as heretofore."

William Rotch continued his account of this episode:

> . . . Yet, after this meeting, the Ambassador [Jefferson] drew up a long petition on the same subject, to endeavor to influence the Min-

ister . . . I believe Necker, accompanied by a letter which I suppose
was a request that it might not be exposed, perhaps with the hope of
working secretly with the Minister, which, if so, was warrantable
and as it was his duty to serve his country in the best manner he
could, and in this step if the Memorial contained nothing but the
truth (which I will not say it did) I justify him; but if secrecy was
intended, this or some other cause disgusted Necker, that instead of
any privacy he sent it, I believe, with a letter also direct to De Ba-
roque [Dunkirk merchants associated with the Rotch firm] and Benjamin's lodgings, for their perusal and answer, which they did and
so effectively refuted all his arguments, that the petition shares the
fate of many others. . . . The Marquis de Lafayette also showed all
his friendship for America in his power in this case, which was very
well. . . .[37]

Jefferson gives additional detail on this development. It bears out
William Rotch's own judgment throughout the situation. Writing to
John Jay, from Paris, he revealed that he suspected the Count de
Luzern as the minister who struck out the clause in the *Arret* which
allowed American oil to come to France duty-free.

. . . As soon as I was apprised of this [he wrote], which was several
days after it passed . . . I wrote to the Count de Montmorin . . . and
had conferences on the subject, from time to time, with him and
other ministers. I found them prepossessed by partial information
of their Dunkirk whale Fishermen; and therefore found it necessary
to give them a view of the whole subject in writing, which I did, in
the piece of which I enclose. . . . I therein entered into more details . . . with M. Necker, as an economist. . . . At a conference, in
the presence of M. Lambert, on the 16th [November 1788] (where I
was ably aided by Marquis de LaFayette, as I have been through the
whole business) it was agreed to except us from the prohibition. But
they will require vigorous assurance that the oils coming under our
name are really of our fishery. They fear we will cover the introduction of English oils from Halifax.[38]

It is easily seen that Jefferson had at first little understanding of
the original motives behind the Rotch efforts to enable American
whaling, through Nantucket, to recoup its forces so as to regain its
former footing in the world market. At the same time, William Rotch,
while appreciating Jefferson's position (as has been shown in his letters) was not aware of the American Ambassador's complete sincerity,

having had numerous opportunities to learn how many men in high position had been petty and vindictive.

Rotch wrote his sons:

> I wish our great men may consider they have not the power sufficient to overturn us in this branch, but it is probably [another] war will do it for them. . . . What I have mentioned respecting Benjamin's meeting with Ministers, Ambassador, etc., thou may keep within our circle as it is not my interest to publish anything in our favor, as truths cannot be received by many at this time; I therefore avoid vindification, having a satisfaction in mind.[39]

It is not so strange a circumstance to find two such strong-minded men as Rotch and Jefferson temporarily at odds over a controversial issue. Neither is it too extraordinary a coincidence to find them basically of the same fundamental opinion on the same question. We need only to take note that both were in near perfect agreement on steps to preserve the American whale fishery.

To show this conclusively, one has only to read the following. It was written by Thomas Jefferson; it might as easily have been written by William Rotch. The excerpt is from a Jefferson letter written from Paris in 1788:

> England fears no rivals in the whale fishery but America; or rather, it is the whale fishery of America of which she is endeavoring to possess herself. It is for this object she is making the present extraordinary efforts, by bounties and other encouragements; and her success so far is very flattering. Before the war she had not one hundred vessels in the whale fishery trade, while America employed 309. In 1786, Great Britain employed 151; in 1787 she had 286; in 1788, 314—nearly the ancient American number—while the latter has fallen to about 80. They have changed places, then; England having gained exactly what America has lost. France, by her ports and markets, holds the ballance between the two countries, and gives the victory by opening or shutting them, to which she pleases. We have still the precious remains of seamen, educated in this fishery, and capable by their poverty, their boldness and address of recovering it from the English in spite of bounties.[40]

What Thomas Jefferson prophesied in 1788, William Rotch by his sagacious action enabled the Nantucketers to accomplish for the American whale fishery through the years 1789-1792. These "precious remains of seamen" were for the most part the Nantucketers. It was of these whalemen that William Rotch was speaking, when he remarked to a member of the Continental Congress, in 1782:

> Can we preserve it the American Whale-Fishery in the present state of things by any other place except Nantucket? The answer was: "No, we cannot."

Now, through prompt action, the fundamental truth of what Jefferson had stated (to which Rotch had dedicated his fortunes and those of his fellow-Islanders) was being surely and fully demonstrated.

chapter xii

~~~◡◡~~~

AMERICA REGAINS ITS WHALING FLEET THROUGH THE ALCHEMY OF REVO- LUTION AND WAR

*Now Bildad, like Peleg, and indeed many other Nantuck-
eters, was a Quaker . . . , and to this day its inhabitants in
general retain in an uncommon measure the peculiarities
of the Quaker. . . . For some of these same Quakers are
the most sanguinary of sailors and whale-hunters. They are
fighting Quakers; they are Quakers with a vengeance.*

—Melville, *Moby Dick*

IT IS SIGNIFICANT to note that for a few years following the first
voyages of the whalers to the west coast of South America, comparatively few ships took the route around the Horn. Instead, the
whaling masters were pursuing voyages to both the west coast of
Africa—Woolwich (Walvis) Bay, Saldanha Bay and Good Hope—and
to the Brazil Banks, River Plate and Falklands in the South Atlantic.
The real penetration of the Pacific was to come with the advent of the
1800's.

The fact that the whaleships rounded the Cape of Good Hope before
they rounded Cape Horn is not generally appreciated. The Nantucketers were in the Gulf of Guinea a decade before the Revolution.
By observing the course of the whales "making their passage," the
whalemen went on to the South Atlantic, then found the Brazil Banks
and the Falkland Islands; sailed across the wide southern Atlantic

164

(rendezvous at St. Helena, where the British East India Company had a fort), and got into Walvis Bay, inside Pelican Point, on Africa's desolate western coastline.

Of this bay (which became a rendezvous for whaleships before the Revolution and continued as such) this excellent description has been given: "Among the indentations of the coast of Western Africa, the Bay of Walwich [Walvis] may be traced on the chart. This bay was much resorted to, in years past, for the right-whale. . . . . The Bay contains good anchorage ground, and shelter for ships, and, at some seasons of the year known to whalemen . . . the coast along its margin is visited by these huge animals in pursuit of food." [1]

Down the coast they went to Fish Bay and Table Bay at Cape Town, and rounding Good Hope, put away up the east coast of Africa, from Algoa Bay to Delagoa Bay. Mozambique Channel was part of the so-called Madagascar Ground, and Fort Dauphin on that island was utilized by the whalemen.

As early as August 1785, William Rotch wrote from London to Nantucket: "Benj'm Clark [in the *Lydia*] has 550 bbls. & stays till next season; he winters at the Cape of Good Hope." [2]

The revival of the whale fishery in America, brought into the fleet ships from New Bedford and Boston districts, and single vessels out of Sag Harbor, Wareham, Hudson, and Connecticut. Of the Nantucket fleet of thirty vessels, at least half went to Africa's Walvis Bay (or as the whalemen called it, Woolwich Bay). The New Bedford fleet, building up fast, followed on. Delagoa Bay, around Good Hope, was another new locality. The Brazil Banks, however, was still the favorite whaling grounds, spreading as it did over a wide area in the South Atlantic. [3]

Arrivals at New Bedford and Nantucket reported the usual whaling incidents. The sloop *Sally,* of Bedford, had lost Captain William Howland, Mate Oliver Slocum and three men while attempting to land at Aricot Harbor, Hispaniola, for provisions. In April 1793, the *Washington, Favourite,* and *Rebecca,* returned from their Pacific voyages with "full ships." In May, the *Warren* and the *Industry* arrived at Nantucket, and reported fourteen other island whalers in the South Atlantic, as well as one New Bedford craft (the *Russell*), three Dunkirk ships, and three familiar craft from Milford Haven.

Tradition has given us a wry tale of the meeting at sea of Captain Frederick Coffin, of the *Hannah and Eliza,* of Milford, and Captain William Swain, in the *Ranger,* of Nantucket.

"How does thee find thy new home, Frederick?" asked Captain Swain.

" 'T will do for a voyage or two," was the reply, "but I miss heading for Dartmouth—at least, on that course I could drop in on the folks at home!" [4]

Where Captain Coffin could go out of his way for one hundred and fifty miles or so while cruising up the Gulf Stream for Nova Scotia, he could not now have shaped his course some one thousand miles to the westward, so that he could "drop in" for a gam at home!

These whalefishers from a common land were going through a period of preparation for the greater struggle ahead. Each ship was a nautical schoolroom, with the foremast hand as anxious to learn as the officers. In the search and discovery of new whaling grounds, new conditions had to be thoroughly learned—the prevailing winds and currents of that section of the sea or coastal region, the type of headlands or shore line, the holding or anchorage ground, the seasons of the year when the whales came into this part of the watery world. This was a training which had been acquired in regular habit down through the years. The whalemen had developed into natural explorers of the sea. They were America's first oceanographers.

How far flung the whaling industry had become may be seen by a survey of their voyages in the early 1790's. The *Alliance,* of Nantucket, Captain Bartlett Coffin, had rounded Good Hope and sailed up the east coast of Africa to Delagoa Bay; the schooner *Swallow,* of Nantucket, Captain Latham Gardner, was at the Falklands; the *Harmony,* of Dunkirk, Captain Jonathan Briggs, was at Table Bay; the *Sea Horse,* of Cape Ann, Captain Mayo, with a dozen other whalers, was at Woolwich Bay (where Captain Mayo reported the sudden sinking of a point of land, which was immediately covered by six fathoms of water). The *Minerva,* of Nantucket, Captain Seth Coffin, was at the Brazil Banks with a fleet of some forty whaleships. The Cape Horn ships have already been enumerated.[5]

With the whalemen from Nantucket so scattered throughout the fleets of the three countries involved, it was natural that immigrants to the island were needed to man the ships. The Macy *History of Nantucket,* states:

> It therefore became necessary to resort to the continent for a considerable portion of each crew, whence there were brought some Indians and a great many negroes. Many of the latter took their residence here, and became the heads of families. They built a cluster of houses near the South part of the Town, which is called New Guinea. Their inebriety and want of economy generally kept them poor, although they made good voyages.[6]

The good Quaker historian could not appreciate that the habits and customs of a generation of islanders could not be adopted or assimilated within a few decades by a race entirely alien to the shores of his native home. The section of the town where the Negroes lived was called New Guinea for a century after, and a street in Nantucket is still designated Angola, after that part of the African coast which was the homeland of that people. As the Quakers were among the first to free their slaves, these Negro whalemen were a free people, having their own churches and for years maintaining their own school. They became excellent whalemen and several advanced to boatsteerers and mates.

The first wave of the French Revolution had come dangerously close to swamping the headquarters of the Dunkirk whaling fleet. Called upon to protect the Quakers from demands by the liberty-crazed Revolutionists, William Rotch and his son Benjamin appeared before the Assembly at Paris and presented a petition, with John Marsillac serving as interpreter.

It was a dramatic moment. With characteristic calmness, his very voice and figure the epitome of the principles he professed, William Rotch stood there as Marsillac read the petition. The galleries were crowded with spectators, and there was a clapping of hands at the conclusion of each subject. Several times Rotch heard hisses, which he believed were expressions of condemnation. But he did not lose his perfect calm. Later he learned the hisses were signs of approval for a point well made.[7]

Mirabeau, then President of the Assembly, heard the entire petition. Rotch stressed the fact that the Nantucket colony had come to

France upon invitation by the French. "In an age signal for the increase of knowledge," he wrote, "you have been struck with this truth: That Conscience, the immediate relation of man with his Creator, cannot be subject to the power of man. . . . You have set a great example to the Nations which continue to persecute for religion. . . . We have come to implore this Spirit of Justice: that we may be suffered without molestation, to conform to some principles, and to use some forms, to which the great family of Friends called Quakers have been inviolably attached. . . . Now that France is becoming the Asylum of Liberty, of equal law and brotherly kindness . . . we hope you will extend your justice and regard to us and our children." [8]

Mirabeau replied in kind, but remarked carefully: "My Brother, if thou hast a right to be free, thou hast a right to prevent any one from making thee a slave. . . . Consider well, whether the defense of yourself and your equals be not also a religious duty." [9]

The petition of the Nantucket Quakers was accepted, however. One wonders whether, if Mirabeau had lived, the course of the world's history might not have been considerably altered. But a month later he was dead.

Rotch, in a letter of May 18, 1792, stated that he was preparing his new ship, the *Ann,* for whaling out of New Bedford, "and will want but some Indian corn for a start." Captain William Mooers took the ship across the Atlantic, but Prince Coleman was her master on her first whaling voyage out of Bedford. (The *Ann* had already made one voyage to the Pacific out of Dunkirk.)

Being so close to the progress of the earth-shaking events in France, William Rotch did not wish to take any more risks with that Revolution's leaders. The *Ospray* had arrived safely from Nantucket, with supplies and mail, and was immediately dispatched to Good Hope. He insured the *Hope* and the *William Penn,* for Cape Horn, for £2,500 each, and the *Penelope,* for Brazil, in an equal sum. He ordered a new ship to be built at New Bedford by George Claghorn (launched October 18, 1793, and named the *Barclay*). [10]

Captain Isaiah Hussey, in the new ship *Benjamin,* had sailed for Good Hope and Captain Daniel Coffin had taken the *Harmony* out, bound for the same region. The *Mary,* returning from her Pacific Ocean voyage, had shipped a heavy sea off the Falklands, and Captain

Whippey had reported her decks swept, her stanchions broken, and the vessel shocked in every part. As soon as repairs were completed, the ship was ordered to America.[11]

In August 1792, Rotch informed his firm that the *Maria* had been fully repaired in England, "her upper works now raised to the height of the quarter-deck . . . giving a better height between decks. Owen Hillman is master, we want boatsteerers." Rotch had written his son Thomas that the *"Maria* was so fine a vessel for her size, I cannot think of breaking her up."

When it became apparent that France and England would soon be embroiled in war, Rotch prepared to save that portion of the whaling fleet registered at Dunkirk. "I have been desirous to get 8, or 10,000 pounds Sterling to England, thence to America," he wrote. "There has been a dreadful massacre in the Capital. John Marsillac (who with his wife is now with us on the way to England) told me he counted 173 dead bodies in the street he passed in the course of ¾ of an hour; which was but a small proportion to what might be seen in other parts." [12]

In mid-December 1792, he wrote to son Thomas:

> It is not impossible there may be a considerable addition to the vessels to Bedford if a war with England of which we fully expect, & might be at hand. I have heretofore wrote thee to draw on the De Bauque for 600 pounds Sterling; when thee can make use of it to advantage which I now confirm.

A few days later, he wrote: "We are now in the midst of war on every hand, it is a very trying experience to us in many ways." Rotch was carefully preparing to leave France and, at the same time, arrange for the news to reach some of his ships so that they could be warned away from the coast when the inevitable war broke out.

On January 19, 1793, Rotch loaded a ship with personal belongings, put his family aboard, and sailed for London, leaving only his son Benjamin in the midst of the rising tide of turmoil. Several other American and English families secreted themselves on board the ship and escaped with Rotch. Two days later, Louis XVI was guillotined and France was again plunged into the throes of a war with Britain.

The old enemy in England, Lord Hawksbury, had ordered all of

Rotch's ships captured, knowing that the war was only a matter of days away. Two of the Rotch fleet were taken in the Channel by British cruisers, but upon arrival in British ports were released. The astute Rotch, anticipating this action, upon his arrival in Britain, had carefully transferred their registries to London.[13]

After a period of considerable anxiety, Benjamin Rotch reached England safely. At this time there came the parting of William Rotch and his son. Benjamin decided to throw in his lot with the Nantucket colony at Milford Haven. But William rejected offers in that direction; he was anxious to get back home to Nantucket.

He had conducted a great experiment, had seen it successfully developed, and it had accomplished its purpose. Now, he saw in America the fruits of the Constitution of the United States—here was the world's hope for freedom and enterprise. He returned to Nantucket in July 1794, after completing the transfer of his larger ships to American registry. But, in 1794, before leaving Britain, he re-established the Dunkirk branch through the De Bauque Brothers. A number of vessels were still kept under French registry, and remained so for twenty years.

William's sons William, Jr., and Thomas, removed to New Bedford, and were joined by him and his son-in-law in 1795. The Rotch firm now bent its collective energies toward making this port the great rival of Nantucket.

So characteristic of William Rotch is a passage in one of his letters, written from Dunkirk in 1791, that it demands quoting. He wrote to his son, Thomas:

> . . . You are now so situated as to possess a privilege which I did not enjoy (though my own fault) and that is, you (Wm. excepted) have no more business than if rightly timed is necessary for both body & mind, for I believe employment is really useful & we are unsafe without it; Idleness I wish may never be the lot of any of my posterity. Now in my youthful days, notwithstanding the heavenly impressions frequently extended to my mind, which I often felt ardent desires I might retain with increase, yet the great and extensive round of business which continually rested on my shoulders, much too much for one person, would seem sometimes . . . take possession, as it were by a storm, of my poor weak mind. . . .[14]

The business of outfitting and sending ships to sea, of refining the whale oil brought home by these ships, of manufacturing candles, and supplying the great cities of the world with the "light of progress," was William Rotch's life. As clerk of the Friends Meeting he kept close to the religious sect which predominated in the island community; as a merchant in the world market he kept in touch with the world's business and politics.

He had dreamed a dream of converting the business of lighting the great cities into a world public utility, an international commodity answerable only to the dictates of supply and demand. He had bitterly learned that the statesmen of nations were not ready for world leadership. He had returned to take up the threads of his former life, for he had never relinquished his control of William Rotch & Sons, of Nantucket. It had been his anchor in the gales of his business adventures.

Arrivals at New Bedford in midsummer, 1793, were the Rotch ships the *Judith,* Captain Paul Ray, of Dunkirk; the *Columbia,* Captain Joseph Bennett, of Dunkirk, and the *Mary,* Captain Pease, whose registry had been switched to New Bedford only a short time before. These were important additions to the growing whaling fleet at New Bedford.

Captain Ray told of the British whaler *Liverpool,* sailing into Woolwich (Walvis) Bay, suddenly showing herself as a letter-of-marque of twenty guns, and capturing the *Phebe,* one of the Rotch fleet from Dunkirk and the *Judith.* There were five other Nantucket ships anchored in the Bay at the time—the *Harlequin, Sally, Harmony, Hero,* and *Fox,* the New Bedford brig *Mary,* a Rhode Island brig, and a ship from Cape Ann—all whalemen. When night fell, Captain Ray cut his cable and escaped. But the pattern of British armed whalemen had been set, and the Ministry was to regret the practise within a few years.[15]

The whaleship *Manila,* bound home for Nantucket, was stopped by a British privateer off Block Island, but Captain Barnard reported he was treated politely and allowed to continue. Early in September 1793, the ship *Eliza* arrived safely at Nantucket from Dunkirk, from which port she had sailed on July 9. Captain Benjamin Coleman had with him Captain Benjamin Bennett and his wife and a French lady. "The day before we left Dunkirk," he reported, "there was great rejoicing, the firing of cannon, and the people in high spirits—Liberty, Equality, Fraternity forever." [16]

On September 19, 1793, the Rotch ship *Three Friends,* under Captain Abel Rawson, of Dunkirk, arrived at New Bedford to report a narrow escape from capture by the same British armed whaler, the *Liverpool,* which was attempting to destroy the Dunkirk fleet. The *Liverpool* put Captain Gardner, of the captured *Phebe,* on board the *Three Friends,* and soon after Captain Rawson promptly effected his craft's escape.

A few days before this Dunkirk whaler arrived at New Bedford, one of her sister-ships, the *Favorite,* put in at Nantucket. Captain David Folger, bound for Dunkirk after a successful Brazil Banks voyage, had reached the mouth of the English Channel when news of the war was shouted to him by a passing ship. Captain Folger immediately bore away for Nantucket. By the time the welcome harbor of his home was reached, half his men were down with scurvy. The *Favorite* had been at sea for more than twelve months and was in sad need of fresh provisions and water. [17]

During the next few weeks, three more of the Dunkirk fleet, like hunted sea birds, found a haven at New Bedford. The *Two Brothers,* under Captain David Swain, arrived in the Acushnet on September 23, 1793, and the *Harmony,* Captain Jonathan Briggs, came in on October 2. Both ships had been in Woolwich Bay and Fish Bay, and had left the African coast when the word of the European war came winging to them from a passing whaleship. The ship *Negar,* Captain John Hawes, appeared in mid-November, having a full cargo of twelve hundred barrels of whale oil and last at Delagoa Bay. [18]

The Nantucket fleet began to return about this time—the *Harlequin, Fox, Leo,* and *Dauphin*—all with excellent cargoes. At New Bedford, several sloops arrived after good voyages to the Bahama Banks and Bermuda Ground.

With the new year of 1794, the whaleship *Benjamin,* of Dunkirk, sailed up the Acushnet and dropped anchor off the New Bedford wharves. Captain Isaiah Hussey had bad news for his fellow-fleet-skippers and crews who had escaped from Woolwich Bay. He had been in Delagoa Bay, up the east coast of Africa, beyond the Cape of Good Hope. On September 2, 1793, a Dutch brig, armed with sixteen guns, entered the bay and captured two of the three Dunkirk whalers there, the *Greyhound*, Captain Obed Bunker, and the *William Penn*, Captain Obed Fitch. Expecting the same fate, Captain Hussey waited the arrival of the boarding party from the brig. He was treated politely by the Dutch captain, who informed him of the war. That night, Captain Hussey got the ship under way and escaped, laying his course for America.[19]

One of the most unusual experiences in escape was that accomplished by Captain Micajah Gardner, in the ship *Edward*, out of Dunkirk. Captain Gardner, a young Nantucket skipper, had been round Good Hope to New Holland, and had a full cargo of oil—fifteen hundred barrels. As was a custom with homeward-bound ships, he touched at St. Helena for news, having been warned by Rotch of the impending war before he left Dunkirk. A boat's crew, under his mate, was sent ashore and was promptly seized. Instead of his own boat returning, several hours later, Captain Gardner was surprised to see another ship's boat come off. The boat hailed him (he learned later it had been taken from the American brig, the *Sea Horse*, Captain Albert Hussey, of Cape Ann). As the boat came alongside, a note was handed up to the *Edward's* decks. It read as follows:

To CAPTAIN GARDNER OF THE *Edward*:
   Sir—France is at war with all the world. The American Ambassador's head has been cut off at Paris—you have no port on earth to put into where you will not be taken—here you shall have generous terms; all your private property, and that of your crew, shall remain your own, the same as if you had never been taken. I have consulted the Lieut-Governor and we have agreed to give you these terms. In witness whereof, I herewith sign and give it under my hand and the Seal of the Honourable East India Company.

ROBERT BROOK,
GOVERNOR GENERAL OF ST. HELENA [20]

Sept. 20, 1793

Suspecting the intentions of the honorable governor of the Honorable Company, Captain Gardner sent a polite reply to Governor Brook. He thanked him for his generous offer, but begged to doubt that France was "at war with all the world," and would therefore not throw himself upon the governor's mercy. He then proceeded to stand off and on the island until the next day, hoping his boat's crew would be released. But only another message from the governor was forth-coming:

> I again inform you that France is at war with all the world—the American States are in alliance with Great Britain. I therefore treat you as an American subject—and demand you enter our port immediately—which, if you refuse to comply with, I shall be obliged to make a representation in the case to the British Secretary of State, and to General Washington. After promising this, if you continue to be obstinate and are taken on any foreign coast, you must undergo all the severity of treatment, by the law of nations, in such cases made and provided.

Captain Gardner now doubted the governor's candor more than ever. His reply was brief and typical of the whaleman: "I shall not enter your port but shall shape my course for America." This he accordingly did, regretfully abandoning his mate and boat's crew as captives on the island.

Captain James Whippey arrived at Nantucket on February 16, 1794, in the Rotch fleet ship *South Carolina.* Of his appearance, Kezia Fanning reported in her diary:

> Capt. James Whippey in a new Brigg ran on the Bar last night. He sailed from France for the Brazels on a whaling voyage owned by himself & Frenchmen; he put in here to escape being taken; he has 500 to 600 bbls. of oil on board. He has been absent 7 years from his family.[21]

The French Revolution and the European war had an alchemists' effect on the whaling industry. When the fire and smoke of the explosion had cleared, a definite result was revealed. Of the Dunkirk fleet, William Rotch had lost eight ships to British frigates, French privateers and the Channel coast (along which they attempted escape) but had salvaged fifteen others, due to the alertness of his resourceful shipmasters. Of the twenty other ships connected with Dunkirk "branch" of American whaling, at least half went over to Britain, with Benjamin Rotch taking several with him to Milford Haven. Some of these eventually returned to Nantucket or New Bedford.

The result of war's alchemy was the great impetus given American whaling by the return of these ships, their masters and crews to New England ports. Opportunity for the world's markets was now heightened by the ability of the fleets to bring in great cargoes of both sperm and right-whale oil. The struggle with Britain for supremacy was now on a more clearly defined basis.

In 1796, the harassed British Ministry sent the frigate *Carysford* to the Cape of Good Hope, establishing General Craig as governor of the Cape Colony. This colony's limits were so laid out as to include Delagoa Bay in its limits, and orders were given to cut off other nations—particularly America—from whaling there. This incident was duly reported by the Boston newspapers of the day with considerable indignation aroused by this typical act of "imperialism" on the part of the British.

Two years later (1789-1800) came the quasi-war with France. This was not so small a war as textbooks would have us believe. France was angry because this nation would not join her in the war with England, as the "Franklin Treaty" of 1778, stipulated, a mutual obligation then having been drawn up to assist one another in any such war. France had furnished money, arms, military and naval assistance in aiding the colonies to gain their independence. When in 1793 she called on us to stand by the treaty, this country stood aloof. The Democrats favored aiding France; the Federalists did not. When the latter put Adams into office in 1796, the new President repudiated the Franklin treaty. France retaliated by ordering the seizure of ships of the country which served England in a neutral trade. The Revolution weakened France in her stand, and when Napoleon precipitated himself into power he wisely abandoned the naval warfare with America.

But the war was costly to our shipping. First to suffer were the whaleships. Six Nantucket ships were captured. The *Federal George,* Captain Latham Gardner, who also owned half the vessel was taken full of oil, homeward bound; the *Nancy,* Zaccheus Swain, master, owned by Thomas and Abishai Delano, was captured with a full cargo of oil in the West Indies; the *Johanna,* Captain Zebdeal Coffin, was taken on her passage home, ship and cargo valued at $40,000; the *Active,* Captain Micajah Gardner, was captured and Captain Gardner and his crew retaken by an English privateer and carried into Halifax. He arrived home owning only his clothes on his back and his ship's manifest. His ship had been on the verge of bringing home the largest cargo of whale and sperm oil—2,380—ever brought back by a whaleship. Captain Gardner died in 1844 at the age of eighty-five. His loss on this voyage was $10,000—his cargo and ship valued at $50,000.[22]

The *Ann* was taken after she left Dunkirk and put a cargo of wine on board at Bordeaux in October 1793, for St. Domingo. Her loss was $20,000.[23]

For years efforts were made, under the French Spoilation Claims, to collect damages. Owners of the New Bedford ships *Fox* were equally unable to obtain financial redress. The *Minerva,* Captain Obed Fitch, was captured on October 5, 1800, on her homeward passage. She had a full cargo, and while still held by a prize crew of Frenchmen was retaken by an English ship and carried into Antigua, West Indies. Captain Obed Fitch, master of the *Minerva,* promptly bought her back again and took her home empty. In a report of the loss of whaling gear, Captain Fitch dutifully noted: "Damage done our whale-boat, $75; 1 deck hatch hove overboard, $10; damage to cable, $100; damage done our hassaw, $20." [24]

Both the *Active* and *Minerva* were owned by Jethro Mitchell & Co., and the value of both ships and cargoes exceeded $100,000. Years of fruitless effort were spent trying to collect claims. The last member of the firm to pass away was Paul Gardner, who had the sad circumstance of having his own corpse attached for debt (1830). His was the last such attachment in Massachusetts, the horrible statute being repealed shortly afterwards.[25]

The *Fox,* of New Bedford, was captured May 5, 1798, by the French frigate *L'Importune,* and condemned at Guadaloupe. She was commanded by Captain Coffin Whippey, one of the Rotch fleet masters, and her cargo was valued at $14,375.87. Captain Whippey arrived home on July 14, according to Kezia Fanning's diary.

The Nantucket shipowners had lost a million dollars in a war that was never declared.

The coming of the new century of the 1800's found the American whaling industry at the threshold of a still greater period of growth. The voyages of the New England whalemen had taken the whaleships from Baffin Bay's icy expanse down the coast of the Americas and adjacent seas; along the Gulf Stream from the Bay of Campeachy to the mid-Atlantic between Europe and Newfoundland's Grand Banks;

from the West Indies to Brazil Banks, River Plate, the Falklands and Cape Horn and into the Pacific to the coast of Peru; from the Guinea coast to Table Bay, thence around to Algoa Bay, Mozambique, Australia, and Desolation Island on the fringe of Antarctic waters.

The New England whalers had ventured into uncharted seas as a matter of choice in doing business on the great waters; they had suffered from the dangers of storm and shipwreck and had been battered by war and piracy. Now they were probing at the outer reaches of the little known seas of the world, where only a handful of the great explorers had preceded them and where they were to prove themselves the true men of the sea. For the time, at least, they had restored the supremacy of American whaling.

PART FOUR

The Sea-Hunters at the Ocean's Frontiers

chapter xiii

~~~~~

WHALES, SEA-ELEPHANTS AND
FUR-SEALS

*. . . Sealing was in many respects nearly allied with whal-
ing. Seals and whales were generally met with on the same
coast; it required as large vessels and as many men in . . .
the former as the latter. . . .*

—Obed Macy, *History of Nantucket.*[1]

URING THE LAST decade and a half of the old century and the
first years of the 1800's, 1785-1810, a new type of seaman made
his appearance in New England. This was the whaleman-sealer, a
combination which created a sea-hunter who was to become among
the boldest of mariners. Embarking on voyages for hunting the
whale, the seal and the sea-elephant, these men literally went to the
very ends of the earth, boldly sailing into the uncharted seas away to
the Antarctic. These "combination" sea-hunts were always a gamble.
Those who had success made fabulous voyages; others met shipwreck
or similar disaster; all had unusual and varied experiences.

The adventures of these sealer-whalemen are of extraordinary interest. In a continual hunt for new rookeries, where fur-seals and sea-
elephants had lived for centuries unmolested by man, these mariners
became nomads of the sea. They made a number of notable contributions toward the geographical history of the world. With the growth
of the trade with China, sealskins were bartered for silks and teas.
Seeking their prey, the sealers went to the Falklands and Patagonia, to

South Georgia; rounded Cape Horn and Cape of Good Hope; sailed to Desolation (Kerguelen) Island after rediscovering the Crozets, then along the high latitudes to Tasmania and New Zealand and the seal islands below these distant lands.

They killed whales in the sea and seals and sea-elephants on the hazardous shores. They voyaged through the South Pacific, along the fringes of the Antarctic circle, and by 1820 were at the South Shetlands —five hundred miles below Cape Horn. Here they established a head-quarters unlike any other yet known and eventually discovered the Antarctic Continent.

Soon after Captain James Cook returned (1775) to Britain with news of the seals at South Georgia, a number of expeditions were planned by the British but were abandoned because of the war. In 1785, how-ever, two vessels were fitted out at London ". . . under the liberty of the British East India Company, but by private adventure," William Rotch wrote from England to Nantucket. They intended to sail "to that part of America where Captain Cook had obtained the skins, (I believe it was near California but cannot fully recollect) that they fetched so high a price in China; some of his officers are going in the ships. . . . Skins are a very fine, delicate quality . . . I intend to inform myself better in this respect & let you know." [2]

Rotch had read Cook's journals and found the furs were sea-otters, valued in China "at the enormous price of $100 per skin," and were obtained in "North Latitude 56° on the northwest coast of America." [3]

The Honorable East India Company enjoyed an unjustified monopoly of British trade in the Far East, so that private British firms could not individually take advantage of Captain Cook's discovery of the fabulous sea-otter. The enterprising Americans promptly entered into the adventure. A few months before, the *Empress of China*, first American craft to Canton, had returned to New York after bringing out a cargo of ginseng, which the Chinese believed was an amazing weed, having many remarkable qualities. Ginseng sold for "nearly its weight in gold." The *Empress of China* (in 1785) and the *Experiment*, second New York craft to sail to Canton, returned with teas, china-ware, silks, nankeens and muslins—also with news of the value of the furs sent down from Asiatic Siberia to China.[4]

The *Grand Turk*, of Salem, returned from Canton on May 22, 1787, with a large profit. But the price of ginseng had dropped. Another commodity that could be sold profitably in China was necessary, as the Chinese market demanded species payment for goods and such sums in cash were out of the question for most New England merchants.[5]

That profitable commodity was found in furs. The Chinese prized the sea-otter, a magnificent animal with a skin five feet by two, of glossy, jet-black fur, which Indians of the American Northwest Coast would trade for iron, muskets, clothes, mirrors, nails and even buttons.

But, although Boston merchants initiated the American fur trade with the China market, Captain Metcalf took the *Eleanora* out of New York in 1788, preceding the *Columbia* and *Lady Washington* to the market by a year, and may have gone on to the Northwest Coast before these Boston ships reached there.

The ship *Columbia* and sloop *Lady Washington* were fitted out by Boston merchants for the Northwest Coast where they hoped that furs which could be obtained would sell in China for the same great profits the Russian furs had brought. After long voyages these two craft arrived late at Nootka Sound. It was not until the summer of 1789 that they got full cargoes and set sail for Canton.

But a dozen other craft had arrived, four of them from Salem. The brigantine *Hope,* sailing in 1790, collected fourteen hundred sea-otter skins on the northwest coast. The *Columbia* was then on her second voyage (starting in September 1790). It was in May 1792, that Captain Gray of the *Columbia* discovered and entered the mouth of the Columbia River.

By 1797, Captain George Vancouver, the exemplary British explorer, listed seven American and eleven British vessels on the northwest coast.

It has been generally overlooked that the first shipment of furs from American ships to Canton were not sea-otter but fur-seal, and came as a result of a set of unusual and far-flung incidents.

William Rotch in London, during the summer of 1785, carefully observing the reaction of British merchants to the prospects of the fur trade with China, was no more watchful and aware of the possibilities than was his brother Francis Rotch, who was then in Boston, having crossed the Atlantic from London some months before. Accompanying him to America was Madam Hayley, the widow of George Hayley.

An article on the vivacious Mrs. Hayley, who was a sister of the celebrated John Wilkes, of London and Parliamentary fame, states that she had a large portion of his intellectual endowments and irresponsibility. She first married Samuel Stork, a West India merchant, then, at his death, became the wife of George Hayley.[6]

George Hayley was a prominent London merchant at the time of his death early in 1784. Of him, Jeremiah Osborn wrote to A. Lopez at Newport, 1767: "Mr. Hayley, the Gent who has been so good as to honor your credit, is a Gentleman been a long time in the American trade, extreem good carracter [and] a large Cappital—they say £100 thousand pos." [7]

It was George Hayley who wrote Lopez in 1775 about the Falkland Islands whaling fleet and of "Mr. Rotch [Francis] whose arrival here will give me great pleasure."

For a number of years since Hayley's death Francis Rotch had "undertook the conduct of the great and extensive concern for his widow. He was her most intimate, councellor, confident, and friend, embarked his fortune with hers." [8]

Mrs. Hayley had written to Christopher Champlin, of Newport, under date of March 11, 1784, that she was intending to leave England in a few days for Boston, in the ship *"United States,* Captain Scott, and among the arrangements that . . . Alexander Champion, Jr., of this city had accepted the principal Agency conducting my affairs while I am abroad. As regards trading with America," Mrs. Hayley further stated, "my situation makes it unnecessary for me to yield to any house whatever in this respect." [9]

In another letter to Champlin, she wrote, under date of August 24, 1784: "I can give you no hope of the duty on oil imported from America being taken off, but on the contrary the Legislature of this Country seem determined to continue it, for the express purpose of encouraging the Fishery from Great Britain. . . . Our friend Mr. Rotch [William] can explain this business to you as I have frequently written him my sentiments on it." [10]

Just when Madam Hayley and Francis Rotch arrived in Boston is not known, but it was probably early in September 1784.

Before sailing for America, Francis Rotch, his Quaker upbringing probably coming to the fore, obtained a marriage license, but delay ensued and the wedding was put off until they arrived in America. Here, further delay was occasioned by circumstances not known— perhaps it was the death of Rotch's parent, Joseph Rotch, in November 1784, or the astute older brother may have advised against it.

The urgency of business in London caused Francis Rotch to return to London in January 1786, and while he was at sea, the faithless Mrs. Hayley married a Patrick Jaffrey, a Boston man who had been hired by Francis Rotch as a clerk. The news of this was sent to Francis at London in July 1786, by his friend Charles Jarvis, of Boston, a brother of Leonard Jarvis, his former partner at New Bedford.[11]

This incident may seem a far cry from sealing, but it has much to do with the first such Rotch expedition after the American Revolution. When William Rotch heard of the proposed fur trade to China from the Northwest Coast, he wrote from London, under date of September 5, 1785: "I wrote Brother Francis discouraging him proceeding on the *Canton's* last destination [the Falklands], he having been interested in the Animals." [12]

In an earlier letter to America, William had mentioned information received from a Nantucket captain in a British ship, who had spoken the *Canton* in February 1785, "on Brazil," and that the *Canton* then had 160 barrels of sperm and Captain Whippey was "for the Islands." The *Canton* at that time was heading for the Falklands, where Francis Rotch had (via London from Nantucket) exiled himself during the American Revolution, with the Rotch-Lopez whaling fleet.

An authority on the sealing trade, A. Howard Clark, unwittingly was the originator of an error which several historians since have perpetuated. As part of his report, he included a portion of the journal of the ship *Neptune,* of New Haven, which sailed on a sealing voyage in 1796. On board the ship was a young supercargo, Ebenezer Townsend, son of the owner, who wrote of his anchorage in the Falklands thus:

> States Harbor derives its name from a ship of that name which lay here two years to obtain sea-elephant oil and hair-seal skins. She was a very large ship, toward 1000 tons, from Boston, fitted from there soon after the Revolutionary War, and the first ship that we know of that took any fur-seal skins. She was owned by Lady Haley, living in Boston. They took about 13,000 fur-seal skins as

an experiment, which were sold in New York at about a half a dollar each, their value not being known. They were afterwards taken to Calcutta, and sold there as sea-otters. From Calcutta, they were taken to Canton by Captain Metcalf of New York, who started from the United States about the same time that Captain Kendricks sailed from Boston. In Canton these skins were sold at about $5.00 each.[13]

Writers following Clark began stating that "Lady Haley, a Boston woman," fitted out the ship *States* for a sealing cruise to the Falklands in 1783—"the first such cruise from America." As had been pointed out, the "Boston woman" was in reality Madame Hayley, of London, in this country with Francis Rotch. The *States* was a Rotch ship. After reaching Boston with Mrs. Hayley and Francis Rotch the ship went to Nantucket, from there she sailed under Captain Benjamin Hussey to the Falklands late in 1784. It was no secret by that time that seals were numerous at the Falklands.

That Francis Rotch was determined to go there again is evident from his brother's letter and from the Jarvis letter, a year or so later (1786), from Boston, which gave him his first inkling of the defection of Mrs. Hayley. Jarvis wrote that this news had been concealed because rumor had it Rotch was negotiating some important business for Mrs. Hayley in London and "would not have done it so well if you were earlier informed." Further, Jarvis wrote, rumor said that "you are indebted to her, and that the remission of that debt has been made you, a return from your services. . . . She told me, when I asked after you, that you were going to the Falklands again, which, she said, you declared were the happiest period of your life." [14]

Upon learning of her marriage, Francis abandoned his plans to embark for the Falklands. Instead he went to Dunkirk with his brother William (which, no doubt, the elder brother had secretly wished). Francis was not to return to America for three decades.

It is obvious that Rotch was the only one in the Hayley firm who knew anything about sealing at the Falklands and that he, and not Mrs. Hayley, dispatched the ship *States,* on that expedition in 1784. Probably, at this time, Francis Rotch was in financial straits and transferred the registry to Mrs. Hayley.

Captain Benjamin Hussey, in the *United States,* after arrival at the Falkland Islands, had put aboard the *Mary* (another Rotch ship) ninety tons of sperm oil. Thereupon, the *Mary,* according to orders given by William Rotch prior to her voyage south, sailed for England, where she arrived on September 1, 1785, with forty tons of oil of her own and "90 tons from the *United States."*

"I need not mention any particulars," stated William Rotch in his letter of September 9, "as this will be accompanied by a letter from Captain Hussey to William [Rotch, Jr.] at Nantucket." [15]

The question as to the identity of this ship *States* is further clarified by the fact that William Rotch had difficulty in getting her oil into Britain duty-free.

"The 90 tons from the ship [*United*] *States,* at the Falklands, entered as oil obtained of British subjects, was protested on information being lodged that she was not navigated according to law," he wrote, "having a greater number of Foreigners than the law admitted, and notwithstanding it is clearly prov'd that the ship had her full compliment of British subjects required by law when she entered the voyage, but some running away required others to ship—those they took being the very men they wish to invite into this country." [16]

It is clear, therefore, that the *United States,* after bringing Francis Rotch and Mrs. Hayley to Boston in the summer of 1784, was sent to Nantucket and there fitted out for the Falklands and her whaling-sealing voyage, under Captain Benjamin Hussey, taking on board Nantucket whalemen to complete the crew, "being the very men they [the British] wish to invite to this country." [17]

If any further proof is needed of the certain identity of the ship *States,* it may be found in a number of letters written during those times. On October 5, 1786, the American merchant Christopher Champlin, at Newport, Rhode Island, received a letter from the De Bauque Brothers stating that a ship called *Le Dauphin* had been dispatched from France for Newport.

Upon the arrival of the ship in Rhode Island, it was the desire of the French firm that Champlin should assist her master, Captain Hayden, of Nantucket, to refit her for the Greenland whale fishery. A letter from Francis Rotch, now settled in Dunkirk, followed, in which he stated: ". . . my friends the De Bauques having bought the ship *United States,* which was Mrs. Hayley's, and meaning to repair her in order to go into the Greenland Fishery, I have advised them to send her to America for that purpose." [18]

A cargo of hemp, iron, and cordage was sent over on the ship and repairs and refitting were paid for out of the sale of the cargo.

Francis Rotch further advised that the ship be loaded with lumber for the return cargo (with whaling equipment) to Dunkirk, but if any unforeseen accident should deprive them of Captain Hayden's services to "give notice of it to my brother William Rotch at Nantucket if he should arrive safe, otherwise to his sons, or the former Captain of this ship Benjamin Hussey, requesting them to provide a suitable captain and men for the fishery if possible in time to save the season." Further, the ship was fully insured in London.

Arriving at Newport in February 1787, in a battered condition, after a long stormy passage, the *States,* or *Le Dauphin,* was promptly refitted, and then sailed for Dunkirk, which port she reached in July 1787. She was sent to the Brazil Banks under Captain Uriah Swain, a Rotch captain, and subsequently made two fine voyages. However, in December 1791, she was wrecked, outward bound. In reporting the incident (January 1792), William Rotch wrote: "Francis Rotch's ship *United States* was cast away all fitted for whaling." Her true owner is thus revealed.

The first cargo of sealskins must have reached Nantucket early in 1786, for the cargo of thirteen thousand skins, sold at fifty cents each to New York—a $6,500 shipment—eventually put on board the brig *Eleanora,* Captain Metcalf, and reached the Canton market, where they were sold for $65,000. One historian states "they were originally mistaken for sea-otter skins." [19] This is hardly creditable, as neither Captain Hussey nor Captain Metcalf can be accused of ignorance, especially in view of the Rotches' knowledge and the experience of the whalemen at the Falklands. The voyages of the *States* and the *Eleanora* inaugurated the Canton fur trade for the sealers.

Of Captain Benjamin Hussey, more should be written. To this whaler-sealer and his contemporaries, Frederick C. Sanford, of Nantucket, gave the following tribute:

> Some of the captains I can remember . . . stout and tall, with splendid address, and some of them with large brains, almost equal

to Franklin. Benjamin Hussey was one of them. . . . I find from my old journals that he was at the Falkland Islands in January, 1786, in Mr. Rotchs' ship *States,* which eventually sailed from Dunkirk. Captain Hussey had a huge head; when he took off his hat I could think of nothing but a half bushel of brains. After plowing the ocean for years, was a victim to Napoleon I, who confiscated this property at Dunkirk [in 1797, when Hussey was living there]. When Napoleon fell in 1815, Captain Hussey took passage in the *Archimedes,* Captain James Bunker, and arrived in France in 1817. He secured some of his property from the government, bought a ship and fitted out to Greenland, where he had previously been whaling; and when he was amidst the ice, he was so injured by the vessel's tiller striking him that he died soon afterwards, aged 80 years and five months! [20]

Sealskins were collected in a far different way from those of the sea-otter. Sealers, instead of being confined to large companies, like the fleet of the Boston Northwest Coast trade, were outfitted by individual groups and firms, from Nantucket, New Haven, Stonington, Salem, New London, Boston, Philadelphia and New York. Sealskins were collected by the men of the vessel going ashore at the rookeries, rather than by exchanging goods by barter with natives. It was a hard, bitter life, in out-of-the-way and remote regions of the world, and the rivalry between American and British sealers was a constant factor. Obed Macy wrote briefly but to the point on the sealers:

> During several years previous to 1790 many profitable sealing voyages were made from England and other places. This induced the people of Nantucket to turn their attention to that business, with a view to prosecute it, if it presented a good prospect of advantage. Sealing was in many respects, nearly allied with whaling. Seals and whales were generally met with on the same coast; it required as large vessels and as many men to engage in taking the former as the latter; the outfits were nearly the same, and the voyages of like duration.[21]

In May 1786, the *Canton,* Captain James Whippey, arrived at Falmouth, England, with oil for William Rotch, who, being then in London and cognizant of the way the British Ministry was maneuvering, ordered the Nantucket vessel to Dunkirk. In the *Canton*'s hold also were from "three to four thousand" sealskins. In September 1786, Rotch reported that he had sold the sealskins to his business associates at Dunkirk, the De Bauque Brothers, for 8 to 9 livres apiece—approximately $20 each. He also asked his sons in Nantucket to send their sealskins to the De Bauques. The *Canton* was to sail out of Dunkirk "on the Fishery" but Captain Whippey was to stop at Nantucket on his return voyage. There was no lack of late news as regards the fur-seal, insofar as Nantucket was concerned.[22]

The schooner *Swallow*, Captain Latham Gardner, sailed from Nantucket early in 1793 for the Falklands. A letter home was reported in the *New Bedford Medley* of July 12, 1793, with the *Swallow* having a total of three thousand skins. Captain Gardner returned home on July 24, 1794, with a great voyage, having sixteen thousand sealskins and also some sperm and whale oil, and sea-elephant oil.[23]

Thus, there were actually three cargoes obtained by many of the whaleships, at this time and for years after. First, was the whale oil itself (both the sperm and right-whale, or black, oil), sealskins and sea-elephant oil. Of all the animal-creatures of the sea, the sea-elephant is the largest which lives both on the land and in the sea. The males average about fifteen feet, although many were near twenty feet. It is from the oddly-shaped extension of this animal's nose that the name "sea-elephant" naturally derives. Due to its huge and unwieldy bulk, the sea-elephant ashore became an easier prey than the seals. Both were killed in the same manner. A crew armed with clubs would surround herds of them on a rocky coasted beach, cut in between the herd of animals and their haven and, taking advantage of the ungainly panic of the beasts, soon club them to death.[24]

Captain Amasa Delano gave an interesting account of sealing. He wrote:

> . . . The method practised to take them was to get between them and the water, and make a lane of men, two abreast, forming three or four couples, and then drive the seal through this lane; each man furnished with a club, between five and six feet long, and as they passed, he knocked down such of them as he chose, which are commonly the half-grown. . . . When stunned, knives are taken to cut and rip them down on the breast from the under jaw. to the tail, giving a stab in the breast that will kill them. After this the hands got to skinning. I have seen men, one of whom would skin sixty in

an hour. They take off all the fat, and some of the lean, with the skin, as the more weight there is to the skin, the easier it will beam. This is done in the same manner in which curriers flesh their skins, after which it is stretched and pegged on the ground to dry. . . . After this they are taken out of pegs and stacked in the manner of salt cod-fish. They will sweat whilst in the pile, so as to render it necessary to open them and give them air, two or three times. After which they may be stacked in a ship's hold, and will keep for years . . . if kept dry.[25]

Skinning the seal was only the first step, which was followed by soaking in salt water and "beaming" or scraping the skins. After a drying-out period, the skins were stacked. Large rats become a nuisance. A sealer reported one morning that the rats had "carried away one of my shoes, which is a great loss to me." [26] As it snowed that day, this was indeed a real handicap.

Shore gangs "worked" the beaches, while the ship was handled by a skeleton crew of shipkeepers, much as when boats were down for whaling. As the industry developed, larger vessels took small tenders, schooner or sloop-rigged, to handle the close inshore tasks, always dangerous in the uncharted coasts and island beaches where the sealers sought their prey.

When the sea-elephant was killed, his thick body-fat, like the whale's blubber, was stripped from him, then cut up into "horse-pieces," about a foot wide. In most cases these blubber sections had to be carried to a place where trypots had been set up, many times over long distances on rocky, muddy ground or slippery beaches. "Backing-it" was the most arduous chore of the sea-elephant hunter. Blubber was tried out on board ship as well as on shore.

The yield of oil varied considerably. The usual season in the Antarctic regions or the islands and coasts in high latitudes was from November through February. In the larger rookeries, or sections of rocky shore where the animals came each year, the crews would build rude huts, where they lived for several weeks as shore parties.

The lives of the sealing gangs were hard and monotonous. There were periods of fierce activity and then dreary waits for the return of the ship or tender to take them off, together with their skins. David Forbes, a young medical student, gives a true picture of his own experience as the leader of one of these shore gangs. At the Falklands in 1796, he wrote:

> . . . Ashore with others to take care of the seal skins, and it being very late in the day, the first thing I thought of was where to take up sleep that night. Searching, I found a few logs which I concluded to make me a little house; though in my search I found a few whale bones which was of great service in building the ruff of my little house.[27]

Food ran short and the party "went to Fox point for sea-elephant oil . . . no food except mussels and maidenweed steeped to drink." Captain Greene arrived in the shallop, bringing food and four thousand more skins to cure. Some geese were shot for a luxurious repast, and several wild hogs were cornered and shot. Forbes reported killing "two loggerhead ducks which weighed 20 lbs. each."

When the *Juno,* of Hudson, Captain Paul Bunker, arrived at States Harbor Forbes recorded: "Held a ball on Captain Bunker's craft . . . music was a flute, drum and violin." The picture of the bewhiskered, oddly-clad sealers gamboling on the decks presents an intriguing scene.[28]

After the sealing season at the Falklands had ended, the *Neptune* rounded Cape Horn and went on to Más Afuera Island, where Forbes noted on May 30, 1798: "This day made a form contract with Captain Greene to go on shore with a crew of ten people and here to seal 20 months . . . employed in getting provisions ashore for us in the fore part of the day."

On the bluffs high above the sea, but still under the shoulder of the great mountain heights, the sealers built a log house. On June 7, the *Neptune* prepared to leave the sealing gang. "Brought a Keg of whiskey," wrote Forbes, "to drink our farewell—tarried all night." The *Neptune* sailed and the shore gang was self-exiled for the next twenty months.

Forbes and his men were busy. During the next four months they killed 27,520 seals and cured the skins. The whaler *Alliance,* of Nantucket, under Captain Hezekiah Barnard, hove to off Más Afuera on October 4, and her master presented the sealers "with oranges and English nuts." Then the *Maryland,* a whaler-sealer, and the *Barclay,* the Rotches' new ship, both from New Bedford came into view. Forbes "played checkers with Captain Barney" of the *Barclay*.

During the next month, Forbes increased his sealskin hoards to 33,340. In February 1799, news of the quasi-war with France came. The beachmaster was forced to barter ten thousand skins for provisions. Among the half dozen ships that hove-to off the island in December 1799, were the *Leo* and *Rebecca*, Nantucket whalers. "Many a look do I cast on the distant ocean to descry our ship & many a sigh for fear she will not come," wrote Forbes.[29]

Interspersed with the details of skins taken and cured are such laconic statements as: "Cartwright dreamed of home last night," or "dreamed of the young virgins." And "killed some goats for fresh meat," and "Davis almost drowned swimming a keg of rum ashore." The barter system was no doubt effective.

Finally, the *Neptune* appeared. After her departure from Más Afuera, on June 9, 1798, she had sailed to Canton, China, sold her fifteen thousand skins at $2 each and put aboard one thousand chest of Bohea tea. On July 11, 1799, she arrived at New Haven—six months from Canton—having been gone two years and eight months.[30]

A contemporary account states: "The *Neptune* . . . left part of her crew on Mac-à-Fuera under Dr. Forbes, who caught another cargo of skins, and the ship immediately returned for them and the skins and went on to China, making the same voyage as the first one, and the richest cargo ever made out of this port." [31]

chapter xiv

~~~

THE FIRST AMERICAN WHALERS
TO DESOLATION ISLAND

*Situated in the center of the southern ocean and far more
remote from either hemisphere than any island is Kerguelen's Land, better known as the Island of Desolation. . . .*

—Dr. Nathaniel Taylor [1]

THE EARLIEST VOYAGES of American ships into the Indian Ocean
were made by the whalers. But it is not realized by maritime
historians that the very first Yankee vessels to penetrate the South
Indian Ocean, nearly to the Antarctic Circle, were the whaler and sea-
elephant hunters. In October 1791, two whaleships sailed from Nantucket—the *Alliance* and the *Asia*. Of the former ship, whaling history
has only a brief notation; of the latter not even her sailing has been
recorded.[2]

Now, after being hidden for over one hundred and sixty years, the
voyage of the *Asia* is at last revealed with the discovery of her logbook. Covered in its original sailcloth, stained but still legible, the log
tells of the long voyage to one of the world's most out-of-the-way
places—Desolation or Kerguelen's Island as it is now known—which
at this period was probably the most remote spot in all the high
southern latitudes.

Sailing from Nantucket on October 6, 1791, the *Asia,* under Captain
Elijah Coffin, and her consort, the *Alliance,* under Captain Bartlett
Coffin, were on combination voyages, whaling, sealing and sea-elephant

194

hunting. Their joint voyage as exploring whaleships constitutes one of the most unusual in whaling history.[3]

Twenty-five days after leaving Nantucket, the two ships were at Palma, in the Canary Islands, an excellent bit of sailing for whaling craft. On November 8, they reached the Cape Verde Isle of Sal, where they spoke Jonathan Coffin, "bound to the bays" (coast of Africa) on a whaling voyage. The *Asia* and the *Alliance* dropped anchor in the island's harbor.

Five whaling craft were anchored here at the time, and all commanded by Nantucket men, their crews also largely composed of islanders. Shipmasters from the old home port and their ships were as follows: Captain Jonathan Coffin in the *Hibernia;* Captain John Sprague, in the *Nancy;* Captain Brown Coffin, in the *Harriett.* All three were from Dartmouth, Nova Scotia, but were not to return to that port. For this was a transitory voyage. Upon their return from Woolworth Bay they were to head for Milford Haven, their new headquarters. How pleasant must have been the gam—a reunion for Nantucketers separated by the twists of fate.[4]

The keeper of the *Asia*'s log was Silvanus Crosby, the mate. He wrote: "The Captains came on Board to Dine with our Capt. . . . We set down and rote letters to Send home. At 12 wayed Anker and Made Sale and Stear'd S by E for Bonavista."

They bypassed this island to stop at the Isle of May, where they put on board five hogs and nineteen goats—later enjoying a quantity of "Orangeis." After a rendezvous at St. Jago, the *Asia* and *Alliance* steered south and on November 16, 1791, crossed the equator at about 25° west longitude. A full month later they made the island of Trinidad in the South Atlantic off Brazil, often used by the whalers going to the Brazil Banks, where wild goats and hogs could be obtained, the latter fat from eating land crabs.[5]

Taking a course southeast by east, the *Asia* sailed across the southern Atlantic and arrived at Table Bay, Cape Town, on January 20, 1792: ". . . saw A great Many Shiping in the Bay. Latt'd in 34°–20″ south. . . ." Here they remained until February first, with parties ashore to see the "folks and fashions." As the *Alliance* had sustained injury to her fore and mainmast (the latter found to be rotting), they put into "Saddinah Bay" to refit, the crews of both whaleships being put to work at this exacting task.[6]

Out to sea again, the ships sailed southeast by east, through seas haunted by the Flying Dutchman and on toward St. Paul Island, one of the two volcanic islets in the southern Indian Ocean. The *Alliance* took some whales but the *Asia* had little luck.

On March 14, 1792, they were at St. Paul Island. At this outpost, where the ancient crater of a volcano forms a natural harbor, holding ground was not safe and sudden squalls, bursting out of the mountains, made it a dangerous anchorage. Mate Crosby recorded:

> Saw a snow [a square-rigged vessel] from Bengal and she was askinning here, and had 15 thousand of skins. Our boat went ashore and got some fish and some seal and come Aboard, then we filled Away and Spoke on Consort and Concluded to stear East.[7]

The *Asia* and *Alliance* then squared their yards for Australia and after running their easting down to April 22 were apprised of the land by the gulls. Soundings gave them 120 fathoms. On April 26 they made the land and two days later the *Asia* got safely to anchor in Shark Bay—"our Captain went ashore aguning But Little or no Grate Game." [8]

An unfortunate accident occurred here. After a long voyage, encountering many storms and squalls, the crew had suffered no injury. But while lying at anchor in Shark Bay, the cabin boy (as all boys of those days) went aloft to help furl the mizzen topsail. The log's entry for April 29, 1792, reads:

> He got up as far as the top and went to Make a Grab at the top, Mist his hold and Come Down by the Lump which will prove his fate. . . . [Next day] Our Boy still no better. [May 2] Our Boy Still Censelefs and [in] Convultion fits.

The *Asia* left Shark Bay on May 6—"all well Except our Poor Little Boy and he will not Remain Long I Believe." Steering to the north, the ship twenty days later sighted Java. Regaining consciousness, the boy slowly grew better all during this cruise, and eventually made a miraculous recovery.

From Java, the ship during July ranged to Prince's Island in the Cocos or Keeling Group, where they put aboard wood, fruit and water, green tortoise and coconuts, "then filled away," west southwest. On this course they sailed for the next twenty-two days, until the island of Mauritius hove into sight on July 29.

On that same day, the *Asia* took a right whale of the humpback species, and the *Alliance* had a boat stove by the same whale. In the business of trying out the whale, it was recorded: ". . . one of our people cut his fingers half off. . . . Sent our boat on shore after our Captain to Stop the Man's Blood that Cut himself, they came off and stopped it, finished trying our wale then went to Breaking out our hole after oil that our Captain sold on Shore." [9]

On August 1, 1792, the logkeeper recorded that no one was allowed on shore "because of the Smallpox that is verry Plenty, Excepting them that has had It." Two more whales were taken near the "Isle of France," as many mariners termed it, and then the *Asia* steered for Madagascar. On August 11, they were close into Cape Ste. Marie, at Madagascar's southern tip, where they dropped anchor in eight fathoms at a small bay, and sent boats after humpbacks. Natives from ashore came out in their canoes. The *Alliance* arrived on August 17. Both vessels took several whales here, one of them at some distance from the ship—"7 or 8 miles of the ship." The ships remained at anchor for two weeks off Cape Ste. Marie. On August 28, two unusual incidents were recorded:

> . . . One of the Native Boats came off A Board our Consort and told us there was a Brig. Cast away where Captain and Crew were without Victles. She was. Cast away the 19th of August. Then our Captain and our Consort carried him some necessaries then he came on Board.

And on the next day:

> . . . Saw 5 boats Coming off on Board of us just Before they got up with us they went on Shore and went into the woods and Blowed *of* there guns *of* and Blowed there horns—As Quick As our Captain Saw that it was git under way as fast as posable (our Captain on Board our Consort), they put of from Shore thinking to have us; the *Alliance* put one anker down. She Slipt her Cable, the *Asia* Being Moored she run a verry grate risk of Being Taking. But she Slipt

her Best Bower and wayed her small Anker; now by this time the Boat is not far of—our Captain haled. Mr. Starbuck not to be Sacrificed By them But to Come with the Boat, But the *Asia* made sale as fast as posable. Then they hove up their chase—they were not more than a Muskit Shot of. At 11 A.M. our Captain came on Board and told us the Chance that we run for our Lives, for they were looking at them with Spye Glases. So end, this 24 hours all well on Board of the *Asia* by the kind hand of Providence.[10]

These two Nantucket whalers were probably the first of their kind in these waters. They spoke no other whaleships during their cruising in this part of the Indian Ocean and they reported the humpbacks tame and numerous. From Madagascar, they sailed up the east coast of that great island. For over six hundred miles, the coast is almost a straight line. North by east, east northeast, east by north ½, north, northeast—these were the courses she took up the longitude 50° to 52° east as far as 12°–11″ south latitude.

As they surveyed this virgin coast, what must have been the thoughts of these whaling nomads, who could fully appreciate that this was the legendary land of the Roc that carried Sinbad the Sailor to the Valley of Diamonds in distant India.

Working away from the northern coast of Madagascar, the two whaleships sailed south and east. It was not until September 27, 1792 (a month from Cape Ste. Marie) that they saw their first ship to windward, "but could not speak her." On the next day, three sperm whales were sighted and one killed and tryed out. On October 4, they saw Mauritius "rite Ahade, at 5 P.M. hove tow under A two-reef Maintopsail."

At Port Louis, they worked the ships in "to the Landing Place and made fast to the Anker on Shore and got a Little supper and then turned in. . . . The Doctor Came off and Nocholated Both our Cruese, for the Small Pox is so Breef that it is Emposable to keep Clear from it it is So Breef that 129 died in one Day." There were other dangers lurking on these coasts besides pirates! [11]

The *Asia* "rigged Awnings over our Decks to make it Cool." For several days "the Smallpox folks complained verry weak, some of them fainted." Captain Bartlett Coffin, of the *Alliance,* was one of those dangerously ill. Whale oil was bartered for corn from the ship *Robert*

Morris. The *Asia* and *Alliance* were hove down or "keeled," their bends scraped and tarred, and preparations made for "our voyage to Desolation." Hundreds of bushels of salt were put aboard for the expected skins, provisions stowed and the rigging set up. A schooner was bought and fitted out as a tender. Given the name *Hunter,* she was put under Simeon Starbuck, the mate. Just before sailing, one of the hands, John Griffin, ran away, and was found on board another ship in the harbor. He was taken aboard in handcuffs.

On November 17, 1792, the *Asia, Alliance,* and schooner *Hunter* sailed from Port Louis, their destination being Desolation (Kerguelen) Island, thousands of miles away to the south, the world's most remote island, four thousand miles from Australia and three thousand miles from Africa, an outpost on the fringe of Antarctic seas.

It was the French explorer Kerguélen-Trémarec who first discovered the bleak shores of this mountainous island in the high latitudes south of "roaring forties." Rightly he called it "Terre Desolation" on that day in 1772. Four years later, 1776, Captain Cook put in at a harbor on the northern end of its forsaken length and called it Christmas Harbor after the day of the landfall. He was the first man to anchor a ship here, Kerguélen having sent a small boat ashore, since he was unable to come to a harbor.

On her voyage down to solitary Desolation, the *Asia* had taken five sperm and was working well in spite of the heavy weather. The *Hunter* broke her tiller, but Captain Starbuck "got it riged again" and kept pace with the ships. In latitude 43°–10″ a northwest gale roared down upon them and the *Asia* was forced to heave to and ride it out under bare poles. The *Alliance* reported a boat stove, "two cabbin windows" broken, and the mizzen staysail split. The *Hunter* again broke her tiller and split the foresail but Captain Starbuck again had it repaired. Now the squalls came frequently, with rain and "hail excessive hard . . . and a Lumbering Swell from the westward." This was followed by "fresh gales and rugged weather," and the *Asia* found it hard to keep a course.[12]

Early in the afternoon on December 17, 1792, the shores of Desolation rose out of the heaving sea to the southwest. Two small islands were given a wide berth and the black shores of Desolation loomed nearer. Here was a volcanic spew of rock, some eighty miles long by twenty miles wide, of the greatest irregularity of shape, featuring precipitous cliffs rising two thousand feet from the sea, many deep bays and inlets. Snowfields and glaciers canted into the foaming seas that dashed continuously and furiously at the forbidding shores, as if eager to display a jealous power over puny man's first attempts to penetrate the almost unknown outpost of ocean's last frontier. Here was the home of the sea-elephant and the seal, unmolested for centuries. Silvanus Crosby wrote:

> . . . at 5 P.M. saw the *Hunter* ahade agoing into the harbour. Middle part Sprang up a breeze at SE we Laying of and on But Could not weather the Bluf which made out the North Side of the harbour Latter part the same tack and half-tack. Next day . . . at 7 P.M. Enter'd into the harbours Mouth then Down Boat and went to towing at 12 o'clock got safe in at anker and got Snug—then turned in. Latter part squally So that we Can't heave up to git to our Moreings So ends this 24 hours all well. on Board the Ship.[13]

The *Alliance* came in successfully the next day. Both ships were now moored in Christmas Harbor. The *Hunter* was hauled alongside the *Alliance* and fitted out for her arduous task of cruising into the innumerable rocky bays for sea-elephants.

In 1852, a young physician, taking to sea life for his health, wrote as follows of this forbidding land: ". . . The coast is indented with small bays . . . rising in abrupt and lofty cliffs surmounted with overhanging precipices, where naught is to be seen save the hoarse-crying sea fowl winging its flight into dusky caverns whence no sound issues except the ceaseless roar of the ocean upon its broken rocks." [14]

Storm of wind and snow was a daily happening. At last the *Hunter* was ready for her cruise along the dangerous coast. On January 9, 1793, "she made sail on Discovery to see if they can find a better harbor . . . we stood Along Shore to the Southward By 3 Long Bays at 7 P.M. cast Anker in 7 fathoms of water in A Bay that we gave the name of Hunter's Bay Saw Elephants all along the Bay Sides."

The next day the hunters went ashore with clubs and lances and began their killing, taking two the first afternoon and twenty-three the next day, despite a northeast snowstorm and fresh gales. The blubber was stripped from the animals, separated from its skin and put in a cask on board the schooner.

But the heavy gales forced Captain Starbuck to take up his anchor and seek a better holding ground for himself and his sloop. On January 16, the schooner set out

in persute of a Better harbour Around the Islands, that lay to the eastward. We run onto a Small Bay and found 10 fathoms of water, Stood out and run acrost the Bay into Another and Sounded and found 20 fathoms water, we tacked Ship and Stood for the Bay again whare we ankered in 10 fathoms water and carried out the small anker. . . . Then we went with the boat around the S.E part of the Island killed Some fowl Saw a parcel of Elephants but could not see any Look over to the other side, and see what it is Conveaneter harbour; then we sounded round the harbour and found a good Bottom from 4 to 15 fathoms water, we found a Small Bay to the SW of here. . . . They may haul the ship a Long side of the Bank Safe from any harm.

These were explorers, the first Americans at this island—these whalemen. "We gave this the name of Mussel Bay," wrote Silvanus Crosby, "for we found aplenty of Mussels and got some of them." The new anchorage ground for the ships "we gave the name of Port Washington. Saw a plenty of elephants all around."[15] The *Alliance* and *Asia* went down to the new harbor, and the *Hunter* resumed her cruising.

During the next nine days, the *Hunter* landed at various places alongshore and killed a total of 369 sea-elephants. In a constant matching of their skill against the elements, Captain Simeon Starbuck and his crew were sailing into uncharted bays and reaches, perilously close to shipwreck on several occasions. One of the most revealing entries was that of February 4, 1793.

. . . at 8 P.M. wayed Anker and run out of the Bay and stear'd to the South ward. Sent the Boats on shore at 2 P.M. Brought 46 Elephants, the weather Looked verry thick we Bore Away to find A harbour then run through A narrow Passage into a Deep Bay that run up SW we run in under the west Shore and tryed to Beat up But we could not; the wind Came down off the high Land So that [we] Could not Carry No Sail then we put her Before the wind and run under an Island that Maid the Lea Side of the Passage and Came to an anker in 13 fathoms water. The Botum Deapened So fast that we was afraid that we Should Drift out; then we carried 2 ankers in shore and Let go in 6 fathoms water then went on Shore and killed an Elephant then came on Board. We Saw rite whales all around not 40 rodds of us. So Ends.

This was one day of a series of running the gauntlet of lee shore and squall. Returning from a successful cruise, the *Hunter*'s crew was surprised to be met at the mouth of Port Washington by "the *Asia*'s boat, she came A Long Side and told us the Sad Nuse of Captain Bartlett Coffin's death . . . after a 9-Days Sickness . . . all the time in great agony and had no relief from pain." On the next day, it was recorded: "At 6 this afternoon cared Captain Coffin on Shore the South Side of the Bay Bewryed him in a Deasent Manner So Ends this Day."

Thus came the end of the voyage for this veteran Nantucket whaling master, who had once sailed the *Maria* out of Dunkirk for William Rotch and taken her to the Falklands. His last command, the *Alliance*, was to see other coasts in these farflung voyages for sea-elephants before her twenty-year career was over.

In Kezia Fanning's diary under date of August 29, 1793, was recorded: "the 3rd of the month letters came from Andrew Pinkham . . . Bartlett Coffin's second mate; he writes that Bartlett died 7th Feb., overstrained and hurt himself in January, died in great agony. Poor Cousin Judith is left a Disconsolate widow."

On the eleventh day of March 1793, the little fleet battened down hatches and began their return voyage to the Isle of France (Mauritius).

We got under way and got safe out of Port Washington harbour, —states the log of the *Asia*—a fine wind at WNW, our consort A following after. 6 P.M. the North point of Stows Island Bore SW by S. 12 Leagues Distance. . . . Then spake our Company. Vessail and Concluded to Stear N.E until we got a good ofen [offing].

All three vessels arrived safely at the Mauritius in April. The *Alliance*, with Captain Hezekiah Pinkham in command, arrived first and the *Asia* reached the harbor on April 6, the *Hunter* not appearing. Casks of blubber, which had been headed up, were started and, once more at sea, the sea-elephant fat was tried out in the warm latitudes. Returning to Port Louis, word was received from Bourbon Island (Reúnion), the companion of Mauritius, that the *Hunter* had arrived there and Captain Starbuck had sold his oil. The schooner reached Port Louis on April 27, where she was sold, and the proceeds of the sale used to buy coffee.

The *Asia* and *Alliance* then began their voyage home. Running to leeward of Bourbon Island, they saw several vessels at anchor before the town of St. Denis, on the north side of the island, as they sailed south and west. On June 30, 1793, they sighted the east coast of Africa at the entrance to that rendezvous of the whaleships—Delagoa Bay. Here eleven whaleships lay at anchor.

"Captain Swain and Captain Hussey came on Board," wrote Silvanus Crosby. "There is 12 Vessels of us and the chief of them are Nantucket Men." [16] This must have been put down with the same laconic pride that characterized these men of the sea. Captain William Swain was in the *Ranger,* of Nantucket; Captain Isaiah Hussey was in the *Benjamin,* of Dunkirk. Another craft here at this time was the *Negar,* also of Dunkirk, Captain John Hawes. These ships narrowly escaped capture in this bay a few months later. Many humpbacks ranged the coast and both the *Asia* and *Alliance* took several, towing them into the bay and up to their ships was a rigorous chore—sometimes as many as four boats being needed to breast the tide. Captain Obed Fitch came in with the Dunkirk-Rotch whaler *William Penn,* and hove to for a gam. Another Rotch ship, Nantucket skipper and crew to sail into the bay was Captain Stephen Gardner in the *Young States.*

One of the unwritten laws of whaling, dating back to colonial times, is described in this period in the *Asia*'s log. The *Alliance* had killed a whale but, the tide running out of the bay, she anchored the captive carcass outside. The *Asia* went out to help tow the whale in. Once outside the bay, two humpbacks were seen and the *Asia*'s two boats struck them.

Not having their regular whaling gear in the boats, the boatsteerers showed true Yankee ingenuity by striking both whales with improvised harpoons—one being a "preventer iron" and the other a "tow iron." One of the whales was killed; the other parted the preventer warp but was killed some time afterwards by a boat from "Captain Hailes ship," a British whaler. The next day, Captain Coffin went aboard the other ship and claimed one half of the whale, as his "preventer iron" was still "fastened" to him. The claim was duly allowed.[17] It was a custom. Nearly a century later, the Supreme Court of Massachusetts rendered a decision in regard to a similar case—common whaling practice determining a judgment in favor of the ship whose harpoon was found in a whale captured by another vessel.

On the eleventh of September, 1793, the *Asia* was warned by Captain William Swain of the presence of an armed Dutch brig. During the day, Captain Coffin sailed over the bay and anchored in front of the exotic town of Lorenço Marques. Here, it was learned that, at the mouth of the bay, the Dutch brig had captured several whaleships.

From Cape of Good Hope, the *Asia* sailed to St. Helena, checked her bearings and continued, passing Ascension Island on November 5, 1793. Sperm whales were taken on her passage at the northern fringe of the Brazil Banks. "A sharpe look-out for land" was kept, while some of the hands employed themselves in "making Nicknacks"— probably scrimshaw, that ancient craft of designing articles from whalebone. On December 4, 1793, the island of Dominica in the West Indies was sighted. It had been good navigating.

While running up along the Leeward Islands, the *Asia* was seized by a British frigate and taken into St. Kitts (St. Christopher). On board the *Asia*, the Nantucket captains held a conference. Here were Captains Coffin, Hussey, Swain, and Gideon Gardner, the latter in the harbor with his vessel, *Prince William*, of Milford Haven. Some of the oil was confiscated by the haughty British prize-master. As an ironical touch to the affair, a British twenty-gun ship was wrecked off the harbor and boats from the *Asia* helped save the twenty survivors of the seventy-six-man crew.[18]

Free from the clutches of this frigate, the unlucky *Asia* sailed for St. Eustatia, where a British frigate promptly impressed several of her men and a boat's crew ran away on shore rather than risk impressment. It took two days to get the hunted whalemen smuggled aboard their own ship. Clear of the harbor, they were forced to return when a bad leak developed on the larboard side forward. Leaking about five hundred strokes an hour, they put in at Turks Islands, and then sailed through the Windward Passage to Môle St. Nicolas, Haiti, a place well known to Nantucket and New England traders. Here the ship was careened and the leak repaired. And so it was not until February 1794, that the *Asia* got home.

That great whaling historian, Alexander Starbuck, thought that the ship *Nancy,* of Bedford, Captain William Swain, which sailed on February 12, 1798, was the first American whaler to Desolation (Kerguelen). He wrote of this voyage, in his *History of the American Whale Fishery:*

> The *Nancy* was the first American whaler to Desolation, only one English vessel there before her. The *Nancy* was captured, homeward bound by the French privateer *Reliance,* and re-captured by the U.S. brig *Eagle.* Value of Cargo $50,000.[19]

Now we know that the *Asia* and *Alliance,* in 1792, with their little schooner-tender *Hunter,* constituted the first whaling and sea-elephant expedition to that remote island.

The British had already established their settlement at Botany Bay (later called Sydney), Australia, in January 1788. In a letter to George Chalmers at London, from Samuel Enderby, Jr., dated January 17, 1789, and quoted in Dakin's *Whalemen's Adventures,* there is the statement: ". . . nothing is wanting to make this Fishery compleat but unlimited right of fishing in all seas, the British Adventurers would soon explore the most distant parts, and the settlements of New Holland would be often visited as there are many whales in the sea." [20]

The letter mentions further that information from America had placed sperm whales about the island of Java and Straits of Sunda, and that some merchants of Boston were fitting out a ship for these waters. It is certain, however, that the *Asia* was the first American whaler of whom we have any knowledge to cover such a tremendous sweep of the Indian Ocean, to the East Indies and Madagascar, and then to the fringe of Antarctic waters at Desolation Island.

Another letter quoted by Dakin concerns the *Britannia,* taking a cargo of convicts to Port Jackson in November 1791, in which her master tried to make the island of Amsterdam, north of Kerguelen, for seals but the weather was against him. The *Britannia* sailed in company with Captain Eber Bunker, formerly of Nantucket, who was in the Alexander Champion whaleship *William and Ann,* the first whaler at New Zealand. "If a voyage can be got upon this coast it will make it shorter than going to Peru," wrote Captain Melville, of the *Britannia.* Norfolk Island, originally a penal colony, was abandoned as such to form a rendezvous for British whalers.[21]

Captain Eber Bunker, in his next voyage in the British *Albion,* made the shortest whaleship voyage to Port Jackson from London, three months and fifteen days. This exiled Nantucket skipper took part in the first settlement of Tasmania. One of Governor King's five chief reasons for settling this island in 1803 was the promotion of the sealing industry. The River Derwent soon became a favorite resort for American whalers as well as British.

It was about the time the *Asia* was sailing her far-flung pioneering voyage in the Indian Ocean that H.M.S. *Pandora,* searching for the *Bounty* and her mutinous crew, was wrecked not far from where the lamented Frenchman La Pérouse had disappeared two years before (1788).

But there has been no one to tell of the long and lonely voyage of the whaleship *Asia,* nor of her consort *Alliance.* But, as recounted by one of that unsung crew, whose canvas-covered logbook journal has been lying in dusty oblivion at the bottom of an old Nantucket trunk for over a century and a half, it speaks for itself.

chapter xv

"OF THE MOST DARING KIND—"
AND "OF SECRECY"

. . . I regret that I am not at liberty to communicate . . . all the interesting facts. . . . In the history of the seal trade, secrecy is what they know has been deemed a part, and a most important part, of their capital.
—J. M. Reynolds [1]

KNOWING OF THE SUCCESS of the Salem ships around Cape of Good Hope to the East Indies, and of the great voyages of the Boston and New York vessels around Cape Horn to the Northwest Coast and to China, it might have been expected that the shipowners of Nantucket and New Bedford would join the rich trade. But the island was part and parcel of whaling, and New Bedford was too closely allied to this Athens of the industry. And so whaling remained their sole business. The only concession whaling made to the new trade with the Far East was through sealing and sea-elephant hunting voyages carried on in the same ship and in the same seas. The growth of both occupations has become legendary—and now they are as dim as all such tales.

In 1786, following the return of the *United States* from the Falklands, Captain Benjamin Hussey, with the first sealskins brought into an American port, several merchants formed companies to engage in the enterprise. The *Swallow,* of Nantucket, Captain Latham Gardner, returned in 1794 with sixteen thousand skins taken at the Falklands, while the *Betsey,* Captain Steele, and *Josephus,* Captain Youte, of New York, also had large cargoes from these islands. Amasa Delano states the *Eliza* was the first craft to take skins from Más Afuera off the west coast of South America to Canton, but Captain Edmund Fanning also mentions that Captain Obed Paddock, of the whaleship *Olive Branch,* of Nantucket, told him how to get ashore and pursue the seal on Más Afuera.[2] The English privateer-mariner Dampier wrote that thousands of seals swarmed about the Juan Fernández Islands, "as if they had no other place in the world to live in—going and coming in the sea all around the island." [3]

Eight hundred miles east southeast of the Falklands were the South Georgia island rookeries, which were worked longer than the Falklands. By 1820, the South Georgia sealers had taken 1,250,000 sealskins from this land of rock, snow and marsh. This great island had been re-discovered by Cook (1775) after being lost for a century following La Roche's finding.

Captain Cook's description, printed in 1784, induced the British sealers to sail to South Georgia, they were soon joined by the Americans. Primarily seeking sea-elephant oil, the whalers brought back to England quantities of fur-seal.

Sandwich Land (South Sandwich Islands), 450 miles south southeast of the South Georgia, discovered by Captain Cook (1775), was also frequented by sealers. They also visited the elusive Gough Island, far to the southeast, and Tristan da Cunha, a South Atlantic mountain-peak island. At Tristan the *Industry,* Captain Patten, took 5,600 sealskins in 1790. Three sealers started a colony here in 1810.[4]

The ship *Neptune,* owned by Ebenezer Townsend, of New Haven, left that port in 1796 to take seals at the Falklands and Patagonia for the China market. Her commander was Captain David Greene (not Eben Townsend, as sometimes given). The voyage was one of the most successful in sealing history (the skins were taken to Canton) but it came perilously close to disaster at the "land of fire"—Patagonia.

The *Neptune* was at the Falklands (Port Egmont) on August 22, 1797, when the ship *Juno,* of Hudson, New York, Captain Paul Bunker, came into that little port. A sloop, the *Betsey,* sailed in company with the *Juno* as a consort, being commanded by Captain Prince Bunker, brother of the ship's master.

Young Eben Townsend, son of the owner and supercargo on the *Neptune*, told of subsequent events.

> . . . Captain Bunker . . . agreed with Captain Greene that they make up a crew and go on to the Coast of Patagonia in the sloop and search for seal. Accordingly, on the 26th . . . with twenty-four men, they sailed in the sloop *Betsey*, with the understanding that, if we heard nothing from them in six weeks, I was to send the shallop over and look for them, as they may have got their vessel on shore. After having been absent 33 days they returned in a passage of twelve days, having left a sealing crew at Cape Mattass, with a whale-boat to shift along the coast if necessary.
>
> On their first arrival on the coast they found a few Spaniards, . . . who told them there would be no difficulty in getting permission from the Commandant at Port Desire to seal.[5]

The two captains, therefore anchored the sloop and took the whale-boat and a crew and rowed some twenty miles to Port Desire. But their plans were roughly halted. Here they found a small Spanish garrison and a suspicious commandant, who informed them that he considered them Englishmen. As Spain and England were at war, this was the signal to declare the Yankee sealers as prisoners.

It was the intention of the Spanish commandant to send an armed launch down the coast to capture the sloop. Captains Greene and Bunker proposed they be retained as hostages and the boat dispatched for the vessel's papers. The Americans were merely sparring for time. They realized that being sent to Montevideo for trial would mean further imprisonment and the loss of their voyage, as English and American ship's papers were so much alike. When the Spaniards sent a party of soldiers to board the *Betsey*, the situation looked black, indeed.

The two sealing masters were determined to make a "bold push" for freedom. To discourage such thoughts, the Spaniards stationed the armed launch down the river a little below the garrison. Townsend describes what happened:

> It looked very dark, for they [Bunker and Greene] were placed inside the garrison [a stockade nine feet high, inside of which was a block house of two stories, a church and large house] and there appeared no chance for escape. However, Greene, who you know is resolute and hawk-eyed, gave a word of caution to keep together.

The Spaniards always keep a padre or priest in their garrisons. When the prayer bell rang at 8 o'clock in the evening, and they all gotten into the small church . . . the wished for time offered.

They [the Yankees] started, and were soon hold of their whale-boat, which had been hauled up. The movement was so quick that it was not known whether an alarm had been given, and after they were afloat (and it was too dark to be fired at) there was little danger but that they could row two feet to one of any boat rowed by the Spaniards. They muffled their oars and got alongside the sloop about midnight, jumped on deck and got possession of the arms, the soldiers being asleep. They then made the soldiers get into their own boat and, knocking out the flints, returned to them their muskets—and treated them to a drink of grog. The soldiers were told to tell their commander that he did not know how to keep Yankees. They then got under way and ran to the Northwest.[6]

On another cruise to Patagonia, Captain Bunker returned with two thousand skins. He had lost the sloop's masthead in a gale and also had a stove by a whirlpool. As an illustration of the comradeships, mention must be made of the help given by Captain Greene to his consort. On a cruise in his shallop to Beaver Islets at the Falklands, Greene sighted a mast on the beach at Big Harbor, and, getting it into the water, towed it to Port Egmont for Captain Bunker's sloop. By this act, he enabled the Hudson skipper to complete a successful voyage.

A phase of the life of a sealer is further reported by Townsend. It gives an insight into what a young man, acting as shipkeeper, thinks about when he is left in solitary charge of the big ship at anchor in Port Egmont:

On the 16th, the shallop sailed for a fort-night's cruise leaving me alone on board, but as it was a good harbor and the ship had good cables, I felt safe. I was then captain, mate and all hands. As I had enough to do, I was not at all lonesome as you may imagine. I was left with a dog, a cat and five kittens, but the dog killed the cat and the kittens died also, being but a day old. I never felt the loss of a cat so much.[7]

The *Neptune* left the Falklands with thirty thousand skins, sailed round the Horn and up the coast of Chile to Más Afuera Island, where she took forty-five thousand more in a period of eight weeks, "finding them much better in quality than we had expected at this latitude." Crossing the Pacific to Canton, the sealers sold their skins, and a cargo of tea, silks, nankeen and teakwood was put on board. Upon arrival home in July 1799, the *Neptune* paid $75,000 in duty fees alone to the treasury of the state of Connecticut—more than the entire civil list of the state! The crew made $1,200 each for their share of the voyage.[8]

According to the statement of Ebenezer Townsend, a New Haven merchant, Elijah Austin, was the first from that city to fit out sealers—this being in the early 1790's. The *Oneida,* Captain Brintnall, had Stephen West, of Nantucket, as her lieutenant (being an armed ship) when she sailed on her sealing voyage from New York in 1800, and her voyage to China and return was made in seventeen months. A merchant-historian, Frederick Coffin Sanford, of Nantucket, declared this voyage to have been so profitable as to be the talk of the counting rooms of the seaports.[9]

Another successful New Haven craft was the *Sally,* under Captain Nathaniel Storer, which sailed from that port on May 22, 1800, and arrived home June 2, 1803. The crew built a shallop at Patagonia, and sealed also in the Falklands and at South Georgia. After drying their skins at "Hurl-Gate Harbor," Patagonia, the *Sally* sailed around Cape Horn for China via the Sandwich Islands, selling forty-five thousand skins at Canton at eighty-seven cents each. In 1882, Captain Peter Storer, then in his ninety-first year, wrote:

> My father, Captain Nathaniel Storer, commanded the *Sally* . . . and he took me with him. I was then 9 years and 9 months old. . . . Only think, eighty-two years ago last January, I was running on the backs of sea elephants, on the island of South Georgia, as they lay in rows on the beach.[10]

No wonder the memory of such an experience was still vivid in the mind of this veteran Yankee sealer.

With the return to Nantucket of such sealers as the *Swallow* in 1794, several expeditions were organized. The British were at South Georgia in 1791 (the *Ann,* Captain Pitman), and other London ships were probably at the Falklands earlier; the ship *Josephus* from New York and her tender were bound for Cape Horn in January 1793; a Boston vessel under Captain Lee sailed for the Falklands on June 1, 1792.[11]

The whaleship *Three Friends,* of Dunkirk, which escaped a British armed whaler at Woolwich Bay, June 1793, lay a course for New Bedford. On board the ship was Captain Isaiah Cahoon, of Providence, who left that port in April 1791, bound on a sailing cruise to Thomson's Island, off the African coast.

He had been marooned there with nine crew-members by his own ship, and was rescued by a Canton ship, the *Canody,* Captain Morehead, and transferred to the *Three Friends.* Several days before being taken from the island, Captain Cahoon's crew of nine sealers had left the island in a small boat for St. Helena, on only a quart of water. He elected to remain but was down to a pint of water when rescued. The small boat and its crew were never found.

The first whaler-sealer out of New Bedford was the ship *Barclay,* which William Rotch had had built at the Acushnet River yard of George Claghorn (who was later to build the famous frigate *Constitution*). Launched in November 1793, the *Barclay,* under Captain David Swain, sailed for Le Havre January 4, 1794, loaded with 238 casks of whale oil, fifty casks of sperm and ninety-nine bundles of whalebone, all consigned to Homberg & Homberg, Frères.[12]

On her return voyage, she brought back William Rotch, his wife and family from England, where they had gone from Dunkirk. The *Barclay* sailed on her whaling-sealing voyage on August 22, 1797, for the Pacific Ocean. On June 26, 1799, she returned to New Bedford with seven hundred barrels of sperm oil, five hundred barrels of whale oil, and reported a catch of twenty-one thousand sealskins, sold at Canton.[13]

In May 1792, Elias Nexsen, of New York, sent out the brig *Betsey,* under a Captain Steele, for a sealing voyage to the Falklands. Edmund Fanning, of Stonington, was first mate, and his description of this expedition is prefaced by the remark: "Our want of knowledge of the sealing business was made manifest at the outset." He tells of coming upon a herd of some three hundred sea lions and, mistaking them for seals, advancing on them, shouting loudly to confuse the animals, with the following result:

> . . . This noise alarmed the lions, so that they immediately rose, and sent forth a roar that appeared to shake the very rocks on which we stood, and in turn advancing upon us in double-quick time, without

any regard to our persons, knocked every man of us down with as much ease as if we had been pipe stems, and passing over our fallen bodies, marched with utmost contempt into the water.[14]

It was in this same New York brig *Betsey* that Fanning, on his first voyage as master, sailed out of his native Stonington, in June 1797, bound for the fur-seal islands and China. At the Cape Verde Islands, the rig of the vessel was altered to facilitate handling her while laying off and on the sea islands. They arrived at the coast of Patagonia, South America, in October, thence to the Falklands, where they anchored in Shallop Cove, New Island, on the southwest side of the group.

It was while at anchor here that Captain Obed Paddock gave him the information about the seals at Más Afuera. Fanning states:

> From information obtained of Captain Paddock . . . I was induced to believe we could at times safely land, and take dry skins, at the island of Massafuero, and not withstanding this was in direct opposition to my previous advises, yet from certain former transactions with Captain Paddock, I was confident that the utmost dependence could be placed upon his word.[15]

Captain Fanning had not been very successful in his sealing operations at the Falklands, and so he was eager to follow the Nantucket sealer's advice. On December 11, 1797, in company with the *Olive Branch,* the *Betsey* left the Falklands. Passing outside Staten Land (Staten Island—Isola de los Estados), Captain Fanning sailed for the south before making his run westward, believing—as he stated—that between 63° and 65° south latitude, a ship "in doubling Cape Horn, will arrive in the South Pacific with less injury to her hull, spars, sails and rigging . . . with less drenching, hardship and fatigue to her crew."

On January 19, 1798, they were off Más Afuera: "The island of Juan Fernandez [Más Tierra] was also in sight, bearing E. by N. Hauled up for Massafuero, and at 10 A.M. was near its northern shore, on which, with the assistance of the glass, numbers of seal were seen." [16]

Captain Amasa Delano, who arrived here two years later in the Boston sealer *Perseverance,* wrote a good description of this island in his *Voyages*:

> Massafuero is . . . nearly circular . . . and about twenty-five miles in circumference. It is clear of any kind of danger, keeping two miles

from the land all around it; but on the southeast side lies a shoal that breaks half a mile distant in bade weather. On the west side is a rock, about one or one and half mile from the shore which does not often show itself. There is likewise a reef off the northwest point, one-half, or three quarters of a mile, which cannot be with safety approached if the wind blows on shore. . . . It has everywhere so bold a shore that anchorage cannot be obtained till within half a mile of it, round most parts of the island. . . . The land is very high, indeed, and can be seen at twenty to twenty-five leagues distance [60 to 75 miles] in clear weather. It is very much excavated, with deep gullies and caverns. . . . The fresh provisions it affords are goats, plenty of good fish, and seals, of which we ate a part. Water can be got in many places, but the best or easiest to be found is on the southeast side, at the place called the landing. . . . Wood can be procured in abundance but with some labor.[17]

From the evidence given by Captain Fanning, it would appear that Captain Obed Paddock, of Nantucket, in his island ship *Olive Branch,* between the years 1795-96 was the first whaler-sealer to land at Más Afuera. This was a veritable treasure island, from whose shores an estimated three million seals were taken in the next twenty years. Captain Delano gives this figure and tells us that he had taken a million seals here himself.

By April Captain Edmund Fanning and his crew of the *Betsey* had taken "a full cargo of selected fur seal skins. . . . The cabin, and finally the fore castle were filled, leaving just space enough for the accommodation of the ship's company; and yet there remaining, in stacks on shore, more than four thousand skins." [18]

To guard these skins, while the *Betsey* made a long voyage to China, a boatswain and a boat's crew were left behind to be picked up within a few months by the *Ontario,* the companion vessel of the *Betsey.* As the ship sailed away, Más Afuera sank slowly beneath the horizon until all that remained in sight was a portion of the top in the form "very similar to that of a shoe."

The *Betsey* sailed for the Marquesas. Making a good passage in the trades, the ship arrived at Hood (Fata Huku) Island, in the Marquesas, on May 17, 1798. As they came up to the island called La Domineque (Hiva Oa), the green foliage of the trees gladdened their hearts, "having been so long estranged therefrom." A double canoe containing eleven native bartered coconuts for nails and small pieces of iron hoops.

Fanning wanted to get into Cook's harbor at La Christiana (Tahuata) Island. A small canoe came off bearing two persons, one of whom was the missionary Reverend William P. Crook, landed at the island several months before by the London Missionary Society ship *Duff,* Captain Wilson. Crook asked Captain Fanning to rescue him.

Dressed in native garb, and thoroughly tanned, the poor missionary did not have to give too long a warning to persuade Fanning that it was dangerous to attempt anchorage in this harbor, called Resolution Bay. A renegade white man in the hills was a menace to all newcomers, as he planned to take by strategem all ships entering the island's quiet harbor. The native chief, much attracted to Crook, promised to warn any white men's ships of the potential danger of the renegade.

It was Crook who informed Fanning of the presence of Washington Islands (north cluster of the Marquesas), to the northwest, and advised going there for refreshment. The *Betsey* accordingly sailed thence, and Captain Fanning believed, from the action of the natives, that this was the first white man's ship they had ever seen. Bits of broken crockery from the galley proved the most valuable article in exchange for fruits and coconuts.

Again, the natives proved treacherous, but Crook's whispered advice gave Fanning ample warning of a planned surprise attack, and the ship worked her way out, with boat crews towing and ship's crew working sweeps, barely escaping a reef as well as the natives who made "the bay ring again with their uproar." A larger craft could never have made such an escape, a point much in favor of the Yankee ships in the islands of the South Seas.

The island was called Hooapoah by the natives. Captain Ingraham, of the Boston Northwest Coast-bound ship *Hope,* had seen these islands several years before, and named them the Washington Islands.

Standing north, the *Betsey* made the island of Nuku Hiva. A half century later this was to become famous as the home of two young Americans—Herman Melville and his shipmate Tobias Green—runaways from the whaleship *Acushnet*. Here, Captain Fanning had a long visit anchoring in the spacious bay, later called, by Captain David

Porter, Massachusetts Bay, and obtaining a plenitude of fresh provisions, roast pig, and water.

On May 30, 1798, the *Betsey* got under way again, heading north by west. On June 11, the lookout at mast's head suddenly called "Land ho!" At the time, the ship under full sail, was going before the wind. The officer of the deck put her helm a lee, and the *Betsey* came up fast into the wind on her starboard tacks. Fanning wrote of this unexpected landfall:

> ... The land was seen stretching along in a direction seemingly about north and south, with the surf on the western board, as a rain shower passed over, and its clearing up enabled us to see it, appearing to be one continued sheet of white foam along the horizon, breaking high, with a tremendous noise, on the coral reef that bound the coast.

These were two barren islands, not laid down on any chart, and the master of the *Betsey* named them Fanning Islands, locating them in 3°-51'-30" north latitude and 159°-12'-30" west longitude. Landing, they found no "Vestige of habitation." A few years later, Captain Donald Mackay, in a vessel sent out by Fanning, found ruins of a stone hut and uncovered fragments of human bone, spear and arrow points, indicating some natives had lived there at some remote time.

On the next day, June 12, another island was discovered about eight miles to the north, this time one with green coconut fronds showing, which Fanning called another new discovery and named Washington Island. "We could perceive no tokens of its being at all inhabited," he wrote. The two islands became well known to the whalemen of New England during the next century. Several days later, the *Betsey* narrowly missed shipwreck on another island or reef, which Fanning thought to be Palmyra Island but was probably Kingman's reef a little to the north of Palmyra.

On July 14, the *Betsey* sighted Tinian Island in the Ladrones or Marianas Islands. As they approached the southwest side of Tinian, where a bay opened to view, the wreck of a large ship was to be clearly observed. Ashore, Fanning met the surviving ranking officer of the wreck (which proved to be a British Indiaman), the mate, a Mr. Swain, of Nantucket, who reported the widow of the captain, her child, a servant woman, and twenty-one men. Their vessel had been wrecked thirteen months before, while on her way from Canton to Port Jackson, Australia.

Mate Swain—Fanning must now expect to find a Nantucketer no matter where he sailed—had erected some neat houses and, under the wrecked ship's sails, had piled "her valuable cargo of silks and teas, &c., and buried in an appropriate grave . . . were the remains of their captain." Leaving the Malay sailors to guard the wreck-cargo, the *Betsey* took on board the others and set sail for Macao, where they arrived on August 5, and landed on the thirteenth. Ten days later, after much delay, Fanning was able to bring the *Betsey* past the Boca Tigris ("the mouth of the Tiger"), at the entrance of the renowned Whampoa River and its guardian forts, and thence to Canton, the trading center of China.

The usages and customs of the port demanded that a "hong" or clearing factory be engaged. A Chinese merchant drew up agreements to pay duties and arrange for the return cargo of teas, silks and nankeens. Captain Fanning left Canton on October 30, 1798, in company with a ship bound for Philadelphia, and making a passage through the East Indies went out through the Strait of Sunda. Off Sumatra, they were attacked by a fleet of piratical proas. Although the Philadelphia ship left them to their fate, Captain Fanning and his crew of the *Betsey* beat the Malays off and escaped.

On January 30, 1799, the *Betsey* rounded Cape of Good Hope; a month later they had passed St. Helena, and on April 18, they came in sight of the welcome shore of Long Island. After putting in at Stonington, the ship passed down Long Island Sound. When the ship docked on April 26, 1799, Captain Fanning proudly recorded that she was the first ship, officered and manned wholly by native-born Americans, ever to circumnavigate the world from the port of New York. Her cargo gave her owners a neat profit of $52,300.

At New Island, in the Falklands, in November 1787, were the *Maria* and *Lydia,* of New Bedford, under Captains Benjamin Paddock and Obed Fitch, of Nantucket, and the *Industry,* Captain William Fosdick. It is well to take note of these veterans of the sea, all in their early thirties. Captain Fitch had lost two ships by capture, homeward bound; Captain Paddock was taking the *Maria* on her fourth voyage in five years; Captain Fosdick had brought the old *Industry* in to refit, having "stove" his tryworks in a protracted storm.[19]

Other ports soon took on sealing adventures. Salem entered the picture with the ships *Minerva* and *Concord* which sailed in October 1799, the former under Captain Mayhew Folger and the latter under Captain Joseph Wyer, both of these masters of Nantucket. Felt's *Annals of Salem* states that Clifford Crowninshield and Nathaniel West owned the *Minerva,* and the *Concord* was owned by several prominent Salem merchants.[20] The latter cleared $42,652.56 on this voyage.

The *Minerva* got her seals at St. Mary's (Santa María) Island, off Concepçion on the Chilean coast, and on Más Afuera, after recruiting at Callao, the port of Lima. She then sailed to Canton with a full cargo of sealskins, and returned to Salem early in May 1802. She was the first vessel from that port ever to circumnavigate the world.[21]

Upon her arrival at Salem in May 1802, the *Minerva* was transferred to Nantucket, where Captain Daniel Jones took her out on a whaling and sealing voyage. He secured twenty-three thousand skins and took them to China, arriving home in August 1804. From this voyage, Captain Jones began a successful mercantile career.

A similar success attended Captain Wyer, in the *Concord.* Arriving at the Falklands, the Salem craft found two other sealing vessels, at Jason Island—the *Mars,* Captain Uriah Swain, of Nantucket, and the *Barclay,* Captain Griffin Barney, of New Bedford. Both masters were fellow-townsmen of Captain Wyer, and they told him of the large numbers of seals at Más Afuera, where both had spent a successful season the previous voyage.

Rounding Cape Horn, during February and March of 1800, the journalist of the voyage, young Nathaniel Appleton, wrote:

> There was carried away our main topmast, top gallant mast and fore top gallant yard, owing to the main top's giving way and slackening the rigging. There was our main topmast and top-gallantmast with the sails in the water together, besides a lee shore on which we expected to drift every moment. If this be Cape Horn, spare me from ever coming again.[22]

Two other Salem craft, the *Rebecca* and the *Rachel,* went sealing in 1803, the former going out to Más Afuera. Then the business from that port lapsed for fifteen years. Perhaps the answer to this unexpected sequel to such excellent voyages by these sealers lies in the fact that the masters and mates of such craft as the *Minerva* and *Concord,* on their next voyages, went out in Boston, Nantucket or New Bedford ships.

Certain it is that Mayhew Folger, when first offered command of the *Minerva,* stated he could not accept unless Reuben Joy, of Nantucket, also went out as his mate as the latter was an experienced sealer. Nantucket merchants purchased three Salem ships—the *Minerva,* the *Essex,* and the *Lady Adams*—all of which went out sealing from that island.

Whether the *Lady Adams* was actually repurchased from Crowninshield, or whether she was originally only chartered by the Salem merchants, is a question. Before and after that 1799-1802 voyage, she sailed out of Nantucket, and continued there until her last voyage from Nantucket to China, under Captain Obed Fitch. The *Lady Adams* met her end in some unknown way in 1823, while on a whaling voyage on the Japan Grounds.[23]

The *Essex,* after some five sealing voyages and one to China, was also to meet an ill fate. She was rammed by a whale and sunk in 1820, and her survivors endured that terrible open-boat voyage described in a later chapter.

Nantucket embarked on sealing with a flourish worthy of her fame. She had ten other vessels in that trade, besides those already noted. Five of these combined sea-elephant hunting with the sealing.

Not all voyages were successful. The *Tryal* was captured by the Spaniards at Valparaiso and condemned; the *Maryland,* Captain Liscomb, of New York, fitting out from Bedford, was captured by the Spaniards but released. Homeward bound, he was again taken, this time by a French privateer, being released after losing two thousand skins in ransom. The *Pegasus,* of New York, was lost on Más Afuera, and two other sealers were wrecked on Patagonia's iron coast.

The sealers were not the type of men to leave personal journals of their experiences. Edmund Fanning was a notable exception. Take the forty-year career of Captain Obed Fitch, as a whaleman which began in post-Revolutionary days. Of him was written in 1888:

Captain Fitch was a fine, majestic figure, over six feet tall, muscular, strong-limbed, his arms when in motion plainly showing his power. It is said that once while bringing a new ship home, they wanted water from alongside, and there being no bucket, he seized a barrel and letting it down drew it up full as easily as an ordinary seaman would a bucket.

He went as second mate of that famous Nantucket ship *Maria,* to the coast of Africa (1787), Captain George Hussey and Micajah Gardner, first mate. Approaching the African coast, near where Riley and Paddock, two of our best captains, were wrecked, the man on the forecastle reported "something" looking strange to him ahead. Fitch, who had the deck, walked forward and, peering under the foresail, at once discovered the land looking white. Quick as a flash, without a word or order, to any one, he sprang to the quarter-deck and put down the helm hard down to the rail, then springing to the yards, swung them around with his powerful arms as quickly as though all hands had been on the ropes, thus putting the ship on the opposite tack; then, pausing to look over her side, he saw the mud coming up, and sea-drift, showing that her keel had struck the bottom. When the ship was safe, Captain Hussey appeared in the gangway and took Mr. Fitch's statement.

Next morning, at the breakfast table, Captain Hussey said playfully: "Mr. Gardner, why didn't you take the deck last night?" "Why, sir," said Mr. Gardner, "I saw Mr. Fitch had it, and that no man was safe around him. I saw he was in earnest." [24]

chapter xvi

⟨⟩

FULL TIDE OF ADVENTURE
WITH THE SEALERS

*Is it not a saying in every one's mouth, Possession is half
the law: that is, regardless of how the thing came into possession? But, often possession is the whole of the law. . . .*

—Melville, *Moby Dick*

IT WAS THE WHALEMEN of New England who first brought American
commerce to the west coast of South America. The Spanish
colonial ports of Talcahuano, Valparaiso, Coquimbo, Callao, Paita and
Túmbez did not welcome the newcomers. Although they drove the
Beaver, of Nantucket, out of Callao in 1792, they grudgingly watched
Captain Bunker, of the *Washington,* hoist the first American flag in
any Spanish Pacific port before he would be driven out.

During the war with Spain, several British whalers captured Spanish
ships near the west coast of South America, and brought their prizes
to Sydney, Australia. One captured vessel, loaded with wheat, was
almost providential to the struggling young colony. In retaliation, the
Spaniards captured a number of the "blubber-hunters." They regarded
the Americans as allies of Britain, because of the common language,
and captured some of the Yankee ships.

The American sealers followed the whale-sealers and were equally
unwelcome. Many of their voyages were carried out with great secrecy
—the hallmark of the sealers. The masters of these vessels were among
the most hardened men of the sea, forced by circumstance to be a law

unto themselves. They were counterparts of the old English buc-
caneers, but they worked harder and under the added hazards of sailing inshore along unknown coasts. The success of their voyages
depended on skins and oil, obtained by searching in the out-of-the-way
recesses of a world they were discovering for themselves. They hunted
in all kinds of weather, were often cold, hungry and wet. They were
bitter, and sentimental, quarrelsome and generous, foolhardy and cal-
culating—a peculiar breed of men, the product of their time.

Some of their experiences were never reported. Often the only narrator was an old man recalling adventures of his youth. A fortunate
exception was the account of the voyage of the *Onico,* a schooner sailing from New London, Connecticut, on October 22, 1799, under
Captain George Howe.[1] She was destined for a storm-crossed year.
Yet, little would be known of it but for a journal kept by William
Moulton, a whaleman of spirit. Moulton protested the blasphemy and
abuse of Captain Howe and bitterly accused him of brutality. He cited
the treatment accorded the Negro cook, whom Capt. Howe "beat un-
mercifully with his fists."

From the narrative it was evident that the *Onico*'s master took a
marked delight in sneering remarks about young Moulton's education.
He declared the dictionary was a "fogee" as he had found only one or
two words on any page that he understood! Early in the voyage the
master pronounced the crew collectively liars, thieves and villains, and
treated them in most respects as such.

The young journalist described the master of the sealing schooner
with a penetrating observation:

> Captain Howe . . . nearly six feet in stature, large boned and lean,
> light complexioned, naturally of a thin, pale smooth visage, sharp
> nose and thin lips; addicted to a sneerful smile; disfigured by a blem-
> ish in his right eye in which he is blind. In his temper capricious,
> jealous and implacably vindictive against whomsoever he has a spleen,
> and his rancour was not known to be in the habit of slumbering for
> want of a victim, during the passage out or whilst, taking seals at
> Staten Land.[2]

At Staten Land, separated from Tierra del Fuego by the Strait of
Le Maire, the sealers had a rendezvous rarely visited by any other
mariners. From Cape St. Anthony at its northwestern extremity,

where Bald Head rose, all around the island to Cape St. John, they had given the rough shore varied names—Ketchell Point, Cape Bartholo-mew, Lee's Harbor, Port Hatches, Tornado Harbor—until New Year's Harbor (so-named by the famed Captain James Cook), was reached.

The *Onico* arrived at Staten Land, January 20, 1800, and at Lee's Harbor, learned that the *Mars,* of Nantucket, lay across the island at Port Hatches. The *Mars* was under Captain Uriah Swain, a man de-scribed by William Rotch as a "smart seaman." With him as first mate was James Cary, another excellent whaleman, soon to make his own mark; as second officer was David Harris and as third officer Joseph Plaskett—all Nantucket men and future shipmasters.

The *Onico* put ashore a gang of men at Lee's Harbor, where the *Mars* had a shore-crew seeking seals, with Mates Harris and Plaskett in command. Moulton was in this crew from the *Onico* and deter-mined to cross the mountains to gain the deck of the *Mars* and throw himself upon the mercy of Captain Swain. Life on board the *Onico* had become almost unbearable. The Nantucket men sympathized with the youth but told him it was foolhardy to attempt such a dangerous journey across the island. But he decided to risk it.[3]

Soon after he began his perilous trip, Moulton discovered he was being followed—by Captain Howe with a gun. Climbing almost per-pendicular ascents, crossing morasses, dodging under cavelike cliffs, narrowly missing being trapped in landslides, he succeeded in escaping from his pursuer (who finally turned back), and reached Penguin Harbor, under Sachem Head. Here he was kindly received by Captain Swain. A few days later, the *Onico* came around into this harbor and Captain Swain, in accord with the law of the sea, upon demand gave up his runaway to Captain Howe.

After sealing here for the season of January-October, the *Onico* rounded the Horn, and arrived at Más Afuera in November. Cruising over toward Juan Fernández (where Alexander Selkirk, prototype of Defoe's Robinson Crusoe, had lived, and where the Chileans now kept convicts), the *Onico* took some seals before returning to Más Afuera. Here they learned from Captain David Ockington, of the Boston sealer *Belle-Savage* lately arrived, that his vessel had been captured by the Spaniards at Juan Fernández (Más Tierra) and had spent three months at Valparaiso recovering her.[4] A similar fate was in store for the *Onico*, but her master hardly expected it.

Leaving a shore-crew on Más Afuera, the *Onico* sailed six hundred miles to the southeast, to the island of Santa María. Here they found on December 6, 1800, the *Minerva*, of Salem, Captain Folger, and her sister sealer, the *Concord*, Captain Wyer; the *Nancy*, of Boston, Captain Hoyt, and the *Perseverence*, Captain Delano. By the end of the season here, the *Onico* had 2,550 skins.[5]

Captain Delano, in his *Voyages*, also tells of Santa María, thus:

> The island forms a kind of half moon, with its points extended to the eastward; but the northerly point stretches much more in that direction. . . . The island has been well stocked with black cattle, with most kinds of quadrupeds, and has had a family living on it for many years . . . but [the family] . . . was compelled to move from it on account of the English who made it a rendezvous in time of war. . . . It is a great place . . . for the American and English ships, as they can get wood and water with little trouble; and on such long voyages it is very convenient to exchange civilities with one another. One ship may be in want of something that another can spare. It is a very pleasant place for the crews to amuse themselves with shooting, fishing, getting bird's eggs, and playing ball. . . . They [the ships] come in from off the whaling ground, from sealing islands. . . . They can get water, and wood, and refreshments. . . . When the weather is clear, the main land will be seen to the eastward coming in from sea, before raising the island, as it is much lower than the main. . . . The distance . . . to the nearest mainland is about three leagues.[6]

Returning to Más Afuera, the *Onico* and her crew found themselves in the midst of another kind of danger. In the absence of the sealing fleet, three Spanish (Chilean) men-of-war had chased the American ship *Pegasus*, of New York, to Más Afuera. Here Captain Luscomb had landed on Christmas Day, 1800, and buried $40,000 in gold and silver.[7]

The Spanish men-of-war, commanded by Don Francisco Parger, searched the *Pegasus*, then landed on the island on New Year's Day, 1801, and rounded up the crews of the sealers stationed there, representing the ships *Mars, Onico, Perseverance, Concord* and *Belle-Savage*.

WHALE FISHERY

Courtesy of Harry Shaw Newman, The Old Print Shop, New York City

Garneray

DESTRUCTION OF TEA, BOSTON HARBOR, IN 1773
From The American Magazine of Useful Knowledge, Boston, 1840

Shipping Paper.

IT is agreed between the Owner s, Master, Seamen and Mariners of the *Ship Essex* of *Nantucket* where *Daniel Russell* Master, now bound on a Whaling Voyage *in the Pacific Ocean and else where*

THAT in consideration of the Shares affixed to our Names, we the said Seamen and Mariners, will perform a Whaling Voyage, from *Nantucket*, and return to *the say Port of Nantucket*. Promising hereby to obey the lawful commands of the said Master, or the other Officers of the said *Ship Essex*; and faithfully to do and perform the Duty of Seamen, as required by said Master, by night or by day, on board the said *Ship Essex*, or in her Boats; and on no account or pretence whatever, to go on Shore, without leave first obtained from the Master or Commanding Officer of said *Ship Essex*: Hereby engaging, that forty-eight hours absence, without such leave, shall be deemed a total desertion. And in case of disobedience, neglect, pillage, embezzlement, or desertion, the said Mariners do forfeit their Shares, together with all their Goods, Chattels, &c. on board the said *Ship Essex*: Hereby for themselves, heirs, executors, and administrators, renouncing all right and title to the same. And the Owner s of said *Ship Essex* hereby promiseth, upon the above conditions, to pay the Shares of next proceeds of all that shall be obtained during said Voyage, agreeable to the Shares set against the names of Seamen and Mariners of the *Ship Essex* as soon after the return of said *Ship* to *Nantucket* as the Oil, or whatever else may be obtained, can be sold, and the Voyage made up by the Owner of said *Ship Essex* or by their agent.

IN Testimony of Our free Assent, Consent, and Agreement to the Premises, WE have hereunto set our Hands, the Day and Date affixed to our Names.

1817	Time of Entry.	NAMES.	Quality.	Witness to Signing.	Shares.
	4 mo 1st	Daniel Russell	Master	John Webster	one seventeenth
1817	4 mo 20	Georg Pollard Junr	Mate	Jno Newbigin	one twenty ninth
1817	4 mo 20	Samuel Joy	seant mate	Pierce Armstrong	one forty seant
1817	4 mo 1	John Ramsdell	Boatsteerer	Walter Folger 3	one sixty seventh
		Henry Bunker	Boat Steerer	Walter Folger 3	one forty eighth
1817	4 mo 2	William Sayer	Sailor	Isaac Austin	one Hundred & tenth
1817	4 mo 2	Thomas Chappell	sailor	Crosby Winslow	one Ninty Fifth
1817	4 mo 2	William H Chase	sailor	Reuben Macy	one Hundred & Twentieth
1817	4 mo 2	William Ramsdell	sailor	David Allen	one twentieth
1817	4 mo 3	Owen Chase	Boatsteerer	Jno Lawrence	one sixty second
1817	6 mo 6	Henry Wm Ramsdell	Carpenter	Nathan Meader	one Ninty fifth
1817	6 mo 6	William Swain	sailor	Nathan Meader	one Ninty fifth
1817	6 mo 6	Barzillai Swain	sailor	Nathan Meader	one Hundred & five
1818	1 mo 1	Eyre Ober	Ship Keeper	George Pollard Junr	Twenty six cents per month
1818	1 month 1	Joseph Underwood	Sailor	Eyre Ober	One Hundred & twentieth
1817	6 mo 6	Benjamin Lawrence	sailor	Nathan Meader	one Hundred & ten
1817	6 mo 6	Obed Hendricks	sailor	Nathan Meader	one hundred & tenth
1817	6 mo 6	Hoxer X Pocknet	sailor	Nathan Meader	one Hundred & thirtieth
1817	6 mo 6	Joseph X his mark Gardner	sailor	Nathan Meader	one Hundred & fifty
1817	5 month 27	For dk Smith	sailor	Elisha Pope	one Hundred & fifteen
1817	5 month 27	Reuben Pocnet	sailor	Elisha Pope	one Hundred & fifteen
may 17		John X Williams	Steward	Samuel Hayris	one Hundred & fifteen
month 12 1817		Henry Jackson cook	Cook	Phillip Hunter	one Hundred & fifteenth

SHIPPING PAPER OF CREW OF THE ESSEX, OF NANTUCKET
From Collection of Nantucket Whaling Museum

Remarks on Board Ship E Carey

Sunday

Nov 9. Commences with fine weather heading East on Southern tack employed In ordinary duties of the Ship So Ends this 24 hours

Monday

Nov. 10th Commences with strong breezes from East, steering by wind to South Emp breaking out the main hold and stowing Salt water to keep the Ship up. set up fore top gallant stay So Ends this 24 hours.

Tuesday

Nov. 11 Commences with good breezes from East Steering a SE course under all sail Emp setting up rigging and other Jobs at 1 P.M. kept off South 4 P.M. saw an Island the name of which I do not know So Ends 5——

Bound to New Bedford.

Wednesday

Nov 12. This day commences with fine weather steering to SW under all sail at so Still saw an Island which appears to be uninhabited sent in two boats for fish at 6 P.M. returned to Ship with Coconuts

CAPTAIN TIMOTHY FOLGER, OF NANTUCKET   J. S. Copley
From the Collection of the Metropolitan Museum of Art, New York City

A CHART OF THE GULF STREAM

Benjamin Franklin after Timothy Folger

From Transactions of the American Philosophical Society

KILLING SEA-ELEPHANTS ON DESOLATION ISLAND

From original drawing owned by Mrs. Lincoln Ceely

W. T. Peters

VIEW IN OTAHEITE, MATAVAI BAY

Walters

THE WHALESHIP SYREN, OF LONDON, ENGLAND
From Collection of Nantucket Whaling Museum

VIEW OF ANTARCTIC CONTINENT

C. Wilkes

Reefs and Islands in the South
Pacific not laid down in the Charts

——————————————————

                                    Lat — Long
Shoal on which the "Griminga" was lost
                        19°·50·S. 161·30·E.
Reef — — — — — — — 26=00 S. 177=00 W
Shoal — — — — — — — 20 = 35.S. 162 = 32 E
Reef — — — — — — — 27 = 00 S. 146=17 W
Reef — — — — — — — 9 = 45.S. 168 = 12 E
Island — — — — — — 11 = 35.S. 165 = 18 W
Reef — — — — — — — 21 = 51.S 175 = 29 W

Reef to the N.W. of Tegees by Capt Carter
                        15 = 44.S. 176 = 25 E

There is a reef bearing from Boscawans island
N ¾ E. to N ½ E. distant about 18 miles it is in
detached peices and breaks heavly when there is
any swell on
  About 15 miles West from Honga Tonga there is
a rock under water an American Ship was lost

EARLY LIFE AT CARLTON.

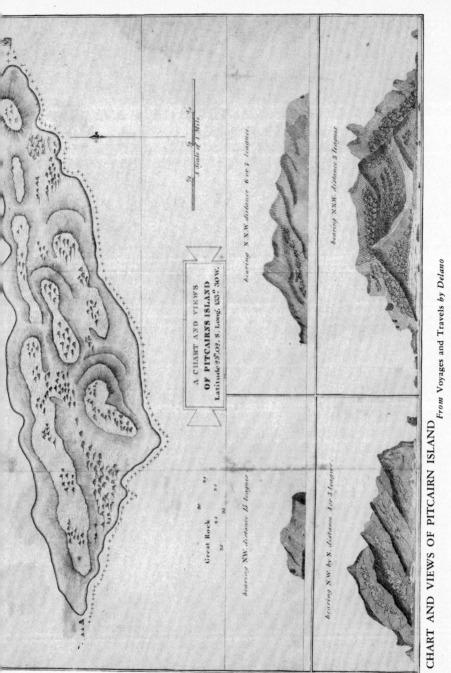

A CHART AND VIEWS
OF PITCAIRNS ISLAND
Latitude 25°.02. S. Long. 133°.30.W.

A Scale of 1 Mile.

Great Rock

bearing N.N.W distance 6 or 7 leagues

bearing N.N.W. distance 3 leagues

bearing NW distance 15 leagues

bearing N.W. by N. distance 4 or 5 leagues

CHART AND VIEWS OF PITCAIRN ISLAND *From Voyages and Travels by Delano*

J. E. Ray

EDWARD CAREY, OF NANTUCKET, OFF NORFOLK ISLAND
From Ship's Log in possession of Nantucket Whaling Museum

After taking a part of each crew, and some sealskins, the three Spaniards sailed away.

While the remaining sealing crews awaited the return of their respective ships, a considerable amount of the *Pegasus'* hidden gold, not found by the Spaniards, was uncovered. Now occurred an orgy of gambling never witnessed there before or since. In the rude huts, covered with the skins of their animal victims, these men of the sea thumbed greasy cards and won and lost money to an amount they had never known and would never know again. One gambling rout lasted thirty-six hours.[8]

The sealing ships returned, accompanied by the *Miantonomah,* of New London, commanded by Captain Valentine Swain, of Nantucket (brother of Captain Uriah), the new vessel being owned by the same merchants as the *Onico.* By this time Moulton saw a chance to escape the clutches of Captain Howe and he appealed to the assembled shipmasters. A court of inquiry was held on board the *Miantonomah,* and it was decided that Moulton had been completely discharged from the *Onico.*[9]

Captain Valentine Swain then advised Moulton to ship with him. But the young former supercargo saw in it a plot by the *Miantonomah*'s master to depose Captain Stowe for incompetence and thus control both New London craft, and so refused the offer. Instead he shipped aboard the *Favourite,* of Nantucket, under Captain Paddock.

Further trouble developed at this point. Captain Uriah Swain, entering into an agreement with Captain Luscomb of the *Pegasus,* sailed for Valparaiso to recover the money taken by Don Francisco Parger. The Nantucketer received permission to sail to Lima and press his claim, but when he arrived at the port of Callao he was detained on the *Mars* for three months. (Frederick C. Sanford claims that Captain Swain recovered the bulk of the money and returned it to the owners of the *Pegasus,* which ship in the meantime was wrecked at Más Afuera.)[10] A loss among the sealers also took place when Captain Delano's blacksmith fell from a cliff seventy feet high and expired in six hours.

At Valparaiso, the *Tryal,* Captain Coffin, of Nantucket, was seized by the Spaniards and sold to the government, its captors. The *Red-*

bridge, of London, Captain Barney, and the *Hannah and Eliza,* of New Bedford (late of Milford Haven), under the unlucky Captain Micajah Gardner, had been seized by the Spaniards at Talcahuano. To cap the climax, the *Onico* was eventually sold at Valparaiso for $2,200 and Captain Howe had to go overland to Santiago for the contract. During the long delay he caught a tropical fever and died, "broken in spirit." [11] Together with the *Leo,* of Nantucket, a whaler, these captured vessels were conveyed to Callao. The *Hannah and Eliza* and *Leo* were later released.

That the sealers were not averse to smuggling is apparent from various sources. The Spaniards, however, were often arbitrary and crude in their methods and showed resentment of Yankee enterprise. Living a hard life, these sea nomads were often guilty of hard practices, and their skullduggery found victims among themselves as well as the Spaniards.

With such dismal happenings, there was reason to expect armed resistance from the sealers or a hasty retreat from their favored haunts at Santa María, Más Afeura, Juan Fernández and the Lobos Islands. And so not all of them were captured. The *Sally,* Captain Storer, of New Haven, which sailed from Más Afuera August 18, 1801, had a great cargo of twenty-three thousand skins which were sold at Canton. Other craft leaving Más Afuera about this time, and safely reaching China included three Nantucket vessels, as well as one Philadelphia and one Boston craft.[12]

On the next sealing expedition to St. Mary's Island the *Favourite* arrived January 25, 1803. William Moulton recorded that here they found several new sealing craft, the *Huron,* Captain Moulthrop, of New Haven; *Dispatch,* Captain Howard of New London; *Rebecca,* Captain Pitts, of New York; *Brothers,* Captain Folger, of Nantucket; *Unicorn,* Captain Porter, of London, bound for the Northwest coast; three Nantucket, one French and one British whaler, all with Nantucket masters. Young Moulton then shipped aboard the *Dispatch,* of New London.[13]

Moulton had one more brush with death before his career as a sealer was done. While at the island of San Lorenzo off Callao, taking off some skins, the boat capsized in the breakers and one of the crew

drowned. The kedge anchor had fallen and held the boat in the breakers until the rope was cut.

"We righted the boat," wrote Moulton,

> and those who could not swim held onto her; those who could held
> on by the feet, or one hand, and swam with the other and towed her
> out from the breakers and rocks. We then collected our oars which
> were floating around and lashed them athwartships, and we endeav-
> ored, but in vain, to get the water out of her. Those of us who could
> swim strove upwards of two hours against the tide, to prevent its
> carrying us out to sea, when Captain Howard, excited by a concern
> for our safety, put out from the ship in the jolly boat and discovered
> our distress and came to our relief after we had been upwards of two
> hours in the water.[14]

On February 1, 1804, while homeward bound, the *Dispatch* spoke
the *Mars,* of Nantucket, five months out of Nantucket, under Captain
Jonathan Barney. She had returned from her Canton voyage (under
Captain Uriah Swain) and Moulton must have realized bitterly how
near he came to being included in a successful voyage—instead of
four years "knocking around" for little or nothing.

There were fur-seal hunters and hair-seal hunters. The hair-seal was
taken on beaches in the same manner as the fur-seal. One of the most
remarkable voyages was made by the ship *Huron,* Captain Moulthrop,
which sailed from New Haven in September 1802, took seals at the
islands of La Mocha, Santa María and Más Afuera. On board the
Huron was a young man named Joel Root, the supercargo, who kept
a journal of the voyage.[15]

Rounding Cape Horn in January, the *Huron* arrived at La Mocha
Island, between 40° and 35° north latitude, off the Chilean coast on
February 8, 1803. Here they sighted a number of hair-seal. Root, with
six men, lowered a whaleboat and started in pursuit, heading toward
the shore. The ship was to sail to St. Mary's Island (Santa María) up
the coast and return to La Mocha to pick up Root's party. His description of the resulting experience is a telling one. It shows how Dame
Fortune often smiles in a peculiar way. It also reveals another danger
facing the sealer.

Once launched in the whaleboat, they found the wind blowing offshore and a strong lee current, which they had not realized. The ship made a long board toward the mainland, leaving the boat to buck this unexpected current. As the wind increased, the whaleboat began to lose headway rapidly, drifting out to the open sea. Root tells the story:

> We continued to pull for the island for six hours, when we judged ourselves three times the distance from the shore that we were when we left the ship. The ship was out of sight and the island nearly so, and the seas running mountains high. Fortunately, we had a fine new whaleboat, twenty-five feet long and an excellent sea-boat. There being no prospect of reaching Mocha under existing circumstances, and fearing that the sea would be too rough, even for our excellent boat, we came to the conclusion to put away before the wind and endeavor to find some other land. We knew that the island of St. Mary's lay somewhere to leeward of us, and we were in hopes to be able to reach there.
>
> We now rigged a jury mast for the boat with one of the oars and made a sail of a pea jacket, lashing the collar to the mast and the skirts to the side of the boat, by means of which we rode briskly over the seas, keeping the boat's stern directly to the wind. Just at night the wind abated and a calm ensued.
>
> Hitherto, we had run directly before the seas, as otherwise the boat could not live. After the seas had a little run down, so that we could safely put the boat's sides to the waves, we began to think of drawing towards the main, which we supposed to be about forty miles distant, with a view of getting sight of it and then coasting about until we came in sight of St. Mary's. Now, seemingly to complete our misery, the mate and myself disagreed as to the course we should steer to bring us in sight of the Main.
>
> Being satisfied myself that the course he wished to steer would carry us further out to sea, I remonstrated, and used the most persuasive arguments in my power to convince him of his error, without effect. He at length told me that he was commander of the boat and that he should steer as he thought best.[16]

Under ordinary circumstances, Root stated he would have considered himself a mere passenger in the boat. But this was a case of life or death. He appealed to the crew and they supported him in his contention that the course set by the mate was wrong. Root then took charge of the boat.

> Having no land in sight nor any compass in the boat, we had nothing to direct us but the heave of the sea, and as we knew that the

wind blew from the south during the gale, consequently the seas must come from that direction. . . . It was clear that we must take the seas in over our starboard side in order to make an easterly course, and yet he insisted in taking the seas on the larboard quarter. The oars were now plied with unremitting diligence, and in the morning we found ourselves in sight of . . . the Main.

Root and his men did not attempt to land, as the surf was high. Skirting the shore they went some fifteen miles to the north, hoping to sight St. Mary's Island, but they came to a point of land making out from shore, where they landed. They did not, of course, realize that St. Mary's lay on the other side of the point, that it appeared to merge with the point. They were weary, having been twenty-nine hours in the boat.

The point where they landed was near a small Indian village called Areppo, about one hundred miles south of Concepçion. Danger was imminent. As soon as they got ashore, the natives surrounded them, took their axes, sealing knives and demanded even the buttons on the men's jackets.

After remaining two days, the white men made their way overland to Arauco, forty miles to the north, the nearest Spanish settlement. Here they were treated kindly and the commandant at Concepçion ordered they be allowed to go to St. Mary's, which they discovered, to their great surprise, was only twenty miles beyond where they had come ashore. But, upon returning to the boat, they found the natives had destroyed the boat to purloin the iron. A party of Chileans then took them to Concepçion, where they were thrown in prison.[17]

This seemed the end of their voyage. Fortunately, the *Huron*, searching for her boat, came into the port of Talcahuano, twelve miles from Concepçion, to look for the missing crew. News of their plight was taken to Captain Moulthrop. He would have been powerless to aid but for the intervention of a Captain Martínez, who arranged to pay $100 for their release. The entire incident was a drab beginning to their sealing expedition but it had a most unusual sequel.

The *Huron* returned to La Mocha Island, landed a party which joined a crew from the sealer *Rebecca*, Captain Pitts, of New York. Sailing for St. Mary's, the *Huron* found several Nantucket whalers and sealers there. Root observed that the seal carcasses along the rookery shores appeared to keep the seals in water from landing. He suggested cleaning the beach, and the result proved his contention.[18]

On April 29, 1803, Captain Moulthrop wanted to go up to the Lobos Islands, but Root, as supercargo, contended the ship should remain at St. Mary's. The captain and supercargo were supposed to consult as to the prosecution of a voyage, and, in case of disagreement, the supercargo, representing the owners, was to make the final decision. Root offered to take charge of a shore party at St. Mary's while the *Huron* sailed for a cruise to the Lobos.

When the ship returned on August 16, Root and his men had taken eight thousand skins. After landing some salt, the *Huron* sailed for La Mocha, to pick up the party left there. During their absence, Root's party secured two thousand more sealskins. On September 25, 1803, the *Huron* sailed for Más Afuera, having nineteen thousand hair-seal pelts on board. Now they were seeking the fur-seal.

Arriving at Más Afuera on October 8, 1803, the *Huron* found parties of men from other sealing craft had been landed. Root and eleven companions joined these, and the *Huron* sailed for New Haven with her cargo. On the island, Root had his men construct a hut covered with sealskins. During the ensuing season, they killed four thousand seals and skinned them—then went into winter quarters to await the return of the ship.

On March 4, 1804, a Spanish warship arrived, issuing an order that all the sealers must leave the island within four months or be thrown into prison. Root went out to the ship, and was surprised to find as its commander none other than Captain Martínez, who had saved him and his men from languishing in the prison at Concepçion, just a year before. Martínez treated the American kindly and when Root returned to shore he gave the sealers there the viceroy's warning, as imparted by Captain Martínez.

The sealers were anxious to get away. The *Huron* was due to arrive soon, and to book passage they sold their skins to Root who paid only $3,400 for nine thousand skins. He piled these skins on the southwest side, "in a convenient place." During the second sealing season he had obtained five thousand more skins for the ship.

On March 7, 1804, the *Huron* arrived to take aboard her crew and skins—as well as the several men on the island from other ships who wanted to get away—and sailed for St. Mary's to get another batch of skins. While they were gone, the Spanish armed vessel returned and captured all but two of the remaining sealers (these hiding in bushes), destroyed the provisions there and took away any skins found. But Captain Martínez, learning of Root's cache, did not disturb it. On meeting Captain Amasa Delano, who carried a message from Martínez, Root learned that the Spaniard had purposely spared the cache.

When the *Huron* sailed for Canton, Root put his own consignment of nine thousand skins on board. They arrived at Canton on November 16, 1804, where Root sold his skins at a profit of $5,000. He invested this in Chinese goods. The *Huron,* disposing of its skins, sailed with a cargo of green teas, and some freight for Hamburg, Germany, where she arrived after a passage of 156 days, including nine days at St. Helena.

At Hamburg, Root sold his Chinese goods and had $20,000 to show for his bargaining. He chartered the ship *George Washington,* of Providence, and sailed for St. Petersburg. Using a letter of credit, he purchased a cargo of "Russian goods" and sailed for New York, where he arrived on October 26, 1806.

After an absence of four years and four months, he arrived home. He found his wife and seven daughters "all in good health, but the children so much altered that I should not have known them had I met them at any other place than their mother's knee." [19]

And so, a sealing voyage begun under precarious conditions ended most successfully and happily. Root does not tell us how he conducted himself before the tribunal at Concepçion prison. But he must have shown a courage and bearing that attracted Captain Don Manuel Martínez. The investment that Root had made in that pile of sealskins at Más Afuera represented not only the shrewdness of the American but the esteem of the Spaniard. Together they meant a fortune for the young supercargo of the sealer *Huron*.

As has been stated, the first whaler to Australia was the British *William and Ann,* commanded by Captain Eber Bunker, of Nantucket, arriving in 1791. It was Captain Bunker who became the first whaler in New Zealand waters, and who took the first settlers to Tasmania in 1805, up the Derwent River.

He made several successful whaling voyages, discovered a group of eight small islands off the Australian coast in 24°–5′ south latitude, which he reported at Sydney in July 1803, commanded the *Governor McQuerie,* first Australian-built ship, and presented King George III with a pair of black swans, probably the first in England from Australia. He retired to a country seat in New South Wales, rounding out a full life. During World War II, Colonel Lawrence Bunker, of General MacArthur's staff, visited Captain Bunker's grave there.[20]

Other Nantucketers commanded British whalers in these waters— Captain Owen Bunker in the *General Boyd* and *Brothers,* Captain Thaddeus Coffin in the *Harriett,* Captain Brown Folger in the *Harpooner*—and others. "Ever since I have been in the service of New South Wales," wrote Surgeon James Thomson in 1804, "I have observed the most of the Commanders of South Sea ships to be Nantucket men." [21]

British whaling in these waters was restricted by the octopus-like monopoly of the British East India Company. In August of 1800, two British whaling firms, Enderby & Sons and Champion & Co., wrote to Lord Liverpool:

> The Americans, hearing that New South Wales is considered within the chartered seas of the East India Company, and that no British merchant can send goods to that colony without risque of seizure, have at times sent small vessels there with investments of goods on their way to India or the Northwest Coast of America, and have benefitted themselves much thereby. . . .[22]

Among the several American ships to benefit from a trade with New South Wales were a number of sealers. From that year when the first American vessel to go into Sydney, the *Philadelphia,* of that port, in 1792, at least one American craft a year visited that port—there being three (Providence) ships in 1794, and three in 1796, 1798, and 1799. There were two Americans in 1800, four in 1801, three in 1802 and 1803 and seven in 1804.[23]

The first of the sealers which port authorities recorded as coming into Sydney was the *Belle-Savage,* Captain Ockington, of Boston, which sailed around Good Hope and got into New South Wales late in 1799. We have already recorded her at Más Afuera in 1800 and 1801, when she sailed for Canton.

The first sealers at the Crozet Islands, one thousand miles east southeast of the Cape of Good Hope, were American craft. A group of five islands, the Crozets were discovered in 1772 by the Frenchman Marion-Dufresne, and lie in longitude 51° to 52° east, and latitude 46°-09″ and 46°-28″ south. They are barren, desolate islands, the haunt of sea-elephants and seals and sea fowl since time immemorial. The largest island, Possession, has a number of rude harbors where the sealers first went ashore, Ship Harbor, on the southeastern coast, being the best of a rough choice.

It appears that the sealer *Favourite,* of Nantucket, Captain Jonathan Paddock, and the *Catherine,* of New York, Captain Henry Fanning, were the first sealers there. Under her veteran master, the *Favourite,* another of Paul Gardner's ships, sailed from Nantucket in 1803 and went to the Crozet Islands for her seals. Fanning in his *Voyages,* claims his brother Henry, in command of the sealer *Catherine,* of New York, was the first sealer at the Crozets.[24] But secrecy was the sealers' watchword. It is easily understandable why the Nantucket and New York vessels worked so carefully to avoid each other. However, it must be noted that the bluff Captain Edmund Fanning was never reticent about advancing his family's claims.

But, basing deductions upon Fanning's own statements, it is apparent that the brig *Union* under Captain Isaac Pendleton, sailed late in 1803 from New York and could not find the Crozets. After this unsuccessful cruise, the *Union* proceeded to the southwestern coast of New Holland, where she ran along shore until she came to Seal Island (so named by Vancouver), in King George III Sound. Few seals were found, however, and consequently the *Union* worked her way along the coast to an island off South Australia which Captain Pendleton named Border's Island. Here seals were found in abundance and a good anchorage charted. Returning to Seal Island, a letter of instructions was buried, according to prior agreement.

While at Border's Island, a "substantial schooner" was constructed, the first vessel built in Australia outside New South Wales. She was named the *Independence.* The *Union* with her new consort sailed on a long cruise which took them through Bass Strait, southeast to South Island, New Zealand, to rediscover the Antipodes. Here were found large quantities of fur-seal, and an officer and eleven men were put ashore to remain a season. The *Union* then sailed to Port Jackson, arriving there in September 1804.[25]

The *Union* was charted at Port Jackson by Simeon Lord (a leading merchant despite his convict's background), to sail for the Fijis for sandlewood. Putting in at Tongatabu, in the Friendly Islands (Tonga Group) to engage an interpreter, the *Union* lost Captain Pendleton and a boat's crew and J. Boston, who was Lord's agent—all were massacred. Warned by the mysterious appearance of a white woman (the sole survivor of a trading vessel) the *Union* escaped.[26]

Mate Wright took the ship back to Port Jackson to report and secure replacements for his crew. Then the *Union* again sailed, this time to her fate, as she was wrecked in the Fijis and all on board who escaped the rocks were killed by the savages.[27]

The sealer *Favourite* arrived at Port Jackson early in 1805, having obtained her seals at the Crozets. Simeon Lord engaged Captain Paddock to sail for the Antipodes to rescue the shore crew left by the *Union*—and also to "rescue" whatever sealskins were there. The *Favourite* sailed on June 11, 1805, and after a long cruise on "the E. coast of New Zealand," she returned to Port Jackson March 10, 1806, with sixty thousand skins. Captain Paddock had picked up that part of the crew of the *Union* left at the Antipodes, together with their seals.[28]

When the *Favourite* sailed for Canton on June 29, 1806, the port returns show only thirty-two thousand on board. However, the account rendered by Daniel Whitney, the supercargo, to Obed Macy, agent, showed that 34,356 skins were sold at Canton for 80 cents, total value $27,484.80 [29]

But the ship's papers show that 87,080 skins were disposed of at Canton, January 8, 9, 10, 1807. As Lord had nineteen thousand of the *Union*'s skins at his Port Jackson store when he engaged the *Favourite* to rescue the boat crew at the Antipodes, it would appear that this shore party had taken 44,080 skins. As payment, two thousand of these skins then became Paddock's. Fanning alleges that Lord sailed in the *Favourite* to Canton, sold the skins rightfully belonging to the *Union*, put aboard China goods which he sold at an eastern port in the United States, and "made off to Europe with the proceeds." [30]

But in the *Favourite*'s papers there is no record of Simeon Lord. He remains either an opportunist or a victim of some unknown circumstance.

Before the *Favourite* arrived at Fort Jackson, to begin her cruising southeast to the Antipodes, another Nantucket sealer, the *Criterion,* Captain Peter Chase, had arrived (April 21, 1805). She also had been at the Crozets and was probably the first American sealer there and took thirteen thousand skins. Upon arrival at Port Jackson she had five boxes of sperm candles and two casks of tobacco in her stores.[31]

On May 27, 1805, the *Criterion* sailed on another of her mysterious voyages. She was back at Port Jackson again exactly one year later, with a full cargo of teas, silks, nankeens and chinaware, obtained at Canton, which her master declared was the sole property of himself and his owners. Despite this deposition, it is known that Simeon Lord had arranged for Captain Chase to sail for the Fijis in June 1805, but Governor King had refused to allow James Aicken (a pilot hired by Lord) to sail in an American ship.

To overcome this was simple. Sailing with the *Criterion* was the British whaler *Harriett*. The commander of the whaler was Captain Thaddeus Coffin, a fellow-townsman of Captain Chase, and once out to sea, Pilot Aicken was transferred to the sealer which immediately sailed for the Fijis and took aboard the sandlewood cargo. Failing to obtain permission at Port Jackson to land any of his cargo from Canton, Captain Chase proceeded to the Derwent River in Tasmania. But here, Lieutenant-Governor Collins also forbade the landing of any of the *Criterion*'s cargo, "although the Article of Tea was one of those comforts of which we had been for some months destitute." There was, indeed, a denial for an Englishman in a primitive land.[32]

In 1806, the *Criterion* took out a cargo from Sydney to America for Simeon Lord, the shipment valued at $30,000. Captain Chase was a shrewd trader as well as a successful sealer.

In returning to Nantucket in 1807, the *Favourite* brought back two Chinese merchants. These were among the earliest of the native Canton trading princes to visit Americans, and they were entertained by Paul Gardner, owner of the ship, and Daniel Whitney, the supercargo. The hong merchants returned to China within a few months, and came back to Nantucket again in 1814. An impressionable young Nantucketer recalled their unusual appearance in the streets of the town: ". . . their rich costumes and cap with red buttons upon the top, marking of a superior position in their own country." [33]

Here, in a Quaker community, which was a miniature kingdom of whalemen, these distinguished Chinese visitors must have felt a nearer kinship of ideas than they could have at any other place in America which they might have selected. But the vision of Paul Gardner and his associates in a lucrative Chinese trade was not supported by other merchants. The island's whole economy, past and present, had been whaling. By choice, as well as tradition, their future was also bound to it.

chapter xvii

~~~~~~~~~~

MUTINEERS' HIDEAWAY

*Captain Folger . . . found there an Englishman of the name
of Alexander Smith, the only person remaining of nine who
escaped in His Majesty's late ship. . . .*

—Lieut. Fitzmaurice, at Valparaiso,
writing to Sir Sydney Smith, at
Rio de Janeiro, October 10, 1808

THE WHALE OIL in the cabin lamp burned brightly, and the lamp
itself threw a soft shadow as the ship rolled in a gentle motion.
Leaning comfortably back in their round-back chairs, the two occupants of this ship's main cabin had talked well into the night, drinking
moderately of the West India rum which came from the squat little
bottle on the side-table and enjoying, with an equal relish, the Spanish
cigars close at hand.

As host, Captain Amasa Delano, of Duxbury, was proud of his ship,
the *Perseverance;* and his guest, Captain Mayhew Folger, of Nantucket, was equally proud of his command, the Salem ship *Minerva.*
Both were sealing craft, now anchored in the roadstead at Santa
María Island, off the coast of Chili, while their crews, for the most
part, were on shore in camps, where they lived while taking quantities
of seal pelts for the Canton market.

It was early in the year 1800, and the two shipmasters often met in
one or the other's cabin to pass the evening. Sometimes, after inter-
vals of separation, the two ships would meet at San Lorenzo, the Lobos Islands or Más Afuera, where they would heave to for a gam. In

later years Captain Delano recalled with pleasure these meetings. He wrote:

> . . . We had an opportunity to be together for months. His [Captain Folger's] company was particularly agreeable to me, and we were often relating to each other our adventures. Among other topics, the fate of the *Bounty* was several times introduced. I showed him a copy of the journal of Edwards [wrecked in the *Pandora* while searching for the missing *Bounty* with her mutineers], which I had taken at Timor, and we were both much interested to know what became of Christian, his ship and party.[1]

Thus, these two sealers—men of the sea—whose voyages took them into the unknown corners of the world, exchanged their own adventures and discussed one of the great sea mysteries of their time—what had happened to H.M.S. *Bounty* since that September day in 1789 when she sailed from Otaheiti under Fletcher Christian, chief mutineer, and disappeared completely? Wrote Captain Delano:

> It is not easy for landsmen, who have never had personal experience of the suffering of sailors at sea, and on savage coasts and desolate islands, to enter into their feelings with anything like an adequate sympathy. We had both suffered many varieties of hardship and privation, and our feelings were perfectly alive to the anxieties and distresses of a mind under the circumstances of Christian's, going from all he had known and loved, and seeking as his last refuge a spot unknown and uninhabited.[2]

Both of these American sailors were to recall their discussions on Más Afuera. When they again met—a decade later—it was the particular topic of their gam.

Captain Mayhew Folger completed his successful voyage on the *Minerva* and made another trip to the South Seas. In the year 1807 (April 5), he sailed from Boston again on a sealing voyage, this time in command of the *Topaz,* owned by Boardman and Pope, and reached the Cape Verde Islands without incident, where a quantity of salt was put on board.[3] Then began one of the most prolonged and discouraging voyages any sealer ever experienced. The *Topaz* was seeking islands never before visited by sealing craft. Captain Folger knew only too well the fabulous cargo awaiting him if he ever discovered such an island. His search, then, was for specks of land in the ocean wastes of the high latitudes. It was to be a voyage of discovery, but not as he planned.

Leaving the Brazilian island of Trinidad, he steered south and in August began hunting for an island known as Grande, said to exist in 47°–40′ south latitude and 38°–43′ west longitude. He searched in vain; and he had a similar disappointment in hunting for a Pepys Island, reported by Cowley (a shipmate of William Dampier). Recording in his log, on August 11, 1807, that he was convinced no land existed "nearer than South Georgia," Captain Folger steered east "in a high Southern Latitude, for the Coast of New Holland, and kept in a track quite unfrequented by former navigators, in hopes of falling in with some new Islands." Of this wide circle of sailing through the great South Atlantic, he wrote that he had "expended so much time in searching for them, that it was past the middle of September before I arrived off Kerguelen's Land, where I went to get a supply of water." [4]

The *Topaz,* in arriving at Kerguelen (Desolation) Island, had sighted its first land since leaving Trinidad four months before. During her voyage she had met storm and heavy seas, Captain Folger reporting, "as heavy a fall of snow as I ever saw," on August 15, and six days later: "Very heavy gales and a tremendous Sea such as I have rarely seen in the course of my peregrinations." [5] The ship had been strained so that she leaked 201 strokes of the pumps an hour and her boats were damaged. Even the bleak shores of frowning Desolation Island were an inviting landfall under the circumstances.

But, with a fortune in skins awaiting him on that island, Captain Folger was compelled by circumstances to lose the opportunity.

> When on that coast and near the entrance of an harbour, [he wrote a year later, and his log so records] there came on a violent snowstorm and violent gale of wind which forced me from the land, and thinking I should save time by running for Vandeman's Land [Tasmania], concluded to stear for that place, where I arrived the middle of October and procured a supply of wood and water in Adventure Bay. [6]

After leaving this bay, Captain Folger, in company with the British armed ship *Porpoise,* went up the Derwent River, "to a small settlement called Hobart-Town, from thence I sent letters to Port Jackson to be forwarded to you with a set of bills." [7] Here, also, is recorded in the log of the *Topaz* that Captain Folger went ashore for a meeting with Lieutenant-Governor Collins, and that some "Rum and Gin" were landed. On Tuesday, November 3, 1807, the *Topaz* sailed from Hobart-Town, but before quitting the land Captain Folger, "brought on board several natives to see the ship and landed them again." Abreast of Adventure Bay he saw a boat pulling out toward them but "supposing it to be a deserter's boat did not shorten sail." [8]

Clearing the southeast shore of Tasmania, Captain Folger again began his hunt for sealing islands. The *Topaz* crossed the Tasman Sea, rounded Stewart Island, off South Island, New Zealand, and sailed for the Chatham Islands, far off the east coast. Here he met Captain Scott in a sealing schooner from Port Jackson, who warned him of the large number of hostile natives in the islands. On the rocks off Pitt Island, the crew of the *Topaz* took the first seals of the voyage—six hundred of them.

On November 26, 1807, Captain Folger sailed south southwest to the Antipodes Islands where his fellow-Nantucketer, Captain Jonathan Paddock, had taken many thousands of skins a year and a half before. Now Captain Folger found "two Sealing Companies from Port Jackson—but not one Seal did I see on the coast. I made a short stay at this island but stood off to the southeast on discovery again." [9]

December dragged out the end of the old year and the *Topaz*'s cruise of discovery in the South Pacific was doomed to suffer the same result as that of the long hunt in the South Atlantic. The only islands seen were "ice islands," great towering bergs in 53° south latitude and 179°–49′ west longitude. Such a fruitless quest was brought to an end by the necessity of procuring water, and in the first month of the new year 1808, Captain Folger reluctantly gave it up, heading to the northward for warmer seas and fresh water—and seals.

Captain Folger now determined to sail for another island which had not been seen since its reported discovery, some forty years before. This island had been discovered in 1767 by Captain Carteret, of H.M.S. *Swallow,* and named for the young midshipman who had first sighted it—Pitcairn Island.

In his course from the high latitudes, southeast of New Zealand, Captain Folger put the ship on an east northeast course, gradually describing an arc and heading due north. It is apparent that he decided to swing west, after discovering that Pitcairn had been put down on the chart too far to the east, as his course by compass on the morning of February 6, 1808, was west by south ½ south. The logbook of the *Topaz* tells what happened:

> Saturday 6th February. First part Light airs at East . . . at ½ past 1 P.M. saw land bearing SW by W½W steared for the land . . . the said Land being Pitcairn's Island discovered in 1767 by Capt. Carteret. . . . At 2 A.M. the Isle bore South 2 leagues dis. Lay off & on till daylight, at 6 A.M. put off with 2 boats to Explore the land and look for Seals. On approaching the Shore saw a Smoke on the land at which I was very much Surprised it being represented by Captain Carteret as destitute of Inhabitants, on approaching Still more the land—I discovered a Boat padling towards me with 3 men in her.

In his whaleboat, Captain Folger looked at the mass of rock that was Pitcairn Island. The smoke which had first caused him such surprise was rising in an almost straight column. Was it a signal for aid? All the information about Pitcairn which he had gleaned from charts, agreed on the fact that it was not inhabited. He looked again at the towering island, then noticed as they drew nearer that there were many groves, green with trees and coconut fronds, occupying this side; also that the seas fringed the island with white surf, so that the shore looked inaccessible.

He turned to gaze at the rude canoe with its three occupants. Were these castaways from a shipwreck? They were dressed like natives—but there was something strikingly different about their features. As he met their own appraising glances, one of them called to him, and the words were in English—an unmistakable British English.

"What ship is that? Where do you come from?" The question was given slowly, deliberately, as if by direction—or memorizing.

"It is the ship *Topaz* of the United States of America," was the reply. "I am Mayhew Folger, her master, an American."

"You are an American? You come from America? Where is America? Is it in Ireland?" [10]

Five years later, Amasa Delano heard the story from his Nantucket contemporary himself. He repeats it:

Captain Folger, thinking he should soonest make himself intelligible to them by sounding out their origin and country, as they spoke English, inquired:

"Who are you?"

"We are Englishmen."

"Where were you born?"

"On that island, which you see."

"How, then, are you Englishmen if you were born on that island, which the English do not own and never possessed?"

"We are Englishmen because our father was an Englishman."

"Who is your father?"

With a very interesting simplicity they answered: "Aleck."

"Who is Aleck?"

"Don't you know Aleck? Well, then, do you know Captain Bligh of the *Bounty?*"

At this question, Folger told me the whole story immediately burst upon his mind. . . .[11]

Here it was—that place of mystery—that unknown spot, where Christian and his companions had sailed the *Bounty* some nineteen years before—Pitcairn, their island of destiny!

All this time of meeting, the three sons of the mutineers were regarding with a rapt curiosity the first people from the outside world they had ever seen. Captain Folger never told of his innermost thoughts on this unprecedented occasion, but perhaps he was thinking of those nights on another solitary island—Más Afuera—when he talked of this mystery with his friend Amasa Delano. Perhaps their conversation of eight years before returned to him: "We had both suffered many varieties of hardships, and our feelings were perfectly alive to the anxieties and distresses of mind . . . of Christian, going from all he had known and loved, and seeking as his last refuge a spot unknown and uninhabited. . . ."

And now he had found the hideaway of the mutineers—he was about to solve a mystery of twenty years.

From the canoe, dipping and rolling in the swells of the open sea, the three young men told Captain Folger that "Aleck" was the only one of the *Bounty*'s crew who remained alive on the island. In the mind of this Nantucket sailing master, there was not only a deep compassion but an awareness of this surviving British Navy man's position. Article 19, of the Articles of War, was a farreaching one. Under it, three of the six men found guilty of the mutiny (after being taken from Tahiti to England) had been hung for their part in it.

"Will you tell Aleck that I will welcome him aboard my ship?"

But when the canoe returned, only the three original islanders were still in it; Aleck, they stated, wished greatly to see the American captain. A few questions brought out the information that the situation ashore was as Folger had surmised. Aleck, with a fatalistic irony, had informed the colony of the penalty under which his life was threatened, and they had persuaded him not to come out—"the women being fearful for his safety."

The logbook of the *Topaz* gives the stark and sober record of the happenings of the next few hours:

> I went on shore and found there an Englishman by the name of Alexander Smith, the only person remaining out of nine that escaped on board the ship *Bounty,* Capt. Bligh, under the command of the arch-mutineer Christian. Smith informed me that after putting Captain Bligh in the long boat and sending her adrift, their commander —Christian, proceeded to Otaheiti, then all the mutineers chose to Stop except Christian, himself and seven others; they all took wives at Otaheiti and Six men as Servants and proceeded to Pitcairn's Island where they landed all their goods and Chattles, ran the Ship *Bounty* on Shore and Broke her up, which took place as near as he could recollect in 1790—soon after which one of their party ran mad and drowned himself another died with a fever, and after they had remained about 4 years on the Island their Men Servants rose upon & killed Six of them, Leaving only Smith & he desperately wounded with a pistol Ball in the neck, however he and the widows of the deceased men arose and put all the Servants to death which left him the only Surviving man on the Island with 8 or 9 women and Several Small Children.[12]

Those are the first written words which record the historic discovery of the *Bounty* mutineers' hide-out; they also represent the first account of the disaster among the mutineer colonists. Many attempts have been made to interpret the story of Alexander Smith. Six years later, upon the occasion of the visits by the first British warships, the *Briton* and *Tagus* (which also sighted Pitcairn two hundred miles out of its position as then placed on the charts), Sir Thomas Staines, commander of the *Briton,* wrote:

. . . A venerable old man named John Adams is the only surviving Englishman of those who last quitted Otaheiti in her [the *Bounty*]. . . . The elder Christian fell a sacrifice to the jealousy of an Otaheitan man, within three or four years after their arrival on the island. . . .[13]

Sir John Barrow calls the letter of Sir Thomas to the Admiralty, "the first official account received of this little colony," and in this the name of Alexander Smith is given as "John Adams." There is no deep mystery for this renaming of the surviving mutineer of the *Bounty*'s escaping crew. When Captain Folger went ashore at Pitcairn to meet the "venerable old man," their conversation had no sooner begun than Smith must have recognized in the Nantucketer a man of sympathy as well as curiosity. Recognizing the fear which Smith undoubtedly confessed, Captain Folger wrote of Smith in his log:

. . . he Immediately went to work tilling the ground so that it now produces plenty for them all and the [re] he lives very comfortably as Commander in Chief of Pitcairn's Island, all the Children of the deceased mutineers Speak tolerable English some of them are grown to the Size of men and women, and to do them Justice I think them a very humane & hospitable people, and whatever may have been the Errors or Crimes of Smith the Mutineer in times Back, he is at present in my oppinion a worthy man and may be useful to Navigators who traverse this imense ocean, such is the history of Christian & his associates.[14]

And so the gray-haired patriarch of Pitcairn became "John Adams," a man prematurely aged, with the marks of years of travail and anxiety etched into the brown of his face; a man who Captain Pipon, in his account, stated: ". . . although in the eye of the law they could only consider [him] . . . a criminal of the deepest dye, yet it would have been an act of the greatest cruelty and inhumanity to have taken him away from his little family. . . ."[15] Pipon recorded the fact that the first man to board the *Tagus* was Thursday October Christian, eldest son of the chief mutineer, who told a story revealing he was fully familiar with the facts of the mutiny. His open countenance and superb physique were admired by all on board.

It will be noted that in the account preserved by the pages of the *Topaz*'s logbook, the Nantucket sealer makes two references to Fletcher Christian; first, "that arch-mutineer," second, "Christian and his associates." Folger also made a third comment, which his friend Delano recounts in his *Narrative*: "Smith told Folger that Christian became sick and died a natural death after which the Tahitian men conspired to kill all the English husbands, and were in turn slaughtered by the women the following night." It is comparatively simple to deduce *why* the Tahitians killed the white men—the quarrel over available wives—but it would seem that the loss of such a leader as Christian determined the timing of the native uprising.

Some eight years later (June 2, 1816), in a reply to a letter of inquiry from Captain Amasa Delano, the Nantucket man wrote:

> ... I stayed with him [Smith] five or six hours, gave him an account of some things that had happened in the world since he left it, particularly the great naval victories, at which he seemed very elated and called out, "Old England forever!" In turn he gave me an account of the mutiny and death of his companions, a circumstantial detail of which could I suppose be of little service to you in the work in which you are at present engaged. The latitude is 23°–2′ south, and the longitude by nine sets of observations, 130° west. Capt. Carteret might well have erred three or four degrees in his longitude, in an old crazy ship with nothing but his log to depend upon.[16]

Sir Thomas Staines and Captain Pipon also observed that Pitcairn was erroneously placed on the charts in 133°–30′ west longitude, which Pipon states puzzled them as to the island's identity.

The letter of Sir Thomas, quoted by Sir John Barrow, mentions that they were astonished to find it inhabited—this despite the fact that, in Valparaiso, Captain Folger gave the information about Pitcairn to Lieutenant William Fitzmaurice and that officer, under date of October 10, 1808, wrote the extraordinary news to Sir Sydney Smith at Rio de Janeiro, who, in turn, forwarded it to the Admiralty where it was recorded on May 14, 1809. This letter of Lieutenant Fitzmaurice gave not only the story of Folger's discovery, but supplied the Admiralty with the name of Alexander Smith as the surviving mutineer, and gave the name of Kendall as the maker of the *Bounty*'s chronometer (presented to Captain Folger)—both facts clearly establishing the truth of the story of the Nantucket sealer.

The *Topaz* remained at Pitcairn all that day and the next, while

Captain Folger "tarried on shore with the friendly Smith and his truely good people." The hull and keel of the burned *Bounty* were still to be seen under the waters of the rocky and treacherous landing place. Among the gifts which were exchanged, Captain Folger received two valuable presents—the *Bounty*'s azimuth compass and Captain Bligh's ship's chronometer.[17]

It was late in the afternoon of Sunday, February 7, 1808, when the sealers again boarded their vessel. As the *Topaz* stood out to sea they looked with a new understanding at the high, rocky island which had been the secret home of a lost ship—the green of the trees and shrubs, clothing the hillsides and showing in lush, tropical grandeur in the valleys, and most of all the marks of the little village perched on a rude eminence overlooking Bounty Bay. And as they gazed from the ship, the little colony of thirty-five souls waved to them a sorrowful good-bye. It would be six years before another ship would chance that way to rediscover them and learn their soul-full story.

The *Topaz* sailed for the coast of South America, and on March 15 drew within sight of Más Afuera. Here, again, was disappointment— seals were very few and at inaccessible places. As several of the crew grew sick with scurvy, Captain Folger resolved to go to Juan Fernández [Más Tierra], further toward the coast, to refresh his crew. Captain Folger's record takes up the story:

> . . . I sent in the Boat with a letter from the Governor, requesting permission to enter his Port, which was readily granted, and promised me every assistance in his power—On the 20th [March] I anchored in the Bay, put the sick on Shore, etc.—On the 22nd, while the crew were variously employed & I was with the Gov. in his house, he made a signal to the officers at his Battery to Fire on the Ship—They Fired Eight 24-pounders at her, wounded our Rigging & Foretopmast, took all hands on Shore & put them to Prison and commenced robbing the Ship of everything they thought proper to take away. They first took all the Clothes on Shores, So that before night there was scarcely one among us all that had a change of clothing. The Gov. then declared to me that I was a Prisoner of War. . . . I was kept a Prisoner on Shore, the chief Mate with one Man was placed on Board under a Guard. They continued . . . robbery until the 14th of April, then arrived a Spanish ship from the Continent with a New Governor. By this time everything of con-

sequence was taken, bread and salt and provisions excepted—even our Boat Anchors & Sealing Clubs they took away.[18]

At Juan Fernández (Más Tierra) the *Topaz* lay at anchor until April 22, when she was taken to Valparaiso under convoy of the Spanish armed ship *Castor*. Upon arrival at that port, another search was made for contraband goods, but the officers conducting the inquiry finally gave Captain Folger a certificate stating that there was no cause for suspicion!

Captain Folger went overland to the Chilean capital at Santiago. For two months and a half he petitioned for the restoration of his ship, and finally received his clearance papers on July 22, 1808. He entered a plea for damages. He wrote to his owners in Boston:

> Whether I shall ever get anything is quite uncertain, for they seem to have no idea of Justice in this Country, tho' to a certainty a greater piece of Piracy never was committed. In the event of getting no Satisfaction here, I shall proceed to Lima. . . . If I fail in getting Satisfaction . . . I can see no other prospect at present but that of selling the Ship, as my People are nearly naked, the ship robbed of everything—Thus stands the business at present, and how it will terminate time must determine.[19]

After another long period of anxious waiting, Captain Folger was able to get provisions for his ship for the long voyage round Cape Horn and home. As the year 1808 was drawing to a close, the *Topaz* came safely into port, after one of the dreariest voyages in the records of the sealers. The difference between great financial success and dismal failure had hinged on the course taken by Captain Folger on his voyage of exploration—for it was primarily a pioneering voyage around the earth's southern frontier. Had his course been south and west of South Georgia instead of east, he would have found the immense rookeries of the unknown South Shetland Islands.

One of the articles stolen by the Spaniards at the Juan Fernández was the *Bounty*'s chronometer, the present of Smith to Captain Folger. Of this timepiece, Amasa Delano wrote: "The chronometer . . ., although of pure gold, was so black with smoke and dust that the metal could not be discovered." [20]

It is to be logically assumed that Captain Folger cleaned the timepiece, as it would probably not have been stolen had it remained in its disguised condition. After being at Juan Fernández, for no one knows how long, the chronometer turned up at Concepçion, south of Valparaiso, where it was bought for three doubloons by an old Spaniard named Castillo, who kept it until his death in Santiago early in 1840.

On May 18, 1840, a Mr. Moirat, of Valparaiso, a watchmaker, received the chronometer from Captain Herbert of H.M.S. *Calliope,* who had purchased it from Castillo's family. Moirat put the timepiece in good order, remarking on the beauty of the workmanship of the original maker. Inside the case was the inscription, "Larcum Kendall, London, 1771." Captain Herbert took the chronometer back to England, and it was presented to the United Service Museum, in Great Scotland Yard, London.[21]

Although the *Bounty*'s chronometer was gone from England over half a century, it never was actually carried completely around the world. When Captain Bligh approached Cape Horn, on his voyage to the South Seas, he was forced to turn back, and went to the Pacific by way of Good Hope. Upon her return to London, the *Calliope* sailed by way of China and Cape Horn, so that the chronometer never actually circumnavigated the globe.

As for the azimuth compass, also from the *Bounty,* presented to Captain Folger, on March 1, 1813, he sent it to Rear Admiral Hotham, commander of His Majesty's fleet on the New England coast, accompanied by a letter stating the facts of his discovery of Pitcairn and her colony.

> This compass I put in repair on board my ship, and made use of it on my homeward passage, since which a new card has been put to it by an instrument maker in Boston. I now forward it to your lordship, thinking there will be a kind of satisfaction in receiving it, merely from the extraordinary circumstances attending it.[22]

During the same year, Captain Mayhew Folger removed from Nantucket with a company of islanders and settled at Kendall, Ohio. He built a grist mill, later became postmaster of Masillon, and died September 21, 1828. His son, Robert Folger, was the oldest practicing lawyer in Ohio at his death in 1897! His grandson was named William Mayhew Folger and, entering the United States Navy, was a

Rear-Admiral at the time of his retirement. When Admiral Folger died, twenty-five years ago, his will bequeathed the logbook of the *Topaz* to the Nantucket Whaling Museum, where it now can be consulted.

The next record of Pitcairn Island was given by Captain Henderson, of the British trading ship *Hercules,* in a letter appearing in the *Calcutta Journal* dated July 15, 1819. Captain Henderson wrote that he had visited the island on January 18, 1819, and that there were then forty-three persons living there—an increase of eight during the decade since Captain Folger's visit. The *Hercules* carried letters to "John Adams" from his brothers in England, as well as a box of books. Captain Henderson reported that an American whaleship had touched at Pitcairn eighteen months before (1817) and left a whaleboat. He did not give the name of the whaler.[23]

In the *Asiatic Journal* for July 1820 is a report of a letter from the Society Islands, stating that a gentleman had published a letter in the *Sydney Gazette* (New South Wales) containing the account of an old Tahitian woman called Jenny who had been removed from Pitcairn by an American whaleship which had "come after Master Folger's ship and the two King's ships and before Captain Henderson." This ship had taken Jenny to the Spanish Main, thence to Nuka Hiva in the Marquesas, thence to the Society Islands where she remained. Clearly visible on her forearm, it was stated, were the letters, "A. S." and the date, "1789."

Whether or not "A. S." stands for Alexander Smith and "1789" the date of the mutiny on the *Bounty,* this account makes the second mention of an American whaler at Pitcairn in 1817. But its identity is still a mystery.

The first census of the inhabitants of Pitcairn was made by Captain Frederick Arthur, the Nantucket captain of the New Bedford whaleship *Russell.* This was the sixth ship to heave-to off that island and put men ashore. On March 8, 1822, Captain Arthur's logbook had the following entry:

> . . . At daylight sighted Pitcairn Island bearing S by E, seven or eight leagues off, stood for it and when we were within about three or

four miles from shore, were boarded by the most interesting crew of young men that we had ever seen; at noon we lay aback near the land. From all I had otherwise read and learned respecting the inhabitants of Pitcairn Island induced me to have the following notice posted up in the fore-part of our ship before we had any communication with the islanders:

"It is the impression of the *Russell's* owners that the most part of her company are from respectable families, and it is desirable that the conduct toward the Islanders should verify that opinion. As the Island has been hitherto but little frequented, they will be less susceptible of fraud than a more general intercourse with the world would justify. It is desired that every officer and man will abstain from all licentiousness in word or deed; but will treat them kindly, courteously and with the strictest good faith. As profane swearing has become an unfashionable thing, even aboard a man of war, it is quite time it was laid aside by whalemen, particularly at this time. As these islanders have been taught to adore their Maker, and are not accustomed to hearing His name blasphemed, they were shocked with horror when they heard the crew of an American ship swear and said it was against the laws of their God, their country and their conscience." [24]

To those who have, in recent years, read much of the wild orgies of whalemen at Pacific Islands, it is well to recall that before the years of the financial peak of the industry—1830-60—the ships which ranged the South Seas were commanded by a superior type of shipmaster. Tradition had given these men of the sea a background of religion and home which made them both God-fearing and self-respecting. It has been too long a mistake to regard the activities of the ships of the later period as characteristic of the earlier years—the true "golden age" of whaling—1783-1830.

Captain Arthur's description of his visit with the islanders has many enlightening aspects:

On our landing, the "Hill of Dificulty" was to be ascended; a job I could not myself have performed in less than two or three hours; it was done in much less time with the assistance of a steady young man named Robert Young, who helped me almost every step. When we arrived at the top, we appeared to be at least 300 feet above the surface of the water, having gone up a zig-zag path. The boat appeared directly under us.

We were then met by the venerable John Adams, who was attended by most of the women and children of the Island, and were welcomed to their shores in the most artless, yet dignified manner. After visiting a while, we were then invited to the village, about half a mile distant, through groves of cocoanut and other trees of large growth, which made an excellent shade. . . . We came to the village, which was situated on a gentle declivity, with a sufficient distance between the houses for a drying and bleaching their clothes. The beautiful prospect, regularity and neatness of their houses, with the joyous welcome of its truely hospitable inhabitants, made the spot enchanting.

Soon after our arrival, a dinner was served up, consisting of two roast pigs, fowls, yams, and plantans, but they declined partaking with us on account of its being their fast day; we concluded to wait until sundown, at which time they would be at liberty to join us. . . . We all sat down together . . . not eating until the chief of our kind entertainers asked a blessing in a very impressive manner.[25]

In a letter written by Captain Arthur and received by a gentleman at Baltimore sometime in August 1822, it was stated:

John Adams assures us, and from what we ourselves saw we have no reason to disbelieve him, that the island was inhabited before; though at what time it is difficult to conjecture. They found after their arrival many places where houses stood, burying places, and images representing the human figure, with other indubitable marks that they were not the first possessors of Pitcairn's Island. It is, however, certain that the aboriginals left at no recent period, and the trees which are growing on the house spots could not have arrived at their present size in less than a hundred years.[26]

During his stay, the commander of the *Russell* made his census, in which he tabulated 6 Adams, 19 Christians, 12 Quintlas, 7 McKays, 6 Youngs, 1 Williams—a total of 51. During the thirty-two years elapsing since the settlement of the island, there had been forty-nine births (two of these since dead), and eleven of the population of fifty-one he recorded as "active young men." These were the sons of the mutineers.

John Adams (or Alexander Smith) told Captain Arthur that when the tragic scene of the murder of the English and Tahitian men had been concluded, there were four white men left—"three of whom died natural deaths; the last one, except John Adams, the only survivor, dying twenty-two years since [1800]." [27] This is a different story from the one he told formerly. Captain Arthur continues in his journal:

> More than thirty years have elapsed since the destruction of the *Bounty;* of course but little remains that came out of her. I saw the copper boilers, the iron vice, an iron mortar, and a number of books, some of which I was presented with. On our arrival at Valparaiso, finding an American squadron there, whose officers frequently came on board . . . and Lieut. Slate appearing desirious of having these books deposited in some of our historical societies, I gave them to him for that purpose.[28]

As for the *Bounty,* and her inglorious ending, Captain Arthur wrote:

> The ship was anchored close in to shore, and they immediately landed everything that would be useful. Christian . . . during the time the articles were landing, was uncommonly ancious that all should be done quickly, that the ship might be immediately destroyed. In about seven or eight days, all had been taken from the ship that was worth preserving—and at about 8 o'clock in the evening, Christian with one other man went on board and set her on fire. She continued burning through the night.[29]

Here was a picture worthy of a great artist: A ship in flames, the glare from which illumined the black, high cliffs of the island, and as the yellow light flared against the lowering, smoke-filled sky, it showed the little group huddled together on shore—their faces like masks as they felt the awful fate of self-exile mounting within them as the flames rose higher and higher into the night.

Captain Beechey, in H.M.S. *Blossom,* visited Pitcairn in 1825. At that time he made a census which showed a total of sixty-six persons on Pitcairn—an increase of fifteen since Captain Arthur's visit in 1822, and of thirty-one since Captain Folger's rediscovery of the island. Of the total of twelve women who had gone to Pitcairn from Tahiti on the *Bounty,* six had died. Beechey recorded five of the remaining six women still living. Could the one remaining unaccounted be the "Jenny" referred to as going away on board that mysterious whaleship which called at Tahiti in 1817? [30]

In 1850 two Nantucket whaleships stopped at Pitcairn—the *Navigator,* Captain George Palmer, and the *Potomac,* Captain Charles Grant

—and both captains put their respective wives on shore. In February 1851, Matthew McCoy wrote to a friend in Nantucket stating:

> We now number in all on the island, man, woman and child, 160 souls, 78 males and 82 females. My brother William died since you left us, and so did the old *Bounty* woman Susannah [the last of the original company]. Mrs. Palmer, the wife of the Captain George Palmer, died at this place on the 27th of September last. Mrs. Grant is still among us and the little boy which was born on the 24th of Dec. last. . . .[31]

Thus the death of the first white woman and the birth of the first white child on Pitcairn are recorded in the same year—both "of Nantucket," while the Pitcairn islander writes at the same time of the death of the last member of the *Bounty*'s original band.

Of all the mariners who touched at Pitcairn Island, the man who first rediscovered it has a claim to that elusive immortality reserved for the great of heart. His voyage in the *Topaz* had been a dismal failure —a sad, long voyage. But, in finding Pitcairn, Captain Mayhew Folger felt something more than the mere satisfaction of a new discovery. In the first shock of his surprise, there was a fierce sense of accomplishment—he had been the one selected by fate to solve the mystery of the *Bounty*'s hideaway.

In the quiet of a summer's day, at his grist-mill in that small Ohio community where he had gone to live "ashore," whenever he listened to the water below, murmuring and sighing as it slipped through the millway, and felt his memories of the sea returning, he must have seen it all again.

There it lay, just ahead of the ship, solitary, almost desolate in appearance, a gigantic black pile of rock rising from the sea—a lonely, unknown refuge; an island, somber and mysterious. Above its craggy top, the sea gulls, circling and swooping, uttered cries strange to his knowing ear. The surf, moaning about its rocky shores, sounded a deeper note from that of other South Sea isles, as if the undercurrent of the brooding and despair, the solemn weeping which must have come from the very hearts of the exiles, was always to linger there— the never-to-be-forgotten, muted dirge of the mutineers.

chapter xviii

~~~~~~~~

"THEIR VERY PURSUITS IN TIMES OF PEACE. . . . RENDER THEM MOST EXPOSED IN TIMES OF WAR"

As the political affairs of the nation drew near to a crisis, the scenes of the Revolution became more vivid in the recollections of the people.

—Obed Macy, *History of Nantucket*

WITH THE ADVENT of the 1800's, the whaleships of Nantucket and New Bedford composed the bulk of the American whaling fleet. With the removal of the firm of William Rotch & Sons, from Nantucket to New Bedford in 1794, the mainland port began its upsurge which within the next three decades, was to carry them to an equal standing with Nantucket. In 1802, Nantucket had twenty-two whaling vessels and New Bedford thirteen. New London, Connecticut, was represented by one vessel and Sag Harbor by two. Adding to this total of whalers, a score of trading craft for Europe and a hundred coasters and the extent of the commerce of the whaling ports became of considerable importance.[1]

It was the custom of masters bound to the Pacific or Indian oceans not to fill their ships in these oceans but to round Cape Horn or Good Hope with well-trimmed holds and take whales in the Atlantic to complete their cargoes. Large cargoes of right whales as well as sperm were being landed. Voyages were lengthened to two and a half years.[2]

Among the first whalers to sail into the western Pacific by way of Good Hope was Captain Micajah Gardner, in the ship *Hannah and Eliza*—a Rotch ship formerly out of Dunkirk but now of New Bedford. Having lost a fortune in the capture of the *Active* by the French in 1799, Captain Gardner left Nantucket owners, as impoverished as himself, to take out the Rotch vessel. Following a trading voyage to Milford Haven in 1800, and an Atlantic whaling voyage the next year, he sailed for the Pacific in April 1804.[3]

Five days out, the whaler was stopped by the British man-of-war *Leander,* and ten of the *Hannah and Eliza*'s crew impressed into His Majesty's Navy. Forced to return to port to replace his men, Captain Gardner sailed again May 23, 1804. The ship made a good passage around Cape of Good Hope. On October 21, 1804, she reached Van Dieman's Land (Tasmania) bearing northeast to east five leagues. Continuing on to the New Zealand whaling grounds, she was the first American whaler on that coast (the *Brothers,* of Nantucket, arrived in July 1805).

They put in at Norfolk Island, a much better place to provision whaleships at this period than Port Jackson with its authoritative regulations. Captain Gardner went ashore on April 19, 1805, with his fellow-townsman Captain James Guinn, commanding the *Ann,* of Milford Haven, a Benjamin Rotch ship. Captain Gardner took aboard at Norfolk Island hundreds of pounds of potatoes, a quantity of "lemmons," and "onnions," eight pigs, thirty bushels of corn, ducks and fowl and fifty pumpkins. It cost $10 to truck the provisions across the island.[4]

In May, the ship was at Broken Bay, fifteen miles north of Port Jackson, where they lay for a week off Broken Beach, with plenty of wood and water. Heeling the ship to "pay her bends," they got her hull ready for the next long cruise. They also made a fid out of the native "beefwood" for the main topmast.

Cruising off the west coast of Australia until October, the ship returned to Broken Bay, going up the Hawksbury River there for two miles. Here she remained until November 20, 1805. Although there was no mention of it in the log, Captain Gardner's papers show that in November, he received a quantity of provisions from Port Jackson.

Among incidents was the smoking of the ship and the disappearance of Thomas Miller, a runaway.[5]

After another cruise on the New Zealand Ground, the *Hannah and Eliza* stood in for Norfolk Island, took aboard provisions and, in company with the *Ann,* made a passage to the Atlantic by way of Cape Horn. On September 24, 1806, the log records speaking a "packet from Bristol bound for Cork, who told us the Hook Light bore N.N.E. by compass." Once again, the close connection between Nantucket and her colonies was maintained—by a ship out of New Bedford, whaling off New Zealand, putting in at Milford Haven, Wales. The *Hannah and Eliza* was a William Rotch ship—the *Ann* was owned by Benjamin Rotch, then at Milford Haven.

Some years later, in July 1821, word reached Nantucket and New Bedford that Captain W. H. Sheriff, of H.M.S. *Andromache,* commanding the British squadron off Callao, Peru, had issued an important notice to the masters of British whaleships. Sheriff announced that, in regard to ships seized by Cochrane's Peruvian revolutionists' squadron, he could not recover them by force, as Commodore Downs, of the U.S. frigate *United States* was doing, until he had evidence that the property seized was bona-fide British. This is a certain indication that several whalers were still sailing out of Milford Haven and London, although owned at New Bedford or Nantucket. The Rotches maintained the Dunkirk connection until the 1830's. Captain Francis Baxter, of Nantucket, was knighted by the King of France because he had brought more whale oil into that country than any other man.[6]

The approach of the war of 1812 found the whaling industry once more imperiled. Young John Quincy Adams may have preferred the British stability to the French Empire's aggression under Napoleon, but Thomas Jefferson preferred neither and his attempts at neutrality aroused violent opposition in the New England ports.

There was a meeting at the whaling port of New Bedford, which pointed out that embargoes might be of value as a temporary measure but were ruinous as a national policy. Idealism always has been a taskmaster in politics and the result of the Jeffersonian theories are too well known to bear repetition. A black border appeared around every page of the *New Bedford Mercury* on January 20, 1809, and an editorial proclaimed "Our Constitution Dead," a greeting to the advent of President James Madison.

A divided nation was the result, and the far-flung whaling fleet found little or no protection by the government at Washington. The case of the *Atlas,* Captain Reuben Joy, is an example. Severely strained by Cape Horn gales, the ship put in at Coquimbo, Chili, in March 1809, to make repairs. After two days, Captain Joy was ordered out of the port, and as the *Atlas* still leaked badly he put in Callao. Although every effort was made to find the leak, the time allowed him in port was not sufficient and he was forced to depart.[7]

All during the cruise for whales up the coast and in the Galápagos Islands, the *Atlas* continued to leak badly. Captain Joy returned to the coast and put in at Paita, Peru, where another effort was made to find the damage below the water line. No sooner was he at sea again than the Spanish privateer *Vulture,* out of Lima, boarded him, seized his papers, took off sixteen of his crew and put aboard a prize-master and ten Spanish sailors. This was on November 6, 1809, and for a month after Captain Joy, his two mates and a boy were kept prisoners on board.

During the weeks of his imprisonment, Captain Joy tried vainly to obtain the release of the *Atlas.* When this was finally granted, he was ordered to sea with the ship's stores broken into and much stolen, sixteen of his men still impressed aboard the *Vulture,* and only himself, his two mates and a boy to work the ship.[8]

History was repeating itself with a vengeance. As the British cruisers ranged the Atlantic coast, the trade with Europe decreased, and the whaleships and ports found the situation steadily worsening. On Nantucket, many families bade goodbye to their island homes, to remove to the continent and comparative safety. The long travail of the Revolution was too fresh in the public mind to admit optimism for the islanders. War was too imminent to risk any delay. Groups of six to eight families at a time began to leave Nantucket, many of them going to Ohio to establish homesteads.

Captain Andrew Pinkham, of Nantucket, wrote to Walter Folger,

Jr., the island's Representative at the General Court of Massachusetts in Boston, as follows:

> It is probable that two hundred of our families will leave us, and amongst them some of our most wealthy people, and what is to become of those who are left behind it is hard for me to conjecture; at all events we shall have plenty of empty houses but that will not support our children.[9]

There was also the same old danger to the American whale fishery—the invitation of Britain for the Yankee whalemen to enter into the English service. Captain Pinkham expressed it thus:

> England has held out such fair prospects for carrying on the whale-fishing, some of our young men have gone there and sent for their families; in fact our situation at the moment appears alarming, in case of war, we are accessible on all points, and have not the means of defending ourselves against an enemy which has reduced the value of our real estate to almost nothing. . . . Should a war ensue, a few ships of war of either of the belligerents would convert all our whale-ships and take us all away together.[10]

This was the feeling of a veteran whaling master who had nearly lost one ship to the European fighters, escaping with a cannon shot through his bulwarks.

The situation in our maritime world at the approach of the War of 1812 was somewhat of a paradox. Nantucket again stood out as the greatest single whaling port in the world—yet she was the least suited geographically to maintain that position. To add to the competition from the neighboring port of New Bedford was the handicap of a narrow sand bar obstructing the entrance to the harbor. Petitions for governmental aid in dredging or erecting breakwaters had dragged over ten years with no result.

With the advent of the year 1808, Nantucket had forty-one ships, nine brigs, twenty-four schooners and forty-one sloops engaged in the whale fishery. Actually those making voyages in the industry were ninety-two vessels, the remaining craft being coasters and traders.[11]

The whale fleet of New England which sailed in 1809, returned in 1811 with excellent cargoes. The ports represented showed Nantucket to have thirty-nine ships in the industry; New Bedford, seven; Sag Harbor, six; Greenwich, Rhode Island, one. Prices averaged a dollar per gallon. Then devastation fell like a thunderclap. War was declared.

For the ships returning from the Pacific after three years of voyaging, there was only the hope that they might hear of the war so that they could seek a near haven. Fully seven-eighths of Nantucket's and New Bedford's mercantile capital was at sea.

The first whaleship taken by the blockading British fleet, following the declaration of war, was the schooner *Mt. Hope,* Nantucket, Captain David Cottle. After burning the schooner and her cargo of oil, the British put the whalemen on board a captured brig and sent them to any port on the mainland they could find. Next to be captured was the *Sally,* Captain Obed Clark, one of William Rotch's Dunkirk ships transferred to New Bedford. She was taken on July 20, 1812, and sent into Bermuda. The loss was estimated by the Rotch firm at $40,000.[12]

At Nantucket, in September 1812, the historian Obed Macy reported in his diary that the people were storing roots and digging peat for fuel, but the swamps being full of water prevented them from getting much. Captain Frederick Starbuck returned from Philadelphia with a partial cargo of flour. "The people came down to the wharf with their money to purchase," wrote Macy, "having been without for some time and were oblidged to return without any. The reason for scarcity is the great quantity shipped to Spain and Portugal and other neutral places . . . and the great call for provisions to support the western armies." [13] The distress of the poor increased as winter began.

Word was received of the capture of the *Aligator,* Captain Owen Swain, homeward bound from the Pacific with a full cargo valued at $40,000. She was sent into St. Thomas, West Indies. "Many were dependent on her voyage for sustenance," commented Macy, "which adds to the distress already experienced." A town meeting convened: "The great exertions of Federalists . . . I am fearful will result to the injury of the best interests of the place." [14] When a cargo of corn arrived on November 11, he wrote: "It is melancholy to see the throng of people with their bags."

The transportation of fuel and provisions was gradually being choked off by the British privateers and cruisers, as the Admirality plan for blocking the coast grew more effective. Of this period, Obed Macy, in his role as a contemporary historian, stated:

British cruisers were so numerous on the coast as to render it very hazardous for the coasters to pass which had usually supplied the market with bread stuffs. Late in the fall no bread stuff could be bought . . . and there was less wood than had been known for many years. Hundreds of the laboring poor might be daily seen in the streets, destitute of the means of subsistence because destitute of employment.[15]

The island of Federalists, the minority party, petitioned President Madison for relief, but the government at Washington was powerless to aid. Several months later, a petition similar in tone was ratified by a town meeting and sent on to Congress with Captain Gideon Gardner as a personal emissary. Nantucket was seeking neutrality for itself and the whale fishery. This was beyond the comprehension of a bewildered government.

The discouraging news of the capture of coasting and merchant vessels augured naught but the worst for the whaling fleet. A reward of $500 was offered to any Martha's Vineyard pilot who would pilot a whaleship safe into Old Town Harbor.

Like a doom, the gloomy predictions of the Nantucketers came to pass. Fate had a cruel sequence in the offing. Ships that had braved the elements during thousands of miles of voyaging fell, one by one, into the hands of the ranging enemy warships.

Few ships escaped. The *Alliance* (that veteran of the first voyage to Desolation Island in 1791) got through the blockade, and Captain Hezekiah Pinkham arrived safely at Newport. The *John Jay* reported herself safe at New Bedford. Having weathered many dangers, the *Mars,* under Captain Fitch, came through the blockade and into Chesapeake Bay in November 1812. After a short voyage of a year and two months, the *Golden Farmer,* of Nantucket, Captain George Swain, arrived at New Bedford with eighteen hundred barrels of oil, "perhaps the greatest ever brought here, valued at $70,000. She is owned by Zenas Coffin (14/20's) and Gilbert Coffin (6/20's). . . . A great favour to a large number of individuals as well as to the whole community. . . ."[16] Like ghosts the ships *Minerva,* Captain Chase, and *Brothers,* Captain Whippey, slipped into home waters from the Pacific, standing up through Vineyard Sound and getting safely into Old Town.

On April 4, 1813, a lookout on the south shore of Nantucket sighted a ship standing in shore. She proved to be the *Leo,* from the coast of Africa, under Captain Tristram Folger, who was then sixty-two years old. Obed Macy wrote: "There is great rejoicing over her arrival beyond anything in its nature I have ever witnessed." [17]

The British seventy-four-gun *Romulus* appeared one day off Nantucket Bar and sent her tender ashore with prisoners taken from several island and Cape ships. But Captain Sylvanus Crosby, arriving safely from New York, reported escaping a pursuit by "running among the rocks" at Brenton Reef, off Newport. Another coasting sloop, the *Yankee,* with Captains Peter Paddock and Daniel Hussey aboard was captured while running the blockade with a cargo of candles.

A prize crew was put aboard, but as soon as the cruiser was out of sight the whaling masters promptly took matters into their own hands. Captain Hussey, armed with a handspike knocked the British sailors down right and left. Captain Paddock, six feet, two inches tall, grabbed the prize master and held him headforemost over the stern quarter until he begged for his life, and surrendered the sloop. The recaptured sloop was sailed into Newport and her former captors turned over to the authorities.

When he returned home, Captain Paddock, an esteemed member of the Society of Friends was met on the "Square" by Captain John Cartwright.

"Friend Peter," queried Captain Cartwright, with a sly grin, "why didn't you drop overboard that fellow you held so long over the quarter?"

"Friend John," retorted Paddock, with not a little embarrassment, "we had lost our boats and I was afraid he would drown." [18]

This was the same Captain Paddock, who in command of the *Lady Adams,* preferred to take a whale at close quarters. Until his death at the age of eighty-nine he carried a scar on his left hand, caused by the force of the blow with which he smashed the British prize-master's musket to the deck while retaking the *Yankee.*

When the *Diana*, Captain David Paddock, of Nantucket, reached New Bedford in June 1813, and the *Samuel*, Captain Prince Coleman, arrived at the same port the following month, they brought alarming advices from the Pacific. News that a state of war existed between the United States and Great Britain had at last reached the fleet—but many shipmasters did not credit it. The *Samuel*, owned by the Cary family at Nantucket, was full of oil, but her sister ship the *Edward*, was reported captured by a Spanish (actually British) privateer. Now that war had broken out, the Peruvians had taken it upon themselves to capture whaleships of either of the belligerents—but as the United States was deemed the weaker maritime power, her whalers were considered a much more logical prey.

To the harassed people of Nantucket and New Bedford, there was no hope—it was merely a question of time when the last American whaleship would be captured or burned, and the rival British would have the great South Seas to themselves.

The British were going to make sure of their vaunted superiority, this time—they had armed their South Sea fleet of whaleships, so that each one constituted, in itself, a letter-of-marque as well as a whaleship.

Unknown to either the despairing people at home or the hunted whalers at sea there was at this very time a good genius preparing to salvage the American South Sea fleet. Rounding Cape Horn during the month of January 1813, the United States frigate *Essex* was heading for the whaling grounds. Under Captain David Porter, the *Essex* was beginning a voyage which was to make his frigate immortal and his exploits one of the most extraordinary of the War of 1812.

PART FIVE

The American Whaleman Becomes a Pathfinder in the World's Greatest Oceans

chapter xix

◥◡◡◢

WHALING MASTERS AND EXPLORERS

*It is impossible to examine the reports of our South Sea
Whaling captains without realizing the value of that mighty
mass of rude materials which they have furnished us. To
have these materials carefully analyzed is the bounden duty
of government.*

—J. N. Reynolds, in
Report of Congress,
September 24, 1828

FOLLOWING CLOSELY after the peace of 1815, the whalemen of Nantucket and New Bedford again took up their "business in the
great waters," this time with renewed determination. The very first
decade after the resumption of whaling saw the creation of an American whaling fleet which was to be the nucleus of that future assemblage
—that myriad number which would characterize the "palmy days" of
the industry—some seven hundred sail.

Natural changes had developed larger ships, costing more than ever
to outfit. These brought home larger cargoes but remained away from
home on an average of three years each voyage. Larger ships and
larger crews brought about an increase in the number of men in
outfitting businesses on shore—boatbuilders, cordage makers, iron and
brass foundrymen, ship chandlers, riggers, etc. Profits became greater;
individual merchant and shipowners' firms became prosperous; the
seaman's "lay" increased considerably.

Obed Macy noted that a "system of long credits" was introduced in

1815 which benefited the industry in a new way, "since more ships and more men were thereby employed." [1] Naturally, some financial failures resulted in over-investment, but the fleet, once more off to a good start, gradually brought in handsome returns. The recovery by the center of the industry—Nantucket—was nothing more nor less than astonishing.

From the less than two dozen ships remaining from her once-proud fleet, Nantucket, during the next five years (1815-1820) expanded her fleet to sixty-one ships and brigs, and by 1822 had increased its fleet to a total of seventy-five ships and seven brigs. Other ports—notably New London, Sag Harbor and Westport—now joined Nantucket, New Bedford and Fairhaven.

The demand for oil was increased by the failure of the British northern fishery. Porter had swept the British whalers from the eastern Pacific, and the Spanish patriot forces controlled several of the ports in Chile and Peru. Most of the whaleships in the Pacific had kept pretty much to the west coast, cruising "on shore" grounds from Cape Horn to the Galápagos Islands. Whales became scarce. As a result, the whaleships in the Pacific began to range farther out into the South Seas, searching for new whaling grounds.

It was Captain George Washington Gardner, Sr., of the *Globe,* of Nantucket, who made the first of the important discoveries. Late in the year 1818, he took a large number of sperm whales a thousand miles off the coast of Peru. These new grounds were thereafter called the "offshore grounds" and were roughly situated between the eightieth and ninetieth degrees of west longitude, around latitude 25° south. Returning in May 1820 with a full ship, Captain Gardner's voyage gave prompt answer to the pessimistic report of Captain George Swain, 2d, who had arrived in November 1819 in the *Independence 1* and gloomily predicted: "No other ship will ever fill with sperm oil in the South Seas." [2] Little had he realized how tremendous a future was in store for the whaleships.

As the whaleships entered the Pacific they headed for St. Mary (Santa Maria) or Valparaiso to "recruit" before beginning their voyaging in this ocean. But, where they once laid a course from Juan Fernández to Paita, then to the Galápagos, and returned south along the same course, now they headed for the offshore grounds, thence along the equator and south to the Society Islands. Of the thirty ships which sailed out of Nantucket in 1819, exactly one half sailed for the Pacific Ocean. In this fleet of fifteen ships were six new vessels.

New Bedford sent out twenty whaleships this same year and five of these went to the Pacific, while Fairhaven sent one vessel to the South Seas. As the total American whaling fleet then numbered sixty-six vessels, it may be seen that less than one third went around Cape Horn. But these were the pioneers for hundreds of other whaleships which followed them into the Pacific. They became the explorers, discovering islands never before seen by white men as well as finding many new haunts of the sperm whale.

The tremendous sweep of the great Pacific had challenged the foremost navigators of Europe for three centuries, and yet only Captain Cook, Admiral Bougainville and a few others had penetrated and written in detail of those portions of the mighty ocean which the whalemen were to explore so thoroughly. From the west coast of South America to the Society Islands the whaleships cruised—south, west and northwest of the Marquesas; or west to the Tonga or Friendly Islands, thence north into the Navigators, Ellice, Kingsmills or Gilbert Islands, and to the Marshall, Caroline and Mariana groups sailed these exploring whalemen. Another route followed was that of sailing up the coasts of Chile and Peru to the Galápagos, then heading for Panama, Lower California and New Albion (California) to San Francisco. Others laid a course westward on the equator, thence northwest to the Sandwich (Hawaiian) Islands, where Honolulu and Lahaina became the great whaling rendezvous.

These whaling fleets which sailed in 1819-20-21 had many adventures. One of the important facts about their voyaging is that several of them entered the central Pacific by different routes, thus contributing, upon their return, some valuable information for the fleets of New England.

Two American whaleships shared the honor of being the first of such craft at the Hawaiian Islands. The *Equator,* Captain Elisha Folger, sailed from Nantucket on October 31, 1818, while the *Balaena,* of New Bedford, Captain Edmund Gardner, left that port two weeks later. These two ships met at Honolulu on Oahu Island on September

29, 1819. They became the forerunners of the whaling fleet which was to make the Hawaiian Islands the most important such group in the Pacific. Both Captains Folger and Gardner were Nantucketers, having once sailed before the mast in the same ship.[3]

From the letters of Captain Gardner it is apparent that the whale-ships sailed north of the Galápagos Islands to the coast of Central America, Lower California and California before crossing the central Pacific to the Sandwich Islands. This is of interest in that it displays the whalemen's knowledge of the migratory routes of the sperm whale.

In November 1857, Captain Gardner wrote from New Bedford to his friend E. D. Gilman, Esq., concerning his arrival at Hawaii. In part, this letter reads:

> Being on the coast of California in the ship *Balaena,* of New Bedford, in company with the ship *Equator,* Capt. Elisha Folger, of Nantucket, scurvy made its appearance in my ship's company, and I came to the conclusion to put off to the Sandwich Islands for refreshments. Left the coast of California Sept. 3d, and arrived at the islands the 29th day of the same month [1819], came to anchor in Kealahekua Bay, Owyhee [Hawaii], in 17 fathoms of water. While at this place I heeled my ship to paint the bends.[4]

It remained for the *Maro,* of Nantucket, in 1819-20, to be the first American whaler to cross the mid-Pacific and, with the *Syren,* of London, became co-discoverer of the greatest of that ocean's famous whaling grounds—"on Japan." Here was a region embracing thousands of square miles, where great schools of sperm whales were found. First information as to the prevalance of whales off Japan's coast (the nearest land, however, was hundreds of miles away) came from Captain Jonathan Winship. This Boston captain, noted for his China voyages and trade in the Sandwich Islands, wrote about it to his friends in Nantucket.[5]

The owners of the *Maro,* in dispatching the ship on her second Pacific voyage, gave specific instructions to Captain Joseph Allen that, upon arrival in that part of the Pacific he was to sail west northwest from the Sandwich Islands. The *Maro* left Nantucket on October 26, 1819, and returned on March 10, 1822, with a full cargo of 2,425 barrels of sperm oil.[6]

Captain Allen discovered an island and a reef north and west of the Sandwich Islands. The reef he named Maro after his ship. Of the island he wrote:

> On the 2nd of June [1820] discovered a new island or rock not laid down on any of our charts—Lat. 25°–3′ North, and by a good lunar we found the Longitude when within 3 miles of the land to be 167°–40′ West—judge it to be 150 feet high, about 1 mile in circumference. It has two detached humps . . . We call it Gardner's Island.[7]

Concerning his voyage "on Japan," Captain Allen wrote:

> On the 22nd of May [1820] we took our anchors at Mowee [Maui, Hawaiian Islands] and steered northwest. . . . We got on Japan the latter part of June—had thick, hazy weather for about three weeks, but by the 2nd of July we had 250 barrels. We took most of our oil from Latitude 36° N. and Longitude 168° E. to 170° West. We went no further west than 168° E. Saw no ships while on the coast but plenty of whales. . . . Left the coast Sept. 17 for the Sandwich Islands, arriving at Mowee on October 27. . . . Shall proceed to the Coast of Mexico [Monterey, California] to spend part of winter and return to Sandwich Islands to recruit. The chance is good to fill the ship in another season on Japan.[8]

Although the shipmaster saw no other craft while cruising on his newly discovered whaling grounds, the *Syren,* of London, under Captain Frederick Coffin, a Nantucket man, was "on Japan" during that same time. Sailing from England in August 1819, the *Syren* arrived off the coast of Japan on April 5, 1820. After a voyage of twenty-three months, the *Syren* returned home with 2,768 barrels of sperm oil.[9]

The *George and Susan,* of New Bedford, under Captain Upham, while rounding Cape Horn into the Pacific spoke the *Maro,* homeward bound. Being advised by Captain Allen of the great numbers of sperm "on Japan," Captain Upham sailed for those grounds. The *George and Susan* was also one of those ships making the eastward cruise from the Sandwich Islands to Lower California.[10] Here was another staunch whaleship, built in the Acushnet River at the foot of Walnut Street, New Bedford, in 1810. Seventy-four years later, in 1884 she was cruising for whales in the Arctic Ocean. Her career rivals that of her sister ships the old *Maria* and the *Barclay,* both of which sailed for more than seventy-five years.

Another of the first whalers to the Japan Grounds was the *Emily*, of London, under Captain Joseph Russell, of Nantucket. Captain Russell took his wife, Mary Hayden Russell, on this voyage. This Nantucket woman sailed from her island home in 1822 to join her husband in London, taking with her a younger son, Charles. Her elder son, William, had shipped aboard his father's ship as boatsteerer.

Mrs. Russell was the first of her sex known to have embarked on a whaling voyage. Her journal is of unusual interest in that it records the courses followed by the whaleships during the decade 1818-28, when they were passing through the Dutch East Indies and on to the Japan Grounds.[11]

Sailing from England early in January 1823, the *Emily* reached the Cape of Good Hope in April. While on the voyage into the South Atlantic, the ship ran into a heavy storm. Mrs. Russell describes the sudden loss of one of the ship's crew thus:

> The moment before the sea struck us, our cabin boy had been trimming our night lamp, and when I knew he had left the cabin to go forward, at the instant my fears for him were excited. A search was made . . . but he was not to be found. Alas! he was gone with the others to render up their account. . . . Our dear William came to my room with the greatest calmness . . . "The hull of the ship seems to have not sustained any injury, but should it be otherwise, and this night is to be our last, we will go trusting in the mercy of God." He then . . . proceded with a lantern to examine the ruin. . . . To his great joy he found all tight. . . . The sea continued to rage with indescribable violence.[12]

The clannishness of the Nantucket whalefishermen has been demonstrated many times. But only to those exiled in another land was the full feeling of homesickness given when these Quaker whalemen met at sea. The sloop *Dispatch,* of Nantucket, Captain Christopher Bunker, was spoken. Mary Russell's journal reported: "Her master proved to be a man well known to my dear Father . . . coming from 'our own native Isle of the Ocean.' He was on that account made doubly welcome."[13]

On board a whaleship the captain had to be the master of his men; the minister to those of his crew in need of guidance; a legal advisor to others; an agent for his owners in port, and a doctor when medical treatment was demanded. But, in the latter case, suppose the patient is one of your own family? Mrs. Russell describes such an instance:

> The evening proving fine, I had a chair placed on deck to see the sun set. My whole mind was engaged in contemplating the magnificence of the sun when I heard a scream from my dear little Charles, who had the minute before left my side. Before I had time to inquire the cause his brother brought him to me with his arm broken just above the wrist joint. Such an accident on the land would have been distressing, but what were my feelings when I saw the child writhing in agony and no surgeon on board. He had been to the cabin and as he was returning [up the companion-way] a sudden lurch of the ship caused him to fall with his weight upon his arm, which snapt it. His dear father, with that fortitude and presence of mind that seldom forsakes him, took him below and, with a man to steady the arm, set it and splintered it up. The dear fellow bore the operation with courage that would have done credit to a man.[14]

There is much of interest in Mrs. Russell's reactions to a whaling voyage. She gives vivid (though unfortunately short) descriptions, as, for instance, on entering St. Simons Bay:

> This little sequestered town . . . looks like something built for the amusement of children. The lofty hills, or mountains, in the background give it such a tiny baby-house look.[15]

How would a mother feel, as watching from the deck of a whaleship she sees her husband and son, both in the same boat, approach and attack a whale? Mary Hayden Russell, of Nantucket, tells us:

> The long-expected cry "There she blows" was heard this morning. It set every one in motion. What a bustle! The first idea it produced was the ship is sinking, unacquainted as I was with such scenes. Here was a new scene to try my fortitude, my husband, my son expos'd to these monsters of the deep. What a comfort at that moment to reflect that they were in the hands of God who was as willing as able to protect them. I could truly say: " 'They that go down to the sea on ships, that do business in the mighty waters, they seeth wonderful works of the Lord.' "[16]

On July 4, 1823, the *Emily* was in sight of Timor. That Captain Russell had been in Copang (Kupang), the Dutch capital, before is shown in Mrs. Russell's notation that ". . . the Governor of Copang and his lady are particular friends of my dear husband." Upon going ashore she found a coach and four awaiting her—the governor's carriage. "Crowds had assembled on the beach to watch the uncommon spectacle, the sight of an Englishwoman. As it is a place where whaleships touch for refreshment, a white man was no novelty, but a female created a wonderful commotion."

The description of the governor's palace could only have been given through the eyes of a woman; and the parting gifts from the governor's wife to Mrs. Russell—a beautiful diamond ring, a golden chain, and a Chinese fan of exquisite workmanship, were fully appreciated by this lone woman. But who else could appreciate them on that whaleship?

Throughout the voyage among the verdant islands Mrs. Russell displays her keen sense of observation. "If all our voyage was to be as pleasant as this, coming to sea might be considered a pleasureable excursion," she wrote, on August 3, 1823. But the dangers of tropic fever lurked behind the lush shores of these inviting islands. Dili, in Portuguese Timor, had been a death trap for several whalers. It was at this island that Captain Moses Bunker in the *Minerva*, of Nantucket, died of "shore-fever." Mrs. Russell records that off Amboyna (Amboina) on a previous voyage (1818-1822) Captain Russell had buried his mate Hezekiah Coffin, "and where he only escap'd the jaws of death himself."

Off the Asia Islands, Mrs. Russell had again to watch, fearful yet fascinated, from the deck of the *Emily* while her husband put off for whales close by the ship. She wrote:

> My dear husband was soon fast to one, and in lancing another he had his boat's head completely broke off and his wrist joint badly sprained. The whales were so near that I could distinctly view the whole scene with a glass. My terror was extreme, and as he had set down low in the stern to keep the boat balanced, I concluded him more hurt than he really was. Under this impression, I was with difficulty kept from fainting. To my great relief, he was soon on board.[17]

From this valuable journal it is shown that the *Emily* had been one of the early ships whaling "on Japan." While off St. David's Islands (Mapia Eilanden) the entry states:

> Last voyage [1818-1822], Captain Russell took two of these simple islanders at their request and after the Japan season he returned one,

the other died. We were soon surrounded by canoes . . . the ship's name and the Captain's were very familiar with most of them.[18]

Captain Russell dressed the king of the island in a white shirt and a new straw hat, and presented him with two hens and a cock to breed. Mrs. Russell reported that the natives' only dress was a strip of cloth around their middle and that "they have a frightful way of frizzing their hair which serves to protect them from the sun."[19] These islands lay off the northwest coast of New Guinea.

An amusing incident was reported in September 1823, when the *Bacchus,* Captain Baker, of Calcutta, from Manila, was sighted and the master came on board the *Emily.* Captain Baker mentioned that he had spoken another whaleship, the *Cape Packet,* of London, also captained by a Nantucket man, whom he could "hardly distinguish from his crew. . . . Perhaps because he was a Yankee!" The British mariner went on: "'Had you been a Yankee, Captain Russell, you would not have seen me on board here, for I detest and despise these Yankees!' Little did he think he was at that time conversing with two of those detestable beings," wrote Mrs. Russell. "I think that when he finds it out . . . it will cause him to discard such useless prejudices for the future."[20]

The value of a woman on board ship might have been debatable in those days, but Mrs. Russell gives one reason why she was of considerable aid to the voyage:

> I have often had reason, since I left Nantucket, to bless the little knowledge I had of medicine, as it has contributed to take a great care off the mind of my husband. He examines the cases and reports them to me; this is his part and I am happy to say that the medicines I have administer'd have never failed of their desired effect.[21]

Under date of October 13, 1823, the *Emily* was at Kemar, in the Molucca Group, where she

> had the pleasure of finding Captain Coffin of the *Syren.* He was just arrived from Japan, where he had been very successful. Mr. Bunker, the chief mate, came on board to see me. He seems in very bad health and has nearly lost the sight of one eye from the effects of a severe wound received from the natives at one of the same Islands.

This entry thus records two facts. First, that the *Syren* was making its second voyage "on Japan" under Captain Frederick Coffin, her Nantucket master, and that most of his officers were Americans, as well. The reference to the wound received by Mate Bunker is explained further by Mrs. Russell:

> It was while the *Syren* was lying off and on the island of Pellew. The natives were very friendly and came on board in great numbers to trade for knives, fish hooks, etc., when without the least provocation they rose upon the ship's company, killed the carpenter and one seaman and wounded several more and for some minutes had possession of the ship, but Captain Coffin succeeded at last in driving them overboard and happily saved themselves from a general massacre.[22]

A further report on this escape of the ship is found in the record of the ship *Elizabeth,* Captain Eber Clarke, of Nantucket, which returned to her home port of New Bedford on April 6, 1824 (six months after the entry in the Russell journal). Captain Clarke told of the *Syren's* narrow escape, two men were killed and Captain Coffin, the mate, a boatsteerer and several of the crew wounded. At the first attack of the natives, the whalemen had raced to the shrouds to climb for safety, afterwards rallying and driving the natives overboard. The attackers and crew both wielded the deadly double-edged blubber knives spades, lances and even harpoons as weapons. Captain Coffin told his brother-islander that his "cook defended his castle alone, driving off every attack with boiling water." [23]

Within the three years following the discovery of the Japan Grounds, more than sixty New England whaleships made voyages to this Pacific field. In 1821 Nantucket sent twenty-seven ships into the Pacific, one third of which went "on Japan," while of New Bedford's twenty-two ships sailing to the South Seas, an equal proportion made their first cruises to this vast region where the migrating sperm, making their passage, were found in such great numbers.[24]

chapter xx

INTO THE UNCHARTED CENTRAL PACIFIC

Our American whaleships generally pass to the Pacific by the way of Cape Horn; others go by the Eastern route. . . . By these adventurous mariners, every part of the Pacific is explored, and many new discoveries are made, which are of great service to the cause of navigation.

—James H. Lanman [1]

THE SEA-HUNTER had now become an explorer in the world's greatest ocean. That indefinable part of his nomadic life—the urge to seek new portions of this wide, wide Pacific—had given him a dual role. He was no longer a mere blubber-hunter, a pursuer of whales; he was also an explorer, whose voyages were now supplementing those of the great navigators of all nations: Cook, Roggeveen, Bougainville, Tasman, La Pérouse, Dampier, Magellan and Drake. Manning a bluff-bowed, unwieldy craft, leather-sheathed, with hemp cables and oil-soaked decks, he steered into uncharted regions and located on the sea maps for the first time islands never before seen and rediscovered others which had been lost for half a century. The story of one of them is the story of most.

Seated in his cabin aboard the ship *Maro,* of Nantucket, Captain Richard Macy wrote a letter to Josiah Hussey, dating it, "Coast of Japan, August 16, 1824." This unusual and self-revealing letter reads, in part, as follows:

Impressed with a strong belief that great numbers of sperm whales existed among the numerous islands in the Pacific, generally known as the Society, Friendly, Feejee and Caroline Islands, I resolved to spend three months among those islands. I steered first for the Society Islands . . . to procure wood and water. The island I selected for that purpose is called Eimeo, and lies 20 miles west of Otaheiti. I entered the harbor on the north side of the Island, which is not to be surpassed for access and safety by any harbor in this ocean. I took my ship 2 miles up the beautiful harbor (entirely land-locked) and tied her to an old tree. The scene that surrounded me was truly romantic. The shores were covered with all kinds of tropical fruit, such as oranges, lemons, limes, cocoanuts, pine-apples, bananas and plantains. The beautiful mountains which encompass the harbour, and exhibit a lofty and majestic appearance, commence within a quarter of a mile from the shore and gradually ascend to the height of 2500 feet, covered with trees from the bottom to the top. I found the natives much more civilized than I had expected.[2]

This is not the language of a rough mariner, but of a shipmaster who possessed that exploring instinct which had been so long a part of these sea-hunters. On December 25, 1823, Captain Macy sailed for the Friendly (Tonga) Islands. While proceeding westward, he discovered three islands not on his charts. He wrote:

I believe them to be a new discovery, in consequence of which I have given them the following names: Elizabeth's Island lat. 21°-.06′South, Long. 178°–36′ West; Eunice's Island, lat. 21°–52′S., long. 178°–47′W., Macy's Island, lat. 20°–52′S., long. 178°–47′W. The land is very low and navigation dangerous, as they are surrounded with coral reefs which extend some distance from them. The islands are inhabited, and are covered with cocoanut and other trees.[3]

These are now called the Tuvanatra Islands and are just below the Eastern Group near the Fiji Islands.

In the journals of Captain Stephen Reynolds (apparently written at Honolulu), now in the Peabody Institute Museum, is reported, under the date of September 9, 1824, the arrival of the whaler *Mercury,* Captain Austin, at the Sandwich Islands.

Captain Austin had spoken the *Maro,* of Nantucket. Captain Macy in his cruise last winter [Dec. 1823] discovered a group of islands in 21° South Latitude, 178° West Longitude . . .

This helps substantiate Captain Macy's letter as well as to reveal the fact that he shared his knowledge with other shipmasters, a characteristic feature of the whalemen (unlike sealers).

Captain Macy's description of his visit to the king of Rotuma Island, north of the Fijis, is an example of his careful preparation against native treachery (shown in the attack on the *Syren*), as well as an exposition of his keen observation:

> Many natives came aboard to trade. . . . I stretched a line across the deck, and suffered no one, except my officers and crew, to go abaft it. I placed, abreast my cabin gangway, two machines which if put in operation would have wounded the whole of them in an instant. However, I had no occasion to make any use of them.[4]

With true Quaker decorum, Captain Macy referred to his cannon as "machines," realizing their value but not desiring to use them unless, like Captain Coffin in the *Syren,* he was suddenly attacked. Finally, assured of a friendly reception by these interesting islanders, he went ashore, and the account of his visit is again best seen by following his own description:

> On land I was immediately surrounded by about 1000 natives. . . . The king took me by the hand and conducted me to his palace, which was a large hut, thatched on the outside and neatly dressed on the inside with mats. The king introduced me to the queen, who was apparently much pleased to see me. I was seated on a clean mat and fanned by a woman on each side of me. The queen spread a table, which was a large wooden tray . . . spread with leaves; and the meal consisted of yams, bread-fruit, tarrow, fish, cocoanuts and other dishes, which were prepared under the immediate inspection of the queen. She handed me each dish separately in a green leaf, taking care not to touch her finger to either. . . .
>
> After dinner I lighted a cigar, which much astonished them. They appeared to be much surprised at my being so *white,* some of them reached over two or three times to touch me with their fingers. After smoking a cigar, I returned to my boat, which I found loaded with vegetables. On my way to the ship, I saw a vast number of canoes, some going to the ship, others returning to the shore. The scene reminded me of our Nantucket *shearing* [the annual sheep-shearing festival at one of the island ponds].
>
> The natives were remarkably clean, cheerful, friendly and hospitable; their complexion is about two shades lighter than the Sandwich

Islanders. They are in a state of nudity, with the exception of a little grass which some of them wear about their loins. They furnished me with everything the island afforded. . . . It was the best recruit I ever obtained since my going to sea.

On the 28th of February, 1824, I left this Island and steered North West for the Coast of Japan.

Such was the visit of an American ship to one of the "high islands" of the South Seas. In this instance it was the first vessel from this country to stop at Rotuma Island, which was to become one of the most popular provisioning places for the whaleships, and a veritable paradise in the Pacific.

Captain Macy's laconic statement that upon leaving Rotuma he "steered to the North West for the Coast of Japan," dismissed with but a few words his voyage of thousands of miles through the uncharted mid-Pacific.

When J. N. Reynolds visited Nantucket in 1828 to interview whaling masters in order to obtain information from them concerning Pacific islands, he wrote of Captain Macy:

> . . . a very intelligent man, he has long been engaged in the whale-fishery and has shown more than usual skill in his observations, as in taking a great many sketches of islands, reefs, coasts, etc., which will be found very useful to the [exploring] expedition.[5]

During his voyages Captain Macy ranged through the Pacific from the Japan Grounds to New Zealand; from South America's west coast to the Loo-Choo Islands; and from California to the fringe of Antarctica. He shared with Captain Jonathan Swain the honor of sighting the first Antarctic land discovered by American mariners—now known as Doughty Island, in about 59°–25′ south latitude, 120°–20′ west longitude.[6] Here he reported passing near enough to see the breakers, noticing many seals and observing the discoloration of the water.

It was the same Captain Richard Macy who first reported correctly that Duke of York Island (Atafu) in the Union Group was inhabited. As a matter of fact, Captain Byron (who is credited with its discovery in 1765), by reporting it as uninhabited, indicated that he probably saw another island. In his famous report to Congress in 1828, Reynolds refers to the conflicting reports about the island and remarks: "I venture the prediction that the whaler [Captain Macy] is correct." [7]

This supposition proved to be accurate, as Captain Macy's discovery of this island, and his description of it were subsequently proven by the visit of the U.S. Exploring Expedition's vessels, *Peacock* and *Flying Fish,* to Duke of York Island on Christmas Day 1840. Commander Wilkes, found it not only to be inhabited but that the natives had pieces of iron and some blue beads. He stated that this, "with the knowledge of trade . . . proved that they had before had intercourse with ships." [8]

Further than this, Captain Macy reported that the natives of Savage Island (Niue—east of the Tonga Group) were not to be trusted, and that the inhabitants of the Wytootacki and Navigator (Samoa) Islands were very fond of large blue beads—as the Exploring Expedition found twenty years after he traded with them. In 1824 when he landed on what he called Armstrong Island, one of the Hervey Group, the natives gave every appearance of never having been visited before:

> They would not allow him to walk . . . but carried him wherever he wished to go. They regarded him as a superior grade of being, and paid him every homage they knew.[9]

Macy was probably the first whaleman to stop at the Navigator Islands, and while in command of the *Harvest,* of Nantucket, in 1827 he discovered a group of wooded islands in the Carolines, now called Nomoi Islands. He also located islands in the Coral Sea, as well as Ujal in the Marshall Group.[10]

This particular sea-hunter deserves considerable mention for his contributions to the geographical knowledge of his time. He has a high reputation as an explorer as well as a whaleman. Of all whaling masters whom Reynolds interviewed, he was the most quoted.

Another of the exploring whalemen was Captain George Barrett, of Nantucket. He took out the *Independence II* on July 23, 1819, went 'round Cape Horn and reached the Pacific in November of that year. After cruising on the offshore grounds, he returned to Valparaiso, fitted out and spent the early season of 1820 in this part of the Pacific and on to the Galápagos Islands. Later in 1820 he was at the Sandwich

Islands where he learned of the new Japan Grounds. He immediately proceeded to that remote region where he cruised two seasons.

On his voyage south from "Japan," Captain Barrett steered east of the Marshalls, skirted the Kingsmills and entered the Ellice Group. His record for November 6, 1821, contains the following discovery:

> At 6 A.M. saw land bearing southeast 5 leagues [15 miles] distant, apparently a group of islands with cocoanut trees on them; at 8 A.M. manned the boat and sent her for the land to get some refreshments for the sick. . . . Found ourselves in the latitude of 9°/18'S., longitude 179°/45' E. by lunar, moderate breeze and pleasant weather.
> Nov. 7. At 6 P.M. the boat returned with a load of cocoanuts, found the land to be a group of islands, encompassed by a reef and inhabited. . . . Two men landed and were treated kindly by the natives. . . . Not finding these islands to be laid down in any charts, we suppose them to be new discoveries, therefore in compliment to Mr. Mitchell, owner of the ship, we named them Mitchell's Group.[11]

This description of Mitchell's Group is substantiated by the description given by Lieutenant Wilkes who visited them in March 1841, while cruising north from Samoa. Wilkes called them

> . . . an extensive ring of small islets, situated on a coral reef surrounding a lagoon. These are so far separated as to give the idea of distinct islands, which has probably led to their having the name of "group." These islets are well covered with cocoanut and other trees, which give them a sufficient elevation to be seen at ten to twelve miles distance. The reef which links these islets is awash, over which the sea breaks with great violence.[12]

This group, now known as Funafuti, was thought to have been the discovery of Captain de Peyster of the British armed brigantine *Rebecca* (late in 1819), who actually discovered Nuku Petau, its neighbor to the north. Captain de Peyster named the islands the Ellice Group, and the name was afterwards used to designate all of the islands from 5° to 10° south latitude and 175° to 180° east longitude. The pretensions of this skipper, who named Ellice Island, "in honor of my friend and benefactor, E. Ellice, M. P. for Coventry," [13] is typical of the sweeping claims made by those mariners who made but a single voyage to these portions of the Pacific and saw but a few islands. They can be contrasted with the whalemen, who cruised regularly through all these island groups and who were the first seamen to chart them accurately and to use them for "wood, water and refreshment."

Two days after his discovery of Mitchell's Group, Captain Barrett discovered another bit of solitary land, placing it in latitude 10°-45' south and longitude 179°-23' east "by a lunar." (He noted his variation at 11° East). Sending two boats to the island "to explore the coast," Captain Barrett reported it to be:

> . . . a small, low, uninhabited island about one mile long, guarded all around by a coral reef, against which the sea broke with great force —the land is not more than 15 feet above the level of the sea, but being covered with high trees makes it appear high; it can be seen 20 miles off in clear weather. The island not being laid down on our charts, we supposed it a new discovery and named it Rocky Island, on account of the many rocks that surrounded it.[13]

The charts today call this Mitchell Island, or by its native name of Nukulailai. Captain Barrett unfortunately died during his voyage home. It is highly probable that his influence on his mate, William Plaskett, had much to do with the latter commander's own explorations during subsequent voyages to the Pacific. Young Plaskett went from a second mate to captain, upon the death of Captain Barrett, but he proved this choice to be no accident.

Captain Jonathan Swain, 2d, in the *Independence I,* sailing out of Nantucket in 1820, discovered an island between the Samoa and the Union Islands, which he called Swain Island. Situated in 170°-45' west longitude and 11°-05' south latitude, it is a high coral island, well wooded with coconut and pandanus trees. When Captain Hudson, of the Wilkes Expedition vessel *Flying Fish,* sought for the island of Gente Hermosa off Quiros, in January 1841, he could not find it. But he did locate Swain Island, which he placed on his chart under that name "after the master of a whaler who had informed him of its existence." [14]

Swain Island is now an accepted part of the United States. By joint resolution of Congress on March 23, 1925, the United States Government decided to extend its sovereignty over Swain's Island, lying some two hundred miles northeast from Apia, Samoa. Since 1856 the island has been continuously owned by the Jennings family, the present owner, Alexander Jennings, having obtained it through inherited rights from his grandfather, Eli Jennings. In 1909 the Gilbert Islands (British) authorities attempted to tax the Jennings family but the action was later rescinded. The island is one and one-half miles long and one mile wide, with a brackish lagoon, and is entirely encircled by a coral reef. It has eight hundred acres planted with coconuts, making copra its principal export. Eli Jennings, the founder of the colony, married a Samoan princess.[15]

In the log of the whaler *General Jackson,* of Bristol, Rhode Island, Captain Stephen R. Crocker wrote on January 28, 1839:

> . . . Steered east, at 6 P.M. sighted land bearing N.W. distant 12 miles at 8 P.M. . . . at 6 A.M. . . . saw D'Wolf Island bearing E. by N., distant 15 miles. . . . At 10 A.M. saw the natives on shore from the masthead. At noon it bore N.W. 5 miles. Lat. by obs. 9°–26' south; Long. 171°–07' west.

In addition to this, Captain Crocker wrote:

> This island was discovered in 1835 on the 14th of February and called D'Wolf Island [William DeWolf, of Bristol, was the owner of the ship]. Low and well-wooded. I have landed and found the natives friendly.[16]

Wilkes' exploring ship *Peacock,* sighted this island five years later [1840] when it was named Bowditch Island (Fakaofo).[17]

Other ships in that pioneering fleet of whalers were also experiencing new adventures. The *Foster,* Captain Shubael Chase, which was built in 1819, sailed on her maiden voyage that year. On January 10, 1822, she was at Easter Island, that mid-Pacific island west of Chile whose great stone images have long puzzled historians. Here the whalemen were treated civilly by the natives. Captain Chase reported that the natives were divided into two parties which frequently went to war, "and when this happened they generally massacred all the prisoners." They furnished him with potatoes and fruit in exchange for whatever he was disposed to give them. He presented them with some seeds of different kinds and taught them how to use them, "at which they appeared to express a sense of gratitude." [18]

A year after the *Foster*'s visit to Easter Island, the *Paragon,* also of

Nantucket, under Captain Henry Bunker, touched at the island for supplies. He reported his visit thus:

. . . obtained sweet potatoes, yams, bananas, plantains, sugar cane, etc., all of which were brought off by the natives of both sexes who swam to the boat lying at the back of the surf, and even for their produce they took nothing but *whale-scraps* which they devoured with great eagerness.[19]

When the renowned Captain Amasa Delano visited Easter Island, he saw the remarkable stone statues,

representing human form of very large size. . . . Captain Cook says they are made of stone, but he does not mention so many as we saw, nor so many inhabitants. It is my opinion that they have populated it fast since Captain Cook visited the place and that they have built many of these statues and buildings.[20]

The opinion of this exceptional Yankee mariner is important. A population increase on Easter Island during the fifteen years between his visit and that of Captain Chase of the *Foster* is further shown by the latter's estimate of between five and six thousand natives on the island.

The *Foster* had a narrow escape from total loss as a result of one of the most unusual accidents ever sustained by a whaleship. Her hull was pierced by the sword or horn of a "horn-fish," which broke off inside the ship, having penetrated two inches of inside timber. By sawing the horn off, the water began to rush into the ship, so that she leaked a thousand strokes of the pumps per hour. Fortunately, the hull was patched so as to allow the ship to return home safely. The horn of this marine fish was brought home by the *Balaena,* of New Bedford, Captain Gardner, in June 1821.

By odd coincidence, another new ship, the *Fortune,* of Plymouth, under Captain Peter Myrick, a Nantucket man, suffered a similar accident. The occurrence was duly reported as follows:

August 5, 1824—The *Fortune* was struck near the floor timbers about midship by a swordfish whose sword went through the copper and thence through ¾ inch white oak plank, a 9-inch white oak timber, and a 2½ inch white oak ceiling, into the hold; then it passed through a white-oak 1-inch stave into an oil cask, leaving the point the distance of an inch and ½ in the oil. The sword broke off 2 or

3 inches from the outside of the ship and remained about 10 months when it was discovered at Talcahuano harbor. During this time she leaked in moderate weather 250 strokes and sailing quick 130 strokes per hour. The part which remained in the ship's hull was about 12 inches in diameter.[21]

The *Fortune* arrived home in September 1825 after a remarkably fast voyage of ninety-four days from Valparaiso.

But the *Loper,* of Nantucket, under Captain John Cotton, was not so lucky. Several years later she foundered at sea, homeward bound, with a full cargo, being on the equator in the Atlantic when she suddenly sank. The crew, led by Captain Cotton, took to their boats and eight days later arrived at Maranhão, Brazil. Insurance on the ship totaled $20,000, while her master and mate were partially insured. The case was tried before several courts, and when the Supreme Court of Massachusetts finally decided in favor of the owners of the *Loper,* it established a precedent in marine insurance decisions.

The legal question was:

> Is it evidence of negligent navigation so as to avoid a policy of insurance if the vessel is lost by a defect—produced by perils of the sea —which is secret and unknown to the master—who sails from the intermediate port with this hidden defect? [22]

From the evidence, it was shown that Captain Coffin had exercised the usual prudence in his care of the ship, and had not "hove her out" when last in port, homeward bound, because there was no indication of a serious injury. How could he have known that his ship had been or was going to be attacked by a horn-fish or bill-fish? The Supreme Court of Massachusetts finally ruled in favor of Joseph Starbuck & Sons, owners of the ship, the first decision of its kind.[23]

The importance of whaling in the commerce of the country was clearly established long before the thirteen colonies formed the United States of America. It was natural enough, however, to find laws and regulations pertaining to coastwise and merchant vessels which had to be re-interpreted when applied to whaleships.

For instance, according to an Act passed by Congress on July 16, 1798, a Hospital Tax was to be collected from vessels of the United States arriving from any foreign port and from vessels licensed for the coastwise trade. When, early in 1822, the brig *Charity,* Captain Barnard, returned to New York from a voyage into the South Atlantic and Antarctic Oceans, with sea-elephant oil and sealskins, Jonathan Thompson, Collector of Customs of New York, immediately requested the payment of the U.S. Hospital Tax. Captain Barnard and owner Delaplaine, protested. In a letter to Collector Thompson, Comptroller Joseph Anderson, U.S. Treasury Department, stated clearly:

> The act, it will be perceived, does not embrace vessels licensed for the fisheries; and *it was decided by my predecessors* that a registered vessel, in such a case, could not be considered as having arrived from a foreign port, within the meaning of the law.
>
> The mere circumstances of a vessel going into a foreign port for provisions is not, according to my views of the subject, such an act as should deprive her of the benefit of the decision alluded to.[24]

The State of New York passed an Act (to provide against infectious diseases) in March 1823. Under Section 34 of the Act, the State Health Commissioner tried to collect Hospital Fees from Captain Israel Paddock of the whaleship *Diana,* just returned from a voyage of nearly three years to the Pacific. The section of the Act authorized the collection of such fees from every vessel arriving from *"any foreign port or place."*

Attorney Anthon, for Thomas Hazard, owner of the *Diana,* and Captain Paddock, contended that whaleships procured their cargoes on the high seas and could not be considered, in the language of the statute, as vessels arriving from any foreign port or place, and further, that this expression referred to such vessels as discharged or procured cargoes in foreign ports—that the whale fisheries, being the nursery of seamen, were protected by law and no tax could be levied unless expressly named. As a support to his argument he offered the letter from the U.S. Treasury Department concerning the brig *Charity*'s case of the year before.

The counsel for the Health Commissioner, Mr. Heddon, insisted that since the U.S. Act contained the words "foreign port" only while the state law had added the word "place" so as to embrace vessels arriving from "foreign ports and places," that the state law was more extensive and hence included the high seas under the word "place."

Judge Hammond, who presided, ruled that such an interpretation could not be admitted—that if the ocean could be deemed, in the strict technical sense of the law, a "place" it must necessarily result that it be under the jurisdiction of the United States. Such an interpretation was fallacious, and, if allowed, would strip the whale fishery of its protection. He considered the interpretation of the law, as given by Comptroller Anderson, U.S. Treasury, correct, and the state law susceptible of no other interpretation, and thereupon gave judgment for the defendant, Captain Israel Paddock.[25]

Had the decision gone to the plaintiff, a precedent would have been established, and the whaling industry would have suffered a considerable set-back. When it is remembered that Great Britain had 132 whaleships in the industry in 1822, and paid over $200,000 in bounties that year, it can be seen that any change in competitive standards would have reacted to the advantage of Britain. At this time half of her ships were captained by American whalemen (principally Nantucketers). Inducements to other whalemen to serve as masters and officers might have tipped the scales again in Britain's favor.

In August 1823, the ship *Factor,* Captain John Maxcy, arrived at Nantucket to bring the news, among other matters, that the *John Adams* had been "spoken" three days 'round Cape Horn, bound for home. The *Adams* reported the death of her master, Captain George Bunker, 2d, and also the disappearance of her mate, Captain Seth Myrick, together with a boat's crew, which had been last seen being towed by a harpooned whale. Peter Green, as second officer, was then bringing the *Adams* home.[26]

The *John Adams* arrived on August 27, 1823, and Peter Green reported that Captain Myrick and the boat's crew had been lost on the previous April second, having last been seen heading into a school of sperm whales. The boat's crew, with Myrick, consisted of Leander Cathcart, of Nantucket; John Collins, of New York; Thomas Morey, of Plymouth; Edward Hinckley, of Falmouth and Caleb Eddy, of Warren, Rhode Island.[27] This complement shows the diverse places in New England which were represented in the whaleships' crews.

But the incident has another interesting angle. Peter Green, the second mate of the ship, upon whom rested the task of taking her home, was a Negro. Despite the fact that he belonged to a race then in slavery, on board a Nantucket whaleship he was an officer and his command, coming as it did through a process of harsh elimination, was nonetheless his—and he was master of his ship. Nantucket Quakers were strong anti-slavery advocates, and a Negro school and church were established on the island early in the nineteenth century.

The emancipation of the Negro on Nantucket went back to the early 1770's, and none other than William Rotch was the leading spirit in the movement. Rotch was one who believed no law in the Commonwealth justified slavery, and when his ship *Friendship* returned from a whaling voyage he directed her master, Captain Elisha Folger, to pay a young Negro named Prince Boston his share or "lay" in the voyage. The reputed owner of the slave, John Swain, brought an action in the Court of Common Pleas to recover the money earned by Boston, but the jury returned a verdict in favor of the defendant. Boston was then manumitted by the magistrates. Swain appealed this judgment to the Supreme Court at Boston. Rotch immediately announced that he would retain John Adams as his counsel in the case, "but Swain, discouraged by the feeling of the people, and the circumstances . . . never prosecuted the appeal. After that period all the slaves on Nantucket obtained their freedom." [28]

The editor of the *Inquirer* stated in 1822, that this "demonstrated the principles from which we hope some may never deviate in any shape whatever." [29]

A few years prior to 1825, while the whaleship *Paragon* was homeward bound, she fell in with the brig *Hunter,* just after crossing the equator in the Atlantic. The brig, bound for Norfolk, Virginia, had lost her captain and her mate had little or no knowledge of his position. Sizing up the situation immediately, Captain Bunker of the *Paragon* reported: "I put a black man aboard who was a navigator and recommended a northwest course." [30]

On board the whaleships of Nantucket and New Bedford, early in the nineteenth century, the Negro was a valuable member of the crew and his advance to an officer's berth was not unusual. When the *Loper* arrived at Nantucket on September 7, 1830, with 2,280 barrels of oil, after having made one of the shortest voyages ever recorded—fourteen months and fourteen days—the owners, including Captain Obed Starbuck, gave a dinner to the almost entirely Negro crew.

Perhaps the most unusual parade ever held on Nantucket preceded the dinner. Captain A. F. Boston, the grandson of the slave Prince Boston, and Samuel Harris, two Negro navigators of note, mounted on horses and carrying boarding knives for swords, led the procession, followed by the crew, shouldering harpoons, whale-spades, lances, and other whaling "craft." [31] Tradition has it that the voices of the singers made the cobbles on Main Street reverberate as the unique parade passed through the market place of the town.

Early in 1822 the editor of the Nantucket *Inquirer* commented:

> The place continues remarkably healthy for the season and business [import of oil] unusually dull. At present there is only one whale-ship in port, out of the 85 owned at Nantucket, and only one whale-ship has arrived and discharged her cargo at the bar this season—a circumstance unbeknown, we believe, in thirty years. On the 25th of October, 1810, there were 48 ships belonging to this port and none in port owing to the embargo and other grievances, all of the ships being at sea.
> Considering the great number of vessels engaged in the traffic at this place, the wharves are deserted. . . . We noticed there were in port here but 2 brigs, 6 schooners, and 36 sloops.

Out of the fleet of eighty-four whaleships at sea, thirty were in the Pacific Ocean. From the port of New Bedford, the ratio was similar, although the numbers were fifteen ships in the Pacific out of twenty-eight.

Nantucket was now on the threshold of her greatest whaling prosperity, while New Bedford was, in turn, getting ready to take over the leadership in the great industry. The next decade (1820-1830) was to see the faltering of the Quaker dominion of the whaling's island headquarters, and although there came a great surge of wealth there also came the choking of that spirit which had given Nantucket its century of supremacy.

As the Society of Friends lost its power, so did that driving spirit of the sea-hunters falter. For Quakerism, the sea, and whaling had become fused into a single spirit. Once one element began to die (although the end of all influence of the three was not yet), the others began to reveal evidences of final conclusion. When the end did come it was complete—like the drawing of a final curtain on the greatest drama ever created out of such elements.

chapter xxi

～～ᴗᴗ～～

ALL ADVENTURES DO NOT END IN GLORY

*. . . I ventured along the beach until I came to the landing.
. . . There were many tracks in the sand and the beach
broken up. . . . I searched around . . . scooped away a few
inches of sand with my hand and came to the face of a
man.*

—William Cary's "Narrative." [1]

N^O GREATER CONTRAST in successive voyages of ships and mariners
may be found than those of the whalers. The *Globe* went from
a highly successful voyage under one master to the terrible mutiny
episode under another; the *Lady Adams* completed great voyages to
China with sealskins, then met a mysterious end somewhere "on
Japan"; the *Essex* performed several excellent voyages, only to be the
ship sunk by a whale—deliberately rammed—an episode which brought
about one of the most tragic of whaling stories.

The whaleship *Oeno* was one of these fated ships. In 1821, she
sailed under Captain George B. Worth, returning in 1825 with a full
cargo. Captain Worth reported the discovery of an island about
eighty miles northwest of Pitcairn, in latitude 23°–05′ west. This
island was low, barren, and had a dangerous reef off its south point.
Captain Worth called it Oeno Island. [2] It is still known by this name.

Then came disaster. Aaron Mitchell & Co. fitted the *Oeno* out again
and early in November 1824, she left Nantucket on her second and

last voyage.[3] Captain Samuel Riddell was embarking on his first command, and had some good officers. He took his ship around Good Hope and into the Indian Ocean, shaping his course south of Australia and Tasmania to New Zealand, where he arrived (at Bay of Islands) on March 2, 1825. Here two men deserted, not realizing, of course, that it was the luckiest possible act.

Having procured wood, water and vegetables, the *Oeno* sailed north in company with the London whaler *Ann,* then bound home, separating from her near French Rock. With strong trade winds the *Oeno* sailed for Wallis Island, intending thence to proceed on to the Kingsmills. On April 13, 1825, they sighted one of the Tonga Group, passing Pysltaat's Island, and continuing north toward Wallis Island.[4]

Leaving the deck at sundown, Captain Riddell gave particular orders to keep a good lookout. Between two and three o'clock the next morning, the helmsman thought he saw white water and called out to Second Officer Drew, but the latter, in the quarterboat, was evidently asleep, as he made no reply. A few minutes later, the helmsman again saw the breaking seas foaming ahead. This time he called out lustily; the second officer tumbled out of the boat in a hurry—but before the crew could get into the rigging the *Oeno* struck heavily on a coral reef bringing up "all standing."[5] Drew immediately got his boat over the side, against the captain's advice, but managed to clear her and stood by until the day broke.

When daylight dawned, it was apparent that the *Oeno* was doomed. She lay nearly on her beam ends with the sea continually breaking over her. The starboard boat got away safely, so that Captain Riddell, two boats and ten men were safe. This left only the weather boat in which the rest of the crew hoped to make an escape.[6] Mate William Shaw and the balance of the crew were thrown into the sea when the tackle falls fouled as they attempted to lower this boat. All hands were saved, however, by the other boats, but the ship's boy, Barzillai Swain, sustained a broken arm.[7]

Leaving the wreck, the men pulled toward the shore of an island, some fifteen miles away, where they landed, after passing through an opening in the narrow reef. As they approached the beach of the island they espied some natives who made hostile gestures and Captain Riddell kept his boats in back of the low surf.

Then came a fateful consultation. Captain Riddell wanted to head for Wallis Island, into the track of the whaleships. First Mate Shaw urged they go ashore here as the natives (who had now ceased their warlike demonstrations) would probably not molest them for a few days. In the meantime, he argued, they could get some articles from the ship, needed for any open-boat voyage to Wallis Island, three hundred miles away. Seeing the white men hesitant about landing, a native came off in a canoe. This was taken as a friendly invitation to come ashore, and the decision was then made to land. It was the beginning of the end of the *Oeno*'s castaways.

They had landed at Turtle (Vatoa) Island, one of the Lau or Eastern Group of the Fijis. Guided by the natives, they were taken to the village where some twenty-five of the islanders lived. The men were tall and muscular, dark-skinned, clad only in a single strip of matting covering their loins, while the women were similarly garbed. Plying the shipwrecked whalemen with food and drink, the natives left them to sleep in comfortable quarters assigned to them in separate huts.

It was all part of a well-conceived plot. While the whalemen slept the natives went off to plunder the ship, burying their plunder on the shore. The natives became most friendly. In fact, Captain Riddell was congratulating himself on being able to remain until the full of the moon, when it was expected that the winds would moderate and they would be able to leave the island.

But the arrival of a fleet of twenty canoes brought a party of "a frightful looking set [of natives] being hideously painted with red and black, and all armed with clubs and spears." [8] These natives were quarrelsome and stole the few possessions of the castaways with an open defiance that was ominous. Captain Riddell hoped that by letting them take what they wished, they would leave without further molesting his crew. But some of the crew tussled with the savages and the situation rapidly came to a crisis.

William S. Cary, the ship's cooper, was keenly aware of the impending disaster. One day he was with Captain Riddell and the two mates and two of the crew in a lookout house, when one of the natives came in "with a sorrowful countenance, as though he had something dreadful to communicate. . . . No doubt, he came to warn us." Cary went on to describe the climax of the tragedy:

Soon after this kind savage left us, we heard a great shout in the valley below us. Captain Riddle started to his feet in alarm, said something as he hurried out of the house, the rest immediately following him. When we got down off the rock, all but myself took the path that led to the town. I took a by path leading across the island (well knowing what was going on in the town). A Sandwich Island boy followed me a part of the way then turned back. When I started I left Captain Riddle standing at the foot of the rocks. Which way he went I never knew. We parted never to meet again.[9]

Running across the island, Cary came to some rocks on the shore and, crawling into a cave, remained hidden the rest of that day and night. He heard the natives searching for him, but his place of concealment was not discovered. That next morning he ventured along the beach, keeping a careful lookout for the natives. When he came to the landing place, he found one of the *Oeno*'s boats which showed evidences that a struggle had taken place there. The beach was "broken up and had evidently been the scene of a scuffle."[10] Cary was prepared for the worst, but he wanted to make certain: "I searched around until I found a place which had been dug with something besides feet. I dug down a few inches with my hands and came to the face of a man. I uncovered one other, but could go no further."[11]

The dreaded facts now definitely established, Cary raced back along the beach until he regained his cave. Here he hid for three days, living on coconut meat and mills from a single nut. Desperately hungry and thirsty, on the third day he crawled from his hiding place and soon after was discovered. Cary slumped to the ground with his head turned so that he would not see the blows he expected would kill him. But, strangely enough, he was not molested and an old man took him under his protection.

Events now moved swiftly. The natives of the adjacent island of Ono returned—the same party which had massacred the whalemen. But the chief of Turtle Island had adopted Cary, thus providing him with a measure of protection. However, the next group to arrive came in canoes from the larger island of Lakemba brought by the news of the plunder from the ship. When these natives left they not only took the plundered articles, but appropriated the surviving white man.

The twenty-year-old Nantucketer was not unwilling to leave Turtle Island, as one of the new party was from the Tonga Islands and spoke a few words of English. Upon arrival at Lakemba Island, Cary, dressed like a native, was the object of much curiosity. It was made known that he was considered "a spirit," otherwise he would have shared the fate of his shipmates. The ability of Cary to clean the rusty muskets, salvaged from the *Oeno,* and to load and fire them, was considered as further evidence of his unusual qualities. The king of Lakemba adopted him and called him his son.

Cary's descriptions of the Fijian customs are of great interest. Among the outstanding incidents was King Toka's grand feast. The big event developed as follows:

> The natives brought provisions from all parts of the island and deposited them on one side of the square before the King's house, and retired to the other to await the performance which was about to take place by visitors from the Friendly and Navigator Islands. They collected provisions enough for two or three thousand people, and when several thousand spectators had collected, the King, with me by his side, was seated on an eminence built of stone on one side of the square.
>
> After all was arranged the actors made their appearance in two parties and took their stations in the square about 25 to 30 feet apart. One of them stepped out into the open square and, brandishing a cocoanut stalk in his hand, cutting many queer capers and challenging any one to come out and fight him. His challenge was promptly accepted by a young native from the same party and a smart fencing match ensued. At last one gave up and the conquerer was greeted by shouts of applause by the spectators. Two others took their places and the sport went on. After one party had their turn, the others came on and fought with their fists muffled in tappah [cloth], which seemed to delight the spectators as much as the club fight.[12]

This description of the Fiji carnival shows considerable similarity to any of the sport contests among so-called civilized races of the world today.

Cary became quite a favorite of King Toka. Nearly a year had passed when a surprising turn of events took place. A party of chiefs from the large island of Ambow visited Lakemba, bringing with them six Philippine sailors, who had mutinied and killed the captain and officers of a Manila brig. Cary learned that two European sailors had been spared. "I was very anxious to go to Ambow," he wrote, "but I made the King believe I would much rather stay where I was." [13] But the King kept him close by during their stay, for fear they would entice him away.

The opportunity eventually came. King Toka was invited to visit Ambow, and so a great variety of presents were prepared for the host.

> Twenty large canoes were fitted for the voyage, and when ready . . . the King went down to the squadron escorted by a large party of chiefs and subjects, five of his wives bringing up the rear and bearing with them the mats to sleep on and cooking utensils. . . . We set sail with a fine breeze . . . made our passage through the reef (which surrounds the Islands) into the open ocean. [14]

One day's journey took them to Emwaller Island, where they spent the night anchored near the shore. The next morning they steered for the island of Engow, where they arrived "with the aid of their paddles," before sunset and again spent the night at anchor. Cary described the ingenious method the natives used for anchoring—diving down and fastening their rope to a piece of coral or rock. Another day and another stop at another island was necessary before they started for the large island of Ambow. It was on the last leg of the journey that a canoe was seen coming toward them, which was said to have been dispatched from Ambow.

As Cary looked anxiously at the approaching canoe, his mind was filled with mixed emotions. Was this visit to Ambow to be but a step toward ultimate rescue? He knew that ships traded there for that strange sea-slug bêche-de-mer, and for sandalwood, both good for the Canton trade, but his knowledge of this traffic also told him that these ships rarely came into the center of the Fiji Group, where he was now located. Despite the hope that he might be able to disinherit himself from King Toka's parental clutches, Cary could not see his rescue as anything in the immediate future.

He watched the canoe coming to meet the squadron from Lakemba, apparently the official welcoming party from the king of Ambow. But when this single canoe drew up alongside King Toka's large craft, the chief native aboard it, apparently the emissary of Ambow, paid no attention to the king. Instead, this tall, half-clothed fellow, sitting motionless among his companions, stared only at the white man who sat at King Toka's side.

Finally the man from Ambow stood up and reached out his hand.

"William Cary," he said, in perfect English. "How are you, William Cary?"

But the survivor of the *Oeno*'s tragic crew was dumb with astonishment.

The stranger waited a little, aware of the shock his words must have created, and then he spoke again.

"Don't you know me?" he asked. And not wishing to prolong it, "Don't you remember a David Whippey?"

"Yes," Cary finally managed to answer. "Yes, I once knew him—he was a townsman of mine and an old playmate in Nantucket."

"Well," said the other, smiling, "I am that David Whippey."

And thus, in the middle of the most savage of the South Sea Island groups, these two young Nantucket whalemen clasped hands and welcomed one another.

David Whippey had sailed from Nantucket in November 1819 on board the whaleship *Francis,* Captain Fitzgerald, but left the ship at Quayaquil, Ecuador, where he shipped aboard the ship *Sydney Packet* for England. In England he found a berth aboard the whaler *Prudent,* and when this ship reached Valparaiso, Whippey left her—apparently not inured to a whaleman's life. His next step was to sign on a merchant ship bound to Sidney, and there went into an English brig trading among the islands for sandalwood.[15]

Whippey like the savage Fijis. He became a favorite of the ruler of Ambow, King Kakombau, and was the only white man ever to become a close friend to this important ruler. Whippey had secured his discharge from his ship and remained at Ambow.

He lived on the island of Ovalau, seven miles from the largest island of the Fiji Group, Viti Levu. The Nantucket man was a chief, and being a prime favorite of the powerful king of Ambow, when he asked that Cary be allowed to go with him to Ovalau, the monarch gave his consent—tantamount to an order.

Ovalau was the little kingdom over which David Whippey ruled. Cary described it thus:

This island was very much like the rest of the group, mountainous, well-wooded, with plenty of water. A considerable portion was under cultivation. It also abounded with beautiful flowers of the most exquisite fragrance and all kinds of tropical fruits. . . . The natives seemed very friendly. . . . Here I spent three days very pleasantly and then returned to Ambow to King Toka.[16]

William Cary's meeting with David Whippey meant his ultimate rescue was assured. The king of Ambow, like other of the powerful native chiefs along the coasts of Fiji's main islands, depended upon Whippey and another white man to help them fight the even more savage tribes which lived in the mountains. Cary joined Whippey in these tribal wars. One of these fights found an army of four thousand natives attacking a large stockade-protected village. After the battle was won by the Ambow party, Cary wrote: "We then marched down to our canoes, taking with us five or six female prisoners and some of the dead bodies for a cannibal feast when we got home." [17]

Cary now looked about for a way to better his lot. With Whippey to advise him, he decided to make his temporary home on the island of Raver, where he soon became the outstanding favorite of that island's king. Here he remained until a message came one day from David Whippey, informing him of the presence of a ship somewhere near them. Whippey planned to take Cary with him and set out to find the vessel. Wrote Cary:

I informed the king of the contents of my letter. . . . I promised to procure him a musket and some powder . . . if he would let me take a canoe and two men to go to Ambow. He was much pleased and promised he would have the canoe and men ready in the morning. I spent a sleepless night. The thought of once more getting on board a ship drove sleep entirely from me.[18]

The search for the ship took Cary some distance to the northeast, but with Whippey guiding the party there was little danger. Finally, the ship was located at Myambooa Bay. She was the *Clay,* of Salem, Captain Benjamin Vandaford, and he welcomed the castaway Nantucketer cordially, engaging him as interpreter to assist in procuring a cargo of sandalwood and bêche-de-mer.

It was now October 1827—two and a half years since the *Oeno* was wrecked off Turtle Island. Cary worked for the *Clay* until she obtained her cargo and sailed for Manila. Rather than make the voyage to the Philippines, Cary decided to remain with Whippey until the *Clay* returned. The ship sailed on February 17, 1828, and on board her Cary placed letters to Aaron Mitchell & Co., the owners of the *Oeno*, informing them of the fate of the ship and her men, and to his sisters in Nantucket.

In July 1828 the *Clay* returned and Cary then began a career as an agent for ships obtaining cargoes at the Fijis. He made a number of voyages to Manila and the Dutch East Indies. On one arrival, the *Clay* brought letters from Manila to Cary.

"Among the letters I found several from home," wrote Cary, "I shall not attempt to describe my feelings on reading these epistles from my sisters, neither can they be imagined by anyone who has not been in a similar situation. It was nearly six years since I had heard a word from home." [19]

During the next year Cary sailed aboard the *Glide*, Captain Henry Archer, another Salem ship. On a voyage to the Sandwich Islands the course lay across the Japan Grounds and, sure enough, they sighted a whaleship, the *Zenas Coffin*, of Nantucket—the first bit of home that Cary had seen in six years.

Cary's journey home was typical of his nomadic existence since leaving Nantucket in 1824. He shipped aboard the *Glide* and the *Perne*, trading ships at the Fijis, then got a berth on the schooner *Charles Daggett*, of Salem, under his old friend Captain Driver, and went to Rotuma Island (the same ship was later cut out at the Fijis). At Rotuma he obtained a cooper's berth on the whaling schooner *New Zealand*, of Sydney, Australia. At the vessel's home port he sailed aboard the schooner *Clementine*, belonging to Mauritius. He finally reached America on the ship *Typee*, Captain Mellet, arriving at Salem on October 27, 1833. Early in November 1833 the wandering whaleman saw the shores of his island home again. He wrote in his journal:

> After an absence of nine years . . . I was received with much joy by my friends and relatives, and I believe heartily welcomed by the inhabitants.[20]

William S. Cary followed the sea the rest of his life, making voyages

out of Nantucket, Hudson, New York, and New Bedford before retiring and settling down at the latter port. He died in March 1883,
being then in his seventy-ninth year, and nearly ten years afterwards
the journal of his adventures was found at the little fishing village of
'Sconset at the east end of Nantucket.

Was Cary the only one of the *Oeno*'s crew to escape the massacre at
Turtle Island? The question will never be answered, but there is one
more bit of evidence which must not be omitted. In March 1831 a
letter arrived at Nantucket from the whaleship *American* which held
some startling news:

> Off Charles Island, Gallapagos Islands: At 6 P.M. got a quadrant
> out of the *Charles,* of London, which formerly belonged to William
> H. Shaw, first officer of the ship *Oeno* of Nantucket, which ship was
> lost five years ago on the Feegee Islands—where this quadrant was
> purchased of one of the natives and has Mr. Shaw's name on the
> case.
>
> Captain Buckle of the ship *Harriett,* of London, states that four-
> teen months ago [December 1829] while at Sidney, he was informed
> by the master of a Russian brig that at the island of Tongataboo he
> saw a young "boy" who said he belonged to the *Oeno,* and that there
> was one man living at the Windward Islands, also belonging to the
> ship, being the only two survivors—the rest having been massacred
> by the natives. The boy seemed very anxious to leave the island with
> the Russian captain of the brig, but the king would not consent.[21]

This was very probably the lad named Barzillai Swain, being the
youngest individual on board the *Oeno*. At the Tongan Group he
would have been as much a slave as Cary had been at Lakemba. Only
Cary was fortunate in having David Whippey. Aaron Mitchell, the
owner of the *Oeno,* requested the government to send the schooner
Dolphin to Tongatabu to rescue young Swain and return him to his
home and widowed mother. But nothing ever came of the request
and the subsequent life of the boy is still a mystery.

But what of David Whippey?

When the United States Exploring Expedition went into the Fiji
Group in 1840, Lieutenant Charles Wilkes met Whippey. Of this ex-
Nantucket whaleman he wrote:

> In passing to the anchorage [at Lerrika], we saw a tiny boat, in
> which was David Whippey, one of the principal white residents here,

with one of his naked children. This man ran away from a ship commanded by his brother. . . . He has now been eighteen years on this island, and is the principal man among the whites. He is considered a royal messenger . . . and is much looked up to by the chiefs. He speaks their language well, is a prudent, trustworthy person, and understands the character of the natives perfectly: his worth and excellent character I had long heard of.[22]

The Nantucket man proved to be a valued guide for the Exploring Expedition. He impressed upon Wilkes the necessity of keeping themselves on guard against surprise attacks. One incident of such an attack occurred while Wilkes was in the Fijis. The natives in the interior of the great islands were considered to be the most savage and resourceful in all of the South Seas. Wilkes lost two of his men in a trap set by the natives, one of the two being his own nephew.[23]

David Whippey not only acted as interpreter for the U.S. Expedition, but his knowledge of the customs and habits of the Fijians proved to be invaluable. It was Toka, the king of Lakemba, who had befriended William Cary, who became the king at Ambow following the old king's death. When the brig *Eliza,* of New England, was wrecked in the Fijis in 1809, firearms were first introduced into the islands, but the white man "Charley," who taught the natives their use and power, fell a victim to his own pupils.[24]

As Whippey's importance in the Fijis was not to be overlooked, he was appointed United States Vice-Consul at the islands. He had already accomplished much in helping castaways from shipwrecks. Between "1828 and 1840, eight vessels, of which five were American, are known to have been lost within the Feejees," wrote Wilkes. "In addition, eleven trading vessels and one English ship of war had been on shore, sustaining greater or less damage within the same space of time." [25] The crew of the French brig *Josephine* suffered the same fate as that of the *Oeno.*

It was during World War II that a Nantucket man, stopping at the Fijis, learned that the descendants of David Whippey were large landowners in the islands. Reporting this information, he also added that he had seen a photograph of the ex-whaleman in the Fiji Museum.[26] In 1946, a letter from Charles Whippey, a great-grandson of David Whippey, gave further facts. When Fiji was ceded to Great Britain in 1874, Whippey acted as the official interpreter on cession day, thereafter retaining his friendly relations with the king. The letter states also:

> David Whippey and my grandfather then took the Wakaya Island in the Fiji group where they resided for a while, and later they bought a large property on Wainunu on the second largest island of Fiji, known as Vanua Levu, comprising approximately 12,000 acres, where they finally settled. I am proud to say we have now reached the sixth generation.[27]

Another great-great grandson of David Whippey, and also his namesake, now practices law in Suva, Fiji, having studied in New Zealand. He once wrote to Nantucket, asking:

> Are there any relatives of the original David Whippey still existing on the island of Nantucket? I am aged 27 years, and . . . being named after the original David Whippey is one of my main reasons for writing in hopes you may be able to put me onto any of his relatives in Nantucket. . . . I am proud to say that the Whippey family is one of the largest, if not the largest part-European families in Fiji.[28]

Perhaps this story of the whaleman who became a South Seasman in reality can be contrasted with the many white renegades who followed after him. Their deeds were a succession of infamous acts, all of which make sad reading. As for Whippey's choice of the wild Fijis as his home in exile, one must read Lieutenant Charles Wilkes' description of those islands:

> So beautiful was their aspect that I could scarcely bring my mind to the realizing sense of the well-known fact that they were the abode of a savage, ferocious and treacherous race of cannibals. . . . Each island has its own peculiar beauty, but the eye as well as mind felt more satisfaction in resting upon Ovolau, which, as we approached it, had more of the appearance of civilization about it than any other.[29]

This was the island where David Whippey established himself as a veritable king of the Fijis. And, among all of his adventures, there could never be one so strange as when from his canoe, surrounded by his savage crew, he gazed across the intervening water at the solitary castaway—the slave of another king—and called to him: "How are you, William Cary? . . . Don't you remember David Whippey?"

chapter xxii

❦❦❦❦❦

AT THE COASTS OF CONTINENTS
AND THE CROSSROADS OF THE
PACIFIC

> . . . *Our Whaling fleet may be said at this very day to whiten the Pacific with its canvas, and the proceeds of this fishery, give comfort and happiness to many thousands of our citizens.*
>
> —Lieut. Charles Wilkes, 1845[1]

FROM THE rounding of the Horn by the first American nor'westmen and whalemen through the first decades of the nineteenth century, there were a hundred American whalers and merchant craft in the Pacific. Yet there was not a single port along the west coasts of either South or North America which a vessel from this country could call its own. This made the gradual building up of American trade with these Spanish-American ports a matter of considerable importance. The whaleships and sealers did it entirely as the result of necessity. It is fair to presume that the influence of the whalemen had much to do with the initial phases of the revolution of the Spanish-American colonies against Spain.

Although the Hawaiian Islands were not so fruitful as others of the South Sea Isles, their geographical situation rendered them the most important group in the Pacific. They became the early cross-roads, stopping places for the Nor'westman and sealers; they grew quickly into the rendezvous of the whaleships whose cruising grounds were in the central, northwest and north Pacific. These whalers developed the islands, created a strong commercial hawser which bound them to our country and which ultimately gave them territorial status.

The first two whaleships—the *Equator,* of Nantucket, and the *Balaena,* of New Bedford—had arrived at the Sandwich Group in 1819.[2] Yet, a large proportion of the 119 whaleships sailing from New England to the Pacific at this time did not go to the Hawaiian Group until the news of the new and fabulous whaling ground "on Japan" spread through the whaling ports. Each year thereafter the number of those whaleships which utilized the attractive islands of Maui, Oahu, and Hawaii grew steadily, so that by 1840 the large percentage of the five hundred American whaleships going to the South Seas visited Honolulu and Lahaina.[3]

Returning in May 1822 from a voyage of only twenty-one months, the *Globe,* of Nantucket, brought in (for the second successive time) more than two thousand barrels of sperm oil. Her master, Captain George W. Gardner, gave an excellent account of the Sandwich Islands, bringing out the many features which made the ports of Lahaina and Honolulu of such value to the whaling fleet.[4]

Captain Gardner reported the following incident: While the *Globe* lay at Oahu on November 12, 1821, a fire was seen ashore. Word reached them that the royal palace and other buildings had been consumed and that the flames were spreading toward the royal fort, containing a thousand casks of powder. Captain Gardner immediately dispatched his crew ashore with buckets and a Nantucket fire brigade was formed. For a moment the racing flames appeared to be gaining; if they reached the fort the resultant explosion would doom the entire village, including a number of large wooden structures erected by the Americans from lumber brought around Cape Horn. He wrote: "By the unparalleled exertion and daring spirit of the Americans who were present, with the watering party from the *Globe* handing buckets, the destroying enemy was stopped in its awful career," and Honolulu was saved.

Captain Joseph Allen's discoveries, within the area dominated by the Sandwich Islands, included Gardner Island and Maro Reef. Disasters came to several whalers in these uncharted waters, however.

The *Lyra,* of New Bedford, discovered a reef and an island which was probably the island of Lysan, northwest of Oahu, but was wrecked not many miles distant from it a few years later (in August 1830).[5]

In 1822 the *Two Brothers* under Captain George Pollard (who had previously lost the *Essex*) was wrecked on a coral reef in latitude 24° north and longitude 168° west. But this time there was no epochal open-boat voyage for Captain Pollard, as he and his crew were rescued the next day by the *Martha,* Captain John Pease, also of Nantucket. The reef still bears the name Two Brothers. When the British whaleships *Pearl* and *Hermes,* on April 26, 1822, piled up on a reef one thousand miles northwest of Honolulu, it also was given the names of the ships it had trapped.[6]

At length the new pattern of the whaling voyages was established. Voyaging to the Hawaiian Group the ships recruited and then went on their several ways. The *Ganges* and *Independence* went "on Japan," thence south, through the Marshalls, Gilberts, Ellices and Fijis to New Zealand; the *Aurora* and *Martha* went "on Japan" and returned; the *Palladium* and *Ploughboy* went to Japan, returned, thence sailed to the coast of California; the *Falcon* and *Lion* were on pioneering voyages through mid-Pacific island groups.

The *Lion* was wrecked on the rocky entrance to Fanning Island, Captain Albert Clark losing a new ship and his cargo of fourteen hundred barrels of oil; the *Falcon,* Captain Benjamin Chase, after being the first whaler to stop at Rurutu in the Cook (Austral) Islands, was lost at this same island in November 1824 when the mate got too near to the harbor reef while the captain was ashore.[7] The *Independence I* narrowly missed a similar fate when she struck an uncharted reef, but managed to limp into Honolulu with her pumps working.[8]

Those long voyages were hard on the crews and sometimes the owners showed little or no appreciation for the toil of months on end. As an example, the troublesome voyage of the *Aurora* demonstrates the courage of the men and skill of the master and officers.[9] Sailing from Nantucket in October 1822 under Captain Seth Coffin, the *Aurora* was only five and one half months out when it was found that the Pacific worms had created such havoc (she was coppered only to the light watermark) that she was compelled to careen and sheath her bends twice during the voyage. With this handicap the ship appeared doomed when she ran on to an uncharted coral reef, thumping for two hours before she was released by kedging. After a successful cruise "on Japan" and filling his ship with oil, Captain Coffin sailed for home. No sooner had they left Honolulu than the old leaks started again and gradually increased as the ship approached Cape Horn. Both pumps were required to keep her free when running before the wind, as at such times she would force the water in at each end of the apron at her stern, notwithstanding that the ceiling was cut away and the leak partially stopped. What rendered the situation more critical, the pumps became so much chamber-worn that bagging them had but little effect.

On the first fair day one of the pumps was hoisted on deck and restored by an ingenious method: The handle of the cooper's long borer was knocked off, holes were punched through the obtuse side and riveted on to a piece of oak plank (of the proper thickness and shape) and then inserted into a lower studdingsale yard with a handle affixed to the latter. Thus the boring was accomplished. The next problem was to get a set of boxes to fit the larger bore. These were made of hardwood, taken on board at the islands. After the pumps were fitted, it was found that one of them would keep her free in good weather.

When the *Aurora* arrived off Pernambuco (Recife), Brazil, anchoring in the outer roads, Captain Coffin planned to go into that port and heave his ship down, but found that she could not enter the harbor without first discharging most of her cargo into lighters. As there was the distinct possibility that once in she might remain in port for all time, Captain Coffin ordered her anchor up, to which some of the hands protested since the ship was leaking and a wintry coast was ahead. But there was no alternative and so the men grudgingly laid hold of the windlass and commenced to heave. One anchor was lost in kedging her out to an offing.

Captain Coffin and his officers utilized one more expedient: When across the equator and still in tropic seas they took advantage of a calm day to heave the ship to and began the unique operation of plugging the leaks from overside. Four Kanackas (South Sea Islanders) and a Nantucket lad dove under the ship and plastered on a substance composed of chalk and slush, thus closing the worst places and reducing the leak from one thousand to five hundred strokes per hour.

One of the foremast hands (then a mere lad) concludes this account with the following comment:

> After being on our coast for fifteen days, parting most of the running rigging, and blowing away the sails, the *Aurora* arrived at Edgartown [Martha's Vineyard] on Christmas Day 1826, after an absence of three years and two months, with 1800 barrels of oil. And neither the captain, officers, nor crew received so much as "I thank you," from the owners and underwriters, although the ship's bottom was eaten to a honeycomb.[10]

The *Aurora* is best remembered for the fact that she was perhaps the first American whaleship to sail into a Japanese port. She arrived on the Japan Grounds early in 1824 and, while in latitude of 30° north and longitude 174° east, sighted the wreck of a Japanese junk.

> There were nine persons still alive on board, nearly in a state of starvation, and three dead, packed in chintz, whom the survivors said died of thirst. The people were taken aboard and the junk set on fire. In running to Jeddo to land them, two sperm whales were taken, and the Japanese eagerly devoured the blubber and lean with a bountiful supply of vinegar. . . . The people were put aboard a fishing schooner off the harbor of Jeddo, and the *Aurora* continued her voyage. . . . Afterwards made two narrow escapes from shipwreck in the night on the low, windward islands. As her headstays were bad, rope taken from the junk replaced them.[11]

Among the first American missionaries to the Hawaiian Islands were those who came to Honolulu on board the whaleship *Henry,* of New Haven, in 1821, under Captain Oriah Coffin. That same year a company at Plymouth, Massachusetts, fitted out that port's first whaleship, the *Mayflower,* Captain David Harris. The first whaler out of Stonington, Connecticut, the *Hydaspe,* sailed in 1822 under Captain Peter Paddock. Thus three ports new to whaling fitted out their first ships and sent them to sea under Nantucket whaling masters.[12]

When Israel Thorndike, a famous merchant of Beverly, Massachusetts, became interested in whaling he secured the services of Captain Alexander Macy, of Nantucket. First taking the *Columbus* out of LeHavre, France, in 1819, Captain Macy returned in May 1820 and sold the ship before sailing for Nantucket. Thorndike engaged him to fit out and command the large ship *Palladium* for sperm-whaling in the Pacific.

The *Palladium* sailed on July 3, 1821. After rounding Cape Horn and recruiting at Coquimbo, arrived at the island of Hawaii on March 19, 1822.[13] Of this landfall, Captain Macy wrote:

> March 20. . . . Heavy showers of rain attended with thunder and lightning. Towards daylight, when the clouds had a little dispersed, we Discovered a Vulcano burning in the mountains.

At anchor in Kealakehua Bay, Captain Macy observed:

> While there, I many times stood on the rock Captain Cook was killed by natives . . . and one of the party that killed him was pointed out to me, and he looked like the man that would be likely to do anything of that kind.[14]

Not being able to get his ship provisioned here, Captain Macy sailed to Maui and, after watering at Lahaina, went over to the island of Oahu. He wrote:

> I had freight taken in Boston to land at Honolulu for the American Missionaries . . . amongst which was the first printing-press ever worked at the Sandwich Islands. This was April 13, 1822.[15]

On April 17, 1822, the *Palladium* sailed for the Japan Grounds with the *Roxana* in company. Just a month later, while in latitude 33°-22′ north and longitude 160°-13′ east, a white bird, called a "heron" by Captain Macy, flew on board and Captain Macy remarked: "This induced me to think we were nigh some land." On May twenty-eighth they sighted a "great quantity of brit [upon which right whales feed] of a reddish couler."

While cruising north and west "on Japan," the *Palladium* on June 10, 1822, spoke the *Carrier,* of New London, under Captain Swain another Nantucket man. She was the first New London whaler to sail into this remote section of the Pacific. On June 17 the *George* and the *Phoenix,* of Nantucket, were spoken in longitude 155°-30′ east and latitude 33°-40′ north, and on the next day the staunch New Bedford pioneer *Balaena* was sighted, Captain Edmund Gardner reporting one thousand barrels—when only eleven months out.

The *Maryland*, of New Bedford, and the *Eliza Barker*, Captain Alley, of New York, were also spoken. The *Barker* had been out twenty-seven months, making her among the pioneer craft "on Japan." She had sailed in April 1820. The *Julius Caesar*, Captain Oliver Fowler, of Sag Harbor, was spoken on August 10, 1822, becoming the first whaler from that port to reach these grounds.

Early in September the *Palladium* was in longitude 177°–50′ east and 36°–32′ north latitude and began a long cruise, by a great circular route, north of the Hawaiian Islands to the coast of California. On November 9, 1822, her logbook reads:

> At one P.M. the weather Cleared and we saw the Land. . . . In the morning we steer'd in E SE into Montarey Bay we saw two white houses on the North side of the bay called Santa Cruize, we run within 5 or 6 miles of the Land sounded 45 fathoms—we then steer'd across for the South side.

Sailing down the coast, the ship made Point Conception and on November 13 was approaching Santa Barbara. While at anchor off here, waiting for a wind, "two canoes came along-side with several Spanish Indians in them of whom we bought some fresh fish, they having nothing else to trade with."

On November 16, the ship "got into the bay of St. Barbary and anchored in 10 fathoms water, with the Mission house bearing NW½N, the west point of the bay WSW, and the center of the Island of St. Nicholas South. . . . We found the Natives quiet and peaceful, but we could get but little vegetation, and wood and water scarce. . . . We got off a bullock from the Shore, one half of the Crew went ashore on Liberty."

It had been a long cruise for the crew, from April to November— eight months without fresh provisions. Among the supplies put aboard were: one bullock, two sheep, 190 pumpkins, sixteen bushels of beans and five barrels of water. While at anchor, Captain Macy welcomed Captain Barney, a fellow-townsman in command of the *Nelson*, of London, as well as the brig *Owyhee* and ship *Fanhill*, both from St. Francisco Bay. The *Owyhee* was one of Josiah Marshall's nor'west-men, a trading type then slowly vanishing from the Pacific scene. It was this craft which, ten years later, brought the first pickled salmon into Boston, which sold for $14 a barrel, but since the U.S. Treasury forced Marshall to pay a duty on it, the attempt to introduce such a delicacy to New England was not made again.[16]

The *Palladium* made another cruise to the Sandwich Islands and "on Japan," before returning to California. Arriving on that coast in October 1823, the ship anchored off "St. Barbary," where the *Mayflower*, of Plymouth, the *Barclay*, of New Bedford and the *Martha*, of Nantucket, were at anchor. Proceeding down the coast to the Maria Islands, the *Palladium* completed her whaling, and then sailed down the longitude to the latitude of the Juan Fernández, where she headed east for Valparaiso and Coquimbo.

Rounding the Horn, the ship arrived back at Boston on October 18, 1824, with two thousand barrels of sperm oil, "and anchored in 3 fathoms off Central Wharf. On the morning of the 19th we took up our anchor and warped the ship up to Russia Wharf and unbent the sails." She had been gone three years and three months. Her log recorded flogging, desertions and incipient mutiny—a typical voyage of its time and kind.

This was the era rightfully titled the "golden twenties," as it solidified the growth of New Bedford and enhanced the position of Nantucket, still the leader in the industry.

Not only had the Pacific fleet done well but the ships whaling in the South Atlantic also made good voyages. One of the most remarkable was that of the *Charles*, of New Bedford, under Captain Joy, which brought back two thousand barrels of oil after being out only seven months and twenty days, sailing to the coast of Patagonia.[17]

From the returns of the various ships which had been in the Pacific, it is apparent that many whaleships were utilizing the large bay at San Francisco early in the 1820's. As has been seen from Captain Gardner's account, the whaleships habitually went to the coast of California before they set sail for the Hawaiian Islands. When the *Ploughboy*, Captain William Chadwick, arrived at Nantucket on May 10, 1824, she was 186 days from San Francisco and spoke of the *Gideon*, Captain Clark, and *Alert*, Captain Ray, of Nantucket, as being at San Francisco in November 1823.[18]

The *Factor*, Captain John Macy, was almost wrecked off San Francisco in November 1825. A sworn statement from the captain estimated the damage to the *Factor* as amounting to $1,200.[19]

Many unknown stretches of the Californian coast were an ever-present danger. Captain Edmund Gardner told J. N. Reynolds in 1828 that, although Captain Vancouver had done a partial survey of the coast from Cedros Island north, there had been no survey south to the lower peninsular.[20] Captain Pease, of the *Hesper,* discovered a reef in 32°–34′ north latitude and 119°–34′ west longitude, and Captain Macy, in the *Palladium,* saw an uncharted island on this coast.[21]

There is a mention of whalers at San Francisco in Beechey's *Voyage*. He wrote of his visit to that harbor:

> As we opened the several islands and stopping places in the harbor, we noticed several American whalers at anchor at Sausalito, not one of which showed their colours; we passed them and anchored off a small bay named Yerba Buena, from the luxuriance of its vegetation, about a league distance from both the presido and the mission of San Francisco.[22]

The coast line of South America, from Ecuador to Chile, held only a few good harbors, like Túmbez, Callao, Coquimbo, Valparaiso and Talcahuano. Due to the revolution of the Spanish colonies, these ports were used by the whalemen under considerable handicap during the 1816-1828 period. One by one the colonies overthrew the despotic rule of the mother country, and on numerous occasions the whalemen were caught between the contending parties.

The experience of one of these whaleships is indicative of the times in which the flames of the South American revolution, smouldering and blazing in sudden bursts, often flared out to singe the sides of the New England whale fleet.

On the evening of March 18, 1820, the whaleship *Hero,* commanded by Captain James Russell, was lying at anchor off the town of Arauco, on the mainland of Chile, in the bay of St. Mary (Santa María), between that island and the main. A boat from the shore brought a message, inviting Captain Russell to dine with General Benevedes, and the whaling master accepted. He was greeted civilly by Benevedes, whom he knew as the commandant representing the Spanish royalists.

Any doubts about Benevedes' intentions toward the whalemen were dispersed when, the dinner over, he suddenly announced that he had intercepted a letter from the *Hero* which proved Captain Russell to be a spy in the employ of Admiral Cochrane, the British leader of the revolutionists' navy. Protests were of no avail; the guest was now a prisoner, and Benevedes promptly threw Captain Russell into jail.[23]

Before the whalemen on board the *Hero* were aware of the situation, several boatloads of soldiers from shore, coming off under cover of darkness, were tumbling over the ship's rail, driving the Americans below. After plundering the ship, the Spanish pirates tied up the crew individually and shut the whalemen up in the forecastle. Whatever they intended next will not be known, as the appearance of a schooner flying patriot colors, coming into the bay, frightened them away. Before they quitted the ship, however, they took off three of the crew and then cut the *Hero*'s cables so that, caught by an in-shore current, she drifted toward the rocky beach.

At this time, a figure emerged from the black depths of the fo'c'sle, leading the *Hero*'s remaining crew. It was Obed Starbuck, the mate, eighteen-year-old nephew of Joseph Starbuck, the owner of the ship. He had worked his bonds free and pried up the forecastle scuttle with a hatchet.

"Come on, boys!" called Mate Starbuck. "Let's get her out to sea!"[24]

The former prisoners leaped to the task. They managed to get sail loosened from the yardarms in the nick of time to keep the *Hero* from piling up on the rocks. Mate Starbuck then took the ship to Valparaiso, where he informed the officers of the frigates *Constellation* and *United States,* then lying there, of the situation at Arauco. It was on August 5, 1821, that the *Hero* returned to Nantucket, Mate Starbuck bringing her safely around Brant Point and being rewarded with the command of the ship on her next voyage. But before she sailed from Valparaiso, word came that the British whaler *Perseverance,* had been similarly treated by Benevedes at Arauco.

In the meantime, Captain Ridgely of the U.S.S. frigate *Constellation,* learned that Captain Hall of the British armed sloop *Conway* had sailed in an attempt to rescue the crews of the whaleships and sealing vessels held captive by the pirate Benevedes.[25] By an odd quirk of fate, Sir Thomas Hardy, in command of the British squadron in these waters, was the same officer who had ordered the bombardment of Stonington, Connecticut, during the War of 1812. Now, he ordered

Captain Hall to rescue the crews of American as well as British ships captured by the Spanish pirates. One of these captured American vessels was the sealer *Hersilia,* of Stonington. Ridgely decided to sail his frigate to Arauco and rescue the American captives.

Word of the proposed operation by the *Constellation* was brought home by the *Atlantic,* Captain Coffin, which arrived at Nantucket in January 1822. This gave hope that Captain Russell and his men might be saved. However, the whaleship *Triton,* Captain Zephaniah Wood, had reported the loss of the captain and a boat's crew from the British whaler *Offley* at Arauco. Captain Hales and his crew, while on shore, were surrounded by Benevedes' men and literally hacked to pieces. One man escaped to tell the horrible details and he only lived a few hours after gaining the safety of the ship.

Such accounts gave little hope for other prisoners of this pirate. Captain Ridgely proceeded on his mission, however, and on April 13, 1821, sighted the New Bedford whaler *Parnasso.* [26] The appearance of this vessel gave the naval commander the idea of using stratagem to catch Benevedes. The log of the *Parnasso* continues the story:

> . . . Finished cutting in the whales and saw a ship to windward. She sent her boat on board and she appeared to be the U.S. Ship *Constellation.* Our captain went on board at 4 returned with 25 of the frigate's men, and we were ordered to proceed to St. Aroque [Arauco] for the purpose of decoying a gang of pirates on board who had, a short time before, attacked the ship *Hero* of Nantucket, robbed her and took her captain and several people out of her. Her second mate was on board the frigate. At 4 A.M. a second boat came on board with arms, a lieutenant, and 3 midshipmen. [27]

Unfortunately, the plan was not successful. Captain Covell, of the Parnasso, took his ship into Arauco Bay and began trying out oil. When the fog of the morning rolled away it showed the *Perseverance* a wreck, where the pirates had run her ashore. Boat crews of navy men were sent to the wreck, but the pirates had a ten-pounder on a rock overlooking the wreck and soon drove the Americans from her. Captain Ridgely did not attempt to land a large party and withdrew from the scene. [28]

Soon after, word came that Benevedes had burned Arauco and retreated into the mountains. It was not until several months had elapsed that the fate of Captain Russell, of the *Hero,* and Captain Clark, of the wrecked *Perseverance,* was learned. Both had been shot in cold blood, as well as had the cabin boy of the *Hero.*

Captain Daniel Bennett and his boatswain had a narrow escape from Benevedes and his men. In the New Bedford whaleship, *Golconda,* they had anchored off Point Romaine, Chile, and finding no one at the coast, had walked inland some distance. Suddenly, they were pounced upon by a party of twenty Spaniards, who took them to Benevedes' camp, some twenty miles farther inland. When their captain did not return, the boat's crew returned to the *Golconda.*[29]

That night, after Bennett and his boatswain were made prisoners, Benevedes' camp was attacked by a company of patriot troops, and in the confusion the two Americans escaped into the brush. As soon as they felt it timely, they started for the seacoast, tracking by night and hiding during the day. The trip was long and difficult, but one can only imagine their dismay when, upon arrival at Point Romaine, they found the ship gone! They walked up the coast to Arauco, to find the town in the hands of the patriots, who treated them kindly. When the ship arrived, several days later, the pleasure of Captain Bennett was mingled with his prayers at his deliverance.

Benevedes was afterwards captured, and so infamous was his reputation that he was drawn and quartered and his head set upon a pike at the gates of Santiago.

A number of other instances found piratical schooners attacking vessels close to the Chile islands. In April 1825, the whaleship *Hysco,* Captain Reuben Coffin, of Nantucket, was boarded by a Spanish pirate off Paita, Peru. As the stranger flew the colors of the Spanish patriot forces, Captain Coffin allowed the schooner to come close aboard, and was taken completely by surprise when two boatloads of well-armed men swarmed over his rail.

The boarders were runaways from the port of Chiloé, and were short of supplies. They robbed the whaleship of provisions, water and charts, and ordered them to stand by during the night. A good breeze sprang up after darkness had set in and Captain Coffin promptly clapped on all sail and got away.[30] But her escape from man-made perils came only a short time before she struck a reef in the Society

Islands and barely made port at Huahine, where she "laid her bones," never to sail again.[31]

Due to the presence of our several warships on the South American coast, the whalemen were offered some protection at such ports as Paita, Callao, Coquimbo and Valparaiso. These frigates and schooners did not get too far from the coast and so their fringe of protection was definitely limited. Nonetheless, Captain Swain, of the whaleship *Lima,* had reason to give heartfelt thanks to an American frigate.

In November 1824, the *Lima*'s larboard boat was struck by a sperm which had been harpooned some distance from the ship. The blow stove the frail craft into kindling, injuring several men, with Captain Swain's son, George, the most seriously hurt. The youth had sustained a crushed right foot and a fracture of the left arm, broken near the shoulder. Realizing the dire need for expert medical care, Captain Swain headed his ship for the nearest port, Callao, where they arrived a fortnight after the accident. There, at anchor, was the frigate *United States,* with the famous Commodore Isaac Hull in command.

The injured boy was taken aboard the frigate, where a series of skilful operations were performed by Doctors Tinslow and Fitzhugh. Mrs. Hull, the commodore's wife, and her sister, promptly took over the nursing duties and, with the whole ship's company to encourage him, the young whaleman slowly regained his shattered health. Four months later he was put aboard the *Lydia,*[32] Captain Allen, and arrived safely at his Nantucket home. Several similar cases could be cited.

Other injured whalemen were not so fortunate. Late in the year 1822, Captain George Clark of the *Parnasso* (who had succeeded Captain Covell, who had gone home sick) was to sustain an injury which came close to ending his short career as a whaling master. The logbook of the *Parnasso* gives us the story in the words of the boat-steerer, John Sampson:

Nov. 23—at 10 A.M. sighted a school of sperm whales, squared the yards . . . at eleven A.M. lowered all three boats . . . at about 12 o'clock our boat being ahead came up with and struck a 50-barrel whale, a moment afterward the waist-boat threw an iron into him, and both boats hauling up on either side in order to lance him, he at that moment raised his tail and struck our boat with such violence as to knock her head entirely off, and as was then supposed, to kill Captain Clark, who hung across the gunwale of the boat without sense or motion.

The boat immediately sunk down under the surface and all hands left her to endeavor to swim to the other boat, which by this time was near us. The Captain was taken up to all appearances dead, he however, gasped soon after and gave signs of returning life. Mr. Chase [First Mate] in the meantime had killed and wafted his whale, but on seeing the signals made by the ship went on board and soon after came off to meet with and help us on board the ship.

We hoisted the Captain up in the boat and carried him below. It appears that the whale struck him on the right side of his face and across the nose, which is at present even with his cheeks. His lips are also cut very bad and he bled copiously from his mouth and nose, but the extent of the injury done his head cannot be ascertained as it is so much swelled as to scarcely retain the appearance of anything human. In getting him aboard he was immediately bled, which seemed to revive him.

Our next object was to pick up the stoven boat and oars; which being done, all hands were called aft by the mate who requested the opinion whether to stay and take in the whale which lay dead near us, or to tack the ship and stand for Payta [Peru] to obtain needed medical aid for the Captain. The last was universally agreed upon.

Captain Clark still remains speechless and the blood still flows from his mouth and nose, a great part of which goes down his throat . . . on the following days he seemed a little to recover the use of his tongue . . . as he pronounced several words but so incoherent and irrational as to be very little understood.[33]

The master of the *Parnasso* was put ashore at Paita, not to return aboard for several weeks. He displayed an erratic disposition for several months, according to the log, on one occasion trading a new whaleboat for an old one, but he stuck to his ship.

After a voyage of two and a half years, the *Parnasso* returned to New Bedford with a "full cargo" of two thousand barrels.[34] Having lost one captain by illness and having nearly lost another, with several men deserting, the ship's company did well to stand by until the voyage was a success.

Perhaps the unusual experience at the time of her entrance into the Pacific, when she was called upon to take part in that abortive sortie to capture Benevedes, induced the crew to believe that she was, after all, a lucky vessel. Whalemen, like all sailors, were great fatalists and superstition had a considerable influence on their lives. Once a ship had displayed an uncanny "bent" to overcome misfortune, she was considered a "lucky ship" and certain to bring them safely home again.

The first whaleships to the coast of Japan had all made splendid voyages, and soon the second fleet to cruise on that fabulous whaling ground also began to return with full ships. In May 1824 the *Alexander,* Captain George B. Chase, of Nantucket arrived at Holmes Hole, bound up the sound, with 2,830 barrels of sperm for the firm of Gardner & Swift—the largest quantity of oil yet brought home. Among other reports, Captain Chase gave a most interesting description of the Society Islands, highly commending Tahiti, Huahine, Moorea and other ports to the whaleships as places for "recruit." [35]

Under the circumstances, the lush islands of Les Sociétés were ideal for provisioning the whaleships. But they were never used to the extent expected. There were two main reasons for this:

First, and most important, the Hawaiian Islands were more strategically situated for whaling ships.

Secondly, the venereal diseases at Tahiti, brought in by the Spanish, French, and English sailors, made that port dangerous to the Quaker whaling masters who did not wish to expose their crews to the "Devil's Curse." Among those warning against Tahiti was Captain Alexander D. Bunker who found a virulent plague raging there when he visited the islands in 1826 in the *Ontario.* The northern islands of the Socities, however, Huahine, Bora-Bora and others, were popular places for provisioning for many years.

In 1822 the Nantucket *Inquirer* noted that seventy-four New England whaleships were in the Pacific during that year, but that the total catch would probably not exceed 32,740 barrels, with few of the craft taking more than 1,500 barrels. This was in direct refutation of articles appearing in various newspapers containing optimistic estimates of the fleet's expected cargoes. But, the editors could at least argue on one important point: The whaling industry had another incalculable worth, independent of its commercial importance—it was a nursery for the hardiest and most expert seamen of its time. These were the second and third generations of sea-hunters in the Pacific.

chapter xxiii

⟨⟨∿⟩⟩

THE WHALE THAT SANK A SHIP

"My God, Mr. Chase, what is the matter?"
I answered, "We have been stove by a whale."

—Owen Chase, Mate of the *Essex*.[1]

O N THE TWENTIETH DAY of November 1820, the whaleship *Essex,*
of Nantucket, was in the Pacific Ocean, just below the equator
in longitude 119° west. On the chart, the ship was approximately equidistant between the Galápagos Islands to the east and the Marquesas
to the west southwest, but actually closer to the latter islands, which
were about twelve hundred miles away.

The three boats of the *Essex* had been lowered and were pursuing
sperm whales when Mate Owen Chase's craft was struck by his whale
and stove. By stuffing their jackets in the holes the men managed to
get her back to the ship. This was the second time within a week that
Mate Chase had been stove by a fractious whale.[2] As he worked on
his boat, now hoisted to the deck of the ship, his mind was on getting
her ready to lower again to return to the attack on the school of sperm.

It was at this moment that Chase observed a large sperm whale
about eighty-five feet long

> lying quietly, with his head in the direction of the ship. He spouted
> two or three times, then disappeared. In less than two or three sec-
> onds he came up again, about the length of the ship off, and made
> directly for us. . . . His appearance and attitude gave us at first no
> alarm, but . . . observing him a ship's length off, I ordered the boy
> at the helm to put it hard up, intending to sheer off and avoid him.

The words were scarcely out of my mouth before he came down upon us with full speed and struck the ship with his head, just forward of the fore chains. He gave us such an appalling and tremendous jar as nearly threw us on our faces. The ship brought up . . . violently as if she had struck a rock and trembled for a few minutes like a leaf.[3]

The whale passed directly under the ship and came up alongside of her to leeward to lay quietly on the surface. Chase thought the creature was stunned by the tremendous blow, and watched it go slowly off. His first concern was for the ship which was now leaking badly. After rigging his pumps, he set a signal for the return of the two boats under Captain Pollard and Second Mate Matthew Joy.

He had scarcely done this when he saw the whale, "apparently in convulsions, on the top of the water, about one hundred rods to leeward. He was enveloped in the foam of the sea . . . and I could distinctly see him smite his jaws together, as if distracted with rage and fury. He remained a short time in this situation and then started off . . . across the bows of the ship to windward."[4]

Owen Chase was thinking only of the *Essex*. He felt that from the way she was settling, she would soon founder and turned his attention to the two remaining boats with the "intention of clearing them away and getting all things ready to embark in them."

At this moment a man on deck called out: "Here he is—he is making for us again!"[5]

The infuriated whale this time struck the *Essex* directly under the cat-head and completely stove in her bows. Passing under the ship again, he went off to leeward and Chase reported, "we never saw him again."

Thus, in the space of a few minutes, the whaleship was rendered a complete wreck. "The shock to our feelings was such I am sure none can have an adequate conception," he wrote the mate. "We were dejected by a sudden most mysterious, and overwhelming calamity. . . . We were more than a thousand miles from the nearest land, and with nothing but a light open boat, as the resource of safety for myself and companions."[6]

The men had time enough to rescue two quadrants, two books on navigation and the small trunks of Captain Pollard and Mate Chase, which with two compasses from the binnacle were all that could be salvaged as the ship slowly sank. Launching their whaleboat, they had barely cleared the ship when "she fell over to windward and settled down in the water."

From the first attack by the whale to the escape from the ship, Chase estimated but ten minutes had elapsed. The men sat at their oars, stunned, utterly silent. The sudden and mysterious disappearance of the ship was discovered by the other two boats, which now came down towards them.

Chase wrote:

> The Captain's boat was the first that reached us. He stopped about a boat's length off, but had no power to utter a single word. . . . I could scarcely recognize his countenance, he appeared so much altered. . . . He was in a short time . . . enabled to address the inquiry to me, "My God, Mr. Chase, what is the matter?" I answered, "We have been stove by a whale." I then briefly told him the story.[7]

The masts of the ship were cut away and she righted. By cutting a hole in her deck, a quantity of bread and some water was taken from her hold, but nothing more. Some of the land turtles caught at the Galápagos Islands, were found and taken into the whaleboats. They proved a life-giving source of food.

For three days the boats lay by the stricken ship hoping that another whaler would appear. But none came, and it was resolved to steer to the south as far as 25° south latitude, there to find the variable winds and work to the eastward toward the South American coast. A quantity of needed material was taken from the wreck, among this being some cedar boards with which the sides of the boats were built up, as they had a low freeboard, and poles and sail canvas with which each boat was provided. Thus, each had a mast and sails, so that they could be maneuvered to the best possible advantage.

Captain Pollard called a council of his first and second mates to determine the course to take and the "best means for our security and preservation."[8] There were twenty whalemen in three boats.

The boats left the scene of the disaster at noon, on the twenty-second, and set sail to the south-southeast. This was in latitude 13' south, longitude 120° west. It was agreed that the three boats should keep together as long as possible, the allowance of food being one biscuit

(1 pound, 3 ounces) and half a pint of water for each man. Mate Chase's boat was in poor condition from being lately stove; it carried six men. Seven men were in Captain Pollard's boat, and the same number in Second Mate Joy's. Provisions enough to last sixty days were on hand. The long chance of being picked up by a whaler (the only craft frequenting those latitudes) was realized to be the one hope for rescue if the voyage exceeded the two months' period expected.

Much criticism has been made concerning the decision to sail south instead of east-southeast for the Marquesas or the Society Islands. To Captain Pollard is attributed the blame for this decision, but this is not borne out by the facts. Chase himself states that a council of three men—Captain Pollard, First Mate Chase and Second Mate Joy— determined the course to be taken. The nearest South Sea Islands were thought to be too dangerous a landfall, being inhabited "by savages, from which we had as much to fear as from the elements." [9] Captain Pollard stated "we feared we should be devoured by cannibals." [10] How ironic a contemplation this became in the light of what happened during the next three months.

Due to the fact that they believed a hurricane season then prevailed around the Sandwich Islands, the officers decided not to sail in that northwesterly direction. Actually, this was the best available course as the prevailing winds and currents would carry them in that direction. As a matter of fact, while they remained by the wreck, they drifted some miles northwest across the equator, so that when Captain Pollard took a sight to get a point of departure, he found they were in longitude 120° west and 0°–13′ north.

"We had no charts from which our calculations might be aided," Chase states in his *Narrative*, "and were consequently obliged to govern ourselves by our navigators alone." [11] Here, Chase reveals how little dependence the whalemen had upon the charts of the Pacific which were then in existence.

"Taking all things with consideration," wrote Chase, "it would be most advisable to shape our course by the wind to the southward, as far as 25° or 26° south latitude, fall in with the variable winds, and then endeavor to get eastward to the coast of Chili or Peru." [12]

And, incredible as it may seem, this is exactly what two boats of the *Essex* accomplished. An open boat voyage of over three thousand miles, in the most fragile of craft—clinker-built whaleboats, built for buoyance and lightness rather than strength and durability. The three boats were to stay together—a feat in itself in case of a storm at night.

On November 27 five days after the leaving the wreck—the Captain's boat was struck by some unknown fish. While repairs were being made, it was necessary to lighten her. Some of the provisions were water-soaked and the men overcome by thirst, and from this time on their extreme suffering increased.

They longed for fresh meat, and schools of dolphins nearby tantalized them, but all efforts to catch one failed. Three days later they killed a turtle, cooking it in its shell, entrails and all, some of the men drinking the raw blood.

The supply of bread that had been wet lasted until the third of December. During the next night the boat of the second mate was lost sight of, but a few hours later the little fleet was reunited and these spells of separation were thereafter quite frequent. This brought up thoughts and discussions as to whether it would not be better to separate.

On the eighth of December they had a sharp gale, and were compelled to unship the masts and abandon all control of the course of the boats. Captain Pollard then realized that he was making no headway to the eastward, the winds and currents continually acting against him. From his observations and by dead reckoning alone he felt that the boats were being taken to the westward. Calculations for his latitude he was able to make and he determined that they were about six hundred miles from the wreck.

By the ninth of December they reached 17°–40′ south latitude, and had become very much exhausted. Mr. Chase had locked in his chest the small supply of bread and guarded it with great care. Good fortune had sent some flying fish against the sails, which dropped into the boats and were quickly devoured, bones, scales, and all.

Wrote Mate Chase: "The privation of water is justly ranked among the most dreadful of the miseries of our life; the violence of raging thirst has no parallel in the catalogue of human calamities." [13]

A week later, the allowance of bread and water was reduced one half. The wind had died out, and the sun was intensely hot. Some relief was found by bathing in the sea; this led to the discovery of barnacles on the boat's bottom, and they were scraped off and eaten with relish. If it had not been for three members of the crew, who could not swim, remaining in the boat, the bathers would have been unable to get back over the gunwales, so greatly weakened had they become. The miraculous discovery of the small shellfish added wonderful nourishment—but lasted only half an hour.

Owen Chase's boat was so leaky that it became necessary to put on a patch. In order to do this effectually, one of his crew named Benjamin Lawrence went overboard and held a hatchet against the wound, so as to enable the men inside to clinch the nails. They were then in latitude 21°-42′ south. It being now calm, rowing was resorted to; but the extremely enfeebled men made but slight headway, and they became much dispirited.

Miles and miles of sea were covered by the boats during that long month. Despite storm, starvation, thirst, leaking boats, and equatorial heat, the little fleet of whaleboats had managed not only to keep afloat but to keep together. Considering the weakened condition of the men, this was altogether remarkable—a tribute to the seamanship and courage of the Nantucket whalemen.

And then, on the morning of December 20, one of the men in Mate Chase's boat suddenly cried out, "There is land!" It was an electrifying moment. Owen Chase said: "There was the blessed vision before us. . . . We shook off the lethargy of our senses. . . . It appeared at first a low, white beach and lay like a basking paradise before our longing eyes."

The feelings of the boat crews may well be imagined. After thirty days and nights of being tossed about by the elements they were again to set foot on stable earth. Landing was made with difficulty, due to rocks. Joy turned to despair as no water could be found.

As soon as the men landed Owen Chase, took an observation and calculated that they were in latitude 24°-40′ south, longitude 120°-40′ west, and from these observations he concluded they were on land called Ducie Island. But they had made a discovery—an island now known as Henderson Island, an uninhabited spot two hundred miles to the west-northwest of Ducie Island. Beyond that to the southwest was the rocky pile of Pitcairn, where, if fortune had so directed, they would have found the colony (discovered a dozen years before by Captain Folger) ready to save them.

The uninhabited speck of land which offered them such limited safety lay comparatively only a few miles northeast of Pitcairn. Wrote Captain Joseph Mitchell, of the whaler *Three Brothers,* who landed here in 1847:

> This is the island that some of the *Essex's* crew landed on. What a pity that they did not know of Pitcairn's Island for they might have been to it in a few days or even one day with a good breeze. . . .[14]

The only sign that showed this island had been visited before was the name of the ship *Elizabeth* cut into a tree.

After several days' search for water, a spring was found which could be used only at low tide, and some of the men drank so much water that their lives were endangered. The island was entirely barren of vegetable growth, except for a small quantity of "pepper-grass." Some fish and a few birds were caught, and a few birds' eggs were found amid the clefts of the rocks. Everything eatable was speedily devoured uncooked.

Realizing that they could not keep alive on such a barren spot, which was far from the haunts of ships, they decided to set sail again. The boats were hauled up on the beach and made as seaworthy as possible with the limited supply of tools which the men had. A meagre quantity of fish was cooked for provisions.

After a week on Henderson Island the three boats of the *Essex* again put to sea. At the last moment three of the crew—William Wright and Seth Weeks of Barnstable, Cape Cod, and Thomas Chapple, of Plymouth, England—decided to remain on the island, rather than face the uncertainty of further open-boat voyaging. Captain Pollard wrote an account of the disaster and placed it in a tin box nailed to one of the trees.

The decision of the three seamen to remain on Henderson Island was not unexpected and although there was little said, it created an inner turmoil. As Chase wrote, earlier in the voyage:

. . . There was a desperate instinct which bound us together; we could not reason on the subject with any degree of satisfaction . . . yet we continued to cling to each other with a strong and involuntary impulse.[15]

Mr. Chase records the sad feelings of the boat crews as, on the twenty-seventh of December, they bade their shipmates farewell and set sail.

It was the intention of Captain Pollard to head for Easter Island to the east-northeast. Many seafaring men have since questioned the judgment of the unhappy shipmaster. First, it is said, after the wreck of the ship he should have set out for the Marquesas—the nearest land from where the *Essex* went down—and in this latter case that he should have steered for the Society Islands, where prevailing tides and winds would have taken him. A week after leaving Henderson Island they found they had gone to the south of their proposed course. Contrary winds and adverse currents soon made the voyage to Easter Island impossible, and so Captain Pollard resolved on the desperate choice of heading for the Juan Fernández Islands and the South American coast, some two thousand miles away to the east. Chase states that their desperate hope lay in being sighted by another ship.

On January 7, 1821, the journal of Owen Chase recorded that the boats were in latitude 30°–18′ south, longitude 117°–29′ west. Three days later the first death occurred—that of the second mate, Matthew P. Joy. Although his condition had been much weakened by the small allotment of rations, his death was the result of complications of which exposure to the elements was the immediate cause.

On the night of the twelfth of January a severe storm came up, during which the mate's boat became separated from the other two. This separation took place in latitude 32°–16′ south and longitude 112°–20′ west. Wrote Mate Chase: "For many days after . . . our progress was attended with dull and melancholy reflections. We had lost the cheering of each other's faces." [16]

The allowance of bread in Chase's boat was now reduced to one and a half ounces per day. One of the crew was caught in the act of stealing bread. Mate Chase presented a pistol to the man's head, the bread was returned, and the unfortunate was let off on his promise never to offend again.

On January 15, a large shark began to follow the boat, making several attacks, but finally left without doing any serious damage. On the sixteenth they were surrounded by porpoises but none could be caught for want of a harpoon; on the eighteenth, whales were spouting around them. Richard Peterson, one of the colored men, died on January 20, and his body was committed to the deep in latitude 35°-07′ south, longitude 105°-46′ west.

On the eighth of February—two months and eleven days at sea— Mr. Chase's diary records:

> Our sufferings were now drawing to a close; a terrible death appeared shortly to await us; hunger became violently; our speech and reason were both considerably impaired.[17]

One of the crew, Isaac Cole, for several days had been alternating between fits of despair and moments of fervent hope, during which he remained for hours at the bottom of the boat or standing in the bow calling encouragement to his shipmates. Suddenly he went mad. Mr. Chase wrote:

> He became about nine o'clock in the morning a most miserable spectacle of madness, calling loudly for a napkin & water, and then, lying stupidly and senselessly at the bottom of the boat again, would close his hollow eyes as if in death. . . . We covered him with some old clothes and left him to his fate. He lay in the greatest pain and apparent misery, groaning piteously until four o'clock, when he died in the most horrid and frightful convulsions I ever witnessed.

While preparations were held next day for Cole's burial, Mr. Chase made the dreadful suggestion. "I addressed them on the painful subject of keeping the body for food. Our provisions could not last beyond three days. . . . It was without any objection agreed to. . . ."[18] Hunger and the craving to live might drive the three of them to cast lots for each other's lifeblood. The proposal to dispose of Cole's remains so as to sustain their own lives was at length agreed to by the three sufferers. Mr. Chase's journal records:

> We separated his limbs from his body, and cut all the flesh from the bones; after which, we opened the body, took out the heart, and then closed it up again—sewed it up decently as we could and committed it to the sea. We now first commenced to satisfy the imme-

diate cravings of nature from the heart, which we eagerly devoured, and then eat sparingly of a few pieces of the flesh; after which we hung up the remainder, cut in thin strips about the boat, to dry in the sun; we made a fire and roasted some of it, to serve us during the next day. In this manner we dispose of our fellow-sufferer; the painful recollection of which, brings to mind at this moment, some of the most disagreeable and revolting ideas that it is capable of conceiving.

He continues:

We knew not then, to whose lot it would fall next, either to die or be shot, and eaten like the poor wretch we had dispatched. Humanity must shudder at the dreadful recital. I have no language to paint the anguish of our souls in this frightful dilemma. The next morning, the 10th of February, we found that the flesh had become tainted, and had turned of a greenish colour, upon which we concluded to make a fire and cook it. . . .[19]

This food lasted until February 15, but during that period they were so strengthened as to take turns at steering the boat "and make a toterable good course." Mate Chase believed they were still three hundred miles from the nearest land—the coast of South America. The continuation of a strong westerly wind was their "only comfort and solace . . . all hope was cast upon the breeze." That night (February 16) Chase dreamed he saw a ship at some distance and woke "with a frenzy . . . I had caught in my slumbers." [20]

That next afternoon, the sight of a heavy cloud "settling down in an E by N from us," indicated to Chase that land was near. He believed himself in the vicinity of Más Afuera Island. "The life blood began to flow again briskly through my veins," he wrote. "We directed our course for the cloud, and our progress that night was extremely good." [21]

The next morning the boy, Thomas Nicholson (Nickerson), lay down to die. Chase endeavored to convince him that it was wicked to abandon reliance on Providence while the least hope remained; "but he felt unwilling to listen to my consolatory suggestions."

About seven o'clock that same morning, Benjamin Lawrence, who had the steering oar, suddenly called, "There's a sail!"

"The earliest of my recollections are," Mr. Chase wrote, "that immediately I stood up, gazing in a state of abstraction and ecstasy upon the blessed vision of a vessel about seven miles off. . . . The boy, too, took a sudden & animated start from his despondency, and stood up to witness the probable instrument of his salvation." [22]

The boat was put on another tack and, with the patched sprit-sail drawing well, sailed a course to intercept that of the ship. It must have seemed an eternity as they approached. But the ship now shortened sail and allowed them to come up to her. Soon the whaleboat with the three survivors were alongside of the brig *Indian,* Captain William Crozier, of London.

Chase tells of the moment:

> I made an effort to assist myself along to the side . . . but my strength failed me altogether. . . . We must have formed at that moment, in the eyes of the Captain and his crew, a most deplorable and affecting picture. . . . Our cadaverous countenances, sunken eyes, and bones just starting through the skin, with the ragged remnants of clothes struck about our sunburnt bodies.[23]

The three survivors were Mate Chase, Benjamin Lawrence and "the boy," Thomas Nicholson. Their first food was a gruel made from tapioca, fed to them in small quantities, and in a few days they had responded enough to the treatment to be able to walk.

The mate's boat had been picked up in latitude 33°–45′ south, longitude 81°–03′ west. At noon on that day (February 18) the island of Más Afuera was sighted. Their twenty-seven-foot whaleboat had been in the open sea nearly three months, and since leaving Henderson Island had been fifty-three days on her course east, east-southeast, and east again. Mate Chase was as near a landfall as he was likely to get in a full-rigged ship. They had covered approximately 3,700 miles.

On February 25, the *Indian* arrived at Valparaiso, where the three survivors were landed "in utter distress and poverty," as Chase described it.

After separating from Mate Chase's boat on January 12, 1821, the captain's and second mate's boats had an even worse experience than that of the mate's. The parting of the three had taken place in latitude 32°–16′ south, longitude 112°–20′ west. The two boats remaining were now bound together by an even stronger bond. There was a fear of separation. Captain Pollard thought Chase's boat had foundered.

Following the death of Second Officer Joy, the command of the third boat had been placed in the hands of the third mate, Obed Hendricks, who was accordingly transferred to the other boat.

The two boats headed on an east-southeast course which they hoped would bring them to Juan Fernández, some two thousand miles away. The captain's boat contained: Captain Pollard, Barzillai Ray, Owen Coffin (nephew of the captain), Samuel Reed (Negro), and Charles Ramsdell. In Mr. Hendrick's boat were Joseph West and four Negro sailors, Lawson Thomas, Charles Shorter, William Bond and Isaiah Shepard.

The meagre supply of food soon gave out. When Charles Shorter, in the third mate's boat, died his body was divided among the survivors in both boats. Captain Pollard stated: "We had no other alternative but to live on their remains. These were roasted to dryness by means of fires kindled in the ballast sand at the bottom of boat. When this supply was spent, what could we do? We looked at each other with horrid thoughts in our minds. . . ." [24]

When Lawson Thomas died, the men were again forced to resort to human flesh to sustain life. Isaiah Shepard, another of the Negro sailor, died, his body being similarly disposed of. In Captain Pollard's boat Samuel Reed died and his body became the only means for sustaining the lives of the surviving four men.

Finally, on the twenty-eighth of January, the two boats were driven apart by the heavy seas. The separation occurred in latitude 35° south and longitude 100° west. Mr. Hendrick's boat was neither seen nor heard from again. In the captain's boat there now remained four men, Captain Pollard, Charles Ramsdell, Barzillai Ray and Owen Coffin.

On the first day of February, 1821, there was nothing remaining in the captain's boat that would aid in keeping the men alive. It was decided that the four should draw lots to see which should submit to death—his body to be used as food. Wrote Pollard. "I am sure we loved one another as brothers . . . yet our looks told plainly what must be done." [25]

The dreadful chance was taken and it became Owen Coffin's lot to die. The executioner's lot was drawn by young Charles Ramsdell.

No sooner had Captain Pollard offered his life in the place of his nephew than Ramsdell, himself only a youth in his 'teens, implored his shipmates to reverse the procedure—that he might give his life for having drawn the executioner's lot. But the pleadings of young Ramsdell were as vain as were Captain Pollard's efforts to induce his nephew to live—Owen Coffin remained steadfast in keeping his bargain and giving his life.

Captain Pollard tells us the story:

> I started forward and cried out, "My lad *if you don't like your lot,* I'll shoot the first man that touches you!" The poor emaciated boy hesitated a moment or two; then, quietly laying his head down upon the guverale of the boat, he said, *"I like it as well as any other."* He was soon dispatched and nothing of him left. . . . But I can tell you no more—my head is on fire at the recollection.

The execution of young Coffin by Ramsdell was the most horrible episode of the tragedy of the *Essex.*

Ten days later Barzillai Ray passed away, and on these bodies the Captain Pollard and Charles Ramsdell subsisted for twelve days.

The indomitable seamanship of Captain Pollard is shown by the fact that on February twenty-third they were in sight of the island of Santa María off the coast of Chile; on the same day, they were sighted by the Nantucket whaleship *Dauphin,* Captain Zimri Coffin, who picked them out of the sea—two survivors who had been sixty days from Henderson Island in their open boat.[26]

Concerning the rescue of Captain Pollard and Charles Ramsdell by the *Dauphin,* an interesting sidelight is revealed by Charles Murphy, of Nantucket. As the third mate of the rescue ship, Murphey kept a journal of the vessel's cruise, the entire account being in rhyme. The following verses from Murphey's journal are typical examples of the quatrains:

> The second month, quite early
>   The three-and-twentieth day,
> From our masthead we did espy,
>   A boat to leeward lay.

> Hard up the helm, and down we went
>   To see who it might be;
> The *Essex* boat we found it was,
>   Been ninety days at sea.

No victuals were there in the boat,
Of any sort or kind,
And two survivors, who did expect
A watery grave to find.

The rest belonging to the boat,
Ah, shocking tale to relate.
For want of food and nourishment
Met an unhappy fate.

We rounded to and hove aback,
A boat was quickly lowered,
We took the two survivors out
And carried them aboard.[27]

Shortly afterwards, the *Diana,* another whaler, sighted the *Dauphin,* and her master wrote in his log:

> At 5 P.M., spoke with the *Dauphin.* . . . On board of this ship, I heard the most distressing narrative that ever came to my knowledge. Capt. Coffin had that morning taken up a whaleboat in which was Captain George Pollard and Charles Ramsdell, believed to be the only survivors of the crew of the ship *Essex* of Nantucket.[28]

When the *Dauphin* arrived at Valparaiso, a few days later, the reunion of the surviving five Nantucketers must have been one of the most touching scenes of the ill-fated voyage of the *Essex.* No time was lost by Captain Pollard in asking for aid in rescuing the three whalemen left behind on Henderson Island.

The U.S. frigate *Constellation,* Commodore Ridgely, was at Valparaiso. After hearing the dramatic story, Ridgely made a bargain with an English shipmaster to go to the rescue of the Henderson Island castaways.

Captain Raine, of the English ship *Surrey,* was the man to whom was entrusted the mission of rescue. The ship, bound for Australia, did not have to alter her course a great deal during her voyage. Captain Raine was given three hundred dollars to effect the rescue.

On April 8, 1821, the three castaways on Henderson Island were startled by the sound of guns. They raced from their shelter and were amazed at the sight of a ship standing in toward the island. Their great joy at being taken off the barren, rocky place can better be imagined than stated. They had been on Henderson 102 days. The *Surrey* brought the three to Sidney. From thence they sailed to London, where the two Americans, Wright and Weeks, were able to take ship for Boston. Several years after his return to England, a short account of Chapple's experiences was published by a London missionary society. The tract refers to him as the "second mate," which was not true.[29]

Captain Raine made Henderson Island in latitude 24°–26′ south, longitude 128°–30′ west. He gave the island the name which it still bears, believing it a discovery of the English whaler *Hercules,* under Captain Henderson. Captain Raine left on Pitcairn Island a copy of a letter telling of his rescue of the *Essex*'s survivors.[30]

From Henderson Island, Captain Raine took the tin box containing Captain George Pollard's letter describing the loss of his ship. There is a typical whaleman's reserve in the bare statement of the details in the tragedy, now in its second phase, which became doubly significant in view of the third and final phase of the tragedy. The letter read:

> Account of the loss of the ship *Essex* of Nantucket, in North America, (written at Ducie's Island Dec. 20), 1820, commanded by George Pollard, junior, which shipwreck happened on the 20th day of November, 1820, on the equator in long. 119° W, done by a large whale striking her in the bow, which caused her to fill with water in about ten minutes. We got what provisions and water the boats could carry and left her on the 22'd of November and arrived here this day with all hands except one black man who left the ship at Ticamus. We intend to leave tomorrow, which will be the 26th, of December, 1820, for the continent. I shall leave with this a letter for my wife, and whoever finds and have the goodness to forward it, will oblige an unfortunate man, and receive his sincere wishes. George Pollard, Junior.[31]

Four of the survivors, Mate Owen Chase, Charles Ramsdell, Benjamin Lawrence and Thomas Nicholson came home on the Nantucket whaler *Eagle,* arriving on August 9, 1821.

Captain Pollard, who was slow to regain his strength, remained at Valparaiso. He took passage for home on the *Two Brothers.*

When the *Eagle* arrived at Nantucket Bar, showing the usual signals that revealed her identity, the wharves were crowded with people. What a moving scene it must have been as they silently watched the handful of survivors from the *Essex* walk slowly up the wharf to their dwellings.[32]

The following were the crews of the three boats and their fates:

First Boat

Capt. George Pollard, Jr. survived
Barzillai Ray, died, body eaten for food
Owen Coffin, shot, body eaten for food
Samuel Reed (Negro), died, body eaten for food
Charles Ramsdell, survived

Obed Hendricks, 3rd Mate, put in third boat
Seth Weeks, Henderson Island, survived

Second Boat

Owen Chase, Mate, survived
Isaac Cole, died, body eaten for food
Benjamin Lawrence, survived
Richard Peterson, (Negro), died, buried at sea
Thomas Nicholson (Nickerson), survived

William Wright, Henderson Island, survived

Third Boat

Matthew P. Joy, 2nd Mate, died, buried at sea
Obed Hendricks, 3rd Mate (transferred from first boat), missing
Lawson Thomas (Negro), died, body eaten for food
Joseph West, missing
Charles Shorter (Negro), died, body eaten for food
William Bond, (Negro), missing
Isaiah Shepard (Negro), died, body eaten for food

Thomas Chapple, Henderson Island, survived [33]

The *Essex* had nine men left from her original crew of twenty-one—the unknown Negro whalemen who went ashore on the coast of Peru, the five men who survived the ordeal in open boats, and the three rescued from the dreary waste of Henderson Island.

A singular fact connected with the five survivors is that they all returned to the sea and rose to the command of vessels. If any human beings had a right to forsake the sea, certainly these men had. But they were men who lived in the tradition of the sea-hunters, of that courage which won over fear.

Captain Charles Ramsdell was the first of the five to pass away. Death came to him on July 6, 1866, some forty-five years after the disaster.

Captain Ramsdell had only one child, a son, Clarence Ramsdell, who died twenty-five years ago. Mr. Ramsdell often remarked that his father would never say much about his experiences, giving only the barest details. This was no doubt due to the sad lot of executioner that had befallen him in the captain's boat, the memory of which must have been most melancholy.

First Mate Owen Chase, became a successful shipmaster. He made several voyages as first officer until 1832, when he was given command of the new ship *Charles Carroll*, built for him at the Brant Point shipyards. He sailed in October 1832, and returned home in March 1836, with a full cargo of 2,610 barrels of sperm oil. Sailing once more in the same year, he brought back 2,678 barrels of sperm, arriving at Nantucket again in 1840. Having acquired a competency, he retired and lived a good many years. He died March 7, 1869, at the good old age of seventy-three. During the final months of his last voyage, he often complained of pain and difficulty about his head, although his reason was never impaired. He lived in the house on the northeast corner of York and Orange streets. Often, when he returned home from a trip to the stores, he would go up into the attic and hide crackers and other supplies—his mind, in his old age, reverting to those terrible scenes of the open-boat voyage.[34]

Captain Benjamin Lawrence died on the twenty-eighth of March, 1879, then being over eighty years of age. He was a young boatsteerer at the time of the *Essex* catastrophe. After making several voyages in ships of his native island, he became master of the bark *Huron*, of Hudson, New York. From 1839 to 1841, he commanded the *Dromo*. Following this voyage he retired from the sea and bought a little farm at 'Sconset. One son was lost at sea, while three daughters and two sons went to California to live. One daughter remained in Nantucket and lived with her father until his death.

Captain Thomas Nickerson (the boy Nicholson) was the last of the survivors to die—February 7, 1883. It is a known fact that Captain

Nickerson, although barely seventeen at the time of the long agony, had a most vivid recollection of the open-boat voyage.

After such a terrible experience it would seem that Captain Pollard would have preferred to remain ashore. Such was not the case, however. His many friends, realizing that he was a fine seaman and a splendid navigator, prevailed upon him to take a ship out again around Brant Point. Certainly, the loss of the *Essex* was no fault of that worthy skipper.

Captain Pollard made his next voyage to the Pacific in command of the whaleship *Two Brothers,* the same ship which had brought him back to Nantucket after the *Dauphin* took him to Valparaiso. Captain Pollard sailed again from Nantucket on November 12, 1821. Five months later, while sailing north of the Sandwich Islands, the ship struck a coral reef and became a total loss. Again Captain Pollard faced the sad ordeal of an open-boat voyage. This time, however, he and his men were picked up a few days later by the Nantucket whaler *Martha,* Captain John Pease.

Captain Pollard arrived home April 27, 1825. He never again went to sea, although he lived to the ripe old age of eighty-one, dying February 7, 1870. During the long years spent ashore he became one of the town's night watchmen.

At the time of his death the *Inquirer and Mirror* said:

> He was still a young man when he retired from the sea and closed the strange and eventful part of his career. For more than forty years he has resided permanently among us, and now leaves a record of a good and worthy man as his legacy to us who remain.[35]

The *Essex* was not the first island whaleship to be wrecked through contact with the creature it hunted. In 1807, the ship *Union,* twenty days out of Nantucket bound on a whaling voyage to the Pacific Ocean, struck a whale at night in mid-Atlantic. So great was the shock that the vessel, under good press of canvas, was brought almost to a complete stop and the men in the forecastle were thrown from their bunks. Captain Edmund Gardner went down into the hold with a lantern. One glance told him the ship was doomed, and so he ordered the men into the boats.

The *Union* sank soon after, and Captain Gardner set out for the

Azores. After seven days and eight nights the boats landed at the island of Flores. Captain Gardner, having saved his quadrant and chronometer, was able to navigate his boats to safety.

In 1826, the sloop-of-war *Peacock* ran into a sleeping sperm whale. The blow, being a glancing one, did not smash in her planking, and she managed to continue her voyage home, although she leaked badly.[36]

The New Bedford whaler *Ann Alexander* was deliberately rammed by a whale in the Pacific Ocean in August, 1851, and soon afterwards foundered. Her crew took to the boats in longitude 102° west and latitude 5° south (eighteen degrees east of where the *Essex* went down) and two days later they were rescued by Captain Richard Gibbs in the island whaler *Nantucket*.[37]

In the early twentieth century, the bark *Kathleen,* of New Bedford, was the victim of an attack by a whale, this time in the Atlantic Ocean. All hands were saved. One crew was in boats only one night, and the other nine days.[38]

It is generally understood that the narrative of Owen Chase formed the basis for the climax of Herman Melville's famous philosophical whaling classic *Moby Dick*. Melville's copy of Chase's story was annotated by the famous author. But did the two men ever meet? In this copy Melville wrote:

> Somewhere about the latter part of A.D., 1841, in this same ship the Acushnet, we spoke the "Wm. Wirt" [later corrected by Melville to read the "Charles Carroll"] of Nantucket. Owen Chase was the Captain, & so it came to pass that I saw him. He was a large, powerful well-made man, rather tall; to all appearance something past forty-five or so, with a handsome face for a Yankee, & expressive of great uprightness & calm unostentatious courage. His whole appearance impressed me most pleasurably. He was the most prepossessing-looking whale hunter I think I ever saw.
>
> Being a mere foremast-hand, I had no opportunity of conversing with Owen Chase (tho' he was on board our ship for two hours at a time) nor have I ever seen him since.[39]

But Owen Chase was not master of the *Charles Carroll* on this particular voyage; it was Captain Thomas Andrews.

Melville further wrote in his copy of the Chase *Narrative* that he had met the son of Owen Chase.

I questioned him concerning his father's adventure; and when I left his ship to return . . . he handed me a complete copy (same edition as this one) of the *Narrative*. This was the first printed account of it I had ever seen. The reading of this wondrous story upon the landless sea, and so close to the very latitude of the shipwreck had a surprising effect upon me.[40]

It is possible that Melville met both father and son. In meeting the latter, as he has stated, he may have confused the fact that he had seen the son first and the father afterwards.

One has only to read the Chase *Narrative* to feel the impact upon such a person as Melville. Wrote Chase: ". . . I began to reflect upon the accident and endeavored to realize by what unaccountable destiny or design . . . this sudden and most deadly attack had been made upon us; by an animal never before suspected of premeditated violence. . . . His aspect was most horrible."[41] And again: "The mysterious and mortal attack of the animal . . ."

It is known for a fact that Melville did meet Captain Pollard. During a visit to Nantucket in July 1851 (after he had written *Moby-Dick*) accompanying his father-in-law, Judge Shaw, the author talked with the whaling master. In a letter to his son, dated July 20, 1851, Shaw reported: "The next day we made various calls and visits. Amongst others, [Melville] met Captain Pollard, who was master of the whaleship *Essex,* which was designedly destroyed by a whale nearly thirty years ago."[42]

Another of Melville's notes in his copy of Chase's *Narrative* reads:

I—sometime about 1850-3—saw Captain Pollard on the island of Nantucket, and exchanged some words with him. To most islanders he was a nobody—to me, the most impressive man, tho' wholly unassuming, even humble—that I have ever encountered.[43]

Captain Pollard had stated: ". . . . Now I am utterly ruined. No one will ever trust me with a whaler again, for all will say I am an unlucky man."[44]

And Melville gives his final picture of the man in *Clarel*:

A Jonah is he? and men bruit the story.
None will give him place in the third venture, came the day
Dire need constrained the man to pace

A night patrolman on the quay.
Watching the bales till morning hour
Through fair and foul. Never he smiled;
Call him and he would come; not sour
In spirit, but meek and reconciled;
Patient he was, he none withstood;
Oft on some secret thing would brood.[45]

Less than a half century ago, a young Nantucket woman, interested in the story of the *Essex,* approached the daughter of one of the men who had survived. The older woman listened carefully to her questioner. Then she said calmly and with finality:

"Miss Mollie, here we never mention the *Essex.*" [46]

Thus the many other details of that voyage against death have long since been locked away forever.

chapter xxiv

⟨⟨≈∽⌣⌣∽≈⟩⟩

THE PACIFIC BECOMES AN
AMERICAN OCEAN

*These Sea Hermits conquered the watery world like so
many Alexanders. . . .*
—Herman Melville, *Moby Dick*

A s an explorer and discoverer in the South Seas, the whaleman
completed his role as a true sea-hunter. He was in direct contrast to the mariner specifically sent out for exploration. The latter,
dispatched with ceremony, under the sponsorship of a generous government or a scientific society, was not circumvented by the commercial
requirements. The whaling master had to fill his ship with whale oil—
that was his primary duty. For the information of himself and his
fellows, he put down on his charts those islands or shoals which he
found.

These whaling-explorers had a personal interest in the islands and
reefs that they discovered and relocated; they charted them for their
own safety as well as for provisioning places for their ships. They had
an occupational use for these islands—a fact which gives their discoveries prior claim over others. Assertions of certain merchants'
skippers as to discoveries were often nebulous, since they sailed in most
cases on a single voyage, and sighted islands at greater distances than
they would have us believe. It is not surprising that whaleman came
to the conclusion that certain Pacific explorers never actually discovered what they claimed. Even Wilkes noted the discrepancies between
certain accounts and the reality.

Besides, crossing the northern Pacific, cruising "on Japan" and through the western Pacific islands, the whalers also ranged south from the "line" or equator islands, to the Cook, Friendly and Navigator groups. One of such whalers was the *Falcon*, Captain Benjamin Chase, and the story of her cruise is typical of the whaleships of the time. Sailing from Nantucket in February 1823, the *Falcon* reached the South Seas in May and cruised through the central Pacific. Captain Chase provisioned his ship in the Society Islands. In April 1824, he reported seeing an island in 21°-17' south latitude and 159°-40' west longitude, called Orotooi by the natives. It had been discovered about six months before by the missionaries from Tahiti, who had left some Tahitian natives there to instruct the newly-found "heathens." The *Falcon* was the first American ship and first whaler at this island, which was described as being very high and seven to eight leagues in circumference.[1]

Sailing from the Society Islands on November 17, 1824, Captain Chase headed for the New Zealand Ground, probably west to Tongatabu before turning south. In January 1825 the *Falcon* had left the Bay of Islands and was at Norfolk Island, that former British convict colony, equidistant between New Zealand and New Caledonia, and much further from Port Jackson, Australia. Here a new bowsprit was fashioned from an island tree: "Some of these trees are 6 feet in diameter and make good spars," wrote Captain Chase.[2]

Again, the *Falcon* made a long voyage through the Fiji, Tonga and Samoa groups before returning to the Society Islands in April 1825. Whales had been scarce and, ill luck continuing during the cruise to the Marquesas, Captain Chase decided to sail for the Austral Islands, where four years before he had been the first whaleman to land at Rurutu.

On September 6, 1825, the *Falcon* reached Rurutu and Captain Chase landed with a boat's crew. Provisioning proceeded in good order but three days later, while Captain Chase was on shore, the ship came too close to the reef. Caught in stays, she struck heavily and stove in her hull. Although the crew managed to work her off, the ship filled rapidly and they were compelled to run her ashore. By working at top speed, a portion of the cargo was saved, but the ship was a total loss.[3]

After remaining ashore a month, Captain Chase and half of his crew were taken off the island by the schooner *Adonis,* a trader bound for Valparaiso. The mate and seven men remained at Rurutu until the whaleship *Chile* took them off with six hundred barrels of oil which had been salvaged from the *Falcon*.[4]

Although the first discovery of the Gilbert and Marshall Islands was made before the turn of the nineteenth century, many of these islands were actually first charted or seen by the American whalemen. It may be noted that neither John Byron, who first charted Nukunau Island in the Gilberts, nor Wallis, who explored the Paumotus (Tuamotu) and Society Groups, had little to report in their cruisings north of the equator. The beautiful island which now bears the name of Uvea Island, was rediscovered by the whalemen, as was Pitcairn Island, first charted by Wallis' consort, Captain Carteret's *Swallow*.[5]

During the years 1787 and 1788, Captains John Marshall and Thomas Gilbert commanded the *Scarborough* and the *Charlotte* on a voyage from England to Australia, thence to Canton, for the British East India Company. On the passage up from Port Jackson, after passing between the New Hebrides and the Fijis, they sighted the islands of Aranuka (on June 17, 1788), Apamama and Kuria, and later an island they named Mathews (so-called also by Duperry, the French explorer, in 1824), and the lower islands of the present Marshall Group, notably Mille, which they called Lord Mulgrave's Range. Captain Gilbert sailed up the Ratak Chain of the Marshalls and then headed west for Canton.[6]

The two mariners whose names are affixed to these groups actually discovered less than half of the islands in them. During the period 1792 to 1820, numerous merchant ships, on their way to China, were in the Marshalls, discovering most of the Ralik (or western) Chain of islands. Among these were Namorik, Kwajalein, Eniwetok, Namu and other Pacific atolls which became famous in the late war. The British brig *Elizabeth,* Captain Patterson, sailed through the Gilberts in 1809, and renamed several of the islands previously discovered by Captains Marshall and Gilbert. The Russian brig *Rurick,* under Kotzebue, the German, was in the Marshalls in 1816 and 1817, and the reports from this voyage are more satisfactory in its details than those of the British.[7]

In the logbook of the ship *Rose,* of Nantucket, Captain James Cary, is the account of the first discovery made by a New England mariner in what the British Captain Bishop had called the Kingsmill Islands.

While the *Rose* was on her way to Canton in 1804, having two thousand sealskins and other goods on board, Captain Cary noted in his log that on March 4 he sighted land at nine o'clock in the morning. An hour later he made a series of observations and found the longitude to be 176°-9′-30″ east of Greenwich.

> This land being not laid down in any of our charts, I suppose it to be a new discovery, therefore I have named it Rose Island. At 1 P.M. fourteen canoes came alongside, brought nothing off for traffic but Beads which they gave us in exchange for Iron Hoops. Latitude by obs. 2°-33′ south.[8]

The next day, March 5, 1804, Captain Cary wrote the following description of his new discovery and the native population:

> . . . Lay to for the canoes which kept alongside until 3:00 P.M. when they all left us and went on shore. By their behavior, we suppose they never saw Foreigners before. They were inoffensive & knew not the use of firearms & seemed pleased with the reception they met with from us. We wore ship, steered North till 4 P.M. when we tack to the westward again. At 6 A.M. were nearly abreast the South part of the Island, when we tack'd North. The Land is bearing from SW to W about 2 miles distant. 1 P.M. tack'd to the South . . . at daylight Rose Island bore NNW. . . . 40 canoes came alongside us. . . . Many natives came on board. . . . They went ashore after cocoanuts when they perceived we prefer'd them to their beads. At 3 P.M. they returned with a quantity which, we purchased for pieces of Iron Hoops. They seem'd strictly honest in their dealings & very much surprised at many things they saw on board the ship.

Coming up the Whampoa to Canton he was in sight of the Grand Lima on April 11. "Could not get a pilot," he wrote in his log, "and being acquainted with the passage concluded to run for Macao, which we saw at 6 P.M."

After remaining a month, taking on board the usual cargo of teas and silks, the *Rose* left the Whampoa on June 8, 1804. Captain Cary had intended to proceed on his voyage by way of the Eastern Passage and Sunda Strait, but owing to the southwest monsoon having set in, he was forced to put away for another route to the Indian Ocean.

On July twenty-eighth the *Rose* anchored under Welcome Island at the northeast of Pitt Passage (Ceram Sea), "after having attempted the passage through Pitts and being rebuked by a southerly wind." Five days later, Captain Cary sent a boat's crew ashore at an island called Salawalti, "for refreshment, when natives arose, cut off 2nd officer Samuel Gelston and two seamen and killed them and badly wounded a third man." [9]

On August eighth Captain Cary took the *Rose* through Dampier Strait and proceeded between New Guinea and New Britain into the Coral Sea, thence to Port Jackson. Sailing south of Tasmania, the *Rose* got at last into the Indian Ocean. But on October 18 she ran into a fierce storm which stove in her larboard bulwarks, from the mizzen to fore shrouds, tore up the caboose and started her deck seams. The ship and cargo were damaged. When they reached Cape Town on October 25, 1804, Captain Cary had an affadavit drawn up "Protesting Against the Sea, Gales of wind and bad Weather which the said ship met with on her passage from Nantucket . . . until her arrival in this port of Table Bay." This "Protest" was duly notarized and signed by two disinterested parties and the ship's officers. The vessel arrived home December 28, 1804. Captain Cary died at Canton on his next voyage and the *Rose* was captured by the British while homeward bound. [10]

It was on a voyage of the *Independence II* in 1825 that Captain Plaskett realized his explorative ambitions. In May 1826 he had recruited at Rotuma, "trading blue, white and green beads, Iron hoops, knives, &c., for yams, plantains, cocoanuts, &c." [11] He further mentioned being on shore "to see the manner & customs of the natives."

Upon leaving Rotuma, the *Independence II* sailed to the north and north by east. A week later an island not laid down on the charts was sighted east by north. Captain Plaskett was anxious to get a closer look at it and, the wind being contrary, he

. . . lowered all four boats and pulled in towards the island within 4 or 5 miles of it. Night coming on, came on board again. . . . At daylight clost to the Land, boat went within hale of the shore But not meeting with a very kind reception came on board again. Latter part calm, spoke several canoes. Latitude by ons. 6°–14' south. Longitude 176°–30' east.[12]

This island (Nanomana) was an actual discovery. Captain Plaskett named it Smut-Face Island, from the appearance of the natives who daubed their faces in black streaks.

Lieutenant Charles Wilkes in March 1841 called it Hudson Island.[13] Sailing north from Samoa, the U. S. Exploring ships came upon Funafuti, and Nukufetau. Then they "fell in with" another island. Wilkes placed it in almost exactly the same latitude and longitude fixed by the whalemen. The *Narrative* continues:

> . . . This discovery I have called Hudson, after Captain Hudson. It was surveyed and found to be one mile and four tenths long, north and south, and nine-tenths of a mile, east and west. This island is inhabited, a few natives being seen on the beach. . . . It is of coral formation, has no lagoon, and can be seen about eight or ten miles. There are reefs . . . on which the surf breaks beavily. They had no communication with the inhabitants.[14]

Steering northwest, the *Independence II* went on to the Kingsmill Ground. On the last day of April 1826, Captain Plaskett was off Nauru (Pleasant) Island, discovered in 1798 by the English Captain Fearn of the *Hunter,* and rediscovered by Captain Mooers in the whaler *Spartan* in 1825.

Some idea of the spirit of exploration which must have been imbued in Captain Plaskett may be obtained by the fact that from the date of his entrance into the Pacific, late in 1825, until he "spoke" the *Japan* off Rotuma in February 1827, he had not sighted a single whaling ship. This fact was reported by the *Japan* at Honolulu in October 1827. It was contained in a message brought home by Captain Bunker of the *Planter,* which arrived at Nantucket in March 1828.[15]

That Captain Plaskett was a careful navigator is shown by his entries during his cruise in the Ellice and Kingsmill Islands. On March 24, 1827, he "got a lunar" and determined that Drummond Island (discovered in 1799 by Captain Charles Bishop in the British brig *Nautilus*) was "laid down wrong" on his chart. Although his latitude was correct, Captain Plaskett was a degree off in his longitude. But he placed Nikunau (Byron) Island correctly in its present position—176°-35′ east longitude and 1°-19′ south latitude.

The next day Captain Plaskett sighted an island "not laid down in the Books and Charts." The log records the discovery as follows:

> The Island bearing SE dist. 7 leagues . . . the eastermost end appeared higher than any other part of it. At 12 Midnight, by a strong current running SW we were set nearly down on it, so that we saw fires burning all along the shore; tacked ship to the NW by W, 4 P.M. tack'd again to E. by S. At daylight the East end bore NE by E, head up for the West Point saw another island bearing NW by W, 8 leagues, not down in the Books and Charts . . . 1°-50′ South Latitude, Longitude by account 175°-20′ East.[16]

To this newly discovered land, Captain Plaskett gave the name Parker's Island, after Robert F. Parker, a prominent Nantucket merchant and a shareholder in the ship. Formerly designated Clerk's Island it is now called Onotoa.

Continuing to display his spirit for discovery, Captain Plaskett steered south, and, after taking several sperm, headed northeast again. On April 12, 1827, he discovered another island not laid down on his charts. This is now called by its native name, Nonouti (formerly Sydenham Island) and had been reported by Bishop, the discoverer of Drummond's Island, as lying south of the latter. The log of the *Independence II* reads:

> . . . Several canoes alongside with cocoanuts and mats for which they exchange Iron Hoops which they were very Eager for. The latitude of this island is 1°-10′ South and longitude 174°-03 East. This island not being down in our Books or Charts we suppose it to be a new discovery. There is a reef runs all around it at the distance of about 3 miles from the shore, and by the appearance of the water it is a shoal. The Island is about 25 miles long, very low, covered with trees, mostly cocoanut. Some of the Canoes are very long and carry a large sail. The Natives go entirely naked. They are rather larger than the common size.[17]

Leaving Nonouti the ship stood away east and southeast and on April 16 Captain Plaskett reported sighting "Lincoln's Island, lately discovered by the *Japan*, Shubael Chase, master, who named it after his mate, John Lincoln." As the *Japan* and *Independence II* had gammed off Rotumah in February, it is probable that Captain Chase had told Captain Plaskett of his discovery as having been made in 1826. The island is now called Tamana or Rotcher Island.

Captain Plaskett returned to Lincoln's Island during his cruise the following week. On this occasion (April 20, 1827) he "lowered away the larboard boat and went inside the reef about 3 miles, rounded it, very shole for the most part." Thus a Nantucket whaleman was the first to discover the island and a fellow-islander the first to chart its reef-enclosed harbor.

Captain Shubael Chase reported another discovery in the Kingsmill Group—in latitude 2°–28′ south and longitude 175°–20′ east—which he called with pardonable pride, Chase's Island. It is now called Arorae. Chase also charted Dundas or Brind's Island, as given by Arrowsmith in his 1821 chart.[18]

In March 1831, Captain Edwards, of the *Harvest,* noted in his log: ". . . at daylight saw Chase's Island in latitude 2°–28′ south, longitude 176°–40′ east . . . run down to it and was visited by the natives in about 30 canoes."[19] The use of the name for the island shows that they were placed on the whalemen's charts as soon as fellow-whalemen had announced their discovery, but due to the length of the voyages the news of discoveries was received for the most part years after the event.

Notwithstanding the fact that the *Independence II* under Captain George Barrett was the first whaleship into the mid-Pacific area of the Samoan, Ellice and Kingsmill groups, and under Captain Plaskett returned to this region in subsequent voyages, another whaleship sailed through these island groups in between the *Independence II*'s voyages. This vessel was the *Loper,* of Nantucket, under Captain Obed Starbuck.

Leaving Nantucket late in 1824, the *Loper* was at Honolulu in March 1825, sailing from Oahu on a cruise along "the line" that same month.[20] On a previous voyage in the *Hero,* Captain Starbuck had cruised "on Japan" and, as the season was not advantageous this time, he decided to cruise on the equator and then to sail south into the Gilbert Islands.

In August 1825, while in longitude 176°–20′ west, Captain Starbuck sighted a low, barren island, not more than half a mile in circumference.[21] Partially covered with a low grass and shrubs, with white

coral beaches that shone dazzling white in the sunlight, this island
(practically on the equator) was named New Nantucket by the shipmaster. Perhaps the name was a combination of homesickness and of
the contrast to the ship's island home. Later this island was called
Baker (its present name) after Captain Michael Baker, of the *Bra-
ganza,* who landed there in 1834.

After leaving New Nantucket Captain Starbuck steered the *Loper*
along the equator into the Gilbert Islands and there found an island
not placed on the charts. This was in longitude 173°–30′ east and latitude 0°–15″ north, and was a cluster of islands which the master of
the *Loper* designated as Starbuck's Group.[22] This is Aranuka Island,
seen by Captain Marshall in 1788, southwest of Apamama, which he
called Hopper Island. In 1841 the United States Exploring Expedition
placed the Aranuka atoll in 0°–11″ north latitude and 173°–39′–20″
east longitude,[23] which compares most favorably with the position
fixed by the whaling master nearly twenty years before.

But Captain Starbuck's next two landfalls were actually to be his
own discoveries. Pursuing his way south-southeast into the Ellice
Group, he sighted and correctly fixed the position of the island of
Niutao, which he called Loper's Island.[24] This is in latitude 6°–07″
south and longitude 177°–40′ east, close to its modern asserted position.

A day or so later, another island was sighted in latitude 7°–30′
south and longitude 178°–45′ east. Captain Starbuck gave it the name
of Tracy's Island, after his mate.[25] It is still so designated on the maps.
The *Peacock* of the Exploring Expedition saw this island in 1841 in
almost the same position, but did not approach it, owing to a contrary
wind and strong current, which Captain Hudson judged would cause
a "waste of time" to attempt to buck.[26]

It remained for Captain Plaskett in the *Independence II,* on August
21, 1827, to substantiate the discovery of his fellow-islander (although
he presumed he was the first to see it). His logbook entry of that date
is of interest since it tends to prove that he was the first explorer to
actually stop at Tracy's or Vaitupo Island:

> . . . At 9 P.M. man on the Fore-yard saw a light ahead soon after saw
> two more. At 10 tack'd ship to S SW, at 1 A.M. tacked again to the
> ENE—at daylight found it to be a small low island about 6 miles

long, Dist. 12 miles; went within 7 miles of it two canoes came off with a few cocoanuts. . . . We learn that they never saw a ship before. The natives name of this island is Voytopo, it is not laid down on the Books or Charts so we call it a new Discovery . . . Lat. 7°–25 south, Longitude 178°–47′ East.[27]

Captain Plaskett lowered a boat to pull in for the island and at sunset returned with the king—"a large, good-looking man, but very dirty, being painted from head to foot with a kind of stuff which looks like soot." The native gave the captain two pigs and several other presents.

Perhaps the most interesting story which developed from Captain Plaskett's cruise through the Ellice Islands was in connection with his discovery of Nui, or Netherlander Island. On November 7, 1827, he discovered the island and hove to about three miles from shore. Three canoes approached from the island. The ship's log recounts the story within a story, as follows:

> . . . We being the first ship they ever saw, they look upon us with wonder and surprise, and after remaining on board about an hour they went on shore again. After learning the particulars from whence we came and where we are bound, this we told them through one of their countrymen who we brought from Rotumah as an interpreter. He had left here thirty years ago in two or three large canoes, together with 60 men & women, in persuit of some other land, of which after being at sea 3 months from their native Isle they fortunately fell in with Rotumah, landed and were treated very friendly, until after about three months they all meet together to form a plan to kill the King, but the Rotumah People perceiving their design soon put a stop to it by killing them all but about a dozen. Latitude of this island 7°–10′ south, Longitude 177°–24′ east.[28]

This is an illuminating entry. It bears out the theory that the natives of the South Sea Islands made long voyages from island to island. In this case, Captain Plaskett's forethought in providing his ship with an interpreter—and a native Ellice Islander, at that—had enabled him to make the discovery of Nui and to reveal the further unusual account of the migration thirty years before—in 1797. As Wilkes observed, after sailing from Swains Island to Samoa, with a constant eight-day westerly breeze:

. . . This will serve to show that there is no real difficulty in the population of Polynesia migrating from west to east during this season of the year, when the trade-winds are almost entirely uninterrupted.[29]

In the summer of 1825, two vessels in the service of the King of the Netherlands crossed the Pacific. Captain Eeg, the commander of the *Pollux,* a sloop, signaled the frigate, *Maria Reygersberch,* that he sighted breakers ahead. At sunrise they saw a low island, two miles distant. Approaching the land in long-boats, they bartered with the natives. They placed the island in latitude 7°–10′ south (using three chronometers) and longitude 177°–33′ east (although their lunar observation was taken some nights before). They called it a new discovery, naming it Eeg or Nederlandich Island.[30] (It is now placed on the charts east of the position given by him).

After the stop at Nui the *Independence II* headed south for New Zealand, since from December to March was the season for storms in this region. After provisioning or recruiting at Rotuma, the ship visited the Wallis and Futuna Islands. On December 21, 1827, the explorer in Captain Plaskett again worked in close collaboration with his whaling responsibilities when he came upon an island northwest by north of Vavau in the Tonga Group. He fixed its latitude in 18°–11′ south and its longtitude 175°–48′ east. Called Fanua Lai by the natives, Captain Plaskett named it Brown's Island for the mate who discovered it, and noted that it was inhabited.[31]

Before he reached the New Zealand Grounds, Captain Plaskett sailed southwest of the Fijis and observed that the islands here were erroneously laid down on the existing charts.[32]

William Plaskett was only twenty-one in 1822 when the death of Captain Barrett advanced him from a second mate's berth to the command of the *Independence II.* After this second voyage in the years 1825 to 1828 (on which the discoveries noted above were made) he took out the *Pacific* on three successive voyages to the Brazil Banks and South Atlantic from 1829 to 1832. His next ship was the *Japan,* formerly commanded by his friend, Captain Shubael Chase, on which he (Plaskett) made a voyage to the Indian Ocean. Later he took the *Clarkson* and the *Napoleon* on Pacific Ocean voyages.

Captain Plaskett was not only an astute mariner and a true explorer, but he was an excellent whaleman as well. During the voyage of the *Independence II,* after taking over command off New Zealand, he took in thirteen hundred barrels of sperm oil, from June 1 to October 16, 1823—a four-month period, averaging over three hundred barrels per month.[33] It was a new record for the industry.

Other discoveries were made in the vicinity of Brown's Island, by another whaling master of Nantucket. Captain William Clark, of the *Winslow,* a New Bedford whaler, discovered two islands in 1823 which he placed on his charts as in latitude 15°–30′ south and longitude 177°–10′ west. He gave these comparatively isolated bits of land, encircled by a coral reef, the name Winslow Islands.

> . . . These islands are inhabited by a race of extremely civil and hospitable people, who furnished Captain Clark with abundant supplies. The inhabitants are generally tall and robust, gentle and even timid in their deportment, and possess no war-like instruments.[34]

Another discovery of Captain Clark, which he called Clark's Island, he fixed in latitude 3°–10′ south and longitude 154°–30′ west.[35] This is Malden Island, reputed to have been discovered by Captain Byron in the *Blonde* on July 29, 1825. A triangular, flat coral formation, five miles long, with a narrow fringing reef, this low, uninhabited island is a desolate spot in the Pacific, well away from the Society and Marquesas Islands.

To the south-southwest, one hundred miles away, is another low coral island, Starbuck Island, which was also discovered by a whaleman.

Late in the year 1823, the British whaler *L'Aigle* was on her way to England from Honolulu, having on board the Hawaiian King Kamehameha II and his Queen. Sailing for Tahiti, the ship was off this low barren island in December, when Captain Valentine Starbuck sighted it, and not finding it on his charts he called it Volunteer Island. When he arrived in England in March 1824 he reported his discovery. This Starbuck was of the Milford Haren, Wales, colony of Nantucket whalemen.

But the island had already been discovered three months before the British mariner saw it. On September 5, 1823, the Nantucket whaleship *Hero,* under Captain Obed Starbuck, on a cruise to the Society Islands, saw the island.[36] A journal of this voyage gives us this account:

> While all hands were busily employed seated on the quarter-deck sewing on sails, the cry of "land" by one of the men who had had occasion to go forward was so unexpected and it being so near that it threw us into considerable confusion. . . . It proved to be an undiscovered island, 8 or 10 feet in height, and 2 miles wide by 10 miles long, with a very white beach. It lay in the form of an angle . . . in latitude 5°–32′ south, and west longitude 155°–55. We made an attempt to land on the west side near the north end, but at this place it was unaccessible . . . the one attempt, merely through curiosity, as it has no other temptation being a dreary waste. It is the abode of nothing save sea foul, although its situation is such that if soon made known may save the lives as thousands.[37]

The fate of another whaleship, the *Independence I,* is also a part of the story of Starbuck's Island. This ship, built in 1817, and out of Nantucket under the command of Captain Isaac Brayton on her sixth voyage to the Pacific, ran into the reef ringing Starbuck Island on the night of December 13, 1835.[38]

The crew lowered away their boats and lay outside the wreck until morning. As the surf was high there was considerable danger in landing, but the crew managed to get twelve casks of beef and pork and some bread and other goods. Although the ship's masts were cut away, hoping that this would make her ride easier, so that more supplies could be taken ashore, the surf beat against the ship so fiercely that the *Independence I* went to pieces in five days.

Since the desolate island offered no protection, rude huts were erected with studding sail yards and sail canvas from the wreck. Less than a week had passed when the plan of launching the boats and heading for the Society Islands was decided upon. Twelve of the ship's company then left the island in three boats under Captain Brayton, First Mate Gibson and Second Officer Whippey. Ten men were left on the island.

Two nights out from the island, a series of heavy squalls with rain separated the boats. Although Captain Brayton's and Mr. Whippey's boats found each other, Mate Gibson's boat had vanished and was not seen again. It was believed to have foundered. The two remaining boats kept together and on the twelfth day out, the high mountains of Bora-bora Island of the Society Group, were sighted some thirty miles away to the leeward. Heartened, the men in the boats bent their energies to gain the land and soon were near Lord Howe Island (Ontong Java). Being unable to land because of the heavy surf, they headed for Harvey Island, where fresh water and provisions were obtained.

It was now two weeks since the boats had left Starbuck Island. Prospects for reaching Tahiti were good, but ill-luck met them when they landed at White Turkey Island. Here the natives stove in the boat of Second Officer Whippey and stole a quadrant, among other articles. Captain Brayton sighted a trading schooner, exchanged their remaining boat to pay for a passage to Tahiti. Remaining on White Turkey island by choice, the four other members of the shipwrecked crew were taken off the island by the whaleship *Mentor,* of New London. But only one of these men, John Davis, of Nantucket, came back with the *Mentor* in August 1836. Second Mate Whippey went ashore at Huahine Island, while the others left at Tahiti.[39]

As for the ten men, self-exiled at Starbuck Island, one may well imagine their great joy when on the morning of January 27, 1836, a lookout screamed, "A ship! A ship!" It was the *Mayflower,* of New Bedford, under Captain Joseph Chase, whose masthead man had seen the distress signals flying on the island. The reaction of the "distressed mariners" is best seen through the words of their shipmates:

> When six long weeks had rolled around
>   Wee saw the *Mayflower* bearing down,
> Which made us all cry out with joy,
>   Some help for us is drawing nigh.
>
> Then on our kneews we then did fall
>   And to the Lord our hearts did swell
> That he was in mercy so kind,
>   As to releas the aking mind.
>
> But we now saw one danger more
>   The boat it could not come on shore
> For the surf was running mountains high
>   And it would be dangerous for to try.[40]

One of the shipwrecked crew, fearful, however, lest the ship should not take them off, plunged through the surf and was lifted into one of the *Mayflower*'s lowered boats. On the next day his companions were similarly rescued, and the ship took them to Tahiti. A brief account of the exploit is found in the logbook of the whaleship *Arabella,* of Sag Harbor, Captain James Pierson, commander:

> . . . 8 P.M. spoke the schooner *True Blue,* 21 days from Tahiti for Hero's Island for the wreck and crew of the ship *Independence,* of Nantucket, which was wrecked on that sand island the night of the 13th of December, 1835, and went to pieces in five days, the mate of the said ship being on board the schooner had been to Tahiti in his boat and had got this vessel. They left the island together, Captain, mate and second mate and he parted from them the second or third night and heard nothing more of them—a sad disaster. Mr. Gibson was 12 days in his boat.[41]

Among the uninhabited islands in this region of the central Pacific is Vostok Island, discovered in August 1820 by Admiral Fabian von Bellingshausen of the Russian exploring expedition who named it after his frigate.[42] During the next year Vostok Island was sighted by Captain Stavers in the *Tuscan* and Captain Thornton in the *Supply* both British whalers. When Captain Benjamin Coffin returned to Nantucket in the ship *Reaper* he reported sighting this island in 1828. He thought it a new discovery and called it Reaper Island, placing it in 9°–55′ south latitude and 152°–40′ west longitude.[43] It was some years before the true position of Vostok was accurately placed on the chart and the Russian explorers' claim substantiated. When Lieutenant-Commander Ringgold, in the *Porpoise,* on the U. S. Exploring Expedition's fleet, visited the island in February 1841 he called it Stavers Island.[44]

Other islands near Starbuck and Vostok are Caroline, Jarvis and Flint islands. Although not as barren, these are uninhabited and some nearly destitute of typical South Sea vegetation. Flint Island is nearest the Society Group, being 390 miles northwest of Tahiti. Although authorities have attributed its discovery to a Captain Keen in 1835, the island, with its shrubs and few coconut palms, was seen and its topographical outline drawn by Captain Samuel Bunker in the whaleship *Alexander,* of Nantucket, in April 1826: "At 6 A.M. saw Flint's Island bearing S E dist. 15 miles, past close to it full of wood." [45]

On this same cruise, Captain Bunker sighted an island "not laid down on the chart, Latt^d 10°–09' south, Long. by Observation 152°– 35' west." [46] This would again appear to be Vostok Island (Captain Bunker called it Alexander or Independence Island). Thus, for the second time, two Nantucket whaling masters discovered the same island "not laid down on their charts" without knowing of its prior discovery by Admiral Bellingshausen.

Caroline Island, in almost the same latitude as Vostok, and two degrees further east, is credited as having been discovered by Captain William Broughton in 1795 in the British sloop *Providence.* He saw it from a distance of six miles and named it for the eldest daughter of the First Lord of the British Admiralty. Captain Thornton of the British whaler *Supply,* called it Thornton Island in 1821. Many of the early whaleships reported it. Captain Stavers landed here in 1828 and left hogs to breed. [47] In 1834, Captain William Cash, of Nantucket, in command of the *Courier,* of New Bedford, reported an island bearing NW by N½N from Flint Island, in latitude 10°–36' south. It was

very low and dangerous, being only seen at a short distance. It is important that this should be known to every navigator in the Pacific, as ships leaving the Society Islands, bound North, frequently make Flint's Island, and this lies in the track of ships bound to the line. Two other shipmasters have seen this Island, in about the latitude above given and were near running their ships on it. [48]

Captain George Ruie, of Nantucket, had three men aloft on "strict lookout for whales," cruising in the whaleship *Fanny* south from Christmas Island. His logbook entry reads:

First part . . . strong breezes and clear weather—ship standing to the W. S. W. Four hands looking out for whales. 4 P.M. saw a low, white island bearing S.W. which is not laid down on any chart we have on board. It extends ½ mile W.N.W. and E.S.E. in latitude 0–21 south and longtd 160–26 west. Ship standing to the southward ——7 A.M. saw a school of sperm whales—lowered all boats but could not fall in with them——9 A.M. the boats returned and were hoistered up. [49]

This was Jarvis Island, discovered only a few months before by Captain Broughton, the British mariner, and so named by him. But the latter saw it only the once; Captain Rule and his contemporary whalemen saw it several times on each voyage. These isolated islands became as familiar to them as their own home landfalls. Nothing better could illustrate the dual purpose of the early whalemen in the Pacific than Captain Rule's above entry.

Captain George W. Gardner who took out the new whaleship *Maria* in 1822 and brought her home with a full cargo in 1825, gave a good account of the attempted rebellion of Prince George Tamoree in the Sandwich Islands.[50] On this same voyage, Captain Gardner discovered the island in the Austral Group which still bears the name he gave it—Maria Island. The extract from his log reads:

> Sunday, December 19, 1824. At 4:3 P.M., saw low land to the SE 3 leagues; tacked ship to the ENE at midnight stood to SSW; at 8 A.M. saw land again. It appeared a small island, 6 to 8 miles in length, 3 miles across. Very low. Lat. 21°–45′ South, Long. 155°–10′ west.[51]

Thus, the whaling masters recorded their discoveries as part of their voyaging. By crossing and recrossing their own sailing routes, they frequented uncharted sections of the Pacific. As the unofficial and nationally unrecognized explorers of their country, they were making the Pacific an American ocean.

chapter xxv

~~~∽∾~~~

THE FIRST RECOGNITION
OF ANTARCTICA

And ice, mast high, came floating by,
As green as emarald.
And through the drifts the snowy cliffs
Did send a dismal sheen . . .
—Coleridge, The Rime of the Ancient Mariner

FOR CENTURIES the continent of Antarctica was the subject of mystery. Captain James Cook, of the British Navy, on his remarkable voyages of 1772-75, circumnavigated the great southern continent without sighting it, although he had reason to believe in its existence. "It is true, however," he wrote as of February 6, 1775,[1]

> that the greatest part of this southern continent (supposing there is one) must lie within the polar circle, where the sea is so pestered with ice that the land is thereby inaccessible. The risque one runs in exploring a coast, in these unknown and icy seas, is so very great, that I can be bold enough to say that no man will ever venture farther than I have done; and that the lands which may lie to the South will never be explored.

The discovery of the Antarctic Continent has been credited to Lieutenant Charles Wilkes of the United States Exploring Expedition, and to Admiral Dumont D'Urville of the French Navy, both of whom approached the ice barrier of the new continent from different positions in January 1840.[2] However, a few years ago American historians advanced belief that the actual discovery of Antarctica's frozen shores

355

probably occurred two decades earlier, when American sealers at the South Shetlands came upon a mountainous, snow-capped land to the south, now known as the Palmer Peninsula.

In 1940, Colonel Lawrence Martin, the Chief of the Division of Maps in the Library of Congress, presented documentary evidence which supports the claim that Captain Nathaniel Brown Palmer, an American sealing master of Stonington, Connecticut, had sighted Antarctica where its peninsula juts out toward the South Shetland Islands, five hundred miles south of Cape Horn.[3] The discovery was claimed to be as of November 1820, when Captain Palmer commanded the sloop *Hero,* one of the Stonington fleet of sealers. The section of the Antarctic peninsula then sighted has been called by a number of geographers Palmer's Land, while the peninsula is now known as the Palmer Peninsula. The logbook of the *Hero* is in the Library of Congress.

On the basis of the log of the Nantucket schooner *Huntress*—found by the present writer beneath the pasted clippings of an old scrapbook—a new claim is advanced here; namely that Christopher Burdick, captain of the *Huntress,* was among the first to recognize the continent of Antarctica as a continental mainland.

The South Shetland Islands were accidentally discovered by Captain William Smith, an Englishman who was making regular commercial voyages from Buenos Aires around Cape Horn to Valparaiso. In the brig *Williams* Captain Smith, whose course had been laid far south of Cape Horn in an attempt to circumvent contrary gales, on February 19, 1819, sighted the islands and on the next day confirmed his discovery, although he did not land. The South Shetlands are a chain of volcanic origin between 61° and 63° South and 53° to 63° West. A strait, fifty miles wide, filled with ice and made doubly treacherous by fog, separates them from the Palmer Peninsula.[4] Later, Lieutenant Edward Bransfield, of the British Naval squadron in the Pacific, was commissioned to accompany Smith on another voyage to the South Shetlands from December 1819 to March 1820. An account of this exploration was composed by Dr. Adam Young, surgeon of the expedition, and printed in the *Edinburgh Philosophical Journal* of April 1821.

The report that there were seals in these islands immediately aroused the interest of both American and British sealers. William Herbert Hobbs, in his exhaustive study, "The Discoveries of Antarctic within the American Sector," states that Smith probably had secretly told British sealers at Buenos Aires of the whereabouts of the South Shetlands, and that the British *Espirito Santo* sailed from that port in October 1819.[5] The American brig *Hersilia,* Captain James P. Sheffield, which had sailed from Stonington, Connecticut, late in July 1819, is supposed to have spoken the *Espirito Santo* at the Falklands and arrived at the South Shetlands about the same time as the British craft —in November 1819. She returned to Stonington in July 1820. Next, a fleet of five vessels left Stonington harbor in the summer of 1820, and several other ports sent out craft as well. Just how many British ships there were is not known, but Captain Burdick in his journal speaks of the British being able to muster eighty men in case there was a pitched battle between the rival sealers.

The mountainous South Shetlands, covered with snow most of the year, where moss, lichen, and some straggling grass are the only growing things, were found to be a great haunt for sea-elephants and fowl as well as seals. The desolate shores did contain several harbors for anchorage purposes, but they were dangerous because of sudden gales, drifting ice, and the great fogs which swept in from the unknown seas to the south. The curious phenomena of hot water springs at two harbors made these fog banks especially thick, adding greatly to the eerie appearance of the rocky shore and beaches.

Captain Christopher Burdick sailed the fifty-foot schooner *Huntress* out of Nantucket on August 4, 1820. Two weeks later he sighted Faial in the Azores, and at five o'clock the next morning hove-to off Pico. "Lowered away the boat and sint it on shore for vegetables. Tacking off and on for boats," he recorded. Continuing his voyage, he made the Cape Verdes on August 28, where he took a cargo of salt on board at the island of Boa Vista. His next passage was across the South Atlantic to the Falkland Islands; on the way (October 26) he spoke to the ship *President,* Captain Cottle, seventy-three days out from Nantucket, and "lowered away the boat and went on board."

On October 31, 1820, the *Huntress* arrived at the Falklands. Captain Burdick carefully noted his approach to the "Western Falklands Island," where, after sailing alongshore, he discovered an opening in the land which appeared to form a bay, with several small islands ahead. His careful seamanship is recorded as follows:

Wednesday, the 1, November [1820]

Begins with moderate Brezes and pleasant at ½ past 12 Being abrest of the opening Concluded to run in close in perceived plenty of kelp in the passage, sent the boat to examine and tacked off. The boat return and reported 2 fathoms in pass & no roks & a Large Sound inside, whre and run in sent the Boat ahead & cros^d the sound to the southward which was six miles wide & 10 fathoms water went in to a snug harbor at 5 P.M. anchored in 2 fathoms. So ends.

. . . took one man with me and went on shore and went onto a hill about 1½ mile high. From it Could Count about fifty islands which formd the sound, the principal part. The smaller islands lay on the South of the sound, the Land I was to anchor under which I supposed to be the main island, proved to be one of those islands, it being very hazy I could not determine whether ther was any islands to the Southward and Westward of me. Got on board at 3 P.M. So Ends.

The Land to the North hindered getting the sun. Suppos^d Lat. 51° 20.

Thursday, the 2 November

. . . All hands employed in Breaking out the hold and shifting the salt room to get at the mainmast. Stong gales. . . . At 11 the gale increasing the schr. hooked her anchor. Let go the small anchor, veered out, 25 & 50 on the other which brought the hawser to with 60 fathoms. At 12 it blew tremendous the schr. heeling well over. . . . Let go the sheat anchor and veared out on him, and then I turned in.

All this time we were lying under the Lee of the Land—¾ mile off in less than 2 fathoms water and good holding ground and smooth, all except the wind had the water right up. At 6 P.M. moderate, took in Sheat Anchor.

Friday the 3 November

. . . Got the fouryard and main Boom up for sheers hoisted our main-mast out of the step, Cut five feet off the heal & steeped it anew which brought the place sprung in the wake of the hardness. At 3 P.M. took a man with me on shore at 6 returned with 14 geese. Saw several seal around the shore in the water.

While in the Falklands, Captain Burdick sighted a small schooner off the mouth of the harbor. He hoisted his colors and, as the schooner ran into the passage, hailed her. "Asking her where from, she answered from West Point. I, thinking she was a-going to anchor, asked no more questions. She tacked soon after and went out without anything more passing between us and was soon out of sight behind the land. . . . She sot no collours." Such were the mysterious visits of rival sealers.

That the Nantucket sealing master, then twenty-seven years old, had more than ordinary curiosity about the geography of his landfalls is evident from his entry at the Falklands:

> Sunday the 5
> Begins with Light [breezes] NW and pleasant. At 8 A.M. started with a Boat's Crew & rowed around the island to the southward and Eastward which I was to anchor under until I came out on the west side it blowing very fresh . . . and very ruff. I landed on a Large Island to the Southward of me and went onto a mountain to see what I coul^d but the Clouds on the mountain hindered me from seeing. Returned to the vessel at 6 P.M. without being much wizer. So Ends this Day.

On November 22, 1820, he left the Falklands, heading for the South Shetlands, this time in company with the New Haven ship *Huron,* Captain Davis, and her shallop, or tender. On November 25 they sighted Staten Island, and Captain Burdick took an observation so as to figure his variations. On November 30, he wrote:

> Begins with moderate breezes and thick cloudy weather attended with snow at 6 P.M. thick fogg hove two being in coullered water. Latter part broken cloudy & a very thick haze to SSE. At 10 A.M. the water being very much discoullered sounded 150 fathoms—no bottom. Lat. 61° 40.

The next day, December 1, 1820, at 4 P.M. the murky weather lifted a little and Captain Burdick made sail. At meridian he made his latitude out as being in 62°-7′ south, and at that time sighted land to the southeast. On December 2, he lay to under the land looking for a harbor. The fog came in so thickly that the larger craft sailed off the shore, leaving the shallop to search for a harbor. A northwest gale drove them to the eastward, but they were back in the vicinity of the land the next day searching for the shallop, which they found the following noon. The small craft had found a harbor. On December 8, Captain Burdick entered in his log:

. . . At 4 P.M. hauled our wind to Beat up the harbor in Co with ship *Huron* of New Haven and her shallop. Middle and Latter part brisk winds. Stood in the Yanky Sound and went into harbor came two at 6 A.M. in 16 fathoms. Landlocked found five Stonington vessels here. So ends sea account.

The five Stonington craft were the fleet commanded by Captain Benjamin Pendleton, consisting of the brig *Frederick,* Captain Pendleton; the brig *Hersilia,* Captain Sheffield; schooner *Hero,* Captain Nathaniel Brown Palmer; schooner *Fregift,* Captain Thomas Dunbar; and schooner *Express,* Captain Ephraim Williams. This was only a portion of the sealing craft at the South Shetlands at this time, as there were an equal number of ships from other American ports and probably as many more British sealers.

The harbor where the fleet lay, Yankee Harbor, was on the southeast coast of Greenwich Island. The business of sealing combined the work of shore crews and boat crews. When a herd was located on the rocky beach, a shore crew was landed to surround and kill them. Then began the skinning operations, after which the sealskins were taken off by the small boats. It is apparent from accounts left by the sealers, such as Captain Burdick's *Journal,* that shipmasters took turns in leading shore crews and boat crews.

The Nantucket and New Haven crews got to work quickly. Captain Burdick reports as of Saturday, December 9, 1820:

> Begins with Brisk wind from NW. sent Mr. Coleman [first mate of the *Huntress*] and eight men on board the shallop . . . the ship sent twenty-two and 2 boats. At 10 A.M. the shallop went out to find a place to land the men for sealing. Latter part brisk gales and rainy. So Ends.

While Captain Burdick remained on board the *Huntress,* clearing out his hold and mending his sails, the shallop of the *Huron* hunted seals along the shores of Greenwich and Friesland (Livingston) Islands. On Wednesday, December 13, Captain Burdick noted:

> Begins with moderate Breezes at NE and Pleasant. At 10 A.M. Capt. Davis and myself with seven men went up Yanky sound to the westward in a boat to see if we could See any place for seals. About 12 miles up the Sound which brought us out on the west side found a Scotch brigg to anchor. She had her men on shore on a

Beech but there was no seal up. Found a passage out to the westward through this Sound, followed it through with our boat it being full of rocks, found seals at 6 P.M. returned to our vessels with fifteen seals. The shallop not returned. So Ends.

It was at this time that the Stonington sealer *Clothier* was wrecked on the northwest shore of Friesland (Livingston) Island. The log of the *Huntress* records this as of Thursday, December 14, 1820:

> Begins with moderate breezes and pleasant. A strange Boat came in which proved a Boat from Capt. Clark's fleet from Stonington and reported the loss of Captain Clark's ship the *Clothier* which run on a Rock in attempting to make a harbor about 15 miles to the westward of where we lay the rest of his fleet had harbored closely by the ship and was saving what they could. Latter part strong gale. So Ends.

Four days later, after weathering a northeast gale accompanied by snow, Captain Burdick made a cruise "around the island called Frezeland," to the south-southwest. On this occasion the Nantucket captain met Captain Johnson, of the schooner *Jane Maria,* of New York. Johnson was one of the most adventurous of the sealing skippers and was to lose his life several years later searching for the land which he expected to find southwest of the South Shetlands. Captain Burdick wrote of the meeting:

> . . . Employed towing to windward to get around the island. At 9 P.M. fell in with Capt. Johnson's fleet of New York from Raged Island looking for Yanky harbor his fleet consists of one Brigg two Schooners and shallop.

Captain Burdick found several large herds of seals at vantage points along the south coast of Friesland (Livingston) Island. He obtained 980 skins and also discovered that the Stonington craft had landed fifty men along a seven-mile stretch of shore. He returned to Yankee Harbor on December 22, 1820, and again met Captain Johnson and his fleet there. The latter had a total of sixteen hundred skins, having arrived at the South Shetlands two months before the *Huntress.* On Christmas Day, Captain Burdick wrote the following in his log:

> Begins with strong Gales at NE with Snow and hail. Me and the Boy busily engaged in scraping the ice from the cables & sides of the vessel. The NE side of our harbor is formed By And Iceburg from

three to five hundred feet high from the surface of the water which Break off in flakes of 4 or 5 hundred tons with a report as Loud as a Cannon. These pieces of ice fall into the water and the wind drives them afoul of us which is very chafing. Latter part moderate. Employed in mending scrivits on the cables. So ends this Day.

In such a dangerous anchorage the *Huntress* lay with the sealing fleet, all with their anchors down, when a gale broke. On one occasion Captain Burdick records: "A large boat as big as two whaleboats which was hauled up on shore was Blown about 30 or 40 rods and stove to pieces." On January 9, 1821, Captain Davis, of the *Huron,* who had "cruised as far to the northeast as the land extended but found no seal to speak of," returned with the shallop. The log of the *Huntress* reads under this date:

> Captain Davis . . . fell in with an English ship and brigg that were castaway, took part of their crews and put them on board an English vessel lying at Ragged Island. Returned to where the men were stationed and brought in 2470 Skins. Took 696 on board being my part. . . . So Ends this Day.

Sealing operations continued to be successful. The shallop returned with 627 skins on January 13, 1821. Captain Burdick took her along the coast of Livingston Island again on a cruise and obtained 981 more skins, but had a difficult time of it when a northeast snowstorm sprang up, followed by a "tremendous gale," forcing him to sail offshore, standing to the "southward and east on a wind . . . with a tremendous sea and perishing cold weather." With the gale increasing, on January 20, at 4 A.M., he sighted President (Snow) Island, the next island southeast of Friesland (Livingston), about three miles ahead. He recorded:

> The gale still increasing, took in the mainsail, whore around and ran between President Island and Frezeland, among a parcel of ledges and hauled round between Ragged Island and Frezeland and anchored in 7 fathoms with both anchors.

The vagaries of South Shetland weather were characteristic of the Antarctic. Upon his return to Yankee Harbor two days later, Captain Burdick remarked that, the wind having fallen away to a calm, he had to lower the boat to tow the shallop into the anchorage.

Some of the most interesting entries in the log now appear:

Thursday, the 25th [January 1821]

. . . A Boat came in belonging to Captain Barnard of Nantucket in Brig *Charity* having been robbed of eighty skins by the English at Sheriffs Cape and drove off the beach. 4 P.M. our Boat came in from a cruise with 52 skins having likewise been drove from the beach at Sheriffs Cove by the English where he said there was plenty of seal. The muskets of all the vessels in the harbor being nine in number and all Americans being notified of the Same all repaired on board ship *Huron*, Capt. Davis, to Consult about what to be done Where we all agreed as one to Muster all our men from our Several Camps and as one body to go on to said beach at Sheriffs Cape and take seal by Fair means if we could but at all Events to take them. So Ends.

Friday, the 26

. . . At 6 A.M. Capt. Bruno of the schooner *Henry* started in a Boat with the First officer of the schro. *Expres* with a circular Letter signed by all the masters to their Respective officers at their Camps to muster all their men save a man at Each Camp and with their Boat to Repair ammediately under the guidance of Capt. Bruno to a Small Bay not far from Sheriffs Cape where Capt. Davis and Capt. Barnard would meet them in the shallop with 5 boats and 33 men . . . the residue of the men from the harbor at 8 P.M.

Capt. Davis and Capt. Barnard started in the shallop they met at the place appointed 120 men, they would have to land and by the best information we can get the English have but about 80 men there. So Ends.

The expected battle between the rival sealers could not have taken place, as Captain Burdick makes no further mention of the subject. It is probable that the British sealers, seeing the large group of Americans determined on using the rookeries, with laudable discretion quietly withdrew.

On the next day, the Nantucket skipper made an important entry in his log. What he wrote is significant of where his true interests lay—in the possibility of discovering new rookeries on land which the American sealers knew lay to the south of the South Shetlands and heretofore not visited by other sealers. He records as follows:

Saturday, the 27

. . . Capt. Johnson came in in shallop from a cruise of 22 days—said he had been to the Lat 66° S and the Long. of 70° West and still found what he took to be Land but appeared to be sollid islands of Ice and Snow. Whether he had found any seal he did not inform nor otherwise than then to say ther was none so far South as he had ben.

This was a very definite report and Captain Burdick promptly took it into account. The next day he observed that the "Stonington shallops" had returned after a cruise of fourteen days to the northward and eastward and had seen no seals. Thus, two possible locations were eliminated. When Captain Davis returned a few days later from a cruise to the westward and brought back 1,720 skins, he had taken care of the shore in that direction. There was only one compass direction left toward which Captain Burdick might sail—south by west, into the unknown seas. This direction he followed two days later.

In the interim he went with several other ship masters to attend the auction of articles from the wreck of the *Clothier* at the place called Clothier Harbor. The master of the wrecked ship, Captain Clark, was a fellow-Nantucketer. On February 1, 1821, he met two well-known sealers here—Captain Winship, of Boston, who had come down on the *O'Cain* three months before, and "Capt. Smith, the man that Discovered this Land first. He had two vessels and 60 men and had got 45,000 skins." Their talk was not recorded, but it may be assumed that Captain Burdick asked many questions of Captain Smith.

On February 12, 1821, Captain Burdick sailed "southward and westward." "Light brezes and Calm, trying to get to the Southward," he entered the first day. Cruising along the southern coast of Livingston Island, he took his first officer, Mr. Coleman, off the bleak shore. The next day, sailing west along shore, they found a rookery and collected 446 skins between them. Later that day he "stood to the southward." On the fifteenth of the month he continued south-southwest. The shallop used by the New Haven and Nantucket captains was named the *Cecelia*. From her deck, Captain Burdick recorded the sighting of Antarctica:

> Begins with Light airs and variable with Calms pleasant wether at Meredian Lat by obs. 63 . . 17 S President Island Bearing North 3 Leagues mount Pisco SW b W dist 7 Leagues the Peak of Frezeland NE ½ W 11 Leagues Deception Island NE by N 8 Leagues and a small low Island SSW 6 Leagues to which I am bound *and Land from South to ESE which I suppose to be a Continent.* Later part

fresh breze at North. At 6 p.m. came to anchor under low island among a parcel of rocks Sent the Boat on shore She returned with 22 Seal So end thes 24 hours.*

The mere fact that Captain Burdick laconically announces sighting "Land from South to ESE which I suppose to be a Continent" reveals that he had sailed the *Huntress* between Hoseason Island and into the present De Gerlache Strait, to an anchoring place where it was easily possible for him to sight the black, rocky, and precipitous shore of the Antarctic Continent with its great, snowy mountain-plateau stretching for miles away.

The atmospheric conditions in the Antarctic favored long-range observation and tended to shorten distances. Burdick mentions sighting Friesland (Livingston) Island more than thirty miles away to the northeast, but it is probable that the peak of Friesland (Livingston) was much farther off, thus placing the continent of Antarctica—twenty miles away—clearly in view. Furthermore, he continued his cruise south for several hours, anchoring at 6 p.m. at an island, some ten miles from the continental shore across De Gerlache Strait. He remained in the vicinity two days, going ashore on both sides of the island and getting sealskins. It was not until February 19 that he returned to Yankee Harbor.

Under these circumstances, it is fair to assume that the Nantucket sealer had no reason to doubt the existence of a continent across the channel from his anchorage. He not only had a long period in which to observe, but he gives bearings which enable one to trace his five-day cruise. Most important of all is the record of the log itself: *"Land from South to ESE which I suppose to be a Continent."*

On the following day Captain Burdick continued:

Friday the 16
Begins with moderate Breezes at NE Got all the men on shore to take seal drove up four hundred and nocked them Down. The wind shifting in to the SW which making a bad harbor where (we) lay took 8 men on board and got under way and shifted her round on the NE side and anchored and at 8 p.m. we had got 400 skins on Board. So Ends these 24 hours.

* *Italics* added.

Saturday the 17

Begins with fresh breezes at NE and thick whether. Sent the Boat on shore . . . returned with 30 skins. It Blowing a hard gale right into the harbor we lay in hoisted in the Boat and got underway and Beat out after clearing the Land. Double refd the sail and stood to Northward. So Ends with hard gale and thick snow.

Sunday the 18

. . . Made President [Snow] Island bearing NE stood close in with it and tacked off to Southward at 4 P.M. more moderate wind canting to South, tacked and steered ENE at 8 made Deception Island. Middle and Latter part Light wind making the best of our way for Yanky harbor.

Wednesday the 28

. . . Capt. Inott of the Ship *Samuel* from Nantucket came into our harbor . . . brought me a package of letters.

Captain Burdick sailed for home on March 11, and arrived June 10.

The controversy over the actual discovery of the Antarctic Peninsula has brought such eminent authorities as Hobbs and Martin, of the United States, and Mill and Gould, of Great Britain, into sharp academic disagreement. The claims of Palmer and Bransfield are contrasted, and the recording of map-makers adds to the confusion. However, certain bits of documentary evidence should be noted. The logbook of Captain Palmer; the newspaper marine-column accounts given by the sealers upon their return, the logs of other sealing craft of the same period, and other contemporary material present overwhelming evidence that several American sealers saw the mainland of Antarctica at the same period that Captain Palmer was at the South Shetland Islands.

The logbook entry in the cruise of the sloop *Hero,* which Colonel Martin believes substantiates Captain Nathaniel Palmer's claim to the discovery of Antarctica, is as follows:

Friday November 17th [1820]

This 24 hours commences with fresh Breeses from SWest and Pleasant at 8 P.M. got over under the land found the sea filled with imense Ice Bergs at 12 hove Too under the Jib Laid off & on until morning—at 4 A.M. made sail in shore and discovered—a strait— Trending SSW & NNE—it was Literally filled with Ice and the shore inaccessible we thought it not Prudent to Venture in ice Bore away to the Northerd & saw 2 small islands and the shore every where Perpendicular we stood across towards friesland [Friesland or Livingston Island] Course NNW—the Latitude of the mouth of the strait was 63–45 S Ends with fine weather wind at SSW.

The island sighted by Palmer and thought by Martin to be Trinity Island is forty miles from the nearest South Shetlands. The strait which he mentions as being filled with floating ice is claimed by Colonel Martin to be Orleans Channel, which lies between the continental mainland of Antarctica and Trinity Island; but it is evident that Captain Palmer did not sail into it. Although Colonel Martin thinks that "it is not clear whether it was the coast of the mainland or the shore of these islands that was considered to be perpendicular," the present writer believes that Palmer had the precipitous shores of islands in mind.

H. R. Mill, the eminent British authority, writing his *The Siege of the South Pole,* believes that Palmer actually saw the littoral around Anvers Island, as did, a decade later, Captain John Biscoe.[6] Certain it is that Palmer's Land was for years attached to an island archipelago, as the many maps cited by William H. Hobbs indicate.[7]

The subsequent voyagings of the *Hero* in January 1821 were uneventful. There is no record of a trip south along Palmer Peninsula as far as Marguerite Bay. Captain Palmer is alleged to have made this important exploration, but the claim was made long afterwards, and his logbook entries make no mention of the land.

J. N. Reynolds, in his Congressional Report of 1828, stated that Captain Benjamin Pendleton "discovered a bay, clear of ice, into which he run for a great distance, but did not ascertain its full extent south." [8] And Captain Edmund Fanning, in his *Voyages,* published first in 1833, credits Pendleton with the actual discovery of Antarctica, declaring that he sighted it first from the peak of Deception Island.[9] According to Fanning, Captain Palmer was sent by Pendleton, who was in command of the Stonington fleet, to investigate the land. Unquestionably he was so dispatched, but his object was to hunt for seals; his log book on November 1820 reveals no suspicion that he had seen the great southern polar continent, if he did actually observe the land mass at all. He merely describes the discovery of a "strait." Fanning's account of the meeting between Captain Palmer and the Russian Vice-

Admiral Thaddeus von Bellingshausen in January 1821, when the Russian explorer was in the South Shetlands,[10] is disappointing. The translation of the Russian navigator's account [11] does not contain the story of the American mariner; nor does it bear any resemblance to the elaborate version given by Captain Palmer's niece, Mrs. Richard Fanning Loper, in 1907,[12] or to that of J. R. Spears a few years later.[13] Palmer's joint voyage with Captain Powell, the British sealer, to the South Orkneys in 1821 is a much more conclusive exploration.

Dumont d'Urville, the French admiral, sighted and named the northeast end of Orleans Channel in 1838. Eduard Dallmann, on his voyage of 1874, merely gave it cursory examination.[14] Both were prevented from exploring the channel by the presence of the ice fields and a heavy fog which shrouded the entire area constantly. The Belgian expedition of 1898-99 further explored the coast; and in 1912 the French Hydrographic Office brought out a map of the South Shetlands showing the results of Charcot's explorations in 1903-05 and 1908-09.[15]

The British base their claim to the Palmer Peninsula, which they call Graham Land, on the voyage of Captain Biscoe, in the brig *Tula,* in 1831-32, as "communicated by Messrs Enderby in 1833." This was a truly magnificent Antarctic circumnavigation. But Biscoe did not even venture as close to the land as did the sealers. The British mariner refers to land sighted as Palmer's Land, thus revealing a contact with sealers, and Mill states that "as a matter of historic justice, it seems to us that Powell's name of Palmer Land ought to be retained for the whole group of islands, and possible continental peninsula south of the South Shetlands." [16]

Captain Burdick made another voyage to the South Shetlands, and then sold the *Huntress* and purchased larger craft for the coasting trade between Nantucket and mainland ports. A brig named after him was his next command. In 1831 he died of yellow fever in New Orleans and his body was brought home in a barrel of pickle for interment in Nantucket. That he was a superior navigator is shown by his log, and his untimely death cut short an enterprising career which might have given other fine logs such as resulted from his remarkable voyage in the *Huntress.*

chapter xxvi

～～い〜つい～ハ

RANGING THE WORLD'S
GREATEST OCEAN

*They may celebrate as they will the heroes of Exploring
Expeditions . . . but I say that scores of anonymous Cap-
tains have sailed out of Nantucket that were as great. . . .
All that is made such a flourish of in the old South Sea
Voyages, these things were but the life-time commonplaces
of our heroic Nantucketers.*
—Herman Melville, *Moby Dick*

CONSIDERING THE BENEFITS derived by the city and town dwellers
of the land from the voyages of the men of the sea, little was
known of the whalemen by their contemporaries. It is surprising how
few who enjoyed the lamps and candles which gave comfort to their
homes, cheerfulness to their gatherings, and particular brilliance to
their social events, took the time to reflect on the hazards of the long
whaling voyages which gave them these advantages.

Personal courage is an uncertain sort of human quality. What might
seem brave to some observers would be considered foolhardy to others.
The whalemen were called upon to face solitude, harsh treatment, salt
provisions, bad weather. They endured monotony as well as sudden
emergency of storm and whale chase. Always there was the long toil
at the oars. And usually there was the climax of each lowering—the
attack on the whale.

There was no parleying with these elements. The confinement in
the dimly-lit forecastle; the shock of lashing gales; the long crawl aloft
to furl frozen canvas; the sight of a dreaded lee shore; the dreary hours

369

at lookouts; the quick and awful battles with giant bull whales—these were the leaven of his shipboard life that demanded self-discipline and basic courage; these were the elements which afforded no compromise.

Some of the unusual emergencies which faced a shipmaster may be gleaned from the following excerpt from the logbook of the whaler *Palladium,* of Boston, under Captain Alexander Macy. A large sperm whale had been killed and towed to the side of the ship. The log continues:

> Rove the cutting tackles and cut off the head and called it along-side and cut in the body . . . commenced boiling. The weather continued moderate until 4 A.M. when it blew a strong gale from the southward. We then put out the fires and sent down the topgallant yards. At 8 o'clock A.M. we parted from the head alongside. We then lowered a boat for the purpose of regaining the head. Set the foresail and close-reeft mizen topsail. Seward P. Morse, seaman, abused the Captain whilst on the topsail yard by damning of him. The Captain, seeing cause to correct the said Morse, he, Morse, made stout resistance and took hold of the Captain and would not loose his hold when the Captain bade him. At the same time William Hunt, a seaman, endeavoured to make a revolt in the Ship by forbidding the Capt'n striking Seward P. Morse, and the said William Hunt attempted to lay viollant hands on the Capt'n but was prevented by the Second Officer. The said William Hunt at the same time, having a long knife in a sheath, slung by his side attempted to draw it on the Capt'n, but was prevented by the officers. . . . About 9 A.M. got three whales lines fast to the head and got them to the ship and commenced boiling again.[1]

Thus, a shipboard drama is conveyed in the language of the whalemen. The account poses a few questions but there is no doubt about the drama. Captain Macy neither lost his own head nor the whale's. Both were worth saving. The whale made seventy barrels.

Macy continued his voyage to a successful completion.

One of the most energetic of these pioneering shipmasters was Captain William Worth. In the War of 1812, he was on the whaleship *Charles* but secured his discharge in order to serve with Porter on the *Essex*. At the war's close, Worth resumed whaling. He became master of the *Rambler,* of Nantucket, in 1822, and made six voyages in this ship and the *Howard* until 1841, when he went into the merchant ship service.[2]

During his whaling career Captain Worth made several South Sea discoveries. On his first voyage (1822-1825) as master of the *Rambler*, of Nantucket, he sighted an island in latitude 7° north and longitude 155°–20' east. Though low, it was well inhabited and thickly wooded. He called it Tuck's Island, for one of the owners of the ship. It is now known as Oroluk or St. Augustin Island, and is in the Caroline Group.³

To the west and north, Captain Worth found other islands not on his charts. These were in latitude 8°–45' north and longitude 151°–3' east and were five in number. He named them Worth Islands. They are now called the Nomwin Islands in the Hall group.

Fair winds and favorable currents took the *Rambler* to the north-northwest. While cruising here for whales, Captain Worth sighted a native canoe in distress. Crouched in the bottom of the outrigger craft were fourteen Polynesians, men and women, utterly exhausted and without food and water, the only survivors of an original party of sixty people. Taking them on board, Worth steered for the Marianas Islands, and a few days later came upon one which modern charts call Agrihan Island. Here the natives were landed. Agrihan was uninhabited and the Polynesians appeared happy at this situation.

The sequel of the story came some years later—eighteen years after (1846 to be exact)—when the *Peruvian,* of New London, under Captain William Brown, came up to Agrihan Island. "I was surprised to find one white man and 17 natives of South Sea Islands there, most of them, women." Captain Brown continued:

> The white man stated he had left the whaler *Rose Flower* some 4 years previous, but as there is no such ship, I suspect him a runaway or survivor of mutineers from some English whaler. . . . The natives informed me they had been left on the island 18 years previous by a Captain Worth, master of a Nantucket whaler. . . . The *Peruvian* was the only vessel which had landed since Captain Worth was here. It would be impossible for me to describe the rapturous feelings they displayed when I told them I knew Captain Worth. . . . They wanted to give me everything they had.⁴

An excellent description of Agrihan Island was written in the log of the *Mentor,* Captain George Newell:

. . . in approaching it, it presents a delightfully enchanting appearance. It is pretty high and covered from the waters edge to the top with trees and shrubs which I believe are always green. It abounds with hogs, fowls, coconuts, real fruit plantains etc., and upon the whole I think I should like to live here better than any place I have seen yet.[5]

William Worth, in his long whaling career, visited other portions of the Pacific. He was at the Tuvana Islands, southeast of the Fijis, just after Captain Richard Macy discovered them. In 1825, he sighted some unknown coral reefs which he called Rambler Reefs. After he had retired from the sea he was called back to command one of the "Stone Fleet" vessels sunk in Charleston Harbor approaches during the Civil War.

Another sequel to Captain Worth's voyages also came nearly twenty years later (1846). Captain John Pease, of Martha's Vineyard, in command of the New Bedford whaler *Chandler Price,* came across the Nomwin Islands, north of Truk in the Carolines, which had been discovered in 1825 by Captain Worth in the *Rambler.*

Captain Pease further noted that two groups of islands (seen the day before), which the map maker Norie had placed on his charts but not named, were incorrectly laid down. This group is also called the Hall Islands. While at the Raven Islands, Captain Pease found four white men and several native women and children as the only inhabitants. His suspicions aroused, he asked and was finally given the story by one of the white men. The skipper of a trading schooner from Sydney had killed all the native males, leaving the four whites as sole proprietors.[6]

Captain Prince B. Mooers of the *Spartan,* of Nantucket, sailing in 1825 through the central Pacific, discovered a reef thirty miles west of Palmyra Island (in longitude 162°-2′ west and latitude 5°-45′ north); rediscovered Nauru Island in longitude 161°-35′ east, just below the equator, and was the first man to sight and get the correct position of the Kapingamarangi atoll, in latitude 1°-10′ north and longitude 154°-30′ east. To trace this voyage westward across the Pacific, picking up the various landfalls, is to follow the course of whaling explorers, "blazing the trail" for future voyagers chasing the sperm.[7]

Admiral Krusenstern, the Russian explorer, writing from St. Petersburg in January 1837, to the "Commander of the Exploring Expedition of the United States" (who was to be Lieutenant Wilkes), stated that the Caroline Islands, though well surveyed by Duperry and Lutke, contained several islands whose positions were not correctly charted while others had only been seen by one navigator. This was a situation of which the whalemen were all too well aware. The *Ann Robinson* lost five of her crew at one of the islands in the little-known Carolines in 1833, all murdered by the natives.[8]

The voyages to and from the Japan Grounds, up and down the islands of the eastern Pacific, followed the pattern set by those early whaling masters. Ships 'round Good Hope went up through the East Indies from Timor to Ternate, thence into the deep between the Philippines and Marianas, or through the Carolines. Returning the ships generally went through the Marshall, Gilbert and Ellice groups, passing either side of the Fijis, thence to New Zealand and Australia.

Before many of the trading schooners entered the Caroline Islands, the whalers had sailed through them. Kusaie, as a "high island," is said to have been Captain Crocker's discovery in the Boston ship *Nancy* in 1804, who named it Strong's Island, but Captain Ray, of the *Hope,* of Salem, has a good claim to that honor. When Captain John Gardner, of Nantucket, took out the whaleship *Atlantic* in 1825, he was bound on a profitable voyage which also saw him discovering several groups. First of these was in latitude 8°-28' north and longitude 144°-35' east, the group now called Faraulep, in the western Carolines.[9]

Captain Gardner's most interesting landfall was the group now known as Kapingamarangi Island seen earlier by Captain Mooers in the *Spartan*. Findlay's Directory of the North Pacific Ocean gives the following description of them.

> The group is composed of a dozen low islands, covered with stunted cocoanut trees, which could not be visible beyond ten miles. They are encircled by a reef which from the mast-head appears to enclose a lagoon. . . . Position of northern islet was determined to be in latitude 1°-4' north and longitude 154°-47'-55" east. . . . They were again seen by Captain Symington in 1864.[10]

Captain Gardner placed the group only a few minutes farther east. He charted them some forty years before Captain Symington saw them. The island called Ebon or Boston, just south of the Ralik Chain of the Marshall Islands, was discovered on May 25, 1824, by Captain George Joy, of the whaler *Boston,* of Nantucket. It is a beautiful atoll, and Captain Hiram Covell, who came upon it in the *Alliance,* of Newport, in 1831, thought he had made a new discovery.

When the German geographer E. Behm made a study of the Pacific Ocean in 1859, he outlined one area in the central Pacific which he designated American Polynesia. Such a name was deserved, although the political significance of those times was directly concerned with the acquisition of islands for the guano companies. This area was also so contained in the *Royal Atlas of Modern Geography* by the British Geographer Alexander Keith Johnson in both the 1873 and 1882 editions. Such a term "American Polynesia" does more than merely imply that the Yankee whalemen visited the islands in it; it recognizes the fact that they contributed to the world's maritime knowledge through discovery of many of these islands.

About thirty-five miles above Baker Island, in longitude 176°–03′ west, is Howland—a barren, uninhabited island which also assumed considerable importance at the time of the controversy over the establishment of air bases there in the late 1930's. It was claimed by the American Guano Company as having been discovered by Captain John Netcher of the New Bedford whaler *Isabella* on September 9, 1842. A correspondent in the *Providence Post* so identified it at about the same time (1859) that Captain Robert Eldridge of the bark *Amazon,* of Fairhaven saw it.

The actual discoverer of this three-mile long island, with its low, growing grasses and shrubs, was Captain Daniel McKenzie, of the New Bedford whaleship *Minerva Smith,* who came upon the island early in November 1827. Captain Shubael Clark, of Nantucket, who was the first mate of the New Bedford craft at this time, wrote:

> Captain McKenzie went on shore and left a bottle with a paper in it, on which was written the day and the date of the discovery, the latitude 0°–47′ north and longitude 176°–35′ west, and the name of Howland Island, after the owner of the ship.[11]

The discoverers of the Phoenix Islands will always be mysterious. Captain Henry Barber, in the ship *Arthur,* on a voyage from Port Jackson to the northwest coast of America in 1794, passed through the northern islands. The name Arthur Island was placed on Arrow-smith's chart in 1798. Captain Barber is credited with naming Drum-mond's Island in the Gilberts.[12] Captain Joshua Coffin's discovery of Gardner's Island will later be noted. But it is unrealistic to con-sider that the whalemen sailed all through this section of the Pacific without sighting these islands. When Wilkes' men in 1840 came upon two which they named Hull and McKean, they found one inhabited by a Frenchman and eleven natives from the Society Islands, seeking turtle, etc.[13]

As for the name of the group: the *Phoenix,* of Nantucket, sailed in 1821, under Captain David Harris and was then the only craft of that name in this part of the ocean. It was followed by the *Phoenix,* of New Bedford. In the March 7, 1825 issue of the *Inquirer,* of Nan-tucket, was a list of island discoveries with no names given, but the latitudes were those of the present Phoenix Islands. The Reynolds report in 1828 lists several more.

Norie, in his map of 1825, lists Canton as Mary's Island, and Reynolds in 1828 calls it Mary Balcourt, and Barney's Island. The *Equator,* of Nantucket, under Captain Joseph Barney, cruised here in 1823-24, and so did Captain Obed Starbuck in the *Loper,* who probably did not have the correct longitude when he plotted the posi-tion of the two islands which he found. Reynolds attributes the dis-coveries to a "Captain Emmett," but gives no date. Enderbury Island may be a corruption of Enderby the name given by an English whal-ing master.

There can be no dispute over the origin of the name Canton Island, formerly Mary's Island. On March 5, 1854, the New Bedford whale-ship *Canton* struck this island's outer shore and became a total wreck. Thirty-two men, under Captain Andrew Wing, landed safely and three weeks later set out in the whaleboats for the Kingsmills. Due to the northerly set of the current, they missed their objective, and for forty-five days they headed west until they arrived safely at the island of Tinian in the Marianas. Not a man was lost, although they suffered great hardships from hunger and thirst. It is estimated that the

Canton's crew sailed four thousand miles in their open boats during their long forty-five-day voyage. When Captain Skinner, of the bark *John A. Robb,* landed at this island several months later, and found the wreck of the *Canton,* he also found a bottle containing a message from Captain Wing, outlining the disaster.[14]

A study of the logbooks will reveal many records left by the sea-hunters to show they were far from being unacquainted with the importance of their geographical discoveries. Their researches into the ocean currents were of invaluable help to Lieutenant Charles Wilkes, and Matthew Fontaine Maury in their studies. For Maury's monumental work none other than Captain Daniel McKenzie, the New Bedford whaleman, was selected to copy in abstract hundreds of whaling logbooks.

Excerpts from the journals of Captains George Chase, Richard Macy, William Plaskett and others have shown pretty clearly how these early whaling masters were aware of the Pacific scene. As a further example, it will not be amiss to quote from Captain Alexander Macy's journal. While on a voyage in the ship *Peruvian,* of Nantucket (in which he reached the Pacific during the summer of 1825), Captain Macy saw land in the west southwest some twelve miles distant, his ship then standing south by east.[15] On the following morning, he saw what looked like two islands. Upon drawing nearer, he found it to be one high island with a valley running between its high peaks. The island was luxuriously clothed in green woods and the white beach sparkled in the sun.

Running close to shore, the *Peruvian* was soon approached by a large canoe which came under its stern and remained there an hour.

"It's inhabitants," wrote Captain Macy, "were of large stature, of ferocious countenance, and well-armed with spears and clubs. Their conduct and appearance was very suspicious and their persons were very different from any natives I had ever seen, their skin being entirely free from scars, punctures or stains."

Soon after, other canoes were seen to leeward, paddling in a direction as though to intercept the ship's course. The maneuvers of these natives appeared so hostile that Captain Macy wasted no time in setting more sail and heading offshore. In their canoes, the natives set up a demonstration, continuing their pursuit until dark.

Whether this was a new island or not, Captain Macy was not sure, but the few articles he saw in the canoes and the character of the natives convinced him they had never met with white men before. He placed the island in latitude 8°–32′ south and longitude 157°–32′ west.

This was Penryhn's Island, discovered by Captain Sever in the British ship, *Lady Penryhn,* on August 9, 1788. But neither Sever nor Kotzebue (in 1816) had approached the island. It was Captain Macy who, rediscovering it thirty-four years after Sever, correctly placed it on the charts. He informed the world, through the medium of the Nantucket *Inquirer,* that "the fact of its being inhabited by people strong and savage may be of importance to such as may hereafter visit it."

This fact was of some consequence. In November 1830, the Salem trading ship *Glide* approached Penryhn "for the purpose of procuring some grass for our live stock, if possible."

Endicott, the third mate, wrote in his journal:

> At 5 P.M. we were near to the shore when the natives came off in great numbers and appeared perfectly savage and fierce, hallowing and shaking spears. The Captain had given orders for every man on board to arm himself. . . . We endeavoured to trade with them and had succeeded in purchasing some cocoanuts when the Captain, in endeavouring to persuade one of the natives to come on board, another native threw his spear at the Captain and slightly wounded him in the neck. He immediately gave orders to fire at them which was accordingly done and 7 or 8 of the natives were killed. We immediately filled our sails and stood on our course, leaving the natives to bewail the visit of civilized people to their uncivilized shores.[16]

The whalemen have often accepted the blame for many South Sea happenings by not taking the trouble to deny alleged practices. In this instance, the contrast between Captain Macy's caution and Captain Archer's near fatal lack of it is obvious.

Another whaling master who sighted and accurately charted Penryhn Island was Captain William Cash in the *Harvest* in 1839. He described the island, as well-wooded with coconut trees principally, and inhabited. Captain Cash, using two chronometers, took the island's position, and found it placed forty miles west of its location on Arrowsmith's chart. While in the *Courier,* of New Bedford, in 1834, Captain Cash deduced that "Bawman's, Roggeveen's and Tenhoven's" islands were further west than their positions on the charts.[17]

But to return to the unknown discoverers of the Phoenix Group: Following the voyage of the *Loper* there in 1823, the next whaleship to announce discovery was the *Ganges,* of Nantucket, under Captain Joshua Coffin 2d. Late in 1825, the *Ganges,* sailing south from Honolulu, sighted a coral atoll which he placed in latitude 4°–30′ south and longitude 174°–22′ west. This is only a few minutes from its latest accepted (U. S. Navy) position, and the name Gardner Island (in honor of Gideon Gardner, owner of the ship), is still retained by geographers.[18]

Many voyagers throughout the Pacific have written of coming upon an island, and yet how many could appreciate them as fully as the whalemen. Here was a typical South Sea atoll, a beautiful, curving strand of white coral, shimmering like a pearl necklace; above, the lush greenery of the coconut and pandanus trees—a jewel set in a blue sea.

When the U. S. Exploring Expedition, visited it, in 1840 (August 19), the sailors were landed and amused themselves in collecting beautiful tail feathers from the exotic tropic birds, "which they twitched from the birds as they sat on its nest." [19] Wilkes noted that the vegetation here was unlike any other of the low islands or Polynesia he had seen, being devoid of low shrubbery. The naval officers made several observations while on the island, determining the compass variation at 7°–26′ east and the dip at 7°–39′ south.

This was not the only island which Captain Coffin discovered on this voyage in the *Ganges.* Proceeding southwest, in the customary track of the whaleships, he probably stopped at the Tonga Islands before heading south for the New Zealand Grounds. In latitude 31°–13′ south and longitude 178°–54′ west, he found, "an island not laid down," in his charts, which he called Coffin's Island.[20] This is south of the Kermadec Islands Group and is probably the one called Curtis Island.

On his next cruise north, from the Tonga Isles, Captain Coffin sighted an atoll—two long, narrow islets, forming a continuous run of reef without any entrance into the lagoon. A village was located on the northern point of one islet, and another situated at the southern part of the west ring of coral.[21] Densely covered with coconut trees, their fronds rising sixty to seventy feet in the air, this island was visible at a distance of about fifteen miles.

The whaling master was greeted by canoes literally loaded with natives. So friendly were they and so eager to trade, that they swarmed into one of the boats preparing to go ashore. One of the natives grabbed a hatchet from the whale boat and jumped into his canoe. The report states:

> Captain Coffin discharged a pistol at some distance over the heads of the natives in their canoes, whereupon they all fell as instantly as if they had received an electric shock; and after lying apparently lifeless for a short time, they all started up, seized their paddles, and rowed off with an astonishing velocity. The natives apparently had no knowledge of fire arms.[22]

To this island Captain Coffin gave the name Great Ganges, placing it in latitude 10°–25' south and longitude 160°–45' west. It is now called Manihiki. Some nineteen miles west by north, Captain Coffin sighted another island called by the natives Rakahanga and by the whaleman Little Ganges Island. He was only two minutes out on his latitude and four minutes off on his longitude in fixing this island at 10° south latitude and 161°–01' west longitude. It was also inhabited.[23]

As these islands were not on his chart, Captain Coffin believed them to be new discoveries. Several years after returning home in 1827, he learned that Captain Patrickson, of the ship *Good Hope,* had sighted the islands in 1822 and had named them Humphrey and Rierson islands. As for Rakahanga, or Rierson (Little Ganges), it was first discovered by Admiral Bellingshausen, the Russian explorer, in August 1820, who wrote: "Inhabitants are treacherous enough to carry branches, as a sign of peace, on one hand, and stones for attack in the other." [24] He named it Grand Duke Alexander Island. From the record, Captain Coffin was the first white man to land at Manihiki or Humphrey (Great Ganges). His position of Rakahanga corresponded with that given by Bellingshausen.

Unfortunately Captain Joshua Coffin died at the comparatively young age of forty-five, before he could carry his explorations further into the Pacific.

In the month of July 1833, Captain Elihu Coffin, while proceeding west-southwest on a cruise from Rakahanga Island (Little Ganges) in the whaleship *Mary Mitchell,* of Nantucket, heard the lookout call, "Land-ho!" Off the larboard bow, "some ten miles distant," was a cloud-like formation on an otherwise clear horizon. Changing his course, Captain Coffin soon came on to an almost perfectly formed atoll. Oval in shape, almost a mile wide, with cocoanut palms rising seventy-five feet in the air, and a coral reef surrounding it with a fringe of foam, this was a South Sea paradise. Captain Coffin placed the island in latitude 11°–30′ south and longitude 165°–35′ west.[25] This is within a few minutes of the position given it by the latest naval observations.

However, in the logbook of the whaleship *Fanny,* Captain George Rule, of London, is the record of the first actual discovery of this attractive island. Captain Rule tells it thus:

> June 7, 1823 . . . At daylight more moderate, made all sail. 6 A.M. saw an Island bearing W. ½ N. distant about 5 leagues—9 A.M. sent the boat ashore—No inhabitance, plenty of wood and fish, saw no fresh water. This island is not laid down on any chart we have on board—It extends about 1½ miles S.S.E. and N.N.W.—a reef runs round the Island with in a 100 rods of the shore—no bottom within a 100 yards of the reef. Latitude 11–48 South, Longitude 165–47 west. At noon the boat returned to the ship.[26]

In justice to its first discoverer, the atoll should be properly called Rule Island. The name given by this whaling master, however, was Lydra Island.

This gemlike island, which Robert Louis Stevenson declared the most perfect he ever saw in his journeys through the South Seas, is now called Nassau Island. Oddly enough this name is taken from the whaleship *Nassau,* of New Bedford, under Captain John Samson, who sighted it in 1835. The log of the ship records, under that date, the following:

> . . . At daylight discovered an Island off the lee quarter bearing N.W. by W. distant 12 miles and run down and went on shore. Found

plenty of fish and plenty of wood growing on the Island. Found no place to land with a boat, the shore altogether iron bound. Found it by observation to be in latitude 11°–20' south and longitude 165°–30' west.[27]

Eighteen days before the *Nassau* came upon the island, the whaler *Awashonks,* of Falmouth, under Captain Prince Coffin, sighted it in latitude 11°–38' south and longitude 165°–06' west. The logbook recorded the following facts:

. . . sent 2 boats ashore, found no inhabitants, saw no landing, with the boats. 4 men swam ashore and found plenty of wood and turtle and Beach La Mer. It is a small low isle not laid down in any book or chart I have on board . . .[28]

Two other whaleships came upon Nassau Island a year later—the *Ranger,* of London, and the *Audley Clark,* Captain Joseph Paddock, of Newport, Rhode Island. Believing it also a new discovery, Captain Paddock named it Newport Island, having come upon it December 28, 1836.

The *Nassau* had sailed into the Pacific early in 1834, and its succeeding months of cruising through the Pacific were typical of the whaleships of that period. Courses followed were from the South American coast to the Marquesas, north to the equator, thence either on to Honolulu or south again to Tahiti.

If the latter route was adopted, the whaleships invariably cruised to the westward, making landfalls from Jarvis or Starbuck islands to Rakahanga, thence to the Friendly (Tonga) Islands. Here, the course would depend on the time of the year. If early in the season, a voyage to New Zealand or north for the line islands or "on Japan" was in order; if mid-year, perhaps it would be another cruise through the 20° to 30° belt of south latitude, touching at the Cook, or Hervey, Islands and heading for Tahiti in the Societies.

On his return cruise in these waters in May 1835, Captain Samson came upon three islands some forty-five miles north of Nassau. Shaped like a native club, the islands were joined together by broad coral reefs. The whole combination extended in an east-west direction and, with another sandy island and a reef, formed a crude triangle. Called by the natives Pukapuka, the whalemen very properly named them the Danger Islands.[29] They are credited to Commodore John Byron—"Foul-weather Jack," who sighted them (at a distance) in his voyage on the *Dolphin* in 1765. However, only the whalers ever used the islands, and were familiar with them for two decades before the missionaries arrived there in 1857.

Captain Samson, of New Bedford, was an excellent navigator and observer. Cruising southwest past these islands in 1835, his rediscovery was at much closer range than Byron's. Captain Samson noted in his log: "The Islands of Danger [are] well inhabited by the worst looking Natives that I have ever seen in the Pacific Ocean." [30] In his one glimpse of them, Bellingshausen in 1820, wrote: "The tortuous ledges of silvery foam thrown up by the surf breaking on the coral shore, connected three wooded islands, all are grown with cocoanut palms." [31]

One hundred and seventy miles south of Nassau is Suvarov (Anchorage) Island, discovered in 1814, by Lieutenant Lazareff in the Russian-American company ship of that name. An irregularly-shaped circular atoll of some twenty-five islets, Suvarov possesses a lagoon which may be entered by vessels drawing up to twenty feet of water. Some of the islets boasted coconut trees which grew as high as one hundred feet. Whaleships utilized them, and the *Gem,* of New Bedford, loaded with oil was once wrecked here, while standing in toward the island.

The *Gem*'s captain and crew reached Samoa, one hundred miles west, and the wreck was sold to a trading firm which sent the schooner *Caroline Hart* to salvage the cargo. Supercargo Livingston not only got the oil but, buried on Anchorage Island, he found a chest containing $15,000 in coins (specie). Later, another man, acting on secret information, went to the island and dug up another chest containing $2,400.[32]

Five degrees south of Suvarov is Palmerston Island (Avaru), also uninhabited when discovered by Captain Cook in the *Resolution* and *Adventure* on June 16, 1774, and again visited in 1777. This was another island supplying provisions for the whalers. Its first colonization began in 1864, when William Masters went there to manage a plantation and took his Penryhn Island wife with him. Today, natives from

Rakahanga and Manihiki occupy Palmerston's green shores and sell the copra for a means of livelihood.[33]

In April 1832, the whaler *Gideon Barstow,* of Mattapoisett, was sailing on a course south and east from the Society Islands when Captain Nathaniel Cary came up to a low island which was not on his charts. It was about fifteen miles long, very narrow, with a dangerous reef from northwest to west northwest, and only twenty-five feet above sea level. After taking several "sights," Captain Cary placed his discovery in latitude 23°–13′ south and longitude 137°–24′ west. "I gave it the name of Barstow Island," wrote the whaling master, in a letter to his family in Nantucket.[34]

Many islands reported by whalemen were not accepted for the charts by some cautious map makers. Others did not learn of the information until years after. In this particular case, no charts recorded Captain Cary's discovery, and ten years later (1842) the whaler *Cadmus,* of Fairhaven, was wrecked on Barstow Island. It was then stated "that this island is believed to have been unknown to Mariners until this unfortunate shipwreck upon it." It is now known as Cadmus or Morane Island.

Captain Driver, of the *Charles Daggett,* of Salem, discovered two islands in the lower Tuamotus—Mururoa and Fangataufa in latitudes 21°–54′ and 22°–12′ south and longitude 138°–51′ west and 138°–42′ west. Beechey claimed discovery of the latter in 1826, calling it Cockburn Island.[35]

On this voyage in the *Daggett,* Captain Driver stopped at Tahiti. Here he found a colony of Pitcairn Islanders, who were desperately attempting to return to their home island. Twelve of them had died, and those remaining were fear-stricken and homesick. In compassion, the Salem skipper offered to take them to Pitcairn. Writing to Messrs. Rogers, owners of the ship, George Nobbs, the self-exiled teacher of Pitcairn, expressed his gratitude for this act, stating: "We sincerely hope it will not prove detrimental to his voyage . . . . We remain your obedient servants, the People of Pitcairn Island." [36]

Much mystery was attached to those islands which like Pitcairn were isolated from the groups. One such island was Nauru or Pleasant Island, just below the equator but far to the west of the Gilberts. Its original discoverer is thought to have been a Captain John Fearn in 1798, who saw it while in the British trader *Hunter,* bound to the Sandwich Islands from Australia.[37]

On January 3, 1801, the *Diana,* of New Bedford, under Captain Jared Gardner, bound to the east along the equator, sighted an island "four or five leagues distant . . . rather high in the middle, the ends sloping down to the water. It appeared to be about 4 leagues (12 miles) from the north to the south. We saw smoke in two or three places, which gave us reason to believe it was inhabited." Captain Gardner placed it in "longitude 167°–13′ east and latitude 00°–17′ south," and called it Rodman's Island.[38]

The story of Alexander Selkirk at solitary Juan Fernández (Màs Tierra) was known to most whalemen, as that island was always a landfall during their Pacific voyages. After months aboard ship, its green hillsides looked inviting, indeed. The American sealers lived there for months at a time.

Perhaps that was how William Davis, of the *Fanny,* felt in December 1822, when he complained of a pain in his back and Captain Rule ordered him to duty, saying "that there was nothing the matter with him. . . . Davis then pointed to Juan Fernández and told the Captain if he thought so he might put him ashore . . . with other insolent language." [39]

Captain Rule was at Christiana (Tahuata) Island in the Marquesas, a few months later, where he "sent ashore the scorbitic patients and got on board, 8 hogs, plantains, bananas, etc." [40] Two apprentice boys and two older hands deserted and Captain Rule hired seven natives to hunt for them. "The deserters cannot be found," he wrote, "and so weighed anchor . . . shipped three natives in lieu of deserters." [41]

From April to July 1823, the *Fanny* cruised across the South Pacific to the Friendly (Tonga) Islands. While taking off water at Middleburgh or Eau Island, the boats' crews were attacked by natives and Captain Rule and two men captured. After much parleying they were ransomed for several muskets, powder and ball and a number of hatchets. Several days later, the ship returned to the island. When several canoes came alongside to trade, Captain Rule captured one with its two occupants. "We lowered a boat after the other canoes, took everything out of them and let them go. . . ." [42]

Two weeks later the *Fanny* again hove-to off Middleburgh Island. "A canoe came alongside with a hog and a few yams as a ransome for the two natives we detained on July 22. We would not let them go without they brought off the muskets . . . at 5 p.m. a canoe came off to the ship with 2 muskets, 2 hogs, 3 pieces of cloth, part of the powder they received and a few yams—they said the other articles were sent to Tongatabo—we sent the two captive natives ashore, made sail and stood to the S.W. . . ." [43]

Such were some of the adventures of the whalers at those islands which had had previous contact with white men.

The master of the *Fanny* was quick to quell insubordination in his crew. One day, while cutting in a whale,

Thomas Croesly being over the side hooking on to the whale, Captain Rule ordered him to hook in—he began to swear and said he never saw such d——d fashions in his life. Captain Rule told him to hold his tongue or he would pound his head with the spade handle. Croesly then said he might do it but he would be d——d if he did not make him pay for it; the Captain then struck him over the head twice with the spade handle; he came off the whale and went aft. . . . [44]

chapter xxvii

~~~◦〜◦〜~~~

"PURSUING THE SPERM WHALE
INTO THE SECRET PLACES OF
THE GREAT SOUTH SEA"

*. . . I have examined the clear and impressive memorial
from the town of Nantucket, which fully comfirms every
statement I have made in regard to the extent of the whale
fishery, although drawn from different sources.*

—J. N. Reynolds [1]

WHEN WE STUDY the Pacific voyages of the great explorers, we
are impressed with certain outstanding facts, the most significant of which is that they seldom if ever retraced their exact course
on the same voyage. The whalemen, however, returned to their old
haunts time and again. Many experiences gave them knowledge of
the islands and their native sailors.

Late in the year 1824, the *Japan,* under Captain Shubael Chase, fell
in with a canoe containing a number of natives from the Kingsmills.
Being many miles at sea, blown from the land, the natives could only
point toward the general direction from which they came. Captain
Chase took them aboard with their canoe, and steered on the course
indicated. To the unmistakable joy of the natives, an island finally
appeared on the horizon. Soon they were returned to their home. On
going ashore, the islanders gathered around Captain Chase in great
numbers, conducting him to the house of their chief, and loading his
boat with fresh provisions.[2]

By the mid-1820's it had become a custom of whaleships to ship Polynesian sailors. At first, the whalers returned the native foremast hands to their own islands. In 1829, the *Harvest* took two natives from Tahuata (Christiana Island), a favorite provisioning place in the Marquesas, and three more from Nuka Hiva. At the latter place, a large canoe with twenty-five natives was seen coming off and rather than risk an attack, Captain Edwards told his crew to stand by. "We loaded our muskets and got our spades ready for use," wrote Third Officer George W. Gardner, Jr. But the Marquesans, this time, proved friendly.[3]

The Nantucket *Inquirer,* for September 18, 1825, reported:

There are probably more than fifty natives of the South Sea Islands employed on board the whaleships belonging to this port. Many are now on the island. They are extremely tractable, free and ingenuous —and if they became vicious the fault is not their own.

One of the most interesting, though short, editorial rebuffs recorded in the *Inquirer* was Editor Samuel Jenks retort to a Boston paper contention that the South Sea Islanders from Nantucket whaleships were engaging in native orgies on the town's wharves at night, during the full of the moon.

The *Boston Recorder* in April 1822, under the head, "Heathen Society at Nantucket," printed in part, as follows:

The place has long been the resort of youths from pagan countries. . . . There reside there twenty Society or Sandwich Islanders who on stated evenings when the sky was clear, assembled in the streets, erected ensigned idols, and in frantic orgies paid their homage to the Host of Heaven. No Barnabas or Paul running among them, saying, "Why do you do such things?"[4]

Editor Jenks commented:

Here is some fact and some fable. We recollect seeing the tawny youngsters alluded to in merry gambols. We are certain, however, that they were at play, like other boys, in innocent frolics. The cream of this Old Wives' tale is that nobody disturbed them while they worshipped the Host of Heaven. But it is hoped that we shall get regulated by and by and that our heathenism will long be eradicated by means of those disinterested missionaries' exertions that are continually making in our behalf.[5]

And, while on the subject of South Sea Islanders and criticisms, it may be well to point out the relationships of the early whalemen and missionaries. In a letter from Reverend Mr. Stewart, in the *Religious Intelligencer,* dated Honolulu, November 24, 1824, it is written:

> . . . We have all had quite a jubilee in a visit from the whaleship *Thames* and our kind friend Captain [Reuben] Clasby. The *Thames* and the *Hydaspe,* Captain Paddack, another of our favorites, arrived at Lahaina on the same day, six weeks hence. . . . Captain Reuben Weeks of the *Enterprise,* of Nantucket, conveyed me to Honolulu from Lahaina and came down five days after the *Thames.* For this gentlemen we entertain a very high regard and we feel a warmth and strength of friendship. . . . It is more than a year since I first became acquainted with him. . . . I felt myself peculiarly happy in being on board the ship of so old and kind a friend. . . . Since our establishment at Lahaina, (8 months since) there have been many arrivals there and probably not less than one hundred and fifty at this port [Honolulu] during the same period. Many of these we see, especially among the whaleships, are interesting young men whose family connections and friends at home are of great respectibility, and are themselves far superior in their advantages and education to the class of ordinary seaman.[6]

How the whaleships brought some of the first missionaries to the Hawaiian islands has already been noted. Also, how Captain Macy took the first printing press to Honolulu on a whaler, and how a whaler's crew helped save that raw, young town from going up in flames. Captain Bunker, of the *Ontario,* listed a gift of $50 to the missionary church, and four whaling masters and their crews, in 1825, joined the "Tabu Association for the Suppression of Immorality," pledging their support. Crew members from a British whaler and the U. S. schooner *Dolphin* created quite a disturbance at Honolulu in January 1826, causing a riot in demanding "the repeal of a restriction which deprived them of the society of females." This has been unjustly connected with New England whaleships of that period.[7]

The number of letters carried by the whaleships around Cape Horn totaled in the thousands each year, and the famed Post Office at Charles (Floreana) Island in the Galápagos Islands was only one of the established centers for this important element—letters from home. In connection with this custom of marine postal service, it will be of interest to read the following notice, of serious content but not without humor:

> Having received sundry letters from Missionaries at the Sandwich Islands enclosed to "the Postmaster," to be by him forwarded by whaling ships from this port, without even the formality of "please forward," I think proper to state that persons wishing to send letters to the Sandwich Islands must pay the postage on them at this office: such will, in all cases, be forwarded—but those who wish the illegal sanction of my name, to evade the payment of legal postage may rest assured that their letters are much more likely to be perused by the General Post Office in Washington, than the Sandwich Islands, even if they have come all the way from Kentucky.
>
> THOMAS MACY, POST MASTER,
> NANTUCKET POST OFFICE [8]

When Captain Richard Macy sailed through the widely spaced Caroline Group in 1826, in the *Harvest,* of Nantucket, he came upon the magnificent Truk or Hogolu Islands. These were named from the highest basaltic island in the chain (also called Truk or "The Land"), which were first discovered by the Spaniard Saavedra, in 1528, and rediscovered by Duperrey in 1824. To the northeast, in latitude 9° and longitude 150° to 151°, Captain Macy discovered some fifteen atolls, beautifully clothed in coconut trees, and enclosed by a reef which he estimated, and correctly, as ninety miles in circumference. These were the Namonurto Islands.

Cruising west toward the Palau or Pelew Islands, Captain Macy "visited another group of islands in 7°-40′ and longitude 144° east. Some of them are well inhabited but not marked on the charts." These were the Woleai (Uleai) and Ifalik Islands which were havens for the Chamorro, or "natives of the soil," who fled the Marianas when the Spaniards came to Guam two centuries before.

Although Captain James Colnet had been dispatched from England in 1793 for the purpose of discovering ports and whaling grounds for the British fleet of South Seasmen, his year's voyage in the *Rattler* was disappointing. In June 1793, Parliament passed an act for encouraging the southern whale fishery, again offering bounties of considerable proportions. Speaker Uniacke, of the Nova Scotian Assembly, warned against such extravagant methods in pursuing the competition with America.

A half-century later, the British superiority in money and ships was gone. Perhaps the best explanation of what had happened is contained in a letter printed in the *Liverpool Times,* June 9, 1846, which Dakin included in his book. It reads, in part:

> You seem surprised that the English whalers should have fallen off whilst those of the Americans should have increased. A few words will explain it—the greater cost of our whalers here, the drunkeness, incapacity and want of energy of the masters and crews. I have know British whalers to be out four years and take thirteen or fourteen hundred barrels of oil and American whalers cruising almost the same ground would probably have captured twice as much. I have little sympathy for Americans, for as a body, I do not believe you could find a more dishonest people, but their energy in bringing the [whaling] trade to the pitch it has arrived at, deserves the highest ecomuim.[9]

Such damning praise is naturally to be expected from the countrymen of Britain's South Seasmen. But to attribute the success of the Americans to their energy alone is to miss completely the true picture of their accomplishments.

There has always been the puzzling question as to why the British, with their traditional background of the sea, never fully realized their potential whaling strength in the Pacific and gradually gave way to the Americans. From 1816 to 1830, the English ships numbered annually some fifty sail, whaling in various parts of the South Seas, with Nantucket men commanding a goodly share of them. But after 1830, they faded rapidly from the scene.

The roving New England and British whaleships sailed up above the Marianas and soon sighted islands in the Ryukyu Islands or the Loo-Choo Isles, as the whalers called them. Those dots on the charts now known as Kito-iwo-jima and Rosa Jima were included in their roamings. Captain Reuben Weeks, of the *Enterprise,* of Nantucket, has two dangerous reefs credited to him as discoveries, and the mysterious Marcus Island, as much unknown in 1942 as in 1824, was seen by both the Sag Harbor whaleship (the name of whose home port it now bears) and by the *Enterprise.*[10] In latitude 31°-45′ north and south longitude 137°–30′ east, southwest from Honshu, Japan's largest island, Captain Clark in the New Bedford whaleship *Elizabeth,* discovered two islands, which are now identified as Bayonnaise Rocks and Aoga-shima.

But of all the discoveries in this region, the best documented are those of Captain James Josiah Coffin, of Nantucket, who in September 1824 was in command of the British Bristol whaleship *Transit.* At the completion of his voyage, Captain Coffin returned to his island home to give a complete account of his discovery of what is now known as the Bonin Islands.

From Captain Coffin's private journal the editor of the Nantucket *Inquirer* printed the following:

> On the 12th of September, 1824, Captain Coffin discovered a group of islands, not laid down in the charts. He found the group to consist of six islands, besides a number of large rocks and reefs. In honour of Messrs. Fisher, Kidd and Fisher, of Bristol, England, he gave to the largest island which is four leagues in length the name of Fisher's Island; the second in size he named Kidd Island; the third, being the most southward of the group, he called South Island, and the fourth, from the abundance of pigeons found on it, he named Pigeon Island.——About four miles east-northeast of South Island lie two high round islands, to which Captain Coffin gave no names.
> Fisher's Island lies from S.S.E. to N.N.W., and Kidd Island, the most western of the group, lies S.E. from the northwest part of Fisher's Island. Between the two last mentioned islands is a beautiful clear bay, two miles wide and five miles up to the head. Captain Coffin sailed up the bay about four miles, where he found, near Fisher's Island, a fine small bay, where he anchored his ship in fifteen fathoms of water. To this Bay, Captain Coffin very properly gave the name of Coffin's Harbour. This harbour is sheltered from all winds excepting W.S.W., and has no current or swell. In three days, Captain Coffin took aboard 5 urns of water of the purest quality and a sufficient supply of wood, both of these essential articles being very abundant.[11]

The transcript from the journal goes on to tell of the quantities of pigeons and turtle which he observed, as well as excellent fish and lobsters, and of the variety of cabbage or such, plant which grew there. He placed the bay or Coffin Harbor in latitude 26°–30′ north and longitude 141° east.

With a reaction characteristic of all men of the sea, especially the whalemen, Captain Coffin could at first think of only the remarkable opportunity the islands offered the whalemen as a provisioning place. The abstract continues:

> For ships employed in the whale-fishery, or bound from Canton to Port Jackson, or the northwest coast of America, they will furnish a valuable place of refreshment. They are about south of Sandown Point on the coast of Japan, and distance may be sailed in four days.[12]

And there was that warmth of feeling which goes with the fulfillment of accomplishment, the deep satisfaction of having been a discoverer of a new group of islands.

> The islands are covered with large and beautiful forest trees, but not a single mark, even of a knife, could be traced upon one of them; nor did it appear that the footsteps of man had ever before been impressed upon any one of these islands.[13]

But Captain Coffin's discoveries did not end here. A few months later, while swinging to the west after a cruise on the Japan Grounds, he sighted a high island—in latitude 27° north and 141°-1' east—well wooded, upon which he landed and obtained some turtle and wood. Eighteen miles north of it, he discovered another high island, with smaller ones near by and a dangerous reef extending from one island to the other. Not being laid down on his charts, Captain Coffin reported the danger of coming too close to their shores, "from our imperfect knowledge of it." [14] These were the islands in the northern group of the Bonins.

Of Captain James Josiah Coffin, Frederick C. Sanford, wrote:

> In the year 1825 we had a gentleman from here who was command at the time of an English whaler from London, who struck a sperm whale and got it on the coast of Japan, the day he was seventy years old. He returned home and died in 1838; that man was James Josiah Coffin, who was a descendant of John Gardner.[15]

Just how many of these early whaleships sailed along the coast of Japan may never be known. But from the reports given by Captain Macy and others—which J. N. Reynolds took down from them by word of mouth and from their journals—while the rest of the world was ignorant of the Loo-Choos and New Islands, the whalemen knew of them. They had observed several as well-peopled, and the inhabitants, like the Japanese, reserved and distrustful of strangers.

Of an island located in 26° north latitude, 126° east longitude, it was reported, ". . . it is well cultivated, all kinds of refreshment may be procured, and a good harbor will probably be found on the southwest part. The inhabitants are peaceable and seem disposed to . . . establish friendly intercourse with foreigners"; of Monmouth Island, one of the Baske Group, the report stated: "The people on the island wear the Chinese costume and appear very friendly. . . . The island abounds with sheep." [16]

When the British Captain F. W. Beechey, with his ship *Blossom,* came upon the Bonins in 1827, he observed: "The southern cluster is evidently that in which a whaleship commanded by Captain Coffin anchored in 1823, who was first to communicate it to this country, and who bestowed his own name upon the port." [17] This Royal Navy man promptly named the group after Francis Bailey, late President of the Astronomical Society. Perhaps, the fact that Captain Coffin was an American and only a whaler gave Beechey the distorted opinion that his name was not worthy of the group he had discovered.

Similarly, when Beechey sailed into the other islands in the Bonins, also discovered by Coffin, he named them Parry's Group. Captain Beechey in his Royal Navy manner, claimed the islands for Great Britain.[18]

In 1830, five white men and some Hawaiians attempted to establish a colony at Port Lloyd. When Commodore Matthew Perry stopped at the Bonins in 1853 only one of the five whites had remained, the others presumably had moved away or were dead. This man was Nathaniel Savory, of Essex County, Massachusetts. He carried on a thriving trade with the whaleships, raising vegetables and pigs, and was known as a distiller of rum.[19] Commodore Perry purchased from Savory a strip of beach one thousand yards wide as a possible coaling station for the U. S. Navy. But the stern-visaged Admiral was too far ahead of his time. Congress failed to follow through in support of his recommendations. Then the Japanese began to appear and soon dominated the islands.

None other than that distinguished man of letter, America's Wash-

ington Irving, wrote to his friend Commodore Perry, shortly after the
latter's return from Japan, observing:

MY DEAR COMMODORE:

The following is the passage in your paper on the enlargement of
geographical science to which I alluded in conversation with you a
few days since. In speaking of the Bonin Islands you observe:

"In respect to these islands it would be of little importance whether
they were occupied by the English or Americans, whether the time-
honored Cross of St. George or the more youthful emblem, the Stars
and Stripes of our own country, floated over their barren hills; yet,
let it be so arranged that the wearied and careworn sailor, of whatever nation, shall find on entering their ports an equally kind and
generous welcome, and I cheerfully take occasion here to remark,
that wherever I have found the British flag, in whatever part of the
world, there have I always found a courteous and hospitable reception."

My dear Commodore, this passage does infinite honor to your
head and heart, and the last sentence is worthy of being written in
letters of gold; as illustrative of that comity which should distinguish
the nautical intercourse of the two kindred nations.

Ever my dear Commodore, Yours most truly,

WASHINGTON IRVING [20]

In the light of our Pacific strategy during the second World War,
how ironic has been the fact that islands so used by the American
whale fleet, a century before, should have become the property of the
expanding Japanese nation. Although she made only meagre contributions to the cause of the Allies in the first World War, Japan obtained a major share in the Pacific booty in securing the German
islands under a mandate. A definite condition was that they should
not be fortified, and in 1922 Japan pledged anew, under the Naval
Limitation Treaty, not to militarize these mandated islands in any
manner. Like a child in a den of wolves, only Guam was retained by
the United States.

The Japanese Mandate included the Marianas, Carolines and Marshalls—a salient that lay like a knife across the sea and air lanes of the
western Pacific, as well as being a first line of defense in protecting
the growing Japanese empire. No foreigners were allowed to inspect
this island network and, in 1935, when Japan withdrew from the
League of Nations, there was no challenge by interested nations over

Japanese claims to them. This diplomatic success of the Japanese was quickly followed by the full-scale war with China. And when the debacle at Pearl Harbor opened the great Pacific war of 1941-45, the importance of the Japanese mandated islands was bitterly realized.

But one man in the Department of State foresaw the possibilities of the Japanese misuse of such a mandate. In 1919, the Third Assistant Secretary of State, later Ambassador to Italy, Breckinridge Long, recommended that the islands be returned (under the League of Nations), to Germany. This was proposed so that the United States might ultimately open negotiations with Berlin for their purchase. Nothing came of Mr. Long's proposal.[21]

Thus, these specific contributions of American mariners to our historical and geographical knowledge of the central and western Pacific were lost completely. They had to be reclaimed in blood by the fighting men of this nation, during the second World War. Just before the war, the heritage of the whalemen in the Pacific found late recognition. When the famous aviatrix Amelia Earhart was lost on her flight toward Howland Island in 1937, the attention of the world was focused on the lonely islets of the central Pacific area. The Japanese carefully screened their fortified islands and, all through the search of this area, refused to allow any visitors there.

Then came the planning of airplane routes across the vast reaches of the Pacific, and the value of these several isolated atolls became an economic as well as a military factor. In 1938, world attention became centered on the vast reaches of the South Seas. Great Britain and the United States became engaged in a friendly diplomatic controversy, each claiming sovereignty, basing claims on rights of discovery and exploration. The islands had now become not only valuable as steppingstones for the air clippers but as an outer, sentinel fringe in the navy's line of defense.

chapter xxviii

⟋⟋⟋◡◡◡⟍⟍⟍

"I SEEK A PASSAGE IN YOUR SHIP—— HOW SOON DOES SHE SAIL!"

Well, my old contemporaries, let us overhaul our memories about things long passed away, some of which we saw and others we heard talk of. Although we sport no titles of nobility . . . we may boast of having descended through a line of seamen, the boldest, the most hardy and adventurous the world ever saw.

—"A Blubber-Hunter's Yarn" [1]

U NFORTUNATELY not many whalemen kept diaries or journals. But the logbooks of their voyages give the skeleton of the full-bodied tale "of a voyage, by God's permission." As most of those preserved were kept by the mate, the picture of life aboard these floating kingdoms of the whaleship are often reported through the eyes of the officers aft.

What manner of men were these sea-hunters? There was something greater in them than what they said; something more eloquent than the starkness of their journals.

Of one of them, it was written in 1876:

We have with us an old salt near his eightieth year, who began his career as a whaleman in 1815 and within my remembrance. In these 62 years since, if one case cane be produced equal to it, in results of obtaining oil—which was the object of his voyages—I am anxious to know it. Fourteen of these voyages he performed as master and four as sailor, boatsteerer and first officer. Sometimes he sailed from Nantucket, at other times from France, Boston, New Bedford and Mattapoisett, meeting with all the hazards usually encountered—losing two gallant ships on coral reefs in the Indian and Pacific Oceans, but crowning the whole activity by obtaining 40,000 barrels of whale and sperm oil.[2]

This man was Captain Nathaniel Cary, of Nantucket.

The nearest to him in the match of game was Captain Clement Norton, of Martha's Vineyard, who commenced his career in the old *Apollo* in 1816, and ended on board the Bremen whaleship *Gustave* in Honolulu Harbor, after obtaining a magnificent voyage of 4,500 barrels of oil. His lifetime total catch was 36,000 barrels.[3]

Some of them went to sea under a cloud of disaster. Captain Charles Rawson was thirteen years old when news came that his father, Captain Stephen Rawson, had been lost with all hands when his ship foundered after being reported within a few days' sail of Nantucket. Two years later young Charles was himself on board a whaler, the *Hope* bound round Cape Horn. In 1815, as boatsteerer on the *Brothers,* Captain Benjamin Whippey, he impressed the officers with his courage and on his next voyage went out as mate of the *William.* While in the *Phebe Ann,* of New Bedford, the master, Peter G. Chase, died and Captain Rawson took command. His subsequent years afloat found him as master of the *Bourbon,* sailing out of LeHavre, France, and two voyages out of Hudson, New York, in the old John Jacob Astor tea ship *Henry Astor.*[4]

On one occasion, Captain Rawson in his whaleboat came up to a great bull sperm whale, which when attacked smashed the frail bow of the boat and capsized her. Regaining the boat, Captain Rawson held on to the bottom by putting his finger into the plug hole. One by one his companions lost their hold and drowned, the sea rolling heavily, and Captain Rawson clung insensible until a boat from the ship finally reached him. In taking him aboard, it was necessary actually to tear his finger out of the hole, stripping the skin and flesh from it. He continued his voyage to a successful conclusion. Upon his retirement at the age of forty-five he had gained a competency.

When Captain William Swain, Jr., died in Auburn, New York, in March 1870, at the age of ninety-three, he had completed a career begun at the age of fifteen aboard his father's whaleship, the *Ranger,* so named for the famed ship of John Paul Jones. Captain Swain sailed most of his early voyages from London for Samuel Enderby & Son, while his brother George took out Nantucket ships. Then, returning to America, he sailed out of Nantucket and New Bedford, retiring from the sea to buy a farm at Auburn in New York State.

Not all of these shipmasters were so favored. Captain Seth Hussey was fifty-two years old when he died of pneumonia on the bleak shores of Staten Land, leaving a widow and two children. Captain Benjamin Coggeshall, unable to regain his strength after being first stricken with illness on the coast of Japan, gave up his command of the *Alabama* at the Bonin Islands and came home by way of Honolulu. After sailing all the way around Cape Horn, the ship he was on was captured by a pirate craft and released after all personal belongings of those on board had been stolen. Despite these vicissitudes, Captain Coggeshall was unable to reach home waters. Just as the vessel, on which he was now a passenger, arrived at Nantucket Bar the stricken man fainted after his first glimpse of his island home in three years. Two days later he was dead.[5]

In 1832, Captain Edward Barnard lost the *Mentor,* of New Bedford, in the reefs of the Pelew Islands, and his crew were taken by the savages and held prisoner for five months. When another ship hove to off the island, the natives held a parley. Three of those surviving the wreck were forced to remain as hostages so that their shipmates could effect an escape. Upon arrival at Nantucket, Captain Barnard tried for years to get the government to send a warship to rescue the hostages. Finally, the *Vincennes,* in 1836, took off two of the captive whalemen. Shipmasters felt all too keenly the responsibilities of the lives of their men in those days of early nineteenth century whaling, especially those who, like Captain Barnard, had to return home and meet face to face the parents of their crew members.

Captain John Tucker, in the *Richmond,* of New Bedford, in 1836 arrived at Cape Town, Cape of Good Hope, with ten of his crew dead of fever and five desperately ill. Captain Josiah Macy, after varied adventurous whaling, left the sea to start a business as commission merchant in New York and became founder of the Seaman's Bank of that city, which institution he considered and proved a necessary one.

Yet, of all the whaling masters few ever approached the record set by Captain Benjamin Worth, of Nantucket, who began his seafaring life at the age of fifteen in the year 1783, and retired in 1824. Within this period of forty-one years he was a whaling master twenty-nine years, and was home during this time only seven years, including every stay at the termination of one voyage and the commencing of another. While at sea, Captain Worth calculated he had sailed, 879,960 miles and circumnavigated the world twice, rounding Cape Horn sixteen times and Cape of Good Hope twice. He had visited over forty island groups in the Pacific and Atlantic oceans, some of them many times, and traversed the entire west coast of South America and as far as the Columbia River on the northwest American coast.[6] During his career he took over twenty thousand barrels of whale oil and, with the exception of having had his ship taken by capture in the 1812 war had never lost a ship or a man. When the island Whigs joined the Bunker Hill procession in 1840, Captain Worth, then seventy years old, commanded a whaleboat float manned by shipmasters.

A volume could be made of Captain Worth's adventures; one will suffice to show his ability and courage. He had taken the whaleship *Brothers* to the coast of New Zealand in the year 1805, the first American whaler in those waters. They were in a deep bay on that coast when a terrific gale suddenly came upon them from out of the sea.[7] All the ship could carry was a close-reefed main topsail and a foretopmast stays'l, and they tried to beat out, but to no avail. Slowly, the *Brothers* was forced toward the dread lee shore, foaming with black, jagged rocks. Captain Worth consulted with his officers and all agreed that it was best to drive the ship ashore while it was still daylight and they could pick out the best available spot.

The dread word flashed through the ship, and several of the Negro sailors immediately crowded aft to appeal to the officers. They were all well aware of the fact that the shore held cannibals as well as rocks and that the natives preferred Negro flesh to that of the white men. "If we do get ashore," they declared, "we shall surely suffer death and be eaten. Try again, try again for the open sea!"

The anguish of face and voice of the Nantucket Negro sailors steeled Captain Worth to make another effort to gain the safety of the ocean. In prompt obedience to orders, the ship was brought to the wind again, the fore and mizzen topsails set, and a reef let out of the main topsail and foretopmast staysail. Like a live thing, the *Brothers* staggered as she caught the onslaught of the wind. Then she steadied and the flight to reach sea-room began.

"You should have seen the tense, almost fierce faces of the men," said Captain Worth, recounting his experience, "and the ship hove down, with the wind howling through her rigging like a legion of devils—and there was the boiling caldron of the rocky shore under our lee. But the sails held, the wind eased up a point or two, and we flew like a bird past that headland and out to sea and safety."

But, even with this danger over, the gale swept the ship mercilessly before it and for two days she fought for her life. At the end of that time she was almost a wreck, with her boats swept away, her tryworks gone, her cabin gangway splintered and part of her bulwarks ripped away. Her commander put away for Port Jackson, New South Wales, where he arrived without further incident.

Now, Captain Worth showed those qualities which distinguished that race of sea-kings—the whalingmaster. Putting all hands to work, he repaired the ship, built new whaleboats, recruited stores, even wove grass rope for hawsers, and again sailed for the New Zealand Grounds. Fifteen months later he was at Nantucket Bar with a full cargo.

Writing of Captain Worth in later years, Frederick Coffin Sanford, of Nantucket, stated: "Folks can hardly believe this story but I heard it from his own lips. He was an elegant sailor and commander, as was his son, Captain Charles Worth who took out London whalemen the *Griffen* and the *Rochester*." Young Captain Worth did not enjoy his father's long success, dying at the age of twenty-eight from the effects of a wound received from a harpoon-barb while going on a whale.

Another revealing episode occurred in the career of Captain Stephen West, one of a family of well-known Nantucket shipmasters. He was in his first command, the *Dolphin,* of New Bedford, in the year 1802, well out on the voyage, when it was discovered that the ship was leaking badly. Instead of putting away for home, Captain West had the pumps manned until he reached Cape Town. Only temporary repairs were made and the *Dolphin* sailed to Delagoa Bay. Here, as Captain West, hoped, a number of whalemen were anchored—French, English and American—most of which were commanded by fellow-townsmen of the young master. Calling for aid, he was supplied with a company of coopers, blacksmiths and other experienced men, the ship repaired, and recaulked about the bow. Again at sea, Captain West soon filled his vessel and sailed for home, being the first craft of the season to arrive home.

This was the start of an eventful career as a whaling master. During the next twenty-five years he commanded the *Martha* for nine voyages, then the Liverpool packet *Pacific,* which was purchased especially for him. In this ship, he took 2,400 barrels in seventeen months' voyage, continuing in her command for another equally successful South Atlantic voyage. His last voyage before retirement saw him bringing in enough oil to make his lifetime total twenty-five thousand barrels of whale oil.[8]

Captain Silas West died in the mouth of a bull sperm whale. Silas was a vigorous whaling master and he met his end in an not unexpected manner. He had once performed one of the most startling feats in the annals of the whale fishery. While in command of the Enderby whaler *Indian* he sighted a school of ten sperm whales off Albemarle Island in the Galápagos Group. Lowering his boat, Captain West was soon in the midst of the school and never slackened his pursuit until all ten were killed.[9]

Captain Samuel Bunker, in the *Alexander,* in 1824, took fourteen whales from a school of sperm in one day, and saved them all. He had a fine voyage, taking six and seven whales one day on a number of occasions, and totaling 2,800 barrels for the voyage. The *Alexander* ranged the Pacific from the Society Islands north to the Kingsmills, thence to the coast of California, the Galápagos and Marquesas groups, to the South American coast.[10]

There is an aura of mystery about some of these grizzled mariners, to whom whaling was a profession which embraced all manner of adventures. Captain Paul West was one of these—a man who was able to take quick advantage of the exigencies of fate and to turn disaster into good fortune. He began his career as a cabin boy of fifteen, and on his next voyage (in the old *Maria,* under Captain Benjamin Paddock) he received $500 as his share in a splendid voyage.

In 1798, Paul West went out as first mate in the *Cyrus,* one of the Rotch ships from Nantucket, still utilizing a Dunkirk registry, with

Captain Archaeleus Hammond in command. While in Delagoa Bay, the *Cyrus* was captured by a British frigate and sent to London. Paul West, sent to England aboard a British whaler, was taken by a French vessel and transported to a French prison. Fortunately, he was almost immediately released by the exertions of the venerable Captain William Mooers, then the Rotch representative at Dunkirk.[11]

Learning that the *Cyrus* was to be sold at London, Paul West went there and identified himself to the prospective purchasers. The result was an invitation to him to take out the ship, which he accepted. She went out armed with eight-pounders, a factor which enabled her to take part in other activities beside whaling.

On one occasion a schooner-rigged vessel was sighted under the lee of the *Cyrus*, "trying to get up to us . . . the wind varying in favor of the schooner enabled her to fetch very near us and from her appearance we had every reason to think her a French privateer," wrote Captain West. Any doubt about the fact that the *Cyrus* was armed is dispelled by the concluding remarks of this day's entry (Sept. 6, 1808):

> . . . Accordingly, got already run down to her with matches to the guns. . . . Spoke and found her to be the *Fly,* of the British government, bound to Portsmouth. Haul'd to the wind and stood off.

The twenty-two-year-old skipper of the *Cyrus* made another excellent voyage to the Pacific, and completed his comparatively short career with one voyage in the British whaler *Charleton*. He returned to Nantucket just before the War of 1812 broke out, and purchased the Captain Uriah Swain house on Liberty Street.

It was no secret that he had gained a fortune at sea. Two successful whaling voyages were lucrative but did not enable him to make a fortune. Family tradition is that he captured a French ship and, finding an important personage on board, demanded and received a ransom in gold.

For the next fifty years he occupied a unique position in the town. He was a director of the Pacific Bank, a founder of several insurance companies and a man whose counsel was much sought.

As for the whaler-privateer *Cyrus*: In a letter written from Nantucket in 1916 Paul West, the great-grandson of Captain Paul, stated:

. . . Somewhere in my memory was the recollection of a picture of
the old whaler *Cyrus* with a lot of guns on her. . . . I have found
that picture. . . . It used to hang in Grandfather West's barn-study,
in Neponset, and on his death went to my aunt Mrs. Flagg . . . and
has just been presented to my son, Paul West, Jr. It shows the *Cyrus*
with nine full-grown cannon on her starboard side, and I presume
there were as many on her port. It shows her going into the harbor
of St. Helena under a British flag with Captain Paul West, Master.
. . . Certainly she did not leave Nantucket so heavily armed.[12]

Whaleship masters who could retire at thirty-four with a fortune
were uncommon but not rare. Captain Obed Starbuck completed three
voyages to the Pacific in less than four years—a remarkable record—
and retired before he was forty. Captain David N. Edwards retired at
forty-three, enjoyed life ashore during the next forty years, preserving
his physical vigor and capacity for service in the community until the
very last.

Some of these veteran sea-hunters met their ends under less happy
circumstances. Having passed through the hazards of their profession,
when age overwhelmed them their minds often reverted to days,
when, as young men, they looked death in the face.

Adventures afloat were not always those of a physical nature. Captain Robert S. Cathcart, out of the *Otter* in 1826, learned that his wife
at home had been unfaithful, took the ship into Santa Catharina and
sold her. This was not so strange as it might seem, as the owner of the
Otter was the "other man" in the case. Cathcart never returned home.
He married a Spanish woman and spent his life on the island (near
the coast of Brazil), where he served as American Consul and
proved a valuable man for his countrymen. Thirty-three years after
his self-exile began, a correspondent of the *Boston Traveler,* on board
the U. S. frigate *Powhatan,* visiting Santa Catharina, wrote the following description of Captain Cathcart:

His native strong sense and shrewd observation make him agreeable in conversation and instructive, and though he has lived so long
amongst an uncultivated and ignorant people when he puts on his
rig, having a noble head and stalwart frame, he can mingle in good
society with a good degree of ease and dignity. He drinks neither
wine or any strong liquors; he never uses a profane or indecent word;
obviously he is a kind husband and father, respected by the people,

not only for his wealth and official position, but for his admitted superiority of mind and character. . . . I inquired for an American newspaper, and was amazed . . . that he did not receive one . . . nor does he have any correspondence with a single mortal in his native land, being almost as ignorant of its condition as was Selkirk in Juan Fernandez of his own. . . . His early misfortune is the secret of his exile.[13]

On Nantucket, one of the most gripping stories has to do with the rainy afternoon when a curtained carriage approached the home of Mrs. Samuel Joy and two stalwart shipmasters got out and knocked at the front door. Before admitting them, Mrs. Joy turned to her two teen-age sons and remarked, quietly, "Thee must prepare yourself for sad news, my sons, I know why these men have come—they are going to tell me thy father has been lost at sea."

No one had a more varied career afloat than Captain Alexander Macy, and this Nantucket man lived to tell the tale. Going to sea as a cabin boy, he was an experienced young whaleman when the War of 1812 put a halt to his next voyage. He shipped as mate on a coasting schooner, under Captain George Chadwick, but the schooner was captured by an English frigate. Soon after, discouraged by the prospects of whaling, young Macy signed on with Captain Gardner who took out a letter-of-marque schooner *Sparta*. After a year of playing hide-and-seek with the British blockading fleet out of New York, the young whalemen went up the North River to Hudson, where some relatives then lived. "They were Quakers," he wrote in later years, "very much opposed to war, and they easily persuaded me to stop there, not approving of my going to sea in an armed vessel." [14]

The war finally over, young Macy returned to Nantucket to ship out with his former captain, James Bunker, aboard the *Tarquin*. On this voyage occurred the strangest adventure of his long career. While off the coast of Brazil, the lookout sighted a ship flying signals of distress. Running down to her, they discovered she was a Brazilian frigate, bound to Santos, with General Livaro and his staff and recruits on board. A bargain was made, in which Captain Bunker agreed to tow the disabled frigate into a Brazilian port if the government would fill his ship with the same quantity of oil he would be otherwise taking while pursuing his voyage.

While the *Tarquin* performed her part of the bargain, the Brazilian authorities showed no disposition to produce the oil. Through an Irishman named Major Cottrell, a soldier of fortune, Captain Bunker received an audience with the Emperor of Brazil. Young Macy accompanied the shipmaster. One of the court rituals required anyone seeking such an audience to kiss the royal hand. Observed Alexander Macy: "Captain Bunker will never kiss the King of Portugal's hand!" [15] But the Quaker shipmaster made an excellent pretense of the ceremony, with the result that the Emperor gave the order for nine hundred barrels of oil to be placed aboard the *Tarquin* at Santa Catharina.

The amount of oil was not enough to fulfill the bargain and Captain Bunker formally protested the breach of contract. A claim was filed through the Brazilian Consulate at Washington. Years passed, and the matter was almost forgotten. Then, thirty-five years later, the Brazilian government awarded a lump sum to settle all claims against that country by American citizens. The *Tarquin* received $6,800, reduced to $5,200 after expenses were paid. Only three members of her original crew remained alive to claim their share—1817 to 1852 was a considerable span—and one of the three was Alexander Macy—boatsteerer.

In contrast to the remarkable success of the *Sarah,* which brought home a cargo valued at $89,000, was the melancholy voyage of the *Harvest* which left Nantucket on October 17, 1844, under Captain George Coffin.[16] Less than a month later she was also wrecked by an Atlantic storm. Her log reported the incident as follows:

Friday, November 13, 1844. Commenced with a very heavy gale from the N. and stormy, heading WNW under 2 staysails, at 8½ p.m. blowing a complete hurricane. Shiped a sea on the starboard quarter which took away the mizzenmast at the deck, all the boats, water butt, round-house, stove the cook house and carried off 9 men by the names of David Brown, boatsteerer, Jacob Reed, Charles D. Chapman, Delos W. Smith, Thomas D. Brown, William Byet, Henry Boston and Antoine Roger, seamen. At midnight the weather cleared and moderated, at daylight commenced clearing the wreck and getting things snug. Latter part a brisk breeze and squally.

On the very next day, Gideon Westerfelt, a seaman whose home was given as Poughkeepsie, New York fell from the jib boom while furling sail and was drowned. Thus, the ship had in twenty-four hours lost ten hands, her mizzenmast and rigging, and all her boats. After a month of trying to regain the home port, the *Harvest* fortunately fell in with the U.S.S. *Decatur,* which helped the exhausted crew to get the *Harvest* into Vineyard Sound and safety.

The *Harvest* refitted and sailed again. No more dreary voyage was ever recorded. Round Cape Horn, through the South Pacific to the Marquesas, thence to the Cook Islands and on to New Zealand. Back and forth cruised the *Harvest,* with no success.

At length, even blackfish were sought. Of several small whales taken one made five barrels and another seven barrels. Shades of the pioneer ships in these waters! It was almost unbelievable that a ship could sail and resail over whaling grounds and sight nothing but blackfish. The year 1845 gave way to 1846 and 1847. Less than one hundred barrels a year had been taken. Writing in the log, the despairing mate stated: "Ship *Harvest* bound to the Eastward, and from there somewhere else God willing."

Day after day, the ship sailed through the South Pacific, from Pitcairn Island to the Juan Fernández Islands, thence north to the Galápagos—and still no whales. On October 5, 1847, the log recorded: "... Today we saw sperm whales for the first time in nine months and seventeen days."

After such an unprecedented cruise, good luck should have been forthcoming—but not so. The log stated: "We lowered the boats and struck two noble sperm, one of them run to the windward until the irons drew; the other, the line got foul and we had to cut from him." On went the *Harvest,* until the logkeeper sadly wrote: "Dec 18, 1847— thirty-four months from home and it is 12 months since we had a whale." Such was the incredible record of the *Harvest.*

In a number of logbooks there are occasional glimpses into the life of those aboard ship. The private journal kept on board the *Maria* (1832-35) by Alexander Hoxie, of Sharon, Massachusetts, is interesting in that it is the record of a landsman making his first voyage a-whaling.[17]

I will note here that all our officers are loved by the crew. Captain Macy is a member of the Methodist Church, and has given orders to have no swearing on board. He has just told the crew to wash up and put on a clean shirt, and when they commence to play he will find work for them to do.[18]

Hoxie affords two more such glimpses—one into a greenhorn's heart, another into the bright face of danger. On October 28, 1832, he wrote in his journal:

Cloudy and could not get the sun . . . the wind continues a gale from the N.E. Everything looks gloomy and disagreeable. Here let the unfidel scoff at religion if he dares. On the mighty deep, the wind roaring through the rigging, the sea rolling mountains high, and our bark tossed to and fro by every rolling billow—who will deny God?

The entry of November 18 tells of one day's experience while getting around Cape Horn:

Latitude 56°-42' south, Longitude 80°-15' west. At 9 A.M. all hands called to tack ship on account of a large iceberg or mountain of ice directly ahead. . . . The weather being thick and foggy prevented our seeing it sooner. It was coming toward us very fast and had it been a little later in the day we should likely have been lost, as it was soon dark. The island of ice rose above the sea 150 to 200 feet—looked frightful enough. Captain Macy had never seen ice in this latitude before. He was considerably frightened.

Young Hoxie made an excellent observer. In taking the first whale he wrote:

. . . The starboard boat put two irons into the monster of the deep and after the lapse of another hour the whale lay a motionless lump on the top of the water. It was to me an interesting scene to be engaged for the first time in fighting with and killing a large whale. He truly made the deep boil like a pot. The whale is very active and very strong. One attacked a Nantucket ship about this latitude a few years since and sunk her, the crew saved themselves in the boats. . . . I was previously fearful my courage would fail me when coming into the whale . . . but I have enjoyed the scene very highly and have established my courage in my own mind at least.[19]

That art peculiar to the whalemen known as scrimshaw, where the sperm whale's teeth and all sizes of whalebone were made use of for carving objects and for engraving pictures thereon, had many exponents. Thoughts of home are reflected in almost every piece—from jagging wheels for piecrusts, clothespins, doll's bed, brushes, canes, umbrella stays and handles, meat choppers, etc., to beautifully designed pictures of fair ladies and whaling ships etched on the smooth teeth. And many South Sea Island curios were brought home to grace the mantlepieces of whalemen's homes. Delicate shells, tapa cloth, sharktooth swords, war clubs, ceremonial masks, models of elaborately carved canoes and even native heads from New Zealand. Of the latter, a story is told of a whaleman being apprehended as he walked up from the waterfront of a great city, carrying a bundle under his arm, which was suspected to contain contraband. Upon examining the bundle it was found to be the shrunken head of a South Sea island chief.

The *Inquirer,* of Nantucket, in October 1822, gives a description of one of these heads:

> A skull brought from New Zealand . . . is now in the possession of one of our neighbors. It appears to have been that of a person about 30 years of age. The skin resembles parchment and is very curiously tatooed. The inside of the skull is perfectly clean and smooth—the teeth in a fine state of preservation, as are the eyelids, ears, lips, nose, etc. The whole structure of the mouth and even the cartilages of the nose are plainly discoverable through the operture of the neck. The sockets of the eyes are filled with a substance resembling sealing wax. The hair about two feet long and very black.[20]

All adventures had their twists, and one experience of a young shipmaster was typical of the rivalry which existed between whaleships from America and England during the early 1830's. While a Yankee whaleship was cruising off the lower Kingsmill Islands in the Pacific in February 1831, she fell in with two British whalers. Just at dusk, a large school of sperm whales was sighted and all three ships lowered boats, the English craft getting four boats each down and the American lowering three. A short time later they entered the school and each boat got fast to a whale.

Twilight dropped its mantle of night quickly, for it was in mid-Pacific. The then-young shipmaster of the *Nantucket* told the story,[21]

Now it was dark and cloudy, the whales, fast and loose ones, all came together in a small space so we could speak one another. Our lines all got a cross and afoul, and we could not tell where the whale was that we were fast to. The English lines were one size larger than ours. When we had a large line across the head of the boat we cut it, and I suppose the English did the same, as I soon found I was cut loose.

I made my line fast to another harpoon and threw it into the first whale I came to. We lanced him and he soon went into his flurry and turned up dead. I lighted my boat lantern hauled up alongside, and found a harpoon on his top-side with a short piece of English line fast to it.

I said to myself that my father was taken prisoner with a cargo of sperm oil by the English in the War of 1812, and now was my chance to get a little back. So with my boat knife I cut the harpoon out and cast it into the deep, and put one of my harpoons in its place in the same hole.

Each one of our boats got a whale, and towed them to the ship which had lanterns in her rigging to guide us. The next day, one of the English captains boarded us and bought about 50 fathoms of our line, pretty well cut up, and reported they had got 7 whales between them in the two British ships.

While cruising off Juan Fernández in October 1821, the *Washington,* of Nantucket, Captain Reuben Swain, 2d, was boarded by two whaleboats, which were believed to have come off to trade. But the crew of one craft was armed. They were a gang of eight convicts attempting to escape from the island then the site of a penal colony. The boats had been taken from the whaleship *Persia,* Captain Cross; being short-handed, Captain Cross immediately bore away for the coast and Valparaiso for help. Finding their scheme to capture the *Persia* thus thwarted, the convicts decided to impress six of the captured whalemen and sail for Más Afeura Island, where they believed there was a better chance to escape. On the way to the companion island of Juan Fernández (Más Tierra), they sighted the *Washington* and under the time-honored ruse as trading or bum-boats, succeeded in getting on board and capturing the Nantucket craft.[22]

Captain Reuben Swain, a veteran whaleman, was not going to lose his ship without a fight. The following night he led a well-planned surprise counter-attack and, in a pitched battle, retook the *Washington*. Fighting with harpoons, lances and boarding knives against cutlasses and pistols, Captain Swain won the fight only after two of the convicts had been killed. Proceeding to Valparaiso Captain Swain restored the mate and crew of the *Persia to* Captain Cross already arrived there and turned the Spanish convicts over to the authorities. Captain Ridgley, in the U. S. frigate *Constitution,* sailed with the *Persia* for Juan Fernández to rescue five other members of the latter's crew and also to restore the governor there his freedom. For his part in the incident Captain Swain was presented a handsome sword and a brace of pistols.

There are three outstanding incidents in which history has substantiated the survival of men who have been in a sperm whale's mouth and lived to tell the tale. In the late eighteenth century, Marshall Jenkins, then residing at Edgartown, Massachusetts, survived such an experience, and it was recorded that he bore the scars of the encounter. Captain Albert Wood, of Nantucket, was another who survived being bitten by a sperm whale.[23]

In the year 1817, Captain Edmund Gardner, then in command of the *Baleana,* of New Bedford, was in his boat attacking a bull sperm when a blow from the gigantic spray knocked the boat end over end. Captain Gardner was precipitated into the air and fell directly into the snapping yaw of the monster. Fortunately, the other boats were near but when the shipmaster's almost lifeless body was hauled out of the water he was believed a dead man. Blood poured from his mouth and his body. On board the ship, the first officer discovered that Captain Gardner had lost his left hand at the wrist and that there was an indentation in the back of his head which all too plainly told of a fractured skull.[24]

The ship was put away to Callao, Peru, the nearest port, and Captain Gardner was taken up into the Peruvian mountains, where the doctors declared his only hope for recovery lay. Captain Gardner did recover, and returned to make several outstanding voyages. As has already been recounted, he was one of the pioneer whalemen to the Sandwich Islands and the coast of Japan.

Shipmasters were often called upon to amputate limbs, which operation they performed with success, following closely the instructions
given in Lot Tripp's *Direction For Mariners on Voyages, Both in Hot
and Cold Climates,* published in 1784 at Hudson, New York. Bleed-
ing for fevers, and even for epileptic fits was often resorted to, and
tourniquets to check the flow of blood when sewing up a wound.
Rollers for pulling teeth, and Epsom salts for all sorts of troubles, were
the usual remedies for the most common ailments.

There was no way, of course, of diagnosing an internal injury, and
many a whaleman suffered lingering and often agonizing illness after
being hurt "inside" as a result of the smashing of a boat by a whale
or a fall from aloft. On the twenty-second of May 1844, the starboard
boat of the *Columbus,* of New Bedford, was smashed by a sperm whale
and one man was drowned and two others painfully cut and bruised.
No mention was made in the logbook at this time of any injury to the
mate, Mr. Cole, who then steered the boat and had the steering oar
splintered and knocked from his hands. On July 22, however, the
logbook reported:

> In the morning Mr. Cole asked the Captain to give him a little
> laudanum, which the captain complyed with, which seemed to re-
> lieve him. While the boats were down, he called to the steward to
> give him a little more laudanum, fifteen drops. I think it was. As
> soon as he had taken it, the steward went on deck and remained but
> a short time, and when he came again into the cabin, he stood at the
> door of the mate's berth but could hear no breathing—he then looked
> at the mate and found he had breathed his last.[25]

There is recorded in the diary of Kezia Fanning, under date of
September 29, 1806, that news had just arrived of the death of Peter
Coffin, cabin boy on board the *Falkland:* "He was taken out of a
boat with a black man, last December, he was under 13."

And there is the brief record of one day when the bark *Vigilant* lay
in the harbor at Juan Fernández and another cabin boy was found
missing:

> Jose, a Spaniard, came on board to trade and left his boat alongside.
> He was down in the cabin, busy talking with Fred when Mr. Worth
> came down and said the boat had gone from alongside. They low-
> ered a boat to go look for it and someone saw the warp was cut, and

someone else said—the crazy boy was missing. They lowered another boat and started to look for him. It was blowing hard and getting dark but Providentially they found him. He was outside the point and had both oars peaked and sat in the stern, with the steering oar, heading out to sea. They hailed him but he sat perfectly still and did not answer them; when they got to him they asked where he was going and he said, to the East. He had nothing in the boat.[26]

There seems to have been many a counterpart to poor Pip, who Melville knew so well and whose admonition still rings: "Lad, lad, thou must not follow Ahab, now!"

chapter xxix

꒰ᵔꔛᵔ꒱

MUTINY AT MIDNIGHT

*. . . and if you make the least damned noise I'll send you to
hell!*

—Samuel Comstock [1]

O F ALL THE MUTINIES which took place aboard the whaleships
the most horrible was that on the *Globe,* of Nantucket, early
in 1824. There have been several accounts of this bloody episode. The
first and most extensive was by two of the survivors, Cyrus Hussey
and William Lay.[2] These two wrote their story in 1828, the year after
they were rescued from the Mulgrave Islands, the only survivors of
a marooned crew, the others having been massacred by the natives.

The story of the mutiny in its stark detail is this: The *Globe,* a
veteran Nantucket whaleship, sailed from Edgartown, Martha's Vineyard, on December 19, 1822. She was owned by Christopher Mitchell &
Co., an old firm of Quaker merchants, and was commanded by
Captain Thomas Worth, of the Vineyard. Mate William Beetle was
also a Vineyard man, as were four of the crew. Arriving at Oahu in
the Sandwich Islands in May 1823, the ship was provisioned and went
for a cruise "on Japan," returning to Oahu, in December 1823.[3] This
was the turning point of the voyage. Here six of the crew deserted and
one was discharged and six new hands were "taken from the beach" to
complete the crew.[4]

The *Globe* sailed from Honolulu on December 29, 1823, and less
than a week later Payne, Oliver, Humphries, Liliston, and Thomas
joined Samuel B. Comstock in plotting a mutiny.[5] On the night of

January 26, 1824, the *Globe* was cruising in company with the *Lyra,* of New Bedford. The boatsteerers, as was customary, had the first night watches. Captain Worth's last order was that the lantern signal for use when a ship came about on a tack, was to be used. This was the beginning of the drama. Comstock took over the deck. Just before midnight the events of the tragedy began as Comstock led his conspirators down into the cabin of the *Globe.* Captain Worth lay in his hammock, fast asleep. The doors of the staterooms were held shut. While Humphries held a lanthorn, Comstock killed the ship's master with a hatchet blow in the head. As by pre-arrangement, Silas Payne at that same moment, opened the door of the first mate's stateroom and stabbed Mate Beetle (asleep in his bunk) with a boarding knife. Beetle was not fatally wounded. Though wrenched from a deep sleep, he put up a good fight for his life. Comstock, however, completed the killing. Comstock then loaded two muskets and fired one of them through the door of the stateroom where Second Mate John Lombard and Third Mate Nathaniel Fisher had barricaded themselves. The shot went through the door panels and wounded Fisher in the face. The mutineers then smashed open the door.[6]

As Comstock entered the cabin he stumbled and was grabbed by Lombard. Fisher pulled the musket from the boatsteerer's hand and pointed it at Comstock's head. But the latter quickly assured him his life would be spared if he dropped the weapon. Fisher, glancing out of the door, saw the lifeless body of Captain Worth sprawled half out of his hammock, his head a gory pulp. His actions certainly indicate that the sight must have unnerved him for he allowed Comstock to regain his gun. Comstock immediately ran the bayonet into Lombard's body several times. He then shot Fisher through the head, killing him instantly.

Comstock organized his beachcombers as a crew, cowed the forecastle hands with threats, and sailed for an island where he could establish himself as a virtual king. First to fall victim to the mutineers was one of their own number—Humphries, the Negro, who was hung for suspected treachery! The *Globe* arrived at the Mulgrave Islands (Milli), in the eastern Marshalls, where the mutineers started putting all available supplies ashore.[7]

A quarrel between Comstock and Payne completed this second

portion of the drama. Payne believed Comstock was inducing the natives to attack. One afternoon he and Oliver lay in ambush and killed Comstock as he returned from the native village. This was on February 16, 1824.

At this time Gilbert Smith the other boatsteerer, determined to cut the ship's hempen cable and escape. He enlisted five men to help him. Among the five were two fellow-Vineyarders, the Kidder brothers; Anthony Hansen, the Cape Cod Indian; Joseph Thomas, one of the men suspected as being as accessory before the mutiny; and George Comstock, the sixteen-year-old brother of the chief mutineer, the murdered Samuel Comstock. These six men did escape in the ship and sailed her across the Pacific to Valparaiso, where they arrived June 7, 1824.[8]

In the meantime, the natives of Milli, incensed at the murder of Comstock and angered by the harsh treatment of their women by Payne and his fellows, suddenly attacked the camp of the marooned men and killed all but two youths—Cyrus Hussey, of Nantucket, and William Lay, of Saybrook, Connecticut. These two young whalemen were captives of the islanders for two years. At last they were rescued by the topsail schooner *Dolphin,* dispatched especially to hunt for them. Upon their return home, Hussey and Lay wrote the narrative of the mutiny which has been the basis for practically all of the recent versions of the *Globe*'s tragic voyage.[9]

But there is other documentary evidence. At Valparaiso, the six crew members made sworn statements to Michael Hogan, the American Consul. Captain Percival took the depositions of both Hussey and Lay at the Mulgraves. At Boston, before the Federal Court, Joseph Thomas was tried and acquitted, and so there is a court record. Finally there is an hitherto unknown account as written by George Comstock, the younger brother of the arch-mutineer.

It is this story of George Comstock, which only recently came to light, that contains so much pertinent material. At the request of Gorham Coffin, of Christopher Mitchell & Co., Comstock had written his narrative. He states:

It is the impression of my mind to set down and note every accident exactly as it happened and not err on either side from the just or unjust part of the work, as well and far as my knowledge would let me go in this case.[10]

In his deposition at Valparaiso, on June 30, 1824, George Comstock had declared that the "most any of the crew had against Captain Worth," was "his not allowing time enough to eat their victuals." [11] Three or four hours before the mutiny, Captain Worth had flogged Joseph Thomas, one of the new hands shipped at Oahu, for remarking that "it would be a dear blow for him," if the *Globe*'s master dared to whip him. Captain Worth immediately took hold of him "by the colar and whipped him with an end of a rope," the rest of the sailors standing in the waist. All hands were silent except Rowland Jones, who asked the others "how they could bear to see the man served that way; after this they went on the forecastle murmuring and saying they would leave her at the first isle they came to." Silas Payne said that if the Captain flogged any more in that way they must tell him to stop. "All this happened in the morning of the day the Mutiny broke out when the officers all were murdered." [12]

Comstock further stated in his deposition that Rowland Coffin, the youngest on board, "told the murderers everything the crew said afterwards," and must have known something of the mutiny, although he took no part in it. George also told of Thomas Liliston going as far as the companionway on the night of the mutiny, "with a hatchet and knife in his hand but gave out and went forward and turned into bed." [13] He also accused Joseph Thomas of having knowledge of the proposed mutiny but of taking no actual part in it. On the voyage of escape in the *Globe,* Thomas was often disobedient and noisy, young Comstock declared.

In his journal Comstock wrote:

> I proceed on with this melancholly tale. . . . Smith it appears had the first watch and then called us, that is the waist-boat's crew. I being one of the number that stayed on board ship when the boats were off, did not belong to any boat but stood a watch with the boatsteerer of the waist boat whose name was Comstock. . . .
> It being my relief at the wheel, I took it to stand from 10 till 12 P.M. The boatsteerer came to me when I first took the helm and told me to keep the ship a good full, which it was my duty to obey without asking any reason, as I knew not if the Capt had told him

too or not. He came to me several times and cursed me because I had the ship in the wind, but I took no notice of this till my helm was up and I took up the rattle to shake it for relief; but I had scarcely begun to shake it when Comstock came to me and said—if I made the least d—d bit of noise he would send me to h—l, this was very alarming to me, suspecting nothing.

I began to rattle but was suddenly checked by a brother in flesh but not in heart; for if he had been he would have put away this wicked design, thinking it would ruin me forever, for little did he think I would ever get home to tell the fatal news.

The younger Comstock then told of the three conspirators who followed Comstock—Payne, Humphries and Oliver—and how they went down the companion. His version of the actual horror of the mutiny follows: [14]

The first that I knew of them having begun their work was an axe which I distinctly heard on deck, and was afterward informed was Comstock when he struck the Capt who lay in a hammock in the cabin, his stateroom being too warm to lie in. At the first stroke he cut the top of his head very nearly off. He repeated the stroke and then run to Paine, who it seems was stationed with a boarding knife to stick the mate [Beetle] as soon as Comstock struck the Capt., which was immediately done. But he boned the knife, which awoke the mate who began thus—(being awoke so sudden) "What—what—what—what—what—what is this! Paine! Comstock! don't kill me! have I not always . . ." Here Comstock interrupted him—"Yes you have always been a dam rascal; you tell lies about me out of the ship, will you! It is a d—d good time for you to beg now, you are too late!" The mate then clinched him by the throat and knocked out the light and Comstock lost his hatchet, but singing out finally for a hatchet, being choked very hard by Beetle the mate. Paine felt for one and accidentally put his hand on one which Comstock took and hit Beetle over the head with it and broke skull, he fell down in the pantry and there lay groaning until Comstock dispatched him.

The stewart [Humphries] held the light all this time and Oliver was cruising around and putting in a blow when it came handy. The 2nd and 3rd mates lay all this time listening but spoke not a word in hopes their lives would be saved. After killing the mate Comstock (leaving a watch at the 2nd mate's door) came up to light a lamp at the binnacle. I then spoke to him and asked if he was going to hurt Smith the other boatsteerer. He said, "Yes," he should kill him and asked where he was. I told him I had not seen him (although he had been aft talking with me) for fear if I told the truth he would kill him or go in pursuit of him. He percieving me shed tears, asked what I was crying about, I informed him I was afraid they would hurt me, he told me he would if I talked that way. This rather silenced me from fear of myself, as I then thought he had most done his wicked deeds, he then left me took his light into the cabin and got ready to attack the 2nd and 3rd mates.

After loading two guns he took one and fired through the door in the direction he thought they were and shot Mr. Fisher through the mouth. He then asked if either of them was shot. Fisher answered "Yes, he was, in the mouth!" Mr. Lumbard asked Comstock if he was going to kill him (previous to his shooting Fisher). He answered him in a joking manner "Oh, no I guess not!" They then opened the door, and Comstock making a pass at Lumbard with his gun missed him and fell into the stateroom. Lumbard collared him but he jerked himself out of their hands, at this time Fisher got his gun and placed the bayonet at his heart but Comstock told him to put it down. He obeyed him in hopes he would spare his life. Comstock took the gun and run Mr. Lumbard through several times, then he told Fisher there was no hope for him, he had got to die (also to remember the scrape he had with him in company of the *Enterprise* of Nantucket, which was as follows—Comstock came to Fisher to play, who being very athletic took Comstock up and handled him very easy. This made him ashamed and he got in a passion and struck at Fisher, who took him up several times and laid him on the deck pretty hard. Comstock then told him he would have his heart's blood for this but Fisher thought nothing of this till it was now brought up). And now to die like a man Fisher turned himself around back too and told him he was ready. Comstock then put the muzzle of the gun to his head and fired which killed him immediately. Lumbard was then begging to spare his life but Comstock told him he was a bloody man he had a bloody hand and would be avenged. He then run him through the body again, and he then begged for water, but Comstock told him he would give him water and then run him through again and left him for dead. It appears by their story as if Comstock the boatsteerer murdered the whole or finished them.

As if there was not horror enough, Comstock the narrator, related how Lombard, by some miracle lived until daylight. Then he was dragged on deck and continued to plead for his life. Utterly mad with the frenzy of their night's work, the mutineers threw the stricken man over the side. With incredible vitality, the doomed Lombard caught hold of the plank-shear on the hull of the ship. Clinging with his death's grip, he called: "Comstock, you said you would save me!" But the head mutineer kicked at the man's fingers until he lost his hold and fell into the sea.

"But he swam very quick," wrote the young brother of the murderer. "After being in the water a minute we see nothing more of him. A boat was ordered to be hoisted out to pursue him, but thinking the crew would take the boat and go to the *Lyra,* they gave orders not to." [15] It was night and escape would have been simple—escape to the dangers of an open-boat voyage would have been preferred.

George Comstock was appointed steward by his brother, probably to guard the food served them. Two days later, George discovered Humphries the former steward loading a pistol. "I immediately went to Comstock and informed him what was going on in the cabin." Humphries was confronted and told of having "heard something which made him afraid of his life." Comstock, Paine and Oliver demanded the story, whereupon Humphries accused "Gilbert Smith, the surviving boatsteerer and Peter Kidder (a man very easily scared), were going to take the ship." [16]

A jury of four men—George Comstock, Rowland Coffin, Silas Payne and John Oliver—pronounced Humphries guilty. It was either that verdict or a similar judgment for Smith and Kidder. The Negro offered no resistance. He was probably too overwhelmed with remorse and terror. Comstock ordered him hung from the foreyard, "with everyone to take hold of the rope and run aft when the signal bell was struck. Humphries murmured: 'When I was born I did not think I should ever come to this. . . .'" The bell was struck "and he was swung to the fore yard without a kick or a groan, he died immediately." [17]

The *Globe* then was headed for the Kingsmill Islands. The natives, however, proved hostile; one canoe was fired upon and several natives wounded. Then the *Globe* sailed northwest and finally reached Lord Mulgrave's Range or the Milli Group of the Marshall Islands. Here the disembarkation, the death of Comstock and the escape of the *Globe* were but subsequent acts in the tragedy.

The *Globe,* with Gilbert Smith and his five shipmates, approached the coast of Chile early in June. Fortunately a ship was sighted which put aboard several hands to help work the whaleship into Valparaiso, where they arrived June 7, 1824. It was a remarkable voyage, a tribute to the navigation of Smith and the seamanship of his mates. Consul Hogan called it a voyage "most miraculously" completed.

After the examination by Consul Hogan, the *Globe's* men were placed under guard on board a French frigate then lying in the harbor, there being no American naval craft present at that time. Hogan seized the *Globe* under his vested authority, placed it under the command of a Captain James King, recruited a crew and ordered her home. The six ex-crew members, held under suspicion of piracy, were not confined to quarters, and Smith served as first mate.

The *Globe* left Valparaiso in July 1824, and made a safe voyage around the Horn, arriving at Edgartown on November 14 of that year. Oddly enough, five days after her arrival, the ship was turned over to Gilbert Smith, as master, who took oath, "as required by law." [18]

News of the mutiny had preceded the ship's arrival by three weeks. The *Inquirer* of Nantucket, printed the first version of the affair, on October 25, 1824, receiving the information from the ship *Bette*. On the day following the *Globe's* arrival at Edgartown, the *Inquirer* printed a garbled account of the disaster, stating in part in its issue of November 15, 1824:

> The only names of the survivors of the Mutiny which we have been able to obtain are Smith, and two sons of Captain Kidder of Edgartown. One of the remaining three is represented as being a lad of 19 or 20 years. It is further stated that Captain Worth was killed with an axe, while asleep in his berth, by Thain, a sailor shipped at the Sandwich Islands. The Mate was shot by the elder Comstock . . . who was later hung at the Mulgrave Islands. The younger brother was compelled to assist at the execution and on his remonstrating afterwards was beaten to death with billets of wood.

The island's newspaper received this news just before going to press and in its next issue of November 22, 1824 apologized for the "imperfect account" it had published. It then printed a column story, "the veracity of which is indisputable." During the examination of Gilbert Smith and his associates, before Magistrate Hussey, at Nantucket, the

Globe quietly crossed the bar, entered the harbor, and was moored at the South Wharf.

For many years there were many weird tales about the fate of the *Globe*. There were actually three ships of that name which went whaling, two from New Bedford. But the old *Globe* of tragic memory had always made excellent voyages. She first sailed out of Nantucket in 1815. In 1825 she sailed under Captain Reuben Swain. When she returned, she was purchased in 1828 for a trading venture to Brazil. This was her last voyage, as Captain George Macy sold her at Santos, Brazil, where she was broken up in 1830. On this voyage Stephen Kidder, one of the ill-fated crew of the mutiny, sailed as first mate.[19]

The return of the *Globe* and her handful of crew in November 1824, set off another chain of events. Gorham Coffin immediately sent several letters to Washington, requesting that a naval craft be dispatched to the Mulgraves to apprehend the remaining mutineers and to save the innocent victims of the plot. Other whaling merchants joined in forwarding a memorial on the subject, requesting immediate action.

Secretary of the Navy Samuel Southard in a reply to Congressman Reed, on January 19, 1825, stated: "I shall send to Capt. Isaac Hull by the first opportunity, directions to send one of the vessels under his command to the Mulgrave Islands, for the object presented in the Memorial. . . . It is impossible to anticipate within what period he will be able to accomplish it."

Secretary Southard's orders to Commodore Hull reached the latter on the west coast of South America early in May. After several weeks of necessary delay, Hull (the old skipper of the famous *Constitution* during 1812) decided to entrust the task to Captain John Percival of the topsail schooner *Dolphin*. Captain Percival was well fitted; his nickname was Mad Jack and he found it was a task to his liking.

The *Dolphin* sailed from the port of Chorillos, Peru, on August 18, 1824.[20] The voyage to the Mulgraves was made by way of the Galápagos and the Marquesas Islands, thence to lonely Caroline Island. Captain Percival steered for Humphrey's or Rierson's islands, lately reported by the Nantucket whaler *Ganges,* but could not find them.

Finally they arrived at the Duke of Clarence Island in the Kingsmills. Here the natives narrowly missed cutting off several boat crews and the *Dolphin* just managed to get away. On November 19, the schooner at last arrived at the Mulgraves.

Captain Percival found evidence of the *Globe*'s landing—a whaleman's lance—soon after he began his search of the Milli Group. These islands were circular in shape—a coral necklace surrounding a lagoon which stretched for miles, across which the natives sailed their canoes with great rapidity.

Meanwhile, both Lay and Hussey were praying for deliverance. They were kept hidden by their captors, who moved them from island to island with skillful planning. As fast as the marines searched one island, the natives would cross and recross the lagoon, so that the procedure was like a great game of checkers, with the natives always one jump ahead. On one occasion, Lay was held under the roof of a hut while a party from the schooner was searching the village.

The finding of several portions of seamen's chests, some ashen poles and other articles from the *Globe,* spurred on the *Dolphin*'s men. A whaleman's mitten was found with the name "Rowland Coffin" marked thereon. This was unmistakable proof that the *Globe*'s men had been here.

At last the arduous efforts of the white men were rewarded. On November twenty-ninth, they came to the islet where the *Globe*'s crew had originally landed and found "a place that was strewed with several hundreds of staves of beef and pork barrels, and old pieces of canvas and cloth. In advancing further, they found a skeleton, lightly covered with sand, and a box containing a few Spanish dollars. . . . There was no doubt . . . that this was the place where the mutineers, and others of the *Globe*'s crew had been left—but where were they now?" [21]

The log of the *Dolphin* records this discovery:

> . . . at 3 Two men of Lt. Homer's party returned to the vessel, bringing intelligence that a skeleton supposed to be the remains of Comstock the chief Mutineer of the Ship *Globe* had been dug out of the Sand beach upon the most-Western Peninsula of Mulgrave island. Also that they had found spars, rigging, part of a sail makers palm, a thimble, staves and several other Things, having no doubt of this

being the place where the Mutineers first landed. Commenced fitting out the launch for a Searching Expedition. . . .[22]

The *Dolphin*'s launch, with eleven men and one junior officer, was placed under the command of Lieutenant Hiram Paulding. This party immediately took the launch through a passage in the reef and into the inland sea—the great lagoon. Cruising along the islets, they came to one where a large body of natives was gathered. Here Paulding decided to investigate. He had his men row the launch until it was just in back of the low surf. At that moment, a person who "was dressed and looked like a native addressed us in our own language," wrote Paulding.[23]

"The Indians are going to kill you; don't come on shore unless you are prepared to fight." [24] Thus spoke the unknown "native" ashore.

The young Lieutenant Paulding gives an excellent description of the scene:

> . . . although we were convinced that this was one of the men we were so anxiously looking for, his sudden and unexpected appearance, his wild attire, and above all, his warning, seemed like an illusion of fancy! His hair was long, combed up, and tied in a knot on the top of his head, round his loins, he wore a large mat, finely wrought, and the use of cocoanut oil, and the action of the tropical sun for nearly two years had made his skin almost as dark as that of the natives.[25]

The man ashore repeated his warning, even described the natives' plot to entice the white men to land and then suddenly attack them with stones. Paulding pondered the situation. Was this one of the mutineers? If he was not, but one of the faithful hands, why had he not made his appearance before? He asked the apparition's name. "William Lay of the *Globe,* of Nantucket," was the reply. Paulding wrote:

> His stature and juvenile appearance answered the description we had of him. I told him to advance to the boat, but he said he was afraid of the natives. . . . I then directed him to run to us and we would protect him; but he declined, saying that the natives would kill him with stones before he got there. During all this time they thought he was arranging for us to come on shore.[26]

Paulding made up his mind quickly. After ordering his men to discharge and reload their pistols, he landed them, swiftly marched to where Lay was standing and not knowing whether he was a mutineer or not, presented a cocked pistol to his breast.

> I repeated the question: "Who are you? to which he replied: I am your man," and burst into tears. I told him then to say to the natives that if they rose from their seats, or threw a stone, we would shoot them all.[27]

Poor William Lay, beside himself with the joy of his deliverance, could only call out half in English and half in native tongue, until Paulding brought him up sharp. There was a moving scene when the old native, who had saved Lay during the massacre of the *Globe*'s marooned crew, had a last parting with the young man. Then Paulding hurried him into the launch.

It was a daring rescue, one that Midshipman Davis of the crew in the launch later declared was the boldest act he ever witnessed. William Lay told Paulding the story of the massacre and informed him that only one other remained alive—Cyrus M. Hussey, a young Nantucketer, who was held captive on another island. Paulding promptly headed the launch for that island, anxious to get there before one of the sailing canoes brought the information of Lay's liberation.

They arrived at the island before the startled natives were aware of their mission. Lay pointed out the native chief, one Lugoma, who was Hussey's captor. Paulding immediately seized him and informed the natives that he would be killed unless the young white captive was freed. The resulting action is best described by Paulding:

> It was a few minutes before he [Hussey] appeared, walking towards us, with his fine yellow hair hanging in ringlets about his shoulders, and his person quite naked with the exception of a piece of blanket tied around his loins. . . . I said to him, "Well, young man, do you wish to return to your country?" His eyes filled with tears as he replied: "Yes, sir, I know of nothing that I have done for which I should be afraid to go home." [28]

On board the *Dolphin,* Captain Percival took statements from both Lay and Hussey. These have recently come to light and corroborate the several depositions made by the *Globe*'s crew at Valparaiso. Lieutenant Paulding also recorded a statement by Lay, which is illuminating:

> After the death of the officers, Comstock made us all live in the cabin with him, where the mutineers used to sing, and carouse, and tell over the story of the murder, and what they had dreamed. Paine and Oliver who could scarcely ever sleep, spoke with horror of their dreams, and of the ghosts which appeared to them at night, but Comstock always made a light of it, and appeared to exult in what he had done. He said once that the captain came to him with his wounded and bloody head, and showed him what he had done, when he told the captain to depart and never come again, or *he would kill him a second time.*[29]

The examination of Hussey, on board the *Dolphin,* as recorded by Captain Percival contains the first account of what happened to the marooned men following the sailing of the *Globe:* [30]

> We were obliged to obey the orders of Payne and Oliver, but they had no written rules for our government. John Oliver became very much attached to liquor and was often intoxicated until I knocked in the head of the spirit cask.—The conduct of Payne to the natives was bad—he went to a distant part of the Island and brought a girl from the natives to live with him, a few nights after, she ran away, he went off with three men armed with Muskets and brought her back, he threatened to shoot her and confined her with feet irons.
>
> Payne was employed [after the sailing of the ship] in taking one Whale-boat to pieces to build upon another and having his tools exposed one night, the Natives stole from the Toolchest a hatchet and two chissels. The day after, he sent four of us after the Indians and the tools stolen; we succeeded in getting the tools and had hold of the Indian when they commenced stoning us, and in this affray Roland Jones was killed. On hearing of the affray Payne was much alarmed went to the tent and prepared the Arms, the natives assembling in great numbers near the tent, armed with Spears Clubs and Stones.
>
> Payne went to the natives and returned with some of them and said he believed he had reconciled them, he did not think they would kill us, he then put into the Arm chest all the Muskets in the possession of the Men, after the natives saw that the men were alarmed they began to plunder from the tent Ironwork, Knives &c, during this time our men were distributed among the natives, a short time after they rose upon the men and killed with their Clubs, spears & stones the following persons, Silas Payne, John Oliver, Thomas Lilis-

ton, Roland Coffin, Columbus Worth and Joe Brown the Sandwich Islander leaving William Lay and myself alive out of the number left upon the Island at the time of the sailing of the *Globe* from this Island.

The *Dolphin* then was steered for the Sandwich Islands, arriving at Honolulu on January 16, 1825, the first American man-of-war that ever entered that harbor. The first news of the schooner's arrival there reached Nantucket, by way of Canton, on August 26, 1826. The report ran thus:

> After a long cruise of five months, we have arrived where there is some indication of civilization, having accomplished the object of our cruise; viz., the taking of the survivors of the crew of the whaleship *Globe* of Nantucket.[31]

This information, so full of hope to the families, was further distorted by the reports:

> Only two or three survivors of the *Globe's* crew were rescued—the rest are reported killed by the natives.[32]

Among those who wrote Secretary of the Navy Southard, for more particular information, was Gorham Coffin, one of the *Globe's* owners, to "relieve the extreme anxiety of friends and relatives at home." [33] No further news was forthcoming.

Under date of September 4, 1826, Secretary Southard reported: "No information has reach the Department of the result of the expedition on which the U.S. schooner *Dolphin* was dispatched to the Mulgrave Islands. Whenever it does, it shall be made public."

The *Dolphin* sailed from Oahu on May 11, 1826, and arrived at Raitera, in the Society Islands on June 7, 1826. She did not reach Valparaiso in Chile until July 23. Having performed the first such voyage of an American ship-of-war, the *Dolphin's* officers and crew were now fully aware of what the whalemen were faced with during their cruising through the Pacific. In their rescue of Lay and Hussey, they had revitalized the Navy's prestige, proving, as Paulding so aptly expressed it, "that no situation was so perilous as to justify dispair."

The schooner soon left to rejoin the frigate *United States* at Callao, and on September 1, 1826, Lay and Hussey were transferred to that vessel under Commodore Hull, which soon after departed for New

York. On April 21, 1827, a year after they were at Honolulu, the two survivors of the *Globe* arrived in the United States.[34]

The *Globe* had returned to Nantucket in November 24, 1824.[35] At this time, Gilbert Smith, George Comstock, Joseph Thomas and the Kidder brothers, were examined by Josiah Hussey. All testified as they had before Consul Hogan, in Valparaiso, five months before. Thomas was arraigned as a part "privy to the intention of Mutiny," and held for the U. S. District Court in Boston. After another six months, he was finally tried and acquitted.[36]

On October 21, 1826, the *Inquirer* of Nantucket reported the arrival of the whaleship *Loper,* "4/ months from Otaheite . . . The U. S. schooner *Dolphin* was at Otaheite when the *Loper* left, having on board two of the surviving crew of the *Globe.*" The following week (October 28) the identity of the two survivors was finally made public. Thus, nearly two years after the *Globe* returned home, the names of Hussey and Lay were at last revealed. This information was contained in a letter from Michael Hogan, at Valparaiso, dated July 30, 1826, which read as follows:

> It affords me great satisfaction to inform you that the U.S. Sch. *Dolphin* anchored her on the 23*rd* inst. having on board two of the youths belonging to the *Globe,* left at the Mulgrave Islands, William Lay and Cyrus M. Hussey, both grown up fine young men, very much liked by their officers. All the rest were killed by the natives, of which no doubt Lt. Commandant Percival has advised; but as this vessel goes direct to Stonington, I conceive it my duty to trouble you with this communication for the information of all concerned.[37]

Much has been made of Joseph Thomas, who returned to stand trial and be acquitted of any part in the actual mutiny. He is mentioned as being a strange almost inscrutable figure, and one authority declares his appearance on the *Globe* is as much a mystery as the character of Comstock, the chief mutineer. But this is not so. From his own testimony, Thomas tells us he went aboard the *Globe* at Honolulu in December 1823, together with Payne, Oliver and the other new hands. He admits his insolence to the captain; describes his flogging for it; denies any connection with the mutiny, and very properly puts the burden of proof on his accusers.[38]

Samuel Comstock did ask Thomas to "go down in the cabin with him," on the night of the mutiny, but Thomas did not commit himself. Thomas also credits George Comstock with the plan to retake the ship following the death of his brother in the Mulgraves. Gilbert Smith takes full credit for navigating the *Globe* back to Valparaiso.[39]

But what of Hussey and Lay? These were mere boys at the time of the disaster, but they returned home marked men. Although saved from the massacre of their shipmates, they became virtual slaves. Their bodies were tattooed from neck to feet. After returning to family and friends, they suddenly disappeared aboard whaleships and never again returned to civilization. Did they quietly escape to Pacific Islands? Did they return to their former homes in the Mulgraves?

Young George Comstock also disappeared from Nantucket. The only story ever current about him comes from San Francisco, many years after the mutiny. One day, a small sailboat capsized in the bay. For hours, two young men who were in her clung to the overturned craft. One finally succumbed; the other was seen by a solitary watcher who lived by himself in a small house overlooking the bay. This watcher put off in a boat and took the young survivor to safety. The rescuer was George Comstock and the man he rescued was his own nephew! [40]

If there was any mysterious figure in all the *Globe*'s complement it was the youngest one on board, Rowland Coffin—at the time of the mutiny only sixteen years old. As the nephew of Gorham Coffin, one of the owners of the ship, he might have asked special privileges. Some of the crew who returned accused him of currying favor with Captain Worth and the officers. But the depositions of George Comstock, Joseph Thomas, and Gilbert Smith and Peter Kidder stated he knew that a mutiny was being planned but did not warn the officers.

Mr. Coffin wrote a vigorous defense of his nephew. He even went so far as to engage the services of Daniel Webster in his behalf if he should be one of those surviving the group of those destroyed by the natives. Wrote Gorham Coffin to Webster:

> I have been induced to make this intrusion from a desire to enlist your talents in behalf of an injured orphan . . . Rowland Coffin . . . an active intelligent youth; his father died at sea some 14 years since while in command of a ship belonging to Boson; his mother poor

and left with 3 children. . . . This boy entered on board the *Globe* as second cooper [Hussey being the first], with a determination to do his duty . . . for which he was stigmatized with the epithet curry-favour (a term of reproach) by those less active.[41]

To show evidence of his nephew's innocence or implication in the mutiny plot, Coffin in his letter to Webster, included a copy of a singular certificate, as follows:

> I, George Comstock, do certify that great jealousy was created against Rowland Coffin, from some of the crew, in consequence of his being taken the most notice of by the Captain, previous to his death, and afterwards, for being much noticed by Samuel B. Comstock. (Signed) George Comstock.

Gorham Coffin's letter further contains scathing indictment of Gilbert Smith and those other five men who escaped with the *Globe*. The shipowner's argument was this: Following the death of Comstock, only two of the actual mutineers remained—Paine and Oliver—and "these two relaxed much in their discipline; the head one of the two to the laying aside his weapons of defense, and going deliberately to work to build a hogsty; the other at work on board the ship." [42]

> Here we had six men, one of whom was an under-officer [Smith], and not one of them with the presence of mind or courage enough to propose calling on the four boys [Hussey, Lay, Coffin and Worth], (everyone of whom was known to be innocent), for assistance to the two mutineers, put them in irons, of which they had plenty, replace everything on board the ship, take on board the two mutineers, & proceed to safety. These are reflections which some of them were capable of making, when they found themselves out of the reach of the mutineers, and how must their want of courage be accounted for, to the satisfaction of the owners of the ship & to the public? [43]

The testimony of Smith and the Kidder brothers before Magistrate Hussey in Nantucket, tended to implicate young Coffin in some knowledge of the proposed mutiny.

This led to Gorham Coffin's shrewd observations of Smith's own conduct.

> Here we view Smith, the only officer at liberty so completely panick struck [at the time of the mutiny] that reason had taken its flight and with it he flies, not knowing whither, but thinks he went into

the forecastle, the sleeping place of the sailors, where he perfectly recollects young Coffin make a statement [of knowing a mutiny was planned]. Smith did not state this at the hearing [before Consul Hogan at Valparaiso]; thence he flies into the forehold . . . and hides, where he had time to reflect that he had acted the fool long enough, leaves his hiding place and goes on deck, where he is accosted by Comstock & asked whether he was for or against them; his reply: "I will do anything you tell me to, if you'll spare my life." [44]

Gorham Coffin wrote similar letters to John Quincy Adams and Secretary of the Navy Samuel Southard. Unknown to anyone but those at the Mulgrave Islands, the unfortunate subject of the uncle's concern was then ten months in his grave.

When the *Globe* was being plundered, her articles moved ashore, and it was known that Comstock intended to burn the ship, it was young Rowland Coffin who declared: "Those transactions were beyond his control, but the stigma of them could be so great on their characters, should they ever return to their country again, that he had no desire to leave that island until taken off a prisoner." [45]

In the extremity of his youth he had tried to make himself a good sailor; he had listened to murmuring that he was currying favor with the officers; finally he was accused of being too friendly with Samuel Comstock.

As for Gilbert Smith: What was the reason he made no attempt as an officer of the *Globe,* to organize the crew and go to the rescue of the other officers in the main cabin? The probable answer is in his own deposition at Valparaiso, when he described his actions on the night of the mutiny:

. . . I was awakened by a disturbance which brought me on Deck without Clothes; then I found the disturbance was in the Cabin, went quickly below, put on my clothes and came on Deck again—went to the cabin gangway. I saw Sam'l B. Comstock with a boarding Knife in his hand at the Stateroom door in which second & third Mate were then. Comstock said to the Second Mate [Lombard], 'Don't you open that door.' He [Lombard] said he would not but he would give him anything he had there to save his life. Then Comstock spoke very loud, swearing his hand; said he was the Bloody Man, he had the Bloody hand and would have revenge. The Second Mate repeated several times: "Comstock! Comstock! what is the matter?" No answer was given by Comstock.[46]

The remainder of Smith's testimony fully indicates his terror. He fled forward and did not recover from his fright, natural enough, until it was too late to save his comrades in the cabin. His own testimony reveals that as the only officer left in the ship, he made no effort to rally the hands in the forecastle, who in turn were helpless without leadership. Smith's only thought was how to preserve his own life. His subsequent actions show this, although his deposition in Nantucket differed from that at Valparaiso and from that of George Comstock.

As for the most controversial figure of all—Samuel Comstock, the harpooner turned murderer—here is a study for the psychiatrists. Born in Nantucket in 1802, he was barely twenty-one years old when he led the bloody mutiny on the *Globe*. His father, Nathan Comstock, was a well-known Quaker schoolmaster, later a cashier in the Pacific Bank. The mutineer's mother, Elizabeth Emmett, was the daughter of a Nantucket Mitchell.[47]

After early schooling at the "Nine Partners" Quaker School, Dutchess County, New York, Samuel B. Comstock went to sea. At the age of thirteen he was aboard the ship *Edwards,* voyaging from New York to Liverpool. In 1817, he made his first voyage whaling, the ship being taken by a Chilean pirate. Returning home to Nantucket, Comstock shipped out on the *Foster,* Captain Shubael Chase, in 1819. This craft cruised in uncharted sections of the Pacific, and it was at this time that Comstock probably got his desire to set up a kingdom of his own on one of the remote South Sea Islands. Two of his shipmates on the voyage—John Lincoln and John Cotten—afterwards became shipmasters. It is recounted that Comstock once requested to be set ashore at an island but was refused by Captain Chase.[48]

When news of the mutiny reached Nathan Comstock in New York, he wrote his relatives in Nantucket. The letter contained one significant sentence: "O, Samuel! Samuel! Heaven forsaken Samuel!" There is no better judgment of this youthful desperado, who, well-nigh singlehanded murdered the officers of the *Globe*.

History and tradition, whether of ancient or modern times, are subjects which require a much different handling from mathematics or others of the exact sciences. The element of probability often proves a troublesome test of fact. But, if this test is patiently conducted, it often brings into a clearer focus the many bits of evidence which make up the historical record. Human nature is that priceless ingredient which must be applied against the facts. Comstock's mind, after months of brooding, had made him a predatory animal—a man crazed by his dreams of a South Sea paradise and goaded by thoughts of revenge. He plotted and executed the deeds of a madman.

That he had some saving qualities is evidenced by several records. Even the attempt by his brother William to glorify his unjustifiable acts had its points.[49] But, by far, the lament of his schoolmate, Henry Glover, of Nantucket, is the most appropriate of all. Glover wrote a poem entitled "The Young Mutineer," stanzas from which ran:

> Tho' beardless his cheek, yet his was a soul
> That knew not a master, that brooked no control;
> Tho' beardless his cheeks, yet his was a hand
> Acquainted with daggers; a voice to command,
> An eye that wept, a heart without fear,
> Were the pride and the boast of the young mutineer.
>
> He lies on the beach of a lone desert isle,
> His dirge the green billows are chanting the while,
> As they in wild tumult, roll over his head,
> And wash the high rock, that marks out his wet bed;
> There lies with a heart that ne'er knew a fear,
> The mangled remains of the young mutineer.
>
> He lies on the beach by a comrade in guilt,
> His forehead was cloven, his best blood split.
> The cries of his victims have risen to God,
> And their wailings were quenched
> In the murderer's blood.
> He fell without mourners, for none dropped a tear
> O'er the mangled remains of the young mutineer.
>
> In years that are coming the seamen will tell
> Of murders and murdered, and murderer's yells.
> The tale, the lone watch of night will beguile
> When they sail by the shores of that desolate isle.
> And their beacon shall be, as they thitherward steer,
> The black rock on the grave of the young mutineer.[50]

The *Globe* mutiny had many consequences. Of paramount importance was the public recognition that a whaleship, although representing in the Pacific Ocean a floating bit of United States property, had no protection by our government once it had left the coast of Peru. The successful cruise of the *Dolphin* gave a new prestige to the Navy. Two years after, Captain Catesby-Jones, aboard the *Peacock* at Tahite, conducted a trial of whalemen accused of mutiny on the whaler *Fortune,* of Plymouth, Massachusetts. He ordered two men to "be punished by thirty-nine lashes with a cat-of-nine tails on the bare back," one other "twenty-five lashes in the same way," and three others to "receive fifteen lashes." [51] This was more severe than punishment hitherto meted out by the whaling masters.

As for the whaleship itself, owners now ordered that boatsteerers should no longer command a watch at night. From time immemorial a boatsteerer or harpooner had been an unofficial officer—now he became a still more ambiguous personage in rank. He lived in the steerage—both in rank and quarters—halfway between foremast hand in the forecastle and officers in the cabin, aft. He was a man apart, selected for his coolness and skill in driving home a harpoon. He originally was designated a "line-coiler," delegated the exact task of putting the whale line in the boat's tubs; then he was specified a "boatsteerer" as, after the whale was harpooned or "fast," he changed places with the mate and took over the steering oar. Now his position on board ship was no less respected and secure—but his authority as an under-officer was curtailed.

chapter xxx

"WE DESIRE YOU TO STEER BY YOUR OWN COMPASS"

As it is not improbable that you will cruise considerably in the Pacific where that ocean is not well explored, the most vigilant lookout will be continually necessary; therefore, no officer must be permitted to retain his post of honour who suffers himself to sleep during his watch upon deck.

—Instructions to Captain David Osborn,
of the ship *Peruvian* [1]

A WHALESHIP, after its fitting out and departure for a three-year voyage, was a veritable floating kingdom. There, between the planks and timbers of a ship of three hundred tons burden, was a monarchy in miniature, over which the captain ruled with a power as absolute as that of any of the emperors of old. The whole deck, from taffrail to the heel of the bowsprit, presented to the eye of the beholder the idea and the picture of an isolated community whose people knew of nothing beyond the bulwarks and to whom everything further off was the same as if it had never existed.

Forward, at the bows, was the barrel-windlass and below the break of the fo'c'sle head, tryworks, that single or double iron (or copper) boiler, embedded in the brick and mortar of its rectangle-shaped support containing the fireplaces and flues. Abaft this was the caboose or camboose, or "office of the doctor," as the hands usually called the cook.

The deck of the whaleship was commanded by the raised quarter-

434

deck where the "king" and his satelites held sway. Gallow-frames
holding spare boats, a house over the main cabin, a binnacle, a tiller or
wheel, were the distinguishing features. With the advent of the 1840's,
houses on the quarter-deck and a wooden porch-like covering became
the accepted design.

Between decks were three distinct and separate quarters; the fo'c'sle
in the bows, where the crew were to spend thirty-odd months in "rent-
free" quarters; the steerage, amidships, the headquarters of the boatsteerers and cooper, and the stowage place for harpoons, lances,
boarding knives and other "craft" peculiar to the whaleship; and aft,
the cabin, where the captain and his officers maintained the seat of
government. Here, individual cabin berths opened into the main cabin,
which was the eating and sitting room for the master of the ship and
his mates.

But of all the outstanding places, the forecastle was the most unusual.
In a space not more than twelve feet square were stowed the bunks
and sea-chests of some sixteen whalemen. In the narrow confines of
such a bed-sitting room these shipmates lived through calm and storm,
day after day, wedged into cramped quarters so that they existed
elbow to elbow. Here was the young whaleman, ambitious, eager; the
old hand, cranky and often morose; the Negro, often happy and content; the Kanacka, a child in his reaction to shipboard routine.

When the voyage was going well, with bellies full and the islands
of the South Seas around, they were a happy lot in the fo'c'sle. Prospects of fresh meat at the west coast ports, and grog; of fruits, and
coconuts, and girls who swam out to meet them at the islands; and
some seventy-barrel-bull-whales somewhere in the wide expanse of the
Pacific—these were the things that cheered them on.

And when the Cape Horn gales froze their fingers and the sails on
the yards, so that the icy canvas ripped off their fingernails; when the
flat, glassy sea made the craft roll in sluggish motion and the blazing
sun of the equator set the tar running out of the deck seams; when
the water grew foul, and the salt beef stank, and whales went off
before they could get within darting distance—that was when the
gloom of the fo'c'sle hung like a curtain of doom. That was when
the hands growled at each other and the officers, and sometimes
engaged in a swift bloody battle over a trifling word or gesture.

But, most of the time the forecastle was a place of comfort and rest —a sanctuary from the deck. Here, the young hand lying in his bunk, listened to the wonderful stories of whaling, or songs about lovers, or joined in a game of cards. Many a weather-beaten sailor, seated on a battered chest, became the center of a ring of listeners as he recounted an experience known only to himself, told with the magic ingredients of authenticity.

Always, in the night watches, there were stories—tales of daring and of faraway places on the "other side of the land," accounts of ships and men, of cities, and women, of islands and girls. Never failing were those yarns about mysterious voices which came from the sea, the doggerel verses, the improvised embellishments of honorable sea tales, and the tales of ghosts of those missing ships. Here, young and old slept, and rested, and dreamed.

The unfortunate opinion that whaleships merely sailed out into the wide ocean, and knocked about aimlessly for three years in their search for whales, is probably the widest divergence from truth that could be supposed. To appreciate how the whaling grounds were carefully charted one has only to follow the courses of the ships, and to observe how they sought certain sections of the oceans at specified times, when they knew whales would be there.

Captain Joseph Gardner, of Nantucket, in command of the *Rosalie,* the first whaleship out of Warren, Rhode Island, noted in his log:

> In the latitude of 2°–12′ south, long 115° to 120° west, from 7th February to the 18th, took eleven whales. The whale's head is principally breaching and [they are] cows, although I have seen 3 large bulls in the same time. The current carried me about 40 miles per day to the westward, being about the full of the moon. Since this longitude there has been no current from this. I stood from 18 miles north to 45 south [of the line] and found whales plenty. I see 3 schools in one day.

He recorded a few weeks later:

> You can cruise down about this time [March] from 20° north latitude to 40° south and in long. as far as 135° west, even to 140° W. and fetch the Sandwich Islands. N. B. Don't leave if you find whales till the 25th of March. A good place to cruise is from 4° 30′ to 5° 30′

south and long. 105° to 107° west in the months of December, and January. Large whales.[2]

Many of the logbooks during the 1820-30 decade reflected the whaleman's knowledge of the migratory habits of the whale. They show his considerable understanding of the ocean currents, along which areas the whales traveled in search of food. Where water temperatures changed but little, the whale appeared to be in largest numbers—areas like the polar seas and the tropics. The months of June and July found the whalemen north of the Sandwich Islands; in September they were back "on Japan" again, and in November cruised on the great circle route, to the coast of California; thence south to the Galápagos Islands and on into the South Pacific.

It was customary to find a whaleship rounding the Horn in late October or early November, recruiting on the west coast of South America, then to the Galápagos or across to the Marquesas or the Society groups. In February and March they stood up toward the equator and Christmas and Fanning Islands. If they did not go on to Honolulu, they would sail to the Phoenix and Kingsmill groups, and in July and August would be headed south to the Ellice and the Navigators. September usually found them sailing east to the south of the Friendly Islands, gradually working northeast to the Austral Islands and thence to the northernmost of the Societies in October. The next cruise would be on the line, or to the Galápagos, then probably north to the coast of California. Such voyages were far from being aimless cruisings.[3]

While on board the ship *Lion,* in 1802, Peter Paddock lost a whale when the line parted. Thirteen years later, in the same part of the Pacific, a whale was killed and in its body was found a harpoon stamped "P. P., Ship *Lion*," proving a whale regularly returns to his old haunts.

Instances where harpoons from other ships were found in a captured whale are not unusual, and, in a number of cases, they were significant in supplying useful knowledge as to the migratory habits of the whale. One of the *Lyra*'s harpoons was found in a whale killed on the Kingsmill Grounds twenty-two years after that ship was wrecked on a reef in the Sandwich Group.

An equally remarkable case was that of the *Catawba*'s harpoon. On November 25, 1855, Captain Swain's logbook recorded:

> ... At 8 A.M. saw whales, large ones, put off and struck one, bow boat went up to him and missed him [lancing] twice, the whale took to running and sounded so we could not get to him. After being fast 8 hours the line parted.[4]

The *Catawba* was then off Charles Island, in the Galápagos Group. Eleven years later the bark *Platina,* of Westport, Captain Otis F. Hamblin, captured a whale ninety miles off Charles Island, and embedded deep in his side was found the head of a harpoon marked with the name *Catawba.* "The shank of the iron projecting out of the blubber of the whale was worn entirely off by the constant friction of the water, but the part beneath the blubber was perfect, as when it was thrown from the hand of the harpooner." [5]

On April 15, 1830, one of the boats of the *Clarkson,* of Nantucket, struck a whale but was forced to cut from her when the fog came rolling across the sea. The ship was then in latitude 30°–25′ north and 172°–24′ east. One of the boats from the New Bedford whaler *Rodman* struck the same whale on April 17, finding in her the *Clarkson*'s harpoon, the ship then being in latitude 31°–04′ north and longitude 170°–1′ east. It was estimated that the whale had run a distance of 320 miles during that time.[6]

The profits derived from a good voyage during this decade (1820-30) make a study in themselves. The *Rosalie,* of Warren, Rhode Island, under Captain Gardner, not only launched that port's whaling business when she sailed in April 1825, but got the enterprise off on the right foot by returning in 1828 (August) with a full ship. The 2,150 barrels of sperm oil sold for seventy-five cents per gallon, making a total of $50,793.73 as the voyage gross return.[7]

The lay system found Captain Gardner, under a ⅟₁₈ share, receiving $2,821.87 for his three years of cruising. First Officer Brown (½₈th lay) received $1,814.06. Second Officer Davis received $1,269.84 and Third Officer Champlin got $923.52. The three boatsteerers (or harpooners) received $725.62 each, the cooper, blacksmith and cook $461.76 each, and the average sailor's lay (at ⅟₁₃₀th) gave him $390.72. The total in "lays" to the officers and crew was $14,289.39, making the new gross for the owners $36,511.36. Out of this came the cost of outfitting the ship, drafts for provisions at South American ports, costs of repairs to the ship, and other items. It was customary to sell ships' voyages in shares—⅛th, ¹⁄₁₆th, etc., and the master of the ship usually had a share under this system.[8]

When a ship cleared for sea, the captain would have a "letter of instruction" from his owners. Some of these were complete, but all of them were evidence of the complete domination of the voyage by the master of the ship. In the letter book of Christopher Mitchell & Co., are a number of these interesting instructions to their captains. One addressed to Captain Elisha Fisher, of the *Maria*, in 1836, is typical:

Sir: Having appointed you to the command of the ship, *Maria*, we wish you to proceed to sea with all convenient dispatch, and as the ship is furnished with everything necessary for you to proceed to the Pacific ocean, we do not think it necessary for you to touch at any port this side of Cape Horn, unless you should be so fortunate as to get oil on your passage before passing the Western or Cape Verde Islands, in which case you can touch at the most convenient port of the islands and ship it home.

On your arrival in the Pacific Ocean, you will consider yourself at liberty to cruise wherever you may think the prospect best for a cargo of sperm oil.

You are at liberty to go into port as often as it becomes necessary to recruit & refit the ship, but you must not prolong your stay for social purposes; and while cruising at sea you will suffer no visiting to interfere with the interests of the voyage. We have had much cause heretofore to complain of visiting & carousing, and expect it will be avoided by you. When in port do not suffer your men to sell their clothes to buy fruit & liquor, but rather give them fruit at the ship's expense, where it is plenty, and at no rate suffer liquor to be brought on board, except in a very small quantity, & that for medical purposes only.

Serious losses have occurred by suffering the officers to neglect a part of their duty, which you must not allow; we mean the practice of leaving the deck in care of boat-steerers, who are not paid for that service. And that you may not misunderstand us in this respect, we repeat that it is our desire that you require the mates to take their regular watch in the night time while at sea, through the whole voyage; it will be no justification for them to omit this part of their duty because it is not practised on board some other ship.

We wish you to bear in mind that perfect order is to be maintained on board the ship by you, & that no quarreling is to be allowed among the officers, nor between them and the crews, as the success of the voyage depends very much on harmony & united exertion.

As master of his ship, a captain, through the very nature of his position, often became autocratic and sometimes despotic. Oddly enough, mates who found the position of captain suddenly thrust upon them turned out to be veritable slave drivers. First Officer Hiram Fisher found himself master of the *Meridian,* of Edgartown, when the ship had returned for the second time to Tarpaulin Cove and Captain Osborn became too ill to take her out to sea.

The log of the *Meridian* was kept by Henry Collins, a young boat-steerer, who held no brief for Captain Fisher. Off Charles Island he reported the following incident:

. . . The captain called John aft and told him to go out and stand on the end of the spanker boom. He went. And the captain called him in and told him to hold onto the rail whilst he whipped him. John told him he would not be shipped for that. They then took him and was a-going to seize him up in the rigging, we all went aft and told [the captain] he should not put him in the rigging, and he swore he would blow our brains out if we did come aft again.[9]

On another occasion, Collins wrote:

When we were heaving in our whales, the Captain told Manuel da Sousa to sing out. He said he did not know how. The captain ketched up the flying jib halyards and struck him with it twice or thrice. Then Manuel took a handspike and was agoing to hit him with it when the captain struck him with it over the head and he did bleed most dreadfully. He then took him aft and was going to seize him up in the rigging and we all went aft and said, "Be you going to kill him or what are you going to do," and he did take him down into the cabin and bound his head up, and so ends these 24 hours of bad usage in 1830.[10]

When it came to making sudden decisions, the ship's master showed good judgment more times than not, as the results proved. On board the *Phoenix,* of New Bedford, Captain Benjamin Worth, in June 1823, the log recorded:

James Smith and Peter Platt, having some dispute about some money . . . Smith struck Platt, and he went to the Captain to get satisfaction, who seized them up in the rigging and gave them one dozen lashes apiece with the cat-nine-tails, Platt on the bare back which cut him shockingly.[11]

This put an effective stop to further fighting during that cruise. Captain Worth no doubt subscribed to the supposition that while it might involve many in investigating a quarrel it took only two to create a fight.

A lad from the mountains of New Hampshire named Addison Pratt had wanted to go to sea since he was fifteen, but waited three more years before he found his way to Nantucket and shipped out aboard the *Rambler,* under Captain William Worth. Early in January 1822, the ship began her voyage of a little over two years' duration. Young Pratt did not return in her, receiving his discharge at Honolulu. He had dislocated his shoulder, having slipped while boarding the ship in a rainstorm. In his diary he left a portrait of Captain Worth which shows a hard master, with a streak of cruelty.

One evening a cask of salt-fish was left open in the galley and one of the "greenies," Joe Davis, helped himself. Although he shared his spoils with his shipmates he did not dispose of the evidence as quickly as they did, and some fish were found in his berth. Captain Worth summoned the boy aft, and proceeded to knock him down with a rope which was as hard as a wooden club.

Then came the flogging—eighteen lashes on the bare back while tied to the rigging by the thumbs. Young Pratt, with justifiable revulsion, reported in his diary:

> Davis told me the blow he received over the head hurt him more than the scourging he received upon his back that left scars he will carry to his grave. And this was all for taking a small fish and dividing among us, where we were hungry. The skipper, because he was off soundings, supposed himself out of reach of the law, and he shall never be called to account for it. I thank my God that he has set a day when he shall judge all such scape gallows. I feel to rejoice that I shall be a witness against him.[12]

In faded handwriting on a piece of old foolscap, in a small keep-sake chest, is an indictment of Captain Worth more damning than a legal document. It reads as follows:

I have every reason to believe that my dear Brother Ammial H. Joy was worn down by the harsh, unmanly treatment he received from a Brute named William Worth, master of the *Howard* of Nantucket, and though he died resigned to his fate September 5, 1834, his memory will be ever dear to me as long as any reason lasts. I am afraid I never can look on Richard Worth's son any better than a murderer, a disfigurer of God's creation—no man, but in shape; in everything else a monster dignified with not a manly virtue, but endowed in with as many vices as Robespierre, Marat, Judas Iscariot, or any other Fiend in human shape . . . and woe be unto him to the third Generation.[13]

One of the best of the short narrative journals of life aboard a whaleship in the early 1820's was that called "Whim-Whams & Opinions," written by Moses E. Morrell, of New York State, on board the *Hero,* of Nantucket, in 1822-24. Upon his return, Morrell left the journal in the hands of his "dear girl," Miss Sarah Snow, with instructions to destroy it as soon as she had read it, as "it was not wrote for the inspection or amusement of any but myself."

The *Hero* sailed out into a wintry sea in January 1822, and Moses Morrell tells of the crew thus:

Most all our hands being unaccustomed to the motion of the ship, those countenances that before had been expressions of pleasure and health, in a moment became dejected, pale and terrific—such a scene is difficult to describe. Literally, it was floating hospital. Some would lay prostrate on the deck, as regardless of the spray as it was of them. Others were lying on their chests, sighing to be home where some friendly hand would administer to their wants, instead of which their shipmates, more accustomed to the boisterous elements, stood and laughed at their calamity.[14]

The *Hero* took two whales on her passage toward the Horn. "After sixty days of buffetting by the boisterous elements," wrote Morrell, "accompanied by hail and snow, we finally succeeded in getting round." Instead of putting in at Valparaiso or some other Chilean port, Captain Obed Starbuck kept the ship headed along the coast, finally putting in at Paita, Peru, after fifteen days at sea. Shore liberty was a welcomed change—even for a day—but the holiday was rudely interrupted. Morrell wrote:

While we were quietly seated in a private house, partaking of fruit, what was our astonishment when we were saluted by a raggamuffin Spaniard carrying something that had the appearance of a musquet.

He addressed us with the words 'largo boardo' ('go on board'). At first we hesitated to obey the summons, but, none of us understanding much of the language so that we could not ascertain the cause of the order, and seeing others come to assist him, we concluded that he was obeying orders from higher authority, and we tamely submitted and marched to the pier.

Here we found 50 or 60 seamen from other ships who had been escorted in the same honorable manner as ourselves, and here we also heard the cause of our being held in durance vile. The case was: an Indian belonging to the our crew had become intoxicated and had engaged in a skirmish with four or five of the Spaniards. The masters of the ships in port had become fearful of serious consequences ensuing, so they had an order issued from the Commandant for us to be sent on board.

At the time my blood boiled with indignation to see a parcel of young men deprived of our liberty when we were peaceably enjoying ourselves (and that civilly) and molesting or injuring no one.[15]

The crew of the *Hero* had better luck when they arrived at Túmbez, a short time later. For the first time in six months, they were greeted by the pleasing sight of green vegetation, although Morrell noted that the indolence of the natives precluded their taking advantage of the rich soil in raising large crops of vegetables for the whaleships. Fruit trees, requiring little care, had been planted and thrived, and this was their chief product.

Reaching the Galápagos Islands, the ship lay to off Hood Island, while the crew went ashore to gather the great land turtle which supplied so many whalers with fresh meat.

The Galápagos turtle, living on the land, had a shell from six to twelve feet in circumference. The neck and head were two or three feet long and, to give themselves a more stately and formidable appearance, they carried their heads erect. Their speed was from one to four feet an hour and they seldom exceeded this rate unless they were pushed by hunger. Though their appearance startled the whalemen, yet they were harmless. Their flesh when cooked was the most delicious of any the whalemen had ever eaten.

The terrapin possessed the strange ability of surviving without any sustenance for nine months, and still retain their fatness and flavor. This makes them of great benefit to those ships which were on long voyages. The men obtained three hundred of them, from twenty to one hundred and fifty pounds each, and though thousands had taken the same quantity, they were yet (1823) quite plentiful. The labor of bringing them four or five miles, over ledges or rocks with nothing to shelter from the rays of the sun, with no water to quench thirst, made it difficult for one man to obtain more than one or two in a day.

The *Hero* sailed for the Japan Grounds, where she took over twelve hundred barrels of sperm, and then once more shaped her course for Oahu. Foremast-hand Morrell's observation on the activities of the American missionaries there is of interest and importance.

> On the Sabbath after there arrival they went on shore and found that there were three missionaries, with their families, stationed at this island. They had been here for three years, had made considerable progress in the education of the natives, built a comfortable church, a framed dwelling house for themselves, and had gained the friendship and esteem of the natives. In the morning the men attended divine Worship in the native tongue. The king, with his wives and chiefs, attended, in addition to a large number of other natives. There appeared to be considerable attention paid to the discourse, and decorum was observed throughout. When the Psalm was sung all joined in with devotion, but with little melody. . . .[16]
> Mrs. Bingham, the wife of the Reverend, stood high in estimation among them. She had been sedulously employed in teaching and improving the manners of the females. It is a proof that whatever station or situation a sensible and amiable woman is in, she can make herself useful. Mrs. Bingham was convincing proof of this for she is as well calculated for spiritual and temporal instruction, and was a great acquisition to the missionary corps.

Homeward bound, the *Hero* touched at Manue Island, one of the Society Group, sixty miles from Tahiti. Here was a different type of native, as Morrell duly noted:

> At this place there is a petty king ruling over about 300 males and females. They are of a lighter color than the Owhyhenians, with handsome features, and are stout, hearty-looking fellows and are individually very hospitable. The missionaries are held in high esteem among them. They are quite proficient in reading and writing. They

have built a handsome, airy church in the native style, to which they all resort in time of worship.

The females are very coy and will run from a stranger if far from their huts. Others, more forward, will indulge you in a few liberties. For anything further, marriage is necessary. Prostitution and bastardry is punished by death. On the whole they have arrived at considerable perfection.

From the renegade conduct of some masters of vessels, who are compelled to touch here, may be apprehended some difficulties arising, as they will be the means of giving the natives a poor opinion of the doctrine and morals that the missionaries inculcate, and in a degree retard their progress and perhaps, if repeated, will be the cause (as at other islands) of shedding innocent blood.[17]

From the Society Islands, Captain Starbuck laid a course for Cape Horn and home. After some time at sea, the young sailor's journal continues:

We are now 4000 miles from Cape Horn without wood sufficient to cook one meal a day for that distance. O Tempera! The greatest beverage to sailors in cold and stormy weather is warm tea. Of course this luxury must be dispensed with and I am of the opinion that ere many days our diet will consist of raw beef and pork.

All hands are now employed in repairing the ship and stopping the breaches in their clothes to stem the chilling blasts of Cape Horn. Trousers that in moderate climes had been condemmed are brought forth. Many who have not the same quality for patches, stop the break with canvas. Shirts that would have disgraced Falstaff's soldiers, that have been kicking under foot mats, are washed and receive first place in our chests.

Ships sailing from warm to cold climates generally carry thermometers to give notice of the approach of ice, land and the variation of the atmosphere, but this article can be disposed of in a whale ship, for the actions of the crew give timely notice of the same.[18]

Those islands of majesty and beauty, named by the Spanish discoverers as the Marquesas, were important provisioning places for the whalemen. Of especial value was Nuku Hiva, that magic island which lured Herman Melville and his friend Toby from the whaleship *Achusnet* in September 1842 to live among the savages. Since the ill-advised actions of Commodore Porter, in the U. S. frigate *Essex*, here in 1814, the natives had often fiercely resisted the efforts at trade by the white men, and there were instances of boats being cut off and their crews massacred.

No one described it as Melville did in *Typee,* but C. S. Stewart, in his cruise on the *Vincennes* in July 1831, gives a fine picture of its enticing beauty.[19]

"The highest peaks of Nukahiva were judged to be between two and three thousand feet above the level of the ocean," he wrote. "Its eastern end is perfectly iron-bound, presenting an uninterrupted succession of bare precipices . . . the headland forming the southeast point . . . a bold lofty promentory, surmounted by a gigantic rock; having a striking resemblance to the ruinous watch tower of some delapidated castle. . . ."[20]

And as for the famous bay:

> Return to yourself a smooth basin eight or nine miles in circumference, stretching in a circular form from the narrow passage between the sentinels, about three miles inland, and terminating at that distance in a curving beach of sand, three-fourths of a mile or more in length. This beach is the front of a valley of the same width, which rises gradually for a couple of miles, and then branching into three or four others more narrow and steep, suddenly terminates on every side in the abrupt acclinties and precipices of a range of lofty mountains which enclose the whole, and descends on either side of the sentinels at the entrance, in bold promontories of rock, thinly covered with green sward.

Three years before Stewart described his landfall here, Captain David Edwards sailed the *Harvest,* of Nantucket, into this bay. Third Officer George W. Gardner told of the incident:

> . . . Luffed to off the Bay at the south part of Nakaheva, saw a large canoe coming off with 25 natives in it backed the main yard and loaded our gun and muskets and got our spades ready as we did not know whether they would be friendly or not. We suffered the canoe to come close to the ship, and 12 of the natives swam on board and appeared very friendly and the canoe went ashore again. We engaged 3 of the natives to go with us on the voyage and lowered a boat and set the others ashore again. Returned on board and stood to the westward under all sails. Latter part no land in sight.[21]

In October 1836, a boat from the *Barclay,* of Nantucket, under Captain Barney, landed at Nuku Hiva, where the natives suddenly attacked

and took the boat. While the crew escaped by swimming, Captain
Barney was held prisoner. Later, he was ransomed by a large quantity
of trade goods to the value of $500.[22]

A similar experience awaited the *Catherine,* of Nantucket, in 1839.
While trading on the opposite side of Nuku Hiva from Resolution
Bay, Captain John Brown was captured by a sudden rush of a large
group of natives. After being held for a day an interpreter announced
he would be released at a price.

Ransom demanded consisted of forty muskets and six kegs of
powder. Captain Brown did not have such a quantity of warfaring
equipment, and was kept prisoner. One of the captured whalemen, a
Spanish boy, freed himself of his bonds, released Captain Brown and
his companions, and all made their escape to the friendly Typees,
eventually regaining the ship. As the *Catherine*'s second officer was
suspected of implication in the natives' sudden attack, he was discharged, and promptly went ashore to join the natives. Captain
Brown's escape was ironic—a few months later he met death while
taking a bull sperm whale. It was safer with the savages.

Of the experiences of the ship *Bengal,* of Salem, under Captain
George Russell, an alert seaman named Ira Poland has left one of the
most informative logs of the early 1830 voyages. The *Bengal* sailed
March 24, 1832. Just a year later she was coming into the famous
Comptroller's Bay, at Nuku Hiva Island. Foremast-hand Ira Poland
wrote:

> . . . Got the guns in order and put 3 lances in each top and made
> all preparation to meet these canibals. . . . 4 P.M. beat up abreast of
> Mr. Stewart's castle and saw several smokes on shore, and the beauti-
> ful streams of fresh water running down [out] of the mountains and
> even breached to falling down where presspiceses [are] 400 to 500
> feet perpendicular . . . the highest mountain from 800 to 1000 feet in
> height and run up to a sharp point above the clouds. Beat up op-
> posite of the port and sailed back through the night and in the morn-
> ing, with smart squalls of wind and rain, and at 9 A.M. came to an-
> chor in 6 fathoms of water. About 200 of the Natives came on board
> of both male and female and a grate many of them entirely naked
> as they were born and . . . could you but see these savages it would
> make your eyes twitch—I think them the most beautiful lined people
> I ever saw . . . We found the *Catherine,* Capt. Chace; *Alliance,* Capt.

Holton; *Cadmus,* Capt. Taber, lying here and there was a British ship lay off and on. Sent a boat in for news.[23]

There is a certain vitality in Poland's description which makes one regret he did not write more. But what he did record, like the above, is enough to make the picture come to life—especially in the islands which were like earthly bits of Paradise to sea-weary whalemen. Three hands deserted, and three natives were shipped to take their places.

Trading was brisk. A musket and a few pounds of powder were exchanged for twenty-one hogs. The king of the "Haipies," and a young chief were on board the ship to dine with the whaling masters. Here was a scene—the cabin table presided over by Captain Russell, with the Marquesan king on his right and the chief of the Haipies on his left, and the fellow-whaling captains all gathered about. A roast pig on the board, with bananas, plantains, oysters, mince pie and tea. And West Indies rum and Spanish cigars afterwards.[24]

From the Marquesas, the *Bengal* sailed on a cruise among the islands, thence to the Sandwich Islands. At Honolulu, seaman Poland had the following pithy comment:

> We understand from Mr. Richards and Mr. Spaulding [that] the Board of Missionaries is to make arrangements for sending three missionaries to the Isle of Nukahiva, but I think they will find it much different times there.[25]

When the *Bengal* returned to Nuku Hiva (after a cruise to the Japan Grounds), Poland had the opportunity to see how his predication had fared. He wrote:

> We understand by the white man here that the Missionaries were very pleased with the place and that the Natives used them well, until they had been here some months, when the English ship *Royal Sovereign* came in and they had a native of this place who had been to England and to the Sandwich Islands, and he came on shore and told the natives that if they let the Missionaries stop there, the bread fruit and coconut trees would all die, and they would have nothing to eat and the Chiefs gave orders to drive them from the Isle.[26]

This was without question an example of native fifth column action, artfully planned and executed. Poland's companion report is equally revealing: ". . . suffered the females to remain on board, they being the best possible remedy for the scurvey."

The *Bengal's* voyage was not as successful as some of her contemporaries. Reason for this is best given in Poland's record:

> . . . In the morning at 5 o'clock found the ship surrounded by sperm whales as far as the eye could reach. Lower'd all 3 boats and the waist boat struck and draw'd and the starboard boat struck and the iron brook and the boats returned on board at 7 A.M. Made sail and pursued on after them with the ship and at 10 A.M. dropped the boats and the waist boat struck her whale and . . . we had a fare chance to take 200 bbls. out of them but things went as they have the whole time. The mate had a good opportunity to strike a 90-bbl. whale but peaked his oars and looked at him, so we had to put up with 18 bbls. —no whalemen no whales this voyage.[27]

It was this same mate who aroused the ire of Poland and his shipmates. The journal gives us a good account of him:

> . . . the thing that shipped as mate flogged the man (that the Captain so hastily took from Mowee) about the decks with a peace of the tackle and threatened to kill him . . . that was unlawful on board of whaleships . . . and he ses "Will you kill me," and the answer, was "yes, I will kill you, dam Son of a Bitch," that if he continues to go in this manner we shall be compelled to give him a New England hug.[28]

Shortly after midnight on the last day of the year 1835, the watch on board the whaleship *William Hamilton,* of New Bedford, Captain William Swain, commander, saw a bright light off the larboard bow. At first, it was believed to be a whaler boiling out her oil, and at daybreak the *Hamilton* steered for it. On coming nearer it was discovered to be a ship low in the water—a mere hulk. The log reads:

> . . . and found it to be the ship *Lydia,* burned to the water's edge. At 4 P.M. came up to the ship. We obtained a number of whale irons, lances, old iron, copper, iron bolts, nails, etc., at 7 A.M. the *Christopher Mitchell* came up. At 6 made fast the chain cables with the cutting falls, at 9 the wreck went down, commenced heaving up the chains; the falls surging around the windlass, we lost the whole; one man by the name of Hall got foul in the falls and went over the bow and took his foot off at the ankle. So ends these 24 hours.[29]

The *Lydia,* of Nantucket, Captain Edward Joy, master, was burned in latitude 11°-15 south, longitude 84°-80' west. By the time the blaze was discovered, the flames had gained such headway that all attempts to fight them were unavailing. An hour and a half later, the crew were forced to get into their boats, saving only a few things. A few hours later they were sighted by the *Washington,* of Hudson, also a whaler, and taken aboard by Captain William Clark, another Nantucket man.[30]

As for what probably happened to the unfortunate man named Hall, who lost his foot at the ankle, a similar accident which befell Third Mate King of the whaler *Norman,* of Nantucket, might point up a surgical parallel. The latter had his right foot mangled when it became entangled in a line fast to a whale. Taken on board, he was stretched out on the cabin table, where Captain Charles Ray cut off the bone just above the ankle and sewed the flap of skin over the end of the bone. Captain Ray then returned to the chase and although the waist boat was stove, finally killed the whale.[31]

Amputations were not common—no more so than on land—but the master of the ship had to be prepared to perform them, and to acquire the knowledge through experience.

There are logbook entries which in only a few words, reflect the mood of the times aboard ship. In 1834, the *Nassau's* log read: ". . . saw plenty of blackfish, porpoises, finbacks, and birds, and everything but women and sperm whales." [32] Captain Samson also noted on the homeward-bound voyage. "Mr. Brownell [the mate] this evening told me that if [he had] had his way he would have 3500 bbls. on board the ship . . . and if I was mad in my life it was at that moment." [33]

In the log of the *Pacific,* of New Bedford, Captain William Reynard, is written under the date of July 4:

> . . . Raised right whale at 8 A.M., lowered two boats . . . but it was no use he sunk at 11 A.M. Hard luck for the 4th. I expect they are all having a good time at home while we poor fellows are pulling to windward just like any other greeser. A hard old 4th of July, long faces and sour looks, while they at home are smiling at their strawberries and cream. So ends our National Day of Independence.[34]

Captain John O. Morse in the *Hector,* of New Bedford (October 1832), commanded a crew of twenty-seven men, the oldest being thirty-two years, only five men over twenty-five years of age, and twelve men of nineteen years. This was practically an all-Martha's Vineyard crew, and two of the officers, Thomas Norton and George Luce, later became famous whalemen.[35]

Some years after, the mate, Thomas Norton, then a shipmaster, told of the attack made by a bull sperm whale on one of the *Hector's* boats. In describing the incident, he stated that the whale himself took the initiative while the boats were approaching him. Mate Norton's boat was first "on," but the moment the harpoon struck the bull sperm, with one flick of his flukes, stove in her bow. By drawing the boat's sail under the bow, the boat was kept free of water and Mate Norton resumed the attack.[36]

In the meantime, Captain Morse came up in his boat and was warned off by Mate Norton. But the ship's master had a long lance which he thought would do the trick and proceeded to the attack. But the sperm was an extraordinary antagonist. Slipping over on his back, he caught the Captain's boat in his mouth and literally shook it to pieces.

Mate Norton's and Second Officer Luce's boats picked up Captain Morse and his men. Norton was anxious to return to the attack. With a picked crew in the remaining undamaged boat, he approached the fighting whale.

Then followed a battle royal: the frail boat carefully advancing, then retreating at "starn all for your lives!" the infuriated whale surging forward, diving to attack from under the surface of the sea, flashing his terrible jaw at the nimbly-handled boat, beating the sea with tremendous blows of his deadly flukes. In a radius of half a mile, the fight continued—until, quickly seizing the opening he had been awaiting, Mate Norton had his boat "wood to blackskin" and with swift probings of his lance, brought a sudden end to the battle. Here was a triumph of skilled whalemen.

The whale made sixty barrels of oil. In cutting him in, two harpoons were found which came from the *Barclay,* of Nantucket, which two months before had attempted to capture him—the mate of that vessel being killed when his "whaleship" smashed the boat.

chapter xxxi

THE SEA-HUNTERS COME INTO
THEIR OWN

*Too much credit cannot be given to our whalers, sealers,
and traffickers in those seas for the information they have
acquired. . . . But, after all their exertions, justice to ourselves as a great people requires that this mass of information should be reviewed . . . and preserved in careful
literary labors for the benefit of all mankind.*

—J. N. Reynolds [1]

B Y THE YEAR 1825 other New England ports were becoming
active in whaling, each sending out several ships. Demand for
oil and bone had increased through the rising prosperity of the country in general. The families of Charleston, New Orleans, Philadelphia,
Baltimore, New York, and Boston were demanding spermaceti candles
as good as those previously marketed in the great cities of Europe.
Whalebone found a ready market for stays, corsets, umbrella ribs, etc.
The establishment of lighthouses along the coast brought another demand for oil. While most of the ships of the smaller ports did Atlantic
whaling from a very early period—Provincetown had several small
schooners sailing to the Azores—a number of whaleships from New
London and other ports followed the Nantucket and New Bedford
craft into the far Pacific. As early as 1802, the new Nantucket bank
was called the "Pacific Bank."

According to a report in *Niles Register* for December 1820, Nantucket at this period had seventy-two whaleships, totaling 20,336 tons. It continued:

> When we consider the numerous other vessels engaged in the coasting trade of the Island, the small number of inhabitants it contains, and the Island itself but a speck on the bordering waters of our Republic; and moreover, that almost the whole of the shipping was captured or destroyed so recently as the last war, we are struck with admiration at the invincible hardihood and enterprise of this little active, industrious and friendly community. . . .

New Bedford, coming to the fore, at this time (1818-1820) had thirty-six whalers, with Sag Harbor the next largest port with seven. New York City, with Jacob Barker and Thomas Hazard leading the way, sent out six whalers, under Nantucket masters and officers. Westport, Massachusetts, with four ships, New London, Connecticut, with three, and Boston and Edgartown, Massachusetts, with two, were other ports represented in New England whaling during this period.

The peak of Nantucket's whaling in the nineteenth century was now approaching. Oddly enough it followed closely on a serious financial depression. Early in the year 1824, the situation had become grave. The Nantucket *Inquirer* reported the fact later, thus:

> . . . little more than a year has elapsed since the oil trade was in a state of unexampled depression. Very many of those hitherto employed in the whale fishery, discouraged by the hopeless project before them, were upon the point of relinquishing their occupation altogether. Had such an event occurred, it would have been a death blow to the interests of the large community, each member of which, is, immediately or remotely, dependent upon the success of this pursuit. Poverty and ruin were inevitable to thousands of individuals, while the nation would have suffered, not only from the measureable extinction of one great source of productive industry, but from the loss of a confessedly valuable seminary for seamen and navigators.[2]

With a sureness based on experience and judgment, a number of shipowners promptly acted to restore the confidence of the people in their industry. By way of encouragement to the adventurers, they offered to guarantee a price for sperm oil far exceeding the then-current price. This action had the quick effect of balancing the fluctuating scale of fortune. Due to the obvious fact that dividends on voyages came at the completion of the ships' whaling, and that no more than two or three ships ever returned together, the oil merchants were able successfully to pursue their plan. As the market was due to pick up after its depression, acting in logical sequence with the law of supply and demand, the Nantucket and New Bedford markets were able to take prompt advantage of increased demands. The *Inquirer* reported in January 1826:

> Immense cargoes of oil have been brought in during the past year, fully realizing the reasonable calculation and hopes of those through whose means the [whale-fishery] trade was revived.[3]

The years 1825-26 saw the port of New Bedford surging to a position where, for the first time, she was on equal terms with Nantucket, the century-old leader in whaling. During the period 1825-1828, the two ports jockeyed for the leading position. On December 31, 1828, the American whale fishery's status was as follows:

For the Pacific Ocean

Sailed from	Year	Now at Sea	Ships	T'tl for Year
Nantucket	1825	" " "	1	
New Bedford	1825	" " "	1	2
Nantucket	1826	" " "	14	
New Bedford	1826	" " "	8	
Plymouth	1826	" " "	1	23
Nantucket	1827	" " "	13	
New Bedford	1827	" " "	14—1 Brig	
New London	1827	" " "	6	
Edgartown	1827	" " "	2	
Falmouth	1827	" " "	1	
Plymouth	1827	" " "	1	
Sag Harbor	1827	" " "	1	
New York	1827	" " "	1	
Newport	1827	" " "	1	
Bristol	1827	" " "	1	41
Nantucket	1828	" " "	20	
New Bedford	1828	" " "	27—2 Brigs	
New London	1828	" " "	2	
Edgartown	1828	" " "	1	
Falmouth	1828	" " "	1	
Bristol	1828	" " "	1	52

TOTAL OUT AT SEA—December 31, 1828—118 ships—3 brigs

For the Brazil Banks

Sailed from	Year	Now at Sea	Ships	T'tl for Year
New Bedford	1827	" " "	2	
Nantucket	1827	" " "	1	3
New Bedford	1828	" " "	22	
Nantucket	1828	" " "	9	31

TOTAL OUT AT SEA—34 ships

For the Atlantic Ocean

Sailed from	Year	Now at Sea	Brigs	T'tl for Year
Nantucket	1827	" " "	1	
New Bedford	1827	" " "	12	
New Bedford	1827	" " "	2 schooners	

TOTAL OUT AT SEA—13 brigs—2 schooners

In Port, December 31, 1828

Nantucket	2 ships
New Bedford	2 ships, 1 brig

Recapitulation

For the Pacific Ocean	" " "	118 ships, 3 brigs
For the Brazil Banks	" " "	34 ships
For the Atlantic Ocean	" " "	13 brigs, 2 schooners
In port, Dec. 31, 1828		4 ships, 1 brig

TOTAL—175 vessels [4]

At this time, December 1828, Nantucket still maintained its proud position as the leader in the importation of whale oil. In the year 1827, New Bedford had a total catch of 38,752 barrels of sperm with Nantucket having 33,063 barrels and all other ports combined 21,248. But in 1828, Nantucket imported 41,073 barrels with New Bedford totalling 25,293 barrels and all other ports, 6,711—a total of 73,077 barrels. This 1828 total was nearly 20,000 barrels less than the previous year. The total imports of 1829 showed little or no increase, but by 1830 the pendulum began to swing toward the peak of the whaling industry.

The position of Nantucket with the dawn of the 1830's, was one which was a tribute to the personal courage of her whalers and the faith of her merchants. During the fourteen years since the end of the War of 1812, Nantucket had lost twenty-five ships through disasters, had sold sixteen to other ports, and broken up eleven which had become old and unseaworthy. This total of fifty-two ships, plus the thirty-eight lost during the 1812 war, brought a total of ninety whaling vessels which Nantucket had lost from her fleet—only sixteen of which had given any return through sale. As for insurance, the amounts were only a fraction of the vessels' worth, especially if they were loaded with oil.

An editorial in the Nantucket *Inquirer* for February 21, 1828, complained that the low price of oil, with the loss of twenty-five ships in thirteen years, had a serious and "paralyzing effect on the community." It expressed the hope that the industry would regulate itself, like many other branches of commerce.

Recovery was strong. In 1828, Nantucket had a fleet of sixty vessels, and in that year thirty-one whalers cleared from the harbor. Although the new ship *Richard Mitchell* was lost at the Western Islands on her outward voyage, and the veteran *Maro* was so badly damaged by a collision at sea that she had to be condemned at Rio, the rest of the fleet all did well. New Bedford in 1828, sent out forty-nine vessels, with twenty-four of these going to the Pacific and the majority of these making excellent voyages.

A new port now made its appearance—Fairhaven, across the river from New Bedford. In 1820, this port had dispatched two whaleships, in 1828 she dispatched eight ships, one of which went out to the Pacific.[5]

Fairhaven was an older settlement than New Bedford. In 1760 one William Wood had set up tryworks and oil sheds near his Acushnet landing place on land purchased from Captain Taber. It was Captain Nathaniel Pope who, in May 1775, recaptured two sloops from the British off the mouth of the Acushnet in an action called the first naval engagement of the Revolution. With the advent of the 1800's and the rebirth of whaling out of New Bedford, the citizens of Fairhaven invested in several vessels. Captains Robert and Thomas Bennett were active members of a family which became identified with Pacific whaling.

Union wharf was built in 1802. Prior to the war of 1812, Fairhaven had only a few large whalers but with the advent of the 1820's her investors built some noble craft. In 1830, eleven ships sailed from Fairhaven; in 1849, the port had fifty ships. Her captains were notable men in their time, among them Captain Thomas Bennett, in the Russian trade; Captain Job Terry, whom Dana described in his *Two Years Before the Mast;* Captain William Washburn, who went hunting with Eskimos; Captain Alexander Winsor, a master of the clipper, *Flying Cloud;* Captain Charles Bryant, who lent helpful advice as to Alaska when Senator Summer was investigating the possibility of purchasing that country; Warren Delano, manager of Russell & Co., of Shanghai, and many others.

New London, after several attempts, finally got into the whale fishery in 1819, when Thomas W. Williams and others sent three vessels to sea. In 1827 the fleet consisted of seven vessels. The industry was continuously prosecuted, so that ten years later in 1837, a total of thirty-six vessels, aggregating 13,500 tons, represented the port. The New London vessel the *Corinthian,* was the first to Heard Island, south of Desolation, landing there in search of sea-elephant oil. Among the first into the Arctic were New London whalers.[6]

Sag Harbor antedated New London as a whaling port. This little community on the eastern end of Long Island, took over the deep-sea industry in this area.[7] In 1834, her fleet totaled fifteen ships. By 1837, twenty-four whalers sailed out of Sag Harbor. A neighboring port—Cold Spring Harbor—began its deep-sea whaling in 1835.

Perusal of accounts and related documents during the early years of the nineteenth century, furnish convincing proof of the Nantucketers' awareness of the importance of the whale fishery not only to themselves but to the nation. Foremost as an advocate of this premise was the able editor of the Nantucket *Inquirer,* Samuel Haynes Jenks. Writing in his paper (November 1822) he stated:

> The practicability of a canal across the isthumus of Darien is daily gaining strength. . . . To no portion of North America could the establishment of an intercurrence through this narrow track be of greater importance than to the inhabitants of Nantucket. The reduction of thousands of miles from the length of a voyage to the South

Seas, merely by excavating a channel of perhaps only 20 miles is a matter of the utmost moment to those concerned in the whale fishery as a saving of at least one-half the time and expense of a voyage, and a total escape from the dangers which attend the doubling of Cape Horn. . . . In fine, this subject is one which ought to affect the whole commercial world.[8]

Surprisingly enough, the editor of the *New Bedford Mercury* disagreed with the Nantucket writer, stating such a canal would result in a great increase in whaleships and "there would soon be no whales in the Pacific."

Having pursued the whale fishery for well over a century without governmental aid, the Nantucket tradition continued to be exercised in its "Kingdom in the Sea." But the dreadful mutiny on the *Globe,* the disaster of the *Essex,* the wrecks of the *Oeno* and *Mentor* and massacre of their crews, and the dangers from the flaring fires of revolution along the South American coast, induced the first requests by the whaling industry for protection. And they sought this protection from the only tangible bit of government then in evidence in the Pacific—the few frigates of the U. S. Navy.

The ever-present dangers from uncharted reefs and islands in the South Seas brought the first petitions by the merchants of Nantucket and New Bedford for an exploring expedition by the government. Editor Jenks of the *Inquirer,* who compiled a list of all discoveries made by the whaleship masters, urged that a report be prepared for such a purpose, so that the Congress could be made aware of the direct contributions made by such discoverers toward the national glory.

But such hopes were not realized. Early in 1828, through an editorial, Editor Jenks commented:

> As the memorials of the citizens of this town and New Bedford, praying that the aid of government be extended, and that appropriation be made to explore the Pacific and South Seas, had no particular reference to sectional interests, but embraced advantages of national character—it might be reasonably expected that a small vessel, if no more, would not have been refused. A glance at the proceedings of Congress in another column, will show that those expectations are not likely to be realized immediately, if ever. Whether the sins of commission or omission, by which the last session of Congress is distinguished, could preponderate, is a question of difficult solution.[9]

From the year 1816 to 1828, the total amount of sperm oil imported into the United States by the New England whalemen was 646,636 barrels, each barrel containing 31½ gallons. This gave an income of $14,258,323.80—averaging the oil at 70 cents per gallon—representing an import of over one million dollars in oil per year over that dozen years' stretch.[10]

Obed Macy was sparing of words but full of fact when he wrote:

> It must be obvious that our whaleships exploring in a more effective manner than twenty national ships would, every part of the vast Pacific. They have discovered many islands, reefs, and shoals, which navigators, sent out expressly for exploring purposes, had passed unseen.[11]

A writer in the *Boston Evening Bulletin* had the same conviction, when he wrote in March 1828: ". . . Our whalemen in the Pacific outstrip competition. . . . Their fame extends to every island from America to Japan and from New Zealand to the coast of Asia. . . . I am told that upwards of one hundred American whaleships are cruising west of Cape Horn." He was conservative—the number was 118.

No petition sent to Congress could be more eloquent than that despatched from Nantucket in February 1828. It reads as follows:

> The subscribers, citizens of Nantucket in Massachusetts, respectfully represent the intercourse maintained between this place and different parts of the world, especially the islands and countries of the Pacific Ocean, has become a matter deserving of the protecting care of national legislation.
> Besides the employment of energy and enterprise by our seamen and merchants, they would represent that they have sixty whaleships, representing 20,000 tons of shipping, requiring $1,000,000 to maintain with attendant industries, and some two thousand seamen. Whether viewed as a valuable nursery for bold and hardy seamen or as employment of capital, or furnishing an article of indispensable necessity to human comfort (whale oil), it seems to your petitioners to be deserving of public care.
> Increased extent of voyages now pursued by whaling and trading vessels, in seas but little explored, has increased continual dangers and losses to our mariners and merchants. Within a few years their cruisings have extended from Peru and Chile to the northwest coast of this continent and to New Zealand and the islands of Japan. Several

vessels have been wrecked on islands and reefs not laid down on any charts; many ships have gone into these seas and no soul returned to tell their fate.

Your petitioners consider it a matter of earnest importance that those seas be explored, and that they should be surveyed in an accurate and authentic manner, with the positions of new islands recently discovered and shoals definitely ascertained.

The advancement of science, and not private interests, but the general interests of the nation, seem to imperiously demand it. They therefore, pray that an expedition be fitted out under the sanction of the government to explore and survey the islands and coasts of the Pacific seas.[12]

New Bedford sent a similar memorial in the month following, "praying that a Naval Expedition be undertaking for the purpose of exploring such portions of the North and South Pacific oceans as present the greatest exposure to these hazards and are most generally resorted to by whalemen."

In an address before Congress about this same time, Honorable John Reed, in whose district Nantucket and New Bedford were included, stated rightfully:

If the great Burke, looked across the Atlantic with astonishment and admiration upon the inhabitants of the little island of Nantucket, . . . surely I, as a representative of the same people, ought to feel my pride rise and my energy, however feeble, called into exercise in support of their right. Nantucket still remains a proud monument of the same perserverance, activity, dexterity, sagacity, and enterprise. They not only pursue their gigantic game, the whale, as in the time Burke spoke, but have since doubled Cape Horn, and traversed the Pacific six thousand miles, north to California, and westerly across the mighty ocean to Asia, on the coast of Japan and New Holland. What peculiar attention have they received? What favours? I am aware that they have participated in the common blessings of our common country, which I do not consider few or small; but, extraordinary and exclusive favours, they have never received.[13]

The speech of Congressman Reed made a definite impression. He held up a chart, on which was traced the extent of the voyages of the whaleships; he also held a copy of the Nantucket newspaper in which was printed (March 7, 1825) a list of islands and reefs discovered by the whalemen in the Pacific. Reminding his listeners that the whalers had not the time nor means to devote to full-scale charting and exploring, he offered a resolution calling for the employment of a government vessel for such a purpose. The resolution was adopted on May 21, 1828.

Then into the picture at this crisis stepped the extraordinary figure of Jeremiah N. Reynolds. A native of New Wilmington, Ohio, he had become imbued with the idea of an exploring expedition by United States vessels, at first advocating the sailing of such a fleet into the Antarctic regions.

Unfortunately, Reynolds became associated for a brief period with one Captain John Symnes, an idealist and theorist. Symnes was lecturing on the theory of concentric spheres and the existence of tunnels at the poles which led into the center of the earth. Such a far-fetched exposition of natural phenomena, under the guise of science, was hardly expected to meet with the approval of most people. Reynolds soon abandoned his connection with the Symnes theory, but his early advocacy was not forgotten by his opponents, and proved later a telling drawback to his plans.[14]

But Reynolds has a definite claim to fame. His persistent exertions in the interest of an exploring expedition finally crystallized the government's procrastinating policy, forcing it into action. His friendship with Edgar Allen Poe influenced that remarkable man in the writing of "Manuscript Found In A Bottle" and the "Narrative of Arthur Gordon Pymn." Among the literary efforts of Reynolds was a short story appearing in the *Knickerbocker Magazine,* in May 1839, entitled "Mocha Dick, or The White Whale of the Pacific." The legend of the white whale was not unknown to whalemen and Reynold's story certainly was not unknown to the author of *Moby Dick.* Reynolds also came close to being associated with Nathaniel Hawthorne, who was recommended as the "historiographer," of the expedition.

Because of his continual efforts on behalf of the exploring expedition, in June 1828, Reynolds was appointed a special envoy by the Navy Department and authorized to gather data and pertinent information of the South Seas from shipmasters and owners. In his report—first submitted September 24, 1828, and reconsidered in January 1835—he states that he repaired "without delay to New London, Stonington, Newport, New Bedford, Edgartown, Nantucket and other places, where information might be found of the Pacific Ocean and South Seas. The whaling captains were ready to communicate such knowledge as they had treasured up or recorded in their numerous voyages. The owners of whaleships were equally anxious to do all in their power to assist me in the object of my visit to them." [15]

Reynolds writes particularly about his visit to Nantucket, where he interviewed "every individual navigator of those seas who could be found at home, with their log-books, and journals and charts. . . . It was pleasant for me to find that all I had heard before was confirmed by a long train of witnesses, and every calculation I had previously made fell far short of the truth."

Due to the scope of his report, Reynolds could not devote space to details, but it would be most valuable today if he had noted the names of all the mariners and interested citizens of Nantucket whom he interviewed. Of those islanders known to have talked with him are Captains George Rule, Jonathan Swain, Richard Macy, Reuben Joy, Jr., Reuben Clasby and George B. Worth. In New Bedford, he saw the inimitable Captain Edmund Gardner as well as Captain Edward Clark and Bennett, and at Newport he met Captain James C. Swain.

But he found a kindred spirit and valuable friend in Samuel Haynes Jenks, the editor of the Nantucket *Inquirer;* a man who had been collecting data on South Sea island discoveries and other whaling material for a number of years. Just how important an individual Jenks was to Reynolds may be easily ascertained by following the course of his editorials from 1821 to 1829. It must be observed that Jenks' compilation of Pacific Island discoveries which first appeared in March 1825, forms the basis for the detailed statement which appears in the Reynolds report for 1828. This important fact has been too long overlooked by historians.

The following letter gives clear evidence of Reynolds' reaction to his Nantucket visit:

To MESSRS. MACY, TUCK, MITCHELL, GARDNER and WEST:
GENTLEMEN:

Be pleased to accept my sincere thanks to your prompt and assiduous attention to my request for information in your possession, relating to the Pacific Ocean and the regions in the pathway of your whaling business; and oblige me by extending these acknowledgements

to all those who have assisted in the cause, for to all I feel deeply
indebted. I expected to find intelligent men among you, but I did
not know, I readily confess, that there was so much information upon
the subject of my inquiries, to be found anywhere, as I have obtained
in this place and in New Bedford. . . .

Distant countries have admired and honoured the daring efforts of
the inhabitants of Nantucket, and have not been backward in propa-
gating these honest impressions; but they could not have known how
much information you had gathered up in these constant and increasing pursuits. What you had done for the general stock of knowledge
was not ever known to your own countrymen; but the time has come
when its amount and value will be duly appreciated. In the expedition that Government are now about fitting out, the explorers will
often have to acknowledge in connexion with the protection of a Kind
Providence, the obligations they are under to you, for pointing out
to them the places of danger, and of comfort, and of subjects of inquiry for the voyage. Your pursuits have acquired a dignity and
praise in addition to their adventurous character. . . .

Most respectfully your obedient servant,
J. N. Reynolds

Nantucket—Aug. 19th, 1828 [16]

One of the most significant paragraphs in the Reynolds Report
speaks the theme of the arguments for the exploring expedition. It is
as follows:

The whole number of vessels in the whale-fishery, with those engaged in the sealing business, far exceeded the number I had given
in my communication to the Naval Committee, and their tonnage is
much greater. There are at least 200 ships employed, being on an
average of 275 tons, some a large as 500 and others under 200 tons.
The average length of their voyages, taking one hundred and seventy-
eight voyages, from 1815 to 1824, was twenty-nine months, and the
average cargo of oil from the same ships was exceeding 1700 barrels.
But it should be observed that the ships are now generally larger
than formerly, the length of their voyages is naturally increasing from
the fact that our whalemen are traversing new seas for the whale.[17]

In October 1828, information reached the newspapers that the Navy
Department was definitely preparing to launch the long-overdue ex-
pedition. The *New York Mercantile Advertiser* reported that: "Lieut.
Alexander B. Pinkham, U.S.N., will be appointed to the command.
Lieut. Pinkham is well known to many of our nautical men as a first

rate seaman and navigator, active and enterprising, possessing strong, robust, constitution, with all the characteristics peculiar to the place of his nativity—Nantucket." [18] The expected plans did not develop, and the expedition lost a valuable leader.

Congress was still delaying the course of events. Under date of February 5 and 6, 1829, President John Quincy Adams requested Secretary of the Navy Samuel Southard to make a detailed report to the Senate upon what plans had been made for the expedition. Southard's reply was favorably worded. But political shoals loomed. President Andrew Jackson was elected and vetoed the project by reason of economy. Before the Jacksonian veto, however, Reynolds had been so far authorized to proceed with plans that he arranged, through Captain Edmund Fanning, for the charters of two brigs.

Thus, the first government-sponsored exploring expedition actually got under way. With Reynolds on board as one of two "scientific" men, the expedition left New York in October 1829. It consisted of the brig *Seraph,* under Captain Benjamin Pendleton, an experienced sealer, and the brig *Annawan* under Captain Nathaniel Brown Palmer. Early in January 1830, they arrived at Staten Land. Sailing into Antarctic seas, for the purpose of making exploratory cruises south of Cape Horn, the expedition was singularly unsuccessful.

In a report, Captain Palmer stated the crews became mutinous due to the ill-success of not making any discoveries and taking few seal. Upon reaching the coast of Chile, the conduct of the crews made it impossible to continue the object of the voyage, and the brigs returned home with just enough hands to navigate them.[19]

Captain Pendleton, also an experienced sealer, commanding the expedition, wrote:

> . . . I am now convinced from experience in this enterprise that an exploring expedition, under private means, never can produce any great or important national benefits, the same must be under authority from the government, and the officers and men under regular pay and discipline, as in the Navy.

The two men of the "scientific corps," A. J. Watson and J. N. Reynolds, were praised "for perserverance and interest they have manifested through out this voyage." Reynolds and Watson were landed at

Arauco, Chile, in July 1830 and explored the country. Watson apparently returned with the expedition, while Reynolds remained at Valparaiso. He was still there when the frigate *Potomac* under Commodore John Downes, arrived in 1832. Reynolds was engaged by Downes as his private secretary, and decided to write the story of that frigate's circumnavigation, especially the landing and attack on the pirate village of Quallah-Battoo, Sumatra. On board the *Potomac* was Lieutenant Reuben Pinkham, of Nantucket, whose journal of the voyage, according to Reynolds, was "placed in my hands," and according to Frederick Sanford was the real basis for the book, *The Voyage of the U. S. Frigate Potomac Around the World.*[20]

While in Chile, Reynolds met many whalemen. Their descriptions of uncharted reaches of the South Seas gave him further inspiration for his renewed campaign for a national exploring expedition. The enthusiasm of the man may be found in his own Report to Congress (1828), reissued in 1835 through Secretary Dickerson, of the Navy.

The failure of the *Seraph-Annawan* Expedition had not been unexpected, and it served as a dash of cold water to proponents. As a result of this experience, Reynolds abandoned his schemes for urging further exploration in the Antarctic and centralized all his energy into the project of an exploring expedition to the Pacific.

Returning home on the *Potomac* with Commodore Downs in 1833, Reynolds busied himself with completing the narrative of the voyage of the frigate. As he had access to official files for this work, he soon met the new Secretary of the Navy Mahlon Dickerson. The two men could not agree, and they took their argument to the public, both using the medium of the *New York Times* and *New York Courier and Inquirer* to present their opinions.[21] Reynolds had originally urged the scientific approach of such an expedition. As he was now advocating it strictly from the view point of "national glory," Dickerson took apparent delight in pointing this and other facts out as examples of inconsistency.

The inevitable result was the "dropping," of Reynolds as a possible "historiographer" for the expedition, and the appointment of Joel R. Poinsett as the official responsible for the conduct of the expedition. The resourcefulness of Poinsett had already been proven by reference to his part in the Chilean Revolution, two decades before. Associated with Poinsett was James Kirke Paulding, who succeeded Dickerson as Secretary of the Navy. Both men were interested in the scientific and other cultural aspects of an exploring expedition rather than commercial prestige.

Reynolds' fading from the picture was not without protest by himself and his friends, among whom was Edgar Allen Poe, who declared that Reynolds had been "shamefully treated." As a matter of fact, if Reynolds had been permitted to go along with the Wilkes Expedition its success might have been much fuller. With all his shortcomings, the man had imagination and fire and his writings would have added immeasurably to the many stilted passages of the resultant volumes. It should be noted that much of Wilkes' observations on the Fiji and Gilbert groups were contributed by ex-whalemen turned beachcombers or "natives," and Reynolds had a background of knowledge of Pacific Islands supplied him by experienced and intelligent whaling masters.

When the first national exploring expedition finally got under way on August 19, 1838, it was some fifteen years late. Under Lieutenant Charles Wilkes, the expedition which performed its historic voyages, from that date until 1841, certainly added much to the scientific and geographical knowledge of the Pacific. Its outstanding accomplishment was the discovery of that part of the Antarctic Continent's mountainous shore line which immortalized the leader and his men.

It is peculiarly significant that Wilkes devotes many pages of his *Narrative* to the importance of the whaling industry.

> The whaling interest, taking into consideration the extent to which it has been carried by our countrymen, may be almost claimed as peculiarly American. . . .
> Our whaling fleet may be said at this very day to whiten the Pacific Ocean with its canvass, and the proceeds of this fishery give comfort and happiness to many thousands of our citizens. . . .[22]
> As it was among the first objects of the Exploring Expedition to render the dangerous path of these enterprising mariners more safe, I trust it will have been perceived that throughout the operation of the squadron, this interest has never been lost sight of.

The excellence of Wilkes' studies of the winds and currents is reflected in his *Narrative*. He hoped his investigations would help to point out the most "feasible routes by which to gain the proper cruising grounds and to define their localities more clearly than has hitherto been done."

Another of his shrewd observations was as follows:

> By a large majority of persons, it is believed that the whale-fishery is a mere lottery, in which success is more owing to good luck than to good management. Those, however, who entertain such opinion are in error. There is, perhaps, no employment on the ocean wherein a sound judgment is more necessary, and no business where success depends more upon the experience, enterprise, and industry of the commander, than in that of whaling.

Unquestionably the Wilkes Exploring Expedition, 1838-42, was eminently successful, but it should have been closely followed up by another and still another. This would have guaranteed a protection for the whaling fleet, as well as insuring the sovereignty of islands in the Pacific which a century later had to be wrested from an enemy nation by force.

While the Exploring Squadron was homeward bound, Captain Seth Pinkham, of Nantucket, in a letter to his friend, Congressman Barker Burnell, voiced the opinion of most whalemen. The letter was written on board the whaler *Henry Astor,* cruising just below the latitude of the Galápagos Islands, and, in part, reads as follows:

> . . . It has become your duty, especially and officially to look after the whaling interest in Congress, and on this important subject, and as a practical man, I beg leave to say a single word. Nearly all the maritime interest of our district is now absorbed in the prosecution of the whale-fishery. This fact is not generally known; indeed it is painful to reflect, that we have at this moment, equipped, and manned four or five hundred sail of the finest ships that swim the ocean; whose canvas whitens every sea, and whose extent of cruising ground is unlimited, and yet our identity is not better known, our bare existence is hardly understood.
> There is no branch of commerce so little protected by our government vessels, and yet no branch needs more protection than these ships which are for so great a length of time beyond the pale of the civil authority.[23]

With the advent of the 1830's came the turning point in the history of New England whaling. Minor ports were now putting two or three more vessels into the business—ports like Falmouth, Massachusetts, Warren and Bristol, Rhode Island, while established ports like New London, Connecticut, and Sag Harbor, Long Island, were increasing their fleets tenfold. The leaders, New Bedford and Nantucket, were at their respective cross-roads. New Bedford was now to surpass her mother-port, like the colonies of ancient Greece outstripping their parent.

New Bedford had the leadership with 245 vessels, while Nantucket still maintained its fleet of seventy-five (having gained in tonnage since 1830 but not in numbers and with increased costs); New London had gained a total of seventy; Sag Harbor could now boast a fleet of seventy-two. In 1857, New Bedford had 329 vessels—half the fleet then whaling, representing an investment of $12,000,000. By that time Nantucket was almost entirely out of the picture.[24]

Nantucket was at the apex of her whaling prosperity, in terms of financial gain, in the mid-1830's. It is of considerable interest to note that the rival port of New Bedford had practically the same population as the island port—7,592 for New Bedford, 7,223 for Nantucket. The mainland port had now the large fleet—seventy-six vessels to sixty for Nantucket. But the island still held the lead in importation of sperm oil—a century and a quarter after Captain Christopher Hussey took the first spermacetti.

This kingdom of whaling at the advent of 1830 was still under the Quaker influence—a fact which more than any other explains its continued prosperity. If the number of men at sea in the whaleships were equally divided among the families, at home, at least one share in the distribution would fall to each family. "Every family . . . had a small expectation, at least, that each arrival would bring some intelligence of a relative or friend . . . should feel a degree of anxiety when information arrived. The whale-fishery as the all important business of the place, makes a strong business bond of connexion . . . what is regarded in one sense as individual prosperity and happiness in a certain degree attaches to all." Thus, stated the editor of the *Inquirer* on November 29, 1828.

Besides her sixty whaleships and ten candle manufactures, ropewalks, stores, etc., the town had four banking institutions and two local insurance companies.

The handicaps to the business of whaling, the threat for future prosperity, did not lay in competition from other ports—it was the physical handicap of a series of sand bars which stretched across that mouth of the harbor, the main ones being four miles long and some twenty yards wide. Petitions for government survey had resulted in a report which proved fully the islanders' contention that the two main bars were of a clay foundation, and could be cut and breakwaters erected, so that the channels so constructed would retain a favorable depth by the scouring action of the tides.

Editor Jenks, of the Nantucket *Inquirer* commented:

> The number of ships employed in the whale-fishery from this island is about sixty, and if $1000 extra expense be incurred in fitting out and receiving the return cargo of each ship, in consequence of having to go to Edgartown and we allow two and a half years as an average time for performing a voyage, it will be seen that this down sustains a loss of $60,000 every two and a half years, or $24,000 annually, which would amount to a MILLION of Dollars in less than forty-two years—a sum considerablly greater than the highest estimate of expense to make an ample harbor at home.[25]

And this estimate was not all that was to be taken into account. Every sum of money paid for loading and unloading, supplying and repairing ships away from home, had an injurious tendency beyond what the merchants sustained by not being able to use all their capital at home—loss of money at Nantucket, loss of business to the local artisans and outfitters.

But, the "enlightened" government under opinionated General Jackson could not see the importance of such action. A dredging machine came to the island to dig a shallow channel through the bar. But it *was not until 1881* that the Federal government took positive steps and voted money to construct a breakwater. This was exactly fifty years too late.

And so, in being forced to lighten their ships in "back of the bar" and to use Edgartown on the Vineyard with its deep harbor, as their port of entry and departure the whalers of Nantucket gradually fell behind their on-coming competitors. The invention of double pontoons or floating drydocks called "camels" early in 1840 gave temporary aid, but these also came too late.

Three catastrophes fell in quick succession on the little island—the Great Fire of 1846, which destroyed the heart of the business section and the wharves; the gold rush of 1849, which took over four hundred of the enterprising young men and sent them to California; the Civil War, which completed the cycle of the collapse of Nantucket whaling. In 1869, the bark *Oak* sailed from the bar, marking the end to nearly three centuries of its great industry.

On May 16, 1828, the venerable William Rotch died in New Bedford, where he had identified himself with his sons and sons-in-law soon after his return from Europe to Nantucket in 1795.

Thus, in his ninety-fourth year passed this combination of the Nestor and Ulysses of the whaling industry. His intelligence and strict adherence to his religious principles had combined with a business acumen to make him one of the outstanding merchants of his time. He had been a pioneer in international history; his sagacity was a tremendous factor in preserving the whale fishery for this nation. In his lifetime he had seen America's golden age of whaling—had contributed in large measure to the success of the two greatest whaling ports of the world, Nantucket and New Bedford.

No better illustration of the dividing line between the "golden age" of whaling and the "age of gold" in whaling may be given than the difference between the crews of the ships before 1830 and after 1835. While the first full century of deep-sea whaling was characterized by the quality of the experienced whalemen who captained, officered and manned the ships, the period, after the first years of the 1830's, was marked by the influx of greenhorns, waterfront toughs, foreign adventurers and unsavory characters, who shipped to escape the law or to a planned desertion. Too few whaleships had officers with patience enough to train such a heterogeneous crew.

With the advent of the 1840's, the number of whaleships increased to a remarkable degree. The shipowners from the port of New Bedford alone were called upon to provide crews for 230 ships, the problem of securing the necessary numbers found the recruits being obtained from every walk of life. Apple-cheeked farm boys from New York State, Vermont and Pennsylvania, stalwart Mid-westerners from Ohio and Illinois, adventure-seeking youths from Virginia and the Carolinas, mingled with waterfront toughs from New York, Baltimore and Boston.

A typical advertisement of the time is:

> There are several whalemen now fitting in our port, and some difficulty is experienced in completing their crews. Active young men from the country and others would now have a good opportunity of obtaining situations on board those vessels, where the wages on perquisites are equal and in most cases superior to those in merchant ships.[26]

Before 1840, many prominent men in the whaling centers were fully aware of the seriousness of conditions aboard whaleships. The increased number of ships had brought about a demand for trained men and more were needed to fill out the ranks of the foremast hands. In 1836, the Nantucket newspaper noted:

> . . . But it cannot be denied that abuses and impositions often to a fearful and fatal degree have latterly encroached upon all the good consequences of the whale fishery. . . . Too many ungovernable lads, runaways from parental authority, or candidate for corrective treatment, too many vagabonds just from the clutches of the police of European and American cities—too many convicts— . . . are suffered to enlist in this service. . . . From materials thus gathered, it is not surprising that revolts, mutinies, and murders, conflagrations and immense destruction of property so frequently arise. . . . The whale-fishery shall not be converted into a mere engine for the repair of cracked reputations and the chastisement of those against the reception of whom even the jail doors revolt.

Captain Charles Starbuck, of the bark *Peru,* commencing a voyage in July of 1851, gives the shipmaster's despairing reaction to such a crew. He recorded in his log:

> I am in hope that we shall have fine weather and see some sperm whales and make a beginning. I think we should all feel well if we could catch a big whale, don't you, but what is for us we shall get and no more. We have got the poorest set of green hands that a ship ever had—dull, O dear, how dull it appears that they will never learn anything. Then there are some cripples amongst them—there

is Hunter, with his arm broke in three places and just at this time down with chills and fever; then there is Tucker that is near-sighted and cannot see an inch before his eyes. Noble follows! just the men that whalers want, for they don't have any work to do and can get along with poor help! They may clear [desert] when we get to the islands, I hope they will and then we shall get some good fellows in their place. . . . The mate is very busy trying to learn his dummies how to steer and learn the compass, but with very little success, certainly he has got some hard cases—his method is a good one, it is this: he drew a map of a compass and gave it to two of them to learn, and stop their watch below until they learn it, and keep them at the wheel through the day. He will fix them I guess.[27]

Always present was the dread homesickness, more keenly felt those first few months from home, with the voyage before them—years of watery wanderings. Captain Starbuck, fully aware of his own lonesomeness, no doubt accentuated by the appearance of his green crew, gives the feeling in his entry for August 26, 1851, as follows:

. . . At 6 P.M. saw another ship and many of us wished ourselves on board of her. O, what poor homesick men, but few of them will ever go to sea again. Home sweet home, and those we have left behind us are constantly in our minds. Little do those on shore know a sailor's feelings, separated from all that they hold dear on earth, with almost a certainty of being apart for three or four long years— enough to make a man's hair grow grey at the thought of it.

The whaling period from 1835 to 1905 embraced the highly lucrative phase of the industry for owners and investors. Its recounting is not a part of this volume which is concerned with the establishment and perfection of the American whaling tradition.

With the return of the Wilkes Expedition in 1841, and the subsequent publication of the voluminous account of that voyage of exploration, the whalemen sea-hunters came into their own. Many people, who had never before realized the extent of the whaling voyages or the dangers and extraordinary hazards connected therewith, now for the first time gained an understanding of the whaling tradition and recognized the scope of their cruisings. Subsequently, the studies of Matthew Fontaine Maury, and his monumental work on the winds and currents of the oceans, brought a new appreciation for the fact that the first true oceanographers were the whalemen.

In years to come the whaleman would enter new fields. When in 1835 Captain Barzillai Folger, in the *Ganges,* of Nantucket, discovered the Kodiak Grounds in the Pacific Northwest the whaling industry began a new great phase. In 1848, Captain James Royce, in the bark *Superior,* of Sag Harbor, was first to enter the Behring Sea and found the bowhead whale in great numbers. His was a pioneering voyage of tremendous significance as it opened the Arctic again to the whalemen —two hundred years after the Davis Straits on the other side of the Arctic world were first found. The first bowhead whales had been taken on the Siberian coast of Kamchatka in 1843 by the *Hercules,* Captain Ricketson; and the *Janus,* Captain Turner, both New Bedford vessels. Captain James Covill, of New Bedford, is credited with discovering the bowheads' value.

It was the whaling tradition reasserting itself, and the spirit of those pioneering mariners who had established that tradition was never more fully revealed. But the story of Arctic whaling is a story in itself. With it the enterprise of American whalemen came into its own and with its ending the last chapter of that extraordinary drama was closed.

The peak of American whaling came in 1846, when six hundred and seventy-eight ships and barks, thirty-five brigs, and twenty-two schooners, composed the fleet. This represented an aggregate capacity of 233,189 tons and a value of $21,075,000. The foreign whaling fleet numbered two hundred and thirty ships, so that the world's combined whaling fleet exceeded nine hundred vessels.

Today, in a world which has become so closely knit in an air age, the limitations of geographical position are not so apparent as they were even a quarter-century ago. But the whaleman of the early nineteenth century gave a concept of internationalism which was far ahead of his time. As a mariner he was a citizen of a watery world; as a man of industry he was a worker who added greatly to the material wealth of his country; as an oceanographer he was a seaman who contributed much to the world's knowledge; as a whaler he was a sea-hunter whose exploits make such a bright page in American history.

NOTES

Chapter I: Whaling Alongshore

1. Massachusetts Historical Society *Collections* (Boston, Mass.), III Series, Vol. VIII, p. 156.
2. Alexander Starbuck, *History of the American Whale-Fishery* (Waltham, Mass., 1878), p. 5.
3. Lorenzo Sabine, *Report on the Fisheries* (Washington, 1852), p. 42. Quoting Mather.
4. *Purchas: His Pilgrimes*, (Hakluyt Society, London), Vol. XIX, Chapter III, "A Relation or Journal of a Plantation Settled at Plymouth in New England," p. 312.
5. *Ibid.*
6. *Ibid.*
7. Starbuck, *op. cit.*, p. 11, quoting Gov. Lovelace, Nov. 28, 1672.
8. Zaccheus Macy, Mass. Hist. Soc. Col., Vol. III, p. 157.
9. Obed Macy, *History of Nantucket* (2d ed. Mansfield, Mass., 1880) p. 40.
10. *Ibid.*, p. 44.
11. Thomas Hutchinson, *Collectons*, "History of Massachusetts," p. 558.
12. Plymouth Colony Records, Vol. VI, pp. 252-53.
13. Starbuck, *op. cit.*, p. 36.
14. James F. Howell, *History of Southampton, New York*, p. 184.
15. Henry P. Hedges, *Bi-Centennial Address at Easthampton, Long Island* (1850).
16. Sir Francis Lovelace, New York Colony Mss., *General Entries*, Vol. IV, p. 123.
17. Howell, *op. cit.*, p. 61.
18. *Ibid.*, p. 62.
19. Hedges, *op. cit.*, p. 21.
20. Starbuck, *op. cit.*, p. 16.
21. Zaccheus Macy, Mass. Hist. Soc. Col., Vol. III, p. 153.
22. Hector St. John de Crèvecoeur, *Lettres d'un Cultivateur Americain* (Paris, 1787), Vol. II, p. 142.
23. Joseph B. Felt, *Annals of Salem* (Boston, 1849), p. 224.
24. Rev. Mr. Upham, *The Inquirer* (Nantucket, Mass.), May 27, 1837.
25. Felt, *op. cit.*, p. 224.
26. Charles E. Banks, *History of Martha's Vineyard* (Boston, 1911), Vol. I, p. 432. Quoting Edgartown (Mass.) *Records*, Vol. I.
27. Banks, *op. cit.*, Vol. I, p. 432.
28. *Ibid.*, Vol. I, p. 434 (Edgartown Records, Vol. I, p. 107).
29. *Ibid.*, p. 436.
30. Daniel Ricketson, *History of New Bedford* (New Bedford, 1858), p. 62.

Chapter II: The Whaleman Sails Out . . .

1. Mass. State Archives, *Domestic Relations*, Vol. I, p. 181.
2. Obed Macy, *op. cit.*, pp. 68, 69.
3. *Ibid.*, p. 49.

4. William Scoresby, *An Account of the Arctic Region,* etc. (Edinburgh, 1820).
5. New York Col. Mss., Vol. XXVII, pp. 65, 66.
6. Starbuck, *op. cit.,* p. 20.
7. Arnold, *History of Rhode Island,* Vol. II, p. 110.
8. Obed Macy, *op. cit.,* p. 48.
9. *Ibid.,* p. 45.
10. Champlin Family Letters, Whetmore Collection, *Commerce of Rhode Island,* Mass. Hist. Soc., Vol. I, p. 70, Henry Lloyd to Aaron Lopez. Rotch Letters, John Carter Brown Library, Brown University, Providence, R. I.

Chapter III: "A People Still in the Gristle . . ."

1. p. 213.
2. *Universal Magazine* (London), 1752.
3. Vol. II, p. 18.
4. Obed Macy, *op. cit.,* p. 49.
5. Felt, *op. cit.,* pp. 225-26.
6. Ricketson, *op. cit.,* p. 68.
7. Christopher Coffin, Log of the *Seaflower,* 1752. Nantucket Atheneum.
8. *Boston News-Letter,* June 28, 1744.
9. Mass. State Archives, Collections of Mss., Maritime, Vol. VI, p. 316.
10. *Ibid.,* Vol. II, p. 400.
11. Peleg Folger, Log of the *Grampus,* 1751. Nantucket Atheneum.
12. Peleg Folger, Log of the *Phebe,* 1751. Nantucket Atheneum.
13. Peleg Folger, Log of the *Mary,* 1752. Nantucket Atheneum.
14. *Boston News-Letter,* Aug. 22, 1765.
15. Starbuck, *op. cit.,* p. 45.
16. *Boston News-Letter,* Jan. 12, 1767.
17. Mass. State Archives, Col. Mss., Maritime, Vol. VI, p. 341.
18. *Ibid.*
19. Obed Macy, *op. cit.,* p. 65.
20. Log of the *Greyhound,* 1753. Nantucket Atheneum.
21. Log of the *Endeavor,* 1762. In possession of writer.

Chapter IV: Business on the Great Waters

1. Mass. State Archives, Col. Mss., Maritime, Vol. VI, p. 243.
2. Starbuck, *op. cit.,* p. 59.
3. Starbuck, *op. cit.,* pp. 43-44 (Log of the *Tryall*), from Ricketson, *op. cit.*
4. Micajah Coffin, Log of the *Sandwich,* 1768. In possession of writer.
5. Obed Macy, *op. cit.,* p. 64.
6. Micajah Coffin, *op. cit.,* 1762.
7. *Boston News-Letter,* April 20, 1768.
8. *Works of Benjamin Franklin,* Vol. III, p. 353.
9. Obed Macy, *op. cit.,* p. 65.
10. De Crèvecoeur, *op. cit.,* Vol. II, p. 116.
11. Frederick C. Sanford Papers. Nantucket Atheneum.
12. *Boston News-Letter,* May 21, 1770.
13. Jefferson, *Report on the Subject of the Cod and the Whale Fishery.* Made to House of Representatives, Feb. 1, 1791. Also printed as part of House Mss. Doc. No. 32, 42d Congress, 2d Session.
14. Burke, "Conciliation with America," in *Select British Eloquence,* Goodrich (New York, 1853), p. 271.

15. Ricketson, *op. cit.*, p. 58.
16. *Ibid.*
17. *Ibid.*
18. Kezia Coffin Fanning *Diaries* (1775-1820), April 21, 1775. Nantucket Historical Association.

Chapter V: The Whalemen Create a Kingdom

1. Thomas Jefferson, *Correspondence and Miscellanies from the Papers of Thomas Jefferson,* Ed. Thomas Jefferson Randolph (2d ed., Boston and New York), "Memoirs," Vol. II, pp. 385, 389: Letter clxx, Jefferson to John Jay.
2. De Crèvecoeur, *op. cit.,* Vol. II, pp. 96, 97.
3. Obed Macy, *op. cit.,* p. 64.
4. *Ibid.,* p. 77.
5. Starbuck, *op. cit.,* p. 57.
6. Zaccheus Macy, Mass. Hist. Soc. Col., I Series, Vol. III.
7. George Churchman, "An Off-Islander's Visit" (in 1781), by George Cadbury, *Proceedings* of Nantucket Historical Association, 1950.
8. De Crèvecoeur, *op. cit.* (Everyman's Library ed., London, 1916), p. 138.
9. *Ibid.,* p. 143.
10. George Bancroft, *History of the United States,* Vol. VI, p. 474.
11. *American Magazine of Useful Knowledge* (New York, 1840), pp. 318-22.
12. Stackpole, E. A., "The Forgotten Man of the Boston Tea Party," *Inquirer and Mirror* (Nantucket, Mass.), Dec. 12, 1938.
13. Bancroft, *op. cit.,* Vol. VI, p. 475.
14. *Ibid.,* p. 476; Frederick C. Sanford, *Inquirer and Mirror,* Oct. 9, 1876.
15. Hutchinson letters, *op. cit.,* Dec. 9 and Dec. 17, 1773.
16. *Ibid.:* Questions proposed by Francis Rotch at Castle William, Boston, Dec. 7, 1773.
17. Bancroft, *op. cit.*
18. Hutchinson letters, *op. cit.,* Dec. 17, 1773.
19. Lord Dartmouth to Francis Rotch, Feb. 15, 1774. Public Record Office, Canadian Office 5. Transcript in Manuscripts Division, Library of Congress.
20. Gift of John J. Locke to Nantucket Historical Society, Nov. 12, 1951.

Chapter VI: Between the Devil

1. George Cabot, of the Committee of House and Senate of Massachusetts, Oct. 29, 1782, quoted by Starbuck, *op. cit.,* p. 254.
2. "Nantucket Before Parliament," *Inquirer and Mirror,* July 24, 1874.
3. March 22, 1775.
4. Fanning, *op. cit.*
5. *Ibid.,* April 29, 1775.
6. *Ibid.,* May 5, 1775.
7. *Ibid.,* May 17, 1775.
8. *Ibid.,* May 23, 1775.
9. *Ibid.,* May 25, 1775.
10. *Records* of the Third Provincial Congress, p. 314.
11. Fanning, *op. cit.,* July 6, 1775.
12. Mass. State Archives, *Petitions,* Vol. 180, p. 86.
13. Starbuck, *History of Nantucket* (Boston, 1925), pp. 188-89.
14. Mass. State Archives, *Petitions,* Vol. 208, pp. 172-73.
15. F. Rotch and A. Lopez to Capt. John Lock, P. R. O., C. O. 5 (Congress, p. 98).
16. Whetmore Collection, *Commerce of Rhode Island.*

17. Starbuck, *Nantucket*, p. 195.
18. *Commerce of Rhode Island*, pp. 39-40.
19. Fanning, *op. cit.*, Aug. 12, 1775.
20. Rotch and Lopez to Capt. Lock, *op. cit.*
21. *Ibid.*
22. *Ibid.*
23. *Ibid.*
24. *Ibid.*
25. Petition of F. Rotch to the Right Honorable Lord Commissioners of His Majesty's Treasury, P. R. O., C. O. 5, Vol. 146, p. 63 b. Transcript in Mss. Div., Library of Congress.
26. *Ibid.*
27. Rotch and Lopez to Capt. Lock, *op. cit.*, Sept. 4, 1775.
28. P. R. O., C. O. 5, Vol. 115, p. 215.
29. Fanning, *op. cit.*, Feb. 12, 1776.
30. P. R. O., C. O. 5, Vol. 40, p. 406. Mss. Div., Library of Congress.
31. *Works of John Adams* (Boston, 1820), Vol. II, p. 63.
32. *American Archives*, Vol. VII, p. 63.
33. Ricketson, *op. cit.*, p. 165.
34. Banks, *op. cit.*, p. 380.

Chapter VII: Salvaging the . . . Ship

1. Fanning, *op. cit.*, Sept. 10, 1778.
2. Banks, *op. cit.*, pp. 380-81.
3. Starbuck, *Nantucket*, p. 210.
4. Obed Macy, *op. cit.*, p. 100.
5. Mass. State Archives, Vol. 222, p. 69.
6. Fanning, *op. cit.*, April 24, 1779.
7. *Ibid.*, Sept. 30, Oct. 1, 1781.
8. Mass. State Archives, Vol. 228, p. 190.
9. Obed Macy, *op. cit.* (1st ed.), p. 116.
10. Mass. State Archives, Vol. 186, p. 370.
11. William Rotch, *Memorandum Written in His Eightieth Year* (Boston, 1916), p. 33.
12. Obed Macy, *op. cit.* (1st ed.), p. 115.
13. Mass. State Archives, Vol. 178, p. 317; Vol. 186, p. 370.
14. *Ibid.*, Vol. 204, p. 17.
15. Obed Macy, *op. cit.* (2d ed.), p. 240.
16. Mass State Archives, Vol. 186, p. 7.
17. *Ibid.*
18. Starbuck, *Nantucket*, p. 254.
19. W. Rotch, *op. cit.*, p. 33.
20. *Journal* of the Continental Congress (March 1783), p. 938.

Chapter VIII: American Whaling in Limbo

1. Quoted in Obed Macy, *op. cit.*, p. 130.
2. *Ibid.*, p. 124.
3. Fanning, *op. cit.*, April 21, 1784.
4. Starbuck, *Nantucket*, p. 383.
5. Letter of William Rotch, Jr., in Starbuck, *Nantucket*, pp. 383-84.
6. *The Gentlemen's Magazine*, London, March, 1783.

7. Record of Micajah Gardner, 1783.
8. Starbuck, *Nantucket,* p. 407.
9. Rotch, *Memorandum,* p. 35.
10. Starbuck, *Nantucket,* p. 386.
11. Obed Macy, *op. cit.,* p. 129.
12. *New Hampshire Gazette and General Advertiser,* Oct. 28, 1785.
13. Starbuck, *Nantucket,* p. 390.
14. *Proceedings* of Nantucket Historical Association, 1934.
15. *The Pollard Papers.* Nantucket Atheneum.
16. *William C. Folger Papers.* Nantucket Historical Association.
17. A. Howard Clark, *The Antarctic Seal Fisheries* (U.S. Fish Com. Report, 1887); Records of the City of Hudson, N. Y.
18. Obed Macy, *op. cit.,* p. 130.
19. *Works of Thomas Jefferson, op. cit.,* "Memoirs," Vol. II, p. 519.
20. *Ibid.*
21. *Continental Journal,* Sept. 15, 1785. Boston Athenaeum.
22. Adams, *op. cit.,* Vol. VIII, p. 288.
23. Murdock, *History of Nova Scotia,* Vol. III, pp. 43-44.
24. *Provincial Archives of Nova Scotia,* Vol. 221, doc. 69; Vol. 222, doc. 12.
25. *Ibid.,* Vol. 302, doc. 20.
26. Parr to Lord Sydney, *P.A.C.N.S.,* Vol. 107M. 503, pp. 159-61. Enquiries with Parr's answers.
27. Parr to Sydney, Sept. 30, 1785, *P.A.N.S.* Vol. 47, doc. 47.
28. Parr to Sydney, *ibid.,* Sept. 20, 1785.
29. Parr to Sydney, *ibid.,* Vol. 47.
30. *Ibid.*
31. John P. Martin, *History of Dartmouth.*
32. Feb. 26, 1785, *P.A.N.S.,* Vol. 301, doc. 78.
33. Sydney to Parr, April 30, 1786, *ibid.,* Vol. 33, doc. 26.
34. *Ibid.,* August 15, 1791.
35. *P. A. C. N. S. A.,* Vol. 170M. 503, pp. 159-61.
36. *Journal of John Townsend,* July to August 1786. Nantucket Historical Association.
37. *Ibid.,* August 10, 1786.
38. *The Nova Scotian,* Halifax, N.S., June 25, 1825.
39. Uniacke to Parr, *op. cit.,* August 15, 1791.
40. *Occasional Letters,* Halifax, N. S., May 16, 1925; *Folios of Mediterranean Passes, P.A.N.S.,* including many for whalers, 1785-91; Hussey & Robinson, *Catalogue of Nantucket Whalers* (Nantucket, 1876); Starbuck, *Nantucket,* p. 394.
41. Parr to Evan Pepean, Under-Secretary of State, August 13, 1788. P. R. O., C. O., August 13, 1788.
42. Margaret Ells, "The Dartmouth Whalers," *Dalhousie Review,* Vol. XV, No. 1 (Halifax, N. S., April 1935).
43. *P. A. N. S.,* Report of Commissioners, 1788.
44. Churchman, *op. cit.,* June 1781.
45. William Rotch, *op. cit.,* p. 36.
46. Letters from William Rotch to Samuel Rodman and William Rotch, Jr., August 2, 1785.
47. *Ibid.*
48. Rotch, *Memorandum,* p. 37.
49. W. Rotch Letters, Aug. 2, 1785.
50. *Ibid.,* Aug. 9, 1785.
51. *Ibid.,* Aug. 18, 1785.

52. *Ibid.,* Nov. 2, 1785.
53. *Ibid.,* March 30, 1786.
54. *Ibid.*
55. *Ibid.,* Sept. 5, 1785.
56. Rotch, *Memorandum,* pp. 40-41.
57. *Ibid.,* pp. 40-41.
58. *Ibid.,* p. 42.
59. Starbuck, *Nantucket,* p. 392.
60. Rotch, *Memorandum,* pp. 43-44.
61. *Ibid.,* p. 45.
62. W. Rotch Letters, March 30, 1786.
63. Rotch, *Memorandum,* p. 51.
64. W. Rotch Letters, June 7, 1786.
65. Obed Macy, *op. cit.,* pp. 246-49.
66. *Ibid.*
67. Rotch, *Memorandum,* pp. 46-47.
68. W. Rotch Letters, May 27, 1786.
69. *Ibid.,* June 7, 1786.
70. Letters to William Rotch & Sons, June 7, 1786. Old Dartmouth Historical Assn., New Bedford, Mass.
71. *Ibid.*
72. Jefferson, *op. cit.,* "Memoirs," Vol. II, p. 392.

Chapter IX: The Whaling Industry . . . the World

1. Adams, *op. cit.,* Vol. VIII, p. 309.
2. *Ibid.*
3. P. R. O. Privy Council, 2/163, pp. 109-13.
4. Adams, *op. cit.,* Vol. VIII, p. 463.
5. P. R. O., P. C., 2/136; also documents in possession of the writer: a letter from Greville to Grenville.
6. Rotch, *Memorandum,* p. 50.
7. *P. A. N. S.,* Vol. 248, doc. 32.
8. P. R. O., P. C., 2/136, pp. 92-113, May 18, 1791.
9. *Ibid.*
10. Flora Thomas, *Builders of Milford* (Pembroke, Wales), p. 4.
11. P. R. O., P. C. 2/136.
12. *Ibid.*
13. *Ibid.*
14. *P. A. N. S.,* Certificate from Gov. Wentworth.
15. *Op. cit.,* Aug. 15, 1791.
16. P. R. O., P. C. 2/136. Grendle to Privy Council.
17. William Rotch to William Rodman, Oct. 24, 1792.
18. Dartmouth Meeting of Friends *Records,* now in custody of the Nantucket Historical Assn.
19. *Ibid.*
20. *Ibid.*
21. *Ibid.*

Chapter X: The "Coup-de-Whale"

1. Jefferson, *op. cit.,* "Memoirs," Vol. II, p. 396.
2. *Ibid.,* p. 391.
3. *Ibid.,* p. 309; W. Rotch Letters, June 7, 1786.

4. *P. A. N. S.*, Vol. 238, doc. 32 (Report of Commissioners to Governor Parr, 1788).

5. Jefferson, *op. cit.*, "Memoirs," p. 400.

6. P. R. O., P. C., 2/136, pp. 92-113, May 18, 1791.

7. *Ibid.*

8. Churchman, *op. cit.*, June 1781.

9. W. Rotch Letters, Sept. 5, 1785.

10. *Ibid.*, Aug. 2, 1785.

11. *Ibid.*, Sept. 5, 1785.

12. *Ibid.*

13. *Ibid.*, Dec. 14, 1785.

14. *Ibid.*

15. *Ibid.*, Nov. 2, 1785.

16. *Ibid.*, Feb. 27, 1786.

17. Sanford in *Boston Advertiser*, Dec. 12, 1871.

18. *Ibid.*

19. *Ibid.*

20. *Ibid.*

21. *Ibid.*

22. *Ibid.*

23. Log of the *Penelope*, 1788, Nantucket Atheneum.

24. W. Rotch Letters, Sept. 6, 1786.

25. *Ibid.*, Oct. 12, 1790.

26. *Ibid.*

27. *Ibid.*, Aug. 9, 1785.

28. *Ibid.*, Nov. 2, 1786.

29. Starbuck, *Nantucket*, p. 185.

30. *P. A. N. S.*, Aug. 17, 1791.

Chapter XI: The Whalemen . . . Cape Horn

1. *Inquirer*, Nov. 28, 1874; Starbuck, *Nantucket*, Obed Macy, *op. cit.*, p. 142.

2. Sanford, *Boston Advertiser*, Dec. 12, 1871.

3. Dakin, *Whalemen's Adventures*.

4. *Ibid.*

5. *Ibid.*

6. W. Rotch Letters, Oct. 19, 1790.

7. *Ibid.*

8. *Ibid.*

9. *Ibid.*, Jan. 25, 1792, Feb. 18, 1792.

10. *Ibid.*, Feb. 3, 1792.

11. *Ibid.*, March 2, 1792.

12. *Ibid.*, March 19, 1792.

13. Rotch, *Memorandum*, p. 42.

14. Dakin, *op. cit.*

15. Adams, *op. cit.*, Vol. VIII, pp. 363-64.

16. *Ibid.*

17. Thomas, *op. cit.*

18. Jefferson, *Cod and the Whale Fishery* (1791).

19. *Ibid.*

20. Starbuck, *Nantucket*, p. 186.

21. *Inquirer & Mirror*, Feb. 8, 1853, Nov. 28, 1874; Obed Macy, *op. cit.*, pp. 142-43; *New Bedford Medley*, March 30, 1793.

22. Josiah Durfy, Log of the *Rebecca*. Marine Historical Association, Mystic, Conn.
23. Obed Macy, *op. cit.*, pp. 143-44.
24. Starbuck, *Nantucket*, p. 186; Log of the *Rebecca*, March 30, 1792.
25. Durfy, *op. cit., New Bedford Medley*, March 30, 1793.
26. *New Bedford Medley*, March 30, 1793.
27. Sanford, *Inquirer and Mirror*, March, 1853.
28. Starbuck, *Nantucket*, p. 186; *New Bedford Medley*, April 15, 1793.
29. Jan. 14, 1853.
30. David Porter, *Journal of a Cruise Made to the Pacific Ocean by Captain David Porter in the U. S. Frigate Essex, 1812-14* (Philadelphia, 1815).
31. Durfy, *op. cit.; New Bedford Medley*, Feb. 23, 1793.
32. *Inquirer and Mirror*, April 16 and 23, 1859.
33. W. Rotch Letters, July 7, 1786.
34. *Ibid.*, Oct. 12, 1790; May 9, 1792.
35. *Ibid.*
36. *Ibid.*
37. *Ibid.*
38. Jefferson, *op. cit.*, "Memoirs," Vol. II, p. 386, Nov. 19, 1788.
39. W. Rotch Letters, Oct. 12, 1790.
40. Jefferson, *loc. cit.*

Chapter XII: America Regains . . . Fleet . . .

1. Joseph C. Hart, *Miriam Coffin* (2d ed., San Francisco, 1872), p. 226.
2. W. Rotch Letters, Aug. 18, 1785.
3. Starbuck, *Nantucket*, pp. 91-92, 187; Obed Macy, *op. cit.*, p. 217.
4. Nantucket tradition.
5. Starbuck, *Nantucket*, pp. 188-90.
6. Obed Macy, *op. cit.* Crew lists of American whaleships at New Bedford, Mass., and Mystic Seaport, Conn.
7. Rotch, *Memorandum*, pp. 53-55.
8. *Ibid.*, pp. 71-72.
9. *Ibid.*, pp. 79-80.
10. W. Rotch Letters, May 16, 1792.
11. *Ibid.*
12. *Ibid.*, Feb. 18, 1792.
13. Rotch, *Memorandum*, p. 66.
14. W. Rotch Letters, Dec. 16, 1791.
15. *New Bedford Medley*, Aug. 23, 1793.
16. *Ibid.*, Sept. 20, 1793.
17. *Ibid.*, Sept. 23, 1793.
18. *Ibid.*, Oct. 4, 1793.
19. *Ibid.*, Jan. 20, 1794.
20. *Ibid.*
21. Feb. 16, 1794.
22. Starbuck, *Nantucket*, p. 91; also original papers in author's possession.
23. *Ibid.*
24. "French Spoilation Claims," Z. W. Pease in an article in *New Bedford Standard*, reprinted by *Inquirer and Mirror*, March 28, 1891.
25. *The Warden* (Nantucket), May 20, 1846.

Chapter XIII: Whales . . . and Fur-Seals

1. P. 142.

2. W. Rotch Letters, Aug. 18, 1785.

3. *Ibid.*

4. *South Street.*

5. Samuel Eliot Morison, *Maritime History of Massachusetts, 1783-1860* (Boston, 1921), p. 46.

6. Sanford, *Proceeding* of the American Antiquarian Society (No. 57, Oct. 21, 1871), footnote p. 28.

7. *Commerce of Rhode Island,* Vol. I, p. 191.

8. Sanford, *Inquirer and Mirror,* Dec. 28, 1876.

9. *Commerce of Rhode Island,* Vol. II, pp. 195-96.

10. *Ibid.,* p. 196.

11. Bullard, *op. cit.,* pp. 60-61.

12. W. Rotch Letters, Sept. 5, 1785.

13. Clark, *op. cit.*

14. Bullard, *op. cit.,* p. 60.

15. W. Rotch Letters, Sept. 9, 1785; Sanford, "A Hundred Years Ago," *Inquirer and Mirror,* Dec. 18, 1869.

16. W. Rotch Letters, Sept. 9, 1785.

17. *Ibid.*

18. *Commerce of Rhode Island* (De Bauque to Champlin), Vol. II, p. 182.

19. W. Rotch Letters, Sept. 19, 1785.

20. Sanford, *Inquirer and Mirror,* Dec. 18, 1869.

21. Obed Macy, *op. cit.,* p. 142.

22. W. Rotch Letters, Sept. 9, 1785.

23. Starbuck, *Nantucket,* p. 188.

24. Clark, *op. cit.,* p. 436.

25. Amasa Delano, *Narrative of Voyages and Travels* (Boston, 1818), pp. 306-07.

26. David Forbes, Diary of the *Neptune,* of New Haven, 1796-99, New Haven Historical Society.

27. *Ibid.,* Oct. 22, 1797.

28. *Ibid.,* Dec. 10, 1797.

29. *Ibid.*

30. *Connecticut Journal* (New Haven, Conn.), July 17, 1799.

31. Charles Peterson New, quoted by Clark in *Antarctic Seal Fisheries,* p. 442.

Chapter XIV: The First . . . Whalers to Desolation

1. Nathaniel Taylor, "Life on a Whaler," *Occasional Publications* (The New London County Hist. Soc., 1929), Vol. II, p. 69.

2. Starbuck, *Nantucket,* p. 186.

3. Silvanus Crosby, Log of the *Asia,* Nantucket, 1791-94. In possession of writer.

4. *Ibid.,* Nov. 9, 1791.

5. *Ibid.,* Dec. 16, 1791.

6. *Ibid.,* Feb. 4-8, 1792.

7. *Ibid.,* March 14, 1792.

8. *Ibid.,* April 22, 1792.

9. *Ibid.,* July 30, 1792.

10. *Ibid.,* Aug. 29, 1792.

11. *Ibid.,* Oct. 5, 1792.

12. *Ibid.,* Dec. 9 and 10, 1792.

13. *Ibid.,* Dec. 18, 1792.
14. Taylor, *op. cit.,* p. 73.
15. Crosby, *op. cit.,* Jan. 19, 1793.
16. *Ibid.,* July 2, 1793.
17. *Ibid.,* July 20, 1793.
18. *Ibid.,* Dec. 10, 1793.
19. Starbuck, *American Whale Fishery,* pp. 196-97.
20. Dakin, *op. cit.,* Introduction, xv.
21. *Ibid.,* p. 8.

Chapter XV: "Of the Most Daring Kind . . ."

1. Jeremiah Reynolds, House Document No. 94, 23d Congress, 2d Session, pp. 36-37.
2. Edmund Fanning, *Voyages and Discoveries in the South Seas, 1792-1832* (Marine Research Soc., 1924), pp. 63, 73-75.
3. William Dampier, *Voyage Around The World,* quoted in Clark's *Fur Seal Industry,* p. 408.
4. Clark, *Fur Seal Industry,* p. 441.
5. Ebenezer Townsend's "Journal of the *Neptune,*" New Haven Historical Society's Papers, Vol. IV, 1888, quoted by Clark, *Fur Seal Industry,* p. 461.
6. *Ibid.,* pp. 462-63.
7. *Ibid.,* p. 461.
8. *Ibid.,* p. 460.
9. *Mirror* (Nantucket, Mass.), Dec. 13, 1859.
10. Clark, *Fur Seal Industry,* pp. 443-44.
11. Durfy, *op. cit.,* Oct. 26, 1793. Starbuck, *Nantucket,* p. 198.
12. *New Bedford Medley,* Sept. 20, 1793.
13. Rotch, *Memorandum,* p. 68. Starbuck, *Nantucket,* p. 194. Clark, *Fur Seal Industry,* p. 442.
14. E. Fanning, *op. cit.,* p. 11.
15. *Ibid.,* p. 63.
16. *Ibid.,* p. 63.
17. A. Delano, *op. cit.,* pp. 303-04.
18. E. Fanning, *op. cit.,* p. 79.
19. Sanford, "The Sea Kings of Nantucket," *Inquirer and Mirror,* Feb. 13, 1888.
20. Clark, *Antarctic Seal Fisheries,* pp. 442-43. Felt, *op. cit.,* May 10, 1802.
21. *Salem Gazette,* May 4, 1802.
22. Nathaniel Appleton, *Voyage of the Concord.* Essex Institute.
23. Sanford, quoted by Clark, *Fur Sealing Industry,* p. 403.
24. Sanford, "Sea Kings," *op. cit.,* Feb. 13, 1888.

Chapter XVI: Full Tide of Adventure

1. William Moulton, *A Concise Extract from the Sea Journal on Board the "Onico,"* of New London, 1799-1804 (Utica, N.Y., 1804).
2. *Ibid.,* pp. 11-12.
3. *Ibid.,* p. 31.
4. *Ibid.,* p. 58.
5. *Ibid.,* p. 61.
6. Delano, *op. cit.,* p. 314.
7. Moulton, *op. cit.,* p. 65.
8. *Ibid.,* p. 66.
9. *Ibid.,* p. 71.

10. Sanford, "Sea Kings," *op. cit.*

11. Delano, *op. cit.*, pp. 289-90.

12. Clark, *Antarctic Seal Fisheries*, pp. 443-44.

13. Moulton, *op. cit.*, p. 106.

14. *Ibid.*, p. 118.

15. Joel Root, *Narrative of a Trading and Sealing Voyage in the Ship Huron from New Haven, Around the World, 1802-1806*. New Haven Colony Historical Society, Vol. V (New Haven, Conn., 1894).

16. *Ibid.*, pp. 155-56.

17. *Ibid.*, p. 156.

18. *Ibid.*, pp. 159-60.

19. *Ibid.*, p. 171.

20. Lawrence Bunker, Letters to his mother, Mrs. Mary H. Bunker, Feb. to March 1, 1945; also in conversation with writer.

21. Dakin, *op. cit.*, p. 25.

22. *Ibid.*, p. 28.

23. Thomas Dunbardin, "Earliest American Voyages to Australia," *The American Neptune*, Jan. 1950, pp. 52-64; Custom House Records of Sydney, Australia, 1791-1825. List sent by Gov. McQuarie at New South Wales to London, dated March 3, 1816.

24. E. Fanning, *op. cit.*, p. 242. Letter to Edward E. Hale, Oct. 2, 1811, *Proceedings* of American Antiquarian Society, No. 57, 1872.

25. E. Fanning, *op. cit.*, pp. 232-33.

26. *Ibid.*, p. 234.

27. *Ibid.*, p. 238.

28. Papers of the ship *Favourite*. Nantucket Whaling Museum.

29. *Ibid.*

30. E. Fanning, *op. cit.*, p. 239.

31. Papers of the ship *Criterion*. Nantucket Whaling Museum; original documents.

32. *An Account of the English Colony in New South Wales*, by Lieut.-Governor David Collins, Viscount Mason Cattereagh, Aug. 31, 1806.

33. Original document in possession of the writer.

Chapter XVII: Mutineers' Hideaway

1. Delano, *op. cit.*, p. 138.

2. *Ibid.*, p. 138.

3. Mayhew Folger, Log of the *Topaz*, 1807-1809. Nantucket Whaling Museum.

4. M. Folger, Letter to Boardman & Pope, Boston, Mass., written at Santiago, Chile, Sept. 10, 1808.

5. M. Folger, Log of the *Topaz*, Aug. 21, 1807.

6. M. Folger, Letter to Boardman & Pope, Sept. 10, 1808.

7. *Ibid.*

8. M. Folger, Log of the *Topaz*, Nov. 6, 1807.

9. *Ibid.*, Dec. 18, 1807.

10. Delano, *op. cit.*, p. 139.

11. *Ibid.*, pp. 137-40.

12. Feb. 6, 1808.

13. Sir John Barrow, *The Mutiny and Piratical Seizure of H.M.S. Bounty* (reprint from The World's Classics ed., 1928), p. 303.

14. Feb. 6, 1808.

15. Barrow, *op. cit.*, p. 309.

16. Delano, *op. cit.*, p. 143.

17. Lady Diana Belcher, *The Mutineers of the Bounty* (New York, 1871), p. 162.

18. M. Folger, Letter to Boardman & Pope, Sept. 10, 1808.
19. *Ibid.*
20. Delano, *op. cit.*, p. 143.
21. Belcher, *op. cit.*, pp. 162-63; also *Nautical Magazine* (London, 1840), Vol. 9, p. 901.
22. Edward Everett Hale, *Stories of the Sea* (Boston, 1880), pp. 227-28.
23. *Asiatic Journal* (July, 1820), Vol. 6.
24. *Ibid.* (October, 1822), Vol. 7.
25. *Inquirer,* Aug. 20, 1822, Sept. 23, 1823.
26. *Ibid.,* Oct. 15, 1822.
27. *Ibid.,* Oct. 22, 1822.
28. *Ibid.,* Oct. 15, 1822.
29. *Ibid.,* Oct. 22, 1822.
30. *Inquirer and Mirror*, Sept. 7, 1935.
31. Letter of Matthew McCoy.

Chapter XVIII: "Their Very Pursuits . . ."

1. Starbuck, *Nantucket*, p. 198.
2. *Ibid.*
3. Micajah Gardner, Log of the *Hannah and Eliza*, 1804-1806. Nantucket Whaling Museum.
4. *Ibid.,* April 20, 1805.
5. Papers of Capt. Micajah Gardner. In possession of the writer.
6. *Inquirer,* July 28, 1821.
7. Log of the *Atlas,* 1808-1810. Nantucket Whaling Museum.
8. Deposition of Capt. Joy, dated Lima, Peru, Dec. 16, 1801.
9. Nov. 19, 1811.
10. *Ibid.*
11. Starbuck, *Nantucket*, p. 273.
12. *Ibid.,* p. 213.
13. Obed Macy's "Diary." Nantucket Historical Association.
14. *Ibid.*
15. *Ibid.*
16. *Ibid.*
17. *Ibid.*
18. William R. Easton, *Inquirer and Mirror*, April 13, 1878.

Chapter XIX: Whaling Masters and Explorers

1. Obed Macy, *op. cit.* (2d ed.), p. 205.
2. Starbuck, *Nantucket*, pp. 428-30.
3. "Life of Captain Edmund Gardner," Inquirer and Mirror, Dec. 14, 1872, Sept. 26, 1898.
4. *Ibid.*
5. Alexander Starbuck, Report of U. S. Fish Commission, Vol. III, p. 76.
6. *Ibid.,* p. 96.
7. Letter from Capt. Joseph Allen to Edward Mitchell & Co., brought home by *Ganges,* Capt. Ray; printed in *New Bedford Mercury,* June 8, 1821.
8. *Ibid.*
9. Thomas Beale, *The Natural History of the Sperm Whale* (London, 1836), p. 149.
10. Log of the *George and Susan,* of New Bedford, Dec. 30, 1821. Old Dartmouth Historical Society Whaling Museum.

11. Journal of Mary Hayden Russell, on board ship, *Emily*, of London, 1823-1825, written for her daughter Marry Ann Mount.

12. *Ibid.*, March 15, 1823.

13. *Ibid.*, Feb. 18, 1823.

14. *Ibid.*, March 18, 1823.

15. *Ibid.*, April 12, 1823.

16. *Ibid.*, June 12, 1823.

17. *Ibid.*, Sept. 3, 1823.

18. *Ibid.*, Sept. 17, 1823.

19. *Ibid.*

20. *Ibid.*, Sept. 22, 1823.

21. *Ibid.*, Sept. 23, 1823.

22. *Ibid.*, Oct. 13, 1823.

23. *Inquirer*, April 10, 1824.

24. Starbuck, *Nantucket*, pp. 230-33.

Chapter XX: Into the Uncharted . . . Pacific

1. James R. Lanman, "The American Whale-Fishery," in Hunt's *Merchant's Magazine and Commercial Review* (New York, 1840), Vol. 3, No. 5, p. 375.

2. *Inquirer*, March 12, 1825.

3. *Ibid.*

4. *Ibid.*

5. Jeremiah N. Reynolds, Report to Secretary of the Navy, 23d Congress, 2d Session, House Document No. 94, p. 30.

6. *Ibid.*, p. 34.

7. *Ibid.*

8. Charles Wilkes, *Narrative of the United States Exploring Expedition* (Philadelphia, 1845), Vol. 5, pp. 6-8.

9. Reynolds, *op. cit.*, p. 32.

10. Reynolds, *op. cit.*, p. 35.

11. Letter from Mate Plaskett of the *Independence II*, *Inquirer*, Oct. 22, 1822.

12. Wilkes. *op. cit.*, Vol. 5, p. 37.

13. *Inquirer*, Oct. 22, 1822.

14. Wilkes, *op. cit.*, Vol. 5, p. 18.

15. Edwin H. Bryant, *American Polynesia and the Hawaiian Chain* (Honolulu).

16. Log of the *General Jackson*, 1836-39. In possession of Paul C. Nicholson, Providence, R. I.

17. Wilkes, *op. cit.*, Vol. 5, p. 18.

18. Report of Capt. Shubael Chase, *Inquirer*, April 18, 1822.

19. Report of Capt. Henry Bunker, *op. cit.*, July 27, 1835.

20. Delano, *op. cit.*, p. 356.

21. Report of the *Fortune*, Sept. 27, 1825.

22. "The Case of the *Loper*," E. A. Stackpole, *Inquirer and Mirror*, 1935.

23. *Ibid.*

24. Report in *Inquirer*, Aug. 23, 1823.

25. *Ibid.*

26. Report of the *Factor*, Aug. 19, 1823.

27. *Inquirer*, Aug. 26, 1823.

28. *Op. cit.*, Feb. 14, 1822.

29. *Ibid.*

30. Report of the *Paragon*, June 27, 1825.

31. *Inquirer*, Sept. 9, 1830.

Chapter XXI: All Adventures . . .

1. William Cary, "Narrative of Voyage of the Barque *Oeno*," of Nantucket. Manuscript now in possession of Earl S. Ray, Nantucket.
2. Report from the *Loper*, Nov. 25, 1826.
3. Cary, *op. cit.*, p. 1.
4. *Ibid.*, p. 3.
5. *Ibid.*, p. 4.
6. *Ibid.*, p. 5.
7. *Ibid.*, p. 8.
8. *Ibid.*, pp. 12-13.
9. *Ibid.*, p. 13.
10. *Ibid.*, p. 14.
11. *Ibid.*, p. 14.
12. *Ibid.*, p. 25.
13. *Ibid.*, p. 28.
14. *Ibid.*, p. 28.
15. *Inquirer*, Feb. 13, 1834.
16. Cary, *op. cit.*, p. 32.
17. *Ibid.*, p. 36.
18. *Ibid.*, p. 53.
19. *Ibid.*, p. 79.
20. *Ibid.*, p. 93.
21. *Inquirer*, March 12, 1831.
22. Wilkes, *op. cit.*, p. 361.
23. *Ibid.*
24. Cary, *op. cit.*, p. 34.
25. Wilkes, *op. cit.*
26. Lieut. George Backus, in interview with writer.
27. Charles Whippey to Lieut. R. H. Smith, U.S.N., Tutuila, Samoa, July 6, 1946.
28. David Whippey to Miss Clara Parker, Nantucket Atheneum, March 8, 1947.
29. Wilkes, *op. cit.*, Vol. 3, p. 46.

Chapter XXII: At the Coasts of Continents

1. Wilkes, *op. cit.*
2. Capt. Edmund Gardner, *Inquirer*, Dec. 14, 1872.
3. Starbuck, *Nantucket;* and files of *Inquirer*, 1821 to 1840.
4. Report of Capt. George W. Gardner, *Inquirer*, May 7, 1822.
5. Capt. Stephen Reynolds, "Journal," Sept. 24, 1824. Peabody Museum, Salem, Mass.
6. Capt. Alexander Macy, Log of the *Palladium*, of Boston, 1821-24. Entry of Nov. 18, 1822. In possession of the writer.
7. Letter of Capt. Benjamin Chase, *Inquirer*, April 29, 1826.
8. Capt. Stephen Reynolds, *op. cit.*, April 1, 1825.
9. "An Old Whaleman," *Inquirer*, March 7, 1851.
10. *Ibid.*
11. *Ibid.*
12. Starbuck, *Whale-Fishery*, pp. 244-46; Obiah Coffin, Log of the *Henry*. New Haven Colony Hist. Soc., New Haven, Conn.
13. Capt. A. Macy, *op. cit.*
14. Capt. A. Macy's "Reminiscences." Nantucket Whaling Museum.
15. *Ibid.*

16. Morison, *op. cit.*, p. 261.
17. Starbuck, *Whale-Fishery*, p. 248.
18. *Inquirer*, May 17, 1824.
19. Document in possession of writer; affidavit of Capt. Macy.
20. J. N. Reynolds, *op. cit.*, p. 27.
21. Capt. A. Macy, Log of the *Palladium*, Dec. 2, 1822.
22. F. W. Beechey, *Narrative of a Voyage to the Pacific* (London, 1830), p. 294.
23. *New Bedford Mercury*, June 15, 1821.
24. Letter of granddaughter of Capt. Obed Starbuck.
25. *New Bedford Mercury*, Feb. 15, 1822.
26. Log of the *Parnasso*, 1820-23. Old Dartmouth Hist. Soc. Whaling Museum.
27. *Ibid.*, April 13, 1821.
28. *Ibid.*, April 14-15, 1821.
29. Log of *Golconda*, 1819-22. Old Dartmouth Hist. Soc. Whaling Museum.
30. *Inquirer*, Nov. 15, 1825.
31. Starbuck, *Whale-Fishery*, p. 251.
32. *Inquirer*, July 11, 1825.
33. Log of the *Parnasso*, Nov. 23-24, 1822.
34. *Ibid.*
35. Capt. George B. Chase, "The Society Islands," *Inquirer*, June 7, 1824.

Chapter XXIII: The Whale That Sank a Ship

1. Owen Chase, *Narrative of the Most Extraordinary and Distressing Ship Wreck of the Whaleship Essex of Nantucket* (New York, 1821).
2. *Ibid.*, p. 22.
3. *Ibid.*, pp. 26-27.
4. *Ibid.*, p. 28.
5. *Ibid.*, p. 29.
6. *Ibid.*, p. 31.
7. *Ibid.*, pp. 33-34.
8. *Ibid.*, p. 47.
9. *Ibid.*, p. 47.
10. Bennett and Tyerman, *Journal of Voyages and Travels* (London, 1830).
11. Chase, *op. cit.*, p. 47.
12. *Ibid.*, p. 47.
13. *Ibid.*, p. 61-62.
14. Capt. Joseph Mitchell, Log of *Three Brothers*, July 7, 1847. Nantucket Whaling Museum.
15. O. Chase, *op. cit.*, p. 68.
16. *Ibid.*, p. 104.
17. *Ibid.*, pp. 115-16.
18. *Ibid.*, p. 118.
19. *Ibid.*, p. 119.
20. *Ibid.*, p. 120.
21. *Ibid.*, p. 121.
22. *Ibid.*, p. 123.
23. *Ibid.*, pp. 123-24.
24. Sir James Barrow, *The Eventful History of the Mutiny of the Bounty*, "Harpers Family Library" (No. XXI, 1832), p. 300.
25. *Ibid.*
26. *Ibid.*

27. Charles Murphey, "Thrilling Whaling Voyage . . . on Board Ship the *Dauphin*" (Mattapoisett, 1877), p. 9.

28. Obed Macy, "Account of the Ship *Diana*," unpublished Mss.

29. *Loss of the Essex* (Religious Tract Society, London), p. 3.

30. *Inquirer*, Oct. 8, 1822; Jan. 7, 1823.

31. *Op. cit.*, Feb. 8, 1822.

32. Sanford, *op. cit.*, April 7, 1870.

33. O. Chase, *op. cit.*, p. 128.

34. Reminiscences of Edward P. Tice, Mrs. Thomas Giffen and James H. Wood, of Nantucket.

35. "The Late George Pollard," *Inquirer and Mirror*, Jan. 8, 1870.

36. *The Old Navy and the New* (Philadelphia, 1891), p. 28.

37. "A Ship Sunk by a Whale," *Littlell's Living Age* (Nov. 29, 1851), p. 415.

38. "Bark Kathleen Sunk by a Whale," related by Capt. Thomas Jenkins (New Bedford, 1902).

39. *The Melville Log, Jay Leyda* (New York, 1951), Vol. I, p. 125.

40. *The Trying Out of Moby Dick*, Howard Vincent (Boston, 1949), p. 47.

41. Chase, *op. cit.*, pp. 37, 38.

42. Leyda, *op. cit.*, Vol. I, p. 452.

43. *Ibid.*

44. Bennett and Tyerman, *op. cit.*, quoted by Forbes, *The Loss of the Essex* (Boston, 1884), pp. 18-20.

45. Melville, *Clarel*, XXXVII.

46. Letter of Miss Mary E. Starbuck, of Nantucket.

Chapter XXIV: The Pacific . . . an American Ocean

1. Capt. Stephen Reynolds, *op. cit.*, Aug. 31, 1824.

2. Letter of Capt. Benjamin Chase, *Inquirer*, April 29, 1826.

3. *Ibid.*

4. *Ibid.*

5. Log of the *Topaz*. Nantucket Whaling Museum.

6. *A Voyage from New South Wales to Canton, in the Year 1788, with Views of the Islands Discovered by Thomas Gilbert, Esq., Commander of the Charlotte* (London, 1789), p. 247. Voyage of Governor Phillips to Botany Bay (London, 1789). This letter contains an account of Capt. Marshall's voyages in an Appendix.

7. *A Voyage of Discovery into the South Seas and Beerings' Straits in the years 1815-18, by Otto von Kutzebue, in the ship Rurik* (English trans., London, 1821, 2 vols.).

8. Capt. James Cary, Log of the *Rose*, 1803-04. In possession of Robert Caldwell, Nantucket, Mass.

9. Affidavit made by Capt. Cary at Cape Town, Oct. 25, 1804. In possession of Robert Caldwell.

10. Obed Macy's "Diary."

11. Capt. William Plaskett, Log of the *Independence II*, 1825-28. Martha's Vineyard Historical Society, Edgartown, Mass.

12. *Ibid.*, April 21, 1826.

13. Wilkes, *op. cit.*, Vol. 5.

14. *Ibid.*

15. *Inquirer*, March 7, 1828.

16. Plaskett, *op. cit.*, March 27, 1827.

17. *Ibid.*, April 12, 1827.

18. *Inquirer*, March 7, 1829.

19. Capt. David Edwards, Log of the *Harvest,* March 12, 1831. Nantucket Whaling Museum.

20. Starbuck, *Whale-Fishery,* p. 250.

21. *Inquirer,* Nov. 25, 1826; *Daily Mercury,* New Bedford, June 20, 1859.

22. *Inquirer,* Nov. 25, 1826.

23. Wilkes, *op. cit.,* Vol. 5, p. 40.

24. *Inquirer,* Nov. 25, 1826.

25. *Ibid.*

26. Wilkes, *op. cit.,* Vol. 5, p. 41.

27. Plaskett, *op. cit.,* Aug. 21, 1827.

28. *Ibid.,* Nov. 11, 1827.

29. Wilkes, *op. cit.,* Vol. 5, p. 18.

30. *Inquirer,* letter to Dr. Brewster from G. Moll, Professor of Natural History in the University of Utrecht.

31. *Inquirer,* March 7, 1829.

32. *Ibid.*

33. *Ibid.,* July 5, 1824.

34. *Ibid.,* Sept. 23, 1826.

35. *Ibid.*

36. Journal of Moses E. Morrell. In possession of the writer.

37. *Ibid.,* Sept. 5, 1823.

38. "The Ship Wreck of the Independence," by two of her crew. In possession of the writer.

39. *Ibid.*

40. *Ibid.*

41. Log of the *Arabella,* Sag Harbor, Feb. 22, 1836. Owned by Misses Clara and Alice Perkins, Riverhead, Long Island, N. Y.

42. Bellingshausen, *The Voyage of Captain Bellingshausen to the Antartic Sea, 1819-21,* Frank Debenham, ed. (London, 1945), pp. xxv-xxvi, 425-26.

43. Capt. Benjamin Coffin's report, *Inquirer,* July 18, 1829.

44. Wilkes, *op. cit.,* Vol. 5.

45. Log of the *Alexander,* April 1826.

46. *Ibid.*

47. Bryant, *op. cit.,* p. 125.

48. Log of the *Courier, Inquirer,* April 6, 1840. New Bedford Whaling Museum.

49. Capt. George Rule, Logbook of the *Fanny,* May 30, 1823. Nantucket Whaling Museum.

50. Capt. George W. Gardner, "An Account of the Sandwich Islands," *Inquirer,* May 23, 1825.

51. *Ibid.*

Chapter XXV: Recognition of Antarctica

1. Capt. James Cook, *A Voyage Towards the South Pole, and Round the World* (London, 1777), p. 231.

2. Wilkes, *op. cit.* Dumont D'Urville, *Voyage au Pôle Sud et dans L'Océanie sur les Corvettes L'Astrolabe et la Zelée executé par order du Roi pendant 1837-40* (29 vols., Paris 1841-45).

3. Lawrence Martin, "Antarctica Discovered by a Connecticut Yankee, Captain Nathaniel Brown Palmer," *Geographical Review,* Vol. XXX (Oct. 1940), pp. 529-52.

4. J. Miers, "Account of the Discovery of New South Shetland," *Edinburgh Philosophical Journal,* Vol. III (1820), pp. 367-80.

5. William Herbert Hobbs, "The Discoveries of Antarctica within the American Sector," *Transactions* of the American Philosophical Society Vol. XXXI (1939), pp. 8-71.

6. Hugh R. Mill, *The Siege of the South Pole* (London, 1905), pp. 161-62.

7. Hobbs, *op. cit.*

8. J. N. Reynolds, Report to the Secretary of the Navy, September 24, 1828, 23d Congress, 2d Session, House Document No. 105, 1835, pp. 26-27.

9. E. Fanning, *op. cit* (ed. Salem, 1924), pp. 306-09.

10. *Ibid.*, pp. 307-09.

11. Bellingshausen, *op. cit.*, pp. 425-26.

12. Mrs. Richard Fanning Loper, article in the *New London Globe,* Jan. 28, 1907.

13. J. R. Spears, *Captain Nathaniel Brown Palmer* (New York, 1922).

14. A. Schuck, "Entwickelung unserer Kenntniss der Länder im Suden von America," *Zeitschrift für wissenschaftliche Geographic,* Vol. VI, pp. 242-64.

15. Jean Charcot, *The Voyage of the "Why Not?" in the Antarctic* (New York and London), 1911.

16. Mill, *op. cit.*, p. 162.

17. Log of the *Hero,* Mss. Division, Library of Congress.

Chapter XXVI: Ranging the . . . Greatest Ocean

1. Capt. Macy, Log of *Palladium,* March 29, 1824.

2. Obituary of Capt. William Worth, *Inquirer and Mirror,* March 14, 1880.

3. "Discoveries of Captain Worth," *Inquirer,* Feb. 7, 1829.

4. *The Friend,* published at Honolulu, Hawaiian Islands, Sept. 1, 1846. Peabody Museum.

5. Capt. George Newell, Log of the *Mentor.* Nantucket Whaling Museum.

6. Report of Capt. Pease, in *The Vineyard Gazette* (Edgartown, Martha's Vineyard), in *Mirror,* June 26, 1847.

7. *Inquirer,* March 3, 1827.

8. *Essex Register* (Salem), Sept. 29, 1834.

9. "The Discoveries of Captain John Gardner," *Inquirer,* May 3, 1828.

10. Findlay, *Directory of the North Pacific Ocean* (3d ed., 1887), p. 996. Name given as Capt. George Ray should be Capt. George Joy (*Salem Mercury,* Oct. 17, 1832).

11. *Inquirer,* Aug. 28, 1859; *National Gazette,* April 27, 1830.

12. *Albany Sentinel,* Aug. 29, 1797. Boston Public Library.

13. Wilkes, *op. cit.,* Vol. 3, p. 368.

14. Starbuck, *Nantucket,* p. 492; *Pacific Commercial Advertiser,* April 16, 1870.

15. Capt. A. Macy, *Inquirer,* April 12, 1828.

16. William Endicott, *Wrecked Among the Cannibals in the Fijis* (Marine Research Society, 1923), pp. 30, 31.

17. Capt. William Cash in *The Polynesian,* Honolulu, March 20, 1841. *Essex Register,* April 16, 1840.

18. Report of Capt. Joshua Coffin 2d, *Inquirer,* Dec. 8, 1827.

19. Wilkes, *op. cit.,* Vol. 3, p. 369.

20. Report of Capt. Joshua Coffin 2d, *op. cit.,* Dec. 8, 1827.

21. *Ibid.*

22. *Ibid.*

23. *Ibid.*

24. Bellingshausen, *op. cit.*

25. Report of Capt. Elihu Coffin, *Inquirer,* Feb. 14, 1835.

26. Capt. George Rule, *op. cit.,* June 7, 1823.

27. Capt. John Samson, Logbook of the *Nassau,* of New Bedford, March 25, 1835. New Bedford Whaling Museum.

28. Capt. Prince Coffin, Log of the *Awashonks,* March 8, 1835.

29. Samson, *op. cit.,* May 12, 1836.

30. *Ibid.*
31. Bellingshausen, *op. cit.*
32. Bryant, *op. cit.*, p. 112.
33. *Ibid.*, p. 116.
34. Report of Capt. Nathaniel Cary, *Inquirer*, Jan. 12, 1833.
35. Letter of Capt. Driver, *Commercial Advertiser*, May 23, 1831.
36. *Ibid.*, Aug. 12, 1831.
37. *Cruise of the Astrolobe*, Appendix.
38. Extract from Logbook of the *Diana*, Capt. Jared Gardner, *New Bedford Courier*, Sept. 21, 1801.
39. Rule, *op. cit.*, Dec. 8, 1822.
40. *Ibid.*, March 29, 1823.
41. *Ibid.*, April 9, 1823.
42. *Ibid.*, July 22, 1823.
43. *Ibid.*, August 8, 1823.
44. *Ibid.*, Sept. 13, 1823.

Chapter XXVII: "Pursuing the Sperm Whale . . ."

1. Jeremiah N. Reynolds to Michael Hoffman, Chairman of the Committee on Naval Affairs, April 7, 1828, quoted April 12, 1828, in the *Inquirer*.
2. *Ibid.*, p. 35.
3. Capt. David Edwards, Log of the *Harvest*, 1828-31. Nantucket Whaling Museum.
4. *Inquirer*, May 3, 1822.
5. *Ibid.*
6. *Inquirer*, Oct. 3, 1825.
7. Lieut. Hiram Paulding, U.S.N., *Journal of a Cruise of the United States Schooner Dolphin* (New York, 1831), p. 225.
8. *Inquirer*, Sept. 3, 1822.
9. Dakin, *op. cit.*
10. Reynolds, *op. cit.*, p. 19.
11. *Inquirer*, Nov. 10, 1825.
12. *Ibid.*
13. *Ibid.*
14. *Ibid.*, Feb. 28, 1828.
15. *Ibid.*
16. Reynolds, *op. cit.*, p. 29.
17. Beechey, *op. cit.*, pp. 11, 520.
18. *Ibid.*
19. Capt. William Worth, *The Sailor's Magazine* (New York), Oct. 1835.
20. Letter of Jane Perry Tiffany, *The New York Times*, April 5, 1946.
21. Interview with Mr. Long, Aug. 12, 1951.

Chapter XXVIII: "I Seek a Passage in Your Ship—"

1. *Inquirer*, May 4, 1842.
2. Sanford, *Inquirer*, June 24, 1876.
3. *Ibid.*
4. Obituary of Capt. Charles Rawson, *Inquirer and Mirror*, Dec. 7, 1878.
5. Death of Capt. Coggeshall, *Inquirer and Mirror*, Sept. 12, 1854.
6. "Career of Captain Benjamin Worth," *Inquirer*, Feb. 28, 1825.
7. Sanford, "The Sea Kings," *Inquirer*.
8. "Another Veteran Gone," *Inquirer*, Dec. 13, 1859.

9. Genealogical records of the West family.

10. Log of the *Alexander*. In possession of writer.

11. "Another Old Citizen Gone," *Inquirer*, March 12, 1862.

12. Paul West II to Alfred Bunker, July 28, 1916.

13. Correspondent to *Boston Traveller*, reprinted by *Inquirer*, Sept. 20, 1860.

14. "Reminiscences" of Capt. Alexander Macy. Nantucket Whaling Museum.

15. *Ibid.*

16. Capt. George Coffin, *op. cit.*

17. Log of the *Maria*, Capt. A. Macy, 1832-35, kept by Alexander Hoxie, of Sharon, Mass. Houghton Library, Harvard University.

18. *Ibid.*, Oct. 14, 1832.

19. *Ibid.*, March 2, 1833.

20. *The Inquirer*, Oct., 1822.

21. "Reminiscences of a Whaling Master," *Inquirer and Mirror*, March 2, 1882.

22. *New Bedford Mercury*, Feb. 15, 1822.

23. Prof. George Wood, Dartmouth College, to writer.

24. Sanford, *Inquirer and Mirror*, as cited.

25. Log of the *Columbus*, 1843-47. Old South Meeting House Boston Marine Exhibits.

26. Log of the *Vigilant*. Old South Meeting House.

Chapter XXIX: Mutiny at Midnight

1. George Comstock, "Narrative of the Mutiny, Capture and Transactions on Board of the Ship *Globe* of Nantucket." Manuscript at the Nantucket Whaling Museum.

2. Cyrus Hussey and William Lay, *A Narrative of the Mutiny on Board the Ship Globe, of Nantucket in the Pacific Ocean, Jan. 1824, and The Journal of a Residence of Two Years in the Mulgrave Islands* (New London, 1828).

3. Comstock, *op. cit.*, p. 4.

4. *Ibid.*

5. Deposition of Peter Kidder at Valparaiso, before U. S. Consul Michael Hogan, June 15, 1824. General Records of the Dept. of State, Consular Dispatches, Valparaiso, Vol. I, National Archives, Washington, D.C.

6. Hussey and Lay, *op. cit.*, p. 24.

7. *Ibid.*, pp. 39-40.

8. Deposition of Gilbert Smith at Valparaiso, June 15, 1824, Consular Dispatches, Vol. I. Letter of Consul Michael Hogan to John Quincy Adams, Secretary of State, Aug. 11, 1824, also in Consular Dispatches, Group No. 59.

9. Hussey and Lay, *op. cit.*

10. Comstock, *op. cit.*, p. 1.

11. Deposition of George Comstock, at Valparaiso, June 9, 1824. Consular Dispatches, Valparaiso, Vol. I.

12. *Ibid.*

13. Comstock, *op. cit.*, p. 7.

14. *Ibid.*, pp. 8, 9.

15. *Ibid.*, p. 10.

16. *Ibid.*, p. 11.

17. *Ibid.*, p. 11.

18. Customs House Record of Edgartown, Martha's Vineyard, at National Archives, Washington, microfilmed by Stuart C. Sherman, Jr., Providence Public Library.

19. William Hussey Macy, *Inquirer and Mirror*, Sept. 27, 1890.

20. Paulding, *op. cit.*, p. 7.

21. *Ibid.*, pp. 119-20.

22. Log of the U.S. Schooner *Dolphin*, 1824-1826. Entry of Nov. 29, 1825. Records of the Naval Dept., National Archives, Washington, D.C.

23. Paulding, *op. cit.*, p. 125.

24. *Ibid.*, p. 125.

25. *Ibid.*, p. 126.

26. *Ibid.*, p. 126.

27. *Ibid.*, pp. 126-27.

28. *Ibid.*, p. 132.

29. *Ibid.*, p. 145.

30. Examination of Cyrus M. Hussey by Captain John Percival on board U.S. Schooner *Dolphin*, Dec. 7, 1825. Transmitted to the Secretary of the Navy, April 2, 1826, by Com. Isaac Hull.

31. *Inquirer*, Aug. 26, 1826.

32. *Boston Patriot* (Boston, Mass), Sept. 2, 1826.

33. Letter of Gorham Coffin to Secretary Southard, Aug. 28, 1826. In possession of writer.

34. *Inquirer*, May 19, 1827. Letters of Capt. Isaac Hull to Samuel L. Southard, Secretary of the Navy, April 21, 1827, while on the frigate *United States*, off New York.

35. Records of the Custom House, Edgartown, Mass. At the National Archives, Washington, Microfilm at Providence Public Library.

36. *Inquirer*, May 22, 1825.

37. *Ibid.*, Oct. 28, 1826.

38. Deposition of Joseph Thomas at Valparaiso, June 30, 1824.

39. *Ibid.*

40. Andrew Gardner Coffin's reminiscenses. From Mrs. B. F. Buchanan, Westport, Conn.

41. Letter of Gorham Coffin to Daniel Webster, Dec. 22, 1824.

42. *Ibid.*

43. *Ibid.*

44. *Ibid.*

45. *Ibid.*

46. June 15, 1824.

47. "The Life of Samuel Comstock," *Inquirer*, Feb. 17, 1883.

48. *Ibid.*

49. William Comstock, *Samuel Comstock, The Terrible Mutineer* (New York and Boston, 1840).

50. Henry Glover, "The Young Mutineer," *Inquirer*.

51. Affidavit of Capt. Thomas Ap Catesby Jones, June 19, 1826. In possession of writer. *Inquirer*, Mar. 24, 1827.

Chapter XXX: "We Desire You . . ."

1. Instructions to Capt. David Osburn of the ship *Peruvian*, Nantucket, by Christopher Mitchell & Co., Aug. 12, 1836. Letter book in possession of *Inquirer and Mirror*.

2. Capt. Joseph Gardner, Log of the *Rosalie*, of Warren, R. I., 1825-28. In possession of Paul C. Nicholson, Providence, R. I.

3. Logbook studies by the author.

4. Capt. Obed Swain, Log of the *Catawba*, Nov. 25, 1855. Nantucket Whaling Museum.

5. *Inquirer and Mirror*, 1866.

6. *Ibid.*

7. Capt. Joseph Gardner, *op. cit.*

8. *Ibid.*

9. Capt. Hiram Fisher, Log of the *Meridian*, 1828, kept by Henry Collins. Entry of January 10, 1829. Paul C. Nicholson Collection, Providence, R. I.

10. *Ibid.*

11. Log of the *Phoenix*.

12. Diary of Addison Pratt. In possession of Nettie Hunt Rancher, Snowflake, Ariz.

13. Document in possession of the author from Whitney C. Riddell.

14. Moses E. Morrell, *op. cit.*

15. *Ibid.*, March 10, 1822.

16. *Ibid.*, Feb. 7, 1823.

17. *Ibid.*, Oct. 6, 1823.

18. *Ibid.*, Oct. 22 to Nov. 15, 1823.

19. *A Visit to the South Seas in the U.S. Ship Vincennes*, C. S. Stewart (New York, 1831).

20. *Ibid.*, Vol. I, pp. 221-23.

21. Capt. David Edwards, *op. cit.*, Nov. 17, 1828.

22. *Inquirer*, June 7, 1837.

23. Log of the *Bengal*, 1832-35, Paul C. Nicholson Collection, Providence, R. I.

24. *Ibid.*, April 3, 1833.

25. *Ibid.*, April 5, 1833.

26. *Ibid.*, May 24, 1833.

27. *Ibid.*, Sept. 14, 1834.

28. *Ibid.*, July 20, 1833.

29. Capt. William Swain, Log of the *William Hamilton*, 1834-37. Entry of Jan. 31, 1835. Paul C. Nicholson Collection.

30. Obed Macy, *op. cit.*, pp. 243-44.

31. Capt. Charles Ray, Log of the *Norman*. Nantucket Whaling Museum.

32. Capt. John Samson, Log of the *Nassau*. New Bedford Whaling Museum.

33. *Ibid.*, April 24, 1834.

34. Capt. William Reynard, Log of the *Pacific*. Entry of July 4, 1866. Old Dartmouth Hist. Soc. Whaling Museum.

35. Capt. John O. Morse, Log of the *Hector*. Old Dartmouth Hist. Soc. Whaling Museum, Oct. 10, 1832.

36. Starbuck, *Nantucket*, pp. 122-23.

Chapter XXXI: The Sea-Hunters . . . Their Own

1. J. N. Reynolds, *op. cit.*, Rep. No. 94, p. 39.

2. *Inquirer*, Jan. 16, 1826.

3. *Ibid.*

4. Starbuck, *Whale-Fishery*, pp. 254-70; *Inquirer*, Feb. 21, 1826; marine columns of Nantucket, New Bedford and New London newspapers.

5. *History of Fairhaven.*

6. C. A. Williams, "Early Whaling Industry of New London," in New London County Historical Society *Papers*, Part I, Vol. II. Published by the Society in 1895.

7. Starbuck, *Whale-Fishery*, pp. 312-40.

8. *Inquirer*, Nov. 26, 1822.

9. *Ibid.*, May 31, 1828.

10. *Ibid.*, Feb. 21, 1829.

11. Obed Macy, *op. cit.*, p. 225.

12. *Inquirer*, March 22, 1828.

13. *Ibid.*, May 31, 1828.

14. Robert F. Almy on "J. N. Reynolds," *Colophon*, 1837 (N. S. 2:227-245).

15. J. N. Reynolds, Report to Secretary of the Navy, 23d Congress, 2d Session, House Document No. 105.

16. *Inquirer,* Aug. 23, 1828.

17. J. N. Reynolds, *Report,* pp. 2, 28.

18. *Inquirer,* Oct. 4, 1828.

19. Report of Capt. Benjamin Palmer in E. Fanning, *op. cit.,* p. 487.

20. J. N. Reynolds, *The Voyage of the U.S. Frigate Potomac Around the World* (New York, 1835).

21. *New York Times,* July, Aug., Sept., 1837; *New York Courier & Inquirer,* Dec. and Jan. 1837-38.

22. Wilkes, *op. cit.,* Vol. 5, p. 484.

23. *Proceedings* of Nantucket Historical Association for 1909.

24. J. P. Williams, *North American Review* (Jan. 1834), pp. 103-108. Grinnell, Joseph in "Speech on the Tariff, with Statistical Tales of the Whale-Fishery" (1844).

25. Oct. 4, 1828.

26. *New Bedford Mercury,* Oct. 25, 1822.

27. Capt. Charles Starbuck, Log of the *Peru,* 1851-55. Entry of July 18, 1851.

INDEX

499